BRITISH SHIPPING LAWS

LAYTIME

By

MICHAEL BRYNMÔR SUMMERSKILL

B.C.L., M.A., F.C.I.Arb., A.C.I.I.

Of Merton College, Oxford, and
of the Middle Temple, Barrister

FOURTH EDITION

LONDON
STEVENS & SONS LIMITED
1989

First Edition 1966
Second Edition 1973
Third Edition 1982
Fourth Edition 1989

Published in 1989 by
Sweet and Maxwell Limited
South Quay Plaza
183 Marsh Wall
London
E14 9FT

Printed in Great Britain by
Butler & Tanner Ltd, Frome and London

British Cataloguing in Publication Data
Summerskill, Michael Brynmôr, 1927–
Laytime.–4th ed.
1. Great Britain. Freight transport. Shipping.
Laytime. Law
I. Title
344.103'967

ISBN 0–420–47970–8

PREFACE

The comparison between our journey through life and the voyage of a ship has attracted people since time immemorial; but they have been aware also of the harsh truth expressed by the late Lord Parker in *North River Freighters Ltd.* v. *President of India*, in 1955: "A ship is a money-earning machine, and time during which she could have earned money was wasted or lost."

Of course we should not pursue too far this parallel between the money-earning characteristics of ships and human beings. Mindful of the value, in a spiritual sense, of being rather than doing, some people might prefer to be compared to houseboats or other pleasure craft. But their story is not this one.

It is often said, after a dispute arises, that the parties could have used clearer words in their agreement. Brokers making a fixture under pressure may consider such advice sensible but unrealistic. Others with more leisure have, on behalf of chartering and shipowning interests, to draft and amend the forms used by brokers. They adapt the forms to new trades, but they often have to cling to phrases whose construction has been hallowed by custom or approved by the courts. It is not surprising that many of the terms used give rise to differences of opinion; and not least in the realm of laytime.

The object of this book is to give some help to all concerned with laytime provisions, whether they be charterers, shipowners, brokers, agents, arbitrators or lawyers. The principles set out are those of English law. So far as possible the cases have been allowed to speak for themselves and the judges to explain the law in their own words. The overwhelming majority of charterparties, wherever they are concluded, provide for London arbitration; and in many other countries considerable attention is paid to decided English cases.

Anyone faced with a laytime problem knows how much we all owe to Scrutton's *Charterparties and Bills of Lading* and to Carver's *Carriage by Sea*; that debt is hereby gratefully acknowledged.

About 50 cases on laytime problems, decided by the English courts since the third edition appeared in 1982, are included in this fourth edition. There were four House of Lords decisions. *Seacrystal Shipping Ltd.* v. *Bulk Transport Group Shipping Ltd.* (*The Kyzikos*) concerned inability to proceed to the berth because of fog, and the words "whether in berth or not." *Lips Maritime Corporation* v. *President of India* (*The Lips*) involved a dispute as to an exchange rate loss in respect of late payment of demurrage. In *Miramar Maritime Corporation* v. *Holborn Oil Trading Ltd.* (*The Miramar*) their Lordships considered whether references to the charterers in the charterparty could be so interpreted as to cause the consignors to be liable for demurrage. In *Société Anonyme Marocaine de l'Industrie du Raffinage* v. *Notos Maritime Corporation* (*The Notos*) the familiar problem of delay in reaching a berth was considered in the light of provisions that demurrage should not count where delay was caused for reasons over which charterers had no control.

There were also eight Court of Appeal and nearly 40 High Court decisions. These dealt with, among other matters, custom house entry; available and workable hatches; shifting expenses; the expression "weather permitting" and the Gencon Strike Clause.

There have been included, for the first time, references to matters decided by London arbitrators, as reported in *Lloyd's Maritime Law Newsletter*. Resistance to publication, on the part of those who have some control, however temporarily, over the supplies of knowledge, has been a recurrent phenomenon. This has been so from the invention of printing, often regarded at the time as fraught with danger, for it could be used to spread new ideas. Authority conceded reluctantly that House of Commons debates could be published (see *Stockdale* v. *Hansard* (1839) 9 A. & E. 1 and the ensuing Parliamentary Papers Act 1840); and its efforts to restrict other publications continue to the present day. The objections by some in London to the regular publication of awards, though not of the same gravity, have much of the same flavour; so the activities of the publishers of the *Newsletter*, or LMLN, have been welcomed by many.

Cases are frequently known by the names of the ships involved. This custom, previously confined almost entirely to Admiralty cases, has been recognised in this edition. The full titles have not, however, been replaced by ships' names; instead, the name is almost invariably stated, in brackets, after the title, usually in the footnotes. In addition, the name is often used in the text, after the initial statement of the title of the case; and the Table of Cases has been more elaborately cross-referenced, as between ships' names and case titles.

As on previous occasions, many people from different parts of the world have provided valuable criticisms which I have endeavoured to incorporate. To them I express my profound thanks. There are those who helped me at the earlier stages of this work, including Glenys Bevan, LL.B., Barrister, who provided stimulating and helpful criticism. There was also the late Edgar Buswell of Bigard Brothers & Buswell Ltd., a friend who gave valuable help, itself the product of many years' experience on the Baltic Exchange. In respect of this edition especially, I owe particular thanks to Peter Barleycorn, John Besman, Basil Eckersley, Richard Faint, B. P. Gunaji, Mark Hamsher, Bruce Harris (at whose suggestion I re-cast the section on the words "reachable on her arrival"), James Higgins, the late Hiro Keswani, David F. H. Marler, Robin Mitchell, Massimo Mordiglia, Albert Morris, Richard J. Reisert, W. S. Tolman, Dr. Johannes Trappe and Sarosh Zaiwalla. I thank my friends from my own firm, including Hugo Wynn Williams, and especially Hugh Wodehouse, with whom I have been able to exchange views on various problems. In addition I thank, for numerous suggestions, and for undertaking the Japanese translation of the last edition, my friends from the Japan Shipping Exchange Inc., including the Executive Director, Hironori Tanimoto, and his colleagues Toshio Matsumoto, Sou Tottori, Taro Arakawa, Osamu Baba, and Masahiro Hojo of Dodwell Protection and Indemnity and Hirosuke Ogawa of Daiichi-Chuo Steamship Co., Ltd. As before, I thank Robert Spicer, M.A., Barrister, for his meticulous preparation of the Index.

Michael Summerskill

London, March 1989

CONTENTS

CHAPTER ONE

INTRODUCTION

CHAPTER TWO

LAYTIME CLAUSES AND THEIR EFFECTS

Contents

Chapter Three

LAYTIME NOT FIXED

Chapter Four

REACHING THE DESTINATION

Contents

CHAPTER FIVE

READINESS

Contents

CHAPTER SIX

MODIFICATION OF REQUIREMENTS FOR BEGINNING OF LAYTIME

CHAPTER SEVEN

INTERRUPTION BY BAD WEATHER

Contents

CHAPTER EIGHT

SUSPENSION OF LAYTIME—OTHER THAN BY BAD WEATHER

Contents

CHAPTER NINE

RELATIONSHIP OF LOADING AND DISCHARGING TIMES

CHAPTER TEN

DEMURRAGE

Contents

CHAPTER ELEVEN

LIABILITY FOR DEMURRAGE

Contents

Chapter Twelve

DISPATCH

TABLE OF CASES

(A page on which the facts of a case are set out, or the case is particularly discussed, is indicated by heavier type)

Table of Cases

Table of Cases

Table of Cases

Table of Cases

Table of Cases

Table of Cases

TABLE OF STATUTES

(INCLUDING U.S.A.)

the parties during which the owner will make and ke..
..........................Bitara to the tenant."

CHAPTER 1

INTRODUCTION

WHAT IS LAYTIME?

LAYTIME is the time during which a ship is lying,[1] for the purpose of loading   **1–01**
or discharging, as distinct from moving, with the object of carrying her
cargo from one place to another.[2] Lord Esher M.R. once said[3]:

> "There must be a stipulation as to the time to be occupied in the loading and in the
> unloading of the cargo. There must be a time, either expressly stipulated, or implied. If it
> is not expressly stipulated, then it is a reasonable time which is implied by the law; but
> either the law or the parties fix a time. Now, when they do fix a time, how do they fix it?
> Why, they allow a certain number of days, during which, although the ship is at the dis-
> posal of the charterer to load or to unload the cargo, he does not pay for the use of the
> ship. That is the meaning of 'lay days.' "[4]

It is the duty of the shipowners to make their ship available to the char-   **1–02**
terers[5] at the agreed place; it is the duty of the charterers to make the cargo
available and to bring it to the ship. The charterers' duty may be expressed
in terms of time, in that the charterparty states how long shall be allotted
for this purpose or provides a method by which the time may be calculated;
alternatively the charterers must bring or take the cargo within a reasonable time. Where that time, which is called the laytime, is exceeded, the
charterers may be called upon under the charterparty[6] to pay liquidated
damages known as demurrage.[7] In the absence of any provision for demurrage they become liable to pay damages for detention.[8] Where the work is
completed within the laytime the shipowners may be liable under the charterparty to pay dispatch money.[9]

---

[1] In modern usage it is normally correct to use the verb "to lay" transitively. The use of the
intransitive verb is restricted by the *Shorter Oxford English Dictionary* (3rd ed.) (otherwise
it is "an illiterate substitute for lie") to nautical expressions. Thus it is possible to say, cor-
rectly, that a ship is laying at anchor. The Charterparty Laytime Definitions 1980 (see
Appendix to this book) state: "6. 'LAYTIME'—means the period of time agreed between
the parties during which the owner will make and keep the ship available for loading/dis-
charging without payment additional to the freight."

[2] This sentence was cited in *Total Transport Corporation* v. *Amoco Trading Company (The
Altus)* [1985] 1 Lloyd's Rep. 423 at p. 427, by Webster J. He also quoted the words of Sir
John Donaldson M.R. in *Mosvolds Rederi A/S* v. *Food Corporation of India* [1984] 1
Lloyd's Rep. 1 (C.A.) (*The King Theras*) at p. 2, who described laytime as a " . . . reser-
voir of time which the charterers draw on for the purpose of loading or discharging. . . . "

[3] In *Nielsen* v. *Wait* (1885) 16 Q.B.D. 67 (C.A.) at p. 70.

[4] For the various types of lay days, including working and running days, see §§ 2–04–2–06
below.

[5] The word "charterers" is used generally henceforward to mean any persons identified with
the cargo interests, such as the shippers, the receivers, or the charterers themselves. The
terms "merchant" or "freighter" are sometimes used.

[6] Liability may also arise under a bill of lading, either by express words in the bill or by reference in the bill to a charterparty. See also Liability for Demurrage, Chap. 11.

[7] See § 10–01 below.

[8] See § 10–37 below.

[9] See Chap. 12 below.

1

1–03   The total time allowed for the lay days is the result of an assessment by the parties of the characteristics of the cargo, the ship and the loading and discharging facilities of the ports. The rate allowed for demurrage usually bears some relation to the amount which the ship can earn.[10] On one view both freight and demurrage can be regarded as payments for the detention of the ship. The detention for the anticipated period of the voyage is recompensed by freight; as Scrutton L.J. said in *Inverkip SS. Co. Ltd.* v. *Bunge & Co.*[11]:

> "The sum agreed for freight in a charter covers the use of the ship for an agreed time for loading and discharging, known as the lay days, and for the voyage";

and as Lord Denning M.R. said of the charterers in *Shipping Developments Corporation S.A.* v. *V/O Sojuzneftexport*[12]:

> " . . . they have brought their laytime and paid for it in the freight . . . "

The detention for extra delay is recompensed by demurrage.[13] Devlin J. discussed these commercial considerations in *Compania de Navigacion Zita S.A.* v. *Louis Dreyfus & Cie*[14]:

> "The shipowner's desire is to achieve a quick turn-round; time is money for him. The object of fixing lay days and providing for demurrage and dispatch money is to penalise dilatoriness in loading and to reward promptitude."

The rate allowed for dispatch is usually one half of the rate agreed for demurrage.[15]

RIGHTS AND DUTIES

1–04   The laytime provision contained in a charterparty, or, in some cases, in a bill of lading, is usually in the form of an undertaking by the charterers for the benefit of the shipowners.[16] It limits the time allowed to the charterers for the performance of their share of the loading or discharging,[17] by providing a fixed period or a method of calculating the time, or alternatively by allowing a reasonable time. For any time beyond that period the charterers are liable in demurrage,[18] and this liability is absolute[19] unless the delay arises through the fault of the shipowners[20] or is covered by an exception in the charterparty or arises because working the ship becomes illegal by the law of the place of performance.

---

[10] The amount due must usually be accepted by the shipowners in full satisfaction of any claim for delay. Mere failure to load and discharge in the given time does not entitle the shipowners to damages other than demurrage: *Suisse Atlantique Société d'Armement Maritime S.A.* v. *N.V. Rotterdamsche Kolen Centrale (The General Guisan)* [1966] 1 Lloyd's Rep. 529 (H.L.). See § 10–08 below.

[11] [1917] 2 K.B. 193 (C.A.) at p. 200.

[12] [1971] 1 Lloyd's Rep. 506 (C.A.) at p. 509.

[13] For the nature of demurrage, see § 10–07 below.

[14] [1953] 2 Lloyd's Rep. 472 at p. 475.

[15] For dispatch, see § 12–01 below.

[16] See the judgment of Dixon C.J. in *President of India* v. *Moor Line Ltd.* [1958] 2 Lloyd's Rep. 205 (High Ct. of Australia) at p. 210, referring to the laytime stipulation in an Australian grain charterparty: "The opening words of clause 9 which deal with the average rate of loading contain a description of stipulation which is usually read as imposing an obligation upon the charterer for the benefit of the shipowner."

[17] For the way in which responsibility for these duties is shared, see § 1–15 below.

[18] For demurrage, see § 10–01 below.

[19] *Love and Stewart Ltd.* v. *Rowtor SS. Co. Ltd.* [1916] 2 A.C. 527 (H.L.); see also § 9–16 below.

[20] See § 10–12 below.

It is possible, though unusual, for circumstances to arise in which the undertaking is regarded as having been given for the benefit of the charterers. In *Dobell* v. *Watts, Ward & Co.*[21] there was such a situation. The charterparty, for the carriage of timber from Quebec to London, stated: "Cargo to be furnished and received by ship at port of loading as fast as vessel can receive in ordinary working hours, and to be received from alongside ship at port of discharge as customary as fast as steamer can deliver in ordinary working hours, Sundays always excepted loading or discharging. Not less than 100 standards a day loading or discharging, and ten days on demurrage over and above the said laying days at £70 per day." By custom of the port of London the ship had to engage stevedores, but the men struck. The charterers claimed damages for delay in the delivery of the cargo and for detention of barges. The shipowners contended that on the true construction of the charterparty the lay days were fixed, and that there was an absolute obligation on the charterers to take delivery of at least 100 standards a day. Wills J. held that the clause was a provision in favour of charterers, and that its effect was to oblige the ship to deliver not less than 100 standards a day; the interests of the shipowners were protected by the terms imposing on the charterers a duty to receive as fast as the ship could deliver. In the Court of Appeal, dismissing the shipowners' appeal, Lindley L.J. is reported[22] as follows:

> " . . . he agreed with Mr. Justice Wills in thinking that the provision as to the 100 standards a day was inserted for the protection of the charterers, and that, according to the true interpretation of these words, the shipowners were bound to discharge the cargo at least at that rate."

CHARTERERS' RIGHTS AND DUTIES

A. Before work has ended[23]   **1–05**
The charterers are entitled to use the whole of the laytime for loading or discharging. They are therefore not in breach of contract if, notwithstanding that they could work the ship faster, they keep the ship for the whole of the laytime. Even if the ship is not being worked, she must remain at the loading port throughout the laytime unless the charterers have refused to provide a cargo. Their refusal constitutes a breach[24] which the shipowners may accept as a repudiation of the contract.

The right to keep the ship   **1–06**
The decision of the High Court in *Petersen* v. *Dunn & Co.*[25] has been cited[26] as an authority for the proposition that the charterers are not in breach if they retain the ship for the whole of the laytime, even though they could work the ship faster. In the reports of the case itself the proposition was not so stated, but if seems that the judge must have considered it to be correct.[27]

---

[21] (1891) 7 T.L.R. 622 (C.A.). The case arose out of the London dock strike of 1889.
[22] At p. 623.
[23] For the charterers' rights and duties after work has ended, see § 1–09 below. As to when work ends, see § 1–11 below.
[24] *Harries* v. *Edmonds* (1845) 1 C. & K. 686.
[25] (1895) 1 Com.Cas. 8.
[26] In the 19th edition of Scrutton on *Charterparties and Bills of Lading,* at Article 156.
[27] His view is borne out by the decision of the High Court in *Margaronis Navigation Agency Ltd.* v. *Henry W. Peabody & Co. of London Ltd.* [1965] 1 Q.B. 300; see § 1–07 hereunder.

A ship had been chartered to carry coal from Ardrossan, the charter-party providing for loading "in the customary manner, say, in twelve colliery working days."[28] She was "to be loaded according to the custom of the port"; "strikes and lock-outs of pitmen and others" were excepted perils. The charterparty further provided: "It is understood that vessel is to be loaded at once, and lay days to count when vessel ready and notice given." A strike occured seven colliery days after notice of readiness. The coal was not loaded (the loading taking two days) until the expiry of the 12 colliery working days. The shipowners argued that the ship could and should have been "loaded at once," and that the charterers, having waited for several days without loading till the strike broke out, were liable for demurrage. The charterers said that there were no working days between the outbreak of the strike and the day on which coal was first sent down to Ardrossan, just before loading began. The High Court held that the charterers were not liable, the loading having been completed within the permitted lay days. Matthew J. said[29]:

> " . . . if the cargo was ready the ship might have been loaded in two days. The charterparty allowed twelve days for the loading, and the plaintiff in effect says that it only allowed seven."[30]

A question thus arises as to whether this decision is an authority for the proposition that the charterers are entitled to keep the ship for all the lay days though they could have loaded in less time. It was argued for the charterers in *Margaronis Navigation Agency Ltd.* v. *Henry W. Peabody & Co. of London Ltd.*[31] that Matthew J. could not have reached his decision, that the charterers were not liable, had he not accepted that proposition. Roskill J. at first instance agreed with the charterers' argument, saying[32]:

> " . . . that it is a necessary inference from the decision is, I think, clear."

1–07   In that case[33] a ship had been chartered to load maize at Cape Town "at the average rate of not less than 1,000 English tons per weather working day of 24 consecutive hours (Sundays and holidays excepted)." Loading began on December 27, and by 5 p.m. on Friday, December 29, 12,588 tons 4 cwts. had been loaded. Further loading was possible on the Friday and Saturday on payment of overtime, but the charterers chose not to complete, and thus to bring the amount loaded to 12,600 tons, until 8 a.m. on Tuesday, January 2, so that January bills of lading would be issued. The shipowners claimed damages for detention from 5 p.m. on the Friday till 8 a.m. on the Tuesday. They argued that the ship had a full and complete cargo on the Friday evening, and said that the principle *de minimis non curat lex* applied to the balance of 11 tons 16 cwts. Roskill J. decided in favour of the charterers. He said[34] of the charterparty:

> " . . . if he" [the charterer] "is entitled to load his cargo in that length of time,[35] what

---

[28] For the meaning of the expression "colliery working days," see § 2–62 below.

[29] At pp. 10–11.

[30] The time available before the strike occurred.

[31] [1965] 1 Q.B. 300 at p. 312.

[32] At p. 325.

[33] The decision by Roskill J. was affirmed by the Court of Appeal ([1964] 2 Lloyd's Rep. 153) which, however, confined itself to the application of the *de minimis* rule. It decided not to interfere with the finding that loading had not been completed on the Friday, and did not consider the question of the right to keep the ship throughout the laytime.

[34] At p. 324.

[35] The time calculable from the rate stated in the laytime clause.

justification is there then for imposing upon him an obligation to load that cargo in some lesser time? One can only impose that restriction upon the charterer's right either as a matter of construction of the contract or as a matter of necessary implication. I can see no possible ground for implying a term to the effect contended for by counsel for the owners. It seems to me, as a matter of construction, that, where a charterparty prescribes that a charterer is to have a fixed time to load (whether it arrives at that time by specifically stating, say 12 weather working days or by a formula expressed by taking a daily rate and dividing it into the total quantity loaded), a charterer is entitled to have that time for loading. The distinction between such a case and the *Nolisement* case,[36] in my judgment, lies in this. A charterer is entitled to have that time to load, but, once he has loaded, he must not use that time for some other purpose. But, so long as he has not completed loading, that time is his, and he is under no obligation to accelerate that rate of loading so as to shorten the time to which he is otherwise entitled."

In other words the charterers are not bound either to work, or to main- **1–08** tain an average loading or discharging rate, on each of the lay days allowed, and are not liable for demurrage or damages for any wasted time, provided that the laytime has not expired and the work has not been completed.[37] The proposition received further support from the Court of Appeal in *Shipping Developments Corporation S.A.* v. *V/O Sojuzneft-export.*[38] Lord Denning M.R. said[39]:

" . . . where the charterers have been guilty of a breach causing delay, they are entitled to apply their laytime so as to diminish or extinguish any claim for the delay, leaving the shipowners to claim for demurrage at the agreed rate for any extra delay over and above the laytime. The reason is because they have bought their laytime and paid for it in the freight, and are entitled to use it in the way which suits them best, and in particular to use it so as to wipe out or lessen any delay for which they would otherwise be responsible . . . "

If they complete the work within the laytime, they will be rewarded under the dispatch provision, if there is one; if they fail to do so, they must compensate the shipowners.[40]

B. After work has ended   **1–09**

Laytime can only be used by the charterers if it is being employed for loading or discharging, or if some loading or discharging remains to be done. When loading has ended,[41] the charterers must release the ship[42] and present the bills of lading for signature within a reasonable time. This duty arises whether or not laytime has ended. Charterers who are in breach of this duty are liable not for demurrage at the charterparty rate but for damages for detention[43] of the ship, because demurrage is due only where the ship is detained for the purpose of working her. The measure of damages is the amount which the parties can reasonably be presumed to

---

[36] *Nolisement (Owners)* v. *Bunge & Born* [1917] 1 K.B. 160 (C.A.), in which it was held that the shipowners can and must issue bills of lading when the cargo is loaded, and that the ship cannot be detained thereafter. See § 1–09 below.

[37] This is the effect of the decisions in *Petersen* v. *Dunn & Co.* (1895) 1 Com.Cas. 8 (see § 1–06 above) and *Margaronis Navigation Agency Ltd.* v. *Henry W. Peabody & Co. of London Ltd.* [1965] 1 Q.B. 300 (see § 1–07 above).

[38] [1971] 1 Lloyd's Rep. 506 (C.A.) (*The Delian Spirit*).

[39] At p. 509.

[40] Usually only by a demurrage payment, and not by damages at large where the shipowners have suffered other damages by the delay: *Suisse Atlantique Société d'Armement Maritime S.A.* v. *N.V. Rotterdamsche Kolen Centrale (The General Guisan)* [1966] 1 Lloyd's Rep. 529 (H.L.). See § 10–30 below.

[41] As to when loading ends, see §§ 1–11–1–13 below.

[42] *Nolisement (Owners)* v. *Bunge & Born* [1917] 1 K.B. 160 (C.A.).

[43] For damages for detention, see § 10–37 below.

have had in mind when they concluded the charterparty. This will usually be the amount which the ship can earn per day in that area or in areas reasonably accessible at that time, less any amounts saved by the detention. As with other breaches of contract, this prima facie rule as to damages does not apply where the parties had in contemplation at the time of the conclusion of the charterparty some special measure of damages, if that measure formed the basis of their contract.

However expeditious the charterers are, they may therefore be liable for wrongful detention of the ship if she is not released when loading or discharging has finished; if accounts have to be settled, bills of lading signed, or some other task completed, a reasonable additional time is allowed for completion of such work.

In *Nolisement (Owners)* v. *Bunge & Born*[44] a charterparty[45] for the carriage of grain from the River Plate provided for loading at the rate of a certain number of tons per day and stated: "otherwise demurrage shall be paid by the charterers." The master was "to sign bills of lading in the form indorsed hereon at any rate of freight that the charterers or their agents require." The ship loaded in eight days, 19 days before expiry of the lay days. Bills of lading and orders as to the port of discharge were not forthcoming until three days after loading ended, as charterers had not decided upon a discharging port. It was agreed that they had a right to keep the ship for 24 hours after completion to settle accounts. Shipowners claimed damages for detention for the two extra days. The Court of Appeal held that charterers were not entitled to detain the ship further, although laytime had not expired. They were obliged to present bills of lading for signature within a reasonable time, which had been agreed to be 24 hours; thereafter they were in breach of contract. But they were entitled to dispatch money for the 19 days saved, which included the two days for which they had to pay damages. Swinfen Eady L.J. said[46]:

> "Under clause 13 demurrage is payable if the steamer is not loaded at the agreed rate. The steamer was in fact loaded at an accelerated rate, and her detention for the two days after being loaded would not give rise to a claim for demurrage under that clause.[47] . . . It is true that, if all the laydays are consumed in loading, there is no breach for which the charterer is liable; but in a charterparty in this form, where the ship is loaded at an accelerated rate, the charterer has no right to say that, as he might have taken more time to load the ship, he can detain her for the rest of the period which he might have occupied in loading without being liable in damages for the detention . . . the damages are such sum as may reasonably be taken to have been in the contemplation of the parties at the time they made the contract as the probable result of the breach of it."

During the laytime, provided that work has not been completed, charterers can load or not; but if work has been completed they must release the ship even if laytime has not ended.

1–10 *Delays*

After loading or discharging has finished, the charterers are not liable for any delay unless it arises from some fault on their part. A delay in naming a discharging port,[48] with a consequent delay in issuing the bills of lading,

---

[44] [1917] 1 K.B. 160 (C.A.).

[45] On the River Plate Charterparty 1914, Homewards (Centrocon) form.

[46] At pp. 168, 170 and 171.

[47] In the rare cases where the demurrage clause provides for demurrage for all detention after completion the demurrage rate would apply.

[48] As in *Nolisement (Owners)* v. *Bunge & Born* [1917] 1 K.B. 160 (C.A.); see § 1–09 above.

may be attributable to the charterers. But delays resulting from failure by shipowners to secure clearances,[49] or from ice,[50] or even from a breach of contract by charterers if the shipowners could have avoided the consequences,[51] have all been held to fall upon the shipowners.

Ice. Delay to the ship as a result of ice where loading or discharging has finished falls upon the shipowners, in the absence of any fault on the part of the charterers.

In *Jamieson & Co.* v. *Lawrie*[52] a ship loaded at Cronstadt. After she was ready to sail bad weather delayed her and she was frozen in for six months. The House of Lords, sitting as an appeal court from a Scottish court, held that the shipowners could recover demurrage up to the moment at which the ship was ready to sail, but neither demurrage nor damages for detention for any time thereafter.

In *Pringle* v. *Mollett*[53] a ship loading a general cargo at Odessa in December was frozen in and unable to leave for London until the end of February. The shipowners claimed demurrage for the 10 days fixed by the charterparty and damages for detention for the rest of the delay. The charterers denied liability for any delay caused by ice after loading had ended. The shipowners argued that the general rule of law was that detention was to be paid by charterers and that the authorities[54] showed that they were not excused from the performance of their covenant by unavoidable detention. It was held that the shipowners must fail. The court is reported as saying[55]: "The detention by the ice was not occasioned by any fault of the defendant. In order to render him liable, the detention must have been for the purpose of loading." Parke B. distinguished the decisions cited by the shipowners, saying that in them loading was impeded; in the present case the detention was not during the loading.

Delay by shipowners' fault. Where charterers delay the ship after the end of loading or discharging, and by doing so are in breach of contract, shipowners are not entitled to demurrage or detention damages if they could have avoided the delay. The payment of harbour dues, for example, even where there is some doubt as to whether shipowners are liable for them, should be made if this will reduce the delay.

In *Möller* v. *Jecks*[56] a ship carried timber from Finland to Lowestoft. After the cargo had been discharged, and the freight paid to the master, the charterers objected to paying harbour dues for landing the cargo. The master could have paid them and departed but instead he refused. As a result, the ship was detained. The shipowners' claim for demurrage was rejected. Willes J. said[57]:

---

[49] *Barret* v. *Dutton* (1815) 4 Camp. 333. Loading had finished but clearances were delayed owing to a fire at the custom house; charterers were held not to be liable for the delay.
[50] *Jamieson & Co.* v. *Lawrie* (1796) 6 Bro.P.C. 474 (H.L.); *Pringle* v. *Mollett* (1840) 6 M. & W. 80. See § 1–10 below.
[51] *Möller* v. *Jecks* (1865) 19 C.B.(N.S.) 332. See § 1–10 below.
[52] (1796) 6 Bro.P.C. 474 (H.L.).
[53] (1840) 6 M. & W. 80.
[54] Including *Barret* v. *Dutton* (1815) 4 Camp. 333 where loading was prevented by frost and the charterers were liable for the delay.
[55] At p. 83.
[56] (1865) 19 C.B.(N.S.) 332.
[57] At p. 340.

"The master might and ought to have paid those charges and sailed out of the harbour, resorting to his remedy against the merchant afterwards. A man has no right to aggravate damages[58] against another by the course of proceeding adopted by the plaintiff here."

1–11 Scope of operation of loading

Time ceases to count against charterers when the ship is no longer detained by the physical problems[59] involved in loading and discharging, and is ready to leave, subject to clearances and other obstacles not the responsibility of charterers.

1–12   As for loading, charterers continue to be debited with time used so long as reasonably necessary operations continue to prepare the cargo. In *C. Wilh. Svenssons Travaruaktiebolag* v. *Cliffe SS. Co.*[60] the scope of the operation of loading was discussed. It was said to involve all that was required—including stowing and, it seems, where necessary, lashing—to put the cargo in a condition in which it could be carried. A ship, chartered to carry pit props from Swedish ports to England, took a list at the second loading port, losing a large quantity of cargo which went overboard. By then the last sling load of deck cargo had been placed on deck but not stowed. The charterers sued the shipowners for the value of the cargo lost. It was held that as at the beginning of loading the ship was seaworthy to receive and hold the cargo, and as at the time of the loss loading had not been completed, all the cargo not having been stowed, there was no breach of the warranty of seaworthiness; the charterers were not entitled to recover. Wright J. pointed out that there were stages of unseaworthiness, the first being on the beginning of the operation of loading, and the next at the completion of loading. The shipowners argued that loading for that purpose meant simply the reception of the goods on board, notwithstanding that some stowage might be necessary. Wright J. said of this argument[61]:

"I think that in a case like this, and, indeed, in most cases, the mere reception or dumping down of the cargo on the ship does not involve the completion of the loading, because I think the operation of loading involves all that is required to put the cargo in a condition in which it can be carried."

He went on to say that some stowage was still needed when the list occurred[62]:

"Some operation of stowing, however, was necessary in respect of each sling—some props would not fall in the right position and would have to be straightened out, and the props generally would have to be arranged so that they would lie as closely as possible together with their round sides as neatly in contact as could be achieved."

Though it was a small operation, taking only a few minutes for each sling load, it remained to be done in respect of the last sling load; loading had not been completed.

---

[58] For mitigation of damages generally where demurrage claims are concerned, see § 8–43 below.

[59] Including stowage (see § 1–12 below); lashing (§ 1–12 below); and bagging (§ 1–13 below). Decisions as to the effect of time spent in opening and closing hatches depend upon the particular charterparty and whether charterers or shipowners do the work.

[60] [1932] 1 K.B. 490.

[61] At pp. 494–495.

[62] At p. 495.

Wright J. said that he did not have to decide whether lashing was a part   **1–13**
of the loading operation, but that he would have held, on the facts, that it
was. He added[63]:

> "Though the lashing is done by the crew, it is done immediately after the stevedores
> have finished their work—the crew were actually engaged in lashing the after-deck cargo
> when this accident occured—and I think that it is an integral part of the operation of
> loading in the case of a vessel situated like this and lying with her deck cargo in an
> exposed roadstead."

In similar circumstances it is therefore probable that time spent in lashing
the cargo would count as time used in loading.

The views of Wright J. were quoted in *Argonaut Navigation Co. Ltd.* v.
Ministry of Food,[64] where grain had to be bagged for stowage in the tween
decks[65] after the charterers had loaded it on board. Holding that bagging
and stowage were part of the loading, Sellers J. said[66]:

> "Often the delivery of cargo on board a vessel is slowed down because of the difficulty
> of stowing certain kinds of cargo or of stowing it in a place particularly difficult of access
> or by reason of its structure or some obstruction. I have never heard it suggested in such a
> case that in assessing the time taken in loading for purposes of demurrage an apportion-
> ment should take place (on some estimated basis, for accuracy would be impossible)
> between time taken in stowing and time taken in bringing the goods to the hold. I can see
> no reason why it should be different with bulk cargo, which has to be trimmed, or, to
> some extent, put into bags for the purpose of safety or for complying with enforceable
> regulations the object of which is safety."

The operation of loading a tanker was considered in *Total Transport Cor-*   **1–14**
poration v. *Amoco Trading Co.*[67] The charterparty, under which crude oil
was carried from Ashtart, Tunisia, to Genoa, provided:

> "10. Pumping in and out. The cargo shall be pumped into the vessel at
> the expense . . . risk and peril of the charterer . . . "; and:
> "11. Hoses for loading and discharging shall be connected and discon-
> nected by the charterer . . . at the charterers' risk and expense.
> Laytime shall continue until the hoses have been disconnected."

A question arose as to liability for time spent in flushing sealines and ballasting a loading barge, an operation which occurred immediately loading
was completed but before the hoses were disconnected.

The sequence was:

August 2	0830	End of loading
	0930	Began to flush sealines and ballast loading barge
	2024	Ballasting ended
	2054	Hoses disconnected

It was held that laytime continued until the hoses had been disconnected. The judge said that, if that was wrong, then by implication time
spent in flushing shore pipelines after loading counted as laytime whether
or not it was required by charterers, and *a fortiori* if it was required by
them. If laytime continued until loading had been completed, then loading
was not completed until 2054 hours because each successive stage of the

---

[63] At p. 496.
[64] [1949] 1 K.B. 14 (*The Argobec*). (Affirmed by the Court of Appeal [1949] 1 K.B. 572). The
charterparty was on the Baltimore Form C.
[65] For time spent trimming bulk wheat, see §§ 1–17–1–18 below.
[66] [1949] 1 K.B. 14 at p. 20.
[67] [1985] 1 Lloyd's Rep. 423 (*The Altus*).

voyage[68] began immediately upon the termination of the preceding stage, and because it could not be said that the ballasting was part of the carrying voyage.

1–15 Fulfilment of charterers' duties

The duties of charterers, so far as they relate to the task of loading, are sometimes said, incorrectly, to come to an end as the cargo passes across the ship's rail.

It is true that in *Harris* v. *Best, Ryley & Co.*[69] Lord Esher M.R. said[70]:

> "By universal practice the shipper has to bring the cargo alongside so as to enable the shipowner to load the ship within the time stipulated by the charterparty, and to lift that cargo to the rail of the ship. It is then the duty of the shipowner to be ready to take such cargo on board and to stow it in the vessel."

Nevertheless, he also stressed that loading was a joint operation; it was

> " . . . a joint act of the shipper or charterer and of the shipowner; neither of them is to do it alone, but it is to be the joint act of both. What is the obligation on each of them in that matter? Each is to do his own part of the work, and to do whatever is reasonable to enable the other to do his part."

In a later case,[71] dealing with discharging, he said:

> "The shipowner has performed the principal part of his obligation when he has put the goods over the rail of his ship; but I think he must do something more—he must put the goods in such a position that the consignee can take delivery of them. He must put them so far over the side as that the consignee can begin to act upon them; but the moment the goods are put within the reach of the consignee he must take his part in the operation."

This comment also emphasises the joint nature of the activity.[72]

1–16 The ship's rail is often mentioned in connection with the question of responsibility for the care of the cargo. The Carriage of Goods by Sea Act 1971 states in its Schedule,[73] however:

> " 'Carriage of goods' covers the period from the time when the goods are loaded on to the time they are discharged from the ship."

Since loading and, by implication, discharging are joint operations, it is difficult to envisage the termination, at the ship's rail, of the responsibility of one of the parties. It is in accordance with commercial usage to regard a party as responsible so long as he is doing, in the words of Lord Esher M.R., "his own part of the work." Neither the Brussels Convention of 1924 nor the Carriage of Goods by Sea Act 1971 contains any reference to the ship's rail.

---

[68] For the four stages, see § 4–02.

[69] (1892) 68 L.T. 76 (C.A.).

[70] *Ibid.* at p. 77.

[71] *Petersen* v. *Freebody* [1895] 2 Q.B. 294 (C.A.) at p. 297.

[72] So also Lord Diplock, referring to the four stages involved in a voyage charterparty (the loading voyage, the loading operation, the carrying voyage and the discharging operation) said: "In all four of these stages acts of performance by the shipowner are called for; in the two voyage stages acts of performance by him alone . . . Loading and discharging are joint operations." See *Oldendorff (E.L.) & Co. G.m.b.H.* v. *Tradax Export S.A. (The Johanna Oldendorff)* [1973] 2 Lloyd's Rep. 285 at p. 304.

[73] Art. 1(e). The Act replaced the Carriage of Goods by Sea Act 1924 as a result of the Carriage of Goods by Sea Act (Commencement) Order 1977 (S.I. 1977 No. 981), on June 23, 1977. The 1971 Act's definition of "Carriage of goods" is the same as that contained in the 1924 Act.

The view that the ship's rail was significant was discussed by Devlin J. in *Pyrene Co. Ltd.* v. *Scindia Navigation Co. Ltd.*[74]:

> "Only the most enthusiastic lawyer could watch with satisfaction the spectacle of liabilities shifting uneasily as the cargo sways at the end of a derrick across a notional perpendicular projecting from the ship's rail."

In that case a fire-tender being loaded by ship's tackle was dropped and damaged before it crossed the ship's rail. No bill of lading had been issued. It was held that the shipowners could limit their liability in accordance with the Hague Rules, as the process of loading had begun.

The charterers' duty is to bring the cargo to or to take it from the ship. They must do the whole of their part of the business of loading or discharging within the laytime. As the cargo is placed on board, it becomes the shipowners' duty to receive and stow it, subject of course to any express charterparty provision by which the charterers assume this duty. The completion of the charterers' own duties as to the loading does not necessarily bring the loading to an end for the purpose of the laytime calculations.[75]

DISCHARGING

Seaworthy trim   **1–17**

Time debited to charterers for the loading operation may include time spent in stowage,[76] lashing[77] and bagging[78] and includes all time occupied in putting the cargo in a condition in which it can be carried. However, time spent at a first discharging port in putting the ship back into seaworthy trim for the passage to the second discharging port does not count unless there are express words to that effect in the charterparty.

In *Chandris* v. *Government of India*[79] wheat was carried from Argentina   **1–18** to India under an Austral[80] charterparty with a seaworthy trim clause which stated: " . . . any expenses incurred by the shipowners at the first port of discharge in shifting, discharging and/or reloading any cargo . . . for the purpose of putting the vessel into seaworthy trim for the passage to the second port . . . shall be paid by the charterers . . . " After a partial discharge of the cargo at Cochin there was a delay of 21 hours to put the ship into seaworthy trim for Bombay. The bulk wheat was trimmed into the lower holds, covered with tarpaulins, and bagged wheat[81] was stacked over it. The shipowners claimed as "expense . . . at the first port of discharge" both money spent on crew overtime and an amount for loss of 21 hours ship's time, or, in the alternative, demurrage. One of their arguments was that the time should count as lay days because it was time occupied in discharging the cargo, in that the discharge could not be said to be completed until the ship was made trim again to proceed on her voyage. The Court of Appeal held that the charterers were liable for the crew overtime money but not for the delay. "Expense" meant money spent out of

---

[74] [1954] 2 Q.B. 402 at p. 416.
[75] See *Argonaut Navigation Co. Ltd.* v. *Ministry of Food (The Argobec)* [1949] 1 K.B. 14 at p. 20; see also § 1–13 above.
[76] See § 1–12 above.
[77] See § 1–12 above.
[78] See § 1–13 above.
[79] [1956] 1 Lloyd's Rep. 11 (C.A.).
[80] Australian Grain Charter 1928.
[81] For time spent bagging grain for stowage, see § 1–13 above.

pocket[82] and did not include loss of time. The alternative argument, that the time should count as lay days, was rejected on the ground that the trimming was no part of the discharging operation, which had already ended. As Morris L.J. said[83]:

> "If the parties had wished to provide that, in the stipulated circumstances , any time occupied at the first port of discharge in shifting cargo for the purpose of putting the vessel into seaworthy trim for passage to the second port should count as part of the lay days, it would have been easy for them so to provide and to use language comparable to that used where in various events they were agreeing that time should for certain purposes count."

1–19   The decision in the *Chandris* case was followed in *Carras (J.C.) & Sons (Shipbrokers) Ltd.* v. *President of India*,[84] where wheat was carried from Beaumont, Texas, to Calcutta, with Madras as the lightening port, under a Baltimore Form C charterparty with a seaworthy trim clause stating: " . . . vessel to be left in seaworthy trim to shift between ports." After unloading ended at Madras there was left a free surface of grain, which rendered the ship unseaworthy; the receivers' stevedores filled 9,900 bags with grain and stowed them on the surface. During the bagging period the harbour authorities ordered the ship to shift to buoys. The charterers said that laytime did not run during that period. They also resisted alternative claims for the shifting expenses, and for running costs and profit during the bagging period, saying that the seaworthy trim provision (a) did not apply at a lightening port; (b) applied only to distribution of the cargo; or (c) was declaratory only and had no legal effect. Mocatta J. first dismissed[85] the contention by charterers that the seaworthy trim provision applied where there were two ports of discharge as opposed to one port of discharge with a lightening port. He rejected[86] the argument that the words "to be left in seaworthy trim" applied only to leaving the ship on an even keel without a list to port or starboard.[87] Nor, he said,[88] were the words merely declaratory. As to laytime, he said[89]: " . . . when all the cargo to be unloaded at a first or lightening port has been landed on the quay, or into lighters when these are used, discharge at such port has, in my judgement, ended, and laytime does not continue to run during the time taken to put the vessel in seaworthy trim. This conclusion follows similar opinions expressed in the Court of Appeal in *The Eugenia Chandris*.[90] . . . " That case had turned upon the words "any expense incurred by the shipowners," which were now absent; the charterers had here to pay to put the ship into seaworthy trim to shift between ports, so far as she had been made unseaworthy by reason of the unloading. The shipowners were entitled to recover the shifting expense; but the charterers were not obliged to bear the running cost and the daily profit.

---

[82] Such expense, incurred in the discharge of the obligation to make the ship fit to meet the perils of the passage to the next port, had been held to fall upon charterers: *Britain SS. Co.* v. *Louis Dreyfus & Co.* (1935) 51 L.L. Rep. 196.

[83] [1956] 1 Lloyd's Rep. 11 (C.A.) at p. 22.

[84] *(The Argobeam)* [1970] 1 Lloyd's Rep. 282.

[85] At p. 290.

[86] At p. 291.

[87] He applied the decision of Mackinnon J. in *Britain SS. Co. Ltd.* v. *Louis Dreyfus & Co.* (1935) 51 Ll.L. Rep. 196. See n. 82 above.

[88] At p. 291.

[89] At p. 291.

[90] *Chandris* v. *Government of India* [1956] 1 Lloyd's Rep. 11 (C.A.) at pp. 17, 19 and 23. See § 1–18 above.

End of discharging   **1–20**

The difficulties involved in deciding when discharging has finished are apparent from the following passage from the judgment of McCardie J. in *Transoceanica Societa Italiana di Navigazione v. H.S. Shipton & Sons.*[91] Shipowners claimed demurrage for delay at London owing to the inferior condition of barley loaded at Alexandria (the bills of lading contained no demurrage provision and did not refer to the charterparty) and part of the charges which as a result they had been obliged to pay to the Port of London Authority. He said[92]:

> "The operation of unloading is a joint operation. The trimmers are in the hold and they are called ship's men and work on behalf of the ship . . . But the operations from the time the grain is elevated from the hold and taken upwards till it gets to the warehouse where it is put into bags and then into craft are done on behalf of the receivers. Therefore although there is one totality of operations, as a matter of fact there is a clear division with respect to the allocation of work."

The receivers were held liable for their proportion of the charges but not for the delay, as there was no warranty that the barley was capable of being handled expeditiously, and in the circumstances they had discharged it in a reasonable time. Though the case does not deal with the termination of laytime, it appears from the judgment of McCardie J. that time runs until the work allocated to the shipowners has come to an end and, further, until the charterers' proportion of the work has been completed, to the extent that the ship can depart.[92a]

Shipowners' duties may include the delivery of the cargo into receivers'   **1–21** barges or lighters,[93] to the quay (either into wagons or on to the open quay),[94] or sometimes, in the case of logs at certain discharging places, into the water.[95]

---

[91] [1923] 1 K.B. 31.

[92] *Ibid.* at pp. 42–43.

[92a] There may be express provision for laytime or demurrage to end when some other event has occurred. In a London arbitration (LMLN 80, November 25, 1982) the ship was to go to two ports, "Leixoes—Hamburg range . . . charters option further discharge port, charterers paying all port costs and laytime counting from taking inward pilot to dropping outward pilot third discharge port." She carried logs and lumber from Sinoe, Liberia, to Leixoes, Santander and Amsterdam. Although the charterers said that demurrage ended on the completion of discharge, the arbitrators considered that the whole of the provision as to the third discharging port showed the intention to have been that time should count, whether as laytime or as demurrage, until the dropping of the pilot.

[93] *Catley* v. *Wintringham* (1793) 1 Peake N.P.C. 202; *Robinson* v. *Turpin* (1805) 1 Peake N.P.C. 203n.

[94] *Hyde* v. *Trent and Mersey Navigation Co.* (1793) 5 T.R. 397.

[95] The expression "discharging" may include a number of operations; see *British Steel Corporation* v. *National Dock Labour Board* [1970] 2 Lloyd's Rep. 137 at p. 141, *per* Cooke J.

CHAPTER 2

LAYTIME CLAUSES AND THEIR EFFECTS

I. TYPES OF CLAUSE

2–01   LAYTIME may be fixed, in which case it is expressly stated, as in "six running days,"[1] or calculable, as in "250 tons per weather working day."[2] It may be unspecified, as in "Cargo to be supplied as fast as steamer can receive and stow," or as in charterparties where there is no reference to the speed of loading and discharging. It is determined by the shipowners and the charterers when the terms of the charterparty are agreed. They take into account their knowledge of the trade, the ports concerned, and the current value of the ship in the chartering market.

2–02   **1. Where laytime is expressly stated**
        When laytime is fixed it can be stated expressly[3]:
        (1) By reference to days.
        (2) By reference to hours.

2–03   (1) *By reference to days*
        These may be described as days, running days or working days.[4]

2–04   A. *Days*
        "The cargo shall be loaded in . . . days and discharged in . . . days."[5]

2–05   B. *Running days*[6]
        "Laytime for loading shall be no more than . . . running days of 24 hours . . . " and "The cargo shall be discharged . . . in no more than . . . running days of 24 hours . . . "[7]
        "Laytime for loading shall be no more than three (3) running days of 24 hours . . . "[8]

2–06   C. *Working days*[9]
        "The cargo shall be
        (A) loaded in . . . discharged in . . .
        or (B) loaded and discharged in . . . full working days . . . "[10]

        [1] See § 2–20.
        [2] See § 2–56.
        [3] The examples are drawn from a number of well-known charterparties and in particular from those issued or approved by the Baltic and International Maritime Council and the General Council of British Shipping.
        [4] See § 2–15 below.
        [5] Often with the addition of such words as "of 24 hours," "of 24 consecutive hours" or "of 24 running hours." See §§ 2–41–2–52 below.
        [6] See also §§ 2–20–2–21 below.
        [7] General Ore Charter Party (Genorecon).
        [8] Iron Ore Charter Party, Vale do Rio Doce Terms 1967 (Riodoceore).
        [9] See also §§ 2–22–2–40 below.
        [10] Scandinavian Voyage Charter 1956 (Scancon).

14

"The cargo to be loaded and discharged . . . in . . . working days reversible, weather permitting . . . "[11]

(2) *By reference to hours*[12] **2–07**
"Cargo to be loaded in . . . running hours[13]
"Laytime . . . running hours Sundays and holidays included."[13a]
"The vessel shall be loaded in . . . running hours . . . "[14]
"Laytime . . . running hours"[14a]
"Cargo to be loaded and discharged in . . . running hours."[15]
"The cargo shall be loaded . . . and discharged in . . . running hours . . . "[16]
"The cargo shall be loaded within the number of running hours as indicated in Box 16"[17]
"The cargo to be loaded in . . . running hours . . . "[18]
"The Vessel shall be loaded and discharged in . . . running hours . . ."[19]
" . . . running hours (Sundays and holidays excepted), weather permitting, shall be allowed the charterers for loading and discharging . . . "[20]
" . . . running hours, weather permitting, Sundays and holidays included"[20a]
"The cargo shall be loaded within the number of running hours as set out in the Loading Scale in force on the date of the Charter Party."[21]
"Laytime . . . running hours Sundays and holidays included."[22]
"Total laytime for load. and disch. in running hours, SHINC[23] . . . "[24]
"Total Laytime in Running Hours . . . "[25]
"The laytime for loading, discharging and all other Charterers' purposes whatsoever shall be the number of running hours specified in Part 1(I)".[25a]

2. Where laytime is calculable **2–08**
Fixed laytime may have to be calculated from the wording of the laytime clause. It may be expressed by reference to:

A. Days or lay days[26] (with no reference to 24 hours).
B. Running days (with no reference to 24 hours).[27]

---

[11] Norsk Hydro-Elektrisk 1923 (Hydrocharter). For "reversible" days, see § 8–09 below.
[12] For "running hours," see § 2–66 below.
[13] Cement Charterparty 1922 (Cemenco), as amended in 1974.
[13a] Intertankvoy 76.
[14] Coasting Coal Charter-Party, 1913 (Welcon).
[14a] Shellvoy 5.
[15] Stone Charterparty 1920 (Panstone).
[16] Fertilisers Charter 1942 (Ferticon).
[17] Uniform General Charter 1922 (Gencon).
[18] Coal Charter 1921 (Baltcon); East Coast Coal Charter Party 1922 (Medcon).
[19] Coasting Coal Charter-Parties 1913 (Welcon) and 1920 (Coastcon).
[20] Tank Vessel Voyage Charter-Party.
[20a] Beepeevoy.
[21] Coal Voyage Charter 1971 (Polcoalvoy), revised in 1976.
[22] Tanker Voyage Charter-Party (Intertankvoy 76).
[23] Saturdays and holidays included.
[24] Gas Voyage Charter-Party (Gasvoy) and Baltic and International Maritime Council Standard Voyage Charter Party for Vegetable/Animal Oils and Fats (Biscoilvoy).
[25] Tanker Voyage Charter-Party (Warshipoilvoy).
[25a] Shellvoy 5.
[26] See §§ 2–15–2–19 below.
[27] See §§ 2–20–2–21 below.

    C. Working days (with no reference to 24 hours).[28]
    D. Days of 24 hours or 24 consecutive hours.[29]
    E. The number of working or workable hatches.[30]
    F. Weather working days (with no reference to 24 hours).[31]

2–09 A. *Days or lay days (with no reference to 24 hours)*[32]
"Scale for loading and Discharging

    up to 1,000 tons—300 tons per day
    10/1400 tons—350 tons per day
    14/1800 tons—400 tons per day
    18/2200 tons—450 tons per day
    If larger by arrangement."[33]

2–10 B. *Running days (with no reference to 24 hours)*[34]
"The steamer shall be loaded at the rate of 500 tons per running day" and various discharging rates for Bristol Channel, Irish, London and Dutch ports.[35]

2–11 C. *Working days (with no reference to 24 hours)*[36]

2–12 D. *Days of 24 hours, 24 consecutive hours and 24 running hours*[37]
"The cargo shall be loaded at not less than the average rate of 1,500 tons for vessels with a summer deadweight of . . . per weather working day of 24 consecutive hours . . . "[38]
"The cargo shall be loaded and discharged within the number of hours/days of 24 consecutive hours stated in Box 19(c) . . . "[39]
"The cargo shall be loaded at the average rate as stated in Box 13 per metric tons per weather working day of 24 consecutive hours . . . " and "The cargo shall be taken from alongside by the Consignees at the port of discharge . . . at the average rate as stated in Box 19 per tons of 1,000 kilos per day of 24 running hours. . . . "[40]
"The cargo to be shipped at the rate of . . . tons and to be discharged at the rate of 500 tons per clear working day of 24 consecutive hours."[41]
"The cargo . . . shall be loaded at the average rate of . . . standards for Deals and Battens . . . standards for Boards and/or Board Ends under 1 in. thick, and . . . standards for other goods, all per workable hatch per weather working day of 24 consecutive hours."[42]

---

[28] See §§ 2–22–2–40 below.
[29] See §§ 2–41–2–52 below.
[30] See §§ 2–53–2–58 below.
[31] See §§ 2–59–2–61 below.
[32] See §§ 2–15–2–19 below.
[33] Phosphate Charter 1914 (Phoscon).
[34] See §§ 2–20–2–21 below.
[35] River Plate Charter-Party 1914 (Centrocon).
[36] See §§ 2–22–2–40 below.
[37] See §§ 2–41–2–52 below.
[38] Australian Grain Charter 1972.
[39] Baltic and International Maritime Conference Standard Ore Charter-Party (Orevoy).
[40] Soviet Coal Charter 1962 (Sovcoal).
[41] Mediterranean Iron Ore Charter Party (C.(Ore) 7).
[42] Soviet Wood Charter Party 1961 (Sovietwood).

"Cargo to be loaded at the average rate of . . . Board Measure Feet/ Cubic Meters per weather working day of 24 consecutive hours . . . "[43]

E. *The number of working or workable hatches*[44]   **2–13**

"The cargo shall be discharged by the Consignees . . . at the average rate of . . . standards per workable hatch per weather working day."

" . . . at the average rate of 1000 metric tonnes basis 5 or more available working hatches . . . "[44a]

"150 metric tons per workable hatch and pro rata with maximum 750 metric tons per weather working day."[44b]

F. *Weather working days (with no reference to 24 hours)*[45]   **2–14**

"The cargo shall be discharged by the Consignees . . . at the average rate of . . . standards per workable hatch per weather working day."

"The cargo shall be loaded at the average rate of 500 tons for cargo in bags and 1,000 tons for cargo in bulk, per weather working day."[46]

"Laytime computed at the rate of . . . tons (2,240 pounds) each per weather working lay day . . . "[47]

II. EXPLANATION AND APPLICATION

A. Days[47a]   **2–15**

The charterparty clauses quoted show that where the laytime is expressly stated,[47b] or calculable, days are variously described as mere "days,"[48] "running days"[49], "working days"[50] or "weather working days."[51]

Where cargo is to be loaded at a certain rate per day, the quantity actually loaded, and not the quantity which should or might have been loaded, is the amount into which the daily rate should be divided.

---

[43] Nanyozai Charter Party 1967.

[44] See §§ 2–53–2–58 below. In a London arbitration (LMLN 129, October 11, 1984) the charterparty provided that laytime for loading should be calculated thus: "150 m.t. per Hook PWWD of 24 consec. hrs." The tribunal said that this gave a more accurate picture of the ship's cargo handling capacity than would a mere reference to the number of hatches or holds.

[44a] As in *President of India* v. *Jebsens (U.K.) Ltd.* [1987] 2 Lloyd's Rep. 354 (*The General Capinpin*). See § 2–55A below.

[44b] As in *Cargill Incorporated* v. *Marpro Ltd.* [1983] 2 Lloyd's Rep. 570 (*The Aegis Progress*). See § 2–55A below.

[45] See §§ 2–59–2–61 below.

[46] Australian Grain Charter 1928 (Austral).

[47] Bulk Sugar Charter—U.S.A., October, 1969.

[47a] The Charterparty Laytime Definitions 1980 (see Appendix to this book) state: "11. 'DAY'—means a continuous period of 24 hours which, unless the context otherwise requires, runs from midnight to midnight."

[47b] The words "discharging 2500/3000 per day," appearing in a booking note relating to the carriage of sugar from Port Sudan to Jeddah, were held to be sufficiently certain, and the minimum rate was applied, in *The Siam Venture* and *The Darfur* [1987] 1 Lloyd's Rep. 147. It was contended, unsuccessfully, that the words were too vague to create an obligation to discharge at a rate which was certain or a rate by which laytime could be calculated. Sheen J. said that no authority was cited in support of the proposition; and he accepted the argument that if there were alternative ways of performing a contractual obligation the plaintiffs could only enforce the contract in the way least burdensome on the defendants.

[48] See §§ 2–15–2–19.

[49] See §§ 2–20–2–21 below.

[50] See §§ 2–22–2–40 below.

[51] See §§ 2–59–2–61 below.

In *Hain Steamship Co. Ltd.* v. *The Minister of Food*[52] a charterparty for the carriage of wheat, maize and rye from the River Plate to the United Kingdom gave charterers the option of shipping other lawful merchandise. The charterparty also provided: "The steamer shall be loaded at the rate of 500 tons per running day." Disputes arose as to the measure of freight to be paid and as to whether laytime was to be calculated, as charterers said, on the basis of the ship's deadweight capacity, or, as the shipowners contended, on the basis of the cargo actually loaded or delivered. It was held that the shipowners were right. The laytime clause was independent of the freight clauses. Tucker L.J. said of the laytime provision[53]:

> " . . . if it was to have the meaning attributed to it by Sir William McNair[54] it would certainly have to read: 'The steamer shall be loaded at the rate of 500 tons per running day, calculated on the deadweight capacity of the ship.' "

It was once customary to speak of "days" without qualification. The expression covered all types of days, whether or not work was normally done then. Disputes arose as to whether such days as Sundays and holidays should count. The phrase "Sundays[55] and holidays excepted"[56] is now almost invariably added to make it clear, if the parties so intend, that such days are not to be counted against the charterers.

As Lord Esher M.R. put it in *Nielsen* v. *Wait*[57]:

> " 'Lay days' are described in a charterparty in various ways; sometimes certain days are fixed for loading or unloading. If those days are described simply as days, then although they are not so called when they are said to be for loading or unloading, nevertheless they are 'lay days.' 'Days' and 'lay days' are really the same in a charterparty."

2–16   *All calendar days are "days"*

The word "days" without more, means "continous days," but an exception is made for Sundays and holidays if there is a custom[58] or express provision to the contrary. It is a custom not to work in most countries on holidays; in most countries with Christian associations on Sunday; and in many other countries on that or another day. It is therefore arguable that such days will be interrupted by virtue of the custom, even though they are not expressly excluded. In such a case "days" would mean working days[59] and only "running days"[60] would be truly consecutive.

Thus in *Brown* v. *Johnson*[61] Lord Abinger C.B. said[62]:

> "I think the word 'days' and 'running days' mean the same thing, *viz.* consecutive days, unless there be some particular custom. If the parties wish to exclude any days from the computation, they must be expressed."[63]

---

[52] [1949] 1 K.B. 492 (C.A.).
[53] At p. 507.
[54] Counsel for the charterers.
[55] Or Fridays where Moslem countries are concerned.
[56] See § 8–03 below.
[57] (1885) 16 Q.B.D. 67 (C.A.) at p. 71. For the facts in that case, see §§ 2–20–2–21 below.
[58] See § 2–17 below.
[59] See § 2–18 below.
[60] See § 2–20 below.
[61] (1842) 10 M. & W. 331.
[62] At p. 334.
[63] So also Lord Esher M.R. in *Nielsen* v. *Wait* (1885) 16 Q.B.D. 67 (C.A.) at p. 73: "With 'running days' or with 'days' only there is nothing to take out the consecutiveness in the mere phraseology."

Days treated as working days. An early example of some "particular custom"[64] altering the ordinary meaning and effect of the word "day" is to be found in *Cochran* v. *Retberg*.[65] A bill of lading for goods carried from the River Elbe to London stated in the margin: "To be discharged in fourteen days, or to pay five guineas per day demurrage." The charterers argued successfully that in the port of London this meant 14 working days, and did not include Sundays and custom house holidays. This resulted in demurrage starting later than it otherwise would have done, as December 21 (St. Thomas's Day) was then a holiday, and Christmas Day and the three days following it were also holidays. Goods could not be landed at the custom house then, though they could be discharged into lighters. There was contradictory evidence from witnesses as to whether "days" meant running days or working days. Lord Eldon said[66]:

> "If no evidence had been offered, but I was to decide on the clause itself, I should have been of opinion that it meant running days . . . As the law however stands, usage may be admitted to establish the meaning of the words used in the margin of the bill of lading; whether the words 'days' used in it, means running days or working-days . . . as the question now stands, it is a matter of general importance to have the opinion of a special jury of the city of London on the usage of trade, with respect to instruments of this description . . . if it is left to the construction of law, I should be of opinion the Plaintiff ought to succeed; if the fact of usage is clearly made out, that the fourteen days mentioned in the bills of lading means working days, that is a construction which excludes Sundays and holidays at the custom-house; there must be a verdict for the defendant."

The jury found for the defendants, ·*i.e.* the cargo interests. This appears to be the earliest recorded case in which the meaning of the word "days" was discussed.

So also in *Commercial SS. Co.* v. *Boulton*,[67] "days" were held to mean   **2–18** working days. The charterparty stated: " . . . loading and discharging the ship as fast as the steamer can work, but a minimum of seven days to be allowed merchants, and ten days on demurrage over and above the said lying days, at £25 per day." The lay days were used up at the loading port, near Riga. If the "lying days" were running days, then a Sunday at the loading port would count, and the ship would have been on demurrage there for one day; if the "lying days" were nor running days, and were working days, then only the lying days were exhausted at the loading port. The ship got into dock in London on a Tuesday at 5 p.m., berthed the next day and ended the discharge at 8 a.m. on the Thursday. The shipowners argued that lying days must mean running days, and that it was the general meaning of the expression unless the term "working days" was expressly used.[68] It was held, in favour of the charterers, that the seven days of laytime must mean working days, so that no demurrage was incurred at the loading port. The court was influenced by the laytime clause taken as a whole, with its words "as fast as the steamer can work, but a minimum of

---

[64] The words used by Lord Abinger C.B. in *Brown* v. *Johnson* (1842) 10 M. & W. 331 at p. 334; see § 2–16 above.
[65] (1800) 3 Esp. 121.
[66] At pp. 122–123.
[67] (1875) L.R. 10 Q.B. 346.
[68] They relied on *Brown* v. *Johnson* (1842) 10 M. & W. 331. There "days" were indeed held to mean running, *i.e.* consecutive, days though the court recognised that custom or express words might alter the situation. See § 4–12 below.

seven days to be allowed merchants . . . "[69] The court held also that the shipowners were entitled to two days on demurrage, *i.e.* the Wednesday and Thursday, although the ship was released at 8 a.m. on the Thursday.[70]

2–19   *Days and working days.* In *Niemann* v. *Moss*[71] a cargo of coals was "to be loaded in Liverpool in fourteen days, and to be discharged, weather permitting, at not less than twenty-five tons per working day (holidays excepted) . . . " Holding that the 14 days were running days, and not working days,[72] Wightman J. said[73]:

> " . . . there is an obvious difference between the time for loading and the time for discharging. The one is so much time as it would take to discharge the cargo at the rate of twenty-five tons per working day; the other is fourteen days, including holidays."

And Blackburn J. added[74]:

> "According to the natural and grammatical construction, the words in the parenthesis are to be referred to the last antecedent, and the only reason against doing so is, that the words 'holidays excepted' are useless, as such days could not be included within the term 'working days.' But such an argument is not of much weight in the construction of documents."

Here the difference between a rate per "working day" for discharge and the mere "days" for loading was significant.

2–20 B. Running days[74a]

The term "running day" is used to distinguish mere days (*i.e.* ordinary calendar days, including Sundays and holidays) from "working days."[75] It is clearer than "days" and from the point of view of the shipowners it is more advantageous than "working" days.[76]

Lord Esher M.R. said in *Nielsen* v. *Wait*[77] that the term "running days" eliminated the unsatisfactory way in which the term "working days" excluded Sundays and holidays. In that case the charterparty provided "Eight running days, Sundays excepted" for loading and discharging. The question was whether in addition to the lightening time at Sharpness, 17 miles from the Gloucester basin, there should be counted the time taken to travel between Sharpness and the basin. The Court of Appeal decided that although "a ship is running . . . every day, day and night,"[78] time would not count when discharging was interrupted.

2–21   *Origin of the term "running days"*

In considering the emergence of the expression "running days," Lord Esher M.R.[79] discussed the use of the term "working days":

> "Merchants and shipowners have thought that this arrangement was not satisfactory to

---

[69] See Lush J. at p. 347.
[70] On the treatment of part of a day as a whole for demurrage purposes, see § 10–48.
[71] (1860) 29 L.J.Q.B. 206.
[72] This calculation would have resulted in the omission of two Sundays.
[73] At p. 207.
[74] At p. 208.
[74a] The Charterparty Laytime Definitions 1980 (see Appendix to this book) state: "15. 'RUNNING DAYS' or 'CONSECUTIVE DAYS'—means days which follow one immediately after the other."
[75] See § 2–22 below.
[76] For running working days, see § 2–39 below.
[77] (1885) 16 Q.B.D. 67 (C.A.) at p. 71.
[78] Lord Esher M.R. at p. 72.
[79] *Ibid.* at pp. 71–72.

them, and that the lay days ought to be counted irrespectively of that custom'', [the custom of a port by which work is not done on certain days] ''so that the charterer should take the risk whether work is done on Sundays or holidays at the ports. They, therefore, introduced a new term, which is 'running days,' . . . What is the run of the ship? how many days does it take a ship to run from the West Indies to England? that is the running of the ship. The run of a ship is a phrase well known. What are 'running days'? It is a nautical phrase . . . the parties are describing the days about which they are talking, namely, days in a port, according to the phraseology which they use with regard to a ship at sea . . .''

Where the word ''running'' is added to ''days'' any exception for Sundays and holidays should be expressly incorporated or justified by a custom. Thus in *Nielsen* v. *Wait*[80] Lord Esher M.R. said:

'' . . . is the phraseology of 'running days' contradicted by proof of a custom, which says that some intermediate days, such as Sundays, are at the port in question to be taken out? It does not seem to me that there is any contradiction. It is an explanation how the running days in that charterparty are to be worked, and they are not to be worked consecutively if the custom is contrary.''

In the absence of an express incorporation or a custom time runs against the cargo interests unless the consecutiveness is impaired, as by the inability of the ship to accept or to deliver her cargo.

C. Working days

2–22

Meaning of ''working day.''[80a] A working day is a period of 24 hours (prima facie starting at one midnight and finishing at the next midnight[81]), in the course of which work is usually done at the port in question, in the sense that the day is not a day of rest,[82] or a holiday.[83]

The use of the expression ''working days''[84] makes it clear that Sundays and holidays do not count, although such days may be excluded where the mere word ''days'' is used, if there is a custom to that effect.[85] Such an exclusion extends to other days on which work is not usually done, such as Fridays in Moslem countries. As Lord Devlin said in *Reardon Smith Line Ltd.* v. *Ministry of Agriculture*[86]:

'' . . . there may, of course, be days in some ports, such as the Mahomedan Friday, which are not working days and yet cannot be described as Sundays or holidays.''

The rule that a working day starts at one midnight and finishes at the next is said to be a prima facie rule because its application may be rebutted by suitable words. Thus, if time is to start at a fixed time after notice of readiness,[87] this rule still applies except that each period of 24 hours starts instead at the fixed time.

During such a period, not comprising a calendar day, a day of rest or a holiday may begin. As such a day must itself last 24 hours, the 24-hour working day is then broken into two parts, one before and one after the

---

[80] (1885) 16 Q.B.D. 67 (C.A.) at p. 73.
[80a] The Charterparty Laytime Definitions 1980 (see Appendix to this book) state: ''14. 'WORKING DAYS'—means days or part(s) thereof which are not expressly excluded from laytime by the charterparty and which are not holidays.''
[81] For the legal authorities, see § 2–26 below.
[82] See Sundays in § 8–06 below.
[83] See Holidays in § 8–08 below.
[84] For running working days, see § 2–39 below.
[85] See *Cochran* v. *Retberg* (1800) 3 Esp. 121 and *Commercial Steam Ship Co.* v. *Boulton* (1875) L.R. 10 Q.B. 346; and see § 2–18 above.
[86] [1963] A.C. 691 (H.L.) at p. 736.
[87] See § 2–23: ''At what time does the first day begin?''

interruption. As Mackinnon J. put it in *Hain SS. Co.* v. *Sociedad Anonima Commercial de Exportacion e Importacion*[88]:

> " . . . the excepted day, running from midnight to midnight, had to be cut out."

2–23 *At what time does the first day begin?*

Laytime usually begins when the notice requirements[89] have been satisfied, though sometimes a further agreed period must elapse. Thus the Gencon charterparty[90] states, at clause 6(c): "Laytime for loading and discharging shall commence at 1 p.m. if notice of readiness is given before noon, and 6 a.m. next working day if notice given during office hours after noon." The addition of a further period has its origin in the need to give the cargo interests time to make adequate preperations.

Of course neither the time at which the notice requirements are satisfied nor the time at which the further period has expired need coincide with the first moment of a calendar day. The day may begin its 24 hours at some time other than midnight. In these circumstances each day will be an artificial or conventional day, as opposed to a calendar day.

An example is to be found in *Leonis SS. Co. Ltd.* v. *Rank (No. 2)*,[91] where time was to begin 12 hours after delivery of the written notice of readiness. Bigham J. said of such a provision[92]:

> "That, in my opinion, alters the construction that would otherwise have been put upon the clause, and it makes the loading time commence at an hour during the twenty-four to be reckoned with reference to the notice given by the captain."

So also in *Hain SS. Co. Ltd.* v. *Sociedad Anonima Commercial de Exportacion e Importacion*[93] MacKinnon J. said of certain days:

> "they are clearly not calendar days. They are periods of 24 hours, because time is to begin 12 hours after a certain notice, and from that moment when time begins you take your consecutive periods of 24 hours as 'running days.' "

2–24 *Working day has 24 hours*

The word "working" in the expression "working day" is a description of the day as a whole, distinguishing it from the days of rest and holidays. It does not result in the working day being calculated as a number of hours longer or shorter than 24.

For example, if the working day is customarily one of eight hours, the charterers could not claim to be entitled to work three calendar days before being debited with one working day.[94]

Lord Devlin said in *Reardon Smith Line Ltd.* v. *Ministry of Agriculture*[95]:

> "How do you ascertain what are normal hours? I should agree that there is no way of

---

[88] *(The Trevarrack)* (1934) 49 Ll.L. Rep. 86 at p. 88.
[89] Reaching the destination, readiness, presentation of notice; see § 4–01 below.
[90] As revised in 1976.
[91] (1908) 13 Com.Cas. 161.
[92] At p. 163.
[93] *(The Trevarrack)* (1934) 49 Ll.L. Rep. 86 at p. 88.
[94] In spite of the decision in *Mein* v. *Ottmann* (1904) 6 Fraser (Ct. of Sess., 5th Ser.) 276 which was not followed in *Reardon Smith Line Ltd.* v. *Ministry of Agriculture (The Vancouver Strike Case)* [1963] A.C. 691 (H.L.). For a case in which a consulting engineer and naval architect's total hours worked were divided into periods of seven hours, each equivalent to a day, for the purpose of calculating fees for days worked, see *Rolland* v. *Alachouzos and Helmville Ltd.* [1967] 1 Lloyd's Rep. 126.
[95] *(The Vancouver Strike Case)* [1963] A.C. 691 (H.C.) at p. 741.

answering that except by enquiring what hours are paid for at normal rates. But I think that answer to be quite unrealistic. Overtime in ports is the rule rather than the exception; and collective bargaining in the labour market often produces a rise in wages by means of a reduction in normal hours." He added[96]: "If the working day means the number of hours normally worked in the port, computation would be difficult if there is a number of different loading ports with different standard hours, or if the lay days are reversible.[97] Even in the case of one trade, such as the grain trade, certainty is not achieved, for it appears that the longshoremen work at normal rates on Saturday morning and the elevator men do not. If the parties use the phrase 'working hours'[98] the court must do the best it can with it, though the parties would be well advised to be more precise. But I can see no justification for the court, unless there is something which in the charterparty demands it, turning the working day into a number of working hours."[99]

Non-working days   **2–25**

It is often tempting to describe a day as a non-working day, because it lacks some attributes of a normal working day. Saturdays[1] fall within this class; there are other days on part or all of which some or all classes of labour may receive overtime, or on which the hours of work may differ from those on other days. These factors do not change a working day into a non-working day if they do not also transform it into a holiday or a day of rest. There is no half-way house. In some countries[2] there is indeed a phenomenon known as the non-working holiday,[3] which is officially listed as such; the question then is whether such a day can be called a holiday or not.

Legal authorities generally relating to "working day"   **2–26**

The English law as to the definition of this term may be regarded as having returned, particularly as the result of the decision reached by the House of Lords in *Reardon Smith Line Ltd.* v. *Ministry of Agriculture*,[4] to the position which it occupied before the Court of Appeal decision in *Alvion SS. Corporation Panama* v. *Galban Lobo Trading Co. S.A. of Havana*.[5] In both cases the charterparties provided for "weather working days," but the courts considered also what was meant by the expression "working day."

A working day must be treated as a day of 24 hours, prima facie[6] beginning and ending at midnight. The alternative view, as expressed in *Alvion*, was that a working day began when normal working hours began and ended when they ended.[7] As Lord Keith of Avonholm put it in the *Reardon Smith Line* case[8]:

"I think there has been a tendancy among the mercantile community to escape from the earlier view that a lay day or a lay working day was a calendar day of 24 hours, and the cases seem to show some support by the courts in this direction. When reference to weather working days was introduced into charterparties the conception of working days being days of so many working hours seemed also more realistic as it made for a certain

---

[96] At pp. 741–742.
[97] For reversibility, see § 9–09 below.
[98] The phrase is rarely used.
[99] But the number of working hours must be considered where, in the case of a charterparty specifying not "working days" but "weather working days," there are periods of bad weather; see § 7–20 below.
[1] Discussed below in § 8–15.
[2] Such as Argentina; see § 8–09.
[3] See § 8–12.
[4] *(The Vancouver Strike Case)* [1963] A.C. 691.
[5] *(The Rubystone)* [1955] 1 Q.B. 430.
[6] The application of the rule may be rebutted by suitable words; see § 2–22 above.
[7] See the summary of the facts of that case at §§ 2–34–2–37 below.
[8] [1963] A.C. 691 (H.L.) at p. 725.

precision in estimating the amount of interruption caused by bad weather in the process of loading or discharging cargo. The fixing of working hours might present some difficulty."

Of the leading cases upholding the present definition of "working day" two were decided by the House of Lords, in 1900[9] and 1963[10]; two by the Court of Appeal, in 1885[11] and 1911[12]; and one by the High Court, in 1938.[13] The cases supporting the alternative point of view were decided by the Scottish Court of Session, in 1904[14]; the Court of Appeal, in 1955[15]; and the High Court, in 1962.[16]

2–27   *Authorities upholding present definition of "working day"*
1. *Nielsen* v. *Wait*[17] a Court of Appeal decision,[18] concerned the construction of the phrase "eight running days, Sundays excepted." Lord Esher M.R. said[19]:

> " 'Working days' mean days on which, at the port, according to the custom of the port, work is done in loading and unloading ships, and the phrase does not include Sundays."

He was primarily concerned with the distinction between days, running days and working days, but there is no suggestion that the expression "working day" should be attributed only to such part of a calendar day as is occupied by work.

2–28   2. *Saxon SS. Co* v. *Union SS. Co.*,[20] a House of Lords decision,[21] concerned the meaning of "colliery working day." Lord Halsbury L.C. said[22]:

> "A working day is, I think, in ordinary parlance to be understood as distinguished from a holiday—including in that term a Sunday or some fixed and usual day for rest and not for work, as a Sunday, Christmas Day, Good Friday, and the like."

So also Lord Brampton said[23]:

> "In ordinary parlance to speak of particular days as working days is to distinguish them from Sundays or recognised and established holidays, and is descriptive of them merely as days on which men ordinarily work in their respective callings; it is a general name applied to such days, and means nothing more."

2–29   3. *British and Mexican Shipping Co. Ltd.* v. *Lockett Brothers & Co. Ltd.*,[24] a Court of Appeal decision, concerned the discharge of Canadian lumber at Iquique, Chile, at a certain rate "per working day." In the High Court Hamilton J. (whose decision was reversed but not on this point) said[25]:

---

[9] *Saxon SS. Co.* v. *Union SS. Co.* (1900) 5 Com.Cas. 381.
[10] *Reardon Smith Line Ltd.* v. *Ministry of Agriculture* [1963] A.C. 391.
[11] *Nielsen* v. *Wait* (1885) 16 Q.B.D. 67.
[12] *British & Mexican Shipping Co.* v. *Lockett Bros. & Co. Ltd.* [1911] 1 K.B. 264.
[13] *Z Steamship Co.* v. *Amtorg of New York* (1938) 61 Ll.L. Rep. 97.
[14] *Mein* v. *Ottmann* (1904) 6 Fraser (Ct. of Sess., 5th Ser.) 276.
[15] *Alvion SS. Corporation Panama* v. *Galban Lobo Trading Co. S.A. of Havana (The Rubystone)* [1955] 1 Q.B. 430.
[16] *N.V. Maatschappij Zeevart* v. *M. Friesacher Soehne* [1962] 1 Lloyd's Rep. 52.
[17] (1885) 16 Q.B.D. 67.
[18] The facts are set out under "Running days," in §§ 2–20 and 2–21 above.
[19] At p. 71.
[20] (1900) 5 Com.Cas. 381.
[21] Some of the facts are set out under the heading "Colliery working days" in § 2–62 below (see n. 63).
[22] At p. 387.
[23] At p. 394.
[24] [1911] 1 K.B. 264.
[25] At p. 273.

" . . . it appears to me that 'working day' in this charterparty means something contra-ditinguished from days which are not working days, a day of work as distinguished from days for play or rest; and I think it is immaterial whether the days for play or rest are so for secular or religious reasons, and whether they are so by the ancient authority of the Church or by the present authority of the state."

This statement was cited with approval in *Reardon Smith Line Ltd.* v. *Ministry of Agriculture*[26] by Lord Devlin, who described it as "a comprehensive definition" and added[27]:

"From this[28] it appears that 'working' is a description of a type of day."

4. *Z SS. Co. Ltd.* v. *Amtorg, New York*,[29] a High Court decision, con- **2–30**
cerned the carriage of coal from Mariupol, U.S.S.R., to Boston, U.S.A.

The ship was "to be loaded at the average rate of 600 tons per weather working day, Sundays, official and local holidays excepted . . . and to be discharged at the average rate of 800 tons per weather working day, Sundays, official and local holidays excepted whether used or not . . . Saturdays and days preceding general or local holidays to count only as three quarters of a day whether used or not. On Monday and the day after general or local holidays, time not to count until 8 a.m. whether used or not." The shipowners contended that it should be assumed that a working day was from 8 a.m. till 5 p.m., and that therefore three-quarters of a day meant a period of six working hours.

Goddard J. rejected this argument. There had been no evidence as to the length of a working day; the provision that time on Monday should not begin till 8 a.m. showed that on other days there was no agreed time as to when it should start; and part of the loading took place at night. He said[30]:

"I am quite satisfied in this case that a 'day' for this purpose means what I call a calendar day—a day of 24 hours."

The use by Goddard J. of the words "for this purpose" might be regarded as having left the way open for a charterparty or port custom to cut down each day to the working hours. Such a reduction to actual working hours is exemplified in the decision by Lord Goddard C.J. (as he had then become) in *Alvion*.[31] Indeed it has been suggested[32] that the decision in the *Z SS. Co. Ltd.* case was based on there being no evidence that "days" meant any particular number of hours or that they should start at one time and end at another.

5. In *Reardon Smith Line Ltd.* v. *Ministry of Agriculture*,[33] the House of **2–31**
Lords considered[34] the construction of the phrase "weather working lay days (Sundays, holidays, and rainy days not to be counted as lay or working days . . .)." Nevertheless its decision can be regarded as authoritative in its definition of "working days." It was held that a working day was a day

---

[26] *(The Vancouver Strike Case)* [1963] A.C. 691 (H.L.).
[27] At p. 736.
[28] Namely, the decision in *British & Mexican Shipping Co. Ltd.* v. *Lockett Brothers & Co. Ltd.* [1911] 1 K.B. 264 (C.A.) and other decisions to which he had referred earlier in his judgment.
[29] (1938) 61 Ll.L.Rep. 97. The court also decided that Saturday in Boston was not an "official" or a "local" holiday; see § 8–14 below.
[30] At p. 101.
[31] *Alvion SS. Corporation Panama* v. *Galban Lobo Trading Co. S.A. of Havana (The Ruby-stone)* [1955] 1 Q.B. 430 (C.A.); see §§ 2–34 and 7–29 below.
[32] By McNair J. in *Alvion* at p. 440.
[33] *(The Vancouver Strike Case)* [1963] A.C. 691.
[34] For greater detail see §§ 7–32–7–35.

of 24 consecutive hours (prima facie from midnight to midnight) rather than the time needed to accumulate 24 working hours. Lord Devlin said[35]:

> " . . . it appears that 'working' is a description of a type of day. Prima facie it is a calendar day of 24 hours just as Sundays and holidays are days of 24 hours, which, when excepted, are taken out of the lay days . . . the character of a day as a working day cannot be determined by standard rates. There is no established authority for that view, which I think stems from the misconception that the 'working day' of the lay time clause has something to do with the hours of the day during which the ship can be compelled to work."

This view of a working day was shared by the four other members of the House of Lords taking part in this decision.

2–32 *Cases supporting alternative view of meaning of "working day"*

As this alternative view did not prevail,[36] the following cases are summarised here partly for their historical interest; partly because they throw a light on the present meaning of "working day"; and partly because it is always possible that a charterparty will be amended to incorporate the alternative method.

2–33 1. In *Mein* v. *Ottmann*[37] the Scottish Court of Session considered the words: "The ship to be loaded in nine working-days, weather permitting, Sundays and holidays excepted . . . . . . Loading time to count from six a.m. after the ship is reported at Customs-House and ready . . . The steamer to work day and night, if required to do so." The ship carried iron ore from Aguilas, Spain, and esparto grass from Oran, Tunisia, in both cases to Glasgow. Two lay days remained for loading at Oran, where each working period was of 12 hours from 6 a.m. to 6 p.m. The parties agreed that laytime there began at 6 a.m. on the day after arrival. The question was whether laytime expired on the following day at 6 p.m., after two working periods, as the shipowners contended, or on the day after at 6 a.m., after 48 actual hours, as the charterers contended. The court held that the shipowners were right. It thus supported the view that a working day consisted of the number of hours worked, and was not merely a calendar day on which, incidentally, work usually took place. Lord Trayner said[38]:

> "In the first place, I think it is wrong to say that a 'working-day' consists of twenty-four hours—that period comprehends both a day and a night. Secondly, if the hours of night were to be comprehended in the 'working day,' I would expect that to be distinctly provided. This charter provides that if necessary at the port of discharge the steamer should 'work day and night.' This provision being made in regard to the discharge, and not in regard to the loading, leads to the conclusion that what was especially stipulated in regard to the one and not to the other was not to be understood, but was excluded where it was not expressed."

In *Reardon Smith Line Ltd.* v. *Ministry of Agriculture*[39] Lord Devlin, speaking of this decision, said[40]:

> "In the Scottish case of *Mein* v. *Ottmann*[41] it was held that a working day was a day of 12 hours, but it does not appear how the figure was calculated. This is the only case cited

[35] At pp. 736 and 742.
[36] See § 2–26 above.
[37] (1904) 6 Fraser (Ct. of Sess., 5th Ser.) 276.
[38] At p. 281.
[39] [1963] A.C. 691 (H.L.). See § 2–31 above.
[40] At p. 737.
[41] (1904) 6 Fraser (Ct. of Sess., 5th Ser.) 276.

before the *Rubystone*[42] in which 'working day,' unless qualified in some way in the charterparty, has been held to be a number of working hours . . . It is, of course, possible, and it is sometimes done, for the lay days to be defined as a number of working hours. Or they may be defined as working days of 24 or some other number of hours, although the authorities are not entirely agreed on what that means. But no authority before *Mein* v. *Ottmann* and the *Rubystone* has been cited for the proposition that the expression 'working day' by itself means a number of working hours; Lord Goddard C.J. in the *Rubystone*[43] treats it as self-evident."

2. In *Alvion SS. Corporation Panama* v. *Galban Lobo Trading Co. S.A.* **2–34** *of Havana*,[44] the Court of Appeal considered the words: "Lay days at the average rate of . . . " [here various quantities of sugar were mentioned, in bags and pounds, applicable to each Cuban port concerned] " . . . provided vessel can receive at these rates per weather working day, Sundays and holidays and Saturday afternoons excepted, shall be allowed to the said charterers (if steamer is not sooner loaded) for loading and waiting for orders." The ship loaded at Cardenas and Havana, the rate applicable being 16,500 100-lb. bags per day. She loaded 90,000 bags at Cardenas and 72,690 bags at Havana. By custom the normal working hours at both ports were 0700 to 1100 hours and 1300 to 1700 hours, *i.e.* eight hours, and, on Saturdays, 0700 to 1100 hours, *i.e.* four hours.

The charterers argued, in the words of the case stated to the High Court, that they "were correct in applying the principle of a day of eight hours and four hours on Saturday to their computation of laytime." The Umpire had made an award in their favour. The alternative laytime statements for Cardenas were, in simplified form, as follows, the two parties agreeing that the ship was preparing her holds from 0700 to 1100 hours on October 1:

Charterers' laytime statement (on the basis of an eight-hour working **2–35** day).
Laytime begins at 1300 hours, October 1.
Time allowed for loading: 5 days, 3 hours, 38 minutes.

1951				D	H	M
October	1	Monday	1300 to 1700 hours (rain stoppage 40 mins)	3	20	
	2	Tuesday	(rain stoppage 15 mins)		7	45
	3	Wednesday	(winch and rain stoppage 1 hr 48 mins)		6	12
	4	Thursday	(winch and rain stoppage 38 mins)		7	22
	5	Friday	(winch stoppage 2 mins)		7	58
	6	Saturday			4	00
	7	Sunday	Time not counting			
	8	Monday	Laytime expires 1616 hours (rain stoppage 15 mins)		7	01
				5	3	38

Loading completed 1645 hours, October 8.
From 1616 to 1645 hours, October 8: 29 minutes.
Demurrage 29 minutes at $1,000 per day or *pro rata* = $20.14 at $2.80 = £7 3s 10d.

A total of 1 day 19 hours 38 minutes, or 43 hours 38 minutes, was actually worked. This yielded five eight-hour periods, which were then

---

[42] *Alvion SS. Corporation Panama* v. *Galban Lobo Trading Co. S.A. of Havana* [1955] 1 Q.B. 430 (C.A.) (*The Rubystone*). See §§ 2–34 and 7–29.

[43] *Ibid.* at p. 445.

[44] *(The Rubystone)* [1955] 1 Q.B. 430. The decision is discussed here so far as it is relevant to the meaning of "working day." Its bearing on the meaning of "weather working day" is discussed in § 7–29 below.

treated as five days; it was not the custom to triple the balance of 3 hours 38 minutes of working time in the same way, though it could be argued that it should be treated as 10 hours 54 minutes.

2–36 **Shipowners' laytime statement** (on the basis of a 24-hour day).
Laytime begins at 1100[45] hours October 1.
Time allowed for loading 5 days 10 hours 55 minutes.[45]

1951				**D**	**H**	**M**
October 1	Monday	1100 to 2400 hours (rain stoppage 40 mins)		12	20	
2	Tuesday	0001 to 2400 hours (rain stoppage 15 mins)		23	45	
3	Wednesday	0001 to 2400 hours (winch and rain stoppage 1 hour 48 mins)		22	12	
4	Thursday	0001 to 2400 hours (winch and rain stoppage 38 mins)		23	22	
5	Friday	0001 to 2400 hours (winch stoppage 2 mins)		23	58	
6	Saturday	0001 to 1200 hours		12	00	
7	Sunday	Time not counting				
8	Monday	Laytime expires 1318 hours. 0001 to 1318 hours		13	18	
				5	10	55

Loading completed 1645 hours October 8.
From 1318 to 1645 hours October 8: 3 hours 27 minutes.
Demurrage 3 hours 27 minutes at $1,000 per day or *pro rata* = $143.75 at $2.80 = £51 6s 9d.

In the shipowners' statement time for stoppages was deducted from (a) the 24 hours in the case of the four full working days; and (b) the hours after the beginning of laytime in the case of October 1.

The case is considered here only in so far as the courts discussed the definition of a "working day."[46]

In the High Court McNair J. held that the charterers were right. He was influenced by the custom that there were eight working hours daily. The Court of Appeal upheld his judgment. Lord Goddard C.J. stressed[47] the differing lengths of day, which could vary according to custom. They could be even more various:

" . . . by the expression 'working day' is meant the part of a day during which work is carried on. Therefore to determine a working day one has to find out what are the customary hours or usual ordinary hours that are worked either at a particular place or in a particular trade."

This was a point which troubled Lord Devlin in the *Reardon Smith Line* case[48]: "How do you ascertain what are normal hours?"

2–37 *Practical difference between 8-hour and 24-hour days*
In *Alvion* v. *Galban Lobo*,[49] Lord Goddard C.J.[50] summarised the shipowners' argument as being that:

" . . . if one takes a day of 24 hours, it means that the men could have worked a good

---

[45] The discrepancy between this time and that in the charterers' statement reflects other differences which are not relevant here and were not referred to the court.
[46] Their consideration of a "weather working day," with particular reference to the problem of interruption by bad weather, is discussed in § 7–29 below.
[47] *Ibid.* at p. 445.
[48] [1963] A.C. 691 at p. 741 (H.L.).
[49] [1955] 1 Q.B. 430 (C.A.).
[50] *Ibid.* at p. 444.

deal longer than they did, and therefore he" [*i.e.* shipowners' counsel] "is entitled to a larger sum of demurrage than has been awarded."

In the light of the decision in the *Reardon Smith Line* case[51] it would seem that the number of hours which the men could have worked was not relevant. The contrast is between the normal hours, however ascertained, and 24 hours as a calendar day, and not as a period throughout which people could have worked.

The differences between shipowners and charterers in respect of the first port were 7 hours 17 minutes for the time used, and 2 hours 58 minutes for the demurrage.[52]

3. In *N.V. Maatschappij Zeevart* v. *Friesacher Soehne,*[53] the High Court considered the expression "working days." A charterparty for the carriage of grain from the United States Gulf to Europe stated: "Steamer to be loaded according to berth terms, with customary berth despatch, and if detained longer than five weather-working days, Sundays and holidays excepted, charterers to pay demurrage at the rate of $800.00 U.S. currency per day, or *pro rata* . . . " The *Leto* was loaded at New Orleans by elevator. Longshoremen there worked 24 hours a day, seven days per week. The shipowners contended that a working day meant the period normally worked, exclusive of overtime; the charterers said that for grain loaded by elevator it was 24 hours long. There was evidence of a standard rate of pay during certain working hours from Mondays to Fridays, and of an overtime rate for all other hours. The problem was not complicated by weather. **2–38**

Elwes J. held that the shipowners were right. A calculation should be made of days consisting of the number of hours worked at standard rates of pay, and not of 24 consecutive hours each. A working day was a period of nine hours.

> "Whether or not the receipt of overtime for some parts of the 24-hour day is wholly and exclusively decisive is not necessary for me to decide, as I understand the case, but that it is a major factor I am persuaded is correct . . . "[54]

In arriving at this conclusion the judge felt bound by the decision of the Court of Appeal in *Alvion* v. *Galban Lobo.*[55]

Running working days **2–39**

The expression "running working days" appeared in the Gencon charterparty[56] until it was amended in 1976, so that the laytime should be calculated in "running hours." The conjunction of the epithets "running" and "working" was unsatisfactory. The term running days has been described[57] as one which eliminates the unsatisfactory way in which the term "working days" excludes Sundays and holidays. Such a situation certainly occurs when the word "running" replaces the word "working." Where the words were used together, they were contradictory, if the usual meaning was imputed to the word "running." A running working day is a working day,[58]

---

[51] *(The Vancouver Strike Case)* [1963] A.C. 691 (H.L.).
[52] The corresponding differences for the second port were 6 hours 30 minutes and 3 hours 30 minutes.
[53] [1962] 1 Lloyd's Rep. 52.
[54] At p. 59.
[55] *(The Rubystone)* [1955] 1 Q.B. 430; see § 2–34 above and § 7–29 below.
[56] Uniform General Charter 1922 (Gencon).
[57] By Lord Esher M.R. in *Nielsen* v. *Wait* (1885) 16 Q.B.D. 67 at p. 71 (C.A.).
[58] See § 2–22 above.

and thus cannot be a Sunday or a holiday; the word "running" was super-fluous except so far as it emphasised that, but for the fact that the ship was at port, she would be running at sea.[59]

2–40   **"Running days . . . Sundays and holidays excepted."** A more readily comprehensible expression is " . . . running days, Sundays and holidays excepted." Thus in *Hain SS. Co. Ltd.* v. *Sociedad Anonima Comercial de Exportacion e Importacion*[60] loading was to take place at the rate of so many "tons per running day . . . Sundays and holidays excepted." It was common ground between the parties that holidays interrupted the running days. In *Burnett SS. Co. Ltd.* v. *Danube and Black Sea Shipping Agencies*[61] the laytime clause[62] referred to loading "at the average rate of 400 units per running day (Sundays and non-working holidays excepted)." Scrutton L.J.[63] said[64]:

> "If the 15 running days include a Sunday it is not to be counted, if they include a non-working holiday, whatever that may be, it is not to be counted, and there is no question that it could not be contended that a Sunday or non-working holiday must be included in the 15 running days, because the charterer had no cargo alongside on the Sunday, or no cargo alongside on the non-working holiday."

So also in *Hain SS. Co. Ltd.* v. *Sociedad Anonima Comercial de Exportacion e Importacion*[65] the charterparty stipulated a loading rate "per running day . . . Sundays and holidays excepted." MacKinnon J. said that, as time was to begin 12 hours after a certain notice, the days were periods of 24 hours and not calendar days. He continued[66]:

> " . . . when you have started at any particular hour counting your consecutive 24 hours, if a Sunday or a holiday comes along you cut that out and omit from the calculation the 24 hours of the Sunday or the holiday."

2–41   D. Days of 24 hours, 24 consecutive hours and 24 running hours
   The following phrases may be found in laytime clauses: "weather working day of twenty-four hours"; "weather working day of twenty-four consecutive hours"[67]; "working day of twenty-four (24) consecutive hours each"[68] and "weather working day of twenty-four running hours"; alternatively the same phrases may be used with the omission in each case of the word "weather," with or without the words "weather permitting."[69]

---

[59] See § 2–20 above.
[60] *(The Tregantle)* (1932) 43 Ll.L. Rep. 136.
[61] [1933] 2 K.B. 438 (C.A.); see also § 7–13 below.
[62] In a Chamber of Shipping Berth Contract, 1911 (Dancon).
[63] Dissenting, but not on this point.
[64] At pp. 447–448.
[65] *(The Trevarrack)* (1934) 49 Ll.L.Rep. 86; see also § 8–23.
[66] At p. 88.
[67] As in *Turnbull, Scott, & Co.* v. *Cruickshank & Co.* (1904) 7 Ct. of Sess., 5th Ser., 265. See §§ 2–50—2–51 below. The Charterparty Laytime Definitions 1980 (see Appendix to this book) state: "17. 'WEATHER WORKING DAY OF 24 CONSECUTIVE HOURS'—means a working day or part of a working day of 24 hours during which it is or, if the ship is still waiting for her turn, it would be possible to load/discharge the cargo without interference due to the weather. If such interference occurs (or would have occurred if work had been in progress) there shall be excluded from the laytime the period during which the weather interfered or would have interfered with the work."
[68] North American Grain Charterparty 1973 (Norgrain).
[69] For the words "weather permitting," see § 6–10 below.

Days (working or weather working) of 24 hours

A working or a weather working day of 24 hours is[70] a conventional as opposed to a calendar day, comprising 24 hours which need not be consecutive.[71] For the purpose of this definition, which may not be of universal application, the day is regarded as being an artificial day, made up of 24 working hours. The hours would be the normal working hours[72] at a port, whether or not the charterers used them. If, for example, the port had an eight-hour day, it would take three calendar days,[73] assuming that no other excepted periods occured, for one working day of 24 working hours to be completed. Such a provision was, so defined, less in the interest of the ship-owners than one which provided for days of 24 consecutive or running hours.[74]

Another method of approach to the expression "[weather] working day of twenty-four hours" in a laytime clause is to deny that there is any difference between this expression and a "weather working day." This solution has the merits of certainty and simplicity, if the parties agree. On the other hand people are usually taken to have intended that the words of their contract should have some effect. On this interpretation perhaps no violence is done to the words "of 24 hours," because a calendar day does in fact have 24 hours; the word "working" is being used to describe the calendar day rather than the 24 hours.

Though the solution has merit, there remain the decided cases.[75] Where similar facts arise, it is possible that a court would come to similar conclusions. Before the cases are presented in detail, their salient features may be summarised as follows:

Forest SS. Co. Ltd. v. *Iberian Iron Ore Co. Ltd.*[76]

"350 tons per working day of twenty-four hours, weather permitting (Sundays and holidays excepted)." The ship was to work at night,[77] and on Sundays and holidays, if required; the time was to count as laytime if used.

Watson Brothers Shipping Co. Ltd. v. *Mysore Manganese Co. Ltd.*[78]

"500 tons per clear working day of 24 hours (weather permitting), Sundays and holidays excepted." The ship was to allow work on Sundays and holidays; half of the time to count as laytime if used.

Orpheus SS. Co. v. *Bovill & Sons*[79]

Eight "working days of twenty-four hours each" to be "exclusive of Sundays, Good Friday, Christmas Day, and bank holidays". The ship could

---

[70] As stated in *Forest SS. Co. Ltd.* v. *Iberian Iron Ore Co. Ltd.* (1899) 5 Com.Cas. 83 (H.L.).
[71] For a day of 24 consecutive hours, see §§ 2–50, 2–51 below.
[72] See § 6–20 below.
[73] As H. Tiberg says, in *The Law of Demurrage* (1979), at p. 420: "If anybody makes a mistake about this, he is liable to find that the laytime is three times as long as he anticipated."
[74] See §§ 2–50–2–51 below.
[75] In particular: *Forest SS. Co. Ltd.* v. *Iberian Iron Ore Co. Ltd.* (1899) 5 Com.Cas. 83 (H.L.): *Watson Brothers Shipping Co. Ltd.* v. *Mysore Manganese Co. Ltd.* (1910) 15 Com.Cas. 159; and *Orpheus SS. Co.* v. *Bovill & Sons* (1916) 114 L.T. 750.
[76] (1899) 5 Com.Cas. 83 (H.L.). See also § 2–44 below.
[77] For the effect of bad weather at night, see § 7–42 below.
[78] (1910) 15 Com.Cas. 159. See also § 2–45 below.
[79] (1916) 114 L.T. 750.

discharge at all hours. The charterparty made no provision for interruption by bad weather.

2–43   The slight differences in the wording of the charterparties in these three cases may or may not affect the outcome of another case with similar wording. It was only in the last case, *Orpheus*, decided by Scrutton J., that charterers failed in their contention that only the usual working hours of the port were to count. In the first two cases, *Forest* and *Watson*, the existence of a provision that time otherwise excluded should count (entirely or as to half) if used, seems to have concluded the argument in favour of charterers. Thus in *Forest*[80] A. L. Smith L.J. in the Court of Appeal attached great significance to the words "unless used." The most important conclusion from the *Orpheus* decision appears to be that the mere words "working days of twenty-four hours each" do not in themselves ensure that non-working hours are excluded from the calculation. If the only other decision were that in *Forest* it might be possible to regard it as complementary to *Orpheus* since the "if used" clause covered all the time outside working hours.[81] Thus such time, which would otherwise have been ignored, was brought into the computation if used.

The *Watson* case is difficult to reconcile with the others, as time outside working hours appears to have been excluded from the computation because the expression "working day of 24 hours" was used.[82] If the mere use of that expression is enough, then it becomes difficult to draw a useful disinction between *Forest* and *Orpheus*.[82a]

2–44   *The cases*

1. In *Forest SS. Co. Ltd.* v. *Iberian Iron Ore Co. Ltd.*[83] the House of Lords considered a charterparty for the carriage of iron ore from Seville to the United Kingdom and elsewhere over a period of 12 months. The charterers were "to be allowed 350 tons per working day of twenty-four hours, weather permitting (Sundays and holidays excepted), for loading and discharging . . . Steamer to work at night if required, also on Sundays and holidays, such time not to count as lay-days unless used." The House of Lords. affirming a majority decision of the Court of Appeal,[84] held that the

---

[80] Reported, as to the Court of Appeal decision, as *Rhymney SS. Co. Ltd.* v. *Iberian Iron Ore Co. Ltd.* (1898) 3 Com.Cas. 316 at p. 319.

[81] The significance of these words was also stressed in *Turnbull, Scott, & Co.* v. *Cruickshank & Co.* (1904) 7 Ct. of Sess., 5th Ser., 265 at p. 269 (Note). See §§ 2–50–2–51 below.

[82] Though Hamilton J. noted (at p. 65) that in the *Forest SS. Co. Ltd.* case the ship was to work if required not only on Sundays and holidays but also at nights. He also referred to the words "weather permitting" which appeared in both cases. If time was interrupted where weather did not permit work, perhaps this suggested that time was not running outside working hours, for the words were inapplicable when no work was being done. For bad weather at night, see § 7–42 below.

[82a] In a New York arbitration, *Aegean Compania Naviera S.A.* v. *Schiavone-Chase Corporation (The Georgios Xylas)*, Society of Maritime Arbitrators No. 1345 (1978), the relevant words were " . . . per weather working day of 24 hours, Sundays and Holidays excepted, even if used." The panel was presented with a choice between the "calendar day" interpretation, as shipowners put it, relying on the *Orpheus* decision, and charterers' reliance on the *Forest* decision. It decided unanimously in favour of the shipowners, saying: "The conceptual inference of a 24 hour calendar day in the application of 'weather working days of 24 hours' is universally accepted in the shipping community on a world-wide basis."

[83] (1899) 5 Com.Cas. 83.

[84] Entitled *Rhymney SS. Co. Ltd.* v. *Iberian Iron Ore Co. Ltd.* (1898) 3 Com.Cas. 316.

charterers were entitled to 24 working hours to load or discharge each 350 tons. In the Court of Appeal[85] A. L. Smith L.J. had summed up the matter as follows[86]:

> "Why were these words ['of twenty-four hours'] inserted? It seems to me for the express purpose of giving to the charterers a fixed period of twenty-four working hours wherein to load or unload each 350 tons of ore, no matter what number of hours might constitute a working day at the port of loading or the ports of discharge. What is the sense of inserting 'of twenty-four hours' if not for this?"

He referred to the provision for working at night,[87] if the charterers so required. In his view this reinforced the charterers' interpretation of the 24-hour clause; nights, Sundays and holidays would not normally count, as they were outside normal hours. Where they were used, the time used was to be counted in the 24 hours. In the absence of such a provision, the use of time outside normal working hours would count against the charterers as part of the 24 hours.

People working for 24 hours. In the House of Lords, Earl Halsbury L.C. said[88]:

> "Surely the parties intended it to be understood as between themselves in respect of that matter that they were only using the word 'day' as meaning a day of twenty-four working hours. There is no such thing as a 'working day of twenty-four hours'; the thing is absurd; nobody supposes people to work for twenty-four hours. That phrase itself shows me that the parties intended to put together the periods of work for the purpose of ascertaining the gross number of hours, which, divided by twenty-four, would be the number of days in respect of which this provision shall apply."

2. The House of Lords decision in the *Forest SS. Co.* case was applied in **2–45** *Watson Brothers Shipping Co. Ltd.* v. *Mysore Manganese Co. Ltd.*[89] The High Court considered the words "to be shipped at the rate of 500 tons per clear working day of 24 hours (weather permitting), Sundays and holidays always excepted: and to be discharged at 500 tons per like day . . . In case charterers can arrange to load or discharge ship on Sundays or holidays, captain to allow work to be done, half such time actually used to count." Ore was loaded at Marmagoa, where plague had caused a scarcity of workmen, as a result of which ships were delayed. There was a working day of $10\frac{1}{2}$ hours. The shipowners claimed demurrage, and one of the disputes concerned the 24 hours provision. Holding that the charterparty could not be distinguished from the one construed in the *Forest SS. Co.* case, where "the parties had created their own charterparty days," Hamilton J. said[90] that quite apart from authority

> " . . . the natural construction of this clause would be that the defendants," [the charterers and the shippers] "who are stipulating it in their favour, are to have, not a day by the calendar or a day which is a working day as distinguished from a calendar day which is a holiday, but a certain number of hours upon which work in the ordinary sense may be done."

---

[85] Which gave more detailed reasons than did the House of Lords.
[86] *Ibid*. at p. 318.
[87] For the effect of bad weather at night, see § 7–42 below.
[88] *Op. cit.*, at pp. 85–6.
[89] (1910) 15 Com.Cas. 159.
[90] At pp. 165–166.

2–46 3. In the third case in which the words of "twenty-four hours" were considered, it was held that they meant a period of 24 consecutive hours. In *Orpheus SS. Co.* v. *Bovill & Sons*[91] a ship had carried grain from Newport News to Avonmouth. Discharge was to be "in accordance with the rules of the Bristol Channel and West of England Corn Trade Association, time to count from arrival off Avonmouth whether berthed or not." There was no provision for interruptions by bad weather. The effect of the Association's rules was that the ship was to be allowed eight "working days of twenty-four hours each" (Sundays excluded) to discharge. The shipowners claimed demurrrage from the receivers and counted time from the moment at which the ship arrived off Avonmouth. Scrutton J. held that a working day of 24 hours meant a period of 24 hours beginning at the time of readiness to discharge, excluding Sundays and certain other excepted days. He said[92]:

> "A day or running day is a consecutive day of the calendar from midnight to midnight. You cut down a running day by speaking of working day. It has been decided in several cases, and the case of *Saxon SS. Co. Ltd.* v. *Union SS. Co. Ltd.*[93] is one example that a working day does not mean the day on which the work is done, but a day on which it can be done, and that a working day ordinarily is twenty-four hours from midnight to midnight, part of it being the time in which work is ordinarily done . . . you may be zealous in discharging a ship and find yourself charged with a whole day, although you had only enjoyed the benefit of part [of] it,[94] and, in my view, that was why the shipowners and charterers began to put in their charters 'working days of twenty-four hours each' meaning that when you were entitled to so many days you would have days of twenty-four hours and not days of six hours, because if you had worked only six hours it would be treated as a whole day. Shortly after that clause began to get into charters a case arose on a complicated charter which went to the House of Lords . . . "

2–47 Scrutton J. was referring to *Forest SS. Co. Ltd.* v. *Iberian Iron Ore Co. Ltd.*,[95] in which case, he said:

> "The House of Lords decided that a conventional day was the right meaning."

He referred to the High Court decision in the *Watson* case,[96] where cargo had "to be shipped at the rate of 500 tons per clear working day of 24 hours (weather permitting)." He said that Hamilton J. "used some language which suggested that it" (the working day of 24 hours) "was to be made up of usual hours of working at the port, and not the hours which were unusual hours, but which the shipowners or charterers could desire each other to work." Hamilton J. seemed to be saying that the fact that the ship must work if asked, while the charterers need not work unless they so chose, did not entitle the shipowners to say that a day consisted of the 24 hours in which they could be called upon to work. Of this part of the judgment of Hamilton J., Scrutton J. said:

> "I find great difficulty in following that passage."

He spoke of the rule

> " . . . you are to take working days of twenty-four hours, but you are to exclude Sun-

---

[91] (1916) 114 L.T. 750.
[92] At p. 752.
[93] See § 2–28 above.
[94] For the present method of apportionment, see § 7–32 below.
[95] (1899) 5 Com.Cas. 83 (H.L.). See § 2–44 above.
[96] (1910) 15 Com.Cas. 159. See § 2–45 above.

days, Good Fridays, Christmas Day and bank holidays, and Saturday if the vessel is only ready to discharge after eight o' clock. There is no provision that you are to exclude anything else. There is no provision as there was in the other cases about what you are to do with the period after the working hours. In *Forest SS. Co. Ltd.* v. *Iberian Iron Ore Co.* you were not to count that; in the other case you have to do so. In this case there is no provision either authorising you to exclude it or saying what will happen if it is worked. In these circumstances it seems to me that it is part of the working day. It is a day on which work can be done between the parties and the parties can require work to be done during that time. I see no reason to exclude it."

Where a "working day of twenty-four hours" is treated as a conventional **2–48** day, there has been doubt as to whether the "hours" should be the actual hours worked or the hours normally worked. It seems that the hours normally worked, though these may include overtime,[97] should count. In *Forest SS. Co. Ltd* v. *Iberian Iron Ore Co. Ltd.*[98] Earl Halsbury L.C. said[99] of the words "working day of twenty-four hours":

> "That phrase itself shows me that the parties intended to put together the periods of work for the purpose of ascertaining the gross number of hours which, divided by twenty-four, would be the number of days in respect of which this provision shall apply."

This could be taken to mean that the actual periods worked, whether during or outside normal working hours, would be counted. A. L. Smith L.J. had said[1] that the charterers were to have "twenty-four working hours wherein to load or unload 350 tons of ore, no matter what number of hours might constitute a working day." In *Watson Brothers Shipping Co. Ltd.* v. *Mysore Manganese Co. Ltd.*[2] Hamilton J. spoke of a "certain number of hours upon which work in the ordinary sense may be done."

The latter stressed[3] the complications which could arise where ports of **2–49** call had different working hours. Lord Devlin in *Reardon Smith Line Ltd.* v. *Ministry of Agriculture*[4] said how difficult it was to speak of normal hours. Overtime was the rule rather than the exception, and there might be a difference between normal hours in the port and normal hours in the trade. He added[5]:

> "But an experienced arbitrator will probably know, from the number of the lay days, the amount of cargo to be loaded and the rate of loading to be expected at the port, how much of the day was expected to be used; and he would naturally assume that work would be done so far as possible during normal hours at standard rates and after that, if necessary, during the hours in which overtime was most likely to be worked."

It seems that when the normal hours are ascertained in connection with the expression "working day of twenty-four hours," the same test should be applied as when the "weather working day" is apportioned.[6]

---

[97] See also *Reardon Smith Line Ltd.* v. *Ministry of Agriculture (The Vancouver Strike Case)* [1963] A.C. 691 (H.L.), *per* Lord Devlin at p. 745.
[98] (1899) 5 Com.Cas. 83.
[99] *Ibid.* at p. 86.
[1] In the Court of Appeal; (1898) 3 Com.Cas. 316 at p. 318.
[2] (1910) 15 Com.Cas. 159 at p. 165. See also § 2–45 above.
[3] (1898) 3 Com.Cas. 316 (C.A.) at p. 318: "The number of hours which constitute a working day vary at the different ports."
[4] *(The Vancouver Strike Case)* [1963] A.C. 691 (H.L.) at p. 741.
[5] *Ibid.* at p. 745.
[6] See § 7–32.

2–50 *Days of 24 consecutive hours and 24 running hours.* A working day of 24 consecutive or running hours[7] is a day of 24 actually consecutive hours, including the hours of night,[8] which is a normal working day,[9] as opposed to a Sunday or a holiday. It can be modified by any apt words, such as "weather" in the case of the expression "weather working day," or the words "weather permitting."[10]

In *Turnbull, Scott, & Co.* v. *Cruickshank & Co.*[11] loading and discharging were to be "at the rate of 500 tons per working day of twenty-four consecutive hours (weather permitting), Sundays and holidays always excepted." The ship had carried iron ore from Spain to Ardrossan, Scotland. The Scottish Court of Session held that "in every twenty-four consecutive hours from the commencement of the loading or discharging 500 tons were to be loaded or discharged if the weather did not hinder it or a holiday or Sunday intervene."[12]

2–51 The charterers were not liable for demurrage in case of delay, *inter alia*, through "stoppage of trains or any case beyond the personal control" of the charterers. The ship was "to work day and night if requested."

The shipowners said that a "working day of twenty-four consecutive hours" meant a day of twenty-four actually consecutive hours, *i.e.* a day in the ordinary sense, so that every hour counted (Sundays and holidays excepted) from the time of readiness to load or discharge until the completion of loading or discharging. The charterers said that it meant an artificial period of 24 hours in each of which the work of loading or discharging was usually performed,[13] the hours of night being regarded as nonexistent. They relied on the decision of the House of Lords in *Forest SS. Co. Ltd.* v. *Iberian Iron Ore Co. Ltd.*[14]

The shipowners claimed demurrage from the charterers, who pleaded the exemption clause. The customary mode of discharge for cargo which had been sold was direct into railway wagons. Delay had been caused by the failure of the railway company to supply enough wagons. The charterers said that this failure was beyond their personal control."

It was held that the shipowners' construction of the expression "working day of twenty-four consecutive hours" was correct. Lord Trayner distinguished[15] the *Forest SS. Co. Ltd.* case,[16] pointing out that there the expression "per working day of twenty-four hours" was interpreted to mean not 24 consecutive hours but 24 working hours. He added[17]:

> "In the clause before us there is the exception that hours when the weather did not permit of loading or discharging were not to be reckoned against the charterers, nor were holidays nor Sundays. But in every twenty-four consecutive hours from the commencement of the loading or discharging, 500 tons were to be loaded or discharged if the weather did not hinder it or a holiday or Sunday intervene. And in my opinion the words

---

[7] With or without the word "weather" before "working."
[8] For the effect of bad weather at night, see § 7–42 below.
[9] For a definition of a working day, see § 2–22.
[10] For "weather permitting," see § 7–10 below.
[11] (1904) 7 Ct. of Sess., 5th Ser., 265.
[12] *Per* Lord Trayner, *ibid.* at p. 273.
[13] Or as he put it, *arguendo* (at p. 270): "a conventional day made up by piecing together twenty-four hours, during each of which there had been or ought to have been work."
[14] (1900) 5 Com.Cas. 83. See § 2–44 above.
[15] At p. 273.
[16] (1900) 5 Com.Cas. 83 (H.L.).
[17] At p. 273.

'working day' in the clause before us are used only in antithesis to the days which were Sundays or holidays."[18]

The Court of Session adopted the views of the Sheriff-substitute in the court below, who had said[19]:

> "I cannot read 'consecutive hours' as equivalent to consecutive working hours, or as meaning anything else than hours following one another immediately and without interval of time."

The Sheriff-substitute had then distinguished the decision in *Forest SS. Co. Ltd.* case[20] on the ground that the charterparty there had referred to "twenty-four hours," and added:

> " . . . the charter-party in that case, after providing that the ship was to work at night if required, provided further that such time was not to count unless used, which in effect limited the 'working day' in the ordinary case to the hours usually worked whereas here the charter-party, while providing that the ship is to work at night if requested, does not contain the further provision that the time is not to count unless used, except in regard to the period between 5 p.m. on Saturday and 7 a.m. on Monday, and the fair inference is that hours not worked on working days were intended to count whether used or not."

The court held that the words "stoppage of train or any cause beyond the **2–52** personal control" of charterers must be construed in the light of the *ejusdem generis* rule. Want of railway trucks was *ejusdem generis* with stoppage of trains. The charterers were not liable for demurrage so far as it arose from the lack of railway trucks. Lord Trayner said[21] that the hours which were not to be charged did not include more than the hours of the ordinary working day during which trucks were usually supplied, but when, in fact, they were not supplied. He added:

> "The defenders[22] say that the hours of night when no trucks were available should also be deducted. I think not. If the charterers had asked for trucks at an unusual hour (wishing to work night and day), and had been refused them, there would have been something to say for their contention. But this is not the case. The hours of the night, therefore, are not to be deducted from the pursuer's claim."

E. Laytime by reference to number of hatches[23]   **2–53**

(1) *"At the average rate of . . . tons per working hatch per day."*
This expression, once described by Scrutton L.J.[24] as an "ambiguous and mysterious clause," obliges consignees to take delivery at the average rate stated in respect of each hatch which still contains cargo. A completed hatch is no longer a working hatch, and must be left out of the calculation.

---

[18] And thus not to limit the time which counted to the working hours.

[19] At p. 269 (Note).

[20] (1899) 5 Com.Cas. 83 (H.L.). See § 2–44 above.

[21] At p. 274.

[22] The charterers.

[23] See examples of laytime clauses at § 2–13 above. The Charterparty Laytime Definitions 1980 (see Appendix to this book) state: "9. 'PER WORKING HATCH PER DAY' or 'PER WORKABLE HATCH PER DAY'—means that laytime is to be calculated by dividing the quantity of cargo in the hold with the largest quantity by the result of multiplying the agreed daily rate per working or workable hatch by the number of hatches serving that hold. Thus:

$$\text{Laytime} = \frac{\text{Largest quantity in one hold}}{\text{Daily rate per hatch} \times \text{Number of hatches serving that hold}} = \text{Days}$$

A hatch that is capable of being worked by two gangs simultaneously shall be counted as two hatches." For the words "PER HATCH PER DAY," see Definition 8 in the Appendix to this book.

[24] *The Sandgate* [1930] P. 30 (C.A.) at p. 32.

In *The Sandgate*[25] a charterparty[26] for the carriage of coal from Cardiff to San Rosario provided: "The cargo to be taken from alongside by consignees at port of discharge, free of expense and risk to the vessel, at the average rate of 125 tons per working hatch per day, weather permitting, Sundays and holidays excepted, provided vessel can deliver at this rate . . ." A marginal note stated: "consignees shall not be obliged to take cargo from alongside . . . at a higher rate than 500 tons a day." The ship had four hatches. The Court of Appeal rejected the shipowners' argument that the ship was to be dispatched at the rate of 500 tons per day. The shipowners said that there was always the same number of working hatches, whether there was coal in them or not. The charterers contended that when, working at the rate of 125 tons a hatch, a hold became empty, the total discharging rate was proportionately reduced while the rate per hatch remained the same. Of the shipowners' argument Scrutton L.J. said[27]:

> "But, if so, there was no need to put in this roundabout phrase of 'per working hatch per day' because, the hatches being the same every day, one could, by putting in a rate per day, have calculated on the same number of hatches every day."

A working hatch was a hatch with cargo in it; whether or not it was worked, it had to be taken into account. Scrutton L.J. concluded[28]:

> " . . . this phrase cannot be read as a roundabout way of saying what might have been said quite simply: 'I will discharge 500 tons per day out of four cargo hatches, 125 tons for each hatch.' What it does mean is to assume that the amount may vary per day, according as there is a working hatch—a hatch which can be worked because there is coal in it. Whether it was a reasonable agreement to make or not, it is not for me to say."

2–54   (2) *"At an average rate of . . . tons per available workable hatch per weather working day."* This expression also has been held[29] to require the charterers to load at the average rate in respect of each hatch which still contains cargo. As with the expression "per working hatch,"[30] a hatch ceases to qualify for inclusion in the calculations when it has been completed. Neither party, in the case where this expression was judicially construed, suggested that there was any relevant difference between the phrases "working hatch" and "available workable hatch."

2–55   In *Compania de Navigacion Zita S.A.* v. *Louis Dreyfus & Cie*[31] a charterparty for the carriage of barley from Algerian ports to the United Kingdom stated: "Cargo to be loaded and stowed free of expense to owners at an average rate of not less than 150 metric tons per available workable hatch per weather working day (Sundays and holidays excepted) provided vessel can receive at this rate." The ship had five holds, each being served by one hatch. The charterers calculated laytime by dividing by 150 the greatest weight of cargo loaded in any one hold. They based their case primarily on the words of Hill J. in *The Sandgate*,[32] where he said[33] of the shipowners:

[25] [1930] P. 30 (C.A.).
[26] A modification of Form A of the Welsh Coal Charter, 1896.
[27] At p. 33.
[28] At p. 34.
[29] In *Compania de Navigacion Zita S.A.* v. *Louis Dreyfus & Cie* [1953] 2 Lloyd's Rep. 472 (*The Corfu Island*).
[30] See § 2–53 above.
[31] [1953] 2 Lloyd's Rep. 472 (*The Corfu Island*).
[32] Reported as *Sandgate (Owners)* v. *W. S. Partridge & Co.* (1929) 35 Ll.L. Rep. 9.
[33] *Ibid.* at p. 13.

" . . . if he took the quantity in the hold which contains the largest quantity and divided that by 125, then that would give you the period in which the discharge had to be carried out, and you would then take into account Sundays and holidays."

The Court of Appeal had not differed from that view.

The shipowners calculated laytime by reference to the number of available workable hatches. With five available and workable hatches, they said, loading should have been at the average rate of 750 metric tons per day. With two such hatches, for example, the average rate should have been 300 metric tons per day. On this basis laytime was shorter and less dispatch would have been due. Devlin J., finding for the charterers, mentioned[34] the differing capacities of the holds:

"Instead of providing simply for a rate per day, it provides for a rate per hatch per day. If all the holds were of equal capacity this refinement would be unnecessary. If they were loaded at the same working rate they would then all be finished simultaneously, and with five holds you might just as well say 750 tons per day as 150 tons per day per hold."

As one hold will be finished before the others, the words under discussion relieve charterers of any duty to speed up the work to maintain the previous total rate. The charterers considered that they had allowed for this by dividing the rate into the largest quantity in any hold. As Hill J. said in *The Sandgate*[35]:

"I suppose worked out most accurately you would take these several quantities" [that is, the quantity in each hold] "and start with 500 and go on reducing to 375" [the rate in that case was 125 tons per working hatch per day], "reducing to 250 and finally to 125, but you get exactly the same result . . . "

Since the *Zita* decision in 1953 there have been five High Court cases in **2–55A** which the questions of workability or availability have been considered. They are:

Maritime Transport Operators G.m.b.H. v. *Louis Dreyfus et Cie*,[35a] with a provision in a sale contract for discharging at "1000 metric tonnes provided minimum 5 hatches or pro rata, if less than 5 hatches available, per working day." The buyers, in an argument dismissed by Parker J., appealed against a decision by the arbitrator that the discharging rate was 800 tonnes per day, only four hatches having been available at the beginning of discharge. It is not proposed to discuss this case in detail. In the last of the five High Court cases since *Zita* Webster J.,[35b] referring to the *Maritime Transport* case, said: "That decision would have been one upon which the charterers in the present appeals could have placed more reliance if the clause had contained the word 'workable' [he also noted that Parker J. did not expressly recognise any distinction between 'workable' and 'available'], had it been decided before the *Giannis Xilas*[35c] and had it not been for the fact that, as it appears, neither *The Sandgate*[35d] nor the *Corfu Island*[35e] was cited. In these circumstances it cannot be regarded as a useful authority on the construction of the clause as a whole. I only cite it, there-

[34] [1953] 2 Lloyd's Rep. 472 at p. 475 (*The Corfu Island*).
[35] (1929) 35 Ll.L. Rep. 9 at p. 13. This decision of the Probate, Divorce and Admiralty Divisional Court is under the name of *Sandgate (Owners)* v. *W. S. Partridge & Co.*
[35a] [1981] 2 Lloyd's Rep. 159 (*The Tropwave*).
[35b] In *President of India* v. *Jebsens (U.K.) Ltd.* [1987] 2 Lloyd's Rep. 354, at p. 357 (*The General Capinpin*).
[35c] *Cargill Inc.* v. *Rionda de Pass Ltd.* [1982] 2 Lloyd's Rep. 511.
[35d] [1930] P. 30 (C.A.). See § 2–55 above.
[35e] *Compania de Navigacion Zita S.A.* v. *Louis Dreyfus & Cie* [1953] 2 Lloyd's Rep. 472. See § 2–55.

fore, as being relevant to the distinction between a rate per day per hatch and a rate (or average rate) per day for the vessel."

Cargill Inc. v. *Rionda de Pass Ltd.*,[35f] with a provision in a sale contract for loading at "150 metric tons per workable hatch and pro rata with maximum 750 metric tons per weather working day . . .";

Cargill Inc. v. *Marpro Ltd.*,[35g] with a provision in the same terms as set out in the earlier *Cargill* case, the sale contract having been concluded just over two weeks later, with different buyers.

President of India v. *Jebsens (U.K.) Ltd.*,[35h] where the four charterparties provided for discharge "at the average rate of 1000 metric tonnes basis 5 or more available workable hatches,[35i] pro rata if less number of hatches per weather working day."

President of India v. *Slobodona Plovidba*,[35j] where again the charterparty provided for discharge "at the average rate of 1000 tonnes basis five or more available working hatches, pro rata if less number of hatches, per weather working day."

2–55B   In *Cargill Inc.* v. *Rionda de Pass Ltd.*[35k] Cargill sold 10,000 m.t. of sugar f.o.b. stowed Antwerp, with shipment to be in two equal quantities, in June and July. Loading was to be at "150 metric tons per workable hatch and pro rata with maximum 750 metric tons per weather working day . . ." Of the five hatches numbers 2 and 3 led into an undivided 'tween deck cargo space above holds 2 and 3. Below hatch 2 was a 'tween deck hatch into lower hold 2; and below hatch 3 were two 'tween deck hatches, one giving access to lower hold 2 and the other giving access to lower hold 3. The largest hold quantities in the July loading were 2,054 tonnes in hold 2 and 1,176 tonnes in hold 3. If the loading time was calculated by considering the hold into which the greatest quantity was loaded, one would divide the 2,054 tonnes by 150 tonnes, and there would be over 13 days laytime.

The buyers said that the hold 2 quantity should be halved, to reflect its capacity to be loaded through two hatches. The largest relevant quantity would then be the 1,176 tonnes in hold 3, and there would be under 11 days laytime. Bingham J., holding that the sellers were right, said of the submissions by the buyers that there was no warrant in the language used for thinking in terms of notional hatches; nor was it legitimate to pay attention to cargo spaces which were not mentioned in preference to hatches which were mentioned. Referring with approval to the decisions in *The Sandgate*,[35l] the *Zita*[35m] case and *The Theraios*,[35n] he said[35o] " . . . these parties have adopted what has, at least over the last half century, become a very well established formula with a known meaning."

[35f] [1982] 2 Lloyd's Rep. 511 (*The Giannis Xilas*).
[35g] [1983] 2 Lloyd's Rep. 570 (*The Aegis Progress*).
[35h] [1987] 2 Lloyd's Rep. 354 (*The General Capinpin*).
[35i] The words "available working hatch" were also considered in a London arbitration (LMLN 127, September 13, 1984). The clause stated: "The cargo is to be discharged at the rate of 240 m.t. available working hatch . . . per weather working day of 24 running hours . . . ."
[35j] LMLN 200, July 4, 1987.
[35k] [1982] 2 Lloyd's Rep. 511 (*The Giannis Xilas*).
[35l] [1930] P. 30 (C.A.). See § 2–53 above.
[35m] [1953] 2 Lloyd's Rep. 472. See § 2–54 above.
[35n] *Lodza Compania de Navigacione S.A.* v. *Government of Ceylon* [1971] 1 Lloyd's Rep. 209 (C.A.). See § 2–56 below.
[35o] *Op. cit.*, at p. 515.

In *Cargill Inc.* v. *Marpro Ltd.*[35p] the sale contract again provided for   **2–55C**
loading at "150 metric tons per workable hatch and pro rata with maximum
750 metric tons per weather working day." Cargill had sold sugar, f.o.b.
stowed, to be loaded at one or two ports at sellers' option in the Dunkirk–
Hamburg range. The sellers nominated Antwerp for 5,000 m.t. and Dunkirk for 4,500 m.t. The ship, which was on time charter, had seven hatches,
serving seven holds. She had previously loaded, at Rouen, a part cargo,
with which Cargill was not concerned.

The sellers claimed substantially more despatch than was agreed by the
buyers. They calculated as follows:

Antwerp: largest quantity loaded in any hold: 2,195.25 m.t., which, at
150 m.t. per day, produced 14.635 days of laytime. Hatches 3 and 4 were
completed by the loading at Antwerp.

Dunkirk: largest quantity loaded in any one hold: 1,579.95 m.t., which,
at 150 m.t. per day, produced 10.533 days. Hatches 1, 2, 6 and 7 were each
workable to the extent of the quantities necessary to complete them.

Total laytime: 25.168 days.

The buyers, on the basis of 9,500 m.t. loaded, and 4 holds being workable and available at both ports, divided the loaded quantity by four, to
produce 2,375 m.t. per hatch, which, at 150 m.t. per day, produced 15.83
days of laytime.

Hobhouse J., finding for the sellers, said that one should first ascertain
which hatches were workable, and when they were workable. One then
calculated how long it would take to load and discharge the relevant cargo
at the agreed rate. He said[35q]: "In most cases the required calculations
could be done by identifying the critical hatch or hold and then calculating
the laytime for that hatch; in exceptional cases, and this is one, more than
one hatch is critical and therefore more than one hatch has to be taken into
account in calculating the laytime."

This case was thus an exception to the general rule, that one has regard
to the hold or hatch with the largest capacity. The right approach was first
to ascertain what hatches were and were not workable during what periods
of time, and then to calculate how long it would take to load the relevant
cargo at the rate of 150 tons per workable hatch. In an interesting distinction between availability and workability, Hobhouse J. said[35r]: "For myself
I am unpersuaded that to introduce the word 'available' either into the
clause or the judicial discussion adds anything of substance. But I am certain that a concept of unavailability cannot be used to detract from the
measurement of laytime by reference to tons per day per workable hatch
or to increase the obligations of the shippers. Lest it be thought that the
word 'available' has to be introduced to cover the situation where a hatch
cannot be worked for reasons other than that the hold is full or empty,
this is neither correct as a matter of English language—the word 'workable' is subject to no such limitation—nor was it the view of Mr. Justice
Bingham who expressly included[35s] in his definition of 'workable' the
words— . . . being a hatch which the party responsible for loading or discharging is not for any reason disabled from working . . . ''

[35p] [1983] 2 Lloyd's Rep. 570 (*The Aegis Progress*).
[35q] *Ibid.*, at p. 577.
[35r] *Ibid.*, at p. 577.
[35s] In the *Cargill* v. *Rionda* case, *op. cit.*, at p. 513.

2-55D   The fourth of the five High Court cases was *President of India* v. *Jebsens (U.K.) Ltd.*,[35t] where the charterparties stated "Cargo to be discharged . . . at the average rate of 1000 metric tonnes basis 5 or more available workable hatches, pro rata if less number of hatches per weather working day." The dispute concerned four charterparties and four ships. In each case charterers said that the rate of discharge would diminish as holds emptied, and that therefore the permitted time was governed by the quantity of cargo in the hold into which the greatest quantity had been loaded, dividing that cargo by 200 tonnes per day for a ship with five hatches. They relied upon a passage from the judgment of Bingham J. in the *Cargill* v. *Rionda* case[35u]: "The use of this expression acknowledges that, holds being of different sizes and containing different quantities of cargo, points will be reached during loading or discharge at which successive hatches will cease to be workable because they are, as the case may be, full or empty, and accordingly the loading or discharging obligation is modified when these points occur. On the proper application of the clause in this form the time permitted for loading is governed by the quantity of cargo loaded into the hold into which the greatest quantity of cargo is loaded."

Webster J. allowed the appeals by charterers from an adverse arbitration award.[35v] He said that although it might be necessary to discharge through some hatches at a daily rate higher than 200 tonnes so as to achieve 1,000 tonnes for the ship, the rate which the ship had to achieve was governed by the numbers of available working hatches. The clause meant only that the average rate was to be 1,000 tonnes if there were five hatches, 800 tonnes if there were four, and so on. There was no reason why a hatch with no cargo in the hold beneath it should be treated as an available working hatch to determine the rate for the ship but not to determine the rate of discharge per hatch. A hatch over an empty hold was not a workable hatch.

2-55E   The last of the five High Court cases on this subject since the *Zita* decision was *President of India* v. *Slobodona Plovidba*,[35w] in which the charterparty stated: "cargo to be discharged . . . at the average rate of 1000 tonnes basis five or more available workable hatches, pro rata if less number of hatches, per weather working day." The charterers said that the discharge rate should diminish as holds became empty, so that the permitted time was governed by the quantity of cargo in the hold into which the greatest quantity of cargo had been loaded. The shipowners argued that laytime was to be calculated by dividing the total cargo tonnage by the daily rate of the ship. It was held that the average discharge rate was to be 1,000 tonnes if there were five available workable hatches, 800 tonnes if there were four, and so on. A hatch with no cargo beneath it in the hold was not an available workable hatch for the purpose of the laytime calculation. A hatch was not unavailable or unworkable simply because no gear was available to load or discharge through it. The charterers' contention was accepted.

[35t] [1987] 2 Lloyd's Rep. 354 (*The General Capinpin*).
[35u] [1982] 2 Lloyd's Rep. 511, at pp. 513–514 (*The Giannis Xilas*).
[35v] That is to say, he allowed the charterers' appeal to the effect that the rate of discharge would diminish as the holds became empty, and that the time for discharge was governed by the quantity in the hold into which the greatest quantity of cargo had been loaded. He dismissed that part of their appeal which was based upon the proposition that the absence of loading or discharging gear was capable of rendering a hatch unavailable or unworkable.
[35w] LMLN 200, July 4, 1987.

(3) *"At the average rate of . . . tons per hatch per weather working day."* **2–56**
Where the words "workable hatch" were absent from the relevant clause,
the result was different from the two cases cited above.[36] In *Lodza Compania de Navigacione S.A.* v. *Government of Ceylon*[37] a charterparty for the
carriage of 4,500 metric tons of lentils from Lattakia to Colombo provided:
"The cargo is to be loaded . . . at the average rate of 120 metric tons per
hatch per weather working day . . . cargo is to be discharged at the average
rate of 12 metric tons per hatch per working day"; and "Vessel has 5 (five)
hatches which shall be at all times available for loading and discharging."
The shipowners contended that they should multiply the daily rate per
hatch by the number of hatches, thus arriving at a daily rate of 600 tons.
The charterers said that one divided by 120 the metric tons loaded in the
largest hold, and that if the largest hold had, say 1,000 tons left in it when
the other holds had been discharged, it would be impossible to discharge
the quantity left at the rate of 600 tons per day out of one hatch.

The Court of Appeal held that the shipowners were right. All three **2–57**
judges emphasised the importance of the word "working" in *The Sandgate*.[38] Salmon L.J. said[39]:

> "In my view it is fairly plain that the decision in *The Sandgate*[39] depended upon the
> word 'working' and would have been in favour of the owners had the clause omitted that
> word, as does clause 17 in the present case."

Megaw L.J. said[40]:

> "There is, if I may say so with respect, good reason why some meaning should be given
> to the word 'working' where it is used to qualify 'hatch'; and there is good reason why
> that meaning should be that the hatch of a hold from which all cargo has been discharged
> is no longer a 'working hatch,' for the purposes of calculating laytime on unloading. But I
> see no good reason why any such connotation should be given to the word 'hatch' *simpli-
> citer*. I see no good reason why the word 'working' should be implied before 'hatch' in
> clause 17 of this charter-party."

Salmon L.J. further explained the matter[41]:

> "Since this vessel has five hatches, the clause seems to me to be a round about way of
> saying that the vessel shall be loaded and discharged at an average rate of 600 tons per
> day, that is to say five hatches at 120 tons per hatch . . . The average rate . . . is only a
> rough average daily rate, negotiated no doubt after taking into consideration all foresee-
> able contingencies and in the light of all the relevant facts, including the size of the vari-
> ous holds . . . "

Problem of availability of holds **2–58**
The word "available" in the phrase "per available working hatch"
affects the calculations in that deduction must be made for the time when
hatches were not available.[41a] It does not affect the initial calculation by
which the number of days is worked out. One criticism made by the ship-

---

[36] *The Sandgate* [1930] P. 30 (C.A.) (see § 2–53 above); and *Compania de Navigacion Zita
S.A.* v. *Louis Dreyfus & Cie* [1953] 2 Lloyd's Rep. 472 (see § 2–55 above) (*The Corfu
Island*).
[37] [1971] 1 Lloyd's Rep. 209 (C.A.). *(The Theraios)*.
[38] [1930] P. 30. (C.A.). See § 2–53 above.
[39] *Op. cit.* at p. 212.
[40] *Op. cit.* at pp. 214–215.
[41] *Op cit* at p. 211. Compare the phraseology used by Scrutton L.J. in *The Sandgate* [1930] P.
30 (C.A.) at pp. 33 and 34, quoted in § 2–53 above.
[41a] See also §§ 2–55A—2–55E above, and the discussions of this concept, and that of workability, in cases since the *Zita* decision.

owners in *Compania de Navigacion Zita S.A.* v. *Louis Dreyfus & Cie*[42] was that the charterers' formula depended upon an unwarrantable assumption of availability. Devlin J. said of this[43]:

> "The formula produces a number of days and hours based on the quantity of cargo actually loaded; it takes the place of a number fixed in advance on the quantity of the cargo estimated to be loaded. Both figures are arrived at on the assumption of good weather and are equally at the mercy of such events as bad weather or the unavailability of hatches. Unavailability is therefore outside the formula and a matter for a separate calculation. You take the formula figure just as you would take a specified number of lay days and make the appropriate deductions, where necessary, for Sundays and holidays and bad weather and unavailability of hatches."

The unavailability must involve interference with the work, and it would not be relevant that a hatch of a completed hold developed a defect. Of such a situation Devlin J. said[44]:

> "It is not irrelevant to observe that the unavailability must be something that matters, that is, must interfere with the work. If, for example, a hatch broke down after a hold had been completely loaded, it clearly would not matter."

The same argument would apply if a hatch broke down at the beginning of loading or discharging, provided that enough time remained to fill the hold at the agreed rate. In an example given to Devlin J. the agreed daily rate per available workable hatch was 150 tons. The largest hold had a capacity of 900 tons and the smallest (No. 1) 150 tons. As Devlin J. put it[45]:

> "If, on Mr. Kerr's figures, No. 1 hatch broke down at the beginning for, say, four days, equally it would not matter, for it would not be long enough to prevent the loading of the hold within the standard time."

2–59   F. Weather working days[45a]

A weather working day is any working day[46] during which weather does not wholly prevent working of the ship or would not wholly prevent working if work were intended.[47] If work is or would have been wholly prevented by weather it is not a weather working day. If there is or would have been partial prevention it is still a weather working day but the charterers are entitled to have it cut down for the purpose of the laytime calculations. The words "weather working days," a deceptively simple form of shorthand, have been explained in a number of cases. They have been described[48] as "an expression which appears to have come into use in shipping matters at about the end of the last century, somewhere about the 90's," and thus after the expression "working days."

---

[42] [1953] 2 Lloyd's Rep. 472.

[43] At p. 477.

[44] *Ibid.*

[45] *Ibid.*

[45a] The Charterparty Laytime Definitions 1980 (see Appendix to this book) state: "16. 'WEATHER WORKING DAY'—means a working day or part of a working day during which it is or, if the vessel is still waiting for her turn, it would be possible to load/discharge the cargo without interference due to the weather. If such interference occurs (or would have occurred if work had been in progress), there shall be excluded from the laytime a period calculated by reference to the ratio which the duration of the interference bears to the time which would have or could have been worked but for the interference."

[46] For "working day," see § 2–22 above.

[47] See § 2–61 below.

[48] By Pearson J. in *Compania Naviera Azuero S.A.* v. *British Oil and Cake Mills Ltd.* [1957] 2 Q.B. at p. 302.

An uninterrupted working day   **2–60**

Authority for part of the definition of a weather working day was provided by the High Court in *Bennetts & Co.* v. *Brown*[49] It established the proposition that a working day on which weather did not prevent working at all was a weather working day. A charterparty for the carriage of coal from New South Wales to Valparaiso provided for discharge "at the average rate of not less than 250 tons per weather working day (Sundays and holidays excepted)." It further stated: "detention through . . . delay by . . . surf . . . not to count in the time allowed for loading or discharging." Shipowners and charterers disagreed as to whether days declared by the port captain to be surf days[50] were non-weather working days, and to be wholly excepted, and as to the extent of any detention through delay by surf. Walton J. said of the phrase "weather working days"[51]:

> "Whether it is perfectly grammatical and perfectly good English is not for me to consider . . . it has a natural meaning, *viz.* a day on which the work of discharge—it might be of loading, but in the present case it is of discharge—is not prevented by bad weather. The phrase might refer to half a day. Half a day might not be weather working and the other half might be weather working[52] . . . I do not think that the charterers can rely upon any custom which would give any meaning different from their natural sense to the words 'weather working day'—they certainly cannot rely upon any custom which would make the captain of the port a kind of arbitrator who should settle conclusively what was a weather working day and what was not . . . "

The judge did not have to consider fractions of a day or the effect of bad weather outside normal port working hours and the difference between a calendar day and a day consisting only of the hours normally worked.[53]

Definition of a weather working day   **2–61**

A weather working day was defined by Pearson J. in *Compania Naviera Azuero S.A.* v. *British Oil and Cake Mills Ltd.*[54] He emphasised that there was no decisive authority, and said[55]:

> "In my view, a correct definition of a 'weather working day' is a day on which the weather permits the relevant work to be done, whether or not any person avails himself of that permission; in other words, so far as the weather is concerned, it is a working day."

This is in effect the definition given in 1908 in *Bennetts & Co.* v. *Brown*[56] but with the addition of the important words "whether or not any person avails himself of that permission." The definition is positive in that it deals with a day on which there is no bad weather. The alternative situation is one in which there is bad weather of a type which could or does prevent work, on all or part of a working day. The judge then dealt with this[57]:

> "In my view, also, the converse proposition must be on the same basis. A day is not a weather working day, it fails to be a weather working day, in so far as the weather on that

---

[49] [1908] 1 K.B. 490.
[50] For "surf days" generally, see § 7–07 below.
[51] *Ibid.* at pp. 496–498.
[52] See *Branckelow SS. Co.* v. *Lamport & Holt* [1897] 1 Q.B. 570; and see § 7–27 below.
[53] As Lord Devlin said in *Reardon Smith Line Ltd.* v. *Ministry of Agriculture (The Vancouver Strike Case)* [1963] A.C. 691 (H.L.) at p. 735, "the learned judge was not directing his mind to the question whether 'day' meant working day or calendar day."
[54] [1957] 2 Q.B. 293.
[55] At p. 303.
[56] [1908] 1 K.B. 490 at p. 496, *per* Walton J.: " . . . a day on which the work . . . is not prevented by bad weather . . . " See § 2–60 above.
[57] At p. 303.

day does not permit the relevant work to be done, and it is not material to inquire whether any person has intended or planned or prepared to do any relevant work on that day. The status of a day as being a weather working day, wholly or in part or not at all, is determined solely by its own weather, and not by extraneous factors, such as the actions, intentions and plans of any person. That interpretation of the expression avoids what seems to me the absurdity of saying that a day afflicted with continual storms of rain, snow and sleet is to be counted as a weather working day if nobody had planned to do relevant work on that day."

2–62 G. Colliery working days

Colliery working day and colliery guarantee. A colliery working day is a day which is an ordinary working day for the colliery, in normal times and under normal circumstances, even though special circumstances, such as a strike,[58] may for the time being prevent work.[59] The expression is found in colliery guarantees. A colliery guarantee is a contract, usually between the colliery and charterers but sometimes between the colliery and shipowners, by which the terms of supply and loading of the cargo are regulated. It has been defined[60]: "A form of contract between charterer and colliery used in British ports. It is obtained from the colliery, which is to supply the cargo and load the ship on terms in accordance with the colliery guarantee. There is usually a clause in all coal charters which provides that the ship shall be loaded according to colliery guarantee terms." The charterparty may refer to, and will usually precede in time, the colliery guarantee.[61] The object of the colliery guarantee, and of the reference to it in the charterparty, is that charterers shall not be liable to shipowners for not supplying coal if their failure arises from circumstances which give no recourse against the colliery owner, who is "the real master of the situation."[62] The charterers are freed from liability by words in the guarantee which exclude from laytime such periods as dock and colliery holidays, time from 5 p.m. on Saturday to 7 a.m. on Monday, and time lost through strikes causing a stoppage at the colliery. The words may also provide[63] that holidays and full-day stoppages shall be deemed to commence at 5 p.m. on the working day preceding, and to end at 7 a.m. on the working day following such holiday or stoppage.[64] It is common to include the words "demurrage to be in accordance with the above scale payable per colliery working day." In such a case demurrage is not payable in respect of Sundays and holidays. The other exclusions apply to lay days and not to days on demurrage.[65]

---

[58] Many of the legal decisions arose out of the general strike in the Welsh coal mines from April to August 1898.

[59] See Lord Russell of Killowen C.J. in *Saxon SS. Co. Ltd.* v. *Union SS. Co. Ltd.* (1898) 4 Com.Cas. 29 at p. 40 in a High Court judgment eventually upheld by the House of Lords: (1900) 5 Com.Cas. 381.

[60] In Kerchove's *International Maritime Dictionary* (2nd ed., 1961).

[61] For the manner of incorporation, see below.

[62] *Per* A. L. Smith L.J. in *Monsen* v. *MacFarlane & Co.* [1895] 2 Q.B. 562 (C.A.) at p. 575; see also *Weir & Co.* v. *Pirie & Co. (No. 1)* (1898) 3 Com.Cas. 263 at p. 267. See also *Shamrock SS. Co.* v. *Storey & Co.* (1899) 5 Com.Cas. 21, and *Thorman* v. *Dowgate SS. Co.* [1910] 1 K.B. 410.

[63] The examples are taken from *Saxon SS. Co. Ltd.* v. *Union SS. Co. Ltd.* (1900) 5 Com.Cas. 381 (H.L.).

[64] *e.g.* Mabon's Day, Cavilling Day, etc.

[65] According to the House of Lords in *Saxon SS. Co. Ltd.* v. *Union SS. Co. Ltd.* (1900) 5 Com.Cas. 381, reversing the Court of Appeal decision in *Clink* v. *Hickie Borman & Co. (No. 2)* (1899) 4 Com.Cas. 292. The colliery guarantee was in the same form in each case.

The incorporation of the colliery guarantee in the charterparty   **2–63**

A charterparty may refer to a colliery guarantee by providing[66] that the ship shall "load in the usual and customary manner a full and complete cargo of Ferndale coal, as ordered by charterers, which they bind themselves to ship subject to colliery guarantee . . . " and stating: "The vessel to be loaded as customary, but subject in all respects to the colliery guarantee."

Colliery guarantee arbitration clause   **2–64**

A reference to the guarantee need not necessarily incorporate its arbitration clause into the charterparty. Thus in *Clink* v. *Hickie Borman & Co. (No. 1)*[67] the Court of Appeal held that the clause was not incorporated.[68] The charterparty provided that the ship should load "in the usual and customary manner, always afloat, in days to be arranged, colliery working days, as per colliery guarantee form, a full and complete cargo . . . " The court was satisfied that such a reference was insufficient to incorporate the arbitration clause. The charterers sought to refer the shipowners' demurrage claim to arbitration. As Sir Nathaniel Lindley M.R. said[69]:

> "Now, if we look at the question from the point of view of the charterparty, I do not think we could possibly hold that it includes and covers this arbitration clause, without a great stretch, whether you look at it in the narrow sense or in the ordinary business sense."

The reference to the colliery guarantee can be wide enough to incorporate its arbitration clause in the charterparty. In *Weir & Co.* v. *Pirie & Co. (No. 1)*[70] the charterparty provided that the ship should "load in the usual and customary manner a full and complete cargo of Ferndale coal, as ordered by the charterers, which they bound themselves to ship subject to colliery guarantee . . . The vessel to be loaded as customary, but subject in all respects to the colliery guarantee." The shipowners' demurrage claim was held by the Court of Appeal to be subject to the arbitration clause. Chitty L.J. said[71]:   **2–65**

> " . . . it would be a very strange thing to say that the words 'subject to the colliery guarantee,' or 'subject in all respects to the colliery guarantee,' are not sufficient to include the arbitration clause."[72]

H. Running hours   **2–66**

Where a cargo is to be loaded or discharged in a fixed number of running hours[73] time runs continously, by day and by night, both during and out of normal hours, except for any times, such as Sundays and holidays, which may be expressly excepted.

---

[66] As in *Weir & Co.* v. *Pirie & Co. (No. 1)* (1898) 3 Com.Cas. 263.
[67] (1898) 3 Com.Cas. 275.
[68] For incorporation see §§ 11–02 and 11–09 below.
[69] At p. 278.
[70] (1898) 3 Com.Cas. 263.
[71] At p. 269.
[72] The colliery guarantee arbitration clause was held by the Court of Appeal to be incorporated in the charterparty in *Monsen* v. *MacFarlane* [1895] 2 Q.B. 562, where the words were "to be loaded as per colliery guarantee in fifteen colliery working days."
[73] For laytime expressed as running hours, see § 2–07 above.

CHAPTER 3

LAYTIME NOT FIXED

3–01 Types of clause
Where laytime is not fixed or calculable, the ship must be loaded and discharged in a reasonable time. The charterers' duty is "to do their best."[1] They must however have their cargo ready to load; they cannot escape that duty merely by arguing that they did their best to provide a cargo.[2] The obligation to load and discharge in a reasonable time is implied in the contract of carriage. It may be governed or qualified by local custom. Lord Selborne L.C. said in *Postlethwaite* v. *Freeland*[3]:

> "If (as in the present case) an obligation, indefinite as to time, is qualified or partially defined by express or implied reference to the custom or practice of a particular port, every impediment arising from or out of that custom or practice, which the charterer could not have overcome by the use of any reasonable diligence, ought (I think) to be taken into consideration."

The parties may express the duty in such phrases as:

"all dispatch as customary"[4]
"with customary steamship dispatch as fast as the steamer can receive and deliver"[5]
"with all dispatch, according to the custom of the port"[6]
"as fast as steamer can deliver after having been berthed as customary"[7]
"as fast as the steamer can deliver as customary"[8]
"as fast as the steamer can deliver in accordance with the custom of the port"[9]
"in the usual and customary time."[10]

---

[1] Bigham J. in *Lyle Shipping Co. Ltd.* v. *Cardiff Corporation* (1899) 5 Com.Cas. 87 at p. 94: " . . . the obligation upon the defendants was to do their best, both in procuring and making use of the wagons."

[2] *Ardan S.S. Co.* v. *Andrew Weir & Co.* [1905] A.C. 501 (H.L.); circumstances beyond control of the shippers could not be relied on to negative their absolute duty to provide a coal cargo.

[3] (1880) 5 App.Cas. 599 (H.L.) at p. 608.

[4] *Castlegate SS. Co. Ltd.* v. *Dempsey* [1892] 1 Q.B. 854 (C.A.) (see § 3–16 below); *Lyle Shipping Co. Ltd.* v. *Cardiff Corporation* (1899) 5 Com.Cas. 87. (See § 3–14 below). The Charterparty Laytime Definitions 1980 (see Appendix to this book) state: "7. 'CUSTOMARY DESPATCH'—means that the charterer must load and/or discharge as fast as is possible in the circumstances prevailing at the time of loading or discharging."

[5] *Hulthen* v. *Stewart & Co.* [1902] 2 K.B. 199 (C.A.). See § 3–13 below. The Charterparty Laytime Definitions 1980 (see Appendix to this book) state: "10. 'AS FAST AS THE VESSEL CAN RECEIVE/DELIVER'—means that the laytime is a period of time to be calculated by reference to the maximum rate at which the ship in full working order is capable of loading/discharging the cargo."

[6] *Postlethwaite* v. *Freeland* (1880) 5 App.Cas. 599 (H.L.). See § 3–11 below.

[7] *Wyllie* v. *Harrison* (1885) 13 Rettie 92.

[8] *Good* v. *Isaacs* [1892] 2 Q.B. 555. See § 3–17.

[9] *Transoceanica Societa Italiana di Navigazione* v. *H. S. Shipton & Sons* [1923] 1 K.B. 31.

[10] *Rodgers* v. *Forresters* (1810) 2 Camp. 483.

48

" . . . deliver the said cargo in the usual and customary manner . . ."[11] **3–02**
"The time for discharging at destination shall be in accordance with
the custom of the Port for Steamers at port of Discharge, except as
hereinafter provided."[12]
"Except as hereinafter provided the time for discharging at destination shall be in accordance with the custom of the port for steamships
at the port of discharge."[13]
"On the Continent the time for discharging shall be in accordance with
the custom of the port for steamships at the port of discharge."[14]

The duty to work the cargo at reasonable speed exists even if the charterparty does not mention reasonable dispatch[15] or if it merely stipulates that
loading or discharging shall be "as fast as master shall require."[16] The origin, as far as English case law is concerned, of the duty to load and discharge at a reasonable speed is to be found in two cases decided in 1810,
Rodgers v. *Forresters*[17] and *Burmester* v. *Hodgson*.[18]
In the examples given above[19] there are three references to dispatch, **3–03**
while in every case there appears either the word "customary" or a reference to "the custom of the port," sometimes known as "c.o.p." The words
"forthwith" and "immediately" have also been used,[20] and can be
employed with or instead of the reference to "dispatch." In addition four
of the clauses refer to the capacity of the ship to help the operation, by such
words as "as fast as the steamer can receive and deliver."[21] The latter
words are not descriptive of the duty of the charterers, though they are relevant to this problem.[22]

"Custom"; "as customary" **3–04**

A reference to custom, or a stipulation that loading or discharging shall
be "as customary," is not necessary in law, as the implied obligation that
the ship will be worked in a reasonable time imports with it the duty to
work in accordance with local custom.[23] The word "custom" in this sense
means a usual practice in the port, and not "custom" in the other legal
sense of a practice so accepted that the parties regard it as a binding and

---

[11] *Ford* v. *Cotesworth* (1868) L.R. 4 Q.B. 127. See § 3–10.
[12] River Plate Charter-Party 1914 (Centrocon). The exceptions relate to Bristol Channel,
Irish and Dutch ports, and London, where fixed daily rates are stipulated.
[13] Australian Grain Charter 1928 (Austral); the exceptions relate to Bristol Channel and Irish
ports, and to Liverpool and Birkenhead, where fixed daily rates are stipulated.
[14] Australian Grain Charter 1956 (Austwheat).
[15] As in *Hick* v. *Raymond & Reid* [1893] A.C. 22 (H.L.). See § 3–12 below.
[16] As in *Sea S.S. Co.* v. *Price Walker* (1903) 8 Com.Cas. 292.
[17] (1810) 2 Camp. 483.
[18] *Ibid.* at p. 488.
[19] In § 3–01.
[20] In *Hudson* v. *Hill* (1874) 43 L.J.C.P. 273.
[21] Sometimes known as f.a.c.
[22] The rate may be limited by the ship's gear; see § 3–20 below.
[23] The existence of a local custom may not help the shipowners if by the exercise of due diligence they could have avoided a delay caused by the custom: *Carali* v. *Xenos* (1862) 2 F. &
F. 740, where goods were delayed by being discharged according to the custom of the port,
and missed the on-carrying ship, which was the last of the season. But the shipowners had
expressly agreed to forward the goods.

integral part of their contract. So Lord Blackburn, in *Postlethwaite* v. *Free-land*[24]:

> "The jurors were told, and I think quite correctly, that 'custom' in the charterparty did not mean custom in the sense in which the word is sometimes used by lawyers, but meant a settled and established practice of the port, and it was then left to them to say whether there was such an established custom . . . "

3–05   Where the parties[25] have employed the words "custom" or "customary," they are taken to refer to the manner of the loading or discharging, and not to the length of time within which it should take place. When the time which should be allowed to charterers is assessed, it is considered in the light of all the circumstances,[26] of which the local custom forms a part.

So in *Smailes & Son* v. *Hans Dessen & Co.*[27] a cargo of pit props was to be supplied to and received from a ship in the manner and at the rate customary at each port during customary working hours, with a further 10 days on demurrage. There was delay at Barry, the discharging port, partly because the customary berths used for pit prop cargoes were occupied when the ship arrived, and partly because of a dispute as to payment of the freight. The shipowners claimed demurrage. The Court of Appeal held that they were only entitled to nominal damages because despite the freight dispute the ship would have suffered the delay. Collins M.R. said of the receiver[28]:

> " . . . all that he is bound to do is to use reasonable care to give the ship the discharge that she is entitled to under the terms of the charterparty. Therefore, his obligation is not as though he had undertaken absolutely to discharge that ship within the given time or any given time—he is only bound to use all reasonable care to see that all the facilities available in the particular port are used for the purpose of giving the ship its due dispatch."

He added later[29]:

> "It seems to me conclusively established upon the undisputed evidence here that delivery according to the custom of the dock was not possible under the existing conditions of congestion in the dock . . . "

3–06   The parties may expunge any reference to custom; if so, it is not possible to imply a term to that effect. This is in accordance with the maxim of construction, *expressum facit cessare tacitum.*[30] Thus in *Maclay* v. *Spillers Ltd. & Baker·Ltd.*[31] the words "any custom of the port to the contrary notwithstanding" appeared in a bill of lading for the carriage of grain to Bristol. The bill stated: "Goods are to be received by the consignee immediately the vessel is ready to discharge, and continuously at all such hours as the Custom House authorities may give permission for the ship to work, any custom of the port to the contrary notwithstanding." The ship-

---

[24] (1880) 5 App.Cas. 599 (H.L.) at p. 616. See also § 3–11 below.

[25] It is important to define "the parties" accurately. A sale contract said that a ship (chartered by sellers) was "to discharge in accordance with the custom of the port." Even where a customary rate was established, the buyers were not liable for demurrage. They were never in contractual relationship with the shipowners, and had not promised sellers discharge in a specified time; *Tradax Internacional S.A.* v. *Pagnan (R.) & Fratelli* [1968] 1 Lloyd's Rep. 244.

[26] See § 3–09 below.

[27] (1906) 12 Com.Cas. 117 (C.A.).

[28] At p. 127.

[29] At p. 132.

[30] So in *Mills* v. *United Counties Bank* [1912] 1 Ch. 231 (C.A.) a deed assigning an equity of redemption which expressed a limited indemnity was held to exclude the wider indemnity which would have been implied at law.   [31] (1901) 17 T.L.R. 391.

owners claimed damages for detention from consignees, as, owing to short-age of labour and congestion of ships, the discharge took six days longer than it otherwise would have done. The Court of Appeal held that there was an absolute obligation on the part of consignees to receive the cargo continuously. Sir A. L. Smith M.R. said[32]:

> " . . . from the time within which it is shown that the ship was ready and willing to deliver the cargo, there is an absolute obligation on the part of the consignee continu-ously to take delivery, any custom of the port to the contrary notwithstanding."

Reasonable time not a fixed time   **3–07**

An obligation to load or discharge the ship in a reasonable time may exist, as has been shown,[33] with or without the use of express words such as "with all dispatch" or "with customary steamship dispatch." Although it is necessary to ascertain what is a reasonable time, it does not follow that the charterparty can then be regarded as one for a fixed time. The circum-stances, both permanent and temporary, which have to be considered, are too many, and too dependent upon the situation of the ship in question, to justify such a conclusion. Thus in *Castlegate SS. Co. Ltd.* v. *Dempsey*[34] it was argued that the words "ten days on demurrage, over and above the said lying days" meant that earlier words, providing for customary dis-patch, fixed a definite time for discharging the cargo. Of this argument Fry L.J. said[35]:

> " . . . this is not one of the class of charterparties which by express language or clear implication define the time to be occupied in the discharge of the cargo. When the time is so defined, it is decided by several cases[36] that the charterer is liable if any event happens which prevents the discharge of the cargo within the specified time. That is not the case here."

In the same vein Lord Herschell said, in *Carlton SS. Co.* v. *Castle Mail*   **3–08**
Co.[37]:

> "There is no such thing as reasonable time in the abstract. The question is whether, having regard to all the obligations of the contract, to its conditions, to its restrictions, and to its limitations, more than a reasonable time has been taken in the performance of any one of these obligations in respect of which the parties have not, by their contract, expressed any limit of time for its performance."

In that case the ship had been chartered to "load in the customary manner (Sundays and holidays excepted) always afloat as and where ordered by the charterers, a cargo of rails." At the loading place, Senhouse Dock, Mary-port, the depth of water was sufficient at spring tides, but not at neap tides, for the ship to load there always afloat. This was within the knowledge of both shipowners and charterers. After loading began, the water began to fall, and the ship had to leave the dock to avoid grounding. After several days she returned with the spring tides and completed her loading. The shipowners claimed demurrage or damages. The House of Lords held that the charterers were not bound to do that which (as was known to the ship-owners) might be physically impossible, namely to order the ship to a berth

---

[32] At p. 219.
[33] In § 3–02 above.
[34] [1892] 1 Q.B. 854 (C.A.). See § 3–16 below.
[35] *Ibid.* at p. 862.
[36] Including *Aktieselskabet Reidar* v. *Arcos* [1927] 1 K.B. 352 (C.A.), *per* Atkin L.J. at p. 363. This rule does not apply if there is an exception clause to the contrary or if the delay results from the shipowners' fault.
[37] [1898] A.C. 486 at p. 491 (H.L.).

where she could then load continuously always afloat. They were not responsible for delay occasioned by natural causes beyond their control. So also, in *Hulthen* v. *Stewart & Co.*[38] where the relevant words were "with customary dispatch as fast as the steamer can receive and deliver," Lord Macnaghten summarised his approach[39]:

> "The words used do not specify, or even, I think, point to definite period of time. What they do point to is the discharge of the cargo with the utmost dispatch practicable, having regard to the custom of the port,[40] the facilities for delivery possessed by the particular vessel under contract of affreightment,[41] and all other circumstances in existence at the time, not being circumstances brought about by the person whose duty it is to take delivery, or circumstnces within his control."

3–09   Reasonable time in the circumstances

In the assessment of what is a reasonable time port custom, the nature of the cargo and of the ship, and "all other circumstances in existence at the time,"[42] are considered. These other circumstances include all factors which govern the speed of loading or discharging,[43] if they are not brought about by or under the control of charterers. It was thought at one time[44] that temporary difficulties and peculiarities could be ignored, but it now seems clear that they must be taken into account. The actual as well as the normal conditions have to be considered. It follows that where a charterparty provides for laytime in indefinite terms, it is not possible at the time of its signature to calculate the loading and discharging laytimes. If circumstances are present which prevent loading or discharging within a reasonable time, then the charterers are not liable for the resultant delay.

3–10   In *Ford* v. *Cotesworth*[45] a ship had to proceed from Liverpool "to Lima or Valparaiso, and there, or so near thereto as she may safely get, deliver the said cargo in the usual and customary manner . . . ." There was provision for laytime, demurrage and despatch at Liverpool, but no such provision with respect to the discharging port, which was Lima. She arrived at Callao, the port of Lima, in February, 1866, took up her berth and was ready to unload on March 1; and after a delay of some days began to discharge. News arrived of the bombardment of Valparaiso by Spanish ships and the authorities refused to allow more cargo to be loaded at the custom house,[46] so that they could empty it, as it would be exposed to the Spanish warships. The ship had to leave her berth for nearly three weeks.

---

[38] [1903] A.C. 389 (H.L.).

[39] At p. 392.

[40] See § 3–04 above.

[41] Note for example the use of such words as "as fast as the steamer can receive and deliver": see § 3–02 above and § 3–17 below.

[42] The words used by Lord Macnaghten in *Hulthen* v. *Stewart & Co.* [1903] A.C. 389 (H.L.) at p. 392.

[43] But not factors which affect the speed with which the cargo is removed after being discharged; *Langham SS. Co.* v. *Gallagher* [1911] 2 Ir.R. 348.

[44] *Ashcroft* v. *Crow Colliery Co.* (1874) L.R. 9 Q.B. 540 and *Wright* v. *New Zealand Shipping Co.* (1879) 4 Ex.D. 165 exemplify this trend. It was held that the unusual circumstances at a port did not justify charterers in their failure to do all that they could have done under normal circumstances.

[45] (1868) L.R. 4 Q.B. 127. The decision was applied in *Sunbeam Shipping Co. Ltd.* v. *President of India (The Atlantic Sunbeam)* [1973] 1 Lloyd's Rep. 482. See § 5–07 below.

[46] Blackburn J. said (*ibid.* p. 132): "The custom-house authorities will not allow any cargo to be landed except through the customs; and in consequence of their dilatoriness, and the general sluggishness of the population, the ordinary discharge of a vessel at Callao is very slow."

The shipowners claimed damages for detention. Blackburn J. said that the Court had decided that their claim failed. The question depended upon what term was implied by law where there was no provison as to the discharging time. He said[47]:

> " . . . the contract, implied by the law, in the absence of any stipulation, in a charterparty, is that each party shall use reasonable diligence in performing his part of the delivery at the port of discharge, the merchant being ready to receive in the usual manner, and the owner by his captain and crew to deliver in the usual manner. So that there is no contract implied by law on the part of the shipowner to allow his vessel to be kept there for the usual time, if by reasonable diligence on the part of the merchant, the cargo might be sooner taken away, and no contract implied by law on the part of the merchant to take the cargo out within such usual time, if he could not by reasonable diligence perform it: though very commonly there are stipulations to that effect."

As to the argument that the charterparty was to be construed as if it provided for a specific number of lay days, the only question being what was the usual and customary time there for such a ship, Blackburn J. added[48]:

> "But we are aware of no authority for saying that the law implies a contract to discharge in the usual time, except what is said in *Burmester* v. *Hodgson*,[49] in which case it was not necessary for the decision. We think that the contract which the law implies is only that the merchant and shipowner should each use reasonable despatch in performing his part . . . If this be so, the delay having happened without fault on either side, and neither having undertaken by contract, express or implied, that there should be no delay, the loss must remain where it falls."

The extent to which the rule can protect charterers was shown in *Post-* **3–11** *lethwaite* v. *Freeland*.[50] A charterparty for the carriage of steel rails and fastenings from England to South Africa stipulated: "The cargo to be discharged with all dispatch according to the custom of the port." Discharge could only be effected by a warp and lighters. These were under the absolute control of a company to which the governmental authorities had transferred all their powers. The ship had to wait 31 working days for her turn. The House of Lords held that the shipowners' claim for demurrage failed: if the charterers had agreed to discharge the ship within a fixed period of time, that would have been an absolute and unconditional engagement. If there was no fixed time they fulfilled their contract by employing the usual methods of dispatch. Lord Selborne L.C. said[51]:

> "If (as in the present case) an obligation, indefinite as to time, is qualified or partially defined by express or implied reference to the custom or practice of a particular port, every impediment arising from or out of that custom or practice, which the charterer could not have overcome by the use of any reasonble diligence, ought (I think) to be taken into consideration."

It is clear from the judgment of Lord Selborne L.C.[52] that charterers **3–12** must use reasonable diligence, but that they will not be held liable for delay if their diligence does not result in the ship being loaded or discharged as fast as usual. This rule applies even where the charterparty or bill of lading contains no such expressions as "with all dispatch," or "in accordance with

---

[47] *Ibid*. at p. 134.
[48] *Ibid*. at pp. 136–137.
[49] (1810) 2 Camp. 488. There was no provision as to unloading time. The London docks were crowded and the ship was delayed 40 days beyond the usual time. It was held that both parties had used reasonable diligence and that charterers were not liable. There was no suggestion that the population of London was sluggish; see n. 46 above.
[50] (1880) 5 App.Cas. 599 (H.L.).
[51] At p. 608.
[52] In *Postlethwaite* v. *Freeland* (1880) 5 App.Cas. 599 at p. 608 (H.L.).

the custom of the port." This follows from the decision of the House of Lords in *Hick* v. *Raymond & Reid*.[53] A ship carried grain from Taganrog in the Sea of Azov to London. The bills of lading were silent as to the time for discharging. Unloading was interrupted by a strike of dock labourers which delayed the discharge far beyond the time which would otherwise have sufficed. It was not possible for the consignees to find any other person to provide or to perform the labour.[54] The House of Lords held that the consignees were not liable in damages for the delay. Lord Herschell L.C. stated that there appeared to be no direct authority as to whether, in assessing what was a reasonable time, one considered normal or extraordinary circumstances. He said[55]:

> "But what may without impropriety be termed the ordinary circumstances differ in particular ports at different times of the year. . . . Could it be contended that in so far as it lasted beyond the ordinary period the delay caused by it was to be excluded in determining whether the cargo had been discharged within a reasonable time? It appears to me that the appellant's[56] contention would involve constant difficulty and dispute, and that the only sound principle is that 'reasonable time' should depend on the circumstances which actually exist. If the cargo has been taken with all reasonable despatch under these circumstances I think the obligation of the consignee has been fulfilled."

3–13   The House thus confirmed[57] that whether the contract of affreightment provided for "all dispatch according to the custom of the port"[58] or was silent as to the time for loading or discharging,[59] then:

1. charterers must employ reasonable diligence[60];
2. shipowners must accept the impediments which arise from custom or practice, and the actual circumstances of the particular voyage.

It was emphasised later by the Court of Appeal that evidence could be produced to show that the circumstances prevented expeditious loading or discharging. Thus in *Hulthen* v. *Stewart & Co.*[61] a charterparty for the carriage of timber from the White Sea to London stated: "The cargo to be loaded and discharged with customary steamship dispatch as fast as the steamer can receive and deliver during the ordinary working hours of the respective ports, but according to the custom of the respective ports." Owing to congestion in the dock there was delay and further delays in getting a berth when she was in dock, and in unloading. The latter took more than the five days otherwise needed. The shipowners sued the indorsees of

---

[53] [1893] A.C. 22.

[54] Consignees are obliged in such a case to arrange for the work to be done in some other way if possible; *Fitzgerald* v. *Lona* (1932) 44 Ll.L. Rep. 212; *Rederiaktiebolaget Macedonia* v. *Slaughter* (1935) 52 Ll.L. Rep. 4.

[55] At p. 29.

[56] The shipowners were appealing from the judgment of the Court of Appeal, reported as *Hick* v. *Rodocanachi* [1891] 2 Q.B. 626 (C.A.).

[57] In *Postlethwaite* v. *Freeland* (1880) 5 App.Cas. 599 (H.L.) (see § 3–11 above) and in *Hick* v. *Raymond & Reid* [1893] A.C. 22 (H.L.) (see § 3–12 above).

[58] As with the charterparty in *Postlethwaite* v. *Freeland* (1880) 5 App.Cas. 599 (H.L.) (see § 3–12 above).

[59] As with the bill of lading in *Hick* v. *Raymond & Reid* [1893] A.C. 22 (H.L.) (see § 3–12 above).

[60] Where laytime is fixed, however, the charterers can insist on keeping the ship to the end of the laytime even if only a small parcel of cargo remains; *Margaronis Navigation Agency Ltd.* v. *Henry W. Peabody & Co. of London Ltd.* [1965] 1 Q.B. 300 (see §§ 1–06–1–08 above).

[61] [1902] 2 K.B. 199 (C.A.).

a bill of lading for demurrage but failed because they were found to have discharged the cargo within a reasonable time. Collins M.R. said[62]:

> "The point, therefore, comes to this—whether the clause that the ship is to be discharged, 'as fast as the steamer can deliver' is to be taken as imparting an obligation to discharge in five days . . . ."

He referred to the line of authorities on the subject[63] and said[64]: **3–14**

> " . . . there is authority that evidence of the circumstances under which the unloading took place can be let in where the undertaking is to use all dispatch in unloading, and even in cases where the undertaking is to discharge as fast as the steamer can deliver. That seems to me to carry this case through . . . it seems to me that the vessel was not detained to any degree of which the shipowner can complain, because it was impossible under the circumstances to get her sooner into the dock, or to unload her faster when she got into the dock."

So also Mathew L.J. said[65]:

> "I should have thought that by this time the mercantile community would have been informed as to the view that lawyers take of this common clause in a charterparty, and if the result is unexpected by the shipowner in this case it should be known that in future it will be perfectly easy to avoid any discussion of the kind if the shipowner and charterer would only insert plain language in the charterparty."

As Romer L.J. put it in *Lyle Shipping Co.* v. *Cardiff Corporation*,[66] when speaking of the words "with all dispatch as customary":

> "I think it is now settled that such a provision means that the discharge shall take place with all reasonable dispatch, and that in considering what is reasonable you must have regard, not to a hypothetical state of things (that is, to what would be reasonable in an ordinary state of circumstances), but to the actual state of things at the time of discharge, and, in particular, to the customs of the port of discharge."

The implication of reasonableness does not extend to the duty of the charterers to have the cargo ready for loading.[67] Such a duty is absolute; failure to perform it is a breach for which charterers are liable unless it resulted from some act of shipowners or was excused by an exceptions clause.

WHAT CIRCUMSTANCES SHOULD BE TAKEN INTO ACCOUNT?

Among the other circumstances[68] which should be taken into account, in **3–15** assessing what is a reasonable time for loading and discharging, are:

1. Strikes;
2. Action of harbour authorities;
3. Illegality;
4. Engagements of consignees and charterers;
5. Limits imposed by ship's gear.

---

[62] At p. 204.
[63] *Postlethwaite* v. *Freeland* (1880) 5 App.Cas. 599 (H.L.) (see § 3–12 above); *Hick* v. *Raymond & Reid* [1893] A.C. 22 (H.L.) (see § 3–12 above); *Lyle Shipping Co.* v. *Cardiff Corporation* [1900] 2 Q.B. 638 (C.A.); *Wyllie* v. *Harrison* (1885) 13 R. 92; *Good* v. *Isaacs* [1892] 2 Q.B. 555 (C.A.).
[64] At pp. 205–206.
[65] At p. 208.
[66] [1900] 2 Q.B. 638 at p. 647 (C.A.).
[67] See also § 3–01 above.
[68] See also those considered in §§ 3–09–3–14 above.

3–16 1. Strikes

One of the "circumstances in existence at the time"[69] may be a strike. In *Castlegate SS. Co. Ltd.* v. *Dempsey*[70] a charterparty for the carriage of deals and sleepers from the Baltic Sea to Garston stipulated that the cargo was "to be discharged with all dispatch as customary, and ten days on demurrage, over and above the said lying days . . . ." By the custom of Garston a dock company undertook the work of discharging. By reason of a strike of the dock labourers the discharge was delayed for four days. The Court of Appeal held that the charterparty had not fixed any definite time for discharging, and that regard must be had to the customary circumstances and the manner of discharging at Garston. The charterers were therefore not liable for the delay. Lord Esher M.R. said of the words "to be discharged with all dispatch as customary"[71]:

> "I should say that the meaning of words such as these, taken by themselves, had been determined by case after case."

He said that the applicable principles were those enunciated by the House of Lords in *Postlethwaite* v. *Freeland*,[72] where the relevant words were "all dispatch according to the custom of the port"; the terms in the two charterparties were exactly equivalent. The words "as customary"[73] referred to the manner and not to the time of discharge. The cargo must be discharged within a reasonable time under the circumstances. Even if the circumstances to be regarded were only those arising out of the application of the custom of the port, the circumstance in question did so arise.[74]

3–17 2. Action of harbour authorities

Where the harbour authorities delay or prevent loading or discharging, charterers are not liable if they are unable to control the actions of the authorities.

So in *Good & Co.* v. *Isaacs*[75] a ship chartered to carry oranges from Mediterranean ports to Hamburg was "to be discharged at usual fruit berth as fast as steamer can deliver, as customary, and where ordered by the charterers." When she was ready to deliver the usual fruit berths were occupied and the fruit warehouses were full. Owing to the action of the harbour authorities she could not begin to discharge for five days. The Court of Appeal rejected the shipowners' demurrage claim on the grounds that (1) the charterers' obligation to unload did not begin until the ship was berthed in a usual fruit berth; (2) she was not so berthed until she occupied a berth by the direction or with the assent of the harbour authorities; (3) the word "customary" must be taken to refer to the discharge and delivery by the ship rather than to the taking of delivery by the charterers or consignees, and to mean that the discharge and delivery must be as fast as the

---

[69] The words used by Lord Macnaghten in *Hulthen* v. *Stewart & Co.* [1903] A.C. 389 at p. 392 (H.L.). See § 3–08 above.

[70] [1892] 1 Q.B. 854 (C.A.).

[71] At p. 858.

[72] (1880) 5 App.Cas. 599. In that case Lord Esher M.R. had been a member of the Court of Appeal, the judgments in which were upheld by the House of Lords.

[73] For "custom" and "as customary" see § 3–04 above.

[74] As to the effect of a strike of dock labourers, see also *Hick* v. *Raymond & Reid* [1873] A.C. 22 (H.L.) and § 3–12 above.

[75] [1892] 2 Q.B. 555 (C.A.).

custom of the port would allow. There was no delay for which the charterers were responsible. Kay L.J. said[76]:

> " 'To be discharged as fast as steamer can deliver, as customary,' means that the discharge and delivery is to be as fast as the custom of the port would allow, and that the shipowner took the risk of a delay in that discharge and delivery owing to the custom of the port . . . ."

He concluded[77]:

> "I think the true result of the evidence is that there was no delay except what was occasioned by the custom of the port, and for this the charterers are not responsible."

3. Illegality   3–18

Illegality, by the law of the country where performance is required, may be one of the relevant circumstances in a decision as to what is a reasonable time for loading or discharging.

In *Ralli Brothers* v. *Compania Naviera Sota y Aznar*[78] a ship had been chartered to carry jute from Calcutta to Barcelona. By a Spanish regulation, made the day before the date of the charterparty and confirmed by royal proclamation before the ship arrived at Barcelona, the freight on jute was not to exceed 875 pesetas per ton. Owing to alterations in exchange rates the freight was, at the date of arrival, in excess of that sum. The receivers refused to pay the excess and the shipowners claimed it from the charterers. The Court of Appeal held that the charterparty was an English contract to be construed by English law, but that as the part of it dealing with the charterers' obligation as to freight had to be performed in Spain, its performance was illegal to that extent, and could not be enforced against the charterers. Scrutton L.J. said[79]:

> " . . . where a contract requires an act to be done in a foreign country, it is, in the absence of very special circumstances, an implied term of the continuing validity of such a provision that the act to be done in the foreign country shall not be illegal by the law of that country. This country should not in my opinion assist or sanction the breach of the laws of other independent states."

4. Engagements of consignees and charterers   3–19

Among the circumstances which may affect the length of time taken to load or discharge are the previous engagements of the shippers, consignees or charterers. Shipowners must accept as reasonable any delay which results from the normal business of such persons.[80] If there is such delay that it cannot reasonably be said to have been contemplated by the parties when the charterparty was concluded, then it constitutes a breach of the charterparty, unless it results from the shipowners' own actions or from the actions of consignees to whom the charterers have sold the cargo.

Delay by consignees rather than by charterers was considered in *Watson* v. *Borner*,[81] where charterers had sold a cargo to the owners of a private wharf, which was the named destination under the charterparty. Discharging time was to begin at 6 a.m. after the ship was ready in berth; for their own convenience the wharf owners, who were receivers under the bills of

---

[76] At p. 564.
[77] At p. 565.
[78] [1920] 2 K.B. 287 (C.A.).
[79] At p. 304.
[80] *Harrowing* v. *Dupré* (1902) 7 Com.Cas. 157.
[81] (1900) 5 Com.Cas. 377 (C.A.).

lading, delayed giving the ship a berth. As the charterers were not responsible for the delay, laytime did not start until the ship reached the berth.

A similar delay was considered in *Ogmore SS. Co. Ltd.* v. *H. Borner & Co. Ltd.*[82] A charterparty provided that the ship should carry iron ore from Cartagena or Porman to "Maryport, Senhouse Dock, and there deliver the same as customary, where and as directed by the consignees." When she arrived at Maryport the purchasers of her cargo had already several ships discharging in the dock. As a result she was delayed and got into berth 12 days after getting into the dock, since a local by-law prevented consignees from having more than three ships discharging in dock at the same time. The Admiralty Court held that the charterers were not responsible for the delay. Gorell Barnes J. pointed out that the charterers had not placed impediments in the way of the shipowners bringing their ship into dock; if they had done so, they would have been responsible for the delay, as if the ship had in fact arrived in dock. As he said[83]:

> "The charterers, however, had sold the cargo to consignees. The position then is that those consignees became agents of the charterers to receive the cargo and pay the freight in accordance with the charterparty and their obligations arose after the vessel arrived in dock. . . . The engagements and actions of the consignees in relation to the other vessels were not entered into or taken by them as agents for the charterers. It was not contended that there was anything unreasonable in the charterers selling the cargo to the particular consignees."

In the circumstances there had been no breach of contract by the charterers.

3–20   **5. Limits imposed by ship's gear**

Charterers may be bound to discharge the ship with reasonable dispatch[84] but their obligation to do so may be linked with, and limited by, the mechanical facilities of the ship. Such a limitation is implied where it is not expressly stated, since charterers cannot be expected to work a ship with reasonable dispatch if the shipowners' own equipment prevents them from so doing. The limitation can be expressed in such words as "provided steamer can deliver it at this rate."

Thus in *Northfield SS. Co.* v. *Compagnie L'Union des Gaz*[85] a charterparty for the carriage of coal from Sunderland to Savona provided for cargo to be taken from alongside at the average rate of 500 tons per day, weather permitting, Sundays and holidays excepted, "provided steamer can deliver it at this rate." Time was to begin whether the ship was in berth or not; there was delay in berthing, and, by a rule of the shore labourers which was also part of the port regulations, cargo could not be discharged until the ship was in berth alongside a wharf. The Court of Appeal, holding that time began when notice was given and the ship was ready to unload, discussed the words "provided steamer can deliver at this rate." The charterers had argued that laytime could not begin where delivery was not possible. Cozens-Hardy M.R. said of the words in the proviso[86]:

> "They only deal with the rate of discharge of the cargo when once the discharge has begun, and are concerned with what I may call the mechanical facilities of the steamer for delivery."

---

[82] (1901) 6 Com.Cas. 104. (*The Deerhound*).
[83] At pp. 110–111.
[84] For the different charterparty clauses embodying this concept, see § 3–01 above.
[85] [1912] 1 K.B. 434 (C.A.).
[86] At pp. 439–440.

So also Farwell L.J.[87]:

> " . . . those words refer to the structural capacity and fittings of the vessel, not to her position in the harbour or to the supply of labour from the shore available for the consignees."

The charterers do not necessarily warrant that the cargo can be handled **3–21** and unloaded expeditiously and effectively by the machinery and appliances in ordinary use at the port of discharge.

In *Transoceanica Societa Italiana di Navigazione* v. *H. S. Shipton & Sons*[88] a ship chartered to carry general cargo from Alexandria to London was "to be discharged as fast as she can deliver in accordance with the custom of the port." The only provision for demurrage was in respect of the loading port. A bill of lading stipulated that the cargo was "to be received by consignees as fast as steamer can deliver in accordance with the custom of the port." The shipowners sued the indorsees of a bill of lading for damages for detention. They did not allege that the parcel of barley in question was not taken as fast as the ship could actually deliver it, but said that it contained sand and stones which choked a pneumatic suction pump and delayed the discharge. McCardie J. said[89]:

> "There was no actual default in that respect[90] by the receivers. They were bound to act with reasonable expedition . . . and they did so."

The shipowners failed because, as he put it,[91] referring to *Acatos* v. *Burns*[92]:

> "One of the questions in the action was whether the shipper of the maize had warranted that the maize was fit for carriage in the vessel, and it was held by the Court of Appeal that where the owner of a vessel has an opportunity of examining goods shipped on board her, no warranty on the part of the shipper of the goods can be implied that they are fit to be carried on the voyage. In my view the principle of that case, and not the principle of the cases as to dangerous goods, is applicable to the facts here."

---

[87] At p. 441.
[88] [1923] 1 K.B. 31.
[89] At p. 38.
[90] In taking the cargo as fast as the ship could actually deliver it.
[91] At p. 40.
[92] (1878) 3 Ex.D. 282 (C.A.). It was held there that a master cannot sell damaged goods, which cannot be carried to the port of discharge, without communicating with their owner. Where they are landed at an intermediate port and sold without the agreement of their owner, the shipowners are not entitled to *pro rata* freight.

CHAPTER 4

REACHING THE DESTINATION

4–01 A CHARTERPARTY may provide for the beginning of laytime in words such as these:

> "Time for loading shall commence to count 12 hours after written notice has been given by the Master or Agent on any day (Sundays and holidays excepted), between 9 a.m. and 6 p.m., to the Charterers or their Agents that the Steamer is ready to receive Cargo, but the said notice to be given at the first port or place of loading only"[1]

or these:

> "Laytime for loading and discharging shall commence at 1 p.m. if notice of readiness is given before noon and at 6 a.m. next working day if notice given during office hours after noon."[2]

Whether or not a charterparty contains a clause similar to either of those mentioned above, certain requirements must usually be satisfied before laytime can begin to count.[3] These are:

1. Reaching the agreed destination[4];
2. Readiness of the ship to load or to discharge[5];
3. Giving a notice of readiness[6] after arrival[7] to the charterers or their agents. Such notice is not usually necessary, however, at the discharging port.

When these requirements are satisfied the ship is said to be an "arrived ship" and, subject to the expiry of any prescribed period after the notice, laytime begins to run.

4–02 The destination, for the purpose of the laytime calculation, may, if stated in the charterparty, be (a) a precise place, such as a particular berth or wharf or (b) an area, such as a port or a dock. A place may have to be named by the charterers, as in "at any safe berth as ordered on arrival . . . at Garston."[8] An area may be stated with a proviso that, on arrival there, the ship is to proceed to a particular part to be nominated by the charterers later, as, for example, "one or two safe loading ports or places in the River Parana"[9] or "one safe port, St. Lawrence river." The effect, for the purpose of finding whether the ship is an arrived ship, is the same as if the location had been expressly incorporated in the original charterparty, and

---

[1] River Plate Charter-Party 1914 (Centrocon).
[2] Uniform General Charter 1922 (Gencon) as revised, 1976.
[3] For clauses modifying the usual requirements as to when laytime begins, see Chapter 6, below.
[4] See §§ 4–02–4–45 below.
[5] See §§ 5–01–5–17 below.
[6] See §§ 5–18–5–35 below.
[7] See § 4–33 below, where the term "arrival" is contrasted with the words "arrived ship."
[8] *Tharsis Sulphur & Copper Mining Co.* v. *Morel Brothers & Co.* [1891] 2 Q.B. 647 (C.A.); see § 4–03 below.
[9] River Plate Charter-Party 1914 (Centrocon).

the ship reaches her agreed destination not when she reaches the larger area or place but when she reaches the named part of it. It follows that a charterparty may be a berth charterparty, a port charterparty or a dock charterparty, either because such a destination is expressly stated at the date of its signature or because there is an express provision for it to be nominated by the charterers.

If there is no provision for such a nomination, the charterers still have a right to direct the ship, when she is ready and at their disposition, to the loading or discharging site, but in this case the ship reaches her agreed destination on arriving at the larger area or place. As Devlin J. said in *Stag Line Ltd.* v. *Board of Trade*[10]:

> "If . . . there is no power of nomination expressly given, and no berth is named[11] so that she goes to the berth ordered by the charterers merely by virtue of the implied right which they have to select the berth, then she becomes an arrived ship when she arrives at the place named in the charterparty, as the port."

The stages of the venture

The manner of allocation of the risk of delay between the shipowners and the charterers arises out of their commercial relationship. The shipowners must arrange for the ship to get to her destination; once she is there and the voyage can be said to be at an end, the risk of delay normally falls upon the charterers, in the absence of provision to the contrary. The essential characteristics of a voyage charterparty have been analysed[12] as follows:

> "The adventure contemplated by a voyage charter involves four successive stages. They are:
> (1) The loading voyage, *viz.* the voyage of the chartered vessel from wherever she is at the date of the charterparty to the place specified in it as the place of loading.
> (2) The loading operation, *viz.* the delivery of the cargo to the vessel at the place of loading and its stowage on board.
> (3) The carrying voyage, *viz.* the voyage of the vessel to the place specified in the charterparty as the place of delivery.
> (4) The discharging operation, *viz.* the delivery of the cargo from the vessel at the place specified in the charterparty as the place of discharge and its receipt there by the charterer or other consignee.
> In all four of these stages acts of performance by the shipowner are called for; in the two voyage stages acts of performance by him alone. . . . So until the vessel has reached the specified place of loading on the loading voyage or the specified place of discharge on the carrying voyage, the contractual obligation to bring the vessel there lies on the shipowner alone; and any loss occasioned by delay in doing so falls upon him. . . . "

So also in a later case[13] Lord Diplock said:

> " . . . while until the *Johanna Oldendorff*[13a] there may have been uncertainty under a port charter as to where within the named port a ship must be in order to complete the voyage stage, there was legal certainty that neither in port nor in berth charter was the voyage stage brought to an end by the arrival of the ship at any waiting place short of the limits of the named port."

---

[10] [1950] 1 K.B. 536 at p. 538, approved by Lord Oaksey in the Court of Appeal [1950] 2 K.B. 194 at p. 195.
[11] *I.e.* in the charterparty.
[12] By Lord Diplock in *Oldendorff (E.L.) & Co. G.m.b.H.* v. *Tradax Export S.A.* [1973] 2 Lloyd's Rep. 285 (H.L.) at pp. 304 and 305 (*The Johanna Oldendorff*). See also § 4–29 below.
[13] *Federal Commerce and Navigation Co. Ltd.* v. *Tradax Export S.A. (The Maratha Envoy)* [1977] 2 Lloyd's Rep. 301 at p. 308 (H.L.). See § 4–35 below.
[13a] *Op. cit.*; see § 4–21 below.

Thus the adventure can be divided into four stages. The loading voyage and the carrying voyage end, respectively, when the ship reaches "the place specified in it [the charterparty] as the place of loading" or "the place specified in the charterparty as the place of delivery." Without some further definition as to the extent of the place of loading or the place of delivery, be it berth or a wharf or a dock or a port,[14] we are unable to say when the ship has reached that place.

The four stages described by Lord Diplock were set out in a different wording by Michael Mustill Q.C. (later Lord Justice Mustill) in a valuable monograph, "Pseudo-demurrage and the arrived ship."[15] He pointed out that shipowners, to make a profit, must aim to have their ships continually engaged either in the actual carriage of cargo, or in proceeding to a place where the carriage can begin. He then said:

> "Anything which interrupts these operations, or causes them to take longer than was foreseen, will cost the shipowner money. With this increase in the accuracy of forward chartering has come the realisation that every cargo voyage includes not one, but at least four, elements each with its own risk of delay to the ship:
> (i) The approach voyage—*i.e.* the passage from the place where the ship ends her previous service to the loading port under the current charter;
> (ii) The time spent at the loading port, either in waiting to load or in actually loading;
> (iii) The carrying voyage, from the loading port to the discharging port;
> (iv) The time spent at the discharging port, either in discharging or in waiting to discharge."

A ship may be prevented from reaching her destination through no fault of the shipowners or her charterers, as, for example, where there is low water[15a] at a bar or congestion. If the charterparty places such a risk on the charterers, the shipowners may recover damages for detention.[16] There is no absolute principle that charterers are liable in damages where arrival is delayed by, for example, the presence of other ships chartered by them; but they might be liable if the delay arose because they had conducted their chartering business in an unreasonable manner. Considerable practical difficulties would of course arise, as the shipowners would have to prove a breach of charterparty and consequent damages.

These are discussed below:

  (a) Berth and wharf charterparties[17];
  (b) Dock charterparties[18];
  (c) Port charterparties.[19]

---

[14] As to which four destinations see, respectively, §§ 4–03, 4–04, 4–06 and 4–07 below.

[15] Published by the Gothenburg Maritime Law Association in 1974, this paper contains the text of a lecture delivered to the Association in 1971. It was amended, for publication, to take account of the views of the House of Lords in *Oldendorff (E.L.) & Co.* v. *Tradax Export S.A.* [1973] 2 Lloyd's Rep. 285 (*The Johanna Oldendorff*). (See § 4–21 below).

[15a] The amount of water may also be relevant to the beginning of laytime. In *John Sadd & Sons, Ltd.* v. *Bertram Ratcliffe & Co.* (1929) 34 Ll.L.Rep. 18 the provision was "Time for discharging to count from first high water on or after arrival providing sufficient water at berth."

[16] *Inca Compania Naviera S.A. and Commercial and Maritime Enterprises Evanghelos P. Nomikos S.A.* v. *Mofinol, Inc. (The President Brand)* [1967] 2 Lloyd's Rep. 338; for the facts, see § 4–35 below.

[17] At § 4–03.

[18] See §§ 4–05 and 4–06.

[19] See §§ 4–05 and 4–07.

(a) Berth[20] and wharf charterparties   **4–03**

Where a berth or a wharf[21] is named as destination, or is to be named later, the ship reaches the agreed destination when she is at[22] that berth or wharf in such a position that she does not need to move further to load or to discharge.[23] As Jenkins L.J. said in *North River Freighters Ltd.* v. *President of India*[24]:

> " . . . in the case of a berth charter (that is to say a charter which requires the vessel to proceed for loading to a particular berth either specified in the charter or by the express terms of the charter to be specified by the charterer) lay days do not begin to run until the vessel has arrived at the particular berth, is ready to load, and has given notice to the charterer in manner prescribed by the charter of her readiness to load."

So also Lord Reid in *Oldendorff (E.L.) & Co. G.m.b.H.* v. *Tradax Export S.A.*[25]:

> "Where a single berth was specified in the charter-party as being the place of loading or of discharge the loading voyage or the carrying voyage did not end until the vessel was at that very berth. Until then no obligation could lie upon the charterer to load the cargo, or to receive it, as the case might be. If the specified berth were occupied by other shipping, the vessel was still at the voyage stage while waiting in the vicinity of the berth until it became available, and time so spent was at the shipowner's expense."

Even if there is congestion, bad weather, or an unfavourable tide, any risk of delay before the ship gets alongside usually falls on the shipowners.[26] Thus in *Tharsis Sulphur & Copper Mining Co. Ltd.* v. *Morel Brothers & Co.*[27] the charterparty provided for a cargo of copper ore to be delivered "at any safe berth[28] as ordered on arrival in the dock at Garston . . . to be discharged when berthed with all dispatch as customary." The shipowners claimed demurrage, because, although the harbour master had ordered the berth at the proper time, there was considerable delay from congestion before the ship went alongside. The shipowners argued first that the charterers were bound to exercise their option to name a berth in favour of an available berth and, secondly, that the voyage came to an

---

[20] One should distinguish a ship loading "on the berth," where the charterers may not know how much cargo they will receive but are responsible to the shipowners for providing a full cargo.

[21] The Shorter Oxford English Dictionary (3rd ed.) defines a berth as "The place where a ship lies when at anchor or at a wharf," and a wharf as "A substantial structure of timber, stone, etc. built along the water's edge, so that ships may lie alongside for loading and unloading." The Charterparty Laytime Definitions 1980 (see Appendix to this book) state: "3. 'BERTH'—means the specific place where the ship is to load and/or discharge. If the word 'BERTH' is not used, but the specific place is (or is to be) identified by its name, this definition shall still apply.

[22] "The original conception of a berth charter was one where a particular berth was named in the charter but the expression has been extended to include the case where the vessel is to proceed to a berth at charterer's option within a port": *per* Sir David Cairns in *Surrey Shipping Co. Ltd.* v. *Compagnie Continentale (France) S.A.* (*The Shackleford*) [1978] 2 Lloyd's Rep. 154 at p. 161. See also § 5–33 below. For earlier cases see *Scrutton on Charterparties* (19th ed., 1984), Art. 72.

[23] For the expression "Time lost in waiting for berth to count . . . " see § 5–02 below.

[24] [1956] 1 Q.B. 333 at p. 348 (C.A.).

[25] [1973] 2 Lloyd's Rep. 285 at p. 305 (H.L.). (*The Johanna Oldendorff*). See § 4–21 below.

[26] For the provision that a berth shall be reachable on arrival, see § 4–33 below.

[27] [1891] 2 Q.B. 647 (C.A.).

[28] The Charterparty Laytime Definitions 1980 (see Appendix to this book) state "4. 'SAFE BERTH'—means a berth which, during the relevant period of time, the ship can reach, remain at and depart from without, in the absence of some abnormal occurrence, being exposed to danger which cannot be avoided by good navigation and seamanship."

end when the ship had arrived at Garston and was placed at the charterers' disposition. Bowen L.J. said[29]:

"The present case is one in which an option is given to the charterer to do that which the charterparty has not done, that is, to name the terminus of the voyage. . . . "

Turning to the shipowners' first argument, he said:

"To limit the option of the charterer by saying that, in the choice of a berth, he is to consider the convenience of the shipowner, is to deprive him of the benefit of his option. The most that can be said is that the charterer does not exercise his option at all unless he chooses a berth that is free or is likely to be so in a reasonable time."

As for the second argument he said[30]:

"The words of this proposition are full of ambiguity. If it means that as soon as the ship arrives at the place where the charterer is to exercise his option, the demurrage days begin, the proposition is too large."

In other cases the option might have to be exercised at a place some considerable distance from the destination, where it could not be said that the duty to unload arose. Lord Esher M.R.,[31] approving of the decision in *Tapscott* v. *Balfour*, said[32]:

" . . . when the charterer has to name a dock or a place in a dock, when he does so, it is as though it had been named in the charterparty, and indicates the termination of the voyage."

The shipowners failed in their claim.

4–04   If the shipowners agree to get to a wharf, so that the expense of lighters can be avoided, and have to wait for the depth of the water to increase, the ship is still pursuing her voyage.[33] The same principle applies in the rare cases where the equivalent of a berth is brought to the ship. In *Postlethwaite* v. *Freeland*[34] a ship moored about a mile outside the East London harbour bar on September 1. The ship was bound to proceed to East London, "to discharge at any safe wharf, where ships can always lie safely afloat. . . . " The discharging of the cargo of steel rails and fastenings would have been possible only when a warp[35] was installed, so that lighters could be run out to the ship. Owing to the great number of ships, she had to wait 24 working days for her turn. There was no provision for lay days; the charterparty merely said: "The cargo is to be discharged with all dispatch according to the custom of the port." The House of Lords held that the shipowners were not entitled to demurrage in respect of the delay. Lord Selborne L.C. said[36] that the ship had been discharged "with all dis-

---

[29] At p. 651.

[30] At p. 651.

[31] (1872) L.R. 8 C.P. 46. See § 4–06 below.

[32] At p. 650.

[33] *Bastifell* v. *Lloyd* (1862) 1 H. & C. 388; a voyage from Llanelly to Rochester, where the shipowners failed in their demurrage claim, and the charterers were found not to have been obliged to send lighters.

[34] (1880) 5 App.Cas. 599 (H.L.).

[35] "A rope or light hawser attached at one end to some fixed object, used in hauling or in moving a ship from one place to another in a harbour, road or river" (Shorter Oxford English Dictionary, 3rd ed.).

[36] At p. 610.

patch according to the custom of the port" and that the charterers were not responsible for the delay. Lord Blackburn said[37] of this conclusion:

> "The parties can, by altering the terms of their contracts in future, avoid any inconvenience that arises from that construction. It is, no doubt, not an easy thing to introduce a new form of contract into mercantile use, but it can be done."

He also said[38]:

> "No question could have been made, if there had been lay-days in the present charterparty, that they would have begun to run on the 1st of September."

(b) *and* (c) *Dock and port charterparties*   **4–05**

A dock and a port have a common characteristic in that each is an area within which is the spot at which the ship will load or discharge. In this sense they may be contrasted with a berth and a wharf,[39] which, when named as destinations in a charterparty, are not only destinations but are also specific spots at which the ship will load or discharge. The principles which apply individually to dock and port charterparties are set out below.[40] They have been expressed especially in decisions which concerned port charterparties,[41] but they seem to be applicable also to dock charterparties. In *Nelson* v. *Dahl*,[42] which concerned a dock charterparty, Lord Brett M.R. set out a general rule which embraced both categories:

> "If the named place describes as before a large space in several ports of which a ship can unload, as a port or dock, the shipowner's right to have the charterer's liability initiate commences as soon as the ship is arrived at the named place, or the place which by custom is considered to be intended by the name and is ready, so far as the ship is concerned, to discharge, though she is not in the particular part of the port or dock in which the particular cargo is to be discharged."

So also Buckley, L.J. in *Leonis SS. Co. Ltd.* v. *Rank Ltd. (No. 1)*[43]:

> " . . . it is difficult to grasp any ground of principle differentiating a dock from that part of a port at which the ship would be so closely proximate to a berth as she would be in a dock. What logical difference can exist? The ship either is not or is an arrived ship when she has not reached a berth. If she is when the named place is a dock, why is she not when the named place is a port and she is at a place as closely proximate to a berth as she would be in a dock?"

The words "as closely proximate" have given rise to some problems, because they could be taken to indicate that the ship in the case of a port charterparty should be as near to the berth as she would be in the case of a dock charterparty. That does not now seem to be so[44]; but the first part of this extract from the judgment of Buckley L.J. serves to illustrate the common factor which links port charterparties and dock charterparties, namely

---

[37] At p. 622.

[38] At p. 618.

[39] See § 4–03 above.

[40] For dock charterparties see § 4–06; for port charterparties see § 4–07.

[41] See §§ 4–07 *et seq.* below.

[42] (1879) 12 Ch.D. 568 (C.A.) at p. 583. See also § 4–42 below, *sub. nom. Dahl* v. *Nelson, Donkin & Co.* (1881) 6 App.Cas. 38 (H.L.).

[43] [1908] 1 K.B. 499 (C.A.) at p. 512. See also § 4–18 below.

[44] Especially since the House of Lords decision in *Oldendorff (E.L.) & Co. G.m.b.H.* v. *Tradax Export S.A.* [1973] 2 Lloyd's Rep. 285, (*The Johanna Oldendorff*). See § 4–21 below.

that the ship reaches her destination on arriving within the port or dock albeit she is not at the berth.

4–06   (b) *Dock charterparties*

Where a dock is named as destination, or is to be named later, the ship reaches her destination on entering that dock. The same principle applies if it is a quay or a roadstead that is named or to be named, or any area of this type, usually greater than a berth but smaller than a port.

In *Tapscott* v. *Balfour*[45] the loading place named in a coal charterparty was "any Liverpool or Birkenhead dock as ordered by charterers." The ship was to load there "in the usual and customary manner." Eight days elapsed between the ship's readiness to enter the dock and her entry; there was a further delay before she went under the spouts or tips. Bovill C.J. said[46]:

> " . . . the shipowner has done all he was required to do when he has taken his vessel to the usual place of loading in the port."

He said of the choice of dock[47]:

> "It seems to me that the effect of such selection was precisely as if that dock had been expressly named in the charterparty originally,[48] and the agreement had been that the vessel should proceed direct to the Wellington Dock, and when there should load in the usual and customary manner. Now, great stress was laid on the words 'in the usual and customary manner.' These words are, however, only part of the ordinary printed form of charterparty, and must be taken, I think, to apply to the mode of loading, and not to the place to which the shipowner undertakes that the ship shall proceed. . . . It would be giving such an expression a very extended construction to say that it applies to the place to which the shipowner undertakes the vessel shall proceed so as to increase his liability to the extent here contended for."

He concluded that the lay days began when the ship entered the dock. As Denman J. put it[49]:

> "on the day when the ship arrived in the dock the shipowner had done all that he was bound to do."

A ship may be held to have arrived whether or not the charterers are ready for her, if she has entered the dock, for whatever reason, and is ready.

In *Davies* v. *McVeagh*[50] shipowners agreed to carry coal from Liverpool to Dublin. The charterparty stated: "Vessel to load in Bramley Moore Dock at Wellington Dock, high level." The ship was admitted into Wellington Dock as a favour because, being empty, she was in danger outside. She was ready to receive her cargo, but owing to the regulations of the

---

[45] (1872) L.R. 8 C.P. 46.
[46] At p. 52.
[47] At pp. 52–53.
[48] The same principle enunciated later by the Court of Appeal where a berth was to be named; *Tharsis Sulphur & Copper Mining Co.* v. *Morel Bros. & Co.* [1891] 2 Q.B. 647. See § 4–03 above.
[49] At p. 55.
[50] (1879) 4 Ex.D. 265 (C.A.).

dock authorities did not berth and begin to load for about a fortnight. A dispute as to demurrage turned upon whether laytime counted from her admission into Wellington Dock. It was held that the shipowners were right. The reason was that the ship had reached her loading place when she was admitted into Wellington Dock. Bramwell L.J. said[51]:

> " . . . I think that it may be laid down that a vessel has reached the place of loading, as distinguished from the spot of loading, when she has entered that port[52] from which her voyage is to commence."

Lord Diplock has said[53]:

> "A dock encloses a comparatively small area entered through a gate. There is no difficulty in saying whether a vessel has arrived in it. As soon as a berth is vacant in the dock a vessel already moored inside the dock can get there within an interval so short for the practical business purpose of loading or discharging cargo it can be ignored."

(c) *Port charterparties*   **4–07**

Arrival at a port. Where a port is named as destination, the ship reaches that destination when she is within the port[54] and at the immediate and effective disposition of the charterers.[55] The cases on this subject are examined below.[56] A crucial passage in the judgment of Lord Reid in *Oldendorff (E.L.) & Co. G.m.b.H.* v. *Tradax Export S.A.*[57–58] reads:

> "Before a ship can be said to have arrived at a port she must, if she cannot proceed immediately to a berth, have reached a position within the port where she is at the immediate and effective disposition of the charterer. If she is at a place where waiting ships usually lie, she will be in such a position unless in some extraordinary circumstances proof of which would lie in the charterer. . . . If the ship is waiting at some other place in the port then it will be for the owner to prove that she is as fully at the disposition of the charterer as she would have been if in the vicinity of the berth for loading or discharge."

This has become known as the "Reid test," an expression used in contradistinction to the "Parker test," as stated by Parker L.J. in the Court of Appeal in *The Aello*.[59] These two conditions, that the ship should be within the port and that she should be at the immediate and effective dis-

---

[51] *Ibid.*, at p. 268.

[52] In this case it was a dock. He said later (at pp. 268–269): "If the defendant's vessel had got into the dock and had afterwards been turned out by the authorities, so far as concerns the defence in this action, she would have been in as good a position for loading as if she had remained inside the dock." This thought is echoed in the events which took place in *Federal Commerce and Navigation Co. Ltd.* v. *Tradax Export S.A.* [1977] 2 Lloyd's Rep. 301 (H.L.) (*The Maratha Envoy*); see § 4–25 below.

[53] In *Oldendorff (E.L.) & Co. G.m.b.H.* v. *Tradax Export S.A.* [1973] 2 Lloyd's Rep. 285 at p. 306 (H.L.) (*The Johanna Oldendorff*). See § 4–21 below.

[54] For the meaning of the word "port," which must here be taken in its commercial sense, see § 4–08 below.

[55] See § 4–11 below.

[56] At § 4–12.

[57–58] [1973] 2 Lloyd's Rep. 285 at p. 291 (H.L.) (*The Johanna Oldendorff*). See § 4–24 below where these words are repeated.

[59] *Sociedad Financiera de Bienes Raices S.A.* v. *Agrimpex Hungarian Trading Co. for Agricultural Products* [1958] 2 Q.B. 385 at p. 401. The Parker test is set out at § 4–31 below.

position of the charterers,[60] and the manner in which they are interpreted, are the result of decisions by the Courts over many years, during which some views have been modified and some decisions overruled. Many of those cases, decided between 1831 and 1977, are examined below.[61] The two conditions are subject to the provisos, that (i) there is no custom of the port to the contrary; (ii) the ship does not, from a stage at which she is still on her voyage and so outside the port, go directly to her specified loading or discharging spot.

4–08   A **"port."** A port may be defined in legal, administrative, fiscal, geographical or commercial terms. The word "port," therefore, may not always have the same meaning. As Bowen L.J. said[62]:

> " . . . you must make up your mind in each particular case as to the sense in which shipowners and charterers would be likely to intend to employ the term 'port.' "

A distinction between the legal and the geographical definitions of a port was made by Lush J. in *Nicholson* v. *Williams*[63]:

> "Ports and havens are not merely geographical expressions; they are places appointed by the Crown 'for persons and merchandises to pass into and out of the realm' and at such places only is it lawful for ships to load and discharge cargo. The assignment of such places to be 'the inlets and gates' of the realm is, and always has been, a branch of the prerogative resting, as Blackstone remarks,[64] partly upon a fiscal foundation, in order to secure the King's marine revenue. Their limits and bounds are necessarily defined by the authority which creates them, and the area embraced within those limits constitutes the port."[65]

The meaning of the term has been discussed in connection with laytime; in cases where advance freight has been due within a fixed time after "final sailing" from the port[66]; and where insurance cover has been linked to "sailing."[67]

---

[60] See § 4–11 below.

[61] See § 4–12 below.

[62] *Sailing-Ship Garston Co.* v. *Hickie & Co.* (1885) 15 Q.B.D. 580 at p. 596 (C.A.). Freight was due 10 days after the ship's final sailing "from her last port." See § 4–15 below.

[63] (1871) L.R. 6 Q.B. 632 at p. 641.

[64] *Commentaries on the Laws of England* (15th ed., 1809), Vol. 1, p. 263: "It is partly upon the same, [the prevention of private fortifications] and partly upon a fiscal foundation, to secure his marine revenue, that the king has the prerogative of appointing ports and havens, or such places only for persons and merchandize to pass into and out of the realm, as he in his wisdom sees proper. . . . " Blackstone then referred (at p. 264) to statutes of Elizabeth I and Charles II which enabled the Crown "to ascertain the limits of all ports, and to assign proper wharfs and quays in each port, for the exclusive landing and loading of merchandize."

[65] The limits are not always specified. See the finding of the arbitrator in *Logs & Timber Products (Singapore) Pte. Ltd.* v. *Keeley Granite (Pty.) Ltd.* [1978] 2 Lloyd's Rep. 1 (C.A.), quoted by Donaldson J. in the High Court, [1978] 1 Lloyd's Rep. 257 at p. 261: "There is no evidence that this port [Lourenco Marques] has any specified fiscal and commercial limits as do most other ports in the world such as Liverpool (Mersey Bar), Hull, etc. Life is simple in warm climates."

[66] *Roelandts* v. *Harrison* (1854) 9 Ex. 444; *Price* v. *Livingstone* (1882) 9 Q.B.D. 679; and *Sailing-Ship Garston Co.* v. *Hickie & Co.* (1885) 15 Q.B.D. 580 (C.A.). As to the last case see § 4–15 below.

[67] *Sea Insurance Co.* v. *Blogg* [1898] 2 Q.B. 398; *Mersey Mutual Association* v. *Poland* (1910) 15 Com.Cas. 205.

Commercial and other meanings of "port." A port is defined for the   **4–09**
present purpose, which is to decide whether a ship has arrived at its destination in the case of a port charterparty,[68] in its commercial sense.[69] This
commercial delimitation may be contrasted with the legal, administrative,
fiscal and geographical limits which may be material for other purposes.[70]
In deciding what should be regarded as the confines of the port in its commercial sense, however, one may take into account the nature of these
legal and other limits. The two concepts are not mutually exclusive,[71] and
evidence of those limits may contribute towards the commercial definition.
Kennedy L.J. said in *Leonis SS. Co. Ltd.* v. *Rank Ltd. (No. 1)*[72]:

> "In the case of a port, and nothing more, being designated in a charterparty as the
> point of destination our Courts have acted in accordance with those dictates of reason
> and practical expediency which ought to be paramount especially in the region of mer-
> cantile business. Just as a port may have one set of limits, if viewed geographically, and
> another for fiscal or for pilotage purposes, so when it is named in a commercial docu-
> ment, and for commercial purposes, the term is to be construed in a commercial sense in
> relation to the objects of the particular transaction."

When has the ship reached the port in its commercial sense? It is not
enough to say that she has done so when she has completed the loading
voyage or the carrying voyage.[73] Nor, as we have seen, is it enough to say
that the application of the non-commercial definitions is inappropriate. A
commercial approach has been adopted frequently by the courts. Brett
M.R. in *Sailing-Ship Garston Co.* v. *Hickie & Co.*[74–75] said of those who
enter into a charterparty:

> "What do they intend? They intend the port as commonly understood by all persons
> who are using it as a port, *i.e.* for sailing to and from it with goods and merchandise.
> What persons are they? Shippers of goods, charterers of vessels, and shipowners. What
> do all these persons in their ordinary language mean by a "port"? What they understand
> by the word is the port in its ordinary sense, in its business sense, in its popular sense—
> *i.e.* the popular sense of such persons. It is also the port in its commercial sense, for, with
> them, business means commercial business."[76]

---

[68] The Charterparty Laytime Definitions 1980 (see Appendix to this book) state: "1.
'PORT'—means an area within which ships are loaded with and/or discharged of cargo and
includes the usual places where ships wait for their turn or are ordered or obliged to wait
for their turn no matter the distance from that area. If the word 'PORT' is not used, but the
port is (or is to be) identified by its name, this definition shall still apply."

[69] As to the use of the term "commercial area" . . . , see § 4–30 below.

[70] See also § 4–08 above.

[71] See, for example, the comments of Palles, C.B., in *M'Intosh* v. *Sinclair* (1877) Ir.R. 11
C.L. 456, at p. 461, cited at § 4–14 below. Lord Dilhorne in *Oldendorff (E.L.) &
Co. G.m.b.H.* v. *Tradax Export S.A. (The Johanna Oldendorff)* [1973] 2 Lloyd's Rep. 285,
at p. 302, said of the Mersey Docks and Harbour Act 1971: " . . . it is unlikely that the
definition of the port of Liverpool did more than define the area which was and had been
regarded as constituting the port and that this was, therefore, an attempt by statute to
define the limits of a port using that word in its commercial sense."

[72] [1908] 1 K.B. 499 (C.A.) at p. 519, in what Lord Reid in *Oldendorff (E.L.) & Co.
G.m.b.H.* v. *Tradax Export S.A., op. cit.*, at p. 288 termed "the leading judgment, perhaps because it is rather less obscure than that of Lord Justice Buckley." See also § 4–18
below.

[73] As to these stages see § 4–02 above.

[74–75] (1885) 15 Q.B.D. 580 at p. 588 (C.A.). See also § 4–15 below.

[76] This passage was cited, and the principles applied, by Hirst J. in *President of India* v. *Olym-
pia Sauna Shipping Co. S.A. (The Ypatia Halcoussi)* [1984] 2 Lloyd's Rep. 455, at p. 457.
The issue for decision was whether calls at three places in the Columbia River were at four
berths within one port, as shipowners contended, or three ports, as charterers, who succeeded, contended.

It was clearly necessary, however, to introduce some element other than the views of the business persons involved, especially as those views might differ. Brett M.R. continued[77]:

> "Then, if you want to find out how far the port extends beyond the place of loading and unloading, what is the next test you would apply? If you find that the authorities, who are known in commercial business language as 'the port authorities,' are exercising authority over ships within a certain space of water, and that the shipowners and shippers who have ships within that space of water are submitting to the jurisdiction which is claimed by those authorities, whether legally or not, whether according to Act of Parliament or not, if you find what are called 'the port authorities' exercising port discipline, and the ships which frequent that water submitting to the port discipline so exercised, that seems to me the strongest possible evidence that the shipowners, the shippers, and the port authorities (that is, the persons connected with the locality), have all come to the conclusion to accept that space of water in which that authority is so exercised and submitted to as 'the port' of the place."

The first of these two passages from the judgment of Brett M.R. has the effect of distinguishing the business and popular understandings of the word "port" from the more technical meanings which can apply, such as the legal or fiscal limits of the port. The latter are usually ascertainable by reference to various enactments or other documents. The business or popular meanings may be more changeable and less capable of being expressed in precise terms at any given moment. If they have been expressed precisely because a judgment happens to have been delivered in respect of a particular port, then that will be of considerable help to the parties.

The second passage from this judgment of Brett M.R. is helpful because it envisages an analysis of the extent to which "the port authorities" exercise authority. Even these words must be treated with caution, because there can be areas of imprecision:

(a) there is not necessarily one port authority,[78] and various authorities may purport to exercise diferring degrees of control;

(b) the "shipowners and shippers" to whom he refers may or may not be submitting to the jurisdiction claimed, and may submit to varying extents with various authorities.

So also in the *Johanna Oldendorff* Lord Morris referred[79] to the powers of the port authorities:

> " . . . if vessels that cannot go straight to some particular place to which charterers will wish them to go are required by the port authorities to wait in a specified area, then within the words of Brett, M.R., that I have quoted from *Sailing-Ship Garston Co.* v. *Hickie*,[80] such ships have arrived at the port."

In addition Viscount Dilhorne[81] entered a caveat about the powers of the authorities by saying:

---

[77] *Ibid.* at p. 590.
[78] Though see Lord Reid's reference to "a port authority" and "its various powers" in *Oldendorff (E.L.) & Co. G.m.b.H.* v. *Tradax Export S.A. (The Johanna Oldendorff)* [1973] 2 Lloyds Rep. 285 at p. 291 (H.L.).
[79] *Op. cit.* at p. 295.
[80] He had quoted words which included the passages from Brett M.R. set out at § 4–09 above.
[81] *Op. cit.* at p. 302.

"Brett, M.R.'s definition . . . and his reference to port discipline may be useful in determining what are the limits of the port in its legal sense but port discipline may be exercised and submitted to over a wider area than the port in its commercial sense."

And Lord Diplock[82] said of the area of a port, comparing it to the area of a dock:

"It may sometimes be less easily determinable, because of absence of definition of its legal limits or variations between these and the limits within which the port authority in actual practice exercises control of the movement of shipping; but I do not believe that in practice it is difficult to discover whether a place where ships usually wait their turn for a berth is within the limits of a named port; or is outside these limits as is the case with Glasgow and with Hull."

Finally, the following comments by Lord Diplock in *Federal Commerce and Navigation Co. Ltd.* v. *Tradax Export S.A.*[83] show that the definition of the word "port" may depend upon the way in which various factors are weighed, and the extent to which some matters may be agreed by the parties:

" . . . it is conceded by Counsel for the charterers that the Weser Lightship anchorage is outside the legal fiscal and administrative limits of the port of Brake. It lies 25 miles from the mouth of the river in an area in which none of the port authorities of Weser ports does any administrative acts or exercise any control over vessels waiting there. . . ."

In deciding whether a ship has arrived at the port, therefore, the courts will consider first the commercial meaning of the term. In ascertaining that meaning, however, they consider not only the views of the business people using the loading and discharging facilities but also the extent of the activities of the various port authorities, whether exercised by virtue or a specific law or regulation or otherwise, and whether acknowledged by the port users or not. This has also involved an acknowledgment that the extents of the legal, administrative, fiscal and geographical boundaries may be taken into account. It can also involve reference to the views of other tribunals.[84]

We have set out above[85] the statement by Lord Reid, in the *Oldendorff* **4–10** case,[86] that, where a port is named as the destination, the ship reaches that destination when she is within the port and at the immediate and effective disposition of the charterers. He also made a distinction between a ship which waits at a place where waiting ships usually lie, and a ship waiting at some other place in the port. In the passage which follows we discuss, first, the expression "at the immediate and effective disposition of the charterer,"[87] and secondly, the concept of the waiting area.[88]

---

[82] *Op. cit.* at p. 306.
[83] [1977] 2 Lloyd's Rep. 301 at p. 307 (H.L.) (*The Maratha Envoy*). See also § 4–28 below at (E).
[84] As, for example, the 1962 decision of a German court about the Weser lightship anchorage, *Federal Commerce & Navigation Co. Ltd.* v. *Tradax Export S.A.* (*The Maratha Envoy*) [1977] 2 Lloyd's Rep. 301 at p. 307 (H.L.), and English and New York arbitration decisions about Rotterdam, in the same case when in the Court of Appeal, [1977] 1 Lloyd's Rep. 217, at pp. 223 (Lord Denning M.R.) and 228 (Stephenson L.J.). See also the Appendix to this Chapter at § 4–48.
[85] At § 4–07.
[86] *Op. cit.* at p. 291.
[87] At § 4–11.
[88] At § 4–12.

4–11   **"at the immediate and effective disposition of the charterer."** To have
arrived at a port for the purpose of the calculation of laytime a ship must
not only be within the port[89]; she must also be at the immediate and effective disposition of the charterers. She is presumed to be at the charterers'
immediate and effective disposition when she has arrived at the contractual
destination. A voyage stage has then ended and the risk of delay has thus
moved, in the absence of provisions of the contrary, from shipowners to
charterers. The ship can be at the disposition of the charterers although not
at the specific loading or discharging spot; nor does she necessarily have to
be, as was once thought, in some area, usually smaller than the port itself,
where ships proposing to load or discharge her type of cargo normally wait.
Thus in *Leonis SS. Co. Ltd.* v. *Rank Ltd. (No. 1)*,[90] Kennedy L.J. spoke of
"that area of the named port of destination on arrival within which the
Master can effectively place his ship at the disposal of the charterer, the
vessel herself being then, so far as she is concerned, ready to load, and as
near as circumstances permit to the actual loading 'spot.' "

The shipowners may not be able to show that the ship is fully at the disposition of the charterers. In *Kell* v. *Anderson*,[91] a ship chartered to go to
the port of London waited 22 miles down river from the Pool. As Lord
Diplock put it in the *Johanna Oldendorff*,[92] referring to what he called
"the empirical decision" in that case[93]:

> "A sailing ship's journey up river from Gravesend would be dependent upon favour-
> able wind and weather. There was no knowing how long it would take her to reach the
> Pool after she had notice that there was room to discharge her cargo there. So she was
> not, while at her moorings, at the disposal of the charterer for discharging her cargo."

He also referred to "the contemporaneous empirical decision in *Brown*
v. *Johnson*,"[94] where, under a port charterparty to go to Hull, the ship
waited her turn inside the dock in which were the discharging berths.
As he put it[95]:

> "As soon as a berth fell vacant she could be warped[96] to it from her moorings without
> any significant delay. So she was at the disposal of the charterers."

The possibility of a greater or smaller delay was also mentioned by
Donaldson J. in the High Court in the *Johanna Oldendorff*[97]:

> "In this context a delay of two or three hours between the nomination of a berth and
> the ship reaching it is wholly immaterial because there will be at least this much notice
> before the berth becomes free . . . "

The proposition that the moment of completion of the voyage coincides
with the moment at which the ship is at the effective disposition of the charterers is one which corresponds with the concept that the adventure con-

---

[89] See § 4–07 above.
[90] [1908] 1 K.B. 499 (C.A.) at p. 521. See also § 4–18 below.
[91] (1842) 10 M. & W. 498. See § 4–12 below.
[92] [1973] 2 Lloyd's Rep. 285 at p. 306 (H.L.). See § 4–21.
[93] The ship was at Gravesend within the legal limits of the port of London but was held not to
have arrived there. See § 4–12 below.
[94] (1842) 10 M. & W. 331. See § 4–12 below.
[95] *Op. cit.* at p. 307.
[96] For "warp" see note 35 above.
[97] [1971] 2 Lloyd's Rep. 96 at p. 100. This passage was cited by Lord Reid in *The Johanna
Oldendorff* (at p. 291) in support of his statement that if the ship were at a place where
waiting ships usually lie, she would be at a position where she was at the immediate and
effective disposition of the charterers unless the charterers could show that some extraordinary circumstances existed.

sists of various stages,[98] *i.e.* (1) the loading voyage; (2) the loading operation; (3) the carrying voyage; and (4) the discharging operation. The law on the subject was set out by Lord Reid in the *Johanna Oldendorff*[99] in the so-called Reid test.[1]

The words "If she is at a place where waiting ships usually lie,[1a] she will be in such a position . . . " must be considered carefully. It seems that they mean only that she will be, to refer to Lord Reid's previous sentence, "in a position . . . where she is at the immediate and effective disposition of the charterer" if she is where waiting ships usually lie. It does not mean that by being where waiting ships usually lie she will be in "a position *within the port*" and at the charterers' disposition.[2] Indeed the same judge also stressed that we cannot say that whenever a ship is in the usual waiting area she has arrived.[3] When the ship is both within the port and at the immediate and effective disposition of the charterers, then it becomes the right and the duty[4] of the latter, subject to any specific exceptions to the contrary, to provide a berth and to begin to load or discharge her. The risk of delay passes from the shipowners to the charterers.

The waiting area 4–12

In *Oldendorff (E.L.) & Co. G.m.b.H.* v. *Tradax Export S.A.*[5] Lord Reid pointed out that the waiting area[6] could be outside the port area. As he put it:

> "We cannot say that whenever a vessel anchors in the usual waiting area for a port she becomes an arrived ship because there are a great many ports where that area is well outside the port area. Glasgow and Hull are examples in this country and we are told of an American port where the usual waiting area is 50 miles from the loading area of the port. All are agreed that to be an arrived ship the vessel must have come to rest within the port."

It followed that the waiting area could be inside or outside the port. He added:

> "Then it was argued that the limits of many ports are so indefinite that it would introduce confusion to hold that a ship is an arrived ship on anchoring at a usual waiting place within the port. But I find it difficult to believe that there would, except perhaps in rare cases, be any real difficulty in deciding whether at any particular port the usual waiting place is or was not within the port. The area within which a port authority[7] exercises its various powers can hardly be difficult to ascertain. Some powers with regard to pilotage

---

[98] See § 4–02 above.

[99] [1973] 2 Lloyd's Rep. 285 (H.L.) at p. 291. See § 4–21 below.

[1] See the passage from his judgment cited at § 4–07 above.

[1a] Bandar Abbas (almost 400 miles from the contractual destination of Bushire), where the ship was waiting to join a convoy, was not regarded as the usual waiting place for the purpose of her becoming an arrived ship, in a London arbitration (LMLN 143, April 25, 1985). In colloquial language, however, it would have been natural to refer to Bandas Abbas roads as the required waiting place so far as convoys were concerned. The arbitrators said that a place so far distant could not be held to be covered by the term "whether in port or not". Compare another London arbitration, (LMLN 155, October 19, 1985), where under an Asbatankvoy form, Sirri Island was held to be a "customary anchorage" so that laytime could begin there when a ship was going to Kharg Island.

[2] Compare the New York arbitration award in *The Polyfreedom* [1965] A.M.C 1826; see the Appendix to this Chapter at § 4–48.

[3] *Op. cit.* at p. 291. As to the "waiting area" see § 4–12 below.

[4] As to the nature of this duty see § 4–46 below.

[5] [1973] 2 Lloyd's Rep. 285 at p. 291 (H.L.) (*The Johanna Oldendorff*). See § 4–21.

[6] As to the term "commercial area" see § 4–30 below.

[7] There is not necessarily only one authority; but the existence of differing powers is recognised in the words which follow.

and other matters may extend far beyond the limits of the port. But those which regulate the movements and conduct of ships would seem to afford a good indication. And in many cases the limits of the port are defined by law. In the present case the umpire has found as a fact . . . that the ship was 'at the Bar anchorage,[8] within the legal, administrative and fiscal areas of Liverpool/Birkenhead.' "[9]

The cases. 1. *Five cases, from 1831 to 1889.* As early as 1831, in *Brereton* v. *Chapman*,[10] a ship going to discharge at Wells was held not to have arrived, for the purpose of counting laytime, until she had reached the quay. The quay was some distance from the entrance to the port. It has been held, for the same reasons, that a ship arrived at Hull on arrival in the dock, and not merely on entering the port. In *Brown* v. *Johnson*[10a] a ship chartered to discharge at Hull entered the dock but was delayed by congestion in reaching her berth. The judge in the lower court held that laytime began when she entered the dock, saying later: " . . . the delay which then arose was inevitable, and neither party was in fault." Lord Abinger C.B., sitting in the Court of Exchequer of Pleas, said[11]:

> "My opinion is, that the lay days under this charter-party commenced from the time of the vessel's coming into dock; it had then arrived at its usual place of discharge. They certainly did not commence at the period of its entering the port, as that might be very extensive; for instance, Gravesend is part of the port of London."

Judgment in that case, which concerned Hull, but where the judge referred to the status of Gravesend, was given in June 1842. In November 1842 Lord Abinger and other judges also, in the Court of Exchequer of Pleas, heard a dispute, *Kell* v. *Anderson*,[12] which concerned Gravesend.[13] A collier from Newcastle was chartered to go to "London, or so near thereto as she could safely get." She was detained for 10 days at Gravesend on the harbour-master's orders, because she was a "metered vessel," the cargo having been sold on arrival and needing to be checked. Gurney B. said[14]:

> "I think the time from which the days are to be calculated is the arrival of the vessel in the usual place of discharge for colliers; that is, in the Pool. If the parties mean otherwise, it is very easy for them to employ words to express their meaning."

4–13   It appears from these three early decisions that a ship was regarded as having arrived at her destination, for the purpose of the calculation of laytime, when she reached the usual place in the port, though not always her

---

[8] See the discussion in the New York arbitration case of *The Polyfreedom*, and the Appendix to this Chapter at § 4–48.

[9] Compare the comment of Bramwell L.J. in *Davies* v. *McVeagh* (1879) 4 Ex.D. 265 (C.A.) at p. 268: " . . . suppose that the defendant's vessel had been lying in the river Mersey, and that the captain had given notice that he was ready to enter the dock and ready to take on board the cargo; I do not think that it would have been open to the plaintiff as charterer, to contend that the vessel was not at the place of loading, that she was not in a proper position, and that the nineteen days did not begin to run." See also § 4–06 above.

[10] (1831) 7 Bing. 559.

[10a] (1842) 10 M. & W. 331. See also n. 68 to § 2–18 above.

[11] At p. 334.

[12] (1842) 10 M. & W. 498. It was relied upon by charterers, but distinguished, in *Seacrystal Shipping Ltd.* v. *Bulk Transport Group Shipping Co. Ltd.* [1987] 2 Lloyd's Rep. 122 (C.A.) (*The Kyzikos*), at p. 126. See also § 6–21 below.

[13] For a decision, not on laytime, as to whether Gravesend Reach was "tidal water" see *The Powstaniec Wielkopolski* [1989] 1 Lloyd's Rep. 58.

[14] At p. 502.

berth, for loading or discharging. In a group of decisions[15] in the latter part of the nineteenth century the courts made it clear that the legal and commercial definitions of a port were frequently different, and that even the commercial definition might vary, according to whether it was needed for laytime or other purposes.

The meaning of the term "port" has been discussed not only in connection with laytime, but also in cases where advance freight has been due upon or within a fixed time after "final sailing" from the port,[16] and where insurance cover has been linked to "sailing."[17]

As Bowen L.J. said[18]:

> " . . . you must make up your mind in each particular case as to the sense in which shipowners and charterers would be likely to intend to employ the term 'port.' "

The need to reach the proper place of discharging was discussed in *Caffarini* v. *Walker*,[19] where there was a dispute as to when laytime began. A ship ordered to the "Port of Newry," Ireland, discharged part of her cargo at The Pool in Carlingford Roads, 10 miles from Newry, where the balance was discharged. The weight of the cargo, the depth of the water and the draught of the ship combined to make the lightening necessary. The Pool was found to be within the port of Newry for custom house purposes. The lay days were held to run from the beginning of the discharge in the Pool; Morris C.J. said[20]: **4–14**

> " . . . it has been proved that 'The Pool' is in the Port of Newry for custom-house purposes, and I do not consider we are called upon to decide whether it is so geographically. The Plaintiff was bound to proceed with his vessel to the Port of Newry—that is my opinion—to proceed to the proper place for discharging his cargo for the Port of Newry, whether geographically within it or not. In the case of *Nicholson* v. *Williams*[21] Mr. Justice Lush shows the distinction between a port as a geographical expression and in its legal sense. . . . I should arrive at the conclusion that all the three places constituted the usual place of discharge for ships of the size of the plaintiffs . . . "

A similar problem arose in *M'Intosh* v. *Sinclair*,[22] also in connection with Newry. Palles C.B. held that the voyage had ended at the Pool and said[23]:

> "The two places together constituted the usual place of discharge."

He also said[24]:

> " . . . evidence that a place is within the limits of a port for customs purposes, fortified, if that be necessary, by evidence of a practice to put out at the particular place, and there deliver into the custody of the merchant so considerable a quantity of the cargo of a par-

---

[15] *Nicholson* v. *Williams* (1871) L.R. 6 Q.B. 632; *Caffarini* v. *Walker* (1876) Ir.R. 10 C.L. 250; *M'Intosh* v. *Sinclair* (1877) Ir.R. 11 C.L. 456; *Sailing-Ship Garston Co.* v. *Hickie & Co.* (1855) 15 Q.B.D. 580 (C.A.); and *Pyman Bros.* v. *Dreyfus Bros. & Co.* (1889) 24 Q.B.D. 152.

[16] *Roelandts* v. *Harrison* (1854) 9 Ex. 444; *Price* v. *Livingstone* (1882) 9 Q.B.D. 679; and *Sailing-Ship Garston Co.* v. *Hickie & Co.* (1885) 15 Q.B.D. 580 (C.A.). See § 4–15 below.

[17] *Sea Insurance Co.* v. *Blogg* [1898] 2 Q.B. 398; *Mersey Mutual Association* v. *Poland* (1910) 15 Com.Cas. 205.

[18] *Sailing-Ship Garston Co.* v. *Hickie & Co.* (1885) 15 Q.B.D. 580 (C.A.) at p. 596. Freight was due 10 days after the ship's final sailing "from her last port." See § 4–15 below.

[19] (1876) Ir.R. 10 C.L. 250.

[20] At p. 252.

[21] (1871) L.R. 6 Q.B. 632 at p. 641. See § 4–09 above.

[22] (1877) Ir.R. 11 C.L. 456.

[23] At p. 466.

[24] At p. 461.

ticular ship as upwards of *two-thirds*[25] of the whole, is evidence that such place is within the port described in the charterparty of that ship. . . . "

and[26]:

> "The place, then, being within the port, the only remaining question is whether it was 'the usual place of discharge,' or, to use the more accurate expression of Parke B. in *Kell* v. *Anderson*,[27] the 'place of discharge, according to the usage of the port . . . for such vessels.' The jury have found that it was the usual place of discharge for vessels of the burthen of the *Mary* to commence their discharge."

The judge stated that the place was "within the port" and then noted the finding of the jury that it was "the usual place of discharge" for such ships. The ship had therefore arrived. The separate attention given to these two issues may be compared with the more recent view[28] that one establishes whether the ship is within the port and then, if she is where waiting ships usually lie, presumes that she is at the immediate and effective disposition of charterers, unless there are extraordinary circumstances, proof of which would depend upon the charterers. If these conditions are satisfied, the ship has arrived. The difference is that in the earlier cases the ship had to be in "the usual place of discharge," whereas now she may be merely "where waiting ships usually lie."[29]

4–15   The Court of Appeal contrasted the legal with the popular, business or commercial limits of a port in *Sailing-Ship Garston Co.* v. *Hickie & Co.*[30] Coal had been loaded at Bute Docks, Cardiff, for Bombay under a charterparty which stated: " . . . the freight to be paid, say two-thirds in cash (less $5\frac{1}{2}$ per cent. for interest and insurance) ten days after the final sailing of the vessel from her last port in Great Britain . . . and the remainder in cash . . . on the right and true delivery of the cargo agreeably to bills of lading . . . " Having cleared at the custom house the ship started on her voyage, proceeding, in tow, down the artificial channel leading from the docks to the River Taff. When about 300 yards out of the channel and into the river, she came into collision with a steamer, and was so damaged that she had to return the next day for repairs. The shipowners claimed two thirds of the freight but the charterers denied liability, saying that the ship had not finally sailed "from her last port in Great Britain." The Court of Appeal, finding for the charterers, held[31] that at the time of the collision the ship was not outside the limits of the port in the popular, business or commercial sense of the word; she had therefore not sailed "from her last port" and no freight was due. Brett M.R. said[32]:

> "Some judges have said, 'In the business sense of the word,' 'In the ordinary sense,' 'In

[25] The italics appear in the law report.

[26] At p. 462.

[27] (1842) 10 M. & W. 498. See § 4–12 above.

[28] As expressed in *Oldendorff (E.L.) & Co. G.m.b.H.* v. *Tradax Export S.A.* [1973] 2 Lloyd's Rep. 285 (M.L.) (*The Johanna Oldendorff*) (see § 4–21 below) and in *Federal Commerce and Navigation Co. Ltd.* v. *Tradax Export S.A.* (*The Maratha Envoy*) (see § 4–25 below).

[29] *Ibid.* at p. 291, *per* Lord Reid.

[30] (1885) 15 Q.B.D. 580.

[31] The collision occurred on December 22, 1884; a writ indorsed with the claim was issued on January 2, 1885; judgment for the charterers was given by Wills J. at the Liverpool assizes on February 23, 1885; and the Court of Appeal delivered judgment on July 3, 1885. Such expedition is now rare.

[32] At pp. 587–588.

the common and ordinary sense.' All these phrases mean very much the same thing. It is not to be the fiscal port. . . . The fiscal port, the limits of which are, of course, always fixed by Act of Parliament, is never in fact taken into consideration by shipowners or merchants employing ships . . . the word 'port' in a charterparty does not necessarily mean an Act of Parliament pilotage port, or, which is the better word, pilotage district. . . . He[33] seems to have been inclined to substitute the words 'the legal port'; but, with deference to him, in my opinion that would not do. The legal port may be fixed by an Act of Parliament about which nobody knows anything."

After eliminating in this way the concepts of a fiscal port, a pilotage port and a legal port, Brett M.R. said[34] that one must find out not only where, in fact, people have had their ships loaded and unloaded, but also how far the port extended.[35]

In *Pyman Bros.* v. *Dreyfus Bros. & Co.*[36] a ship was chartered to go "to **4–16** Odessa or so near thereunto as she might safely get."[37] On December 22 she reached the outer harbour at a point at which she was as near as she might safely get to a loading berth. The master gave notice of readiness to load.[38] Loading was practicable in the outer harbour and in the inner harbour, but only alongside or at a quay berth. The harbour-master made the ship wait for her regular turn. The charterers were willing to load when she got to a quay berth in the inner harbour, where the cargo was stored. There was no custom by which ships were not considered ready to receive cargo until moored alongside a quay. The charterers began loading at a quay berth, in the inner harbour, for which she had received orders two days earlier, on January 10. It was held that laytime began on December 22, when the ship reached the outer harbour. Huddleston B. said[39] that the solution was to be found in a passage in a judgment delivered by Brett L.J. in *Nelson* v. *Dahl*[40]:

"If the place named be of the larger description, as a port or dock, the notice may be given, though the ship is not then in the particular part of the port or dock in which the particular cargo is to be loaded; but if the place named is of the more limited description, the notice cannot be given until the ship is at the named place, though the ship is in the port or dock in which the named place is situated."

Huddleston B. went on to say[41]:

"Had the contract been that the ship was 'to proceed to the inner harbour at Odessa and load,' she could not be said to have arrived within the meaning of the charterparty till January 8, when she reached the inner harbour, and the arbitrator would have been wrong. But the contract is that she is 'to proceed to Odessa and load.' This is satisfied by her arrival in the outer harbour at Odessa on December 22."

---

[33] Wills J., who had also held that the ship was still within the port.
[34] At pp. 589–590. See the second passage quoted from his judgment at § 4–09 above. It was cited with approval by Lord Morris and Viscount Dilhorne in *Oldendorff (E.L.) & Co. G.m.b.H.* v. *Tradax Export S.A.* [1973] 2 Lloyd's Rep. 285 (H.L.) (*The Johanna Oldendorff*) at pp. 293–294 and 300 respectively. See also § 4–21 below.
[35] An almost exactly similar problem, also concerning a ship in tow from the Bute Docks, but ending in her going aground in the artificial channel, had been considered in *Roelandts* v. *Harrison* (1854) 9 Ex. 444. It was held that she had not finally sailed.
[36] (1889) 24 Q.B.D. 152.
[37] For the meaning of this phrase see § 4–38 below.
[38] As to why notice is needed see § 5–18 below.
[39] At p. 155.
[40] (1879) 12 Ch.D. 568 at p. 581 (C.A.). For this case, *sub. nom. Dahl* v. *Nelson, Donkin & Co.* (1881) 6 App.Cas 38 (H.L.), see § 4–42 below.
[41] At pp. 155–156.

And as Mathew J. added,[42] speaking of the charterers' rights to select the loading place:

> "They had only to indicate the place to which she was to go for her cargo, and she would have been there immediately."

4–17   2. *Five later cases, from 1908 to 1977.* The five subsequent leading cases which define the word "port" are *Leonis SS. Co. Ltd. v. Rank Ltd. (No. 1)*[43]; *Sociedad Financiera de Bienes Raices S.A. v. Agrimpex Hungarian Trading Co. for Agricultural Products*[44]; *Shipping Developments Corporation S.A. v. V/O Sojuzneftexport*[45]; *Oldendorff (E.L.) & Co. G.m.b.H. v. Tradax Export S.A.*[46]; and *Federal Commerce and Navigation Co. Ltd. v. Tradax Export S.A.*[47] In these cases the distinction between commercial and other limits was emphasised; and the problem of laytime and the waiting ship was discussed.

4–18   In *Leonis SS. Co. Ltd. v. Rank Ltd. (No. 1)*[48] a ship chartered to carry wheat was to "proceed as ordered . . . to the under-mentioned place or places, . . . *viz.* . . . at one or two safe loading ports or places in the river Paraña . . . " with "the option of loading the entire cargo at Bahia Blanca." Time was to begin 12 hours after written notice was given by the master. She was ordered to Bahia Blanca, where she arrived off the pier, anchoring in the river "only a few ship's lengths off the pier,"[49] because there were other ships alongside. The master then gave notice of readiness to load. The ship was delayed in getting a berth owing to the crowded state of the port. The Court of Appeal held that laytime began 12 hours after the notice, and not from the time the ship obtained the berth alongside the pier. Buckley L.J. referred to the judgment of Bovill C.J. in *Tapscott v. Balfour*[50] and said[51] of his words:

> "In those words I find an expression of the meaning to be given to what has been called the commercial ambit of the port as distinguished from the whole port in a geographical or maritime sense. It means, not the whole part, but such part of the port as is a proper place for discharging, whether the vessel has reached a berth or not."

So also Kennedy L.J. said,[52] after discussing the effect that custom might have on the question:

> "In the absence of any proof of a custom of this kind—and I may note in passing that no evidence of such a custom was given in the present case—the commercial area of a port, arrival within which makes the ship an arrived ship, and, as such, entitled to give notice of readiness to load, and at the expiration of the notice to begin to count lay days, ought, I think, to be that area of the named port of destination on arrival within which the master can effectively place his ship at the disposal of the charterer, the vessel herself being then, so far as she is concerned, ready to load, and as near as circumstances permit to the actual loading 'spot.' "

---

[42] At p. 157.
[43] [1908] 1 K.B. 499 (C.A.). See § 4–18 below
[44] [1961] A.C. 135 (H.L.) (*The Aello*). See § 4–19 below.
[45] [1971] 1 Lloyd's Rep. 506 (C.A.) (*The Delian Spirit*). See § 4–20 below.
[46] [1973] 2 Lloyd's Rep. 285 (H.L.) (*The Johanna Oldendorff*). See § 4–21 below.
[47] [1977] 2 Lloyd's Rep. 301 (H.L.) (*The Maratha Envoy*); see § 4–25 below.
[48] [1908] 1 K.B. 499 (C.A.).
[49] The words of Kennedy L.J., *ibid.* at p. 524, citing the judgment of Channell J. in the court below [1907] (K.B. 344 at p. 351).
[50] (1872) L.R. 8 C.P. 46 at p. 52., where he said that the shipowner had done all that was required when he had "taken his vessel to the usual place of loading in the port." See § 4–06 above.
[51] At p. 513.
[52] At p. 521.

Kennedy L.J. also distinguished small ports from large ports,[53] saying[54]:

> "In the case of a small port 'port' may or may not mean the whole of the geographical port. In the case of a widely extended area, such as London, Liverpool or Hull, it certainly signifies some area which is less than the geographical port, and which may, I think, not unfitly be called the commercial area. . . . "

In *Sociedad Financiera de Bienes Raices S.A.* v. *Agrimpex Hungarian* **4–19** *Trading Co. for Agricultural Products*[55] the *Aello* had been chartered on the Centrocon form to load maize "at one or two safe loading ports or places in the River Paraña . . . and the balance of the cargo in the port of Buenos Aires," and to carry the cargo to Hamburg. The traffic control system prevented maize ships from proceeding beyond the Free Anchorage near a point in the roads called Intersection,[55a] within the legal limits of Buenos Aires, but 22 miles (three hours' steaming time) from the dock area, until they had obtained a "giro" or permit. Grain was not loaded or discharged at Intersection. The giro was issued by the customs authority on the ship's application when the Grain Board certified that cargo had been allocated. As there was congestion the port authority decided that before a giro was issued, not only must the Board's certificate be obtained, but a cargo must be available. The *Aello* arrived in the Free Anchorage on October 12; the shippers obtained the certificate on October 13, but did not have a cargo ready to be loaded until October 29. The charterers contended that the *Aello* was not an arrived ship until October 29. The shipowners argued that if this were so it resulted from a breach of an absolute obligation to provide a cargo in time.

The House of Lords held, by a majority of three[56] to two,[57] that the *Aello* was not an arrived ship until October 29, because when in the roads whe was not within the commercial area.[58] This decision was reversed by the House in the *Oldendorff* case.[59] The charterers, it was held, were in breach of an absolute obligation, of which they were not relieved by showing that before October 29 they had taken all reasonable steps to provide a cargo. The following quotations from the speeches of the majority indicate the principles applied. Lord Keith summarised his approach by saying[60]:

> "I have no reason to think that the question cannot be answered satisfactorily by an application of the principles elaborated in *Leonis SS. Co. Ltd.* v. *Rank Ltd.*[61]. . . . The ship was no doubt as near as she could get to 'the actual loading spot' for some time after her arrival at the anchorage but that, in my opinion, is immaterial. A point 'as near as circumstances permit to the actual loading spot' must, in my opinion, be within the port in its commercial sense, apart from stipulation in the charterparty. . . . The fact that oil vessels or other types of vessel might load or discharge in the roads is nothing to the point. There may be different commercial areas in a port for different types of vessel and cargo, or a vessel may have to load or discharge outside a port. . . . I reach the conclusion that the *Aello* was not an arrived ship when she anchored in the roads."

---

[53] See also Donaldson J. on "a small port, such as Tuapse" and "a large port, such as London" in *Shipping Developments Corporation S.A.* v. *V/O Sojuznefiexport (The Delian Spirit)* [1971] 1 Lloyd's Rep. 64 at p. 69. As to that case, see § 4–20 below.
[54] At p. 520.
[55] [1961] A.C. 135 (H.L.). (*The Aello*).
[55a] Being the intersection of the rivers Parana and Uruguay.
[56] Lord Keith of Avonholm, Lord Jenkins and Lord Morris of Borth-y-Gest.
[57] Lord Radcliffe and Lord Cohen.
[58] For a general discussion of the term "commercial area" see § 4–30 below.
[59] [1973] 2 Lloyd's Rep. 285 (*The Johanna Oldendorff*). See § 4–21 below.
[60] At pp. 187–188.
[61] [1908] 1 K.B. 499 (C.A.).

Lord Jenkins said that both sides agreed that the question whether the *Aello* became an arrived ship at the Free Anchorage, or when she entered the inner harbour, was to be resolved by applying the general principles laid down in the *Leonis* case.[62] He outlined those principles and said[63] that their effect was to impute to the parties

> "the intention that the shipowner will (in point of geographical position) have per-formed his duty of making the vessel available to load at the port in question when he has brought it to the 'commercial area' of the port, that is to say, the area in which the actual loading spot is to be found and to which vessels seeking to load cargo of the relevant des-cription usually go, and in which the business of loading such cargo is usually carried out. . . . The judgments, as I think, clearly postulate as the 'commercial area' a physical area capable (though no doubt only within broad limits) of identification on a map. When the given ship enters that area and positions herself within it in accordance with the requirements just stated, she is (in point of geographical position) an arrived ship: until she does so she is not an arrived ship, and lay days and demurrage are to be calculated accordingly. . . . I think the true view is that these vessels were awaiting access to the commercial area of the port as distinct from being in the commercial area of the port and awaiting access to the actual loading spot in that area."

Lord Morris of Borth-y-Gest spoke[64] of the unassailability of the auth-ority of *Leonis*[65] and said[66]:

> " . . . if it can reasonably be said that a ship which is required to go to a port in order there to load has reached the commercial area of the port within which are the loading spots for her specified cargo, so that she next awaits details as to her particular loading spots and directions as to proceeding to them, then it can also fairly be said that she has arrived at her destination. . . . "

He agreed[67] with the view of Parker L.J. who in the Court of Appeal[68] had said:

> "The commercial area was intended to be that part of the port where a ship can be loaded when a berth is available, albeit she cannot be loaded until a berth is available."

4–20   In a later case a member of the House of Lords[69] said of the views of the majority in *The Aello* (Lord Keith, Lord Jenkins and Lord Morris): "The majority of this House thus accepted Lord Parker's definition of 'commer-cial area' and in doing so in my opinion they gave a different interpretation to *Leonis* v. *Rank* from that given prior thereto."

The Court of Appeal in *Shipping Developments Corporation S.A.* v. *V/O Sojuzneftexport*[70] considered what one judge[71] later called "a classical example of the difficulties created by a decision such as that in *The Aello*." *The Delian Spirit* had been chartered, in 1963, to carry oil from "one or two safe ports Soviet Black Sea, at Charterers' option" to Japan. The char-

---

[62] *Ibid.*
[63] At pp. 207–208.
[64] At p. 211.
[65] [1908] 1 K.B. 499 (C.A.).
[66] At p. 216.
[67] *Ibid.*
[68] [1958] 2 Q.B. 385 at p. 401. This has been called the Parker test. See, for example, Lord Diplock in *Federal Commerce and Navigation Co. Ltd.* v. *Tradax Export S.A.* [1977] 2 Lloyd's Rep. 301 at p. 305 (H.L.) (*The Maratha Envoy*); and § 4–27 below, at (B). It should be compared with the Reid test, as stated by Lord Reid in *Oldendorff (E.L.) & Co. G.m.b.H.* v. *Tradax Export S.A.* [1973] 2 Lloyd's Rep. 285 at p. 291 (H.L.) (*The Johanna Oldendorff*); see § 4–21 below.
[69] Viscount Dilhorne in *Oldendorff (E.L.) & Co. G.m.b.H.* v. *Tradax Export S.A.* (*The Johanna Oldendorff*), *op. cit.*, at p. 301.
[70] [1971] 1 Lloyd's Rep. 506. (*The Delian Spirit*).
[71] Lord Reid in *The Johanna Oldendorff*, *op. cit.*, at p. 291. See § 4–21 below.

terers were allowed "120 running hours . . . for loading and discharging." The charterparty also stated: "The vessel shall load and discharge at a place or at a dock alongside lighters reachable on her arrival, which shall be indicated by Charterers . . . "; and "The laying days shall commence from the time the vessel is ready to receive or discharge her cargo, the Captain giving six hours' notice. . . . " She was ordered to Tuapse, a small port,[72] where, giving notice of readiness, she remained anchored for just over five days in the roads. She was then ordered to go alongside a loading berth inside the breakwaters which surrounded the harbour. The berth was 1¼ miles from her anchorage. Free pratique was granted[73]; loading began and was completed in less than a day. The jetty at which she moored had berths for four tankers; if the berths were all occupied, tankers had to remain anchored in the roads.

The shipowners first contended that the time at anchorage (allowing for six hours' notice) was laytime. In 1964, before the matter was resolved, another judgment[74] became available. Its finding that charterers were in breach of a duty to load at a place "reachable on her arrival, which shall be indicated by Charterers . . . " encouraged the shipowners to re-formulate their claim. They claimed damages for detention in respect of a failure by the charterers to find such a place on arrival: alternatively they claimed demurrage. The claim for damages was described[75] as having "a looking-glass quality which would have delighted Lewis Carroll," as the shipowners were "busily contending that the motor tanker *Delian Spirit* was not an arrived ship before she berthed at Tuapse, whereas the charterers contend that she became an arrived ship several days earlier when she anchored in the roads."

In the High Court[76] Donaldson J. had held that the charterers were in breach and that the ship had arrived at her contractual destination at the anchorage. "The geographical situation of the vessel," he said[77]; "was in fact almost identical with that in *Leonis* v. *Rank* . . . save that two breakwaters lay between her and the jetty." In *The Aello* those concerned did not have to consider a port as small as Tuapse.

The Court of Appeal, allowing an appeal by the charterers, had agreed that she was an arrived ship while at the anchorage, though free pratique had not been granted[78]; but it held that, although they were in breach of the duty to find a place on arrival,[79] no damages should be awarded for delay. Denning M.R. said[80]:

> "The present case seems to me to fall within the *Leonis* and not *The Aello*. The *Delian Spirit* had put down anchor as near as she possibly could get to the jetty where she had to go. The only reason she could not get in was because the berths were all occupied by other tankers at the time. She waited at the allotted customary and usual place for

---

[72] For one distinction between small ports and large ports, see Kennedy L.J. in *Leonis SS. Co. Ltd.* v. *Rank Ltd. (No. 1)* [1908] 1 K.B. 499 (C.A.) at p. 520, and § 4–18 above. For a map of Tuapse port, with scale, see [1971] 1 Lloyd's Rep. 506 at p. 513.

[73] For free pratique see § 5–11 below.

[74] *Sociedad Carga Oceanica S.A.* v. *Idolinoele Vertriebsgesellschaft m.b.H.* [1964] 2 Lloyd's Rep. 28 (*The Angelos Lusis*). See § 4–33 below as to "reachable on her arrival."

[75] By Donaldson J. in [1971] 1 Lloyd's Rep. 64 at pp. 65–66.

[76] [1971] 1 Lloyd's Rep. 64.

[77] *Ibid.* at p. 69.

[78] This aspect of the problem is discussed at § 5–11 below.

[79] As to this duty, and the consequences of a breach thereof, see § 4–16 below.

[80] At p. 509.

tankers waiting to get in. It was the only place. She was not allowed to wait inside the breakwater. She waited within a distance of 1¼ miles from the jetty. She herself gave notice of readiness."

He approved of "the classic test of Lord Justice Kennedy."[81] Fenton Atkinson L.J.[82] agreed that the ship had arrived for the purposes of laytime when anchored in the roads. Sir Gordon Willmer relied on (a) the acceptance of the notice of readiness "without question by the officials acting on behalf of the charterers"[82] which was material as "the view of shipping persons present at the time must obviously be treated with great respect"[83]; (b) the fact that the ship was at the appointed anchorage, and so within what Kennedy L.J.[84] called the " . . . area of the named port of destination on arrival within which the master can effectively place his ship at the disposal of the charterer . . . "; and (c) the ship being, as Kennedy L.J. put it, "in a place where ships waiting for access to that spot usually lie."[85]

4–21   In *Oldendorff (E.L.) & Co. G.m.b.H.* v. *Tradax Export S.A.*[86] the *Johanna Oldendorff*, chartered on the Baltimore Berth Grain Form C, loaded wheat and soya beans in bulk in the U.S.A. She was to go to "London or Avonmouth or Glasgow or Belfast or Liverpool/Birkenhead (counting as one port) or Hull" at the option of the charterers, who directed her "to proceed to the port of Liverpool/Birkenhead to discharge." The charterparty stated:

"Time to count from the first working period on the next day following receipt during ordinary office hours of written notice of readiness to discharge whether in berth or not."

The ship arrived at the Mersey Bar light ship and pilot station on January 2, 1968 at 1630 hours, lying there at anchor over night. She then moved to Prince's landing stage, mooring there at 1030 hours on January 3. She was ordered by the port authority to leave, and arrived back at the anchorage off the light ship at 1440 hours. The shipowners gave notice of readiness at 1435 hours. The ship left the anchorage on January 20 at 1506 hours and berthed at East Tower, East Float, Birkenhead, on January 21 at 0315 hours. The question was whether laytime began (a) at 0800 hours on January 4; or (b) at 0800 hours on January 22 (the day after she berthed); or (c) at 0800 hours on January 23. Evidence was given that the Bar anchorage, 17 miles from the nearest discharging berth, was the usual place where grain ships lay while awaiting a berth. The umpire held that laytime began at 0800 hours on January 4. In the High Court[87] Donaldson J. held that the ship had not arrived either when she reached the Bar anchorage or when she reached the Prince's landing stage.

The Court of Appeal, upholding the High Court's decision, held[88] by a

---

[81] In *Leonis SS. Co. Ltd.* v. *Rank Ltd. (No. 1)* [1908] 1 K.B. 499 at p. 521 (C.A.). For the passage in question, see § 4–18 above.
[82] At pp. 510, 512. On acceptance and rejection of notices of readiness, see § 5–35 below.
[83] At p. 512.
[84] See [1971] 1 Lloyd's Rep. 64 at p. 69.
[85] Viscount Dilhorne, in *Oldendorff (E.L.) & Co. G.m.b.H.* v. *Tradax Export S.A. (The Johanna Oldendorff)*, *op. cit.* at p. 302, commented on these two judgments: "The interpretation put on the *Leonis* by the majority in the *Aello* case was thus not applied. If that interpretation was correct, then, in my opinion, the *Delian Spirit* was wrongly decided."
[86] [1973] 2 Lloyd's Rep. 285 (H.L.).
[87] [1971] 2 Lloyd's Rep. 96.
[88] [1972] 2 Lloyd's Rep. 292.

majority[89] that (1) the ship had not arrived at the Bar anchorage because (a) she had not reached the commercial area of the port; (b) the relevant waiting area must be in the commercial area; and (c) the commercial area must be that part of the port where she could be discharged when a berth was available; (2) the words "whether in berth or not" applied only when a ship was already an arrived ship.

The House of Lords allowed the appeal by the shipowners. It held[90] that **4–22** (1) for a ship to have arrived she must, if she could not go immediately to a berth, have reached a position within the port where she was at the immediate and effective disposition of the charterers: a place where waiting ships usually lay[90a] constituted such a position unless there were some extraordinary circumstances the onus of proof of which would fall on the charterers; if the ship were at some other place in the port, the shipowners must prove that she was as fully at the disposition of the charterers as if she were in the vicinity of the discharging berth; (2) the ship arrived when she reached the Bar anchorage, so that laytime began at 0800 hours on January 4. The House applied the decision in *Leonis* v. *Rank*[91] and overruled its own decision in *The Aello*.[92] The leading speech was given by Lord Reid, who formulated what has become known as "the Reid test."[93]

Lord Reid's judgment can be summarised by the following quotations from it:

> "Until the decision of the Court of Appeal in *Leonis Steamship Co.* v. *Rank Ltd.*[94] . . . the law was in some confusion . . . the question at issue in *Leonis* was very different from the question in the present case. There it was whether the ship did not arrive until she was actually at the loading berth or whether it was enough that she had arrived in the immediate vicinity; and it was held that it was enough that she had come within a few ships' lengths of the pier. Here it is admitted that the vessel would have been an arrived ship if she had been allowed to wait anywhere in the dock area of the port but it is said to make all the difference that she was required to wait in a more remote area of port."[95]

> "It has always been held that the Court of Appeal in *Leonis* laid down general principles which must be followed: The difficulty has been to find out what those principles are. Lord Justice Buckley and Lord Justice Kennedy each delivered long judgments and Lord Alverstone, C.J., agreed with both. So he must have thought that there was no substantial difference between them. And that has been the view of almost all the many Judges who have since then had to consider the matter. The judgment of Lord Justice Kennedy has generally been regarded as the leading judgment, perhaps because it is rather less obscure than that of Lord Justice Buckley. . . . I would adopt the general view hitherto held that there is no substantial difference between them.[96]

He continued[97]:

> "So I turn to enquire what principles Lord Justice Kennedy intended to lay down . . .

[89] Buckley and Roskill L.JJ.; Lord Denning M.R. dissenting.
[90] [1973] 2 Lloyd's Rep. 285.
[90a] For a reference to this concept in a London arbitration, where a ship waited for a convoy at Bandar Abbas, 400 miles from her destination, see LMLN 143, April 25, 1985, and § 4–11 above, at n. 1a.
[91] [1908] 1 K.B. 499 (C.A.). See § 4–18 above.
[92] [1961] A.C. 135 (H.L.); see § 4–19 above.
[93] It was so described by Lord Diplock, for example, in *Federal Commerce and Navigation Co. Ltd.* v. *Tradax Export S.A. (The Maratha Envoy)* [1977] 2 Lloyd's Rep. 301 at p. 305 (H.L.). See § 4–25 below.
[94] [1908] 1 K.B. 499. See § 4–18 above.
[95] *Op. cit.* at p. 287.
[96] *Op. cit.* at p. 288.
[97] *Op. cit.* at pp. 288–289.

[Lord Reid cited certain passages,[98] and then continued.] Then . . . there comes a passage,[99] which to my mind is even more important than those which I have already quoted. 'What Brett L.J. meant by the words "usual place at which loading ships lie,"[1] as what Bovill C.J. also meant by "the dock or roadstead where loading usually takes place," is the area in the port within which vessels whose obligation and purpose is to receive a cargo lie; *in other words* [my italics] that which I have ventured to describe as the commercial port, or the commercial area within the port, which is usually occupied by such vessels. . . .'

"This appears to me to make it perfectly clear that Lord Justice Kennedy meant that the commercial area includes the area within the port at which waiting vessels lie. It is true that in *Leonis* that area was close to the loading berth and it may be that in 1907 it was unusual for the waiting area to be at any great distance from the loading berths; ships were smaller, congestion may not have been so great and communication between ship and shore was not so rapid. So there was no reason for Lord Justice Kennedy to have prominently in mind a case where the waiting area was distinct from the loading berth. But he was not basing his judgment on distance. He was basing it on commercial good sense and I find it quite incredible that if he had been faced with a case where, although the waiting area was distant, that had no commercial significance and the ship was as fully at the disposal of the charterer as if she had been within a few hundred yards, he would have decided the case the other way.

"In *The Aello*[2] the facts were unusual. The usual waiting place for vessels arriving at the port of Buenos Aires was close to the loading berth but owing to temporary congestion the port authority decided that ships which arrived and had no cargo waiting for them must wait at a point which, though within the limits of the port, was some 22 miles from the loading area. So the *Aello* had to wait there, and Mr. Justice Ashworth, the Court of Appeal and the majority in this House decided that while here she was not an arrived ship . . . "

Lord Reid then quoted from the judgment of Lord Justice Parker in *The Aello*[3]:

"The commercial area was intended to be that part of the port where a ship can be loaded when a berth is available, albeit she cannot be loaded until a berth is available."

Lord Reid went on[3a] to comment on the so-called Parker test:

"Although Lord Justice Kennedy clearly based his judgment on what he thought was commercial good sense, I do not find in the judgment of Lord Justice Parker any consideration of that matter. If he had held that while waiting at the intersection 22 miles away the *Aello* was not as effectively at the disposition of the charterers as she would have been if in the usual waiting place that would certainly have justified his decision: but that matter does not seem to have been discussed. He admitted that if the test stated by Lord Justice Kennedy is read literally the *Aello* satisfied it but he based his refusal so to read it on the fact that throughout his judgment Lord Justice Kennedy was contrasting an area where loading takes place with the actual loading spot. Of course he was doing that because he was quite properly thinking of the facts of the case before him. But . . . he was also doing a good deal more. I am quite unable to agree that the concluding part of the above quotation from the judgment of Lord Justice Parker is an accurate reflection of the views expressed by Lord Justice Kennedy. If it were, it would lead to the absurd conclusion that the decision of a case must be different if on the one hand the usual waiting area is just inside that part of a port where a ship can be loaded or on the other hand just outside that part of the port, although this slight difference of location would make no practical difference in any commercial sense to any one."

4–23   Lord Reid gave brief extracts from what had been said by others who had dealt with the case. He quoted Mr. Justice Donaldson[4]:

---

[98] Including those from the judgment of Kennedy L.J. (at pp. 520 and 521 of the *Leonis* decision) set out at § 4–18 above.
[99] *Leonis Steamship Co.* v. *Rank Ltd. (No. 1)* [1908] 1 K.B. 499 at p. 523.
[1] In *Nelson* v. *Dahl* (1879) 12 Ch.D. 568 at p. 582 (C.A.). See also § 4–05 above.
[2] See § 4–19 above.
[3] [1958] 2 Q.B. 385 at p. 401 (C.A.).
[3a] At p. 289.
[4] In the High Court; [1971] 2 Lloyd's Rep. 96, at p. 100.

> "If the present case had fallen to be decided in 1957,[5] it would have been perfectly clear that the vessel had 'arrived' when she reached the bar anchorage. She was then at the disposition of the charterers within the legal limits of the port of destination and in a position in which vessels usually lie while awaiting a discharging berth."

And he added:

> "Unfortunately the authoritative view of the law has changed since 1957. I say 'unfortunately' because the law as it now appears to be[6] is that a ship is only arrived when she is in 'that part of the port where a ship can be loaded with the relevant cargo when a berth is available, albeit she cannot be loaded until a berth is available.' (See Scrutton,[7] (17th ed., 1964), at p. 124)."

Lord Reid then quoted[8] from the two majority judgments in the Court of Appeal,[9] namely:
Lord Justice Buckley[10]:

> "With a sense of regret similar to that expressed by Mr. Justice Donaldson, I feel constrained to accept that this Court and the House of Lords in *The Aello* did interpret the decision in *Leonis* v. *Rank* in a manner different from that in which it had theretofore been interpreted and in that sense changed the law . . . "

and Lord Justice Roskill[11]:

> "It is now over 12 years since *The Aello* was finally decided. It is widely known that it was not a popular decision either in St. Mary Axe or the Temple. It is also widely known that its application has from time to time caused difficulty not only to brokers but also to arbitrators and umpires and indeed to Judges."[11a]

In what can be regarded as a summary of his conclusions, and a defini- **4–24** tive statement of the law as it now stands as to what contitutes an arrived ship, Lord Reid then said[12]:

> "I would therefore state what I would hope to be the true legal position in this way. Before a ship can be said to have arrived at a port she must, if she cannot proceed immediately to a berth, have reached a position within the port where she is at the immediate and effective disposition of the charterer. If she is at a place where waiting ships usually lie, she will be in such a position unless in some extraordinary circumstances proof of which would lie in the charterer . . . If the ship is waiting at some other place in the port[13] then it will be for the owner to prove that she is as fully at the disposition of the charterer as she would have been if in the vicinity of the berth for loading or discharge."

Lord Reid then said that he would allow the appeal by the shipowners and hold that laytime for discharge began at 0800 hours on January 4. The ship was therefore held to have arrived when at the Mersey Bar anchorage. The other Judges[14] agreed with Lord Reid.

---

[5] Before the High Court decision in *The Aello*.
[6] *i.e.* at the time of his judgment, in 1971.
[7] *i.e. Scrutton on Charterparties*. The extract was itself a repetition of the words used by Parker L.J. in the Court of Appeal in *The Aello* (see § 4–19 above). The passage in the 17th ed. in which these words were quoted gives them as the definition of "the commercial area of the port," an expression which is absent from the corresponding passage in the 19th ed. (1984, p. 142) which refers only to "the port."
[8] *Op. cit.*, at pp. 290 and 291.
[9] [1972] 2 Lloyd's Rep. 292. He also referred briefly to the minority judgment of Lord Denning M.R.
[10] *Ibid.* at p. 302.
[11] *Ibid.* at p. 311.
[11a] Rank and power of comprehension thus marching hand in hand.
[12] *Op. cit.* at p. 291. Part of this important passage is also cited at § 4–07 above.
[13] *i.e.* other than at a place where waiting ships usually lie.
[14] Lord Morris of Borth-y-Gest, Viscount Dilhorne, Lord Diplock and Lord Simon of Glaisdale. For comments by the first three of these Law Lords see § 4–10 above.

4–25   In *Federal Commerce and Navigation Co. Ltd.* v. *Tradax Export S.A.*[15] the *Maratha Envoy*, chartered on the Baltimore Form C,[16] was to carry corn and soya bean meal from Chicago to "one port out of Amsterdam or Rotterdam or Antwerp or Ghent or one (1) safe port German North Sea." The charterers ordered the ship to the River Weser. The charterparty did not include the Weser Lightship clause, by which a ship ordered by the authorities to anchor at the Lightship can tender notice of readiness at an anchorage near the Lightship, as if she has arrived at her final port.[17] The ship anchored at the Lightship, the charterers asking her to lighten at Brake and go to Bremen. It was decided that she would at least show herself at Brake. She went up river, turned off Brake and returned to the Lightship. There was neither an available berth nor any waiting place there and anchoring in the river was forbidden. The ship did not obtain health or customs clearance. When she got back to Bremerhaven, notice of readiness was tendered and rejected. The charterers then nominated Brake for discharge. The ship made a second excursion up river, obtaining health clearance but not customs clearance. This excursion was later variously described as "showing her chimney," "a charade," and "a voyage of convenience." She turned back again; notice of readiness was given and again rejected. She eventually berthed at Brake. It is significant that these events took place in 1970, when (as Lord Denning M.R. put it in the Court of Appeal)[18] "the law was as thought to be finally declared by the House of Lords in *The Aello*. According to that decision, *The Maratha Envoy* was not an arrived ship when she was at the Weser lightship." The House of Lords decision in *The Johanna Oldendorff* was made in 1973; it decided *The Maratha Envoy* in 1976.

The shipowners contended that the *Maratha Envoy* had arrived upon one of the two excursions, and demanded damages for waiting at the Lightship, because of charterers' failure to give discharging orders promptly. The importance of this case lies mainly in the decision of the House of Lords to reaffirm its decision in the *Johanna Oldendorff*, and to continue to reject *The Aello*, rather than in its establishment of new law. It also showed that it can be difficult to apply the so-called "Reid test" set out in the *Johanna Oldendorff*.[19] It is sometimes easier to say that a ship is at the usual waiting place than to say that she is within the port.

4–26   In the High Court[20] Donaldson J., deciding for charterers, held that in a commercial and legal sense ships were in the port of Brake when off the quay, but that the excursions did not cause the ship to be arrived because her voyage had not ended.

The Court of Appeal,[21] allowing the shipowners' appeal, held:

---

[15] [1977] 2 Lloyd's Rep. 301 (H.L.).

[16] This was the same form as that used in the chartering of the *Johanna Oldendorff*; see § 4–21 above.

[17] The Weser Lightship clause has taken various forms. One version states: "If vessel is ordered to River Weser port and is unable to berth immediately on arrival River Weser on account of congestion, vessel shall be permitted to present notice of readiness to discharge at anchorage off Weser Lightship or any other waiting berth in the River Weser and laytime to count accordingly, but time used for steaming from waiting berth to discharging berth not to count as laytime."

[18] [1977] 1 Lloyd's Rep. 217, at p. 221.

[19] See § 4–24 above.

[20] [1975] 2 Lloyd's Rep. 223.

[21] [1977] 1 Lloyd's Rep. 217.

(1) (unanimously) that the ship had arrived at the Weser Lightship;
(2) (by a majority) that it was an implied term that arrival at the Light-ship should take effect as if it were arrival in the port of Brake;
(3) that the words "whether in berth or not"[22] permitted notice of readiness at the usual waiting place even though the ship had not reached a berth; indicated that the Lightship was part of the port of Brake; and emphasised that this was a port and not a berth charter-party[23];
(4) (by a majority) that the "excursions" showed that the shipowners, having reached the final stage of the voyage,[24] were ready to do all that was required of them and were at the immediate and effective disposition of the charterers.

Lord Denning M.R., said[25]:

> "By making the dramatic trip up the river and back the shipowners have exposed the law to ridicule. For, although the charter was a port charter—and although it contained an express stipulation that the shipowners could give notice of readiness 'whether in berth or not'—nevertheless the law says that the shipowners cannot give notice of readiness until she has actually reached a berth. So by a process of interpretation, the law has turned this port charter into a berth charter: and altered the whole incidence of waiting time."

A crucial issue was whether the Court could decide that the ship had **4–27** arrived when she was still outside the port. The issue of principle[26] was whether the ship had ended her voyage by doing all that she could do; or had to get within the area known as "the port." Lord Denning continued[27] (but we must remember that this decision of the Court of Appeal was reversed by the House of Lords):

> " . . . there is no decision which binds us to hold that a vessel cannot be an arrived ship until she gets within the limits of the ports . . . I think that, at the present day, a vessel should be held to be an arrived ship when she has reached the usual waiting place for the port, even though it may be a few miles outside the limits of the port itself.[27a] The reason being that she has completed her carrying voyage and is at the disposition of the char-terers as effectively as if she was inside the port itself in the vicinity of a berth."

The House of Lords[28] allowed the charterers' appeal. The only full judg-ment was given by Lord Diplock, the four other Law Lords stating that they agreed with him and had nothing further to add. As this is an area of the law in which there is some possibility of disagreement, it is important to set out the more significant parts of this judgment.

(A) *The freight market and the allocation of risks of delay*

> " . . . the freight market for chartered vessels still remains a classic example of a free market . . . there is an inter-relationship between rates of freight, demurrage and dis-patch money and clauses of the charter-party which deal with the allocation between the

---

[22] See also the discussion of these words at § 4–29 below.
[23] As to berth charterparties see § 4–03 above.
[24] As to the concept of stages see § 4–02 above and the passage there cited from *The Johanna Oldendorff*.
[25] *Op. cit.* at p. 221.
[26] Which still has been disputed, despite the decision in *The Johanna Oldendorff*; see a pamphlet by Donald Davies, a well-known London arbitrator, entitled "The 'Arrived Ship' Concept," published by Lloyd's of London Press Ltd., 1977.
[27] At pp. 222 and 223.
[27a] But not, it seems, 400 miles. See a London arbitration (LMLN 143, April 25, 1985) and § 4–11 above, at n. 1a.
[28] [1977] 2 Lloyd's Rep. 301.

charterer and shipowner of those risks of delay in the prosecution of the adventure contemplated by the charter-party which, being beyond the control of either party, have
been conveniently called 'misfortune risks' as distinguished from 'fault risks' . . ."[29]

(B) *The Johanna Oldendorff as a decision which produced more certainty than the Aello:*

" . . . in *E.L. Oldendorff & Co.* v. *Tradax Export S.A. (The Johanna Oldendorff)*[30] . . . the purpose of this House was to give legal certainty to the way in which the
risk of delay from congestion at the discharging port was allocated between charterer and
shipowner under a port charter which contained no special clause expressly dealing with
this matter . . . The allocation of this risk under this kind of charter-party depends upon
when the vessel becomes an 'arrived ship' so as to enable laytime to start running and
demurrage to become payable once laytime has expired. Legal certainty on this subject
had been impaired by the earlier decision of this House in *The Aello*[31] . . . which had laid
down a test ('the Parker test') of what was an 'arrived ship' under a port charter. The
Parker test had in the years that followed turned out in practice to be obscure and difficult to apply to the circumstances of individual cases. So the *Johanna Oldendorff* was
brought up to this House for the specific purpose of re-examining the Parker test with a
view to replacing it by one which would provide greater legal certainty . . . this House
substituted for the Parker test a test which I ventured to describe as the 'Reid test,' which
in its most summary form is stated by Lord Reid . . . thus[32]:
"Before a ship can be said to have arrived at a port she must, if she cannot proceed
immediately to a berth, have reached a position within the port where she is at the
immediate and effective disposition of the charterer . . . "[33]

4–28 ### (C) *Burden of misfortune risk in a port charter depends on port limits:*

"A vessel ordered to wait outside the port is not an arrived ship. In the course of my
own speech I spoke throughout[34] of a waiting place *within* the port and this qualification
was a necessary consequence of the analysis of the four stages of the adventure[35] contemplated by a charter-party which led to my acceptance of the Reid test as correct . . . [The
Reid test] allocates the risk to the charterer when the waiting place lies within the limits
of the port; but to the shipowner when it lies outside those limits. In a berth charter, on
the other hand, it had long been settled law that, in the absence of express provision providing for some other allocation of the risk, the risk is allocated to the shipowner
wherever the waiting place lies."[36]

(D) *Transfer of misfortune risk:*

He then[37] referred to the use of standard clauses to allocate the risk of
delay. These clauses,[38] which generally provide for the transfer to the charterers of all or part of the risk, are discussed below.[39]

---

[29] *Ibid.* p. 304. There has been some disagreement as to whether in practice such an inter-
relationship exists. See, for example, the pamphlet by Donald Davies, *op. cit.* at n. 26, at
para. 17: " . . . freight and demurrage rates tend to move together according to the state of
the market and cannot be used in the bargaining manner postulated by his Lordship
(freight rate up to cover sufficiently the expense of waiting at the owner's risk, and down if
the charterer takes the waiting risk)." For another view, see the opinion of the dissenting
New York arbitrator in *Maritime Bulk Carriers Co.* v. *Garnac Grain Co. Inc. (The Polyfreedom)* [1975] A.M.C. 1826. (See the Appendix to this Chapter at § 4–48).
[30] [1973] 2 Lloyd's Rep. 285 (H.L.).
[31] [1961] A.C. 135 (H.L.). See § 4–19 above.
[32] *Op. cit.* at p. 535.
[33] *Op. cit.* at pp. 304 and 305.
[34] See, for example, the passage cited at § 4–02 above.
[35] For the four stages, see § 4–02 above.
[36] *Op. cit.* at p. 305.
[37] *Op. cit.* at p. 305.
[38] Such as "Time lost waiting for a berth to count as lay time" or as "loading time" or "discharging time," or clauses, including the Weser Lightship Clause (see § 4–25, n. 17), dealing with individual ports.
[39] See Chap. 5.

(E) *Weser Lightship anchorage area not part of the port:*
Lord Diplock continued[40]:

> " . . . it is conceded by Counsel for the charterers that the Weser Lightship anchorage is outside the legal fiscal and administrative limits of the port of Brake. It lies 25 miles from the mouth of the river in an area in which none of the port authorities of Weser ports does any administrative acts or exercise any control over vessels waiting there. It was held by a German Court in 1962 that a ship waiting at the Weser Lightship anchorage is not an arrived ship. A similar decision was reached by Mr. Justice Donaldson in *The Timna*[41] . . . and approved by Lord Justice Megaw when the case came before the Court of Appeal[42] . . . Counsel also concedes that the charterers, shippers and shipowners who use the Weser ports would *not* regard the waiting area at the Lightship as forming any part of them . . . "

(F) *The four stages of a voyage charter and the need to arrive within the* **4–29** *limits of the port:*

> "As I endeavoured to explain in *The Johanna Oldendorff* the basic nature of the adventure contemplated by a voyage charter has remained unchanged. Its four stages include two voyage stages which end either at a named port (port charter) or at a berth in a named port (berth charter); and while until *The Johanna Oldendorff* there may have been uncertainty under a port charter as to where within the named port a ship must be in order to complete the voyage stage, there was legal certainty that neither in port nor in berth charter was the voyage stage brought to an end by the arrival of the ship at any waiting place short of the limits of the named port."[43]

(G) *The "whether in berth or not" clause:*
He then[44] referred to the printed clause in the charterparty stating: "Time to count from the first working period on the next day following receipt . . . of written notice of readiness to discharge, whether in berth or not." These last words, "whether in berth or not," are, with the comments of Lord Diplock thereon, who said that they were "surplusage in a port charter," discussed below.[45]

"Commercial area" **4–30**
The term "commercial area" has been used frequently to describe that part of the legal or geographical area of a port in which a ship can be loaded or discharged so that the ship has arrived when she reaches it, although she is not loaded or discharged at the particular spot where she is waiting. As we have seen above, there were two cases in the middle of the nineteenth century[46] in which it was held, in port charterparties, that ships chartered to Hull and to London had not arrived until they entered, respectively, the dock and the Pool of those ports. They had to be in an area where ships loaded or discharged, and not merely where ships waited. This was equivalent to saying that they had not reached the ports in question. In a later case,[47] it was held that a ship had arrived for the purpose of the computation of laytime when she was at such part of the port as was a proper place for loading, even though not at a precise spot where it would occur.

---

[40] *Op. cit.* at p. 307. Part of this passage is also cited as § 4–09 above.
[41] *Zim Israel Navigation Co. Ltd.* v. *Tradax Export S.A.* [1970] 2 Lloyd's Rep. 409.
[42] [1971] 2 Lloyd's Rep. 91.
[43] *Op. cit.* at p. 308. See § 4–02 above for the four stages of the venture.
[44] *Op. cit.* at pp. 308 and 309.
[45] See §§ 6–19 to 6–21.
[46] *Brown* v. *Johnson* (1842) 10 M. & W. 331; *Kell* v. *Anderson* (1842) 10 M. & W. 498. See § 4–12 above.
[47] *Leonis SS. Co. Ltd.* v. *Rank Ltd. (No. 1)* [1908] 1 K.B. 499 (C.A.). See § 4–18.

Kennedy L.J. spoke[48] of "the commercial area of a port, arrival within which makes the ship an arrived ship." He said that it ought to be "that area of the named port of destination on arrival within which the master can effectively place his ship at the disposal of the charterer, the vessel herself being then, so far as she is concerned, ready to load, and as near as circumstances permit to the actual loading 'spot.' " In saying this he thought that the ship could not be said to have arrived at the port until she was in such an area. It could thus be an area within, and an area which ['was part of, the port defined in its legal or geographical sense, but it was the same as the port in its commercial sense. As he said later in his judgement,[49] the area within which lay ships whose obligation and purpose was to receive a cargo was "that which I have ventured to describe as the commercial port, or the commercial area within the port, which is usually occupied by such vessels." Perhaps the expression "commercial port" as opposed to "legal port," "geographical port," "fiscal port," etc., is clearer and leads to less confusion than the words "commercial area within the port." The ship did not arrive at the port, for the purpose of the calculation of laytime, until she was in what is described as a commercial area.

4–31   So also in the *Sociedad Financiera de Bienes Raices S.A.* case[50] Parker L.J. in the Court of Appeal said: "The commercial area was intended to be that part of the port where a ship can be loaded when a berth is available, albeit she cannot be loaded until a berth is available." The ship was therefore held not to have arrived at the port of Buenos Aires although she was within its legal limits. A risk of ambiguity, or at least difficulty of interpretation, arises as a result of the use here of the word "port." Strictly speaking it must have been employed to indicate the legal port (within whose confines the ship was in that case) or some concept of port other than the commercial port. If the commercial port can be something within, and thus smaller[51] than, the port as defined for one or more other purposes, then how is its extent measured? It is clearly not confined to the precise spot which the ship will occupy when being worked. Indeed that position may not be known, and may be one of several possible berths. As Donaldson J. said once[52]:

> "Such a rule [he had been citing the reference in *The Aello* to 'that part of the port where a ship can be loaded with the relevant cargo'] is much more difficult to apply because it involves a decision on whether the waiting place is in the same or a different part of the port from that in which the loading or discharging berths lie."

In a similar manner Lord Jenkins in the House of Lords in the *Aello*[53] described the commercial area as "the area in which the actual loading spot is to be found and to which vessels seeking to load cargo of the relevant des-

---

[48] *Ibid.* at p. 521. See also a reference to these comments at § 4–18 above.

[49] At p. 523.

[50] [1958] 2 Q.B. 385 at p. 401 (*The Aello*). See § 4–19 above. This decision was reversed by the House of Lords in *Oldendorff (E.L.) & Co. G.m.b.H* v. *Tradax Export S.A.* [1973] 2 Lloyd's Rep. 285 (*The Johanna Oldendorff*). See § 4–21 above.

[51] "In the case of a widely extended area, such as London, Liverpool and Hull, it ['port'] certainly signifies some area which is less than the geographical port, and which may, I think, not unfitly be called the commercial area": Kennedy L.J. in *Leonis SS. Co. Ltd.* v. *Rank Ltd. (No. 1)* [1908] 1 K.B. 499 at p. 520 (C.A.).

[52] In the High Court in *Oldendorff (E.L.) & Co. G.m.b.H.* v. *Tradax Export S.A. (The Johanna Oldendorff)* [1971] 2 Lloyd's Rep. 96 at p. 100.

[53] [1961] A.C. 135 at p. 207.

cription usually go, and in which the business of loading such cargo is usually carried out."

The risk was that a ship might be held to have arrived, when this principle was being applied, if the distance from her waiting spot to the alternative possible loading spots was not very great,[54] but not to have arrived if they were some miles apart. Thus in *Shipping Developments Corporation S.A.* v. *V/O Sojuzneftexport*[55] the *Delian Spirit* waited where tankers anchored, outside the breakwater, within the bounds of the outer roads and $1\frac{1}{4}$ miles away from the jetty. It was held that she lay within the commercial area of this small port of Tuapse and that the case fell within the *Leonis* rather than within the *Aello*.[56]

The umpire[57] in *Oldendorff (E.L.) & Co. G.m.b.H.* v. *Tradax Export S.A.*[58] said:

> " . . . the hazy penumbra of the 'commercial area' seems to me to have clouded reason . . . But if we must live with the doctrine of 'commercial area' there is no reason why it be put in a shrine."

He held, subject to the ruling of the Court as to the law, that the ship in question had arrived at the port when she reached the Mersey Bar anchorage. This was 17 miles away from the spot where the ship berthed and discharged.

The House of Lords in *The Johanna Oldendorff* moved away from the **4–32** concept of a commercial area as that area smaller than the legal, fiscal or geographical area of the port in which waiting ships lie. A port has still to be defined commercially, but a different significance was attached to the presence of a ship in an area where waiting ships usually lay.[58a] Such presence creates a presumption that she has "reached a position within the port where she is at the immediate and effective disposition of the charterer."[59] Lord Morris[60] recognised that ships at the Mersey Bar anchorage were remote from any of the recognised activities of a port, but said that the waiting area came within what was said by Kennedy L.J.,[61] adding:

> "In such a case as the present the phrase 'commercial area' may not be a very helpful one for if used it covers the major part of the area of the legal limits of the port. In other cases the phrase if used may relate, as indeed it did in *Leonis* v. *Rank*, to an area less than the area of the legal limits of a port but it would denote an area within which waiting areas were not far removed from docks or wharfs or other places where cargoes were discharged."

In more general terms, without indicating that the term could be useful or

---

[54] As in *Leonis SS. Co. Ltd.* v. *Rank Ltd. (No. 1)* [1908] 1 K.B. 499 (C.A.) ("a few ship's length off the pier"). See § 4–18 above.

[55] [1971] 1 Lloyd's Rep. 506 (C.A.). See § 4–20 above.

[56] *Sociedad Financiera de Bienes Raices S.A.* v. *Agrimpex Hungarian Trading Co. for Agricultural Products* [1961] A.C. 135 (H.L.).

[57] Richard Clyde.

[58] [1973] 2 Lloyd's Rep. 285 (H.L.) (*The Johanna Oldendorff*). His remarks are quoted at p. 290 of the report.

[58a] An area may be a usual waiting place in one sense (*e.g.* waiting for a convoy) but not so as to cause the ship to have arrived, even with the words "whether in port or not". See LMLN 143, April 25, 1985, and § 4–11 above, at n. 1a.

[59] See § 4–07 above.

[60] *Op. cit.* at p. 295. His comments on the term "commercial area" are relevant although he distinguished *The Aello* rather than overruled it.

[61] *Leonis SS. Co. Ltd.* v. *Rank Ltd. (No. 1)* [1908] 1 K.B. 499 (C.A.). See § 4–18 above.

more useful when the waiting area was "not far removed" from the loading or discharging spot, Viscount Dilhorne[62] said:

> "I hope that after this case the expression 'commercial area,' which has caused so much trouble, will not have much, if any, weight attached to it in relation to the question whether a ship has arrived."

4–33   **"Reachable on her arrival":[63] "arrival" compared with "arrived ship"**

A ship may be regarded as having arrived so that the risk of delay falls on charterers although she has not yet become an arrived ship for the purpose of the laytime clause, and although the cause of the delay is beyond the control of charterers. Such a situation may arise where the charterers have to name a place which the ship can reach when she arrived. If they fail to do so they will be liable to pay damages suffered by the shipowners, unless there exist appropriate words which relieve them of that liability. The shipowners are entitled to claim damages for actual time lost; the laytime exceptions do not apply until laytime has begun.

The distinction between an arrival which causes the risk of delay to pass to charterers and an arrival which is one of the ingredients which allows laytime to begin[64] has been discussion in two High Court cases, *Sociedad Carga Oceanica S.A.* v. *Idolinoele Vertriebsgesellschaft m.b.H.*,[65] and *Inca Compania Naviera S.A. and Commercial and Maritime Enterprise Evanghelos P. Nomikos S.A.* v. *Mofinol Inc.*,[66] in one Court of Appeal case, *Shipping Developments Corporation S.A.* v. *V/O Sojuzneftexport*[67]; and in one House of Lords case, *Nereide S.p.A. di Navigazione* v. *Bulk Oil International Ltd.*[68]

In each of these four cases, the Courts were concerned with a laytime commencement clause, and a clause providing that charterers shall designate and procure certain facilities reachable on the arrival of the ship. We shall call the latter the reachable on arrival clause. Some of these cases, as we shall see, involved certain standard clauses from the Exxonvoy 1969 form of charterparty. We now set out the wordings, subject to the caveat that not all of the cases were subject to these provisions.

The laytime commencement clause

The laytime commencement clause, which was Clause 6 of the Exxonvoy 1969 form, and headed "Notice of Readiness", stated:

> "6. Notice of Readiness. 'Upon arrival at customary anchorage at each port of loading or discharge, the Master or his agent shall give the Charterer or his agent notice by letter, telegraph, wireless or telephone that the Vessel is ready to load or discharge cargo, berth or no berth, and laytime, as hereinafter provided, shall commence upon the expiration of six (6) hours after receipt of such notice,[68a] or upon the Vessel's arrival in berth (*i.e.* finished mooring when at a sealoading or discharging terminal and all fast when loading or discharging alongside a wharf), whichever first occurs. However, where delay is caused to

---

[62] *Op. cit.* at p. 302.

[63] The Charterparty Laytime Definitions 1980 (see Appendix to this book) state: "5. 'REACHABLE ON ARRIVAL' or 'ALWAYS ACCESSIBLE'—means that the charterer undertakes that when the ship arrives at the port there will be a loading/discharging berth for her to which she can proceed without delay."

[64] For the requirements see § 4–01 above.

[65] [1964] 2 Lloyd's Rep. 28 (*The Angelos Lusis*).

[66] [1967] 2 Lloyd's Rep. 338 (*The President Brand*).

[67] [1971] 1 Lloyd's Rep. 506 (*The Delian Spirit*).

[68] [1982] 1 Lloyd's Rep. 1 (*The Laura Prima*).

[68a] For cases on the six hours clause see §§ 9–52 and 9–53 below.

> Vessel getting into berth after giving notice of readiness for any reason over which Charterer has no control, such delay shall not count as used laytime."

An earlier version of Clause 6 stated: "The lay-days shall commence from the time the vessel is ready to receive her cargo, the Captain giving six hours notice to the Charterers' agents, berth or no berth." There was thus no provision as to delays caused for any reason over which the charterers had no control.

The reachable on arrival clause

As with the laytime commencement clause there was an earlier version of the reachable on arrival clause. This version, numbered Clause 6, contained slightly different wording and punctuation. It was succeeded by Clause 9 of Exxonvoy 1969, the first sentence of which stated, under the heading "Safe Berthing-Shifting":

> "The vessel shall load and discharge at any safe place or wharf, or alongside vessels or lighters reachable on her arrival,[69] which shall be designated and procured by the Charterer, provided the Vessel can proceed thereto, lie at, and depart therefrom always safely afloat, any lighterage being at the expense, risk and peril of the Charterer."

The second and third sentences dealt with shifting, and are not relevant here.

The Exxonvoy 1969 form was succeeded in 1974 by the STBVOY form, as the result of a formal request by EXXON. Some brokers considered that the STBVOY form, which did not contain a reachable on arrival clause, imposed too many obligations upon shipowners. As a result the Association of Ship Brokers and Agents (U.S.A.) Inc., or ASBA, issued the Asbatankvoy 1977 form, which was essentially the same as the Exxonvoy 1969 form. Under its Clause 9, the equivalent of Exxonvoy's later Clause 9, there is a reachable on arrival provision.

We can now turn to the four cases mentioned above. In the *Sociedad* **4–34** *Carga Oceanica* case[70] the *Angelos Lusis* was chartered for a voyage from Constanza "or so near unto as she may safely get (always afloat)." The laytime commencement clause under consideration contained no exception from liability for charterers with respect to reasons over which they had no control.[71] The reachable on arrival clause was in the same terms as that in the Exxonvoy form, but there was no comma after the word "arrival."[71]

She anchored at Constanza roads and was permitted to enter the port five days later, when a berth was available.[72] The charterers contended that "reachable on her arrival" meant arrival in the port, and that they need not nominate a loading berth until the ship entered its commercial area. It was held that they were in breach and that shipowners were entitled to damages for detention. Megaw J. said that the provision that the ship should load "at a place . . . reachable on her arrival" was intended to be a stipulation giving the shipowners some contractual right which they

---

[69] For the significance of this comma see n. 79 below.
[70] [1964] 2 Lloyd's Rep. 28.
[71] Lawton L.J. said in *Nereide S.p.A. di Navigazione* v. *Bulk Oil International Ltd.* [1981] (*The Laura Prima*) 2 Lloyd's Rep. 24 (C.A.) at p. 27, referring to *The Angelos Lusis* case; " . . . it is pertinent to note that there were no punctuation marks linking the words 'reachable on her arrival' solely with lighters." See also § 4–35 below. For further comments by this judge on punctuation see § 4–35 below, at n. 79.
[72] For a "ready quay berth" as ordered, see *Harris and Dixon* v. *Marcus Jacobs & Co.* (1885) 15 Q.B.D. 247 (C.A.). The charterers are liable in damages if they fail to name a berth ready for loading when the ship arrives.

would not otherwise have, and to impose on charterers a contractual obligation of value to the shipowners. He added[73]:

> "If the words 'on her arrival' have the meaning for which the charterers contend, the owners have got nothing: the provision might as well not be there . . . If it is to be assumed that the general requirements of the port authority at Constanza are what the umpire has found them to be in this case, that is, that a vessel may not enter the port until a berth is available, then there is no place within the port where vessels ordinarily lie awaiting their turn to load. Thus a vessel under a port charter could not become an 'arrived vessel' in this sense until a berth had actually become available . . . The parties, in using the words 'on her arrival,' did not have in mind, or at least did not have solely and exclusively in mind, the technical meaning of 'arrival' in respect of an 'arrived vessel' in a port charter-party: they had in mind her physical arrival at the point, wherever it might be, whether within or outside the fiscal or commercial limits of the port, where the indication or nomination of a particular loading place would become relevant if the vessel were to be able to proceed without being held up . . . "

He said that the decision in *Roland-Linie Schiffahrt G.m.b.H.* v. *Spillers Ltd.*[74] supported the shipowners' contention; the judge had been prepared to find that a ship outside the limits of the port of Hull "was to be treated as having arrived at the port of Hull"[75] although she would not be an arrived ship. The decision by McNair J. in *Carga del Sur Compania Naviera, S.A.* v. *Ross T. Smyth & Co. Ltd.*[76] could be distinguished because it related not to a clause such as the present one but to a clause[77] expressly concerned with laytime.

4–35   The second High Court case in which the words "reachable on her arrival" were discussed was *Inca Compania Naviera and Commercial and Maritime Enterprises Evanghelos P. Nomikos S.A.* v. *Mofinol, Inc.*[78] Oil was carried from the Persian Gulf to Lourenco Marques under an Exxonvoy form which stated: "The vessel shall load and discharge at a place or at a dock or alongside lighters reachable on her arrival, which shall be indicated by charterers, and where she can always lie afloat . . . " The reachable on arrival clause was in the same terms as in *The Angelos Lusis*, except that there was a comma after the word "arrival."[79]

The shipowners had undertaken that the ship, the *President Brand*, would "arrive at Lourenco Marques with a maximum draft of 32'5"." She

---

[73] At pp. 33–34.

[74] [1957] 1 Q.B. 109 (*The Werrastein*). See § 6–35 below.

[75] *Ibid.* at pp. 119–120.

[76] [1962] 2 Lloyd's Rep. 147 (*The Seafort*). See § 6–19 below.

[77] "Time at second port to count from arrival of vessel at second port, whether in berth or not."

[78] [1967] 2 Lloyd's Rep. 338, at p. 347 (*The President Brand*).

[79] See the clause as set out above, under the heading "The reachable on arrival clause." It was thus in the usual printed Exxonvoy form. In *The Laura Prima* [1981] 2 Lloyd's Rep. 24, at p. 27, Lawton L.J. described the clause in *The Angelos Lusis* as being the same as that in *The President Brand*, "save for an intrusive comma after arrival." In one sense the comma had the right to be present, and was not an intruder. As he summed it up: "A comma comes after 'wharf' and another one after 'arrival.' " He mentioned this in the course of saying that the Court of Appeal, which found in *The Laura Prima* in favour of the charterers (see § 4–37 below) did not question the reasoning of Megaw J. in *The Angelos Lusis*; but it noted that the clauses were different, the other difference being that there was no equivalent to the last sentence, or the words of exception, in the laytime commencement clause; and "Further, Mr. Justice Megaw did not have to consider the effect of the 'reachable on her arrival' clause upon the laytime clause." He added later (at p. 28) that the comma after 'wharf' could be disregarded because it did not make commercial sense, but that the Court's decision on the punctuation point did not affect its decision on the appeal.

arrived at the pilot station, which was outside the commercial limits of the port,[80] and where it was usual to report, and gave a cabled notice of readiness. Owing to her draught she did not cross the bar until four days later, in the early morning; she then anchored again to wait for a berth, and gave another notice of readiness. The berth became available later that day but her shift was delayed till the next day as pilots were not allowed to handle her during the hours of darkness.

The shipowners, saying that the charterers had failed to provide a place reachable on arrival, claimed detention from the time of anchorage at the pilot station to the beginning of the shift; or alternatively demurrage on the basis that the initial notice of readiness was valid. The charterers said that the word "arrival" meant that the ship must have become an arrived ship and that she became an arrived ship only on anchoring after crossing the bar.

Roskill J., saying[81] that independently of the decision in the *Angelos Lusis*[82] he would construe "arrival" in the popular sense of that word, stated[83]:

> "I think as a matter of ordinary common sense if one asked two businessmen if a ship had arrived at Lourenco Marques when she reported at the pilot station in that way and in those circumstances they would answer: 'Yes, she has arrived there,' notwithstanding that she had not yet got within the commercial limits of the port."

It made no difference that the maximum draught clause was not a warranty by charterers; or that it was not their fault that there was not enough water, any more than if there had been a ship occupying the berth at the material time.

The judge summarised his decision by saying[84]:

> "It may be (and I think the present case is such a case) that the breach arises without what one might call fault on their [the charterers'] part but the ultimate question is what does this charter-party provide concerning the respective liabilities of owners and charterers if the ship cannot cross the bar owing to shortage of water[84a] and then proceed to a berth. My answer to that as a matter of construction of the four words in Clause 6 is that liability for that loss of time falls upon the charterers and not the owners. In the result, therefore, I think that the charterers are liable inasmuch as the discharging berth was not reachable at the time when the vessel was held up at the bar owing to shortage of water."

As to the period of time lost, and recoverable as detention by the shipowners, he said that the charterers' liability ended when the second notice

---

[80] See p. 349 of the report. The judge concluded, on the agreed facts, that the pilot station was outside the commercial limits, but stressed that he should not be taken as determining what were the commercial limits.

[81] At p. 348.

[82] See § 4–19 above.

[83] At p. 349.

[84] At p. 350.

[84a] In *K/S Arnt J. Moerland* v. *Kuwait Petroleum Corporation of Kuwait (The Fjordaas)* [1988] 1 Lloyd's Rep. 336, at pp. 341–2, Steyn J. said that he found it difficult to see how insufficiency of water could be described as a physical obstruction. He added: "And, if insufficiency of water may amount to a breach of the 'reachable on arrival' provision it is difficult to see why, for example, fog (as a species of bad weather) should not fall within the clause . . . I regard the analysis of Roskill J., which has stood unchallenged for some twenty years, as entitled to great weight. Thousands of voyage charter-parties must have concluded on the basis that the interpretation of 'reachable on arrival' in *The President Brand* is correct."

of readiness was given; after that, subject to a six hours' notice provision, laytime ran.

4–36   Damages not always available for charterers' breach.

There may therefore be an "arrival" of the ship sufficient to bring into operation the duty of the charterers to provide a place "reachable on her arrival," although she is not an "arrived ship." In such a case shipowners may be able to recover damages. Where, however, there is an "arrival" for the purpose of the beginning of laytime or demurrage, shipowners cannot claim damages in addition to counting time.

This proposition was borne out in the Court of Appeal decision in *Shipping Developments Corporation S.A.* v. *V/O Sojuzneftexport*,[85] where a tanker had been ordered to load at Tuapse. The charterparty again stated: "The vessel shall load and discharge at a place or at a dock or alongside lighters reachable on her arrival, which shall be indicated by charterers, and where she can lie always afloat . . . " The "reachable on her arrival" clause was thus in the same terms as in the *Inca Compania Naviera S.A.* case. She remained at anchor in the roads for five days. The shipowners claimed damages for detention for the charterers' failure to find such a place reachable on arrival. The Court of Appeal, though holding that the ship had arrived when at the anchorage,[86] rejected the claim for damages.

4–37   The beginning of laytime

Lord Denning M.R. said[87]:

> "It would be most unjust that the charterers should be made liable twice over. The answer is given by a long line of cases[88] which establish that where the charterers have been guilty of a breach causing delay, they are entiled to apply their laytime so as to diminish or extinguish any claim for the delay, leaving the shipowners to claim for demurrage at the agreed rate for any extra delay over and above the laytime."

Fenton Atkinson L.J. distinguished the two meanings of "arrive" by saying[89]:

> "While in certain circumstances which I do not think it is necessary to attempt to define on the facts of this case you can have an arrival of a ship within clause 6 [the 'arrival' clause] before that ship becomes technically an arrived ship for laytime purposes, and therefore the charterer who has failed to provide a berth at the time of such arrival will become liable for damages for detention, once the ship becomes an arrived ship in the technical sense the position is different, and in my judgment the charterer gets the advantage of the laytime provided. . . . "

So also Sir Gordon Willmer[90]:

> " . . . the shipowners here cannot count their time twice for the purpose of advancing

---

[85] [1971] 1 Lloyd's Rep. 506 (*The Delian Spirit*). See § 4–20 above for the views of the Court of Appeal as to when this ship became an "arrived" ship.

[86] See § 4–20 above.

[87] At p. 509.

[88] He cited the cases, starting with *Petersen* v. *Dunn & Co.* [1895] 1 Com.Cas. 8 (see § 1–06 above) and ending with *Inca Compania Naviera S.A. and Commercial and Maritime Enterprises Evanghelos P. Nomikos S.A.* v. *Mofinol, Inc. (The President Brand)* [1967] 2 Lloyd's Rep. 338. (See § 4–35 above).

[89] At pp. 510–511.

[90] At p. 512.

such claim as they have. The loss of time involved in the case may no doubt have been due to two causes; but there was only one loss of time."

The words "reachable on her arrival" were also considered by the House of Lords in *Nereide S.p.A. di Navigazione* v. *Bulk Oil International Ltd.*,[91] where the *Laura Prima* was chartered, on the Exxonvoy 1969 form,[92] to carry oil from Marsa el Hariga, Libya, to Sarroch, Sardinia. The ship arrived at the customary loading anchorage at 0140 hours on November 27, 1978, and gave notice of readiness, which expired at 0740 hours on the same day. There was congestion, all possible loading berths being occupied by other ships, and she could not berth until 1630 hours on December 6. The shipowners said that demurrage began at 0740 hours on November 30, 72 hours after the expiry of the notice of readiness, and ended when loading was completed on December 8. Alternatively, they claimed damages for detention.

The charterers relied on the last sentence in the laytime commencement clause, by which delay in getting into berth after notice of readiness for any reason over which they had no control was not to count as used laytime. The umpire, accepting their argument in respect of the demurrage claim, found as a fact that the sole cause of the delay in getting into berth was the unavailability of a berth, caused by the presence of other ships. He said: "[The charterers] were not responsible for this situation, nor was it in any way within their control." As for the alternative claim for damages he held that, although the charterers were in breach of the reachable on arrival clause (clause 9), they could offset against any such claim the time lost during any periods which, by reason of the laytime commencement clause (clause 6), were exempted from counting as laytime.

In the High Court Mocatta J. held[93] that the shipowners' demurrage claim succeeded. He said that the last sentence in clause 6 only applied if charterers, pursuant to clause 9, had designated and procured a safe place or wharf or vessels or lighters reachable on the ship's arrival. Then, if some intervening event occurred, causing delay over which charterers had no control, the last sentence of clause 6 would apply. The Court of Appeal found unanimously[94] that the charterers' submission was right.

Lawton L.J. said[95]: "It fits into the scheme of the charterparty. It enables the last sentence of cl. 6 to be read as we think commercial men would read it and to be reconciled with cl. 9 since, when the reasoning in *The President Brand*[96] and *The Delian Spirit*[97] is applied, the period of detention for breach of cl. 9 will come to an end with the allowed period of laytime extended by delay caused for any reason beyond the charterers' control if that is what the evidence establishes. In many cases the evidence

---

[91] [1982] 1 Lloyd's Rep. 1 (*The Laura Prima*).
[92] The laytime commencement clause and the reachable on arrival clause were in the form set out at § 4–33 above. The same clauses were considered in *Sametiet M/T Johs Stove* v. *Istanbul Petrol Rafinerisi A/S* [1984] 1 Lloyd's Rep. 38 (*The Johs Stove*), where *The Laura Prima* was applied, despite an attempt by charterers to rely on an exceptions clause.
[93] [1980] 1 Lloyd's Rep. 466 at p. 468.
[94] [1980] 1 Lloyd's Rep. 466.
[95] [1981] 2 Lloyd's Rep. 24, at p. 28.
[96] *Inca Compania Naviera S.A. and Commercial and Maritime Enterprises Evanghelos P. Nomikos S.A.* v. *Mofinol, Inc.* [1967] 2 Lloyd's Rep. 338. See § 4–35 above.
[97] *Shipping Developments Corporation S.A.* v. *V/O Sojuznefteexport* [1971] 1 Lloyd's Rep. 506 (C.A.). See § 4–36 above.

will not do this, and when it does not cl. 9 will apply as it did in *The Ange-los Lusis*."⁹⁸

The House of Lords, unanimously reversing the decision of the Court of Appeal, held⁹⁹ that the shipowners were right. As the charterers had not procured a berth within the six hours specified in clause 6, the commencement of laytime clause, there had been no berth which could have been reached on arrival within clause 9, the reachable on arrival clause.

"Berth" in the last sentence of clause 6 meant a berth which had already been designated and procured by the charterers in accordance with their obligations under clause 9. The charterers' argument involved reading "berth" in the last sentence of clause 6 as "any berth" and not the "designated and procured berth" required under clause 9. But it was axiomatic that charterparties, like other contracts, must be construed as a whole, and it was impossible to ignore the opening words of clause 9¹ in construing the last sentence of clause 6.² Lord Roskill added³: "I would only add that the case seems to have proceeded in the Courts below upon the footing that there was a conflict between cll. 6 and 9 which required reconciliation. With regret, I am unable to see any such conflict. Properly construed, in the manner which I have suggested, these clauses are in no way in conflict. I would regard them upon this construction as complementary one to the other."⁴

An unsuccessful attempt was made to treat clause 6 of the STB form of charterparty as being equivalent to the *Laura Prima's* reachable on arrival clause. This occurred in *Société Anonyme Marocaine de l'Industrie du Raffinage* v. *Notos Maritime Corporation*.⁵ Lord Goff said⁶: " . . . I do not think that *The Laura Prima* is of assistance in the present case, since the charterparty in that case was in materially different terms, containing as it did an express warranty by the charterers that loading and discharging places for the vessel would be 'reachable on her arrival.' "⁷

---

⁹⁸ *Sociedad Carga Oceanica S.A.* v. *Idolinoele Vertriebsgesellschaft m.b.H.* [1964] 2 Lloyd's Rep. 28. See § 4–19 above.
⁹⁹ [1982] 1 Lloyd's Rep. 1. See also *Palm Shipping Inc.* v. *Kuwait Petroleum Corporation* [1988] 1 Lloyd's Rep. 500 (*The Sea Queen*) for a judgment by Saville J., following *The Laura Prima*; the case involved cls. 6 and 9 of the Asbatankvoy form, loading at Mina al Ahmadi, and an unsuccessful attempt by charterers to distinguish *The Laura Prima*.
¹ "The vessel shall load and discharge at any safe place or wharf, or alongside vessels or lighters reachable on her arrival, which shall be designated and procured by the Charterer . . . "
² "However, where delay is caused to Vessel getting into berth after giving notice of readiness for any reason over which Charterer has no control, such delay shall not count as used laytime."
³ At p. 6.
⁴ On the causes of obstruction see Steyn J. in *K/S Arnt J. Moerland of Arendal Norway* v. *Kuwait Petroleum Corporation of Kuwait* (*The Fjordaas*) [1988] 1 Lloyd's Rep. 336 at p. 342. He said: "In my judgment the distinction between physical causes of obstruction, and non-physical causes rendering a designated place unreachable, is not supported by the language of the contract or common sense; it is in conflict with the reasoning in *The Laura Prima*; and it is insupportable on the interpretation given to that provision in *The President Brand*. Quite independently of authority I believe it to be wrong." The judge rejected the proposition that "reachable on arrival" ought to be interpreted as "reachable without delay due to port congestion." This proposition had been set out by Schofield in "Laytime and Demurrage," 1986, at pp. 249–252, and by Davies in "Commencement of Laytime," 1987, at pp. 46 to 55.
⁵ [1987] 1 Lloyd's Rep. 503 (H.L.) (*The Notos*). See § 10–55 below.
⁶ *Ibid.* at p. 507.
⁷ For the text of cl. 6 of the STB voyage charterparty see § 10–55 below.

(d) *Modifying words.* **"Or so near thereto [or "thereunto"] as she may**   **4–38**
safely get." Words such as "or so near thereto [or "thereunto"] as she
may safely get"[8] have the effect of giving shipowners an alternative contractual destination, if the ship is unable, by virtue of an obstruction that
cannot be overcome by them by reasonable means, to reach the named
destination without waiting an unreasonable time. By reaching the
alternative destination the ship becomes an arrived ship. Obstacles which
may prevent her from reaching the destination have included ice,[9] blockades,[10] congestion[11] and tides,[12] but the hindrances need not be physical
ones.[13] It is a question of fact whether an obstruction will cause an
unreasonable delay. The circumstances of the voyage, such as the trade,
the time of year, the type of ship, and the port, have to be considered. A
view has to be formed in the light of the facts which were known or which
should have been known before the delay, or at any rate all the delay, has
occurred. The court has to ignore subsequent developments which may
indicate that an action was misconceived. As Scrutton J. said in *Embiricos
v. Reid (Sydney) & Co.*[14]:

> "Commercial men must not be asked to wait till the end of a long delay to find out from
> what in fact happens whether they are bound by a contract or not[15]; they must be entitled
> to act on reasonable commercial probabilities at the time when they are called upon to
> make up their minds."

Nevertheless they must make proper inquiries, from those with special
knowledge, such as ship's and charterers' agents, as to the extent of the
delay. The application of the words "or so near thereto as she may safely
get" is now considered in connection with the following obstacles:

    (i) Ice[16];
    (ii) Blockades[17];
    (iii) Congestion[18];
    (iv) Tides and other water conditions.[19]

---

[8] Used, for example, in the Uniform General Charter (Gencon) 1922 and 1976 versions and
also, with slight variations in wording, in many other charterparties. Other phrases may be
used so as to delay the beginning of laytime. In *Plakoura Maritime Corporation* v. *Shell
International Petroleum Co. Ltd.* [1987] 2 Lloyd's Rep. 258 (*The Plakoura*) the words, in
the Shellvoy 4 form, were: " . . . laytime . . . shall commence when the vessel is in all
respects ready to load or discharge and written notice thereof has been received . . . and
the vessel is securely moored at the loading or discharging place." Leggatt J. held that the
words meant "all fast at the spot where the actual process of loading or discharging was to
occur" and not merely upon arrival at the port.
[9] See §§ 4–39 and 4–40.
[10] See § 4–41 below.
[11] See § 4–42 below.
[12] See § 4–43 below.
[13] *Dahl* v. *Nelson, Donkin & Co.* (1881) 6 App.Cas. 38 (H.L.). See § 4–42 below.
[14] [1914] 3 K.B. 45 at p. 54. The case concerned the frustration of a charterparty for the carriage of grain on a Greek ship from the Sea of Azov to the United Kingdom, through the
Dardanelles, where the Turks were detaining Greek ships.
[15] In the case of the present clause it is a question not of release from a contract but of release
from an obligation to go to the primary destination.
[16] At §§ 4–39 and 4–40.
[17] At § 4–41 below.
[18] At § 4–42 below.
[19] At § 4–43 below.

4–39   **(i) Ice.** Where a ship is prevented by ice from reaching her contractual destination, a question arises as to whether she must wait until the ice melts, and then proceed, in order to become an arrived ship. If the situation could have been reasonably anticipated when the charterparty was concluded, then she may be obliged to wait.[20]

The Court of Appeal reached this conclusion in *Metcalfe* v. *Britannia Iron Works Co.*[21] A charterparty provided for the carriage of railway bars from England to Taganrog, in the Azov Sea, "or so near thereunto as she may safely get." On arrival in mid-December at Kertch, a considerable distance to the south of Taganrog,[22] the master found the Azov Sea blocked by ice until the ensuing spring. He discharged the cargo and sailed. The Court of Appeal held that the shipowners were not entitled to full or *pro rata* freight. Brett L.J. said[23]:

> " . . . we must hold, as a condition precedent to the recovery of anything as freight under the charterparty, that the goods shall have been carried to the port of destination, or as near thereto as the ship can safely get . . . "

As to whether the ship got as far as she safely could, Lord Coleridge C.J. said[24]:

> "It is not necessary to say more than that the obstruction was only temporary, and is such as must be incidental to every contract for a voyage to a frozen sea, and it cannot be said that in all these contracts the words 'at that time' or 'then and there,' are to be inserted after the words 'as near thereto as the ship can safely get.' "

4–40   In the court below all three judges had supported the proposition that "the ship must get within the ambit of the port, although she may not be able to enter it. There is no pretence for saying that Kertch is within the ambit of the port of Taganrog."[25] This view restricts the rights of shipowners. In the *Metcalfe* case there was no doubt that they had taken their ship as near as she could then safely get. As Lord Coleridge C.J. said, the clause did not contain such words as "at that time." It followed that the phrase must be interpreted as if it read "as near thereto as the ship can safely get at the most favourable time." Presumably this duty exists unless the voyage is frustrated. Where the delay is likely to be such that the voyage would become entirely different from that for which the parties had contracted, the contract is frustrated. In *Metcalfe* the charterparty had been concluded in November for a voyage to the Azov Sea, and the parties must be taken to have been aware of the risks of ice.[26]

To decide whether an obstacle is permanent or semi-permanent, so that the shipowners can take their ship "so near thereunto as she may safely get," it may be necessary to consider its likely duration in comparison with the length of the voyage. In *Grace* v. *General Steam Navigation Co.*,[27] though the case did not concern the application of these words, the High

---

[20] A similar conclusion may be reached in the case of tidal harbours or rivers; *The Curfew* [1891] P. 13. See also § 4–44 below.

[21] (1877) 2 Q.B.D. 423.

[22] In the High Court it was assumed that the distance was about 30 miles; on appeal it was stated and admitted that the distance was 300 miles by sea and 700 miles by land.

[23] At pp. 430 and 431.

[24] At p. 426.

[25] They relied on the decision in *Schillizzi* v. *Derry* (1855) 4 E. & B. 873. See § 4–43 below.

[26] As to what should reasonably be foreseen by the parties when they conclude their contract, see also Lord Watson in *Dahl* v. *Nelson, Donkin & Co.* (1881) 6 App.Cas. 38 at p. 63 (H.L.); see § 4–42 below.

[27] [1950] 2 K.B. 383.

Court rejected the time charterers' contention that the presence of ice was temporary. They ordered a ship to go from London to Hamburg with flour, and to return with timber. She was damaged by ice in the River Elbe on the voyages to and from Hamburg. The shipowners claimed damages. The charterparty provided for the ship to be employed "only between good and safe ports." It also stated: "If on account of ice the master considers it dangerous to remain at the loading or discharging place for fear of the vessel being frozen in and/or damaged, he has liberty to sail to a convenient open place and await the charterers' fresh instructions." The High Court held that at the time Hamburg was not a safe port. Devlin J. discussed the question of temporary obstacles[28]:

> " . . . it is contended that the condition of unsafety was temporary only. . . . The arbitrator . . . noted the charterers' contention that the obstacle was temporary only, and must be taken by his finding to have decided against them. The period of the ice danger compared with the duration of the charterparty and the shortness of the voyage to Hamburg clearly justifies this conclusion. . . . "

(ii) Blockades. If a blockade makes access to the port impossible, the **4–41** words "so near thereto as she can safely get" will help shipowners it if is not likely that the blockade will be lifted within a reasonable time. If the words apply, they can take the ship to another port. The port must, as the clause says, be as near as the ship can safely get to the contractual destination. Where the clause is differently worded, or where there are special circumstances, the port may not be the nearest port to the destination.

Hong Kong has been held to be "the nearest safe and convenient port" to Yokohama, though the facts were unusual. In *Nobel's Explosives Co.* v. *Jenkins & Co.*[29] dynamite and other explosives were shipped at London for Yokohama under a bill of lading which stated: " . . . if the entering of or discharging in the port shall be considered by the master unsafe by reason of war . . . the master may land the goods at the nearest safe and convenient port." The bill also contained the exception "restraint of princes." War broke out between China and Japan during a call by the ship at Hong Kong. The master landed the goods there, as he feared confiscation of the cargo by Chinese warships in and round Hong Kong. The High Court held that the risk of seizure amounted to a "restraint of princes" and also rendered access to or discharge at Yokohama "unsafe." As for the words "nearest safe and convenient port," Mathew J. said[30]:

> "It was said that this clause was only intended to apply where difficulties arose upon the vessel's arrival at the port of destination. But I see no ground for this narrow construction. The object was to enable the master to guard against obstacles which might prevent the vessel from reaching her destination in due course. There is no reason to suppose that it was intended to limit his discretion to the case where the information reached him on his arrival off the port of destination."

(iii) Congestion. Shipowners may rely upon the words "or so near thereto **4–42** as she may safely get," and take the ship elsewhere, if the congestion seems likely to last for an unreasonable time.

Thus in *Dahl* v. *Nelson, Donkin & Co.*[31] a ship carrying timber from the Baltic Sea was to go "to London Surrey Commercial Docks, or so near thereto as she can safely get," and there discharge. Application for a berth

---

[28] At p. 392.
[29] [1896] 2 Q.B. 326.
[30] At p. 33.
[31] (1881) 6 App.Cas. 38 (H.L.).

was made nearly three weeks before the ship arrived at the dock gates, when it appeared that five weeks or more would elapse before she was discharged. The shipowners then discharged the cargo into lighters at Deptford Buoys. The House of Lords held that the ship had completed the voyage when she reached the dock entrance. The delay was unreasonable and the shipowners were entitled to insist that the charterers take the cargo elsewhere at the charterers' expense. As Lord Watson said[32]:

> " . . . seeing that, on the 4th of August, the authorities could not undertake, within a month, or any other given time, to admit the *Euxine* into the dock, and that even on the 23rd of August they were not in a position to give a more definite or satisfactory undertaking, it appears to me to be safe to conclude that the length of time for which the *Euxine* must have waited in the port of London, in order to discharge in the Surrey Docks, would have been in excess of any delay which either the shipowner or the charterer, at the time of entering into the charterparty, could reasonably have contemplated."[33]

The problem of congestion was also considered in *The Varing*.[34] The ship was to discharge her timber cargo at Garston "or so near thereto as she may safely get." Congestion prevented entry and she anchored at the usual place of waiting, Sloyne Channel. The receivers insisted that the timber should be discharged on the railway company's storing ground and sorted there; the company said in effect: "we cannot take any ship which claims that its cargo was to be sorted and stowed on our storing ground." As a result the ship was refused admission to the dock. Scrutton L.J. said[35]:

> "The liability and rights of a ship in that position have been laid down once and for all in *Dahl* v. *Nelson*[31] and an infinite number of differences arise which give opportunities to industrious counsel to cite a number of other cases which are not the case before the court, and to express in what respect they differ or agree with the case before the court. But, after all, one goes back to *Dahl* v. *Nelson*,[31] and as I understand the decision of the House of Lords, it is this, when you are chartered to go to a discharging place and cannot get there, you are bound to wait a reasonable time before having recourse to the clause 'or as near thereto as she can safely get.'"

4-43   **(iv) Tides and other water conditions.** Where tides or other water conditions such as the depth of a river prevent access to the destination, shipowners may be able to rely on the words "or so near thereto as she can safely get," and load or discharge elsewhere. Just as in an icebound sea a ship may have to wait until the ice melts,[36] so also she may have to wait until normal spring tides.

In *Schilizzi* v. *Derry*[37] a ship was to go to Galatz, "or so near thereto as she may safely get," to load grain for Europe, "all and every other dangers and accidents of the seas, rivers and navigation during the voyage excepted." She arrived off the mouth of the Danube, 95 miles from Galatz, on November 5; the water was unusually low on the bar at Sulina, and she

---

[32] *Ibid.* at p. 63.
[33] As to what should reasonably have been contemplated, see also *Metcalfe* v. *Britannia Iron Works Co.* (1887) 2 Q.B.D. 423 (C.A.) and § 4–39 above.
[34] [1931] P. 79 (C.A.). See § 4–02 above for the question of liability where arrival is delayed by other ships chartered by the same charterers; and § 5–38 below for discussion in *Aktieselskabet Inglewood* v. *Millar's Karris and Jarrah Forests Ltd.* (1903) 8 Com.Cas. 196 of the occupation of three out of four practicable berths by such ships; and § 10–03 below for the similarity between damages in such cases and demurrage.
[35] At pp. 86–87.
[36] *Metcalfe* v. *Britannia Iron Works Co.* (1877) 2 Q.B.D. 423 (C.A.). See § 4–39 above.
[37] (1855) 24 L.J.Q.B. 193.

could not pass. On December 11 the weather forced her to go to Odessa as the nearest safe port, where she took in another cargo and sailed for England. On and after January 7 she could have crossed the bar, gone up to Galatz and loaded. It was held that the shipowners could not rely on the exception clause and put an end to the contract.

Lord Campbell C.J. said[38] of the words "or so near thereto as she could safely get":

> " . . . the meaning must be that she should get within the ambit of the port,[39] though she may not be able to enter it. It might as well be said, that if the ship had been stopped in the Dardanelles she had got as near Galatz as she safely could . . . It was, no doubt, not safe for the ship to keep on and off at the mouth of the Danube, but she might have gone to Odessa or Constantinople and there waited until the bar was passable. If the master had done this, is it not quite clear the defendants[40] would have been entitled to demand a cargo at Galatz, or at one of the other ports?"

Crompton J. added[41]:

> "It would be very dangerous to hold that a mere temporary obstruction such as this put an end to the contract."

4–44 In *The Curfew*[42] a ship was to "load, always afloat, a full and complete cargo" at North Dock, Swansea. She could have completed loading "always afloat" but there was a risk of her being neaped; the shipowners therefore moved her to another dock to complete, to prevent her being delayed a week in getting out of North Dock. They claimed freight, the charterers counterclaiming the cost of carrying the balance of the cargo to the other dock. The Probate, Divorce and Admiralty Divisional Court held that the shipowners were liable for that cost. The fear of detention did not justify removal of the ship. Butt J. said of the risk of detention[43]:

> "It did not render the steamer to complete her loading while afloat in the dock; it only rendered the performance of the contract by the plaintiffs[44] more onerous to them by reason of the loss of the use of their vessel during the neap tides."

4–45 In establishing whether an obstacle is permanent or semi-permanent, so that shipowners can rely on the words "so near thereto as she may safely get," the courts have considered not only the time factor but also other circumstances such as the amount of cargo to be worked, the expense, and other methods of loading or unloading the cargo.

In *Athamas (Owners)* v. *Dig Vijay Cement Co. Ltd.*[45] a Gencon charterparty for the carriage of cement from Sika, India, provided for discharge in part at Saigon with the balance "at one safe place, always afloat, Phnom-Penh, or so near thereto as she may safely get and lie always afloat . . . " The pilotage authorities refused to accept the ship for pilotage to Phnom-Penh (in Cambodia, 250 miles from Saigon and 180 miles up the River Mekong) because, with her draught, a minimum speed of 10 knots was needed to navigate the river safely. Pilotage would not have been allowed for approximately another five months. The shipowners discharged the Phnom-Penh cargo at Saigon and claimed demurrage. The Court of

---

[38] At p. 197.
[39] This had been doubted by Lord Blackburn in *Dahl* v. *Nelson, Donkin & Co.* (1881) 6 App. Cas. 38 at p. 51 (H.L.).
[40] The shipowners.
[41] At p. 198.
[42] [1891] P. 131.
[43] At p. 138.
[44] The shipowners.
[45] [1963] 1 Lloyd's Rep. 287 (C.A.).

Appeal held that shipowners were entitled to demurrage for the time spent in discharging Phnom-Penh cargo at Saigon. The Court said that one had to bear in mind that the obstacle was sufficiently permanent, taking into account the carrying and earning capacities of the ship; that less than a quarter of her cargo was involved; the prohibitive expense of storing the cargo until it could be carried to Phnom-Penh; and that the cargo could have been lightered from Saigon to Phnom-Penh. Saigon was the nearest reasonable practical place of discharge. Sellers L.J. referred to earlier decisions[46] as to the words "so near thereto as she may safely get" and criticised the use by Lord Campbell C.J. in *Schilizzi* v. *Derry*[47] of the words:

> " . . . the meaning of the charterparty must be that the vessel is to get within the ambit of the port, though she may not reach the actual harbour."

The charterers had relied on these words when arguing that the clause contemplated a situation in which the ship went to a bar or bank close to a harbour, and that it must be restricted to similar circumstances. Pearson L.J. discussed the way in which the application of the clause had to be limited, and referred to the decided cases.[48] He concluded[49]:

> "This examination of the authorities has not yielded any precise definition of the range of proximity or vicinity within which the substitute destination must lie in order to be, in relation to the named destination for the ship, 'as near thereto as she may get.' I do, however, derive from these authorities an impression that the range is fairly narrow, and that in an ordinary case a subsitute destination 250 miles by water from the named destination would be outside the range of proximity. This, however, is an extraordinary case in that Saigon, though 250 miles by water away from Phnom-Penh, is nevertheless the nearest Port to Pnom-Penh at any rate for the purpose of unloading the cargo concerned. . . . The question is largely one of degree and to be decided mainly on a basis of commercial knowledge and experience."

WORK BEFORE LAYTIME

4-46 Shipowners may contend that laytime has begun although there has not been compliance with the requirements as to when time should start. This contention is sometimes made when work begins before the expiry of some fixed period stipulated by the charterparty, as in the words: "Laytime for loading and discharging shall commence at 1 p.m. if notice of readiness is given before noon, and at 6 a.m. next working day if notice given during office hours after noon ."[50] Loading or discharging before the fixed period has expired is insufficient evidence in itself of an agreement to vary that

---

[46] *Schilizzi* v. *Derry* (1855) 4 E. & B. 873; *Metcalfe* v. *Britannia Iron Works Co.* (1877) 2 Q.B.D. 423 (C.A.) (ice; see § 4–39 above); and *Dahl* v. *Nelson Donkin & Co.* (1881) 6 App.Cas. 38 (H.L.) (congestion): see § 4–42 above.

[47] (1855) 4 E. & B. 873. See § 4–43 above.

[48] The three cases mentioned above at n. 42 and: *Capper & Co.* v. *Wallace Brothers* (1880) 5 Q.B.D. 163 (draught too great to reach Koogerpolder at end of canal; ship held to be "as near thereto as she may safely get" at Nieuwediep, 30 miles away); *Hayton* v. *Irwin* (1879) 5 C.PD. 130 (draught too great to reach Hamburg; ship held to be "so near thereto as she may safely get" at Stade, about 30 miles away); *Horsley* v. *Price* (1883) 11 Q.B.D. 244; *Custel & Latta* v. *Trechman* (1884) 1 C. & E. 276 (Taganrog and Tuapse blockaded; Constantinople held not to be as near "as she could safely get"); *East Asiatic Co. Ltd.* v. *SS. Toronto Co. Ltd.* (1915) 31 T.L.R. 543 (Hull, 200 miles from Amsterdam, said, but in an *obiter dictum*, not to be "so near thereto as she may safely get").

[49] [1963] 1 Lloyd's Rep. 287 at p. 302.

[50] In the Uniform General Charter (Gencon) (1976 revision).

stipulation.[51] It must be shown, if laytime is to begin earlier, that the parties agreed to vary their contract to that effect.

The Court of Appeal considered, in *The Katy*,[52] the problem which **4–47** arises when work begins before the time agreed for the beginning of laytime. Fourteen running days were allowed for loading and discharging; there was no provision as to when laytime should begin. On Saturday the ship got into her loading berth at 10 a.m. and the charterers worked her from 1 p.m. to 4 p.m. The Court of Appeal held that they had, by their action, agreed that time should count for the whole of that day. As Lord Esher M.R. said[53]:

> "The captain said 'Come—agree with me to take delivery'; and they did agree to take delivery, and they did it. Is that, or is that not, agreeing to treat Saturday as one of the lay days? . . . They agree to treat is as a lay day; and if it once is a lay day, to my mind it does not signify how much of it was left. The whole of that day is a lay day, and if they neither did nor could take delivery during half of it, still it is a lay day."

Though the Court of Appeal was satisfied in *The Katy*, the House of Lords adopted a different approach in *James Nelson & Sons, Ltd.* v. *Nelson Line (Liverpool), Ltd.*[54] The question was whether loading during holiday periods but with the master's consent overrode the express provision; "Sundays and holidays excepted." It was held that the mere fact of such working could not vary the express term. Lord Loreburn L.C. said[55]:

> "In my view, it is a question, not of law, but of fact, whether or not there was an agreement varying . . . the terms of the charterparty and providing that the holidays in question should count as lay days. I am unable to see any evidence of such an agreement. Very likely it was convenient to both sides to do what was done. I do not believe it entered into the heads of either that they were making such an agreement as is suggested. At all events, there is no proof of it, and therefore the charterparty, which excludes holidays, must prevail."

This conclusion is in accordance with the general principle that a variation of a contract requires the same elements as are needed in the original contract.[56] The House of Lords considered that they were absent in the *Nelson* case. It is a question of fact whether the parties made a new agreement to vary the charterparty. In *Pteroti Compania Naviera S.A.* v. *National Coal Board*[57] an Amwelsh charterparty stated: "Time to commence 24 hours, Sundays and holidays excepted, after vessel is ready to unload and written notice given." The ship berthed at 0200 hours, began to discharge at 0230 hours, and tendered notice of readiness at 0900 hours. The owners failed in their contention that laytime began when discharging began. They argued that the object of the notice was to give the charterers time to prepare,[58] but that the charterers were ready many hours before the notice. Diplock J. said that it was the first time that the question had arisen in England as to when time began in such a situation. The mere beginning of the discharge was evidence neither of a waiver of the notice clause nor of a new agree-

---

[51] *Pteroti* v. *National Coal Board* [1958] 1 Q.B. 469. See § 4–47 below.
[52] [1895] P. 56.
[53] *Ibid.* at p. 63.
[54] [1908] A.C. 108.
[55] At p. 113.
[56] Namely, offer, acceptance, consideration and the intention to create legal relations; see, for example, *Stead* v. *Dawber* (1839) 10 A. & E. 57.
[57] [1958] 1 Q.B. 469.
[58] As to why notice is needed, see § 5–18 above.

ment. There were advantages to both sides in starting to discharge early, but he, said[59]:

> "Whether one advantage outweighs the other in any particular case I do not know, and I do not think it matters. As I say, I think that there are advantages to both sides; and in those circumstances I am not prepared to infer any waiver of what I think are the plain terms of the clause itself."

APPENDIX TO CHAPTER 4

4-48 *Arrived Ship—A New York Arbitration*

The House of Lords in *The Johanna Oldendorff*[60] reversed its decision in *The Aello*[61] and established the Reid test,[62] of which certain essential words are: "Before a ship can be said to have arrived at a port she must, if she cannot proceed immediately to a berth, have reached a position *within the port*[63] where she is at the immediate and effective disposition of the charterer. . . . " In *The Maratha Envoy*[64] the House followed strictly the principles which it had already laid down. All concerned wished to ensure legal certainty. There may be some scope for dispute as to how one should define the "port" within which the ship must be, and as to how wide can be the area within which the various port authorities can exercise their various powers.[65]

4-49   Lord Denning M.R. and Stephenson L.J. referred, in their judgments in the Court of Appeal in *The Maratha Envoy*,[66] to the decision of New York arbitrators in *Maritime Bulk Carriers Corporation* v. *Garnac Grain Co.*[67] The arbitrators had to decide whether a ship had arrived at Rotterdam. The *Polyfreedom* was chartered on the Baltimore Form C to carry grain from Port Cartier, Quebec, to "1/2 safe berths Rotterdam including Botlek." Laytime was to begin, subject to such usual requirement as entry at the custom house, "whether in berth or not." On June 29, 1973, she arrived off the Hook of Holland. She anchored there to await the discharging berth arranged by charterers at G.E.M. Installation Botlek, which was then occupied by another ship. On the same day the pilotage service told the Master that the berth was occupied and that the ship must wait. No other berth was available. She was also entered at the custom house and obtained free pratique on that day.

4-50   She was within an area designated as "Recommended Anchorage" which was not within the legal, fiscal or geographical limits of the port. Notice of readiness was tendered on June 29 but the charterers' agents declined to accept it. Their telex message included the words: "We leave it entirely to Master/owners to decide to keep the vessel waiting in open sea until availability of nominated discharge berth for entire risk/account/

---

[59] At p. 477.
[60] *Oldendorff (E.L.) and Co. G.m.b.H.* v. *Tradax Export S.A.* [1973] 2 Lloyd's Rep. 285. See § 4–21 above.
[61] *Sociedad Financiera de Bienes Raices S.A.* v. *Agrimpex Hungarian Trading Co. for Agricultural Products* [1961] A.C. 135. See § 4–19 above.
[62] *Op. cit.* at p. 291.
[63] Italics supplied. For the sentences which followed see § 4–24 above.
[64] *Federal Commerce and Navigation Co. Ltd.* v. *Tradax Export S.A.* [1977] 1 Lloyd's Rep. 217. See § 4–25 above.
[65] See § 4–09 above.
[66] [1977] 1 Lloyd's Rep. 217 at pp. 223 and 228.
[67] [1975] A.M.C. 1826 (*The Polyfreedom*).

expense of the vessel, or to bring the vessel to a waiting berth within official Rotterdam territory, in which case shifting from waiting berth to discharge berth will be for vessel's account. Notice of readiness will only be accepted after vessel being definitely moored within Rotterdam territory."[68] The ship was ordered to and arrived at the discharging berth on July 4.

The owners argued that it followed from the decision of the House of **4–51** Lords in *The Johanna Oldendorff*[69] that the ship had arrived on June 29. They quoted Lord Reid[70]:

> "The area within which a port authority exercises its various powers can hardly be difficult to ascertain. Some powers with regard to pilotage and other matters may extend far beyond the limits of the port. But those which regulate the movements and conduct of ships would seem to afford a good indication."

Shipowners' counsel, referring to *Sailing-Ship Garston Co.* v. *Hickie & Co.*[71] cited Bowen L.J.[72]:

> "Another matter which ought to be considered is the authority exercised, and the **4–52** limits within which that authority is exercised, not for fiscal purposes, but for purposes connected with the loading and unloading, the arrival and departure, of ships; the mode in which the business of loading and unloading is done, and the general usage of the place. Taking all these things together, you must make up your mind in each particular case as to the sense in which shipowners and charterers would be likely to intend to employ the term 'port.' "

The evidence as to the discipline exercised by the various Rotterdam **4–53** port authorities was that:

1. The Harbour Master of Rotterdam said: "The anchorage is not a part of the harbour of Rotterdam, nor of the municipality of Rotterdam. The Rotterdam harbour authority exercises no power over the anchorage." He also said that "recommended" and "not recommended" anchorage areas were officially outlined on charts of the harbour and the adjacent sea area.
2. The State Harbour Master for the Rotterdam Waterway Authority said that under the Waterway regulations ships lying at the anchorage could not enter the waterway if they could not proceed to a designated berth.
3. The government Pilotage Service, at the Hook of Holland, observed and recorded the arrivals and departures of ships anchored in the sea area adjacent to the port.
4. The Rotterdam customs authority issued permits to discharge while ships were at the Anchorage Area.

The arbitration panel of three, agreeing that the ship was outside the **4–54** legal, fiscal and geographical port limits, asked itself: "Does this geographic imaginary line drawn up by the Dutch government authorities for totally different purposes, mean that under the terms of this particular Charter Party, the *M/V Polyfreedom* had not arrived at Rotterdam?"[73]

---

[68] As to apparently premature notices of readiness see § 5–27 above.
[69] [1973] 1 Lloyd's Rep. 285.
[70] *Ibid.* at p. 291. This part of his judgment is cited at greater length at § 4–10 above.
[71] (1884) 15 Q.B.D. 580 (C.A.). See § 4–15 above for the facts and for a similar comment by Brett M.R., on which shipowners' counsel in this arbitration also relied.
[72] *Ibid.* at pp. 595–596. See also § 4–08.
[73] *Op. cit.* at p. 1831.

The panel considered several English cases.[74] The majority found, though there was conflicting evidence, that ships at the anchorage were subject to some discipline by port authorities. With respect to the decision in *The Johanna Oldendorff* they said[75]: " . . . conditions at Liverpool . . . were only different in that the anchorage where the ship was obliged to wait was within the legal, fiscal and administrative limits of the port of Liverpool/ Birkenhead. However, that anchorage is about equidistant from the berth where *Johanna Oldendorff* discharged her cargo as is the Botlek/G.E.M. installation from the anchorage where *M/V Polyfreedom* was waiting. The Charter Party requirements were identical for the commencement of lay-time. Both ships were at the usual place where vessels awaiting berth lie and both ships were at the disposal of Charterers."

4–55   The majority stated[76]:

> "Under a port charter party containing a 'whether in berth or not' provision, if a vessel has reached a point as close as she may reasonably arrive to the designated discharging berth, and can prove that it was not possible or practical to get nearer, then the physical and geographical location of the waiting point (provided it is within the usual waiting area) is of no importance. The Owner of the vessel has at that point in time executed the requirement of the contract to the extent required to place the ship and cargo at Charterers' disposal. Clearly this requires that the vessel be able, immediately she is required to do so, to proceed on charterers' instructions to the discharging berth, without causing any delay to Charterers at that time."

In these, the final sentences of the reasons, the majority stated that the shipowners had executed the contractual requirement "to the extent required to place the ship and cargo at Charterers' disposal." It is submitted that in English law it is vital that both requirements, *i.e.* as to arrival at the port and as to the ship being at the charterers' disposition, should be clearly and separately achieved.

4–56   The dissenting arbitrator, finding in favour of the charterers, stressed the importance of the Reid test[77] in the *Johanna Oldendorff*. As a result, he said, the ship, in order to tender notice should first arrive in Rotterdam at a position within the port where she was at the immediate disposition of charterers. He cited the certificate issued by the Rotterdam Harbour Master, as to the anchorage not being part of either the harbour or the municipality of Rotterdam, and as to the Rotterdam harbour authority exercising "no power over the anchorage." He concluded that the port authorities had no control over ships at the anchorage other than to forbid them to enter the port if no discharge or lay berth was available. The possibility of non-availability of a berth in Rotterdam on account of commercial congestion was a well-known fact in the trade. Some shipowners preferred to charter with grain houses which accepted notice of readiness at the Hook of Holland, receiving a somewhat reduced freight rate.[78] Others inserted in the destination clause the term "as close as she can get" or the Genwait

---

[74] Including *Sailing-Ship Garston Co.* v. *Hickie & Co.* (1885) 15 Q.B.D. 580 (C.A.) (see § 4–15 above); *Sociedad Financiera de Bienes Raices S.A.* v. *Agrimpex Hungarian Trading Co. for Agricultural Products (The Aello)* [1961] A.C. 135 (H.L.) (see § 4–19 above); and *Oldendorff (E.L.) & Co. G.m.b.H.* v. *Tradax Export S.A.* [1973] 2 Lloyd's Rep. 285 (*The Johanna Oldendorff*) (see § 4–21 above).

[75] *Op. cit.* at p. 1835.

[76] *Ibid.* at p. 1836.

[77] See § 4–24 above.

[78] See the comments on this question in Lord Diplock's judgment in *Federal Commerce and Navigation Co. Ltd.* v. *Tradax Export S.A. (The Maratha Envoy)* [1977] 2 Lloyd's Rep. 301, at p. 304, cited above at § 4–25.

clause,[79] published by the Baltic and International Maritime Conference in 1968.

The shipowners, he said, were not caught unawares. They bargained for and accepted the arrival clause in the charterparty. He concluded that the *Polyfreedom* did not meet the minimum requirements for being considered an arrived ship on June 29. He added that he hoped that shipowners and charterers would adopt the relevant clause of the Norgrain charterparty[80] or allocate equal liability for such a loss of time, "thus reverting to the principle of tendering notice within the commercial limits of the port."

The decision in *The Polyfreedom* in favour of the shipowners was mentioned by Lord Denning M.R. in *Federal Commerce and Navigation Co. Ltd.* v. *Tradax Export S.A.*,[81] though it is important to remember that the Court of Appeal decision there was reversed, in the charterers' favour, by the House of Lords.[82] Pointing out that the anchorage in that case was not within the legal, fiscal or geographical limits of the port of Rotterdam, Lord Denning said[83]: **4–57**

> "It was held, by two to one of the arbitrators, that under a port charter-party containing a 'whether in berth or not' provision, the vessel was entitled to give notice of readiness when she was anchored at that point . . . [Lord Denning then quoted part of the award, including the sentence: 'Those doing business in Rotterdam either must take steps to ensure that all vessels can be accommodated within the Port as and when they arrive, or accept the costs for delaying such ships outside the geographical and fiscal limits officially in force'] . . . In coming to their decision the arbitrators relied much on the decision of the English Courts, especially *The Johanna Oldendorff*[84] . . . As the commercial men in the United States pay us the complement of relying on our decisions, so should we return the compliment. The merchants and shipping men on both sides of the

[79] Its Code name is Genwait. Entitled the Baltic Conference General Waiting for Berth Clause, 1968, it states:

> "(a) If the loading berth is not available on Vessel's arrival at or off the port of loading or so near thereunto as she may be permitted to approach, the Vessel shall be entitled to give notice of readiness on arrival there with the effect that laytime counts as if she were in berth and in all respects ready for loading provided that the Master warrants that she is in fact ready in all respects. Actual time occupied in moving from place of waiting to loading berth not to count as laytime. If after berthing the Vessel is found not to be ready in all respects to load, the actual time lost from the discovery thereof until she is in fact ready to load shall not count as laytime.
>
> (b) If the discharging berth is not available on Vessel's arrival at or off the port of discharge or so near thereunto as she may be permitted to approach, the Vessel shall be entitled to give notice of readiness on arrival there with the effect that laytime counts as if she were in berth and in all respects ready for discharging provided that the Master warrants that she is in fact ready in all respects. Actual time occupied in moving from place of waiting to discharging berth not to count as laytime. If after berthing the Vessel is found not to be ready in all respects to discharge, the actual time lost from the discovery thereof until she is in fact ready to discharge shall not count as laytime."

[80] The North American Grain Charterparty 1973, issued by the Association of Ship Brokers and Agents (U.S.A.) Inc. (A.S.B.A.). The first sentence of Clause 17(b) states: "Waiting for Berth. If the vessel is prevented from entering the commercial limits of the loading/discharging port(s) because the first or sole loading/discharging berth or lay berth or anchorage is not available, or on the order of the Charterers/Receivers or any competent official body or authority, and the Master warrants that the vessel is physically ready in all respects to load or discharge, the time spent waiting at a usual waiting place outside the commercial limits of the port or off the port shall count against laytime."

[81] [1977] 1 Lloyd's Rep. 217 (C.A.) (*The Maratha Envoy*).

[82] [1977] 2 Lloyd's Rep. 301.

[83] At pp. 223–224.

[84] [1973] 2 Lloyd's Rep. 285 (H.L.).

Atlantic use the same standard forms of contract, and the same words and phrases. These should be interpreted in the same way in whichever place they come up for decision. No matter whether in London or New York, the result should be the same. The Courts of this country have in the past done much to form it and develop it. Let us not fail in our time. So on this point let us follow the lead given by New York."

4–58 Stephenson L.J. also commented[85] on the decision:

"I do not go so far as to say with Lord Denning, M.R., that for the purpose of deciding whether a ship has completed its carrying voyage in these days it does not matter whether she waits outside or inside the named port provided that she is at the immediate and effective disposition of the charterers. That is what a majority of American arbitrators have said in *The Polyfreedom* . . . and I should like to say so too. Brake is not the only port whose geographical and legal limits are disputed and may lead to differences of judicial opinion. Buenos Aires is another example . . . To say what those arbitrators have said would get rid of such disputes and differences and of such attempts to qualify as an arrived ship, by voyages which add nothing to the ship's readiness to discharge, as were made by this ship and others."

[85] At p. 228.

CHAPTER 5

READINESS[1]

A SHIP is ready to load, in the sense that shipowners can give a proper **5–01** notice of readiness,[2] when she is available to charterers, so far as they can then use her. She must be available in the legal sense,[3] in that no laws or regulations stand in the way of access by charterers, and in the physical sense, in that access to the ship and her holds is possible.[4] As Lopes J. said in *Groves, Maclean & Co.* v. *Volkart Brothers*[5]:

> "A ship to be ready to load must be completely ready in all her holds . . . so as to afford the merchant/charterer complete control of every portion of the ship available for cargo."[6]

The same rules apply to readiness to discharge[7] as in the case of the loading operations. Diplock J. said in *Government of Ceylon* v. *Société Franco-Tunisienne d'Armement-Tunis*[8] that the shipowners had argued that there was no authority that the same principle applied to discharging. He added:

> "Well, someone has got to decide whether it does or whether it does not. I can, in this respect, see no reason for distinguishing between loading and discharging. It seems to me common sense that the same principle as regards availability of holds would apply to discharging as to loading, and I propose, at any rate temporarily, to fill the gap in the authority upon this subject. I take the view, therefore, that the charterers are right in their contention that lay time did not begin to run until all the flour cargo was accessible. . . . "

Both the ship's gear, so far as it is reasonably necessary for loading or discharging, and the holds must be made available. If there is some difficulty, as a result of which work is partly or wholly obstructed, a question may arise as to whether the ship is ready. If, for example, a ship is completely ready, save that one of the winches has broken down, then she is not ready for the purpose of the notice of readiness. Where port regulations prevent the use of ship's winchmen, on the other hand, or if shore winchmen are not available, a ship is probably ready in spite of the impossibility of working the winches. She is not ready if her hatches are not all available, unless perhaps there are special reasons[9] why they should not be so at the beginning of loading.

---

[1] For reaching the agreed destination, see § 4–01 above; for giving a notice of readiness, see § 5–18 below.

[2] For which see § 5–17 below. As to the effect of a premature notice, see § 5–27 below.

[3] See § 5–09 below.

[4] See § 5–14 below.

[5] (1884) C. & E. 309.

[6] They need not be afforded complete control of portions of the ship needed for bunkers; see *Darling* v. *Raeburn* [1907] 1 K.B. 846 (C.A.) and § 5–16 below.

[7] See § 5–02 below as to whether notice is needed.

[8] [1962] 2 Q.B. 416 at p. 426 (*The Massalia*).

[9] Such as reasons of safety.

5–02 Readiness as far as ship is concerned
The ship does not have to be so positioned physically that, given the order for loading or discharging to begin, work could start at once. There has merely to be readiness as far as she is then concerned. The ship might be in the middle of the port[10] and at a place where work is not, or cannot be, done, but still be ready.[11] Such a situation arose in *Armement Adolf Deppe* v. *John Robinson & Co. Ltd.*[12] A grain ship entered a dock at Avonmouth and moored at the buoys; the hatches were not removed. There were no express words empowering the charterers to name a berth, and laytime was to begin whenever she was ready to discharge. The consignees could have discharged her at the buoys but that was most unusual and they did not wish to do so. The Court of Appeal, supporting the shipowners, held that she was ready; the charterers were not in a position to work the ship; but laytime had begun.[13] As Scrutton L.J. put it[14]:

> "I should be surprised to find that in practice it was ever thought necessary for the ship as soon as she entered the dock to rig her discharging gear, and get men to do her part of the discharging on board, before her time could begin to run, though it was well worth that, at the place where she was, discharging would not take place. Such a reqirement would be quite unbusinesslike."

A ship may be ready to discharge, so that a notice of readiness may properly be given, where it is contemplated in the charterparty that discharging will be partly into lighters and partly at a berth or berths.

5–03 The requirement that the ship has to be ready as far as she is concerned involves a distinction between mere routine formalities, which do not prevent her being regarded as ready, and matters which will cause delay.[14a] In *Compania de Naviera Nedelka S.A.* v. *Tradax Internacional S.A.*[15] a ship was chartered on the Synacomex form to carry maize from Varna to Famagusta. The charterparty stated:

> "6 . . . Before tendering notice Master has to take necessary measures for holds to be clean, dry without smell and in every way suitable to receive grain to shippers'/charterers' satisfaction."
> "21 . . . Master is allowed to give the notice of load readiness . . . when ship is arrived on the road of loading port."

The Master gave notice on November 22 when the ship came into the roads, within the geographical limits of the port. She could not then be inspected, as there was rough weather and the inspectors could not get out

---

[10] Provided that she has reached her contractual destination.
[11] It is enough that she is ready to discharge in the manner contemplated by the charterparty. This may be by an initial discharge into lighters, with a subsequent discharge at the berth. See *Clerco Compania Naviera S.A.* v. *Food Corporation of India (The Savvas)* [1982] 1 Lloyd's Rep. 22 (C.A.), *per* Ackner L.J. at p. 25 (see § 8–49 below) and *N.Z. Michalos* v. *Food Corporation of India (The Apollon)* [1983] 1 Lloyd's Rep. 409, *per* Bingham J. at pp. 414–415 (see § 8–52 below).
[12] [1917] 2 K.B. 204 (C.A.). Applied in *Gerani Compania Naviera S.A.* v. *General Organization for Supply Goods* [1982] 1 Lloyd's Rep. 275 (*The Demosthenes V.*) (*No. 1*). See § 5–04.
[13] The decision was cited by Lord Denning M.R. in *Shipping Developments Corporation S.A.* v. *V/O Sojuzneftexport* [1971] 1 Lloyd's Rep. 506 at p. 510 (C.A.) (*The Delian Spirit*) to show that a notice of readiness may sometimes be given without free pratique. See § 5–12. See also § 5–03 and § 5–04 as to where more than routine formalities have to be completed and § 5–27 as to whether notice must be correct. [14] At p. 212.
[14a] But she must be ready to discharge all the cargo; *Unifert International SAL* v. *Panous Shipping Co. Inc. (The Virginia M)* LMLN 237, December 3, 1988.
[15] [1973] 2 Lloyd's Rep. 247 (C.A.) (*The Tres Flores*).

to her until November 27. Then she was found to have pests in the cargo spaces and to be unfit for loading until she was fumigated. Fumigation took place on November 30. The Court of Appeal held, supporting the charterers, that the ship only became ready to load[16] on November 30. Lord Denning M.R. said that Clause 6 laid down a condition precedent to the validity of the notice of readiness and added[17]:

> "That condition precedent was not fulfilled until the fumigation had been completed on November 30, and therefore the notice of readiness could not validly be given until that time . . . One thing is clear. In order for notice of readiness to be good, the vessel must be ready at the time that the notice is given, and not at a time in the future. Readiness is a preliminary existing fact which must exist before you can give a notice of readiness.[18]

He then made a distinction in respect of routine formalities:

> "In order to be a good notice of readiness, the Master must be in a position to say: 'I am ready at the moment you want me, whenever that may be, and any necessary preliminaries on my part to the loading will not be such as to delay you.' Applying this test[19] it is apparent that notice of readiness can be given even though there are some further preliminaries to be done, or routine matters be carried on, or formalities observed. If those things are not such as to give any reason to suppose that they will cause any delay, and it is apparent that the ship will be ready when the appropriate time arrives, then notice of readiness can be given. In the present case there were pests in the hull such as to make the ship unready to receive cargo. Fumigation was not a mere preliminary, nor a routine matter, nor a formality at all. It was an essential step which had to be taken before any cargo could be received at all. Until the vessel had been fumigated, notice of readiness could not be given. It has always been held that, for a notice of readiness to be given, the vessel must be completely ready in all her holds to receive the cargo at any moment when she is required to receive it. It was said by Mr. Justice Lopes in *Groves, Maclean & Co.* v. *Volkart Brothers*[20] . . . and accepted in *Noemijulia Steamship Co. Ltd.* v. *Minister of Food*."[21]

This distinction, between conditions precedent to the validity of a notice **5–04** of readiness and routine formalities, was also made in *Gerani Compania Naviera S.A.* v. *General Organisation for Supply Goods*.[22] There was a notice of readiness clause and further clauses which stated: "Owners to supply sufficient vacuators . . . " and "Owners to guarantee minimum six (6) vacuators at discharging port. . . . " Staughton J. upheld the shipowners' contention that the case was not like the *Compania de Naviera*

---

[16] In *Eurico S.p.A.* v. *Philipp Brothers* [1986] 2 Lloyd's Rep. 387 (*The Epaphus*) infestation was discovered in a rice cargo when the hatches were opened at the discharging port; the buyers, who would have been liable for demurrage, argued that the ship was not ready. Staughton J. said, at p. 394, that the *Nedelka* case was inapplicable: "Here, it is not a question of loading but discharging. The ship, as a ship, was fit and ready to do her part . . . the problem was the insects in the buyers' cargo." His judgment as to this issue was supported by the Court of Appeal: [1987] 2 Lloyd's Rep. 215.

[17] *Ibid.* at p. 249.

[18] He referred to the judgment of Atkin L.J. in *A/B Nordiska Lloyd* v. *J. Brownlie & Co. (Hull) Ltd.* (1925) 30 Com.Cas. 307 at p. 315 (C.A.). See also § 5–06 below. But see also § 5–20 and § 5–27 below, as to whether the notice must be correct when it is given.

[19] This test was applied by London arbitrators in a case concerning a prior entry manifest at Bombay; LMLN 90, April 14, 1983; see also § 5–10 below, at n. 50.

[20] (1884) C. & E. 309. He was referring to the words of Lopes J. cited at § 5–01 above.

[21] [1951] 1 K.B. 223 (C.A.). See also § 5–07 below.

[22] [1982] 1 Lloyd's Rep. 275 (*The Demosthenes V*) (No. 1). This case, and the earlier case of *Government of Ceylon* v. *Société Franco-Tunisienne d'Armement Tunis* [1962] 2 Q.B. 416 (*The Massalia*) were said by Evans J. in *Transgrain Shipping B.V.* v. *Global Transporte Oceanico S.A.* (*The Mexico 1*) [1988] 2 Lloyd's Rep. 149, at p. 153, to be, until the case before him, the only reported cases concerning readiness to discharge.

Nedelka case[23] and that there was nothing to link the obligations as to vacuators with the notice of readiness provision. He said[24]: "The vacuators were essentially, as I see it, equipment which was to emerge from the shore when the operation of discharge was to commence. The ship [*The Demosthenes V*], as a ship, was ready. All that had not been done was to supply the equipment which the owners were to supply for the purposes of discharge."

In view of this conclusion it was not necessary for the Judge to decide what he considered to be a more difficult issue: "that is, if the ship was not, in point of her physical state, ready to discharge on May 27 [when notice of readiness had been given], whether the notice is still valid because she could have been made fit within such time as the charterers could conceivably have required her to start discharging."[25] Referring to the two relevant Court of Appeal decisions,[26] he said that it was not altogether easy to discern the line between them. He concluded[27]: "I would be prepared for my part to hold that this case is within the *Armement Adolf Deppe* principle, rather than that laid down in the *Compania Nedelka* case . . . I would be prepared to describe the supply of vacuators in the present case as normal and usual preliminaries, at any rate in the case of a vessel which was to be discharged in that way, in contrast with the fumigation in the *Compania Nedelka* case."

5–05   *Readiness: two types*

A ship may be ready in the sense that charterers cannot cancel her under the cancellation clause, but not ready for the purpose of enabling shipowners to give an effective notice of readiness.[28] An example of the contrast between the two types of readiness was given by Kennedy L.J. in *Leonis SS. Co. Ltd.* v. *Rank Ltd. (No. 1)*[29]:

> "The charterer has an option to cancel should the vessel not be ready to load by 6 p.m. on March 15. She did not in fact reach the berth at the pier until March 30. On March 29 she first left her anchorage to go alongside another vessel which had the inner berth alongside the pier. Could the charterers at any time between March 15 and March 28, whilst the *Leonis* was lying at her anchorage, have said to the owners, 'Your ship is not ready to load, and, therefore, we cancel the charterparty?' It appears to me very difficult, if not impossible, to suppose that such a thing could be within the intention of the parties."

He concluded that the charterers could not have cancelled and that the ship was ready at the anchorage in the sense required for laytime to run.

A ship may be ready to receive stiffening, but not ready for the purpose of preventing cancellation under the cancellation clause. In *Lyderhorn Sailing Ship Co. Ltd.* v. *Duncan Fox & Co.*[30] there was a charterparty to load nitrate at Iquique and Caleta Buena, Chile. Laytime was to begin the day after the master gave notice of readiness. Stiffening of nitrate was to be supplied on receipt of 48 hours' notice from the master. The cancelling

---

[23] [1979] 2 Lloyd's Rep. 247 (C.A.) (*The Tres Flores*). See § 5–03 above.
[24] [1982] 1 Lloyd's Rep. 275 at p. 279.
[25] *Ibid.*
[26] *Armement Adolf Deppe* v. *John Robinson & Co. Ltd.* [1917] 2 K.B. 204 (see § 5–02 above) and *Compania de Naviera Nedelka S.A.* v. *Tradax Internacional S.A.* [1973] 2 Lloyd's Rep. 247 (*The Tres Flores*) (see § 5–03 above).
[27] *Ibid.* at pp. 279–280.
[28] On why notice is needed, see § 5–18 below.
[29] [1908] 1 K.B. 499 at p. 527 (C.A.). See § 4–18 above.
[30] [1909] 2 K.B. 929 (C.A.).

clause referred to readiness: "Should the vessel not have arrived at her loading port and be ready for loading . . . on or before noon of January 31, 1908, charterers to have the option of cancelling this charter." When the ship arrived at Iquique she had the remainder of a cargo of coal to discharge; by January 27 she had discharged as much as could safely be unloaded without some stiffening. She could not have discharged it all by January 31. The master gave notice to the charterers' agents that he needed nitrate for stiffening, but they would not supply it without his agreement to redeliver it if the charterparty were cancelled. The charterers cancelled on the cancelling date. The Court of Appeal held that the ship was not ready within the meaning of the cancelling clause.

The distinction between the two types of readiness was discussed in *A/B*   **5–06** *Nordiska Lloyd* v. *J. Brownlie & Co. (Hull) Ltd.*[31] A charterparty for the carriage of coal from the Humber to Germany gave an option to cancel if the ship was not ready to load from any cause on or before Tuesday, April 3 at 6 a.m. If prevented from entering the harbour or docks by congestion she was to be treated as ready from the first high water on or after arrival and entitled to give written notice. She arrived off Hull on Saturday, March 31. The port was so congested that she could not enter the docks. As Monday, April 2, was Easter Monday notice of readiness could not be given until 9 a.m. the next day. The charterers claimed the right to cancel as notice had not been given before 6 a.m. The Court of Appeal, supporting the shipowners, held that notice of readiness to load was irrelevant to the cancelling clause. The test was the actual readiness of the ship. All three judges stressed that the particular wording of the charterparty, by which the ship was "to be treated as a ready ship" in such circumstances, precluded cancellation. Whether the readiness was constructive (as here) or actual, it was not necessarily the same as the readiness required to entitle the shipowners to give a notice of readiness. As Atkin L.J. said[32]:

> "I reserve any questions that may arise on other charterparties except to say this, that it appears to me that notice of readiness is a different and distinct act and a later act than the act of being ready; and for my part I find it difficult to see how you can give a notice of readiness until there is a preliminary existing fact, namely, readiness,[33] and therefore the mere fact that you are required or asked to give notice of readiness seems to me to assume that there is something in existence of which you are giving notice, namely, that the ship is ready, which would appear to be a condition the existence of which, one way or the other, is necessary for determining the right of the charterer to cancel."

Cancellation on the ground that the ship was not ready was considered   **5–07** by the Court of Appeal in *Noemijulia SS. Co. Ltd.* v. *Minister of Food.*[34] A charterparty to carry grain from Argentinian ports granted the charterer "the full reach and burthen[35] of the steamer including 'tween and shelter decks, bridges, poop, etc. (provided same are not occupied by bunker coals and/or stores)." The charterer could cancel if the ship were not ready to load at the first loading port by a specified time. The ship gave notice of readiness to load but the charterers cancelled on the ground that she was not ready. Her number three lower hold contained some bunker coal, and

---

[31] (1925) 30 Com.Cas. 307 (C.A.).
[32] At p. 315.
[33] As to the effect of a premature notice, see § 5–27 below. See also the approving comments of Roskill L.J. in *Compania de Naviera Nedelka S.A.* v. *Tradax Internacional S.A.* [1973] 2 Lloyd's Rep. 247 (C.A.) (*The Tres Flores*) cited at § 5–32, n. 7, below.
[34] [1951] 1 K.B. 223.
[35] As to the meaning of "full reach and burthen," see § 5–15 below.

she had no main mast or after derricks. The Court of Appeal held that the shipowners were right. It was for the charterers to show, if they claimed that a reserve bunker space should be made available for cargo, that it could not reasonably be required for bunkers. As they had not done so, that hold was not a space which the shipowners had to make ready for loading. The loading gear, unlike the cargo space, did not have to be placed at the disposal of the charterers; they had to show that at the date of cancellation the shipowners must be unable to comply with their obligation to load such cargo as they were entitled to ship.

Tucker L.J. pointed out[36] that the charterers were to have "the full reach and burthen of the steamer including 'tween and shelter decks" and other places. The proviso as to the "same"[37] not being occupied by bunker coals and/or stores applied to number 3 lower hold. That hold contained reserve bunker coal and was so designated in the capacity plan. As for the loading gear, he said[38]:

> " . . . in principle a charterer who has cancelled on the ground of unreadiness to load by reason of the insufficiency of the loading gear, in a case where the obligation to load is on the shipowner and where there is more than one port of loading and different kinds of cargo which may be loaded at the option of the charterer, must at least prove that at the cancelling date the ship was in such a condition that the shipowner would necessarily be unable to comply with his obligation to load some cargo which the charterer was entitled under the charterparty to call upon him to take on board at the first or some subsequent port. It is, in my view, not enough for him to show that at the cancelling date the shipowner *may* be unable to load some particular cargo; he must prove that he could not do so."

5–08   Charterers must act with reasonable diligence to enable the ship to become an arrived ship. In *Sunbeam Shipping Co. Ltd.* v. *President of India*[39] a ship was prevented from becoming an arrived ship by the charterers' delay in obtaining a document called a "jetty challan." The *Atlantic Sunbeam* was chartered to carry bulk fertiliser from the United States Gulf to one or two safe berths or ports on the east coast of India. She was ordered to Madras, where she discharged part of the cargo, and to Calcutta. She arrived and anchored off Sandheads, an anchorage off the River Hooghly, on June 16, 1967, and waited there until June 23, when the pilot boarded her and she went to Calcutta. She was not free to go up the river and could not become an arrived ship until, among other procedures, (i) the shipowners had lodged with Calcutta customs papers constituting what was known as a "prior entry"[40] (this was done on June 13); and (ii) the

---

[36] At pp. 233–234.

[37] Whether "same" referred to "full reach and burthen" or to the " 'tween and shelter decks . . . etc."

[38] At pp. 237–238. He referred particularly to *Vaughan* v. *Campbell Heatley & Co.* (1885) 2 T.L.R. 33 (C.A.) (ship not lined as usual and necessary to protect wheat or flour cargo: charterers not entitled to cancel as ship to be "ready" to load, not necessarily "fit" to load); *Grampian SS. Co. Ltd.* v. *Carver & Co.* (1893) 9 T.L.R. 210 (mats for cotton seed, wheat, beans, maize or other grain need not be laid down to make a ship ready to load: enough that mats were ready if needed: charterers not entitled to cancel); *Armement Adolf Deppe* v. *John Robinson & Co. Ltd.* [1917] 2 K.B. 204 (See also § 5–02 above); and *Sun Shipping Co. Ltd.* v. *Watson & Youell Shipping Agency Ltd.* (1926) 42 T.L.R. 240 (shifting boards not in position though needed at first loading port; not ready to load for purpose of calculating lay days).

[39] [1973] 1 Lloyd's Rep. 482 (*The Atlantic Sunbeam*).

[40] For prior entry rules, entitling ships to be entered at the custom house, see § 5–10 below.

consignees had obtained the jetty challan from the port commissioners. There was no question of congestion.[41]

In the High Court Kerr J., applying the decision in *Ford* v. *Cotesworth*,[42] said[43] that it showed clearly that an objective test, *i.e.* what would be a reasonable time considered objectively without reference to the position of the parties, was the wrong approach, and that the right approach was that each party should act with reasonable diligence. He then said[44]:

> "A requirement of a high standard of initiative, let alone any excessive zeal, cannot be implied in a situation of this nature, however much one would like to see it used. Something of that kind would require an express term. If, for instance, there were two procedures in a certain port whereby a vessel's documentation can be dealt with, one on paying an expedition fee or taking some special steps, and the other one the ordinary procedure, then it seems to me that the charterers would be under no obligation to use the speedier and unusual procedure. It therefore follows that in my view the term to be implied in this case is to the effect that the charterers were bound to act with reasonable dispatch and in accordance with the ordinary practice of the port of Calcutta in doing these acts which had to be done by them as consignees to enable the ship to become an arrived ship. In that connection the burden of proof, as in all cases of allegations of breach of contract, rests on the plaintiff, in this case the owners. But the arbitrators are of course entitled to draw inferences adverse to the charterers if there are unexplained periods of delay or inactivity."[45]

Legal readiness. The ship must be legally available, in that the necessary   **5–09** permits have been obtained and no laws or regulations prevent charterers having access to the ship for his work. She must usually have free pratique,[46] be free from any quarantine restrictions,[47] and be fully documented unless the parties have either dispersed with any of these requirements in their charterparty or waived them. The documentation may be stipulated by national or local laws, or established at the discretion of the authorities. The documents needed in most ports are the certificate of registry, bills of lading, charterparty, manifest, official log-book, ship's articles, list of dutiable stores, loadline and wireless installation inspection certificates, and in some ports a bill of health.[48]

The ship is not ready if failure to meet these requirements results in her not being available to the charterers to whatever extent they require her. Thus where a police permit, the absence of which would not delay loading, was not obtained, a ship could still be regarded as "ready."[49]

---

[41] For documentation generally see § 5–09 below.

[42] (1868) 4 Q.B. 127. See § 3–10 above.

[43] *Op. cit.* at p. 487. He also referred to *Watson* v. *Borner (H.) & Co. Ltd.* (1900) 5 Com.Cas 377 (C.A.) (see § 3–19 above) as to charterers' duty to act with reasonable dispatch in the ordinary course of business, and as showing that they did not have a duty to go out of their way to take special measures to help the other party.

[44] *Op. cit.* at p. 488.

[45] In this case he felt himself unable to discover whether that was the test which had been applied by the arbitrators (who had made an award in the form of a special case in favour of shipowners) or whether they had applied some other test. Nor could he see how the calculation as to the "wasted days" had been computed. He remitted the case to the arbitrators for them to reconsider the issues in the light of the implied terms which he had spelt out, and to make appropriate findings of fact against the background of that implied term.

[46] See § 5–11 below; but see § 5–12 as to notice of readiness in the absence of free pratique.

[47] See § 5–13 below.

[48] See free pratique at § 5–11 below. See also the references to customs papers and a "jetty challan" in *Sunbeam Shipping Co. Ltd.* v. *President of India* [1973] 1 Lloyd's Rep. 482. (*The Atlantic Sunbeam*) at § 4–53 above.

[49] See *Sociedad Financiera de Bienes Raices S.A.* v. *Agrimpex Hungarian Trading Co. for Agricultural Products* [1961] A.C. 135 (H.L.) at pp. 175, 180, 186 and 220. (*The Aello*).

5–10 *Custom House Entry*

There appears to have been very little litigation of a general nature in connection with the requirement that a ship should, at the time of the notice of readiness, have been entered at the custom house. In some Indian ports "prior to entry rules" entitle ships to be entered at the custom house prior to arrival, so that they can begin to discharge upon arrival, at which point they are presented for the purpose of final entry. There have been differing decisions in the English courts as to whether the preliminary entry constitutes entry at the custom house for the purpose of the beginning of laytime.[50]

5–11 *Free pratique.* Pratique has been defined[51] as: "Permission or licence granted by the port medical authorities to a vessel upon arrival from a foreign port after quarantine inspection,[52] to communicate with the shore"; and as: "A certificate issued in British ports by the medical officer of health upon declaration made by the captain or the ship's doctor on arrival at quarantine station that no member of the crew or passenger is suffering from any contagious disease. Also called certificate of health. Without this document the vessel cannot report at the custom house." The same authority has also defined radio pratique: "The permission granted by medical authorities to some of the larger passenger vessels whereby they may enter certain specified U.S. ports without stopping at quarantine. A request by radio giving all particulars regarding the sanitary conditions on board must be made from 12 to 24 hours before the expected arrival in port." A clean bill of health, once essential for free pratique, is now unusual except if the ship has called at ports where contagious diseases are prevalent.

5–12 The grant of free pratique, even where as in most cases there is no reference to it in the charterparty, is usually regarded as essential to the readi-

[50] See *N.Z. Michalos* v. *Food Corporation of India* [1983] 1 Lloyd's Rep. 409 (*The Apollon*) (" . . . before this notice [of readiness] can be given Vessel also having been entered at the Custom House . . . whether in berth or not") and *Food Corporation of India* v. *Carras Shipping Co. Ltd.* [1983] 2 Lloyd's Rep. 496 (*The Delian Leto*) (" . . . time to count from 24 hours after receipt of Master's written notice of discharge . . . vessel also having been entered at custom house . . . "). In the former case Bingham J. said, at p. 412: "Although the language of the charter-party did not expressly refer to entry under the 'prior to entry' rules, it was, in my judgment, both the correct and the commercial construction of this contract that the vessel was indeed entered at the time when entry was necessary and required in order to permit discharge." For the custom that at Indian ports prior entry can be lodged before a ship's arrival, and the prior entry manifest filed with customs, see a London arbitration, LMLN 90, April 14, 1983. But see also *President of India* v. *Davenport Marine Panama S.A.* [1987] 2 Lloyd's Rep. 365 (*The Albion*), where the words "entered at Customs House" and the Indian Customs Act 1962, ss.30 and 31, were construed, and "entered" held to mean final entry, not the filing of an entry inward application. In *President of India* v. *Diamantis Pateras (Hellas) Marine Enterprises Ltd.* [1987] 2 Lloyd's Rep. 649 (*The Nestor*) Leggatt J. followed *The Albion*. For other cases see § 6–23 below. For consideration of the 1962 Act and an Indian decision favouring shipowners see *Union of India* v. *Great Eastern Shipping Co. Ltd.* (*The Jag Leela*), LMLN 242, February 11, 1989.
[51] *International Maritime Dictionary*, by de Kerchove (2nd ed.). *La pratique* means, strictly speaking, practice or experience, and, by extension, circulation. Thus *libre pratique* or free pratique means that the ship and those on it can circulate freely within the port.
[52] See § 5–13 below.

ness of the ship[53]: but its absence has been held not to disentitle the master from giving notice of readiness.[54] In *Shipping Developments Corporation S.A.* v. *V/O Sojuzneftexport*[55] notice of readiness was given while the ship was at anchorage in the roads at Tuapse, but free pratique was not given until she got to her berth. It was argued that the notice of readiness was not valid. Distinguishing *The Austin Friars*,[56] Lord Denning M.R. said[57]:

> "I can understand that, if a ship is known to be infected by a disease such as to prevent her getting her pratique, she would not be ready to load or discharge. But if she has apparently a clean bill of health, such that there is no reason to fear delay, then even though she has not been given her pratique, she is entitled to give notice of readiness, and laytime will begin to run. That is supported by the case of the hatch covers, see *Armement Adolf Deppe* v. *John Robinson & Co. Ltd.*[58] . . . I hold therefore that the notice of readiness was good."

Its absence means that the ship is not ready enough to prevent charterers cancelling under the cancelling clause. In *Smith* v. *Dart & Son*[59] a charterparty for the carriage of oranges from Spain to England stated: " . . . should the steamer not be arrived at first loading port free of pratique and ready to load on or before the 15th of December next, charterers have the option of cancelling or confirming this charterparty." As a result of winds and heavy seas, and a stay at a port of refuge, the ship was not granted free pratique at the first loading port by that date and the charterers cancelled. The charterparty contained an exceptions clause which included the words " . . . all dangers of the seas . . . during the said voyage always excepted." It was held that the cancellation was justified. A. L. Smith L.J. said[60]:

> "The question is whether the exception in the charter as to dangers applies to the whole contract of voyage together with the option clause, or only to the contract of voyage. I am of opinion that it applies only to the contract of voyage."

He added[61] that the exceptions clause was put into the charterparty in favour of shipowners, whereas the option or cancellation clause was inserted in favour of charterers.

> "It is an absolute engagement that if he does not get there the charterers may cancel."

Quarantine. Where a quarantine[62] restriction is imposed, so that work is **5–13** prevented or charterers are prevented in some other way from obtaining

---

[53] Though the charterparty may dispense with the requirement, employing such words as "whether in free pratique or not." This phrase occurred in *Surrey Shipping Co. Ltd.* v. *Compagnie Continentale (France) S.A.* [1978] 2 Lloyd's Rep. 154 (*The Shackleford*) (see § 5–33 below), though the case did not turn on this point.

[54] The circumstances in each port have to be considered. Of one port Roskill L.J. said "In other words in Lourenco Marques—whatever else it may be in other parts of the world— the obtaining of free pratique is not what, if my memory serves, in some of the cases has been called 'an idle formality' "; *Logs & Timber Products (Singapore) Pte. Ltd.* v. *Keeley Granite (Pty.) Ltd.* [1978] 2 Lloyd's Rep. 1 (C.A.) at p. 3. See also § 6–39 below.

[55] [1971] 1 Lloyd's Rep. 506 (C.A.) (*The Delian Spirit*). See also § 4–20 above.

[56] (1894) 10 T.L.R. 633. See § 5–13 below.

[57] At p. 510.

[58] [1917] 2 K.B. 204 (C.A.). See § 5–02 above.

[59] (1884) 14 Q.B.D. 105 (C.A.).

[60] At p. 109.

[61] At p. 110.

[62] Quarantine is defined in the *Shorter Oxford English Dictionary* 3rd ed., revised (1956), as "A period (originally of forty days) during which persons who might spread a contagious disease (esp. travellers) are kept isolated; commonly, the period during which a ship, suspected of carrying contagion, is kept isolated on its arrival at a port. Hence, the fact or practice of isolating or of being isolated in this way; the place where infected or isolated ships are stationed."

access to her, the ship is not regarded as being ready. Thus in *White* v. *Winchester SS. Co.*[63] a ship was sent into quarantine on arrival from Port Said; the Scottish Court of Session, holding that laytime did not begin until she was ready, said that she was not ready while she was in quarantine.

The continuation of quarantine restrictions may also prevent a ship from being ready for the purpose of a cancellation clause. So, in *The Austin Friars*,[64] health regulations provided that no one could board or leave the ship until the health officer had visited her. The charterers had the right to cancel "if the steamer does not arrive at port of loading, and be ready to load on or before midnight of October 10." She arrived at 2300 hours that day but the health officer's visit took place on October 11. She was held not to have been ready for the purpose of the cancelling clause. It has been said[65] of this decision: "It was a very special case," and that it did not warrant the proposition that notice of readiness without free pratique was invalid.[66]

5–14   **Physical availability.** The cargo interests must be allowed physical control of the ship, including access to the holds, so far as that is necessary for them to perform their part of the joint operation of loading or discharging. This right is expressed by saying that their rights extend to the "full reach and burthen of the ship."

5–15   *"Full reach and burthen"; "Whole reach or burthen."* These archaic words[67] were discussed in *Weir* v. *Union SS. Co. Ltd.*[68] A charterparty for two or three round voyages provided for the ship "to be placed, with clear holds, at the disposal of the charterers, at the port of New York, they having the whole reach or burthen of the vessel, including passenger accommodation, if any." Sand ballast had been used to supplement the water ballast, and the charterers deducted hire equivalent to its cost. The shipowners argued that the taking of extra ballast would have constituted a breach of their obligation to give "the whole reach or burthen." The House of Lords held that the references to "clear holds" and to "the whole reach or burthen," taken together, amounted to an undertaking by the shipowners that the charterers should have the "full space of the vessel proper to be filled with cargo." The shipowners were responsible for the cost.

Lord Davey said[69]:

> " . . . if you find that the owners are responsible for the safe navigation of the ship they must have the right and the power to do whatever may be necessary to enable them to discharge that responsibility. In other words, you must read such expressions as 'with clear holds' or 'the whole reach or burthen of the vessel' as meaning the full space of the vessel proper to be filled with cargo. . . . I observe that the charterers are not obliged to ship a full cargo or any cargo, and it was therefore within the contemplation of the parties that the vessel might have to sail in ballast."

Shipowners cannot be in breach of their duty to offer the "whole reach

---

[63] (1886) 23 Sc.L.R. 342.
[64] (1894) 10 T.L.R. 633. Discussed in *Compania de Naviera ,Nedelka S.A.* v. *Tradax International S.A.* [1973] 2 Lloyd's Rep. 247 (C.A.) (*The Tres Flores*). See § 5–03.
[65] By Lord Denning M.R. in *Shipping Developments Corporation S.A.* v. *V/O Sojuzneftexport* [1971] 1 Lloyd's Rep. 506 at p. 510 (C.A.) (*The Delian Spirit*).
[66] See § 5–12 above.
[67] "Burthen" means burden, or carrying capacity.
[68] [1900] A.C. 525 (H.L.).
[69] At pp. 532–533.

or burthen" merely by providing proper ballast. In *Japy Frères & Co.* v. *R.W.J. Sutherland & Co.*[70] the Court of Appeal discussed a time charterparty provision that the whole reach and lawful burden were to be at charterers' disposal. One hundred tons of cement had been placed in the bottom of the *Thöger*[71] as permanent ballast, so that the deadweight capacity was reduced. The clause relating to deadweight stated: " . . . supposed to carry about 600 tons—but no guarantee given—deadweight on Board of Trade summer freeboard, inclusive of bunkers." There was a similar provision, including the words "without guarantee," in a voyage charterparty concluded by the time charterers. The court held that shipowners had discharged their obligations by giving to time charterers the whole reach and lawful burden of the ship as she in fact existed at the date of the time charterparty. As Bankes L.J. said[72]:

> " . . . the clause refers to the reach and burthen of the vessel as then existing. . . . I cannot agree that where such a permanent alteration as this has been made in the vessel the owner is committing a breach of his contract if he does not remove it. . . . "

Bunkers. So far as the holds are needed for bunkers, charterers cannot   **5–16**
complain that a ship is not ready because they cannot use that part of the ship, as they are not normally entitled to load in the space. In *Darling* v. *Raeburn*,[73] however, the shipowners had, at the first port of discharge, taken on board a large quantity of bunker coal intended for use upon a prospective voyage to be begun after the final discharge. As a result the ship had to be lightened before she could get over the bar at the next port of discharge. The charterers claimed the cost of lighterage. The Court of Appeal held that the shipowners were not entitled to load more bunker coal than was reasonably necessary for seaworthiness upon the voyage. The shipowners had to reimburse the charterers. Lord Alverstone C.J. said[74] that a limit must be placed upon the rights of a shipowner:

> " . . . he is not entitled to burden the undertaking or adventure of the charterer by using the space reserved to him for a purpose which has no connection whatever with the voyage on which the vessel is engaged."

Nevertheless shipowners may carry not only the bunkers needed for the voyage and a margin for contingencies but another margin "to provide for the fact, if it be a fact, that when the vessel gets to her ultimate destination she may be left there without coal, and not be able to get any."[75] But charterers can maintain that the ship is not ready if cargo from the previous voyage is on deck, unless it is intended to play a part in the new voyage. Thus in *London Traders Shipping Co. Ltd.* v. *General Mercantile Shipping Co. Ltd.*[76] a large quantity of coal from the previous voyage was stored on deck between the bulwarks and the raised coamings. It had been bought by the shipowners as bunker coal for the homeward voyage from South America. The Court of Appeal held that the ship was ready to load maize, though the charterers had given notice of cancellation under the cancelling

---

[70] (1921) 26 Com.Cas. 227.
[71] Described by Scrutton L.J. at p. 234 as "a small tramp steamer of considerable antiquity." Lloyd's Register for 1917 (the year of the charterparty) refers to the *Thöger*, 459 g.r.t., built in 1889 at Lübeck.
[72] At p. 232.
[73] [1907] 1 K.B. 846 (C.A.).
[74] At p. 850.
[75] *Per* Buckley L.J. at p. 852.
[76] (1914) 30 T.L.R. 493 (C.A.). See also § 5–07, n. 38.

clause, saying that the charterparty required the outward cargo to be discharged before the ship could be ready. As Phillimore L.J. pointed out[77]:

> " . . . the decision of the court must not be deemed to whittle down the general duty of the shipowner to have all outward cargo discharged when he presented his vessel to receive the homeward cargo, unless in special circumstances, or when dealing with a particular cargo the loading and unloading could continue simultaneously."

None of the coal was cargo at the cancelling date.

5–17   *Ballast.* Similarly part of the holds may be needed for ballast. If so the ship may still be regarded as being ready. In *Vaughan* v. *Campbell Heatley & Co.*[78] ballast was required to keep the ship upright but she was held to be ready to load.

5–18   **Giving a notice of readiness**[79]

Why notice is needed. Charterers must have notice of the readiness of the ship[80] at the loading port.[81] This requirement is one aspect of a common law rule that where the acts of one party are not within the knowledge of the other, then such obligations of the other as are dependent upon knowledge of these acts do not begin until he has or should have that knowledge. As Lord Abinger C.B. said in *Vyse* v. *Wakefield*[82]:

> " . . . where a party stipulates to do a certain thing in a certain specific event which may become known to him, or with which he can make himself acquainted, he is not entitled to any notice, unless he stipulates for it; but when it is to do a thing which lies within the peculiar knowledge of the opposite party, then notice ought to be given him."

So in the case of a charterparty the readiness of the ship at the loading port will usually be within the peculiar knowledge of shipowners, who must give notice to charterers.

Similarly in *Makin* v. *Watkinson*[83] it was held that notice must be given of a state of affairs which, upon its being known, would oblige the other party to act. Channell B., following *Vyse* v. *Wakefield*,[84] said[85]:

> " . . . we ought to import into the covenant the condition that he shall have notice of the want of repair before he can be called on under the covenant to make it good."

---

[77] At p. 494.

[78] (1885) 2 T.L.R. 33.

[79] For reaching the agreed destination, see § 4–01 above; for readiness, see § 5–01 above.

[80] The Charterparty Laytime Definitions 1980 (see Appendix to this book) state: " 'NOTICE OF READINESS'—means notice to the charterer, shipper, receiver or other person as required by the charterer that the ship has arrived at the port or berth as the case may be and is ready to load/discharge."

[81] For notice at a discharging port, see § 5–26 below. In *Transgrain Shipping B.V.* v. *Global Transporte Oceanico S.A.* (*The Mexico 1*) [1988] 2 Lloyd's Rep. 149, at p. 153, Evans J. said that in the case of loading, but not discharge, a term that notice was to be given was implied by law. This was "the position at common law", according to McNair J. in *Graigwen (Owners)* v. *Anglo-Canadian Shipping Co. Ltd.* [1955] 2 Lloyd's Rep. 260 at p. 266.

[82] (1840) 6 M. & W. 442 at p. 452; this concerned an insurance policy and the failure of the person who effected it for the assured to let him know that it would be null and void if the assured went outside Europe.

[83] (1870) L.R. 6 Ex. 25; the case concerned an action for non-repair of main walls, etc., against a lessor who had not received notice of want of repair.

[84] (1840) 6 M. & W. 442.

[85] As: "the Master shall give written notice of readiness."

It follows from these cases that where a person is otherwise aware of the state of affairs, the other party is not obliged to give notice. It is sufficient, unless there are specific words in the charterparty to the contrary,[86] that charterers be aware of the readiness of the ship. In addition, if the ship is ready, notice can be given before laytime is fixed to start.[87]

Owners' duty to inform   **5–19**

The decision in *Makin* v. *Watkinson*[88] was mentioned with approval in *Kawasaki Kisen Kabushiki Kaisha* v. *Bantham SS. Co. Ltd.*[89] No statement of the deadweight of a time chartered ship was delivered by shipowners to charterers. As a result the charterers were late in their payment of the first month's hire, the amount of which depended on the deadweight. The shipowners claimed the right to withdraw the ship. It was held that they were not entitled to do so. Branson J. said that the charterers were not obliged to make their own independent enquiries—by way of an application to the builders, for example—about the deadweight. He said[90]:

> "I think that there must be implied into the contract an obligation on the owners to inform the charterers of that which was within their knowledge and not within the knowledge of the charterers—namely, the correct amount of the deadweight capacity—in order to enable the charterers to put themselves into a position to discharge their obligation to pay the chartered hire."

Giving notice when in doubt   **5–20**

Sometimes a master is doubtful as to whether he may or should give notice. The following robust advice[91] may help him:

> "I have considerable sumpathy with the master in his predicament. It is a good working rule in such situations to give notice of readiness and to go on giving such notices in order that, when later the lawyers are brought in, no one shall be able to say: 'If only the master had given notice of readiness, laytime would have begun and the owners would now be able to claim demurrage' . . . "

It does not follow that one or more of those notices will be valid. Their validity will depend upon other circumstances, such as the readiness of the ship at those times[92] or the attitude of charterers.[93]

Form of notice. Charterers may have notice of the readiness of the ship   **5–21**
from shipowners, or be otherwise aware of her readiness. If they do not notice and are not otherwise aware of the readiness of the ship, laytime does not begin.

If notice is to be given in a particular form, the mere notice or awareness of readiness is not enough. Shipowners must adhere to the method prescribed; it might be a requirement, for example, that notice should be

---

[86] *Ibid.*
[87] But see also "Work Before Laytime," at § 4–46 above.
[88] (1870) L.R. 6 Ex. 25. See § 5–18 above.
[89] [1938] 1 K.B. 805.
[90] At p. 812.
[91] Given by Donaldson J. in *Zim Israel Navigation Co. Ltd.* v. *Tradax Export S.A.* [1970] 2 Lloyd's Rep. 409 at p. 411 (*The Timna*). For the same judge on rejection of notices, see § 5–35 below.
[92] See §§ 5–01–5–17 above.
[93] See § 5–22 below.

given in office hours[94] or in writing.[95] Failure to adopt the prescribed method will usually prevent time from beginning. In *Gordon* v. *Powis*[96] the charterparty provided: "Captain or owners to telegraph advising probable arrival, and at least eight clear days' notice shall be given previous to requiring cargo." It was held that for the master to have telegraphed that he had left Philadelphia, the last port on the previous voyage, for Quebec, did not amount to a notice. Day J. said[97] of the telegraphic notice of departure:

> "That is something entirely distinct from the telegraphic notice as to probable arrival and that is not a notice requiring cargo. It is a provision precedent that such notice should be given, and it is in substitution of the 24 hours' notice."

Absence of notice may prevent time from running. In *Stanton* v. *Austin*[98] the shipowners alleged failure to load under a charterparty for the carriage of coals from Sunderland to Calcutta. The ship was to proceed direct to the South Dock, Sunderland, and there load, in the usual and customary manner, at any colliery they named. The charterers pleaded that they had no notice of the ship having proceeded to and arrived at the South Dock, and being ready to receive cargo. It was held that this was a good defence, though the shipowners argued that it was the duty of the charterers to watch for the ship, and that their undertaking to load was absolute. So also in *Fairbridge* v. *Pace*,[99] where the ship was entered at the custom house but no notice of readiness was given to the charterers, it was held that the charterers were not liable for failure to provide a cargo. Rolfe B. said[1]:

> "The question is, did the captain, or did he not, fail to get a cargo by reason of the default of the defendant? . . . Of the arrival of the ship the agents of the defendant may have been bound to take notice; but of the time at which the [inward] cargo was discharged they could know nothing, and they were therefore, entitled to notice of that fact from the captain."

In the absence of a notice provision does time begin if the shipowners give no notice and the charterers should be, but are not, aware of the readiness of the ship? The shipowners argued this in *Stanton* v. *Austin*[2] but the point was not decided by the court.

Of *Stanton* v. *Austin* Scrutton L.J. said in *A/B Nordiska Lloyd* v. *J. Brownlie & Co. (Hull) Ltd.*[3]:

> "I can quite well see that in charters worded in different ways at least two questions of importance may arise. One is whether it is enough that the charterer knows of the presence of the ship from other circumstances although he has no notice from the shipowner.

---

[94] In *Pacific Carriers Corporation* v. *Tradax Export S.A.* [1971] 2 Lloyd's Rep. 460 (*The North King*), notice of readiness was given on a holiday. See also § 8–10 below, at n. 40.

[95] The Charterparty Laytime Definitions 1980 (see Appendix to this book) state: "24. 'IN WRITING'—means, in relation to a notice of readiness, a notice visibly expressed in any mode of reproducing words and includes cable, telegram and telex." In a London arbitration (LMLN 151, August 15, 1985) a tribunal was divided, where notice was cabled, as to whether some time ought to be allowed for transmission time. The majority decided that the use of the word "cable" meant that landlines were used, and that three hours represented an appropriate delay between sending and receiving.

[96] (1892) 8 T.L.R. 397.

[97] At p. 397.

[98] (1872) L.R. 7 C.P. 651.

[99] (1844) 1 C. & K. 317.

[1] At p. 318.

[2] (1872) L.R. 7 C.P. 651.

[3] (1925) 30 Com.Cas 307 at p. 313. See § 5–04 and the meanings of "readiness."

That question, in my view, is not decided by *Stanton* v. *Austin and Others*[4] and remains open for decision in some other case which raises the question on a charter which does not exclude the point; and I think another question may arise on charters worded differently from this, whether generally upon the cancelling clause the owner ought to tender the ship to the charterer.''

Charterers aware of readiness. A question can arise as to whether time **5–22** begins where there is no provision for written notice and charterers (a) are aware; or (b) should be, but are not, aware of the readiness of the ship. It seems that if they are aware of her readiness (the contingency envisaged by Scrutton L.J. in the *A/B Nordiska Lloyd* case[5]) the courts will hold this to be sufficient to enable laytime to begin.

So in *Franco-British SS. Co.* v. *Watson & Youell*[6] a charterparty provided for the loading of wheat and/or grain and/or merchandise at Galatz. Written notice of readiness was given at the charterers' office at a nearby port[7] on a Saturday before a Bank Holiday Monday. Orders to go to Galatz were given on Wednesday, and the ship waited there a further six days before being ordered to a dock. No written notice was given at Galatz but the charterers, who were also the ship's agents, were aware of the arrival and the readiness to load on the Thursday. Loading time was to begin "from the morning after the ship's arrival and report at the Customs, she being then in free pratique and ready to load in all her holds, and notice of readiness given. . . . " It was held that verbal notice was enough. Horridge J. said[8]:

"There is no request that notice in writing should be given and, therefore, verbal notice would be sufficient. . . . When she came to Galatz the captain would have to see the charterers, as the ship's agents, with reference to passing her through the Custom House and other matters, and under these circumstances it seems to me impossible to say there was not material on which the umpire could find that the charterers had notice of readiness of the ship to load. . . . I cannot say time did not run because the master did not go up into the office and say formally: 'I give you notice my ship is ready to load.' "

It seems that even where charterers are not also the ship's agents it could also be successfully maintained, subject to proof, that they had notice of readiness.

Charterers' agents may be uncertain as to whether the notice is valid. Of that uncertainty it has been said[9]:

"Just as it is a good working rule for masters, when in doubt, to give notices of readiness, it is an equally good working rule for charterers' agents to reject them if there is any conceivable doubt as to their validity."

So also a judge has said[10]:

" . . . both parties acted on the basis that the vessel was an arrived ship. The master gave notice of readiness to load, and that was accepted without question by the officials acting on behalf of the charterers. That is a not unimportant point. . . . "

---

[4] (1872) L.R. 7 C.P. 651.
[5] See § 5–21 above.
[6] (1921) 9 Ll.L.Rep. 282.
[7] Braila, where inward cargo was being discharged.
[8] At p. 284.
[9] By Donaldson J. in *Zim Israel Navigation Co. Ltd.* v. *Tradax Export S.A.* [1970] 2 Lloyd's Rep. 409 at p. 411 (*The Timna*). For the same judge on the giving of notice, see § 5–20 above.
[10] Sir Gordon Willmer in *Shipping Developments Corporation S.A.* v. *V/O Sojuzneftexport* [1971] 1 Lloyd's Rep. 506 at p. 512 (C.A.) (*The Delian Spirit*).

5–23   The charterparty will usually fix a date before which laytime cannot begin, combining this with a stipulation as to the cancelling date, in such terms as "Laydays/cancelling March 15/25." Where notice is given before that date the notice period starts to run at once. If it has expired by the date in question laytime begins on that date. If only part of the period has elapsed by then, laytime begins as soon as the rest of the period has been exhausted. Though there appears to be no English authority as to this, it appears that it is the general practice in the shipping industry to calculate laytime on this basis. In *Frota Oceanica Brasileira, S.A.* v. *Continental Ore Corporation,*[11] a New York arbitration, the charterparty provided for time to count from 8 a.m. on the day after the ship was reported and in free pratique, but laytime was not to begin before November 15, 1970. At 2400 hours on November 11 the ship arrived at her loading port, was granted free pratique and tendered notice of readiness. The shipowners, allowing for the fact that November 15 was a Sunday, said that laytime began at 8 a.m. on November 16. The charterers contended that notice could not properly be given until November 16 (as it could not be given on the Sunday), so that laytime began at 8 a.m. on November 17. The tribunal supported the shipowners. Another New York arbitration tribunal reached the same conclusion in *Trave Schiffahrts G.m.b.H. K.G.* v. *Amoco Transport Co.*[12] So also in *Burmah Oil Tankers Ltd.* v. *Marc Rich & Co. Inc.,*[13] involving an Exxonvoy 1969 charterparty, a ship was to load crude oil at Kharg Island with February 12 as the earliest date for loading. She arrived at the anchorage and gave notice of readiness at 0100 hours on February 10, berthing at 0720 hours on February 15. The arbitrators supported the shipowners' contention that laytime began at 0001 hours on February 12. The six-hour period after the notice of readiness had already elapsed.[14]

5–24   *Notice only at first loading port*

Notice of readiness is needed at a sole loading port, even in the absence of an express stipulation to that effect,[15] although, as we have seen,[16] awareness by the charterers of readiness is sufficient to constitute notice to them. Notice is not needed, however, at later loading ports, unless the charterparty requires it.[17] The reason for this rule is that if there has been a call at the first loading port, charterers are aware that the ship has begun to

---

[11] [1973] A.M.C. 2315 (*The Frotanorte*).

[12] Society of Maritime Arbitrators, Award No. 1288 (1978) (*The Schleswig-Holstein*).

[13] Society of Maritime Arbitrators, Award No. 1506 (1981) (*The Atlantic Empress*).

[14] For the six hours' notice period see also § 6–43A below. A London panel of arbitrators (LMLN 103, October 13, 1983) decided that a proper notice can be given before the time at which laytime may begin. The notes for the fixture stated "lay days 22/30 July." The Gencon form has no printed clauses relating to the beginning of laytime. In the charterparty, as finally drawn up, the ship was described in clause 1 as "expected ready to load under this charter about 22 July 1980." Cl. 6 gave the cancelling date as July 30. Notice of readiness was given on July 21. The arbitrators decided that July 22 must be taken as the date at which lay days could begin. They considered that those who drafted the Gencon form must have thought that the statement as to the date of expected readiness in cl. 1 was sufficient for that purpose. However, a valid notice could be given before that date. The notice was therefore valid, and laytime began on July 22.

[15] For the reasons set out in § 5–18 above.

[16] See § 5–20 above.

[17] As to notice of readiness not being needed when the ship is already on demurrage see *Pagnan & Fratelli* v. *Tradax Export S.A.* [1969] 2 Lloyd's Rep. 150 (concerning a discharging port) and see § 10–49 below.

fulfil her obligations. They must be presumed to be following her course and to be making loading preparations accordingly. Notice of readiness was held not to be necessary at second and third loading ports in *Burnett.* v. *Olivier & Co., Ltd.*[18] A charterparty provided for a voyage from three eastern Mediterranean ports to the United Kingdom. The laytime clause stated: "Lay days to commence on the day following notice of readiness to load. . . . " The main issue was whether notice of readiness was necessary at each port of loading. It was held that it was only necessary at the first port. Branson J. said[19]:

> "It seems to me that it is not by any means clear that had the question been asked when the charterparty was being agreed, 'Are we to have a notice at every port?' the ship-owners would have said, 'Oh, yes, of course,' because the giving of notice involves an extra day's delay for the ship, and once the ship has been tendered and notice of readiness given she is under the orders of the charterers. That being so, it seems to me, if I have to assume what is the business of the matter, that the charterers should know near enough without a fresh notice of readiness at what time they are to have their cargo ready at the port to which they have ordered the ship to go."

The judge therefore treated the clause as being, as he said,[20] a "provision for only one notice of readiness."

Notice at later loading ports **5–25**

It does not follow from the decision in the *Burnett* case[21] that notice of readiness will never be necessary at ports other than the first loading port. It is always open to the parties, by apt words such as "lay days *at each loading port* to commence on the day following notice of readiness to load" to agree that there shall be notice at each loading port. In the absence of such words the courts will apparently take the view that business efficiency requires notice only at the first port.

Notice not usually needed at discharging port **5–26**

Notice to receivers. If notice of readiness to discharge is to be given to the receivers of cargo, the charterparty or bill of lading must expressly so provide; alternatively there must be a custom to this effect. In the absence of such provision or custom shipowners are not obliged to give notice of readiness. Receivers must look for the ship.[22] Even an express provision for a notice period may relate only to cases where laytime has not expired; demurrage would run from the moment of the ship's arrival at the discharging port.[23]

The principle applies both between shipowners and bill of lading holders and between shipowners and charterers. Thus Brett L.J. in *Nelson* v. *Dahl*[24]:

> "The right of the shipowner is that the liability of the charterer as to his part of the joint act of unloading should accrue as soon as the ship is in the place named as that at which the carrying voyage is to end; and the ship is ready so far as she is concerned to

---

[18] (1934) 48 Ll.L.Rep. 238.
[19] At p. 240.
[20] *Ibid.*
[21] (1934) 48 Ll.L.Rep. 238; see § 5–25.
[22] *Harman* v. *Clarke* (1815) 4 Camp. 159; *Harman* v. *Mant* (1815) 4 Camp. 161; *Houlder* v. *General S.N. Co.* (1862) 3 F. & F. 170.
[23] *Pagnan & Fratelli* v. *Tradax Export S.A.* [1969] 2 Lloyd's Rep. 150.
[24] (1879) 12 Ch.D. 568 at p. 583.

unload. The shipowner, however, is not bound to give notice that his ship is so arrived and is so ready.''

A bill of lading may state that a particular person is ''to be notified.'' So in *E. Clemens Horst Co.* v. *Norfolk & North American Steam Shipping Co. Ltd.*[25] through bills of lading stated: ''Party to be notified; E. Clemens Horst.'' The bills were issued at San Francisco for the carriage of hops by rail to Philadelphia and thence by ship to London. The shipowners did not advise the ''Party to be notified'' of the name of the ship or of the arrival of the hops and delivery was delayed. The receivers brought an action for damages against the shipowners, as a result of a fall in the market price of hops. The shipowners said that they were under no duty to notify, and that the phrase indicated a business practice, not an obligation.

The High Court held that the receivers were entitled to damages. Kennedy J. said[26]:

> ''I am of opinion that under the through bill of lading there was a contractual obligation on the defendants to give the notification to the plaintiffs. Notification properly sent by post would, I think have been sufficient, even if the letter, although posted to the plaintiffs, did not arrive. But the defendants have not proved that they posted a letter of notification to the plaintiffs.''

Though receivers must look for the ship, shipowners must not make it difficult or impossible for them so to do. In *Harman* v. *Clarke*[27] a ship was entered at the custom house as *Die Treue* instead of *The Treue*. It was held that this was insufficient to mislead reasonably diligent receivers, but that where a description was misleading, the receivers would be excused for their unawareness of the readiness of the ship.

5–27   *Whether notice must be correct*
A notice of readiness is a notice to charterers of certain facts, in whatever form may have been prescribed. These facts are the arrival of the ship at her contractual destination,[28] or ''so near thereto as she can safely get,'' and her readiness to load or to discharge.[29] Sometimes notice of readiness is given prematurely, when, for example, the ship is not fully ready to load, or, on discharging, the cargo is inaccessible, or when one of the requirements as to the beginning of laytime has not been satisfied.[30] The notice is not premature if only mere routine formalities remain to be completed, however.[31] A clause may read: ''Lay days at first loading port to commence twenty-four hours, Sundays and holidays excepted, after receipt by charterers or their agents of master's written notice during ordinary working hours, that steamer is entered at the Custom House and in all respects ready to load.'' In that case does the notice have to be given again when it can be a true notice, or does it become valid by virtue of the changing situation? One judge[32] has said: ''The authorities on that point are perhaps a little sparse.'' Certain general conclusions on this subject are set out

[25] (1906) 11 Com.Cas. 141.
[26] At p. 146.
[27] (1815) 4 Camp. 159.
[28] See § 4–02 above.
[29] For readiness to load, see § 5–01 above.
[30] As in *Surrey Shipping Co. Ltd.* v. *Compagnie Continentale (France) S.A.* [1978] 2 Lloyd's Rep. 154 (*The Shackleford*); see § 5–33 below.
[31] See § 5–03 above.
[32] Staughton J. in *Gerani Compania Naviera S.A.* v. *General Organisation for Supply Goods (The Demosthenes V) (No. 1)* [1982] 1 Lloyd's Rep. 275, at p. 280. See § 5–04 above.

below.[33] The answer to the question depends generally upon whether charterers rejected or did not accept the notice,[34] accepted it,[35] reserved their position, waived the requirement, or were estopped from asserting their rights. As a matter of practical policy, if there is any doubt it is desirable to give notice early and to go on giving notice.[36]

In *Graigwen (Owners)* v. *Anglo-Canadian Shipping Co. Ltd.*[37] a charterparty provided for the carriage of lumber from "six . . . berths British Columbia range . . . Victoria and/or Vancouver and/or New Westminster to be first port or ports if required by charterers. . . . " It stipulated: "Lay days at first loading port to commence twenty-four hours . . . after receipt by charterers or their agents of master's written notice during ordinary working hours, that steamer is entered at the Custom House and in all respects ready to load. Charterers have the privilege of using the twenty-four hours' notice period, same not to be counted as lay days." McNair J., holding that, as shipowners contended, it was a port charterparty, said[38]:

> "Clearly, although the clause only relates the commencement of the lay days to the giving of notice, the facts stated in the notice, namely, the entry at Customs House and readiness, must also be true at the time when the notice is given."

This passage must mean that where the facts are not true when written notice is given, then the period of 24 hours cannot begin to run. So also in *N.V. Bodewes Scheepswerven and N.V. Kuva* v. *Highways Construction Ltd.*[39] Judge Block said:

> " . . . there is a twenty-four hour delay . . . from the moment when the master can go ashore and tell the agents or the receivers at the discharging port that his steamer is actually ready for loading or unloading . . . "

The notice provision in *Government of Ceylon* v. *Société Franco-Tunisienne d'Armement-Tunis*[40] was: "Time to commence at 2 p.m. if notice of readiness to discharge is given before noon, and at 8 a.m. next working day if notice given during office hours after noon." The *Massalia* had been chartered to go "to Colombo (one good and safe berth)." Notice of readiness to discharge was given at 0900 hours on the day of her arrival in the outer anchorage of the port of Colombo. A berth became available, and discharging began, six days later. Owing to the stowing above the flour of another cargo with which the charterers were not concerned, but which the shipowners had liberty to carry, the whole of the flour was not freely accessible for discharging until 0400 hours three days later.[40a] Discharge was completed after six more days, or 15 days after arrival. But for the **5–28**

---

[33] At § 5–34.

[34] See *Compania de Naviera Nedelka S.A.* v. *Tradax Internacional S.A.* [1973] 2 Lloyd's Rep. 247 (C.A.) (*The Tres Flores*) (§ 5–03 above).

[35] As in *Sofial S.A.* v. *Ove Skou Rederi A/S* [1976] 2 Lloyd's Rep. 205 (*The Helle Skou*); see § 5–35 below.

[36] See Donaldson J. in *Zim Israel Navigation Co. Ltd.* v. *Tradax Export S.A.* [1970] 2 Lloyd's Rep. 409 at p. 411, (*The Timna*) cited in § 5–20 above. See also § 5–35 below.

[37] [1955] 2 Lloyd's Rep. 260.

[38] At p. 266.

[39] [1966] 1 Lloyd's Rep. 402 at p. 406 (*The Jan Herman*). See § 6–40 below. The case was heard in the Mayor's and City of London Court.

[40] [1962] 2 Q.B. 416 (*The Massalia*).

[40a] "It is possible, though unclear from the reports, that the charterers had already began to discharge those parts of the flour cargo which could be reached before the whole of the cargo became inaccessible and the notice took effect": Evans J. in *Transgrain Shipping B.V.* v. *Global Transporte Oceanico S.A.* (*The Mexico 1*) [1988] 2 Lloyd's Rep. 149, at p. 154.

unavailability of a berth the *Massalia* would have been discharged nearly six days earlier. The shipowners invoked the "time lost in waiting" clause.

The High Court held that, because notice of readiness had been given on the day of arrival, no further notice was needed when all the flour became freely accessible. Laytime therefore began then, having been in suspension until readiness. It was not necessary to repeat the notice, or to treat the notice as if it had not been given until 0400 hours on the day of readiness, with time beginning at 1400 hours. The shipowners, however, had, in calculating the time lost in waiting for a berth, begun at 1400 hours and not on 0900 hours on the day of arrival, so that in a different form they had allowed the notice period to apply. Counsel for shipowners said[41] of the notice of readiness: "It was then [*i.e.* on the day of arrival] inchoate but took effect as soon as the condition as to readiness was fulfilled." Diplock J. noted[42] the concession made by the shipowners, and said that he therefore did not have to decide whether the time waiting for a berth started at that later hour. He then considered whether on the day of readiness laytime began at 1400 hours. He held that it began at 0400 hours, which was the moment of readiness, and said:

> "I think there is a good deal to be said for either view on this interesting problem of arithmetic. There is no authority on it that I know of; certainly no one has drawn my attention to it. There is authority[42a] that, when notice of readiness is given (as this one was) before the vessel was in fact ready, no further notice of readiness is required. On the whole, I see no reason why I should treat the position as if a further notice of readiness had been given at 0400 hours on the Saturday. There was a notice of readiness already given. It could not take effect until the vessel was in fact ready for discharge, and, as the charterers were in fact discharging the cargo at the other hatches at that time, and so needed no notice to get ready, I do not think I shall be doing any substantial injustice if I take the view, which *prima facie* I think would be the correct one here, namely, that lay time started at 0400 hours . . . "[43]

5–29   One view of the decision in the *Graigwen* case[44] is that a written notice must be repeated when the ship becomes fully ready; but there can be situations in which an invalid notice is regarded as becoming effective at the moment of true readiness. This is borne out by the *Massalia* case,[45] where notice was treated as having taken effect as soon as the conditions of readiness were fulfilled. It seems, however, that there may have to be special circumstances. In a later case[45a] a judge set out the facts in *The Massalia* and said that the charterers had waived or been estopped from asserting the full extent of their rights under the notice clause.

A second conclusion which could have been drawn from *Graigwen* was that until a notice becomes effective any prescribed period of delay, if specified in the charterparty as due to run from the notice of readiness, cannot begin to run. Its expiry would thus be a second pre-condition (the

---

[41] At p. 423.

[42] At p. 427.

[42a] Not cited by Diplock J.; and not traced: see Donaldson J. in *Christensen* v. *Hindustan Steel Ltd.* [1971] 1 Lloyd's Rep. 395, at p. 399 and Evans J. in *Transgrain Shipping B.V.* v. *Global Transporte Oceanico S.A.* (*The Mexico 1*) [1988] 2 Lloyd's Rep. 149, at p. 154. The charterers in the latter case said (*ibid* at p. 152) that this passage in the judgement of Diplock J. was wrong. See also Roskill L.J. at n. 59 below.

[43] As to when notice can be given, see §§ 5–18 and 5–27 above.

[44] [1955] 2 Lloyd's Rep. 260. See § 5–27 above.

[45] [1962] 2 Q.B. 416. See § 5–28 above.

[45a] *Transgrain Shipping B.V.* v. *Global Transporte Oceanico S.A.* (*The Mexico 1*) [1988] 2 Lloyd's Rep. 149, per Evans J., at p. 155.

first being an effective notice of readiness) of the beginning of laytime. This is so irrespective of the length of the period between the actual and effective times of the notice of readiness.

This conclusion seemed as a result of the *Massalia* decision to be less justified than had previously been thought, though the facts there were special.[46] If the conclusion had been strictly applied laytime would have begun at 1400 hours on the day of readiness, since the notice became effective at 0400 hours on that day. It was held to have begun at 0400 hours, apparently as a result of (a) the shipowners' concession in respect of the "time lost in waiting," allowing it to begin at 1400 hours and not 0900 hours on the day of arrival (of this it may be said that this is a different category of "time," and that it is doubtful whether a concession as to that time could alter a subsequent laytime calculation); and (b) the view formed by the court that the delay period was not required as the charterers "needed no notice to get ready." One may compare this with situations in which the awareness of charterers that the ship is available has excused shipowners from giving notice of readiness,[47] though not where there is an express stipulation for notice to be given.[48]

The notice given on behalf of shipowners may itself concede that the ship **5–30** is not yet ready, and, furthermore, that a future time named therein is one at which she is expected to be ready.

Thus in *Christensen* v. *Hindustan Steel Ltd.*[49] a charterparty on the Gencon form for a voyage from Vizagapatam to Odessa stated: "5. Time to commence at twenty-four hours after 1 p.m. if notice of readiness to load is given before noon at twenty-four hours after 8 a.m. next working day if notice given during office hours after noon." Clause 6 dealt with the commencement of discharging laytime but was in the unmodified Gencon form and so did not have inserted, at two places, as in the loading clause, the words: "twenty-four hours after." There were two more relevant clauses:

> "24. The notice of readiness at the port of loading and discharging to be served during normal office hours. Time shall not count between noon on Saturday and 8 a.m. on Monday, nor between noon on the last working day preceding a legal holiday and/or port Labour Holiday and 8 a.m. on the first working day thereafter even if used."
> "33. The Master is to give Charterers' Agents at Vizagapatam three days and twenty-four hours' notice of vessel's readiness to load."

The ship discharged at Vizagapatam under another charterparty between October 26 and 28; at 0900 hours on the 28th (a Saturday) the master gave a notice of readiness that she would be in all respects ready to

---

[46] As was said in *Christensen* v. *Hindustan Steel Ltd.* [1971] 1 Lloyd's Rep. 395, by Donaldson J. at p. 399: " . . . this decision [in the Government of Ceylon case] turned upon very special facts and does not cast doubt upon the general rule that a notice of readiness is wholly ineffective if, subject to minimal qualfications, the vessel is not ready to discharge at the time at which it is given." As to the question of minimal qualifications see *Companian de Noviera Nedelka* v. *Tradax International S.A.* [1973] 2 Lloyd's Rep. 247 (C.A.) (*The Tres Flores*) and § 5–03 above.
[47] *Burnett SS. Co. Ltd.* v. *Olivier & Co. Ltd.* (1934) 48 Ll.L.Rep. 238. See § 5–24 above.
[48] "It is difficult to see how the view which Mr. Justice Diplock formed that 'no fresh notice was necessary' should lead to the conclusion that he reached that 'no notice period was to run' "; this was the comment of Staughton J. in *Gerani Compania Naviera S.A.* v. *General Organisation for Supply Goods (The Demosthenes V) (No. 1)* [1982] 1 Lloyd's Rep. 275, at p. 280. See also §§ 5–03 above and 5–32 below.
[49] [1971] 1 Lloyd's Rep. 395.

receive cargo at 0000 hours on Sunday the 29th. The charterers argued that clauses 5 and 33 called for two notices of anticipated readiness followed by one notice of actual readiness so that there was an additional postponement of the beginning of laytime for 24 hours after the final notice. They also argued that as notice of readiness for the purpose of clause 5 had to be served during office hours, it was to be treated as being effective at 0800 hours on the Monday, with 24 hours then running from 1300 hours that day until 1300 hours on Tuesday the 31st. The holiday provisions then postponed the beginning of laytime until 0800 hours on Thursday the 2nd.

5–31   Donaldson J., assuming that the arbitrators had found that the ship was ready at 0000 hours on the Sunday, agreed[50] with the shipowners that Clause 5 called "for the same twenty-four hours" notice of anticipated readiness as was required by Clause 33 with time to commence 24 hours later than it would have done if the clause [Clause 5] had not been modified and a notice of actual readiness had been called for." Notice of readiness was given on Saturday before noon so that laytime would have begun 24 hours after 1300 hours on Sunday, but for the exclusions in clause 24, so that it began at 0800 hours on Monday the 30th. He said[51]:

> "The owners . . . can point with force to the fact that when the charter-party was concluded on October 21, 1967, the vessel was already at Vizagapatam to the knowledge of the charterers (see line 5)[52] and that accordingly one would expect less rather than more notice than usual. In these circumstances, I have no real doubt that the owners' construction is to be preferred. It is true that the notice gave fifteen and not twenty-four hours of anticipated readiness to load, but this is no detriment to the charterers since laytime would have begun at exactly the same time if the master had given notice anticipating readiness at 0900 hours on October 29. It would have been otherwise if the master had given notice of a time more than twenty-four hours ahead."

5–32   Referring to the *Christensen* case,[53] Staughton J. said in *Gerani Compania Naviera S.A.* v. *General Organisation for Supply Goods*[54]: "There the charterparty provided for a notice of readiness and the master tendered a notice stating that the vessel would be ready at a point in the future, not that she was then ready . . . so it was, on its face, not a notice of readiness." In the *Gerani* case the Judge had concluded that there had been a valid notice of readiness,[55] so that it was not necessary to decide whether the notice was valid when given. The shipowners had contended that a fresh notice must be given. The Judge referred also to the *Government of Ceylon* case[56] and to *Compania de Naviera Nedelka S.A.* v. *Tradax Internacional S.A.*,[57] where Roskill L.J. had said[58]: "Notice of readiness that the ship will be ready to load at some future time is a bad notice."[59]

---

[50] *Ibid.* at p. 400.
[51] *Op. cit.* at p. 400.
[52] Line 5 of the charterparty mentioned this fact.
[53] [1971] 1 Lloyd's Rep. 395; see § 5–30 above.
[54] [1982] 1 Lloyd's Rep. 275, at p. 280 (*The Demosthenes V (No. 1)*). See also § 5–04 above.
[55] See § 5–04 above.
[56] [1962] 2 Q.B. 416 (*The Massalia*); see § 5–29 above, at n. 48.
[57] [1973] 2 Lloyd's Rep. 247 (C.A.) (*The Tres Flores*). See § 5–03 above.
[58] *Ibid.* at p. 275.
[59] Roskill L.J. had continued " . . . it was so held in *Aktiebolaget Nordiska Lloyd* v. *J. Brownlie & Co. (Hull) Ltd.* ((1925) 30 Com.Cas. 307; [see § 5–06 above] per Atkin L.J., at page 315. The contrary statement by Diplock J. in *Ceylon Government* v. *Société Franco-Tunisienne D'Armement—Tunis* [1962] 2 Q.B. 416, 428, must, I think, with all respect to the Judge, be taken to have been made *per incuriam*."

Staughton J. concluded[60]: "The point did not actually arise in the *Compania Nedelka* case because there was no argument there—as far as I can see—as to whether an old notice became validated when the ship was ready, or whether a fresh notice had to be given. It seems to me by no means easy to decide between those authorities, and I do not do so. But I just say this. I would require a good deal of persuading to reach the view that the charterers, who had had notice of this ship's arrival, were entitled to allow her to sit there for a period of (as it turned out) just over two weeks, and not pay demurrage or bear the cost of the time that had elapsed, merely on the ground that they had not received notice from the shipowners that another three vacuators could be obtained within a matter of hours."[61]

Waiving a requirement   **5–33**
The receivers may, on behalf of the charterers, waive one of the requirements for the beginning of laytime. In *Surrey Shipping Co. Ltd.* v. *Compagnie Continentale (France) S.A.*[62] a charterparty on the Baltimore Form C, for the carriage of grain from the U.S. Gulf to Constanza, stated:

> "Notification of the vessel's readiness at port of discharge must be delivered . . . at or before 4 p.m. . . . on official working days, vessel also having been entered at the Custom House and the laydays will then commence at 8 a.m. on the next business day, whether in berth or not, whether in port or not,[63] whether in free pratique or not."

The ship arrived at Constanza roads, anchoring at the usual waiting anchorage, and immediately giving notice of readiness, which the receivers accepted, their agents stating also a few days later:

> "Your time should count as per ch/party terms from arrival"

Congestion prevented the ship from proceeding to a discharging berth. She remained at the anchorage for six weeks, when she went to a berth for bunkers and obtained free pratique and customs clearance. She then moved to a lay-by berth for three days, and thereafter went to her discharging berth. The Court of Appeal found in favour of the shipowners' contention that laytime began at 8 a.m. on the next business day after arrival. Sir David Cairns said[64]:

> "The receivers must have authority to make some commercial decisions on behalf of charterers. They must be able to decide whether the vessel and its equipment are in a state of readiness to begin discharge of the cargo. As a matter of commercial practicality I consider that they must have implied authority to waive a condition as to the commencement of laytime . . . I think it is to be assumed that the receivers would know that customs entry could not be obtained at Constanza until after berthing . . . If the notice of readiness was accepted with ignorance of what the effect would be under the charterparty I do not consider the charterers can take advantage of that ignorance."[65]

---

[60] *Op. cit.* at p. 281.
[61] For the charterparty clauses see § 5–04 above. The notice of readiness, later held to be valid, was given on May 27. The first three vacuators were put on board on May 29 and three more were put on board on June 15.
[62] [1978] 2 Lloyd's Rep. 154 (*The Shackleford*). See also § 8–47 below.
[63] For this infrequently used expression, see § 6–26 below.
[64] *Ibid.* at pp. 159–160.
[65] For an arbitration in which the *Surrey Shipping* case was distinguished, there being no evidence that shipowners were prejudiced, see LMLN 206, September 26, 1987.

5–33A   The circumstances in which an invalid notice might become a valid notice were discussed in *Transgrain Shipping B.V.* v. *Global Transporte Oceanico S.A.*[65a] There were two charterparties for the same ship, and to the same charterers, for the carriage of 5,000 m.t. of maize and about 500 m.t. of beans, respectively, from Argentina to Angola. Parts of a completion cargo overstowed the maize and the beans. The ship went to other discharging ports and then to Luanda, giving notice of readiness on January 25. The maize, then inaccessible, became accessible on February 6. The beans became accessible on February 19, on which day discharge of both cargoes began. Evans J. said: (1) charterers were "entitled to insist that the laytime cannot begin until the notice has been given,"[65b] but if they waived that right laytime would begin; (2) "the circumstances in which no further notice is required are limited to those where there are further dealings between the parties, after the invalid notice is given, which result in the charterers' losing the right to insist that a valid notice should have been served"[65c]; (3) in the absence of special factors (facts which established that the obligation was varied by agreement, or was waived in whole or in part, or that charterers could not insist upon compliance or precise compliance) a master must give a further notice of readiness because "there is nothing to prevent the charterers from relying upon the contractual requirement that notice must be given before the laytime can begin, and an invalid notice is a nullity"[65d]; that was not a rule of law but the requirement of the clause on its sensible and true construction; (4) the notice became effective when the maize became accessible for discharge, on February 6, and laytime began at 0800 hours on February 7.

Evans J., discussing *The Massalia*, emphasised the special nature of its facts, pointing out that a single notice was given to the charterparty cargo and any other cargo; it was neither accepted nor expressly rejected; other cargo was discharged before the charterparty cargo became fully accessible; no substantial injustice was done by requiring charterers to continue immediately with discharging the flour; and they did not expressly accept the orginal notice as being valid at that time. He concluded[65e]: ". . . these facts. . . amply justify the conclusion that the charterers cannot thereafter insist that the laytime for discharging should not begin until either a further notice was served (not suggested by the charterers of *The Massalia*) or until a further notice period had expired. Put another way, they waived or were estopped from asserting the full extent of their rights under the notice clause."

[65a] [1988] 2 Lloyd's Rep. 149 (*The Mexico 1*).

[65b] *Ibid.*, at p. 153

[65c] *Ibid.*, at p. 154

[65d] *Ibid.* Evans J. noted the view expressed by Donald Davies in *Commencement of Laytime* (1987), at para. 73. The writer had said: " . . . the law should be that no further notice of readiness is required when a notice has already been given. As soon as the necessary facts come into existence then the earlier notice, which is deemed to be lying inchoate, becomes good . . . In support of this premise the writer prays in aid *The Massalia* . . . and the practice of virtually all commercial maritime arbitrators in the City of London." The judge also noted that Donald Davies had said that he was thereby taking "the opposite view" from that expressed in the 3rd edition of "Laytime", and repeated here. Evans J. said (at p. 155): "In my view, Mr. Summerskill is correct in saying that [as Donald Davies put it in describing Summerskill's view] absent special factors (such as particular circumstances, waiver, estoppel) a master has to give a further notice of readiness." As at November 1988 notice of appeal had been given in this case.

[65e] *Op. cit.*

Comments on the Graigwen,[66] Government of Ceylon,[67] Christensen,[68] **5-34**
  Surrey Shipping,[69] Gerani[70] and Transgrain[70a] cases
Unless charterers, or receivers on their behalf, waive one or more of the
conditions as to the commencement of laytime, or are estopped from
asserting the full extent of their rights under the notice clause, the following conclusions can probably be drawn from these six cases:
  1. If all the requirements of readiness,[71] apart from minimal qualifications,[72] are not satisfied when the notice is given, the notice is ineffective.[73]
  2. In the situation envisaged in 1. above, notice would have to be given
again, upon the readiness requirements being met, subject to what is stated
in 4. below.
  3. If there is an express provision for a further waiting period to elapse
after notice and before laytime can begin, then that further waiting period
will have also to elapse after the requirements of readiness have been satisfied.
  4. Despite 2. above, it has been held in special circumstances that notice
did not have to be repeated when the readiness requirements had been
met. But in that case[74] there was provision for one notice of readiness with
a postponement period (of 24 hours) for the purpose of laytime and for
other more general notices of readiness (three days and 24 hours). It was
then held that only one notice (apart from the three days' notice) was
required; and that notice could be given less than 24 hours before readiness
if no detriment was suffered by charterers by way of an earlier beginning to
laytime, and if the postponement period was still allowed to operate. But it
has been said[75] of that case: " . . . this decision turned upon very special
facts and does not cast doubt upon the general rule that a notice of readiness is wholly ineffective if, subject to mimimal qualifications, the vessel is
not ready to discharge at the time at which it is given." (See 1. above).
  5. The requirement, as set out in 3. above, as to a further waiting period
after the readiness requirements have been satisfied, may be dispensed
with. This can happen, for example,[76] where some reciprocal concession is
made by shipowners delaying the beginning of the "time lost in waiting"
period.[77]
  The distinction between (a) a notice being rejected; (b) a notice being **5-35**
neither rejected nor accepted but, as was said in the case in question, "left"

---

[66] See § 5–27 above.
[67] See § 5–28 above.
[68] See § 5–30 above.
[69] See § 5–33 above.
[70] See §§ 5–04 and 5–32 above.
[70a] *Transgrain Shipping B.V.* v. *Global Transporte Oceanico S.A. (The Mexico 1)* [1988] 2
  Lloyd's Rep. 149.
[71] For these, see §§ 5–01–5–17 above. As for free pratique, see § 5–11 above.
[72] See § 5–03 above.
[73] See Donaldson J. in *Christensen* v. *Hindustan Steel Ltd.* [1971] 1 Lloyd's Rep. 395 at
  p. 399.
[74] *Government of Ceylon* v. *Société Franco-Tunisienne d'Armement-Tunis* [1962] 2 Q.B. 416
  (*The Massalia*). See § 5–28 above.
[75] In *Christensen* v. *Hindustan Steel Ltd.* [1971] 1 Lloyd's Rep. 395, by Donaldson J. at p. 399.
[76] *Government of Ceylon* v. *Société Franco-Tunisienne d'Armement-Tunis* [1962] 2 Q.B. 416
  (*The Massalia*). See § 5–28 above.
[77] But see the critical judicial comments, in two cases, as to the views of Diplock J. in the
  Government of Ceylon case, set out at § 5–32.

with charterers; and (c) a notice being accepted, was discussed in *Sofial S.A.* v. *Ove Skou Rederi A/S*[78] Shipowners, under a berth charterparty on the Gencon form, carried milk powder from Antwerp to Kandla, India. Laytime was to begin at 1 p.m. if notice of readiness to load was given during office hours before noon. The ship, which had previously carried bagged fish meal, was to be presented "with holds clean and dry and free from smell." She berthed on January 22, 1974, giving notice of readiness on the next day, before noon. The charterers began loading on January 24 but had not then ascertained whether the ship was "clean and dry and free from smell." She was not free from smell; the loaded cargo had to be discharged and the ship cleaned. She moved to a buoy for this purpose and returned to her berth on January 28. Shipowners said that notice of readiness was effective when given so that laytime began at 1 p.m. on January 23. They agreed that the ship was not ready to load but contended that by loading charterers lost their right to reject the notice. Charterers said that they had not waived that right, and that they had rejected the notice when loading stopped and it was decided to discharge cargo.

Donaldson J. held that the shipowners were right. He said[79]:

> "There have been many cases of notice of readiness being rejected as premature and subsequently accepted: see for example *The Tres Flores*,[80] . . . but I think this is the first case in which charterers have accepted such a notice and later claimed to reject it. I do not think that they can do so. As Mr. Hallgarten[81] pointed out, the contrary view would enable a charterer to reject a notice of readiness and start laytime all over again if he discovered some lack of readiness in the ship at a late stage in loading. And this would be the case even if the cargo did not have to be discharged. A notice of readiness which is rightly rejected is a nullity, save to the extent that, with the express or implied agreement of the charterers, it may be left with them instead of being re-served and will then take effect when it truly represents the facts. But this notice was far from being a nullity. It was the key which unlocked the holds of the vessel and allowed loading to begin. And it was the charterers' act which created this position. Whether it is labelled as waiver or estoppel or something else, I do not consider that the charterers can resile from this position, save upon grounds of fraud. . . . "

---

[78] [1976] 2 Lloyds Rep. 205 (*The Helle Skou*).
[79] *Ibid.* at p. 214.
[80] *Compania de Naviera Nedelka S.A.* v. *Tradax Internacional S.A.* [1973] 2 Lloyd's Rep. 247 (C.A.) (*The Tres Flores*). See § 5–03 above.
[81] Counsel for the shipowners.

CHAPTER 6

MODIFICATION OF REQUIREMENTS FOR BEGINNING OF LAYTIME

Clauses modifying the usual requirements as to when laytime begins   **6–01**
The usual conditions for the beginning of laytime[1] are that the ship should have arrived at the agreed destination; that she must be ready to load or to discharge; that notice of readiness should have been given on or after arrival to the charterers or their agents; and that any prescribed period after the notice should have elapsed. These conditions may be modified by express terms which can advance or delay the moment at which laytime begins. As Scrutton L.J. said in *United States Shipping Board* v. *Frank C. Strick & Co. Ltd.*[2]:

> "The point in dispute is one which has been the subject of bargaining ever since I have been concerned with shipping cases, and that is, on whom is the risk of waiting for turn,[3] or waiting for a berth, to fall."

In the following year he said[4]:

> "As long as I can remember there has been controversy between shipowner and charterer as to who is to bear the risk of waiting at a port for a berth."

The terms which may modify the usual conditions include the following expressions:

1. *"Time lost in waiting for berth to count as loading or discharging*   **6–02** *time, as the case may be,"* or *"as laytime."*[5]
2. *"Whether in berth or not."*[6] These words may be found in a number of laytime provisions, such as "Time to commence when steamer is ready to unload and written notice given, whether in berth or not"[7]

---

[1] They are set out in § 4–01 above and thereafter discussed in detail.
[2] (1924) 30 Com.Cas. 210 at p. 224.
[3] For turn time and similar expressions, see § 6–28 below.
[4] In *Van Nievelt, Goudrian & Co. Stoomvaart Maatschappij* v. *Forslind & Son Ltd.* (1925) 30 Com.Cas. 263 at p. 267.
[5] In cl. 6(c) of the Uniform General charter (Gencon) as revised in 1976. Similar forms of words, as set out in the 1922 Gencon revision, were considered in *North Freighters Ltd.* v. *President of India* [1956] 1 Q.B. 333 (C.A.) (*The Radnor*) (see § 6–03 below); *Government of Ceylon* v. *Société Franco-Tunisienne d'Armement-Tunis* [1962] 2 Q.B. 416 (*The Massalia*); *Ionian Navigation Company Inc.* v. *Atlantic Shipping Company S.A.* [1970] Lloyd's Rep. 215 (C.A.) (*The Loucas N*) (see § 6–04 below); *Nea Tyhi Maritime Co. Ltd. of Piraeus* v. *Compagnie Grainière S.A. of Zurich* [1975] 2 Lloyds Rep. 415 (*The Finix*) (see § 6–14 below); and *Aldebaran Compania Maritima S.A. Panama* v. *Aussenhandel A.G. Zürich* [1977] A.C. 157 (H.L.) (*The Darrah*). See § 6–03 below.
[6] The Charterparty Laytime Definitions 1980 (see Appendix to this book) state: "26. 'WHETHER IN BERTH OR NOT' or 'BERTH NO BERTH'—means that if the location named for loading/discharging is a berth and if the berth is not immediately accessible to the ship a notice of readiness can be given when the ship has arrived at the port in which the berth is situated." For a brief discussion of this definition see *Seacrystal Shipping Ltd.* v. *Bulk Transport Group Shipping Co. Ltd.* [1987] 2 Lloyd's Rep. 122 (C.A.) (*The Kyzikos*) by Lloyd L.J., at p. 126.
[7] Considered in *Northfield SS. Co.* v. *Compagnie L'Union des Gaz* [1912] 1 K.B. 434. See § 6–19 below.

or "Time at second port to count from arrival of vessel at second port, whether in berth or not."[8]

3. "Time . . . to commence on being reported at custom house."[9]

4. "Whether in port or not."[9a]

5. "In regular turn." One clause read: "The cargo to be loaded . . . in regular turn as customary . . . commencing when written notice is given of steamer being ready to load . . . "[10] There are other similar expressions relating to the turn of the ship.

6. "Demurrage in respect of all time waiting."[11] These words may be sufficient to entitle the shipowners to demurrage even where the ship is not an arrived ship.

7. "To be loaded as per colliery guarantee" combined with a provision in the colliery guarantee[12] for the ship "to load in . . . days after the ship is ready in Dock at . . . "[13]

8. "Time to count twenty-four hours after arrival at or off the port."[14]

6–03   1. *"Time lost in waiting for berth to count as loading or discharging time, as the case may be," or "as laytime."*

This expression, used in the Gencon charterparty,[15] may cause waiting time to be counted against charterers as time used even though the ship has not reached her contractual destination and though the master has not given notice of readiness.[15a] Thus in a berth charterparty, where the port is stated but the berth is to be named, the waiting period after arrival at the port is to count. This may be so although the ship is still awaiting her berth and unable to give notice of readiness[16] so that laytime has not begun.[17]

---

[8] Considered in *Carga del Sur Compania Naviera* v. *Ross T. Smyth & Co. Ltd.* [1962] 2 Lloyd's Rep. 147 (*The Seafort*). See § 6–20 below.

[9] Considered in *Horsley Line Ltd.* v. *Roechling Brothers*, 1908 S.C. 866. See § 6–23 below.

[9a] See § 6–27 below.

[10] Considered in *U.S. Shipping Board* v. *Frank C. Strick & Co. Ltd.* [1926] A.C. 545 (H.L.). See § 6–31 and generally §§ 6–28 and 6–35 below.

[11] Cl. 2 of the Australian Grain Charter 1928 (Austral) considered in *Roland-Linie Schiffarht G.m.b.H.* v. *Spillers Ltd.* [1957] 1 Q.B. 109 (*The Werrastein*). See § 6–37 below.

[12] For colliery working days and colliery guarantees, see § 2–62 above. See § 6–39 below.

[13] Discussed in *Monsen* v. *Macfarlane* [1895] 2 Q.B. 562 and *Thorman* v. *Dowgate SS. Co.* [1910] 1 K.B. 410. See § 6–39 below.

[14] Discussed in *Borg (Owners)* v. *Darwen Paper Co.* (1921) 8 Ll.L.Rep. 49. See § 6–43 below.

[15] Uniform General Charter, revised in 1976. The 1922 revision stated: "Time lost in waiting for berth to count as loading time," and "Time lost in waiting for berth to count as discharging time." Both versions have the same effect. For the Shellvoy 3 words (now superseded: see n. 16) "Whether or not the specific berth or other loading or discharging spot is available and accessible, if the vessel is nevertheless ordered by Charterers to wait before proceeding thereto, laytime shall commence" (etc.), see *Cosmar Compania Naviera S.A.* v. *Total Transport Corporation* [1982] 2 Lloyd's Rep. 81 (*The Isabelle*). In that case the order to wait was given by the port authorities and the shipowners' claim failed.

[15a] But the words may be overruled by suitable contradictory words, especially where the former are printed and the latter specially agreed. See *Navrom* v. *Callitsis Ship Management S.A.* [1987] 2 Lloyd's Rep. 276 (*The Radauti*) and § 8–79, n. 13a below.

[16] As to when notice can be given, see § 5–25 above. Some charterparties provide for such a contingency. The Shellvoy 5 charterparty provides that if the ship does not proceed immediately to the berth time shall begin to run six hours after (i) she is lying in the area where she is ordered to wait, or, in the absence of an order, in a usual waiting area and (ii) written notice has been tendered and (iii) the specified berth is accessible. The circumstances in which a berth "shall be deemed inaccessible" are those set out in cl. 13(1)(a) of the charterparty. The Asbatankvoy charterparty provides that notice of readiness can be given upon arrival at the customary anchorage, "berth or no berth."

[17] For berth charterparties generally, see § 4–03 above.

Speaking of a berth charterparty, Donaldson J. said[18]:

> " . . . the moment when she becomes an arrived ship and when she ceases to wait for the berth will be nearly contemporaneous, since she ceases to wait when she moves off towards the berth and becomes an arrived ship when she reaches the berth."

For a period of just over 20 years, in five cases, the Courts were concerned with the precise manner in which the time lost in waiting for a berth was "to count as loading or discharging time." Was it a special sort of time, governed by an independent code, or should it be treated in the same way as if it were laytime, and as if laytime had begun?

In *North River Freighters, Ltd.* v. *President of India*[19] the *Radnor* had   **6–04** carried soya beans from "one safe berth Dairen (Manchuria)" to Madras and Calcutta. The charterparty provided, by clause 17, that lay days should begin 24 hours after notice of readiness to load had been given. Another clause stated: "Time lost in waiting for berth to count as loading time."[20]

When the ship anchored in the quarantine anchorage at Dairen customs and port officials sealed the radio, took away a number of ship's documents, and banned communication with the shore. Seven days later the ship was taken to a berth (though not loaded there) and on the following day the master was able to give notice of readiness. The Court of Appeal held that the shipowners were entitled to count the eight days although notice had not then been given. Singleton J. said[21]:

> "The clause as to time wasted is independent[22] of Clause 17.[23] It is inserted to avoid questions which have arisen in many cases which have been before the courts. The risk of time wasted in waiting for a berth is put upon the charterers whose agents are, or ought to be, familiar with local conditions. The clause might have provided simply that time lost in waiting for a berth should be paid for at the rate of £600[24] a day. As drawn, it gives the charterers an advantage, for they may save on loading time some, or all, of the time lost in waiting for a berth. The time lost is to count as, or to be added to, loading time in order to ascertain the position between the parties."

He stressed[25] that the need for notice, under clause 17, only arose when the ship had arrived at her agreed destination.[26] It was a berth charterparty[27]: " . . . the master could not give the notice envisaged in Clause 17 of the charterparty until the vessel arrived at the nominated berth. Upon the charterparty, she had to proceed to 'one safe berth Dairen.' " He therefore rejected the charterers' argument that the "time lost in waiting" clause could not operate until notice had been given, and that time could not be lost until time (*i.e.* laytime) had begun to run.

---

[18] In *Ionian Navigation Company Inc.* v. *Atlantic Shipping Company S.A.* [1970] 2 Lloyd's Rep. 482 (*The Loucas N.*) at p. 486. See § 6–04 above.

[19] [1956] 1 Q.B. 333 (C.A.). (*The Radnor*).

[20] This was the 1922 version of the Gencon charterparty. See § 6–02 above.

[21] At p. 340.

[22] It was the word "independent" which, in the opinion of Lord Diplock in *Aldebaran Compania Maritima S.A. Panama* v. *Aussenhandel A.G. Zürich* [1977] A.C. 157 (*The Darrah*), was to cause problems. See n. 31 below.

[23] In *The Darrah* (*ibid.*) Lord Diplock said (at p. 166) of Singleton L.J. that in saying this "All his mind was directed to was one provision in the laytime clause which made its commencement dependent on the giving of notice of readiness."

[24] The charterparty demurrage rate.

[25] At pp. 340–341.

[26] As to when notice can be given, see § 5–25 above.

[27] Jenkins L.J. and Parker L.J., though inclining to this view, found it unnecessary to decide whether it was a berth or a port charterparty, though they supported the shipowners.

He said[28] of the "Time lost in waiting clause":

> "In my opinion, the provision as to notice in clause 17[29] does not affect the question arising under clause 5[30] of the charterparty, and the lack of a notice under clause 17 does not avoid the owners' rights in regard to time lost through waiting for a berth. The notice is something which has to be given for the purpose of calculating lay days. That calculation is independent of the provision in clause 5,[31] though the one has to be added to the other to reach the true position under the contract."

6–05 Here the Court of Appeal did not equate the time lost in waiting with laytime, but emphasised the independence of the laytime clause, in which the excepted periods were mentioned, from the waiting time clause.

Ten years later, in *Metals and Ropes Co. Ltd.* v. *Filia Compania Limitada*,[32] the words "Time lost in waiting for berth to count as discharging time" were considered in the case of a charterparty for the carriage of scrap metal from the United Kingdom to Italy. The ship anchored in the roads outside the commercial area of Genoa on a Saturday, no berth being available. Notice of readiness was given on the Monday, though the ship was not then an arrived ship; on the Tuesday she berthed and discharging began. The charterers relied on a provision that time was not to count between noon on Saturday and 8 a.m. on Monday. McNair J. decided, however, that time which would have been excluded from laytime if the ship had been in berth must be included in the calculation of time lost in waiting for a berth.

He concluded[33]:

6–06
> "Whilst I feel that there is great force in the contention . . . that the construction placed on these Clauses in the case of *North River Freighters, Ltd.* v. *H.E. The President of India* has in effect the result that the Respondents [the shipowners] are financially better off, and that in fact from the commercial point of view the only time which was lost because the ship was waiting for berth was between 1 o'clock on the Monday and 1 o'clock on the Tuesday, because all earlier times and been inevitably lost to the ship owing to her arrival after office hours on the Saturday, yet I am not able to give effect to that contention in view of the guidance I have received in this matter, which is binding upon me, in the *North River Freighters Ltd.* case."[34]

A similar conclusion was reached by the High Court and the Court of Appeal in *Ionian Navigation Company Inc.* v. *Atlantic Shipping Company S.A.*[35] *The Loucas N.* was chartered on the Gencon form for a voyage from Caen and Antwerp to Houston, New Orleans and Tampa.

---

[28] At p. 341.

[29] The clause which dealt with laytime.

[30] The waiting time clause.

[31] As to this Lord Diplock said in *The Darrah* (*op. cit.*, at p. 168): " . . . one starts with an unconsidered reference by Singleton L.J. in *The Radnor* . . . to the 'time lost' clause as being 'independent' of a clause in the charterparty which, while it did contain the only stipulation as to laytime that was relevant to the question for decision in the case, *viz.* when laytime commenced, also contained other stipulations as to what was to be reckoned as included in permitted laytime, with which the Lord Justice was not concerned."

[32] [1966] 2 Lloyd's Rep. 219 (*The Vastric*).

[33] *Op. cit.* p. 226.

[34] Lord Diplock said in the *Aldebaran* case (*op. cit.*) at p. 167 that McNair J. formed this view "with unconcealed reluctance," and he added: "He was, in my view, mistaken in thinking that he was so bound (by the *North River Freighters* case). It was a matter to which the Court of Appeal in *The Radnor* had not directed their minds at all."

[35] [1971] 1 Lloyd's Rep. 215 (C.A.). Though the contentions of the parties, and the decision of the Court of Appeal, are set out here, it is important, in reading them, to recall that the decision was overruled by the House of Lords in *Aldebaran Compania Maritima S.A. Panama* v. *Aussenhandel A.G. Zürich* [1977] A.C. 157 (*The Darrah*); see § 6–09 below.

The charterparty provided, in clause 5: "At each loading port . . . Time lost in waiting for berth to count as loading time"; and in clause 6: "At first discharging port . . . Time lost in waiting for berth to count as discharging time." Clause 39, the Centrocon Strike Clause, stated: " . . . if the cargo cannot be discharged by reason . . . of a strike . . . of any class of workmen essential to the discharge of the cargo, or by reason of obstructions or stoppages beyond the control of Charterers on the barges and/or railways or in dock or other discharging places, the time for . . . discharging, shall not count during the continuance of such causes . . . " The ship waited outside the commercial areas of Caen for just over a day and of Houston for seven weeks until berths became available. At Caen and Houston all the berths were occupied; at Houston there was also a strike of stevedores during the initial part of the period, and congestion caused by a strike for the rest of the period. The charterers had argued that no time was lost as a result of the strike, even if the ship had been able to go to a berth, she could not have begun to discharge.

In the High Court Donaldson J. decided[36] that time had been lost by the **6–07** ship at both ports in waiting for a berth, and that the "Time lost" provision was independent of the Centrocon Strike Clause. Of the judgment of Donaldson J. it was said[37]:

> "Donaldson J. had treated *The Radnor* . . . as establishing that under the Gencon charter there were two independent codes—a 'laytime' code to be applied in calculating laytime and a 'time lost' code which was not subject to any of the exclusions of periods from the reckoning which were applicable to laytime. Under the 'time lost' code, time lost once it had started was like demurrage; it ran continuously until the waiting period ended. This ratio decidendi received the express approval of the Court of Appeal."

The Court of Appeal held that the strike clause, though it said that time should not count, did not apply to the time lost in waiting for berth, although the latter was to count as discharging time.

Lord Denning M.R., dealing with the contention by the charterers that **6–08** time at Houston ought not to count because, if the ship had been in a berth, she would have been unable to discharge, said[38]:

> "If anyone had asked the master of this vessel, when she was waiting outside Houston: 'What are you waiting for?' he would say: 'I am waiting for a berth.' No matter what was the cause of the waiting; no matter whether it was a strike or congestion, or anything else at the port, he would say that he was waiting for a berth."

As for the word "obstructions" in the Centrocon Strike Clause, it had been determined[39] that it covered congestion by reason of which a berth was not available. It was argued that at both ports the cargo could not be worked by reason of obstructions, so that time should not count during that continuance. Lord Denning said[40]:

> " . . . I think that we should hold that clause 39, the strike clause, is dealing with a situation after the ship has arrived and is ready to load or to discharge, as the case may be. The charterers can rely on the clause to exempt them from responsibility for strikes or obstructions, and so forth, after she is an arrived ship . . .

---

[36] [1970] 2 Lloyd's Rep. 482.

[37] By Lord Diplock in the *Aldebaran* case (*op. cit.*) at p. 167.

[38] At p. 218.

[39] In *N.V. Reederij Amsterdam* v. *President of India* [1961] 2 Lloyd's Rep. 1 (C.A.) (*The Amstelmolen*). For the facts, see § 8–40 below. For a criticism by Lord Denning M.R. of that case, see § 8–40 below.

[40] At p. 218.

6–09   Against the background of these three cases there was nevertheless a change of view when the matter was considered by the House of Lords in 1977. Where the words "Time lost waiting for berth to count as laytime" are used in a port charterparty, and an arrived ship is unable to reach her discharging berth, the time so lost must now be subject to the same exclusions as if laytime itself was running. There is thus one time code; the concept of two different time codes, one for time lost and not subject to laytime exceptions, and another for laytime and subject to those exceptions, was abandoned.[41] The House of Lords established this proposition, overruling the decision of the Court of Appeal in the *Ionian Navigation* case,[42] in *Aldebaran Compania Maritime S.A. Panama* v. *Aussenhandel A.G. Zürich*.[43]

6–10   The *Darrah* was chartered on the Gencon form, as revised in 1922,[44] to carry cement from Novorossisk to Tripoli, Libya. Clause 4 stated: "Time to commence at 2 p.m. if notice of readiness to discharge given before noon. Time lost in waiting for berth to count as laytime."[45] Clause 20 provided for discharge "at the rate of 625 metric tons per weather working day of 24 consecutive hours, Fridays and holidays excepted." Clause 21 said: "At discharging port, time from noon Thursday or noon on the day before a legal holiday until 8 a.m. the next working day not to count, even if used." The ship reached Tripoli roads, where she was within the port and an arrived ship,[46] on January 2, 1973, and gave notice of readiness. Because of congestion she did not reach her discharging berth until January 9 at 8 a.m. Discharge began at once and ended on the 24th. The shipowners treated the whole of the waiting time as if it were laytime. The effect was that demurrage would be due to them rather than dispatch due to the charterers.

6–11   The House of Lords found in favour of the charterers, so that only the weather working days counted. Lord Diplock expressed the dilemma when he said[47]:

> " . . . it would at first sight seem startling that notwithstanding that the charterer under a voyage charter had completed the discharging operation within the laytime permitted by the charterparty and paid for in the freight, the shipowner should be enriched by an amount equivalent to 10 days' demurrage merely because the absence of a vacant berth at which the vessel's cargo could be discharged had prevented the charterer from using some of the days that would otherwise have been available to him for that purpose, though he would have been under no contractual duty so to use them provided that he could complete the discharging operation within the permitted laytime."

---

[41] Roskill L.J., in the Court of Appeal in *Aldebaran* (see later in this section) referred to *Dick Hampton (Earth Moving) Ltd.* v. *Lewis* [1975] 3 W.L.R. 357, at p. 356, in which Ormrod L.J. quoted Mr. Justice Frankfurter: "A phrase begins life as a literary expression; its felicity leads to its lazy repetition; and repetition soon establishes it as a legal formula, indiscriminately used to express different and somewhat contradictory ideas." (*Tiller* v. *Atlantic Coast Line Railroad Co.* (1943) 318 U.S. 54 at p. 68). The references to independent codes are a good illustration of that principle.

[42] [1971] 1 Lloyd's Rep. 215 (*The Loucas N.*). See § 6–04 above.

[43] [1977] A.C. 157.

[44] Nothing turned on the differences between the 1922 and 1976 revisions.

[45] The word "laytime" replaced the words "discharging time" which were in the printed form. The House of Lords indicated that this amendment made no difference; see § 6–11 below.

[46] In accordance with *Oldendorff (E.L.) & Co. G.m.b.H.* v. *Tradax Export S.A.* [1973] 2 Lloyd's Rep. 285 (H.L.) (*The Johanna Oldendorff*). See § 4–21 above.

[47] *Op. cit.* at p. 164.

He then reviewed[48] what he called the judicial history. He said that the House of Lords was not bound by the Court of Appeal decision in the *Ionian Navigation* case as to the construction of the "time lost" clauses in the Gencon charterparty. He added[49]:

> "I have already expressed my own opinion that the construction placed upon the "time lost" clause in the cases which followed *The Radnor*[50] . . . to which I have referred was wrong and that in the computation of time lost in waiting for berth there are to be excluded all periods which would have been left out in the computation of permitted laytime used up if the vessel had actually been in berth. So, in the case of an arrived ship under a port charter there is no conflict between the laytime provisions and the time lost provisions."

He concluded by saying that the alteration to "counted as laytime" from "counted as discharging time" made no difference to the meaning.[51]

The berth and the cargo for which the ship is waiting   **6–12**

Time lost in waiting for a berth must arise in respect of the cargo in question, and not some other cargo which the ship may also have. In *Agios Stylianos Compania Naviera S.A.* v. *Maritime Associates International Ltd.*[52] there were two charterparties[53] on the Gencon form for the simultaneous carriage of vehicles and cement (which was wholly overstowed by the vehicles) from Constanza to Lagos. Demurrage was at the rate of $1,500 per day with "time lost in waiting for berth to count as discharging time." The ship waited for a berth from May 14 to May 29, 1971, completed discharge of the vehicles on June 1, and immediately began to discharge the cement. The shipowners were awarded demurrage from the vehicle charterers and then claimed demurrage from the cement charterers, counting against charterers in each case the period from May 15 to May 29.

Donaldson J. held that "time lost waiting for berth" in the cement char-   **6–13** terparty meant "time lost waiting for the cement berth." That conclusion was supported by the decision in *Government of Ceylon* v. *Société Franco-Tunisienne D'Armement-Tunis (No. 2)*[54] that "cargo" in that charterparty meant the flour. Speaking of charterers' counsel he said[55]:

> "He goes on to submit that none of the time spent, lost or wasted[56] before the vehicles

---

[48] *Op. cit.* at p. 166. The cases which he considered were: *North River Freighters Ltd.* v. *President of India* [1956] 1 Q.B. 33 (C.A.) (*The Radnor*) see § 6–03 above); *Metals & Ropes Co. Ltd.* v. *Filia Compania Limitada* [1966] 2 Lloyd's Rep. 219. (*The Vastric*) (see § 6–07 above); *Ionian Navigation Co. Inc.* v. *Atlantic Shipping Co. S.A.* [1971] 1 Lloyd's Rep. 215 (C.A.) (*The Loucas N.*) (see § 6–04 above); and *Nea Tyhi Maritime Co. Ltd. of Piraeus* v. *Compagnie Grainière S.A. of Zürich* [1975] 2 Lloyd's Rep. 415 (*The Finix*) (see § 6–14 below).

[49] *Op. cit.* at p. 168.

[50] *The North River Freighters Ltd.* case.

[51] See also Viscount Dilhorne, at p. 170: "I do not think that it has any significance." He also (at pp. 173–174) found support for his view in *Rederiaktiebologet Transatlantic* v. *La Compagnie Française des Phosphates de L'Océanie* [1926] 32 Com.Cas. 126 (C.A.), which involved the adding of time "not consumed in loading" to the discharging time. See §§ 9–11 and 9–12 below.

[52] [1975] 1 Lloyd's Rep. 426.

[53] For another case involving two charterparties for simultaneous carriage see *Sarma Navigation S.A.* v. *Sidermar S.p.A.* [1982] 1 Lloyd's Rep. 13 (C.A.) (*The Sea Pioneer*) at § 10–26 below. The *Agios Stylianos* case was distinguished, because the facts were different in two important respects.

[54] [1960] 2 Lloyd's Rep. 352 (*The Massalia*). See §§ 5–26 above and 6–17 below.

[55] *Op. cit.* at p. 431.

[56] The words "spent" and "wasted" were not in the charterparty.

had been discharged was spent, lost or wasted waiting for the cement berth. This is right. The vessel was waiting for a vehicle discharging berth. Once the vehicles had been discharged the cement charterers had the right and duty to nominate a berth, but this did not arise at any earlier point of time. In fact, they nominated the same berth, but, so far as the charter was concerned, they could have nominated one or two other berths in Lagos."

Time therefore ran from 0800 hours on the day after June 2.[56a]

6-14   Cases following The Darrah

In *Nea Tyhi Maritime Co. Ltd. of Piraeus* v. *Compagnie Grainière S.A. of Zürich*[57] grain was carried, under a Centrocon charterparty from the River Plate, to "one or two safe berths, one safe port in the Democratic People's Republic of Korea". It was provided: " . . . the time for discharging shall commence from 1 p.m. if notice is delivered . . . before noon and from 8 a.m. following working day if delivered during office hours in the afternoon, but time lost in waiting for berth to count as discharging time." Nampo was nominated; the ship arrived in the roads on June 7, 1973. Notice of readiness was tendered on Saturday, June 9, at 1830 hours, and accepted on Monday, June 11, at 0800 hours. The ship began to shift from the roads to a quay berth at 2300 hours on July 5.

A dispute arose as to whether, as the charterers said, the period from the tendering of the notice of readiness until the ship began to shift was covered by the laytime provisions, with laytime beginning on Monday, June 11 and Sundays and non-weather working days being excepted. The shipowners contended that the "time lost in waiting" provision meant that time ran continuously from arrival at the roads.

6-15   The Court of Appeal, following the House of Lords decision in *The Darrah*[58] decided that the charterers were right. It was not necessary for the Court to give, and it did not give, any reasons other than those stated by Lord Denning M.R.[59-60] In saying that the charterers' appeal from the High Court judgment must be allowed, he pointed out that it had been

---

[56a] Although shipowners are discharging a second cargo, they may rely on the expression "time lost in waiting for berth," as between themselves and the interests involved in the first cargo, so long as no berth is available. In a London arbitration, LMLN 71, July 22, 1982 the tribunal considered a charterparty for the loading of a part cargo of fertiliser. It contained the Centrocon Completion Clause, which provided: "Owners have the liberty to complete with other . . . merchandise from port or ports to port or ports en route for owners' risk and benefit, but . . . same not to hinder the . . . discharging of this cargo." Although, because of over-stowage of other cargoes, the ship was not ready to discharge until nearly three weeks after her arrival, a fertiliser berth only became available when three more weeks had elapsed. It was held that the shipowners were entitled to succeed in their demurrage claim. It would seem, it was said, that *Re Ropner Shipping Co. Ltd. and Cleeves Western Valleys Anthracite Collieries Ltd.* [1927] 1 K.B. 879 (see § 10-66 below) would have been decided in favour of the shipowners if it had been shown that the charterers were unable to work the ship during her period of unavailability. If that were right, and if it were also correct that (a) "time lost" provisions might operate even when a ship could not give a valid notice of readiness, and (b) time lost was to be counted as if it were laytime, it followed that all the time should count. This also seemed to be a commercially just result as the ship would have waited for a fertiliser berth as long as she did in any event, and the charterers lost nothing by her other activities. If the charterers had thought that the Centrocon Completion Clause gave them inadequate protection they should have sought other remedies at the time of fixing, such as a demurrage rate not reflecting the full value of the ship.

[57] [1978] 1 Lloyd's Rep. 16 (C.A.) (*The Finix*).
[58] [1977] A.C. 157. See § 6-09 above.
[59-60] *Op. cit.* at p. 18.

made in June, 1975, and that the House of Lords judgment in *The Darrah* was given in July, 1976, and said: "The point was, however, under discussion in *The Darrah* . . . As a result it was clear that the decision in this Court both of the umpire and the Judge was wrong." It was this decision in the High Court which was considered by the House of Lords when they took the opposite view, in favour of the time lost being subject to the usual laytime exceptions, in the *Aldebaran* case.[61]

The decision of the House of Lords in *The Darrah*[62] was again applied in *Magnolia Shipping Co. Ltd. of Limassol* v. *Joint Venture of the International Trading & Shipping Enterprises and Kinship Management Co. Ltd. of Brussels*.[63] The Commercial Court, having decided that the words "weather permitting working day" had the same effect as the words "working day weather permitting," considered the words:

> "Berth occupied: When no cargo berth available on arrival roads, the master will cable . . . date and time of arrival roads to the Agents and this time will be treated as if vessel had tendered notice of readiness alongside the berth and time will count accordingly."

The shipowners said that as the phrase "weather permitting" constituted words of exception time could only be excluded from laytime if discharge was prevented by the weather. They said that as the ship was not in berth she was *ex hypothesi* not engaged in discharging. The charterers said that allowance should be made for time notionally lost. Brandon J., deciding in favour of the charterers, said that the argument for the shipowners was contrary to the whole basis on which the House of Lords had decided the *Aldebaran* case. He added[64]:

> "What the House of Lords was saying is that the object of this kind of clause is to put both parties in the same position when a berth is not available as they would have been in if it had not been available.

Shipowners failed again in another case, *Navrom* v. *Callitsis Ship Man-* **6–16** *agement S.A.*,[65] in which clause 6 of a Gencon charterparty, with the words "Time lost in waiting for berth to count as lay time," was contrasted with a general exceptions clause. The latter read: "33. Force majeure; strikes or lock outs of workmen at shippers' factory on railways barges trucks lorries at the loading or discharging port or elsewhere, war, or effects of war, revolution, civil commotion, breakdown on or stoppage of railways barges trucks or lorries, interruptions, stoppage or shortage or destruction of goods in transit or fire tempests inundations, earthquakes, unavoidable accidents to machinery or other unavoidable hindrances in transportation, loading, discharging or receiving the goods, restraints of established authorities or any other causes or hindrances happening without the fault of the charterers, shippers or suppliers of cargo, preventing or delaying the manufacturing supplying loading discharging or receiving of the cargo are excepted and neither charterers nor shippers should be liable for any loss or damage resulting from any such excepted causes and time lost by reason thereof shall not count as lay days or days on demurrage. The same shall apply to any delay caused by the ship or crew."

The *Radauti* had carried bagged wheat flour from Rotterdam to Tripoli,

---

[61] See § 5–11 above.
[62] [1977] A.C. 157.
[63] [1978] 2 Lloyd's Rep. 182 (*The Camelia* and *The Magnolia*).
[64] *Op. cit.* at p. 185.
[65] [1987] 2 Lloyd's Rep. 276.

Libya. She anchored in the roads at Tripoli and gave notice of readiness on the next day, but did not obtain a berth for nearly two months. Shipowners claimed that demurrage began when the laytime expired, and that clause 33 had no effect. Charterers argued that clause 33 prevented laytime from beginning until the ship berthed.

Staughton J. said first that it was well established that if there were a conflict clause 6, which was mostly in printed form, must yield to clause 33, which was specially agreed by the parties. Secondly, there was the Court of Appeal authority in *The Amstelmolen*[66] that the word "obstructions" in the Centrocon Strike Clause was apt to cover congestion which prevented the ship from entering a berth, despite the presence of the words "whether in berth or not." The Judge could see no significant difference where the words were, as in this case, "Time lost in waiting for a berth to count . . . " Furthermore, the shipowners' contention was the one which succeeded in the Court of Appeal in *The Loucas N*[67] which was overruled in *The Darrah*.[68] He continued[69]:

> "In the latter case the dispute was not about an exceptions clause which could be said to apply to congestion in the port, but about an express exception of non-working days. So theoretically it would have been open to the House of Lords to uphold the decision in *The Loucas N* but distinguish it in the result. But in my judgment the House of Lords plainly did not take that course. It follows that clause 6 in the present case does not override clause 33. If, on a fair reading of clause 33, the charterers are exempted from liability for the consequences of congestion in the port, it may well be that in consequence the printed clause has little or no content, but that is the result of the decisions to which I have referred."

The Judge also considered the argument that the exceptions clause must be confined to events which happen when a ship had already reached a berth. There were passages in *The Darrah*[70] and the *Magnolia Shipping* case[71] which would, taken literally and wrenched from their context, support that contention. He said[72]:

> "If lay time is to be calculated in the same way as if the vessel had reached a berth, an obstacle which prevents the vessel ever reaching a berth cannot be an exception which stops time running. But neither Lord Diplock nor Brandon J. was considering such an exception: they were concerned with non-working days in one case and with rain in the other. I do not believe that they intended to rule that obstacles which prevented the vessel reaching a berth could not, if provided for in the exceptions clause, stop waiting time from running. Indeed, the fact that *The Loucas N* was overruled in *The Darrah*, as Brandon J. mentioned and I agree, is authority to the contrary since *The Loucas N* was concerned in part with congestion as well as in part with a strike."

6–17   Should time lost in waiting be counted at the beginning or added at the end of the lay days?

There are two cases which deal with the problem; it seems that the later of them, in which it was decided that waiting time should be counted as it occurred, is the better authority.

---

[66] *N.V. Reederij Amsterdam* v. *President of India* [1961] 2 Lloyd's Rep. 1; see § 8–40 below for the facts. See also § 6–04 above and n. 29.

[67] *Ionian Navigation Company Inc.* v. *Atlantic Shipping Company S.A.* [1971] 1 Lloyd's Rep. 215; see §§ 6–04 and 6–08 above.

[68] *Aldebaran Compania Maritime S.A.* v. *Aussenhandel A.G. Zürich* [1977] A.C. 157. See § 6–09 above.

[69] *Op. cit.*, at p. 279.

[70] *Ibid.*

[71] [1978] 2 Lloyd's Rep. 182; see § 6–16 above.

[72] *Op. cit.* at p. 280.

First, the High Court held in *Government of Ceylon* v. *Société Franco-Tunisienne d'Armement-Tunis*[73] that time lost in waiting should be added at the end of the lay days. Diplock J. said[74]:

> "The last matter which I have to decide is whether one adds the time lost in waiting for a berth at the beginning or at the end of the lay days. That sounds to an arithmetician as if the sum must come to the same, but in this particular case I understand that it makes a difference of a day, because, if one adds it at the beginning, the Sunday, October 28, is excluded from the laytime and therefore counts as demurrage.[75] If, on the other hand, one adds it at the end, then the Sunday comes during laytime and does not count. So it does make a difference of 24 hours. Without giving any reason, I hold that it should be added at the end."

The dates in that case were complicated by the fact that there was a part cargo destined for parties other than the charterers.[76]

Secondly, in *Ionian Company Inc.* v. *Atlantic Shipping Company S.A.*, **6–18** the High Court[77] held that time lost in waiting should count "from moment to moment as the time is lost."[78] Pointing out that in the *Government of Ceylon* case it had been a subsidiary point, Donaldson J. said[79]:

> " . . . I consider that it should be brought into account as and when the delay occurs. It is, of course, quite separate from the time allowed for loading and discharging[80] but the extent of the delay in waiting for a berth affects the yardstick which has to be applied in determining how much chronological time remains available for the completion of these processes. Furthermore, it affects the computation of demurrage, since once the laytime is exhausted, demurrage accrues day by day without regard to the exceptions affecting laytime itself such as Sundays, holidays and strike days, at least in the absence of an appropriately worded clause. Receivers of cargo, who may or may not be the charterers, are entitled to know at the time when they have to take delivery whether the ship has any laytime left and how much, since their bill of lading contracts may make them liable to pay the proportion of demurrage apportionable to their cargo. Equally the owners need to know the position at the time in order that they may exercise a lien for demurrage."[80a]

2. *"Whether in berth or not"*   **6–19**

The inclusion of the words "whether in berth[81] or not in a port charter-party" cause laytime to begin whether the ship is in berth (a berth being available) or not in berth (a berth not being available).[82] The mere

---

[73] [1962] 2 Q.B. 416 (*The Massalia*). See §§ 5–26 and 6–13 above.

[74] At p. 428.

[75] Because the time waiting for the berth, added to the discharging time used, would by that date already have exceeded the laytime.

[76] For the facts, see § 5–26 above.

[77] [1970] 2 Lloyd's Rep. 482 (*Loucas N.*). See § 6–04 above.

[78] *Op. cit.* at p. 487. The point was not raised before the Court of Appeal ([1971] 1 Lloyd's Rep. 215), both sides agreeing that time was to be counted as and when it occurred.

[79] *Ibid.*

[80] Though the concept of two independent codes, one for time lost and one for laytime, has now been abandoned; *Aldebaran Compania Maritima S.A. Panama* v. *Aussenhandel A.G. Zürich* [1977] A.C. 157 (H.L.) (*The Darrah*). See § 6–09 above.

[80a] This matter has also been considered in a New York arbitration, *Niver Lines* v. *C. M. McLean Ltd.* (*The Paros*) Society of Maritime Arbitrators No. 1669 (1982). In this case, of a charterparty on an amended Gencon form, the panel considered *The Massalia* [1960] 2 Lloyd's Rep. 352, and *The Loucas N.* [1970] 2 Lloyd's Rep. 482. It said that waiting time should be counted chronologically in computing laytime and demurrage. The view expressed in *The Loucas N.* was considered to be preferable.

[81] Sometimes abbreviated to the acronym "wibon."

[82] *Northfield SS. Co.* v. *Compagnie L'Union des Gaz* [1912] 1 K.B. 434 (C.A.); and *Seacrystal Shipping Ltd.* v. *Bulk Transport Group Shipping Co. Ltd.* [1989] 1 Lloyd's Rep. 1 (H.L.) (*The Kyzikos*).

addition of the words "whether in berth or not" does not permit ship-owners to count time where the ship has not arrived at the port.[83]

The Court of Appeal considered the expression in *Northfield SS. Co. v. Compagnie L'Union des Gaz*.[84] A ship chartered on the North-East Coast (Tees to Berwick) Coal Charter form, 1896,[85] carried coal from Sutherland to Savona where she was to "deliver her cargo alongside any wharf and/or vessel and/or craft as ordered, or so near there unto as she can safely get where she can safely deliver,[85a] always float . . . " The laytime clause stated: "Time to commence when steamer is ready to unload and written notice given, whether in berth or not." At Savona, all on one day, the ship arrived, was moored inside the port and harbour, and gave notice of readiness to unload. All berths alongside the wharves were occupied; this fact is of crucial importance.[85b] As a result of their own rules, sanctioned by the port authorities, the shore labourers would not work until she berthed alongside a wharf. The charterers contended that she was neither ready to unload nor an arrived ship until three days later, when she got a berth and began to discharge. The Court of Appeal rejected this argument. It held that laytime, as a result of the "whether in berth or not" clause, began when she moored, was ready to unload and had given notice. Farwell L.J. said[86]:

> "There was no berth vacant at Savona at which the steamer could be unloaded until four days after her arrival, and accordingly she did not get a berth until the fifth day . . . In my opinion the words 'whether in berth or not' were inserted to meet this very case. I do not think it possible to read them as equivalent to 'although she be moored alongside a vessel or craft and not in berth.' Want of space to berth is of very frequent occurrence, and the parties appear to me to have expressly provided for it; and this disposes also of the contention that the ship was not 'ready to unload.' She was ready so far as she was concerned, and the fact that she was not in a berth is rendered immaterial by this clause."

Under the charterparty time was not to run where "strikes, lock-outs, civil commotions, or any other causes or accidents" prevented or delayed discharging. The Court of Appeal said that the conduct of the shore labourers was not *ejusdem generis* with "strikes, lock-outs, civil commotions." But a clause such as the Centrocon Strike Clause would have helped the charterers if the facts had fallen within it, although the words "whether in berth or not" were used.[87]

6–20   Although the words "whether in berth or not" are used, the ship must in other respects have arrived, unless express words make this unnecessary. The words were considered by the High Court, in a charterparty on the Baltimore Form C, in *Carga del Sur Compania Naviera, S.A. v. Ross T.*

---

[83] *Carga del sur Compania Naviera, S.A. v. Ross T. Smyth & Co. Ltd.* [1962] 2 Lloyd's Rep. 147 (*The Seafort*); and see § 6–20 below. As Lloyd L.J. said in the Court of Appeal in *Seacrystal Shipping Ltd v. Bulk Transport Group Shipping Co. Ltd.* [1987] 2 Lloyd's Rep. 122 (*The Kyzikos*), at p. 125: "Nobody suggests that notice of readiness can be given while the vessel is still at sea (I say nothing as to the effect of 'whether in port or not,' which was also included in the charterparty, but as to which we heard no argument)."

[84] [1912] 1 K.B. 434.

[85] Of which the equivalent today is the East Coast Coal Charterparty 1922 (Medcon).

[85a] In speaking of this case Lord Brandon said, in the *Kyzikos* case in 1988 (see n. 82 above), at pp. 5–6: " . . . a ship was chartered under what would today be called a berth charterparty."

[85b] See §6–21 below.

[86] At p. 440.

[87] For the Centrocon Strike Clause, see § 8–38.

Smythe & Co. Ltd.[88] The *Seafort* carried grain from Vancouver to London and Hull. The clause entitling the charterers to discharge at a second port said: "Time at second port to count from arrival at second port, whether in berth or not." The ship anchored at Spurn Head Anchorage, 22 miles from Hull, the usual place for ships of her size to wait for a berth. She berthed at the silo berth in King George Dock, Hull, 10 days later. The charterers, resisting a demurrage claim and demanding dispatch, contended that time did not count until arrival of the ship in the dock area, where ships of her size discharged. The High Court held that arrival at Spurn Head Anchorage did not constitute arrival at the port of Hull, and that the provision for time to count whether in berth or not was irrelevant. McNair J. said[89]:

> " . . . the matter is concluded against the shipowner by the decision of the House of Lords in *Sociedad Financiera Raices S.A.* v. *Agrimpex Hungarian Trading Company for Agricultural Products*[90] unless the present case can be distinguished from that case by the inclusion in clause 9 of the words 'whether in berth or not' . . . it is clear that the vessel, on arrival at Spurn Head, had not even reached the legal, administrative or fiscal limits of the port of Hull, and it is quite impossible to give to the words 'whether in berth or not' the effect of extending the words 'arrival at second port' to include a place which is not within the limits of the port, whether legal, administrative or fiscal."

The judge considered that his decision was consistent with the judgment about Spurn Head Anchorage delivered by Sellers J. in *Roland-Linie Schiffahrt G.m.b.H.* v. *Spillers Ltd. and Others.*[91] There also it was held that the ship had not arrived; but the words were such[92] that it was not necessary for the ship to reach the port for the shipowners to recover demurrage.[93]

In *Oldendorff (E.L.) & Co. G.m.b.H.* v. *Tradax Export S.A.*[94] the   **6–20A** words "whether in berth or not" were held not to entitle shipowners to count laytime from anchorage in a usual waiting place outside the commercial area of the port of Liverpool or Birkenhead. No berth was available for the ship when she arrived at the discharging port. The application of the phrase had for 50 years been limited to cases where the ship was already an arrived ship. It did not mean "whether in port or not"[95] or "whether arrived or not." Roskill L.J. said in the Court of Appeal[96]: "The phrase 'whether in berth or not' was designed to convert a berth charterparty into a port charterparty and to ensure that under a berth charterparty notice of readiness could be given as soon as the ship had arrived within the commercial area of the port concerned so that laytime would start to run on its

---

[88] [1962] 2 Lloyd's Rep. 147 (*The Seafort*).
[89] At pp. 153 and 154.
[90] [1961] A.C. 135 (H.L.) (*The Aello*).
[91] [1957] 1 Q.B. 109 (*The Werrastein*). See § 6–37 below.
[92] An Austral charterparty had been used. See "Demurrage in respect of all time waiting" at § 6–36 below.
[93] The parties can choose words which cause time to start earlier. Thus a sale contract in *Gilbert J. McCaul & Co. Ltd.* v. *J.R. Moodie & Co. Ltd.* [1961] 1 Lloyd's Rep. 308 stated: "The basis of discharge is understood to be custom of the port in all cases except in the event of the vessel being ordered to Glasgow where time will commence at Tail of the Bank and Hull where time will count at Spurn Head." See also § 6–38 below.
[94] [1973] 2 Lloyd's Rep. 285 (H.L.) (*The Johanna Oldendorff*). See § 4–21 above.
[95] As to which see § 6–27 below.
[96] [1972] 2 Lloyd's Rep. 292 at p. 312. In the *Kyzikos* case (see n. 82 above) Lord Brandon said (at p. 5): "In evaluating the observations of Roskill L.J. . . . it is essential to appreciate that he made them, and made them only, with reference to a case where no berth was available for the ship concerned on her arrival at the port of discharge."

expiry. It has no proper place in a port charterparty." Lord Diplock, in *Federal Commerce and Navigation Co. Ltd.* v. *Tradax Export S.A.*[97] said: "The words italicised ['whether in berth or not'] are surplusage in a port charter. Their presence, however, is readily explicable. The parties took a printed form[98] appropriate to a berth charter as respects both loading and carrying voyages, and used it for an adventure in which the destination of the carrying, though not the loading voyage, was a range of named ports, not berths. The effect of this well-known phrase in berth charters has been settled for more than half a century. Under it time starts to run when the vessel is waiting within the named port of designation for a berth there to become vacant. In effect it makes the Reid test applicable to a berth charter. It has no effect in a port charter; the Reid test is applicable anyway."[99]

6–21   The phrase "whether in berth or not" enables shipowners to give a valid notice of readiness, if the ship has reached the port, and is "at the immediate and effective disposition of the charterer,"[99a] provided that it is the non-availability of a berth which prevents her further progress. In *Seacrystal Shipping Ltd* v. *Bulk Transport Group Shipping Co. Ltd.*[1] the *Kyzikos* carried steel from Italy to Houston, Texas. The charterparty, on the Gencon box form, stated "Time lost in waiting for berth to count as loading time. . . . Time to count . . . WIPON/WIBON/WIFPON/WCCON[1a] . . ." and that time lost in waiting for a discharging berth was to count as "discharging time."

At Houston a berth was available when notice of readiness was given, and at all material times thereafter; but fog prevented the ship from reaching it. The charterers contended that the shipowners were not entitled to give notice until she berthed, or until she left her anchorage, on her way to the berth.

The first question was whether a valid notice of readiness could be given; the second question was whether the ship could be said to be at the immediate and effective disposition[2] of the charterers at that time. The House of Lords allowed the appeal by charterers from the judgment of the Court of Appeal,[3] and so restored the award of the High Court judge, Webster J. The latter, finding for the shipowners, had considered that the ship was not waiting for a berth to become available, but was waiting for the fog to clear.

In the Court of Appeal Lloyd L.J. agreed that the provision, "whether in berth or not," was originally included in berth charterparties to cater for the case where the port was congested and a berth unavailable; but the wording did not limit its operation to such an event. If a limit were to be

---

[97] [1977] 2 Lloyd's Rep. 301 at p. 308 (*The Maratha Envoy*). See § 4–25 above.
[98] The Baltimore Form C.
[99] He added that a full discussion of the clause and of the previous authorities was to be found in the judgments of Buckley L.J. and Roskill L.J. in the Court of Appeal in the *Johanna Oldendorff*, [1972] 2 Lloyd's Rep. 292 at pp. 302–303 and 313–314. For the Reid test see § 4–22.
[99a] For this phrase see the discussion of *The Johanna Oldendorff*, beginning at §4–21 above, and especially §4–24.
[1] [1989] 1 Lloyd's Rep. 1 (H.L.) (*The Kyzikos*).
[1a] Whether in port or not/whether in berth or not/whether in free pratique or not/whether cleared customs or not.
[2] For this expression see § 4–11 above.
[3] [1987] 2 Lloyd's Rep. 122.

imposed, as to when notice of readiness should be given, it was better that it should be by reference to the place at which it might be given than to the reason why the ship was unable to proceed to her berth.

In the House of Lords Lord Brandon, delivering a speech with which the other Law Lords agreed, referred to the question of law formulated by the High Court for consideration by the Court of Appeal. This was: "whether the provision 'whether in berth or not' has the effect of converting a berth charterparty into a port charter-party in circumstances where a berth is available for the vessel." He said[3a] that the formulation, though generally succinct, tended to telescope the legal issues. The view put forward by the charterers and accepted by Webster J. was that the provision covered cases where the reason for the ship not being in berth was that no berth was available, but not cases where a berth was available and the only reason why the ship could not proceed to it was that she was prevented by bad weather such as fog. The other view, advanced by the shipowners and accepted by the arbitrator and the Court of Appeal, was that the phrase covered cases where a ship was unable to proceed to a berth either because none was available or because, although a berth was available, the ship was prevented by bad weather such as fog from proceeding to it.

Lord Brandon said that the propostion that the inclusion in a berth charterparty of the phrase "whether in berth or not" had the effect of converting it into a port charterparty appeared to have had its origin in the judgement of Roskill L.J. in the *Johanna Oldendorff*.[3b] It was essential to appreciate that Roskill L.J. had made those observations only with reference to a case where no berth was available for the ship on her arrival at the port of discharge. Lord Brandon continued[3c]: "It follows that, when he said that the phrase 'whether in berth or not' was designed to convert a berth charter-party into a port charter-party, he was saying it only in relation to a case where no berth was available for the ship on arrival. He had no reason to consider whether the words which he used would have been appropriate in a case where a berth was available for the ship on arrival but she was prevented by bad weather such as fog from proceeding to it."

He turned then to two cases in which the phrase "whether in berth or not" had been used. The first was the *Northfield* case,[3d] decided in 1912. All the berths were occupied, and Farwell L.J. had said[3e] that the phrase was presented to meet that very case. The second was the *Federal Commerce* case.[3f] He noted that Lord Diplock had said that the words were surplusage in a port charterparty, and that they caused time to run "when the vessel is waiting within the named port of destination for a berth there to become vacant." There seemed to have been no reported case in which it had been contended that the phrase covered a case where a berth was available for a ship but she was prevented by bad weather from proceeding to it.

Lord Brandon concluded that the phrase had, over a very long period, been treated as shorthand for "whether in berth (a berth being available)

[3a] [1989] 1 Loyd's Rep. 1, at p. 4.
[3b] Lord Brandon then quoted the two sentences from the judgment of Roskill L.J. which are set out in §6–20A above.
[3c] *Op. cit.*, at p. 5.
[3d] See §6–19 above.
[3e] [1912] 1 K.B. 434 at p. 440.
[3f] *The Maratha Envoy.* See §6–20A above.

or not in berth (a berth not being available)." He noted that the parties had not amended the provisions "Time lost in waiting for berth to count as loading time" and "Time lost in waiting for berth to count as discharging time." The inference was that the introduction of the acronym "wibon" was not intended to modify those provisions. It was found in association with the acronyms "wipon", "wifpon" and "wccon." These were all directed at the problem of congestion rather than that of delay by bad weather. It was reasonable to infer that the acronym "wibon" was similarly directed.

As to three matters upon which Lloyd L.J. had relied, Lord Brandon commented as follows. First, although there were no words which qualified the phrase "whether in berth or not," the authorities to which he (Lord Brandon) had referred showed that its purpose was to deal with the problem that no berth was available. Secondly, it had been said that the traditional view[3g] was that the phrase enabled a valid notice to be given as soon as the ship arrived in the port. This was the case where no berth was available when the ship arrived, but not otherwise, because, as he said, "the question of the effect of the phrase in that situation has never previously arisen for decision by any court." Thirdly, as to the importance of certainty in relation to a commercial contract, he said that, although it was desirable, he could not see that a decision that the phrase only took effect when a berth was not available provided any less certainty than a decision that it also took effect when a berth was available but unreachable by reason of bad weather.

Lord Brandon concluded by saying[3h]: " . . . I am of opinion, having regard to the authorities to which I referred earlier and the context in which the acronym "wibon" is to be found in the charter-party here concerned, that the phrase "whether in berth or not" should be interpreted as applying only to cases where a berth is not available and not also to cases where a berth is available but is unreachable by reason of bad weather."

6–22   Though the object of the words "whether in berth or not" is to advance the moment at which laytime begins, where a berth is unavailable, the same words may be neutralised by apt words of exception. In *Reardon Smith Line Ltd.* v. *East Asiatic Co. Ltd.*[4] those words[5] were: "If the cargo cannot be loaded . . . by reason of obstructions or stoppages beyond the control of the charterers . . . in the docks, or other loading places . . . the time for loading . . . shall not count during the continuance of such causes. . . . " A ship arrived at Dairen to load soya beans for Europe and gave notice on the next day. A loading berth was not available until 13 days later, and she was sent away on the day thereafter, not being allowed to resume loading for four more days because the government required the berth for landing troops and stores. The shipowners, claiming demurrage, argued that the words "whether in berth or not" obliged the charterers to provide a berth, and that if they failed to do so the lay days ran against them. The High Court held that the charterers were excused by the excep-

---

[3g] This is of course correct if the views of persons other than judges are not to be regarded as forming part of "the traditional view." Lord Brandon cited these last words five times, and without qualification, twice from the judgment of Lloyd L.J. and three times himself, before saying that no such view had been established because the question had not arisen in a court.

[3h] *Op. cit.*, at p. 8.

[4] (1938) 62 Ll.L.R. 23.

[5] As in the strike clause of the River Plate Charter-party 1914 (Centrocon).

tions clause. Branson J. said[6] that he was bound by the Court of Appeal decision in *Leonis SS. Co. Ltd.* v. *Joseph Rank Ltd.*[7] He said[8]:

> "To my mind that clause can have no effect on the construction to be put on the exceptions in clause 11 [the exceptions clause]. All that that clause is doing is to indicate the time at which a notice of readiness shall be given in order to fix when the lay days shall begin to run, and what it is saying is that that notice may be given, whether the ship is in berth or not, and the existence of that clause cannot, to my mind, have any effect in enabling me to put a different construction upon the exceptions clause than that which was adopted in *Leonis SS. Co. Ltd.* v. *Joseph Rank Ltd.*"[9]

3. *"Time to commence on being reported*[10] *at custom house"*[11]   **6–23**

Where the words are appropriate, time may begin even where the ship is outside the legal and commercial area of the port.

In *Horsley Line Ltd.* v. *Roechling Bros*[12] a charterparty for the carriage of pig-iron from Middlesborough provided that the ship should "proceed to Savona or Genoa, as ordered . . . and there deliver the same . . ." Time for discharging to commence on being reported at the custom house." The ship anchored in the Savona roads and was reported to the custom house on the same day. The roads were the usual place for ships to lie while the harbour was full. The parties agreed that the roads were outside both the geographical limits of the port and what was known commercially as the port. It was not the custom to discharge in the roads. There was a delay before the ship could get into the harbour, and a further delay before she could berth there. The shipowners claimed demurrage, contending that by the custom of the port ships were allotted berths according to the order of reporting on arrival in the roads. The charterers said that until the ship got within port limits she was not an arrived ship. The Court of Session held that time began when the ship was reported. Lord Low said[13] of the shipowners' contention as to port custom:

> "If that be so, then the report to the custom-house which the *Dalmally* made when she had anchored in the roads is the report referred to in the charterparty, and accordingly she must then be regarded as having been an 'arrived' ship within the meaning and for the purposes of the charterparty."

---

[6] At p. 27.

[7] (1970) 13 Com.Cas. 295.

[8] At p. 27.

[9] (1907) 13 Com.Cas. 295 (C.A.).

[10] Section 492 of the Merchant Shipping Act 1894 states (in connection with Delivery of Goods and Lien for Freight): "The expression 'report' means the report required by the customs laws to be made by the master of an importing ship."

[11] For a combination of a custom house provision with a 24-hour clause (for the latter see § 6–39 below) see the charterparty in *Graigwen (Owners)* v. *Anglo-Canadian Shipping Co. Ltd.* [1955] 2 Lloyd's Rep. 260: "Lay days at first loading port to commence twenty-four hours . . . after receipt by charterers or their agents of master's written notice during ordinary working hours, that steamer is entered at the custom house and in all respects ready to load." See § 6–40 below. For some cases as to custom house entry in India see § 5–10, n. 50 above.

[12] 1908 S.C. 866. An earlier example of a similar provision appears in *Macbeth* v. *Wild & Co.* (1900) 16 T.L.R. 497, where the words were: "Lay days shall commence when the steamer is reported at the Custom House, and in free pratique—unless the loading or delivery has sooner commenced . . ." The ship was to go "to a safe berth at Middlesborough-on-Tees as directed." Bigham J. held that time began when she was in the port, in free pratique and had reported, though still without a berth.

[13] At p. 876.

So also Lord Ardwall[14]:

> " . . . although when there is no express stipulation on the subject in the contract, lay-days will not be held to commence to run till the ship becomes what has been called an 'arrived ship,' yet the parties may contract otherwise, and as in this case and the *Machra-hanish,* fix the date of arrival in the Harbour roads as the commencement of the lay-days, thus throwing on the charterers the risk of the vessel failing to get a harbour berth for some time after arrival in the roadstead off the port."

The view taken by Lord Ardwall, that time began although she was not an arrived ship, seems more consistent with the English authorities[15] than that of Lord Low, that she must be regarded as an arrived ship, despite the latter's qualification[16] that she had arrived "within the meaning and for the purposes of the charterparty."

6–24   The words "For each lightening vessel at Calcutta, time to count from 24 hours after receipt of Master's written notice of readiness to discharge . . . vessel also having been entered at Custom House and in free pratique, whether in berth or not" have been considered by the U.S. District Court, Southern District of New York. In *Venore Transportation Company* v. *President of India*[17] a charterparty provided for the *Venore* to carry wheat grain from Philadelphia, Pennsylvania, to Calcutta, India. The shipowners chartered four smaller ships to lighten her at Madras and carry her cargo to Calcutta. The words quoted above were in the main charterparty but referred to the laytime of the lightening ships. These ships were delayed for periods of 35 to 40 days at Sandheads, an anchorage off the mouth of the River Hooghly. This was 123 miles from the commercial limits of the port of Calcutta, but it fell under the jurisdiction of the Commissioners of the Calcutta Port Trust. Notice of readiness was given there. It was held that whether or not the ships were "at Calcutta" laytime had not begun. Harold R. Tyler, Jr., D.J. said[18]: " . . . this contention need not be resolved since at least one other condition precedent to the running of the laytime had not been fulfilled at the time the notices were sent from Sandheads. As the evidence reveals, the lightening vessels were not and could not have been 'entered at Custom House' until some time after they had entered the commercial limits of Calcutta . . . the report of arrival at Sandheads is of no legal effect *vis-à-vis* Calcutta Customs and confers no rights upon vessels other than a rotation number." He noted that the result might have been different if laytime had to begin when the ship was reported at the custom house, as in *Horsley Line Ltd.* v. *Roechling Bros.*[19]

6–25   A requirement that the ship shall have been entered at the custom house has been ignored for the purpose of deciding when laytime shall begin. In *Alcon Ltd.* v. *Finagrain Compagnie Commerciale Agricole et Financière, S.A. Genève,*[20] a New York arbitration, the relevant clause stated: "Notifi-

---

[14] At p. 878. He relied on the case of *The Machrahanish*, read to the court by counsel from the *Shipping Gazette* of April 4, 1906.

[15] Including especially *Leonis SS. Co. Ltd.* v. *Joseph Rank Ltd. (No. 1)* [1908] 1 K.B. 499 and *Sociedad Financiera de Bienes Raices S.A.* v. *Agrimpex Hungarian Trading Co. for Agricultural Products* [1961] A.C. (H.L.) (*The Aello*). See also §§ 4–18 and 4–19 above.

[16] 1908 S.C. 866 at p. 876.

[17] [1973] 1 Lloyd's Rep. 494.

[18] At p. 498.

[19] 1908 S.C. 866. See § 6–23 above.

[20] Society of Maritime Arbitrators No. 1212 (1978) (*The Aquagem*). The facts were substantially the same as in the *The Konkar Pioneer* arbitration, (1977) A.M.C. 1794, Society of Maritime Arbitrators No. 1047, in which the same conclusion was reached.

cation of the vessel's readiness at discharge port must be given to the office at Agroexport, Bucharest, or their agents 'Navlomar,' Constanza . . . vessel also having been entered at the Custom House and the laydays will then commence at 8 a.m. on the next business day, whether in berth or not whether in port or not, whether in free pratique or not." It was held that those concluding expressions prevailed over the requirement of custom house entry, "a procedure that is routinely granted after the vessel has berthed and is in free pratique." The dissenting arbitrator[21] said that the words "Vessel also having been entered at the Custom House" were very clear: "If they had no meaning, why would they be written in the charterparty as part of a special typewritten clause? The clause could very well have read ' . . . whether in berth or not, whether in port or not, whether in free pratique or not, whether entered by Customs or not' . . . they [the parties] chose to make Custom House entry a condition precedent to the starting of the laytime." It seems that the majority opinion is in accordance with English law on the subject.

A berth charterparty may provide that (a) laytime begins following customs clearance and notice of readiness, whether the ship is in berth or not; and (b) notice of readiness may be given, and laytime may count, when the ship is at a place where customs clearance cannot be obtained. In such a case it has been held that the second of the two provisions is effective, and that laytime begins. In *Compania Argentina de Navegacion de Ultramar* v. *Tradax Export S.A.*[22] a ship was to carry grain, under a Centrocon charterparty, from the River Plate "to one safe berth, Seaforth Dock Liverpool." Time was to count **6–26**

> "from the first working period on the next business day following vessel's custom clearance[23] and receipt of writen notice of readiness during ordinary office hours by Charterers' agents from 0900 hours to 1700 hours from Monday to Friday, unless a holiday whether in berth or not."

The charterers had an option to discharge at a "second safe wharf or berth." It was further provided:

> "In the event that vessel is unable to berth immediately upon arrival, on account of congestion, vessel is to present notice of readiness . . . from arrival at Mersey Bar and time is to count accordingly. . . ."

The ship arrived at the Mersey Bar anchorage where it was not possible to obtain customs clearance. The shipowners gave notice of readiness, which was rejected on the ground that clearance had not been obtained. They ordered the ship to a lay-by berth in Seaforth Dock and gave a second notice, which was accepted. Mocatta J., finding for the shipowners, said that it was unreasonable and uncommercial to require the notice of readiness to be given from the lay-by berth. He concluded[24]:

> "I take the view that the argument advanced on behalf of the owners is the right one and that this being a berth charter and the discharging berth being unavailable owing to congestion at the time that the vessel reached Mersey Bar, cl. 50 [the clause which referred to Mersey Bar] did come into operation."

The first notice was therefore valid.

[21] Who was also the dissenting arbitrator in the *Konkar Pioneer* arbitration.
[22] [1978] 1 Lloyd's Rep. 252 (*The Puerto Rocca*).
[23] A ship is usually said to "report" to the customs authorities on her arrival, but to "clear" them on her departure. The parties here agreed that the word "clearance" referred to the arrival.
[24] *Op. cit.* at p. 257.

6–27   4. *"Whether in port or not."*

The frequently used expression, "whether in berth or not" has been considered above.[25] The words "whether in port or not" are less frequently used. It has been said[26] that the earliest case which the parties had found was *Compania de Naviera Nedelka S.A.* v. *Tradax International S.A.*,[27] and that the only one where specific attention had been directed to the words was *Surrey Shipping Co. Ltd.* v. *Compagnie Continentale (France) S.A.*[28] Donaldson J. had said in the High Court[29]:

> "The words 'whether in port or not' cover the possibility, if such there was, that a bunkering or other berth might be 'at' but not 'in' the port of Constanza, and also the possibility of any change in the regulations allowing customs entry while a vessel lay in the roads. The words 'whether in free pratique or not' show that the obtaining of free pratique is not a condition precedent to giving notice of readiness."

6–28   5. *"In regular turn"*

The old expression "turn"[30] refers to the sequence in which ships are taken, usually by the port authorities, for loading or discharging. A ship is often described as being "in turn" when she is awaiting her turn. As Morris J. said in *The Themistocles*[31]:

> "The vessel might arrive at the wharf reserved to shippers, might be admitted in free pratique and give notice that she is ready to load, and might then have to wait to be told at which precise berth she is to load. The vessel would then be in turn."

"Turn time" is the period from arrival until the ship is brought forward to be given a loading or discharging place. "Regular turn," an expression often found in coal charterparties, means that ships, whether all ships or merely ships of one class, are taken for loading or discharging in order. The order may be that in which they were reported to the authorities, usually at the custom house; or the order of their arrival; or the usual order adopted by receivers for that kind of ship. Time will not count during the turn time. "Free of turn" or "free turn" means that time counts during the turn time; laytime begins when the ship reaches her contractual destination and is ready, notice of readiness having been given,[32] irrespective of the fact that she is waiting her turn.

Without the presence in the laytime clause of such expressions as "in regular turn," "take its turn," "limited turn" and "in berth in turn," laytime begins, in the case of a port charterparty when the ship arrives at her contractual destination, is ready, and gives notice of readiness.[33] Congestion does not relieve charterers by preventing laytime from beginning,[34] in the absence of express words. Thus the Phosphate Charter Party, 1950

---

[25] See § 6–19 above.

[26] *Pagnan (R.) & Fratelli* v. *Finagrain Compagnie Commerciale Agricole et Financière S.A.* [1986] 2 Lloyd's Rep. 395 (*The Adolf Leonhardt*), by Staughton J., at p. 402.

[27] [1973] 2 Lloyd's Rep. 247 (*The Tres Flores*); see § 5–03 below.

[28] [1978] 2 Lloyd's Rep. 154 (C.A.) (*The Shackleford*); see § 5–30 below.

[29] [1978] 1 Lloyd's Rep. 191, at p. 197.

[30] The context is important: thus "regular turn" may mean "regular turn of the colliery" rather than "regular turn of arrival" as in *Barque Quilpué, Ltd.* v. *Brown* [1904] 2 K.B. 264 (C.A.). See also § 6–29.

[31] (1949) 82 Ll.L.Rep. 232 at p. 237. See also § 6–32 below.

[32] In the absence of any other clause modifying the usual requirements as to when laytime begins: for such clauses, see § 6–02 above.

[33] See § 4–01 above.

[34] *Randall* v. *Lynch* (1810) 2 Camp. 352: *Brown* v. *Johnson* (1843) 10 M. & W. 331 (see § 4–12 above); and *Tapscott* v. *Balfour* (1872) L.R. 8 C.P. 46 (see § 4–06 above).

(Africanphos) states: "The vessel will be loaded in turn not exceeding 48 running hours, Sundays and legal or local holidays included . . . " Where it is agreed that the ship shall be taken "in regular turn," then the beginning of laytime is postponed.

In *The Cordelia*[35] a charterparty for the carriage of phosphate from the Thames to "the Nob near Topsham in the river Exe, or to Topsham Quay, as ordered on arrival," provided for the ship to "deliver . . . in regular turn with other seagoing vessels at the average rate of thirty tons per weather working day." The ship, though ready to deliver, was kept waiting some days at the Nob while another ship, consigned to the charterers and already there, was being discharged by lighters sent by the charterers. The Probate, Divorce and Admiralty Divisional Court held that the shipowners' demurrage claim must fail, as the words "in regular turn" meant one ship at a time. Sir Gorell Barnes P. said[36]:

> "It looks to me as if the plaintiff expected that his vessel find a string of barges when she got to the Nob. I am afraid the plaintiff could not reasonably expect more than that he should have his vessel discharged in regular turn with other seagoing vessels which were being discharged in turn with usual despatch. The terms of the charterparty do not justify the plaintiff in expecting more than that."

Relevance of type of ship. Charterers may distinguish between various **6–29** kinds of ships when arranging the "turn" if discrimination is an established practice. It is sometimes the practice to take ocean sailing ships in turn, while interposing certain coasting ships. Furthermore, the ship may be taken in turn, but the delay may be such that shipowners consider that there has been a breach of charterers' implied obligation not to do anything to prevent or to delay performance by shipowners. If shipowners are shown to have been aware, at the time of the conclusion of the charterparty, of a probable delay, then they have no claim against charterers.

So in *Barque Quilpué, Ltd.* v. *Brown*[37] a charterparty for the carriage of coal from Newcastle, New South Wales, to South America provided that the ship should "in the usual and customary manner load in regular turn from Brown's Duckenfield Colliery, or any of the collieries the freighters may name." The ship arrived on August 3, but many other ships, entitled to priority over her, were waiting to load. She berthed on October 6, and completed loading on October 9. The Court of Appeal held that the charterers were not liable for the detention of the ship. They had not chartered more ships to load than they did in the ordinary course of their business. Vaughan Williams L.J. said[38]:

> "Cases have been cited which, I take it, shew that prima facie the words 'in regular turn,' unless there is something to lead to a different conclusion, mean 'in regular port turn'; but none of these cases show that 'in regular turn' cannot mean 'in regular colliery turn' as distinguished from 'regular port turn' . . . both parties must have comtemplated that the ship would be loaded in accordance with the 'colliery turn' . . . The evidence shews that 'regular turn' means the regular turn amongst ocean sailing ships, and that being so it is plain that the *Quilpué*, although she was detained for sixty-seven days, did get her 'regular turn.' "

---

[35] [1909] P. 27.
[36] At p. 31.
[37] [1904] 2 K.B. 264 (C.A.).
[38] At pp. 270–271.

The Court also held that the shipowners must have known not only that the charterers would have prior engagements which might delay the colliery turn of that ship, but also that a delay of from 40 to 50 days was not impossible or even unusual in loading at Newcastle.

6–30   **Losing turn.** If the ship is in her place, ready, and does not get her turn, charterers are responsible for further delay, unless it is not caused by any fault of theirs. If the ship is not or ceases to be ready, the charterers are not usually responsible.

So in *Taylor* v. *Clay*[39] a ship was to carry coal from Port Talbot to America and be loaded in turn. The master and crew worked the ship in a manner contrary to the directions given by the harbour-master, so that she was damaged and lost her loading turn. The charterers were held not to be liable for the delay. Lord Denman C.J. said[40]:

> " . . . the terms of this contract imply only that she was to have her turn when she was ready to take it. Her turn was not come if she was not in a situation to take advantage of it."

But where the missing of the turn is caused by charterers, whether through their failure to procure cargo or otherwise, shipowners can hold them responsible.[41] In *Jones* v. *Adamson*[42] a ship was chartered to go to a foreign port for a cargo and "there, in the usual and accustomed manner, load in her regular turn." When her turn came she was not ready owing to the charterers' fault, and was detained for 11 days; when her turn came round again there was a wind which, since the harbour was crowded, caused the harbour-master to refuse her permission to load so that she was detained for three days. It was held that the charterers were liable for all the detention, though they had argued that the second period was too remote a consequence of their fault. Cleasby B. said[43]:

> "It was not a question of one turn or two turns, but the contract was that the ship should load in her regular turn, and the breach of it caused a loss of fourteen days . . . The proximate cause of the detention for the three days was in default of the defendant in not performing his contract to load in regular turn, and not any great catastrophe caused by vis major."

Perhaps this should be regarded only as an example of loss of a turn through the fault of charterers. It might not justify the proposition that loss of the second turn is also a risk which they should bear, except in the rare cases where the onset of bad weather at a particular time was reasonably foreseeable at the time of the contract.[44]

---

[39] (1846) 9 Q.B. 713.

[40] At p. 724.

[41] Unless the charterers are protected by an exceptions clause. But the clause was not wide enough to protect them in *Fenwick* v. *Schmalz* (1868) L.R. 3 C.P. 313, where the words were: "in regular and customary turn (except in cases of riots, strikes or any other accidents beyond their control.)" and snowstorms were held not to be "accidents."

[42] (1876) 1 Ex.D. 60.

[43] At p. 61.

[44] For the measure of damages for breach of contract, see, among many authorities, *Hadley* v. *Baxendale* (1854) 9 Ex. 341; *Victoria Laundry (Windsor) Ltd.* v. *Newman Industries Ltd.* [1949] 2 K.B. 528 (C.A.); and *Monarch SS. Co. Ltd.* v. *Karlshamns Oljefabriker (A/B)* [1949] 196 (H.L.).

Relation to notice of readiness. Even in a port charterparty the beginning **6–31** of laytime is postponed, in spite of the ship having arrived, being ready, and having given notice, if she must await her "regular turn."[45] The notice and the turn provisions may be so closely linked as to suggest that laytime begins when notice is given. Much confusion and subsequent litigation can be avoided by the use of clear words and phrases.[46]

In *United States Shipping Board* v. *Frank C. Strick & Co. Ltd.*[47] a charterparty for the carriage of coal from Delagoa Bay to Suez stated: "The cargo to be loaded . . . in regular turn as customary at the rate of 1,000 tons per day . . . commencing when written notice is given of steamer being . . . ready to load." The ship arrived at Delagoa Bay and anchored within the commercial limits on July 30, giving notice of readiness on the following day. The only loading berth was occupied by another ship until August 26. The shipowners failed in their demurrage claim. The House of Lords held (Viscount Haldane and Lord Sumner dissenting) that the obligation to load in turn at the agreed rate became binding when the notice of readiness was given, but operative only when the turn arrived. It was the wait for the regular turn and not the loading time which was "commencing" when notice was given. Viscount Cave L.C. referred to earlier cases dealing with ships' turns[48] and said[49]:

" . . . our Courts have uniformly given effect to those expressions having a bearing on the question of lay days. In most, if not all, of the cases[50] the ship in question was an arrived ship and ready to load, but it was nevertheless held or assumed that the commencement of the loading or unloading days was by the terms of the contract postponed until the ship's 'turn' arrived . . . "

Of the words "commencing when written notice is given of steamer being . . . ready to load," he said[51]:

" . . . I think that the true meaning of the clause is that the obligation to load in turn at the specified rate is to become binding when the notice to load in turn is given, although that obligation cannot become actually operative until the turn arrives. In other words, to the three conditions for the commencement of the lay days enumerated by Kennedy L.J. in *Leonis Steamship Co. Ltd.* v. *Rank*[52]—namely arrival of the ship, readiness to load

---

[45] See § 6–28 above.
[46] As was emphasised by Scrutton L.J. in *United States Shipping Board* v. *Frank C. Strick & Co. Ltd.* (1924) 30 Com.Cas. 210 at p. 224: " . . . each side could have made the meaning they contend for perfectly clear by the addition of some perfectly well-known words which are repeatedly used in charterparties."
[47] [1926] A.C. 545 (H.L.).
[48] *Robertson* v. *Jackson* (1845) C.B. 412 (detention "from the time of the vessel being ready to unload and in turn to deliver": see § 6–33 below): *Leidemann* v. *Schultz* (1853) 14 C.B. 38 ("on arrival there be ready forthwith in regular turns of loading to take on board" coal and coke: see § 6–34 below.): *Lawson* v. *Burness* (1862) 1 H. & C. 396 (coke "to be loaded in regular turn"); *The Cordelia* [1909] P. 27 ("in regular turn": see § 6–28 above.); *Kokusai Kisen Kabushiki Kaisha* v. *Flack & Son* (1922) 10 Ll.L.Rep. 83, 635 (C.A.) ("in regular turn"); and *Miguel de Larrinaga S.S. Co.* v. *Flack & Son* (1925) 20 Ll.L.Rep. 268.
[49] At p. 555.
[50] He relied especially on the High Court decision in *Miguel de Larrinaga Co.* v. *Flack* (1925) 20 Ll.L.Rep. 268, where the facts and charterparty wording were similar. Roche J. said of the dock charterparty in that case (at p. 270): "In the ordinary case she would not be an arrived ship until she got into dock, but . . . the obligation to load at a certain specified rate per day did not arise until the vessel was 'in turn,' that is to say, was at the pier, and was there to load as customary."
[51] At pp. 556–557.
[52] [1908] 1 K.B. 499 (C.A.).

and notice of such readiness . . . there is added by the terms of this charterparty a fourth condition—namely, the arrival of the turn."[53]

It was said above[54] that laytime may begin when notice is given, but much depends on the wording. The House of Lords has held[55] that laytime did not begin until the turn arrived; but in *Moor Line, Ltd.* v. *Manganexport G.m.b.H.*[56] the High Court held, in favour of the shipowners, that laytime began when the ship was ready. A charterparty provided for the carriage of iron ore from Nicolaieff, U.S.S.R., to U.S. ports. By clause 2 the ship was to load "in usual turn with other steamers loading ore for account of same charterers, when, where and as soon as ordered . . . " Clause 6 stated: "Time for loading to count from 6 a.m. after the ship is reported and ready, and in free pratique (whether in berth or not) in accordance with Clause 2 . . . " The ship waited 10 days after free pratique was granted and notice of readiness given to get her "usual turn." It was held that time began to count at 6 a.m. after the notice was given, despite the reference in clause 6 to clause 2 . Branson J. said[57]:

> " . . . if the words 'in usual turn' and so forth were really intended to govern the time at which the time for loading was to commence, one would expect to find that set out in Clause 6, which is the clause dealing with that very point, but they are not there."

If the parties had said in Clause 6 "Time to count from so many hours after the ship is on turn" the clause could have been construed otherwise.

6–32   **Turn delay limited.** The delay in the beginning of laytime, imposed by the provision for the ship to take her regular or customary turn, may be limited by appropriate words. Such a limitation may be created by such words as "in turn not exceeding 48 (or 24) running hours."

In *The Themistocles*[58] a charterparty for the carriage of phospate from Sfax and Casablanca to Finland stated: "The vessel to be loaded . . . in the customary manner alongside the wharf reserved to shippers, at the berth they indicate and according to their orders, in turn not exceeding 48 running hours not included [various periods were then excluded] . . . even though work should have commenced earlier, and after the vessel has been admitted in free pratique and notice been given to shipper that she is ready to load . . . "; and "Lay days to count as soon as the vessel has reached the end of her turn from 8 a.m. or 2 p.m. after the vessel being admitted into the port in free pratique and ready in all respects to load has occupied the loading berth . . . " At Sfax the ship berthed and began loading, no time being lost in waiting her turn. The High Court held that the time allowed for turn ceased to run as soon as she berthed and was ready to load, laytime counting immediately. Morris J. said[59]:

> "If the charterers are correct, there would seem to be no reason for the employment of the word 'turn.' The period might be continuing to run when the vessel was in no sense

---

[53] Lord Sumner (dissenting) regarded this application of the words "in regular turn" as an inroad on the rule in *Leonis SS. Co. Ltd.* v. *Rank Ltd. (No. 1)* [1908] 1 K.B. 499 (C.A.). He said (at p. 571) that they should apply only to the mode and not to the time of loading.

[54] In § 6–26.

[55] *United States Shipping Board* v. *Frank C. Strick & Co. Ltd.* [1926] A.C. 545 (H.L.). See this section above.

[56] (1936) 55 Ll.L.Rep. 114.

[57] At p. 117.

[58] (1949) 82 Ll.L.Rep. 232. The decision is also an authority on dispatch; see § 12–11 below.

[59] At p. 237.

being kept waiting. Nor would any meaning be derived from the words 'not exceeding 48 running hours.' "

Special meanings of "turn." It has already been shown that the meaning **6–33** of the terms "turn" and "regular turn" can differ according to the context in which they are found.[60] Thus "regular turn" may indicate the order of arrival, or the order in which the collieries can provide cargoes, or some other order.[61] A special meaning may be attached to such an expression in a particular trade or at a particular port. If so, the parties are bound by that meaning, as they are taken to have contracted with reference to it.

In *Robertson* v. *Jackson*[62] a ship was to carry coal from the Tyne to Algiers. She was to be discharged at a daily rate but if that was exceeded the charterers were to "pay for such detention at the rate of 5l. [£5] per diem, to reckon from the time of the vessel being ready to unload, and in turn to deliver." The coal was being shipped for the receivers under a contract with a French government department. Offical regulations required to be unloaded at a particular spot, and in a given order. It was held that evidence was admissible to show that the words "in turn to deliver" had by the usage of that trade acquired a special meaning. Tindal C.J., giving judgment for the charterers in respect of the shipowners' claim for damages for detention, found that there was a generally understood meaning of the words. The government regulations formed part of the port regulations. He said[63]:

> "Taking, therefore, the interpretation of the words to be, turn of delivery in conformity with the regulations of the port of Algiers, the question really becomes one of parcel or no parcel—was the regulation under which this delivery took place, a regulation of the port or not? And we think, upon the evidence, it was."

Similar conclusions have been reached in other cases, by the courts hold- **6–34** ing that the parties are bound by special meanings of such expressions as "in regular turn" or "in customary turn," where they are generally known and accepted in the trade. The other cases include:

Leidemann v. *Schultz*.[64] The ship was to "be ready forthwith, in regular turns of loading, to take on board a full and complete cargo" of coal and coke at Newcastle. By Act of Parliament "regular turns," with reference to coal, meant in turn at the spout. It was held that this interpretation applied to the charterparty, and that evidence was admissible to prove a practice to load coke in turn in the same manner. Jervis C.J. said[65] that the case was "very similar in principle to that of *Robertson* v. *Jackson*."[66]

King v. *Hinde*.[67] A sailing ship was chartered to load coal at White-haven, "regular turn" being allowed for loading. By port custom steam ships were loaded before sailing ships, even when the latter arrived first; the shipowners were aware of this custom, and their ship was delayed while several steam ships which had arrived earlier were loaded. Their own ship was loaded in order of arrival of sailing ships, this also being a port custom. It was held, when they claimed demurrage, that the phrase "regular turn"

---

[60] See § 6–28 above.
[61] *Barque Quilpué, Ltd.* v. *Brown* [1904] 2 K.B. 264 (C.A.). See § 6–29 above.
[62] (1845) 2 C.B. 412.
[63] At p. 428.
[64] (1853) 14 C.B. 38.
[65] At p. 51.
[66] (1845) 2 C.B. 412. See § 6–33 above.
[67] (1883) 12 L.R.Ir. 113.

had to be construed against the background of the customs of Whitehaven; that their ignorance of such customs was immaterial; and that their claim failed.

Hudson v. *Clementson.*[68] The charterers agreed that the ship would, for her voyage from Sunderland to Cartagena, "with all possible dispatch load in the south dock, in the customary manner . . . a full and complete cargo of coke, to be loaded in regular turn." It was held that evidence was not admissible to show that, by port custom, shipowners were bound to wait their turn according to a list kept by a coke manufacturer.

6–35   **Customary turn.** The application of the expression "customary turn" is limited to the order in which ships reach the place of loading or discharging, and does not, without other express words, refer to delay in bringing the cargo to them.

In *The Sheila*[69] a ship had been chartered to load, at jetties in Fowey, "in the customary manner a full and complete cargo of china clay and china stone in bulk . . . customary turn by Great Western Railway as for steamers at Fowey to be allowed the merchants (if the ship not be sooner dispatched) for loading the said cargo at Fowey." Loading was delayed because the G.W.R., acting for the charterers, failed to forward enough trucks to the jetties. Resisting a demurrage claim, the charterers argued that the words "customary turn by Great Western Railway" meant that the shipowners had agreed that (1) the ship was to take her turn to get to the jetty where she was to be loaded, (2) she was to accept customary turn as to the manner of loading after she had got there, *i.e.* that everything should be done according to the customs of the G.W.R. In the Divisional Court sitting in Admiralty Bucknill J. said[70]:

> "The word 'customary' does not seem to me to apply at all to the mode of loading which they choose to adopt in loading ships which come to their jetty, but in my opinion it applies only to the ship's getting to the loading place—the customary turn for loading."

6–36   6. *"Demurrage in respect of all time waiting"*

The words "demurrage in respect of all time waiting" appear in the Austral charterparty.[71] Under the destination clause[72] the ship is to proceed to "one safe port . . . or so near thereunto as the Vessel can safely get . . . and there deliver the cargo . . . at any customary dock, wharf or pier as ordered by the Charterers or their agents, where the Vessel can safely lie . . . " This is followed by a proviso: "Provided always that if such discharging place is not immediately available, demurrage in respect of all time waiting thereafter shall be paid at the rate mentioned in clause 17."[73] The result is that demurrage may accrue although the ship has not yet arrived at the port, if she is in other respects ready and has done everything possible to satisfy the conditions governing the beginning of laytime. The situation can be compared with that arising if laytime is to begin when the

---

[68] (1886) 18 C.B. 213.
[69] Decided on December 3, 1907; the report consists of an extended note inserted after the report of *The Cordelia* [1909] P. 27 at p. 31.
[70] At p. 34.
[71] Australian Grain Charter 1928. There is a similar clause in the Australian Grain Charter, 1972 (Austwheat).
[72] Cl. 2.
[73] Cl. 17 is another printed clause in the Austral form of charterparty, setting out a demurrage rate of three pence per gross register ton per running day.

ship is "reported at Custom House."[74] Just as in such a case[75] the parties can fix the time of arrival outside the port as marking the beginning of laytime, so such a time can mark the beginning of demurrage. Though demurrage normally succeeds the expiry of laytime, the parties can agree that time before the beginning of laytime should attract a demurrage rate.[76]

Spurn Head. In *Roland-Linie Schiffahrt G.m.b.H.* v. *Spillers Ltd.*[77] the **6–37** *Werrastein* carried bulk wheat under an Austral charterparty[78] from Sydney, New South Wales, to Hull. The charterparty contained the Austral form of discharging clause with a proviso relating to "demurrage in respect of all time waiting."[79] At Hull grain could only be discharged at the King George Dock, but its berths were occupied when the ship reached the Humber. There was neither room to wait in the Dock nor a safe anchorage in the vicinity of the docks. She was ordered by the port authorities to anchor at Spurn Head, 22 miles from, and outside the geographical, legal and fiscal limits of, the port. She waited a week at the anchorage, which was one of three customary waiting places for large ships to anchor while awaiting entry to the docks. The shipowners claimed demurrage in repect of that period, saying that "demurrage" in the proviso meant "as if on demurrage." The charterers contended that the risk of loss resulting from the congestion fell on the shipowners and that the words "demurrage in respect of all time waiting thereafter" only applied after a discharging place had been ordered by the charterers.

The High Court held that the shipowners were entitled to demurrage for the waiting period. Sellers J. said[80]:

> "In my view, the proviso deals with waiting time (due to the discharging place being unavailable) before the lay days commence to run, and provides for just such an occasion as has arisen here . . . The ship has to face the hazards of the voyage whereby she may be delayed by storm, fog, tides and many other events. But for clause 2[81] the waiting at the anchorage would likewise have fallen on the ship, for it would seem that the earliest time, on any view, that she could have become an arrived ship so that time for discharge would run against the charterers or their agents would be when she entered the King George Dock, and she could not have done that before she in fact did enter."

The *Roland Linie* decision favoured shipowners whose ships were delayed at the Spurn Head anchorage; and depended on the Austral proviso: "demurrage in respect of all time waiting . . . shall be paid." In *Carga del sur Compania Naviera S.A.* v. *Ross T. Smyth & Co. Ltd.*[82] the High Court decided against shipowners whose ship was delayed at the Spurn Head anchorage and held that the ship was not an arrived ship; the judgment turned on the words in the Baltimore Form C: "Time at second port to count from arrival at second port, whether in berth or not." In the former case the proviso could be, and was, taken to embrace the situation where the ship had not arrived. In the latter case the words on which the

---

[74] See § 6–23 above.

[75] See *Horsley Line Ltd.* v. *Roechling Brothers*, 1908 S.C. and § 6–23 above.

[76] Their freedom so to do was emphasised by Singleton L.J. in *North River Freighters Ltd.* v. *President of India* [1956] 1 Q.B. 333 (C.A.) (*The Radnor*) at p. 340. See § 6–03 above.

[77] [1957] 1 Q.B. 109 (*The Werrastein*).

[78] Australian Grain Charter 1928.

[79] As set out in § 6–36 above.

[80] At pp. 120 and 121.

[81] The clause which contained the demurrage provision.

[82] [1962] 2 Lloyd's Rep. 147 (*The Seafort*); see also § 6–20 above.

shipowners relied unsuccessfully were themselves concerned with "arrival at second port."[83]

6–38   **Leith Roads.** In *Gilbert J. McCaul & Co., Ltd.* v. *J.R. Moodie & Co., Ltd.*[84] the *North Devon* had carried oats from Australia to Liverpool and Leith. An Austral charterparty[85] said that delivery was to be "at any customary dock, wharf or pier as ordered by the Charterers or their agents" and added the proviso: "Provided always that if such discharging place is not immediately available, demurrage in respect of all time waiting thereafter shall be paid . . . " The ship arrived at Leith Roads, outside the commercial but within the legal, fiscal and administrative limits of the port. She berthed three weeks later. The shipowners claimed demurrage from the receivers, as the bills of lading incorporated the charterparty. The Scottish Court of Session held that the receivers were liable. They, as buyers, then claimed to be indemnified by their sellers under London Corn Trade Association Contract. The contract provided, *inter alia*: "Vessel to discharge according to the custom of the Port." The High Court held that the sellers were not liable. Any custom of the Port related only to matters arising after the ship had arrived, and she was not an arrived ship at Leith Roads. Diplock J. said[86] that the decisions in *North River Freighters Ltd.* v. *President of India*[87] and in the *Roland-Linie* case[88] drew a clear distinction between waiting time and discharging time, and added[89]:

> " . . . on the true construction of the London Corn Trade Association Contract, the provision 'Vessel to discharge according to the custom of the Port' relates only to matters arising after the vessel has become an arrived ship. It follows, therefore, that the buyers are entitled to be indemnified by the sellers for the amount they have paid for the waiting time."

6–39   **7. *"To be loaded as per colliery guarantee"*[90]**
This elderly clause is combined with a provision in the guarantee for the ship "to load in . . . days after the ship is ready in Dock at . . . " Where the guarantee states the time from which lay days count, the beginning of laytime is governed by this collateral document. Thus in *Monsen* v. *Macfarlane & Co.*[91] the charterparty, for the carriage of coal from the Royal Dock, Grimsby, provided for loading as per colliery guarantee in 15 colliery working days. The colliery guarantee obliged the colliery company to load in 15 colliery working days "after the said ship is wholly unballasted and ready in dock at Grimsby to receive her entire cargo . . . Time to count from the day following that on which notice of readiness is received." The ship gave notice of readiness when she arrived in the dock.

---

[83] For both sides agreeing that laytime began at the Spurn Head Anchorage, but disagreeing as to whether certain time there should count as shifting time, see *Compania Naviera Termar S.A.* v. *Tradax Export S.A.* [1966] 1 Lloyd's Rep. 566 (H.L.) (*The Ante Topic*) and § 8–48 below.
[84] [1961] 1 Lloyd's Rep. 308.
[85] Australian Grain Charter 1928.
[86] At p. 317.
[87] [1956] 1 Q.B. 333 (C.A.) (*The Radnor*). See § 6–03.
[88] [1957] 1 Q.B. 109 (*The Werrastein*). See also § 8–48 below.
[89] At pp. 317–318.
[90] The meanings of the expressions "colliery guarantee" and "colliery working day" have been explained in §§ 2–62–2–66 above.
[91] [1895] 2 Q.B. 562 (C.A.).

The Court of Appeal held that laytime began on the day after, and not when she arrived at the customary loading place inside the dock, to which access had been delayed by congestion. As Lord Esher said[92]:

> "All that the shipowner could do was to get his ship ready, so that when she was under the spout she would be able at once to receive the coal. He must place the ship as near to the spout as the harbour-master would permit her to be, and have everything on board ready for the reception of the coal, and when she is in that place and condition he is to give notice of readiness to the charterer that he may get his coal ready for shipment. Notice must also be given to the harbour-master. It seems to me, therefore, upon the construction of this charter, coupled with the colliery guaranty, that the lay days begin to run on the day after that on which notice of readiness is received by the charterer, and after that everything is at the risk of the charterer."

8. *"Time to count twenty-four hours after arrival at or off the port"*[93]

A clause which stipulates a period, such as 24 or 48 hours from arrival at or off the port, after which time is to count, may delay or advance the beginning of laytime. It may delay it where, for example, under a port charterparty the ship has arrived at the port, is in all other respects ready and has given notice. It may advance the beginning of laytime where under a port charterparty the ship is off the port but is delayed in berthing owing to congestion.[94]

The operation of the clause has been held[95] to be affected by the rights **6–40** of charterers to name a loading or discharging place; but the charterers may put themselves in the wrong if they cause such a place to be inaccessible to shipowners.[96]

In *Aktieselsabet Inglewood* v. *Millar's Karri and Jarrah Forest Ltd.*[97] a ship was to go "to Fremantle, or so near thereto as she may safely get, and there load as customary, always afloat, at such wharf, jetty or anchorage as the charterer's agent may direct," a timber cargo. Laytime was to begin "24 hours after written notice has been given of ship being wholly clear of ballast and ready to take in cargo." Notice of readiness was given when she was at an anchorage where she could have been loaded by lighters. She was ordered to the jetty, where all four practicable berths were full, three being occupied by ships which the charterers were loading. The High Court held that laytime began 24 hours after the notice of readiness. Kennedy J. said[98]:

> "When the charterers in this case ordered the *Inglewood*, as they did, to load at the jetty, the jetty became the place of loading,[99] as though it had been originally named in

---

[92] At p. 569.

[93] Discussed in *Borg (Owners)* v. *Darwen Paper Co.* (1921) 8 Ll.L.Rep. 49. See § 5–43 below.

[94] See *Logs & Timber Products (Singapore) Pte. Ltd.* v. *Keeley Granite (Pty.) Ltd.* [1978] 2 Lloyd's Rep. 1 (C.A.); § 6–40 below.

[95] In *Aktieselskabet Inglewood* v. *Millar's Karri and Jarrah Forests Ltd.* (1903) 8 Com.Cas. 196. But see also *Graigwen (Owners)* v. *Anglo-Canadian Shipping Co. Ltd.* [1955] 2 Lloyd's Rep. 260, below.

[96] See § 4–02 above for discussion as to liability where arrival is delayed by other ships chartered by the same charterers, and § 4–42 above for consideration in *The Varing* [1931] P. 79 (C.A.) of the problem of congestion in relation to the words "so near thereto as she may safely get"; and § 10–03 below for the similarity between damages in such a case and demurrage as described in *The Varing, ibid.*

[97] (1903) 8 Com.Cas. 196.

[98] At p. 200.

[99] The judge considered himself bound by the Court of Appeal decision in *Tharsis Sulphur & Copper Mining Co.* v. *Morel Bros & Co.* [1891] 2 Q.B. 647, as followed by Collins J. in *Sanders* v. *Jenkins* [1897] 1 Q.B. 93. See also § 4–03 above.

the charterparty; and in the absence . . . of special circumstances, the lay days could not commence until the *Inglewood* was ready to take in cargo at that place. . . . "

Having stated this principle, which was adverse to the shipowners, he then considered the "special circumstances" and said[1]:

"If a ship is prevented from going to the loading place, which the charterer has the right to name, by obstacles caused by the charterer . . . the lay days commence to count as soon as the ship is ready to load, and would, but for such obstacles or engagements, begin to load at that place."[2]

The charterers could have loaded the *Inglewood* with lighters at the anchorage when notice given; alternatively they could have ordered away from the jetty (at least there was no evidence that they could not have done so) one of the three ships which they were loading there.

If charterers can name a specific place, is laytime not to begin until the ship reaches that place? The presumption that it is not to begin may be displaced, especially where there is a clear distinction between the provisions defining the place of arrival and the provisions defining the beginning of laytime. Such a distinction was made in *Graigwen (Owners)* v. *Anglo-Canadian Shipping Co. Ltd.*[3] Lumber was carried from British Columbia to United Kingdom ports. The ship had to load at six berths in a range of ports. The laytime clause stated: "Lay days at first loading port to commence twenty-four hours . . . after receipt by charterers or their agents of master's written notice during ordinary working hours, that steamer is entered at the custom house and in all respects ready to load. Charterers have the privilege of using the twenty-four hours' notice period, same not to be counted as lay days." At subsequent loading ports there was no provision for a 24-hour notice period. The High Court was primarily concerned with those subsequent loading ports, but its conclusions are relevant to any similar clause, whether or not it contains a 24-hour notice provision. It held that although the words relating to berths indicated that it was a berth charterparty,[4] so that notice of readiness could not be given until the ship was in berth, laytime began 24 hours after the notice given at the first loading port. As for the other ports, the situation was the same except that there was no 24-hour notice period. McNair J. distinguished the decision in *Atkieselskabet Inglewood* v. *Millar's Karri and Jarrah Forests Ltd.*[5] In this case, as opposed to the earlier case, he said[6]:

" . . . the termini of the approach voyage are defined by reference to berths, whereas the provisions relating to the commencement of the laytime are related to the ports . . . "

6–41   The beginning of laytime may be advanced by specific words which dispense with the requirements of the usual laytime commencement clause in certain circumstances. Congestion may provide such an occasion. There may be such words as

---

[1] *Op. cit.* at p. 201.

[2] He relied on the principles enunciated by Lord Halsbury L.C. in *Watson* v. *H. Borner & Co.* (1900) 5 Com.Cas. 377 at p. 379; by Gorrell Barnes J. in *Ogmore SS. Co. Ltd.* v. *H. Borner & Co.* (1901) 6 Com.Cas. 104 at p. 110; and by Bigham J. in *Harrowing* v. *Dupré* (1902) 7 Com.Cas. 157 at pp. 165–166.

[3] [1955] 2 Lloyd's Rep. 260. See also § 5–25 above as to the question of the correctness of a notice of readiness.

[4] For berth charterparties generally see § 4–03 above.

[5] (1903) 8 Com.Cas. 196. See § 6–40 above.

[6] [1955] 2 Lloyd's Rep. 260 at p. 268.

"If through congestion at the port of Discharge and loading steamer is kept waiting off the port lay days are to commence to count as per Clause 6 [the charterparty clause dealing with the beginning of laytime in normal circumstances], but not until 36 hours from arrival (Sundays and holidays excepted)."

These were considered in *Logs & Timber Products (Singapore) Pte. Ltd.* v. *Keeley Granite (Pty.) Ltd.*[7] Under a charterparty on a C. Ore 7 form a ship carried granite blocks from Lourenco Marques to Yokohama. The laytime commencement clause stated:

"Time for loading to count from 8 a.m. after the ship has reported as ready and in free pratique whether in berth or not . . . "

The ship anchored at the Lourenco Marques pilot station, about 16 miles from the inner anchorage, and gave notice of readiness on July 12, 1974. Owing to congestion she remained there until August 1, when she moved to the inner anchorage and obtained free pratique. At that port free pratique involved clearance by all authorities, including the immigration officials. It was granted only when a ship had reached the inner anchorage, when the local agents brought on board customs, health and immigration representatives. The Court of Appeal, affirming the judgment of Donaldson J. in the High Court,[8] supported the shipowners' contention that the grant of free pratique was not a condition precedent to the beginning of laytime where, as here, the congestion clause was applicable. As Roskill L.J. said[9]:

"It seems to me, looking at the charterparty as a whole, that it is plain that the burden of waiting time through congestion, as a result of which the ship cannot get to the inner anchorage to commence loading, is cast by this clause upon the charterers . . . The parties have chosen to advance the time for the commencement of laytime and, in those circumstances, it seems to me that laytime commences to count notwithstanding that the ship has neither reported nor is ready nor has received free pratique under cl. 6 [the clause dealing with the beginning of laytime under normal circumstances]."

Even where the beginning of laytime is not expressly postponed until the **6–42** expiry of 24 hours after arrival, the charterparty may have this effect. Thus in *N.V. Bodewes Scheepswerven and N.V. Kuva* v. *Highways Construction, Ltd.*[10] rock asphalt was to be carried from Sète to London and the freight agreement stated: " . . . twenty-four hours' notice to be given to Shippers' Agents at loading port, and to Receivers at discharging port, of steamer being ready to load or discharge respectively." The cargo was "to be loaded, stowed and discharged . . . in one w.w. day SHEX for loading and three w.w. days SHEX for discharging, not reversible." In respect of each port notice was given, on the day before arrival, that the ship would arrive on the next day. The shipowners, relying on the *Aktieselskabet Inglewood* and *Graigwen* cases,[11] argued that a postponement of the beginning of laytime should be stated in the clause dealing with laytime. The Judge[12] summarised the argument of the cargo interests thus[13]:

---

[7] [1978] 2 Lloyd's Rep. 1 (C.A).
[8] [1978] 1 Lloyd's Rep. 257.
[9] *Op. cit.*, at p. 3.
[10] [1966] 1 Lloyd's Rep. 402 (*The Jan Herman*). See also § 5–25.
[11] See § 6–40 above.
[12] In the Mayor's and City of London Court.
[13] At p. 406.

" . . . the notice is to be of the steamer being ready to load, not about to be ready to load, but being actually and in fact ready to load and it seems difficult to know how a master could give 24 hours' notice because, be it marked, it is not 'at least 24 hours' notice' it is '24 hours' notice, and he is 24 hours out of that port and a number of considerations might be met with which would prevent him getting into port and berthing and being ready to load 24 hours after he had made a radio signal out at sea somewhere."

The judge, accepting this argument, said[14]:

" . . . there, is a 24-hour delay, because otherwise those words are meaningless, from the moment the master can go ashore and tell the agents of the receivers at a discharging port that his steamer is actually ready for loading or unloading . . . "

6–43   **Excepted periods.** Where there is merely provision for a 24-hour or other fixed period to elapse between arrival at or off a port or other place and the commencement of laytime, the period runs from arrival although it may include time which would be excepted from laytime.[15] The provision may of course cover such a contingency, stating that such periods as Sundays and holidays are not to count during the notice period. If the notice period ends during an excepted period, then the beginning of laytime is postponed until the excepted period has ended.

In *Borg (Owners)* v. *Darwen Paper Co.*[16] a charterparty for the carriage of wet wood pulp from Sweden to Grimsby provided that laytime was to count 24 hours after arrival at or off Grimsby. The latter part of the 24 hours fell on a Bank Holiday, and the receivers contended that the notice period could not run then, as the object was to give them a chance to prepare for the discharge. The High Court rejected the argument. Rowlatt J. said[17]:

"Now the time which has to elapse before the time of discharge begins is a totally different matter from the rate of discharge, and is not the time which has to be counted after the discharge has begun, and I do not see why, if the 24 hours, which means 24 hours by the sun, are to be qualified, it should not be expressly done."

6–43A   **The six hours' notice period.** So also where laytime is to begin at a certain time or a certain number of hours after notice of readiness is given, the notice period may run although the earliest time at which laytime may run has not yet arrived. The Asbatankvoy form contains the words: "Upon arrival . . . the Master or his agent shall give . . . notice . . . and laytime . . . shall commence upon the expiration of six (6) hours after receipt of such notice, or upon the Vessel's arrival in berth . . . whichever first occurs." It was held in a New York arbitration, *Burmah Oil Tankers Ltd.* v. *Marc Rich & Co. Inc.*[18] that laytime began at the earliest time stated in the charterparty, the six running hours having run and expired during a period in which laytime could not run.

6–44   **Ending at a fixed time.** The provision for a 24-hour or other notice period may be combined with a provision that laytime is to begin at a certain hour, usually on the day of expiry of the notice. Much will depend upon its wording. In *Metalimex Foreign Trade Corporation* v. *Eugenie Maritime Co.*

---

[14] *Ibid.*
[15] For excepted periods when time waiting for berth is to count, see § 6–06 above.
[16] (1921) 8 Ll.L.Rep. 49.
[17] At p. 50.
[18] Society of Maritime Arbitrators Award No. 1506 (1981) (*The Atlantic Empress*). See § 5–21 above.

Ltd.[19] a charterparty for the carriage of iron ore from Kakinada, India, to Rijeka stated: "Time for loading to count from 8 a.m. 48 hours after the Ship is reported and ready . . . and for discharging from 8 a.m. 24 hours after Ship is reported . . . " At each port notice was given at 9 a.m. At the loading port time was said by the shipowners to begin at 9 a.m. two days later and by the charterers to begin at 8 a.m. three days later. At the discharging port the shipowners said that time began at 9 a.m. one day later, the charterers saying that it began at 8 a.m. two days later. The claim by the charterers for dispatch was held to be time-barred, so that the views expressed by McNair J. are *obiter dicta*. He considered that the shipowners were right and said[20]:

> " . . . the purpose of this is quite clearly to secure that the charterers get the dual protection suggested by the shipowners, namely, 48 hours clear before the loading time shall start, and that the expiry of the 48 hours shall not start at some inconvenient time, and one should, accordingly, read 'from 8 a.m.' as 'not earlier than 8 a.m.' "

The result might have been different if the clause had stated: "Time for loading to commence at 8 a.m. . . . " rather than "Time for loading to count from 8 a.m."

---

[19] [1962] 1 Lloyd's Rep. 378.
[20] At p. 388.

CHAPTER 7

INTERRUPTION BY BAD WEATHER

WHAT KIND OF WEATHER INTERRUPTS TIME?

7–01 THE WORD "weather" has a wide meaning. According to the *Shorter Oxford English Dictionary*,[1] it includes: "Atmospheric conditions prevailing at a place and time, combination produced by heat or cold, clearness or cloudiness, dryness or moisture, wind or calm, high or low pressure, electrical state, of local air and sky. . . . " When a phenomenon falling within this definition has the effect of preventing work from being done, or would have that effect if anyone had been working (they having not worked for some reason other than the weather), then laytime is interrupted if the laytime clause refers to weather working time. Weather may be beautiful but bad.[1a] In *Dampskibsselskabet Botnia A/S* v. *C.P. Bell & Co.*[2] Bateson J. said:

> "Mr Pilcher[3] says that this was not bad weather, that ice is present very often in beautiful weather; but I think in this charterparty it is bad weather when ice prevents loading."

The natural phenomena which may constitute bad weather can also include earthquakes, snow, storms[3a] and surf.[4] It has not been decided whether bore tides constitute weather.[5]

7–02 **Ice**

The fact that the weather is almost certain to be bad, and that this is known at the date of the charterparty, is irrelevant. This is shown by the decision in *Dampskibsselskabet Botnia A/S* v. *C.P. Bell & Co.*,[6] where pit-props were to be loaded in Finland at a specified rate "per weather working day." The ship was ordered to Mollersvik, Middle Finland, which was normally blocked by ice from about the middle of November. At first cargo

---

[1] 3rd ed. The sense in which a word is used by the majority of people may be considered by a court; *Re Levy, ex p. Walton* (1881) 17 Ch.D. 746 (C.A.), *per* Jessel M.R. at p. 751: "The grammatical and ordinary sense of the words is to be adhered to, unless that would lead to some absurdity, or some repugnance or inconsistency with the rest of the instrument, in which case the grammatical or ordinary sense of the words may be modified, so as to avoid that absurdity and inconsistency, but no further." So also Swinfen Eady L.J. in *Beard* v. *Moira Colliery Co.* [1951] 1 Ch. 257 (C.A.) at p. 268.

[1a] This passage was referred to in a London arbitration (LMLN 64, April 15, 1982), the Umpire then considering whether high swell could be regarded as weather. As to this see § 7–08 below.

[2] [1932] 2 K.B. 569 at p. 575. See § 7–02 below.

[3] Counsel for the shipowners.

[3a] For a reference to storm, but in the context of the Asbatankvoy form and a possible interruption of demurrage, see a London arbitration (LMLN 166, March 13, 1986) and § 10–53 below.

[4] *Bennetts & Co.* v. *Brown* [1908] 1 K.B. 490. See also § 7–09 below.

[5] *Compania Crystal de Vapores of Panama* v. *Herman & Mohatta (India) Ltd.* [1958] 2 Q.B. 196. See § 7–03 below.

[6] [1932] 2 K.B. 569.

could be towed out in the form of rafts but later in November ice formed and loading was impossible. The ship sailed with a part cargo, because the charterers told the master that they could load no more. The port was then closed for the winter. The shipowners were held not to be entitled to dead freight. Bateson J. said that the issue was the meaning of the phrase "weather working day"; he rejected the view advanced by the shipowners. This was that ice was not weather but was merely the result of weather, just as trees blown down by the wind and blocking road transport were not weather but the consequence thereof. He said[7]:

> "I think that the formation of ice by cold which prevents the loading is weather, and that the meaning of the phrase 'weather working day,' between business men dealing with this kind of charterparty, must relate to prevention from loading by ice . . . Mr Willink[8] pointed out that if ice is not weather, the waves which are produced by the wind, and so prevent lighters or rafts from settling alongside vessels, could not be said to be weather, because it was waves and not wind. Perhaps that is somewhat analogous. I think weather means loading weather, and if you have ice which prevents you loading you are stopped from loading by the weather unfit for loading."

The shipowners were not entitled to dead freight, as the charterers' otherwise absolute obligation to load was qualified by the words "weather working day." The judge rejected the shipowners' argument that the words related only to the rate for loading; he decided that the words also qualified the charterers' obligation to load a full cargo. But it seems that the existence of weather bad enough to stop loading, and so to stop laytime running, does not of itself extinguish the obligation to load a full cargo. In the *Botnia* case the nature of the trade and the length of the delay seem to have affected the interpretation of the charterers' obligation.

Fear of bad weather 7–03

Bore tide. Mere fear that loading or discharging will be interrupted or prevented is not enough. In *Compania Crystal de Vapores of Panama* v. *Herman & Mohatta (India) Ltd.*[9] a charterparty for the carriage of scrap from Calcutta stated: "Cargo to be loaded and stowed free of expense to the ship at the average rate of 400 tons per weather working day." The Calcutta harbour master ordered a shift from the loading berth to buoys, and then allowed her to return to berth. The shift was ordered because he feared that she could become dangerous during the bore tides, which were expected and materialised while she was at the buoys. Loading was discontinued during her six days at the buoys. Shipowners argued that whereas ice was the result of atmospheric and meteorological conditions, tides were predictable and occurred whether the weather was good or bad. Charterers contended that bore tides were entirely different from ordinary tides, as they were associated in the Orient with hurricanes and typhoons. The High Court held that, assuming that a bore tide was "weather," the mere threat of bad weather could not make a day a non-weather working day. As Devlin J. said[10]:

> "I shall assume, without deciding it, that a bore tide is weather within the meaning of this clause. But no case has been cited to me in which a mere threat of bad weather has been held to make a day not a weather working day and certainly no case where the threat of bad weather has affected not the operation of the actual work of loading, but

[7] At pp. 574 and 575.
[8] Counsel for the charterers.
[9] [1958] 2 Q.B. 196.
[10] At p. 203.

the safety of the ship in a particular place in which she was. In my judgment, the expression 'weather working day' cannot be construed so widely as to cover the circumstances of this case."

Two points arise from this passage. First, the judge made no finding that a bore tide was "weather." Secondly, a threat of bad weather is not enough if it is a threat to the safety of the ship. It might be enough if it is a threat to "the operation of the actual work of loading," but no authority was cited and the judge did not decide the point, which thus remains open.

7–04 Bad weather where no work intended

Bad weather may occur when work is not intended or contemplated, during normal working hours,[11] while laytime is running. There are various possibilities. The normal working hours may have begun, but the day's work itself may not yet have started; work may have stopped for lunch; or there may be a shortage of labour. If so, bad weather interrupts laytime[12] if, had work been contemplated or possible, the weather would have prevented it. This is so if the laytime clause refers to weather working days, weather working days of 24 hours,[13] or weather working days of 24 consecutive (or running) hours[14]; but not where the words "weather permitting"[15] are used.

7–05 *Rain need not "stop play"*

In *Compania Naviera S.A.* v. *British Oil and Cake Mills Ltd.*[16] a charterparty for the carriage of grain from Philadelphia to Great Britain stated: "Cargo to be received at destination at an average rate of not less than 1,000 tons per weather working day (Sundays and holidays excepted . . .)," and "lay days in loading and discharging to be calculated on the basis of 24 hours per day." The shipowners contended that deductions for rainy periods were only to be made where rain had stopped work; they said that the phrase was equivalent to "rain stops play."

At Avonmouth there had been enough rain to prevent unloading operations if they had been started or intended. The receivers' arrangements were such that no such operations were being conducted or were intended. The High Court held that a weather working day was day on which the weather let the relevant work be done whether or not any persons availed themselves of the opportunity. The shipowners argued successfully that laytime should be interrupted during the rainy periods. They relied on (1) Lord Goddard C.J. having expressly refrained in the Court of Appeal from deciding the point in *Alvion SS. Corporation* v. *Panama Galban Lobo Trading Co. S.A. of Havana*[17]; (2) a remark in that case by McNair J.[18]:

" . . . one has to consider, as regards a particular day, whether during the working

---

[11] For the effect of bad weather outside normal working hours, see § 7–46 below.
[12] As to the manner of assessing the interruption where there is bad weather during only part of the normal working hours, see § 7–25 below.
[13] See § 7–41 below.
[14] See § 7–44 below.
[15] See § 7–10 below.
[16] [1957] 2 Q.B. 293.
[17] [1955] 1 Q.B. 430 at p. 449, when he said: "No question is raised in the Special case as to whether Charterers are bound to have cargo ready on a day or at a time when weather prevented work, so I say nothing about this." See also § 2–34 and § 7–34.
[18] In the High Court; *ibid.* at p. 438.

hours the weather does, *or would*,[19] interfere with the loading or discharging, as the case may be";

and (3) a dictum in a dissenting judgment by Scrutton L.J. in *Burnett SS. Co. Ltd.* v. *Danube and Black Sea Shipping Agencies*[20]:

> "What about weather? The charterer is to have 15 days for loading. Supposing it rains on the 15 days, is he to have only 15 days for loading or is he to have any more? That is very frequently dealt with by the clause saying that the charterer is to have so many weather working days. In that case it is quite clear that it would be no answer to say to the charterer, it is true that Monday was not a weather working day, but inasmuch as no cargo was alongside the ship on that day it must count as a weather working day."

He added[21] that a charterer could reply:

> "I am under no obligation to have cargo there every minute of every day. I do not break my contract if on a particular day I have no cargo either alongside or contracted for, so long as in the fixed period of 15 days I load the ship."

In the *Azuero*[22] Pearson J., holding that the charterers were entitled to   **7–06** deduct all rainy periods, whether during working hours or not, said[23]:

> "A day is not a weather working day, it fails to be a weather working day, in so far as the weather on that day does not permit the relevant work to be done, and it is not material to enquire whether any person has intended or planned or prepared to do any relevant work on that day.[24] The status of a weather working day, wholly or in part or not at all, is determined solely by its own weather, and not by extraneous factors, such as the actions, intentions and plans of any person."

So where laytime has begun bad weather in normal working hours[25] interrupts laytime[26] if it (a) prevents work or (b) would, if work had been contemplated, have prevented work.

Work may be prohibited or brought to an end by order of a port or other authority even though the weather is not bad enough to prevent it. Thus Indian and Italian port authorities have issued documents[27] showing that there was bad weather, and on which charterers have sometimes relied to justify a contention that laytime was interrupted. In such a case laytime is not interrupted unless some other clause provides for an interruption in the event of work being prohibited. The document is merely evidence from which it may or may not be concluded that the weather was bad enough to prevent the working of the ship. As Walton J. said in *Bennetts & Co.* v. *Brown*,[28] where charterers relied on a declaration by the port captain at Valparaiso that certain days were surf days:

> " . . . they certainly cannot rely upon any custom which would make the captain of the port a kind of arbitrator who should settle conclusively what was a weather working day and what was not . . . "

---

[19] Author's italics.
[20] [1933] 2 K.B. 438 at p. 448 (C.A.). See also § 2–40 and § 7–18.
[21] At p. 448.
[22] [1957] 2 Q.B. 293.
[23] At p. 303.
[24] But it would be relevant to enquire whether the words "weather permitting" or even "weather permitting working day" were used. See §§ 7–10 and 7–14 below.
[25] For the meaning of the expression "normal working hours," see § 7–26 below.
[26] As to the manner of indicating the interruption on the timesheet see § 6–31.
[27] Italian port authorities register weather conditions affecting loading and discharging. In Bombay the Chamber of Commerce declare what are non-weather working days.
[28] [1908] 1 K.B. 490 at pp. 497–498. See §§ 7–07–7–09 below.

SURF DAYS

7–07   A surf day defined
A surf[29] day is a day on which the surf on a beach is so heavy that lighters cannot load or land cargo there without unusual difficulty and delay.[30]

Such a state of affairs does not necessarily result in laytime being interrupted where the laytime clause contains such words as "weather working day"[31] or "weather permitting"[32] A charterparty may, however, provide expressly for the problem of delay by surf, especially where loading or discharging is to take place at a place often affected by surf. Such a provision if suitably worded may also give the cargo interests some relief as to laytime in respect of activities occurring before the loading or after the discharging, such as the bringing forward for shipment or the removal of the cargo.

7–08   Laytime not necessarily affected
Inability of lighters to load or land their cargo at a particular place without unusual difficulty and delay does not necessarily affect the calculation of laytime. The responsibility of the ship begins with the taking from, and ends with the delivery into, the lighters; these operations can often continue whatever the conditions at the beach. A shortage of lighters does not usually put shipowners in breach of their obligations. If surf delays the working of the ship the laytime calculation will not be affected, in the absence of some special provision relating to the surf. If, however, the ship's cargo gear cannot be used or lighters cannot be accepted alongside because of the conditions of the sea, the position may be different. Even then it might be argued that surf, or indeed a heavy swell,[33] though a type of weather or a product of weather, does not affect laytime.[33a]

Effect of custom
A local custom to stop work on surf days does not necessarily govern the meaning of express words in a charterparty. In *Holman* v. *Peruvian Nitrate Co.*[34] a number of "working days" was allowed for discharging outward

---

[29] "Surf" is defined in the *Shorter Oxford English Dictionary* (3rd ed.) as "The mass or line of white foamy water caused by the sea breaking upon a shore or rock."
[30] *Per* Walton J. in *Bennetts & Co.* v. *Brown* [1908] 1 K.B. 490 at p. 496, as to landing.
[31] See § 7–24 below.
[32] See § 7–10 below.
[33] "When the Mistral and Tamentane winds blow from the Provençal and Languedoc coasts of France a heavy swell occurs in Bejaia; if, when that swell occurs, vessels remain in the port there can be a risk of rupturing hoses and possibly of damage to the vessels"; so spoke Robert Goff J. in *Cosmar Compania Naviera S.A.* v. *Total Transport Corporation* [1982] 2 Lloyd's Rep. 81 (*The Isabelle*), at p. 83. The phenomenon is known as the Ressac.
[33a] An issue in one London arbitration, LMLN 64, April 15, 1982, was whether delays during discharge caused by high swell at various times over five days entitled charterers to deduct such periods from laytime. Discharge was to be within a certain number of working days. After referring to an earlier passage in this book, as to the definition of weather (§ 5–01 in the 2nd edition), the Umpire said:
"There appeared to be no direct authority, nor was any cited to me, as to whether 'high swell' is 'weather.' 'Weather' certainly includes 'storms.' 'Swell' is a phenomenon of the high seas and has been defined as 'a slow, steady, continuous undulation of the sea unbroken by waves *after a storm*.' It is the product of bad weather. . . . I . . . found that 'high swell' was covered by 'weather' and that the charterers were entitled to except such periods from laytime."
[34] (1878) 5 Ct. of Sess., 4th Series, 657.

cargo and loading homeward cargo at Iquique, Chile. On certain days work in the open roadstead could not be carried on as a result of surf, and by local custom work was stopped by order of the captain of the port. The Scottish Court of Session held that these days were "working days."

Surf clause in charterparty   **7–09**

In *Bennetts & Co.* v. *Brown*[35] the High Court considered the words "Detention through . . . delay by . . . surf . . . not to count in the time allowed for loading or discharging." At Valparaiso the port captain declared that certain days were surf days, the lighters being unable to discharge on the beach as frequently as they normally did. The operation of discharging into the lighters was not prevented, Walton J. summarised the matter as follows[36]:

> "I am of opinion that by terms of the charterparty the parties have agreed that, if surf interferes with the discharge and causes detention, the detention shall not be taken into account in the time for discharging. Now by 'surf' they must, I think, have meant surf on the beach, and the detention they must have had in their minds must have been detention, not in discharging the cargo into the lighters, but in landing the cargo from the lighters on to the beach, and I come to the conclusion that that exception does apply . . . "

In such a situation the parties are neither bound by the declaration of the port captain nor obliged to exclude surf days from the category of weather working days. Instead they must calculate, as the court did in *Bennetts & Co.* v. *Brown*,[37] how much detention took place, and exclude it from the time allowed.

"Weather Permitting"; the development of judicial views from 1887 to 1983   **7–09A**

In *Stephens* v. *Harris & Co.*,[38] where ore was carried from Bilbao to Middlesbrough, the laytime clause stipulated: ". . . four hundred tons per working day (Sundays and holidays excepted), weather permitting, are to be allowed for loading the said ship at Bilbao, and the ore to be received, on arrival at port of discharge, at the rate of not less than three hundred tons per working day (Sundays and holidays excepted), weather permitting . . . " While the ship was at her loading berth, and waiting to receive cargo under a spout, wet weather caused heavy floods. The ore became so wet that delay occurred in loading it into the railway trucks; the floods caused delay in transit on the railway; and as a result of cholera the men loading the trucks, and some railway men, left work. The ship was detained at Bilbao five days beyond the lay days. Ore brought down by rail to the wharves was never loaded by the other method available, namely, by lighters direct from places higher up the river.

The Court of Appeal held that the bad weather must, if the charterers were to rely on the words "weather permitting," hinder the loading itself. As Lord Esher said[39]:

> "I do not think that the word 'weather' can be confined to weather affecting the water, but I think it would apply to weather which affects the putting of the ore on board . . . "

---

[35] [1908] 1 K.B. 490. As for the references in that case to the meaning of the phrase "weather working day," see §§ 2–60–2–61 above.
[36] *Ibid.* at p. 498.
[37] [1908] 1 K.B. 490.
[38] (1888) 57 L.J.Q.B. 203 (C.A.).
[39] At p. 208.

So also Bowen L.J.[40]:

> "What is meant is weather, not miles away, but at the place where the ship is, which interferes with the loading."

and Fry L.J.[41]:

> " . . . it must refer to the weather at the place of loading . . . "

7–10   The conclusion to be drawn from this decision is not, as has sometimes been said, that the weather must delay or stop the loading of the ship in question. It is that the relevant weather is that at the place of loading. As was said later by Sir John Donaldson M.R.[42]:

> " . . . the Court was considering a case in which the vessel was at the berth and the effect of the weather was not. It did not consider the converse case in which the effect of the weather was at the loading berth and the vessel was not."

7–11   In a later case, *The Glendevon*,[43] "the effect of the weather was indeed present at the loading berth and the vessel was elsewhere, but the issue was dispatch, not laytime or demurrage."[44] Nevertheless, the words "weather permitting" were considered, and the case is an example of the wish of shipowners to show that work must be actually prevented. A charterparty for the carriage of coal from Newcastle to Lisbon stated: "The steamer to be discharged at the rate of two hundred tons per day weather permitting (Sundays and holidays excepted) . . . and if sooner discharged to pay at the rate of 8s. 4d. per hour for every hour saved." The parties disagreed as to whether dispatch was due in respect of a Sunday and a Fête Day saved. The shipowners argued that days during which weather would not have permitted discharge were on the same footing, and that if charterers were right all these differing types of day should be excluded, though discharge had finished. Jeune P. said[45]:

> "I confess I am unable to see any answer to that argument, and the results would be so extraordinary as to be unintelligible. It would come to this, that after the ship was discharged, the charterer would have the right to say that on a large number of days, it might be even weeks or months, he was prevented by the weather from discharging, and therefore he was entitled to add these in as days of twenty-four hours, for each hour of which he was entitled to have 8s. 4d. That is an absurdity."

He therefore held that the shipowners were right and that dispatch was not due for the disputed days.

This conclusion could be seen, and was for some time seen, as supporting the requirement that, where the words are "weather permitting," there must be actual obstruction of work by the ship in question, but it is better to restrict it to its special context.

7–12   The next development occurred in *Reardon Smith Line Ltd.* v. *Ministry of Agriculture*,[46] where laytime was expressed in "weather working days." Lord Devlin, however, referred to the meaning of the phrase "weather

---

[40] At p. 210.
[41] At p. 211.
[42] *Dow Chemical (Nederland) B.V.* v. *B.P. Tanker Co. Ltd.* [1983] 1 Lloyd's Rep. 579 (C.A.) (*The Vorras*) at p. 582. See § 7–16 below.
[43] [1893] P. 269. For the issue of dispatch see § 12–15 below.
[44] The quoted words are again from the judgment by Sir John Donaldson, M.R., in *Dow Chemical (Nederland) B.V.* v. *B.P. Tanker Co. Ltd.* [1983] 1 Lloyd's Rep. 579 (C.A.) (*The Vorras*), at p. 582. See § 7–16 below.
[45] *Ibid.* at p. 273.
[46] [1963] A.C. 691 (H.L.) (*The Vancouver Strike Case*). See § 2–31.

permitting." Speaking of the old rule that part of a day was a whole day,[47] he said[48] that in the earlier approach to a weather working day "There was no investigation to see to what extent the weather actually prevented work. If that was what was wanted, if the weather was to be treated as if it were an excepted peril excusing work only when it was actually operating, words [*i.e.* 'weather permitting'] could, of course, be found to do it. In *Stephens* v. *Harris & Co.* . . . . the Court of Appeal held that the phrase 'weather permitting' in the laytime clause had that effect. I see no reason to doubt the authority of that decision although there has been some controversy about it."

As for *Stephens* v. *Harris & Co.*[49] and the *Reardon Smith* case,[50] Sir **7–13** John Donaldson M.R. later commented[51]: "You can look to see whether the loading process is in fact prevented by the weather or you can look to see whether it is the weather which is the actual cause of the particular vessel not being loaded. In *Stephens* v. *Harris* and in the *Vancouver Strike* case, both questions would have received the same answer. In neither case was the loading process affected by the weather. The loading process was at a standstill because there was no cargo (*Stephens* v. *Harris*) and because the elevators could not be worked (*Vancouver Strikes*) . . . Lord Devlin did not have to consider a case in which (a) weather was the sole cause of the loading process being at a standstill or not available, and (b) there was a different or additional reason why the particular vessel was not able to be loaded, namely that she was not in the berth."

A further stage was reached in the history of the words "weather permit- **7–14** ting" in *Magnolia Shipping Co. Ltd. of Limassol* v. *Joint Venture of the International Trading & Shipping Enterprises and Kinship Management Co. Ltd. of Brussels.*[52] Two ships carried sugar from Cuba, one going to Lattakia and the other to Tartous, both in Syria, under a charterparty which stated: "Lay days for discharging to begin twenty-four hours after captain reports ship's arrival and readiness to deliver cargo . . . " The cargo was to be discharged " . . . at the average rate of 750 metric tons per day of 24 consecutive hours per weather permitting working day." Clause 6 stipulated: "Berth occupied: When no cargo berth available on arrival roads, the master will cable . . . date and time of arrival roads to the Agents and this time will be treated as if vessel has tendered alongside the berth and time will count accordingly." In each case when the ship arrived in the roads no cargo berth was available. Notice of readiness was tendered and laytime began. During a further delay before she reached berth rain fell to an extent which would have prevented discharge if she had been in berth. The charterers contended that the words "weather permitting work- ing day"[53] had the same effect as the expression "weather working day," so that they meant a day on which work was permitted by the weather whether it would have been carried out or not.

[47] See § 7–29 below.
[48] *Ibid.* at pp. 739–740.
[49] [1887] 57 L.J.Q.B. 203 (C.A.). See § 7–10 above.
[50] [1963] A.C. 691 (H.L.) (*The Vancouver Strike Case*). See also § 2–31.
[51] In *Dow Chemical (Nederland) B.V.* v. *B.P. Tanker Co. Ltd.* [1983] 1 Lloyd's Rep. 579 (*The Vorras*) at p. 583. See § 7–16 below.
[52] [1978] 2 Lloyd's Rep. 182 (*The Camelia* and *The Magnolia*).
[53] The Judge (at p. 184) said that this language was "not very happy." The original printed words were "per weather working day." The word "permitting" was typed in the margin with a line showing that it was to be inserted between the words "weather" and "working day."

Brandon J. held that the shipowners' interpretation was correct.[54] He said[55]:

> "It was contended for the shipowners . . . that the expression meant the same as the expression 'working day weather permitting,' that is to say that it meant a working day which counted unless work was actually prevented by the weather—a day on which work would have been done but for the weather preventing it (see *Stephens* v. *Harris*).[56] The contention for the charterers involves treating the words as words of description. In my view, the intention was to produce the same result as would be produced by the words 'working day weather permitting'."

7–15   In *Gebr. Broere B.V.* v. *Saras Chimica S.p.A.*[57] the decisions in *The Darrah*[58] and the *Magnolia Shipping* cases[59] were applied. Cargo was carried under four charterparties, in each case between the same shipowners and charterers, from Sarroch, Sardinia, to Le Havre. The charterparties provided:

> "5 [specified number] running hours weather permitting shall be allowed Charterers for loading and discharging. . . . "

Laytime was to begin when a ship was ready to receive cargo, the master giving six hours notice of readiness. The dispute in each case covered the calculation of laytime between expiry of notice of readiness at Sarroch and completion of loading. During that period the port authority closed the port owing to weather conditions, so that the ship was either unable for a time to get into her berth or, having reached it, had to leave it for a time. The shipowners contended that the words "weather permitting" only interrupted or extended the fixed period when weather in fact did not permit loading. The charterers said that the fixed period was extended by any period during which bad weather would not have permitted loading if, contrary to the facts, the ship had been in berth.

Parker J., finding for the charterers, said that in *The Darrah*, concerning a port charterparty, there was also a provision that time lost waiting for berthing should count as laytime. The House of Lords had held that in calculating the time so lost the ship must be treated as if she were in berth. Lord Diplock had in that case referred to the concept of two time codes, one for time lost and not subject to laytime exceptions and another for laytime and subject to those exceptions.[60] He had said, of that concept:

> " . . . it gives to the shipowner the chance of receiving a bonus dependent upon whether (a) his ship is lucky enough to be kept waiting for a berth and (b) is so kept waiting during a period which includes time which would not have counted against permitted laytime if the ship had been in berth."

Though that case had concerned congestion Parker J. concluded that the observation applied with equal force to the case before him. Weather which would have interrupted loading came into the same category as Sun-

---

[54] Though the case was decided in favour of the charterers in view of the wording of cl. 6 on the authority of *The Darrah*; see § 6–16 above.

[55] *Op. cit.* at p. 184.

[56] The decision of Brandon J. was said to be "based upon a misreading of *Stephens* v. *Harris*" by Sir John Donaldson M.R. in *Dow Chemical (Nederland) B.V.* v. *B.P. Tanker Co. Ltd.* [1983] 1 Lloyd's Rep. 579 (*The Vorras*) at p. 584. See also § 7–16.

[57] [1982] 2 Lloyd's Rep. 436 (*The San Nicolas*).

[58] *Aldebaran Compania Maritime S.A. Panama* v. *Aussenhandel A.G. Zürich* [1977] A.C. 157 (H.L.); see § 6–09 above.

[59] [1978] 2 Lloyd's Rep. 182; see § 7–14 above.

[60] See § 6–09 above.

days and holidays, if they were excepted. Of the decision of Brandon J. in the *Magnolia Shipping* case,[61] he said[62]:

> "He held, however, that although it was impossible for work actually to be prevented by weather because the vessel was not in berth, cl. 6[63] and the decision in *The Darrah* resulted in the exclusion from laytime of any period during which, had the vessel been in berth, rain would have prevented discharge which would otherwise have taken place."

The Court of Appeal, in *Dow Chemical (Nederland) B.V.* v. *B.P.*   **7–16**
Tanker Co. Ltd.,[64] attempted to decide the proper status of the decision in *Stephens* v. *Harris & Co.*,[65] and also commented on the earlier cases generally. Under a charterparty on the Beepeevoy 2 form the *Vorras* carried petroleum products from Skikda, Algeria, to Rotterdam. The charterparty stated:

> "15 [Amount of laytime] 72 running hours weather permitting."

When the ship arrived at Skikda on December 15, 1980 and tendered notice of readiness, the loading berth was occupied by another ship, which left it on December 16. The port then closed, owing to bad weather, until December 20, when another ship occupied the berth, leaving it on December 26. The port was again closed because of bad weather, and the Vorras went on the berth on December 28, completing loading on January 13, 1981.

The shipowners said that laytime ended at midnight on December 21, and was not extended by the bad weather, as the weather did not prevent loading when she was not on the berth. The charterers contended that the weather extended the expiry of laytime if it was such as to prevent loading, whether the ship or another ship or no ship was on the berth. The High Court found in favour of the charterers,[66] and the Court of Appeal came to the same conclusion. Sir John Donaldson M.R. said, refreshingly[67]:

> "Authority apart, I would have no doubt that the charterers were right."

He then reviewed the authorities.[68]

The substance of the decision can be expressed in the following words from his judgment:

> "The words are '72 hours, weather permitting.' The essence of the owners' argument is that this phrase means '72 hours, unless the weather prevents the vessel from loading.' There would be something to be said for this if the antonym for 'permitting' was 'preventing.' But it is not. It is 'prohibiting.' If the phrase is to be inverted, it reads '72 hours unless the weather prohibits loading.' In my judgment the weather prohibited any vessel of this general type from loading and it is nothing to the point that owing to the presence of another vessel in the berth, the prohibition was not the operative cause which prevented the vessel from loading. I would construe '72 hours, weather permitting' as meaning '72 hours when the weather was of such a nature as to permit loading.' "

---

[61] [1978] 2 Lloyd's Rep. 182; see § 7–14 above.
[62] *Op. cit.* at p. 439.
[63] By which time was to count though the ship was not in berth; see § 7–14 above.
[64] [1983] 1 Lloyd's Rep. 579 (*The Vorras*).
[65] (1887) 57 L.J.Q.B. 203 (C.A.). See § 7–10 above.
[66] Unrep.
[67] *Op. cit.* at p. 582.
[68] Namely: *Stephens* v. *Harris* (1887) 57 L.J.Q.B. 203 (see § 7–10 above); *The Glendevon* [1893] P. 269 (see § 7–11 above); *Reardon Smith Line Ltd.* v. *Ministry of Agriculture* [1963] A.C. 691 (H.L.) (see § 7–11 above); the *Magnolia Shipping* case [1978] 2 Lloyd's Rep. 182 (see § 7–14 above); and *Gebr. Broere B.V.* v. *Saras Chimica S.p.A.* [1982] 2 Lloyd's Rep. 436 (*The San Nicolas*) (see § 7–15 above).

7–17 Descriptions and Exceptions

The expressions "words of description" and "words of exception" have been used,[69] the latter, as Sir John Donaldson M.R. put it,[70] "importing a causative connection with the delay." He said that he was not sure how much such a classification added to clarity, but commented:

> "Prima facie, any clause defining laytime is descriptive and any clause providing that time shall not count against laytime so defined . . . is exceptive. If it matters, I would classify the expression '72 running hours, weather permitting' as descriptive."

Kerr L.J. said,[71] in agreeing that the shipowners' appeal should be dismissed:

> "I would also regard the words 'weather permitting' as descriptive rather than exceptive if a choice has to be made between these terms."

7–18 An unambigous weather clause

A clause dealing with bad weather may be so expressed that there is no doubt that the weather must prevent work.

In *Burnett SS. Co. Ltd.* v. *Danube & Black Sea Shipping Agencies*[72] a berth contract for the carriage of grain from the Danube stated: "Should any time be lost while steamer is in a loading berth owing to work being inmpossible through rain, snow or storm . . . the amount of actual time so lost during which it is impossible to work owing to rain, snow or storm . . . to be added to the loading time . . . " In two loading ports rain occurred at intervals and to such an extent that it would have been impossible to load cargo had cargo been alongside. The charterers had not then booked cargo with shippers. The Court of Appeal upheld by a majority a decision by MacKinnon J. that charterers must prove both that loading became impossible through rain and that as a result they lost loading time. Greer L.J. said[73] of the charterer:

> "He did prove that there were hours of time, amounting in all to two days, in which work was impossible through rain, but he did not prove that that resulted in any loss of time by him, because on the facts as found[73a] he was not there ready to utilise the time, and, therefore, he cannot say that he has established that it was the impossibility of loading that caused him to lose that time."

In a dissenting judgment Scrutton L.J. said[74] that the charterers need only show that during the lay days there was time during which work was impossible:

> " . . . such time is to be added to the running days which the charterer has for loading on the assumption that he can work on them."

BAD WEATHER

7–19 Effect of bad weather at different times

Just as it is necessary to define the word "weather"[75] so it is necessary to examine the ways in which different periods of time are affected by bad

---

[69] By Brandon J. in the *Magnolia* case, for example; see § 7–14 above.
[70] In the *Dow Chemical* case, *op. cit.* at p. 584.
[71] *Op. cit.* at p. 585.
[72] [1933] 2 K.B. 438 (C.A.). See also § 2–40 above.
[73] At p. 451.
[73a] By the sole arbitrator in his award.
[74] At p. 449.
[75] See § 7–01 above.

weather. There may be bad weather before or after laytime has begun; before or after work has begun, or while it is beginning or ending; during normal working hours or during time usually worked as overtime; at night or otherwise outside normal working hours[76]; on Saturdays,[77] on Sundays and holidays[78]; or at other special times.[79]

The periods to be considered may thus be summarised as follows:

    A. Bad weather before laytime begins.
    B. Bad weather after laytime begins.

I. *Bad weather in normal working hours*   **7–20**

    1. Weather working days (or "weather permitting working days")[80];
    2. Working days of 24 hours;

      (a) working days of 24 hours (weather permitting);
      (b) weather working days of 24 hours.

    3. Working days of 24 consecutive (or running) hours;

      (a) weather working days of 24 consecutive (or running) hours;
      (b) working days of 24 consecutive (or running) hours (weather permitting).

II. *Bad weather at night or otherwise outside normal working hours*   **7–21**

    1. Weather working days (or "weather permitting working days");
    2. Working days of 24 hours:

      (a) working days of 24 hours (weather permitting);
      (b) weather working days of 24 hours.

    3. Working days of 24 consecutive (or running) hours;

      (a) weather working days of 24 consecutive (or running) hours;
      (b) working days of 24 consecutive (or running) hours (weather permitting).

III. *Bad weather on Saturdays*

IV. *Bad weather on Sundays and holidays*

V. *Bad weather during other specially excepted periods*

BAD WEATHER BEFORE LAYTIME BEGINS

Before laytime has begun the ship may still be on her way to her destina-   **7–22** tion, in which case bad weather can have no affect on any laytime calculations. If the ship is delayed at sea, any loss of time is for the account of shipowners. If she is delayed by bad weather outside and before reaching her contractual destination, whether that be a berth, port or other place,

---

[76] See § 7–45 below.
[77] See § 7–54 below.
[78] See § 7–56 below.
[79] *e.g.* specially excepted periods such as "Friday after 5 p.m. to Monday at 8 a.m."; see § 7–57 below.
[80] See § 7–14 above.

charterers are not responsible since they have not caused the delay. If they have brought about a delay, by, for example, creating congestion through an unreasonable and abnormal amount of chartering,[81] they may be liable to pay detention damages to shipowners. If bad weather would have prevented work during part or all of that period, had she not been otherwise delayed, charterers are nevertheless liable. The reason for this is that the excepted periods apply to laytime which has already begun to run[82]: they do not affect a claim by shipowners for damages for detention. Similarly where laytime has not begun, although the ship has reached her destination, bad weather has no effect on the laytime calculation. The same rule applies where work is beginning, for example by hatches being opened, or where work has begun,[83] if laytime has not begun. Laytime can only be interrupted if it is running.

BAD WEATHER AFTER LAYTIME BEGINS

7–23   I. Bad weather in normal working hours

After laytime has begun there may be bad weather which interrupts or prevents work or would, had work been intended or contemplated, have interrupted or prevented it.

The effect of bad weather in normal working hours depends upon the wording of the laytime clause. The clause may refer to:

  1. Weather working days[84];
  2. Working days of 24 hours, in either of the following forms:

    (a) working days of 24 hours (weather permitting)[85];
    (b) weather working days of 24 hours.[86]

  3. Working days of 24 consecutive (or running) hours, in either of the following forms:

    (a) weather working days of 24 consecutive (or running) hours[87];
    (b) working days of 24 consecutive (or running) hours (weather permitting).[88]

7–24   1. *Weather working days*[89]

  (a) **Bad weather during all normal working hours.** If bad weather entirely prevents work during normal working hours,[90] or would have prevented it

---

[81] It must be their own chartering, and not that of receivers; *Watson & Co.* v. *H. Borner & Co. Ltd.* (1900) 5 Com.Cas. 377 (C.A.). The congestion must be more than could reasonably have been contemplated, when the charterparty was concluded; *Harrowing* v. *Dupré* (1902) 7 Com.Cas. 157.

[82] For the meaning of the words "time lost in waiting for berth to count," and the effect of excepted periods during such time, see § 6–02 above.

[83] As it may do, where laytime has not begun, if for example a notice period has not yet expired. See *Pteroti Compania Naviera S.A.* v. *National Coal Board* [1958] 1 Q.B. 469, and § 4–46 above.

[84] See § 7–24 below.

[85] See § 7–41 below.

[86] See § 7–42 below.

[87] See § 7–44 below.

[88] See § 7–45 below.

[89] This expression is defined at § 2–59 above. For "weather permitting working day" see § 7–14 above.

[90] For the meaning of "normal working hours," see § 7–26 below.

if work were intended or contemplated,[91] and the laytime clause refers to weather working days, then the day is not counted in the laytime calculation, as it ceases to be a weather working day.[92]

As Lord Keith of Avonholm said in *Reardon Smith Line Ltd.* v. *Ministry of Agriculture*[93]:

> " . . . where there is total interference by weather with work being done during working hours which might otherwise have been done the day will not be computed as a lay day."

(b) Bad weather for part of normal working hours. Bad weather may be **7–25** such that it prevents work, or would prevent it if work were intended or contemplated,[94] for part of the normal working hours.[95] If so the mere definition of a weather working day as one during which weather does not wholly prevent working if work were intended[96] is not enough. The day has been partially affected by weather.[97] For example, at a port with a normal working day of eight hours there may be rain during part of the eight hours and part of the remaining 16 hours[98] during which no work is contemplated by the charterers. Where the charterparty is based on "weather working days," the day is treated as a calendar day of 24 hours,[99] in the sense that one day is debited to the charterers every calendar day, and not every three calendar days. But the day is treated as consisting of the numbers of hours usually worked, including overtime where normal, for the purpose of making an apportionment between the parts affected and those not affected by bad weather.

Fractions of a weather working day **7–26**

Normal working hours. To calculate the fraction of the calendar day to be debited to charterers, the normal working hours must be established. It might be normal to work overtime.[1] The length and normality of the work-

---

[91] See *Compania Naviera Azuero S.A.* v. *British Oil & Cake Mills Ltd.* (*The Azuero*) [1957] 2 Q.B. 293; see § 7–05 above.

[92] See §§ 2–60–2–62 above and the judgments of Walton J. in *Bennetts & Co.* v. *Brown* [1908] 1 K.B. 490, at pp. 496–498, and Pearson J. in *Compania Naviera Azuero S.A.* v. *British Oil and Cake Mills Ltd.* (*The Azuero*) [1957] 2 Q.B. 293 at p. 303.

[93] [1963] A.C. 691 at p. 726 (H.L.).

[94] See *Compania Naviera Azuero S.A.* v. *British Oil & Cake Mills Ltd.* (*The Azuero*) [1957] 2 Q.B. 293, see also §§ 7–05 and 7–06 above.

[95] For "normal working hours," see § 7–26 below.

[96] See § 7–05 above.

[97] For the duty of charterers to establish, on the balance of probabilities, that for the period claimed not to be weather working days the weather did not permit working, see *Freedom Maritime Corporation* v. *International Bulk Carriers S.A.* [1985] 2 Lloyd's Rep. 212, at pp. 214–215 (*The Khian Captain*).

[98] For the effect of bad weather during non-working hours, see § 7–45 below.

[99] *Reardon Smith Line Ltd.* v. *Ministry of Agriculture* (*The Vancouver Strike Case*) [1963] A.C. 691 (H.L.); and see "working day" in § 2–22 above.

[1] "Overtime in ports is the rule rather than the exception; and collective bargaining in the labour market often produces a rise in wages by means of a reduction in normal hours"; Lord Devlin in *Reardon Smith Line Ltd.* v. *Ministry of Agriculture* (*The Vancouver Strike Case*) [1963] A.C. 691 at p. 741 (H.L.).

ing hours might depend on the port, port trade, trade, ship or other factors.

Normal working hours are the hours during which it is customary for labour to work the ship in question, in the trade[2] or with the cargo in question, at that particular area of the port, and at that time. In *Reardon Smith Line Ltd.* v. *Ministry of Agriculture*[3] Lord Devlin spoke of the need to make a "reasonable apportionment" of the day and contrasted this phrase with the phrase "equitable view," as employed by Lord Russell of Killowen C.J. in *Branckelow SS. Co.* v. *Lamport & Holt*[4]:

> " . . . a reasonable apportionment should be made of the day— Lord Russell of Killowen based this decision on an 'equitable view'—according to the incidence of the weather upon the length of day that the parties were working or might be expected to have been working at the time."

The decision is one fact, and so may be made by an arbitrator:

> "I do not mean that the arbitrator must deal in half days or even quarter days, if he has the material before him that will enable him to do better . . . an experienced arbitrator will probably know from the number of lay days, the amount of cargo to be loaded and the rate of loading to be expected at the port, how much of the day was expected to be used, and he would naturally assume that work would be done so far as possible during normal hours at standard rates and after that, if necessary, during the hours in which overtime was most likely to be worked. I should regard such an apportionment as entirely a question of fact and should not, as at present advised, be prepared to recognise any principle of law that would allow the court to interfere with it."

Any apportionment must therefore be made with regard to the normal working hours; this involves a study of the circumstances of the particular case.

7–27 *Normal working hours—other views in the Reardon Smith case.* Lord Devlin said[5] that his thoughts as to how weather working days should be computed were not strictly relevant as weather was not a factor in the case. Nevertheless the views of the House of Lords must be regarded as having considerable persuasive effect. They may be summarised as follows:
Viscount Radcliffe[6]:

> " . . . the basic calculation in such cases should be determined by ascertaining what part of the calendar day was used, if loading was actually being done, or could reasonably have been used, if there was in fact no loading. The proportion which this bears to the working hours of the ship should be charged to the shipper."

On this basis the normal working hours are taken to be "the working hours of the ship while in the particular port." This coincides with the view of Lord Devlin, in that it is agreed that the criteria should be the activities of the parties and the ship and the port in question.

---

[2] Lord Devlin said *ibid.* at p. 741: "If it means in the trade, the grain trade or whatever else it may be . . . what happens if there is a cargo of general merchandise? This would make the lay days difficult if not impossible to calculate." Presumably even in the case of general cargo, it might be possible to find out the number of hours normally worked for such a cargo.
[3] [1963] A.C. 691 (H.L.) at p. 744.
[4] [1897] 1 Q.B. 570 at p. 573. The words quoted here are those of Lord Devlin.
[5] At p. 743.
[6] At p. 724.

Lord Cohen[7] and Lord Evershed[8] stated that they concurred with the views expressed by Lord Devlin.

Lord Keith of Avonholm[9] did not consider separately the fixing of the number of working hours for the purpose of dealing with interruptions by bad weather. However, he discussed the question when considering whether a working day should be treated as a day of 24 hours (with which view he concurred) or as a day of so many working hours. He then referred[10] to the number of working hours:

> "The fixing of working hours might present some difficulty. But it would be a question of fact to be resolved, I think, largely on the rules of practice at any particular port. That working hours might vary at different ports would be, I think, immaterial. Nor where there was a general practice of working at overtime rates need 'working hours' be confined to hours worked at standard wages."

Lord Keith then adopted the view that a weather working day was a calendar day of 24 hours.

Twenty-four normal working hours? There seems no reason why it **7–28** should not be found as a fact that there are 24 normal working hours per calendar day in a particular trade at a particular port. There would then be no need to apply a fraction[11] to the figure of 24; the number of hours during which work was possible and not prevented by bad weather would be the number debited to the charterers.

In *N.V. Maatschaapij Zeevart* v. *M. Friesacher Soehne*[12] a charterparty provided for the carriage of heavy grain, milo, and soya beans from the U.S. Gulf to the Antwerp-Hamburg range. It stated: "Steamer to be loaded according to berth terms, with customary berth dispatch, and if detained longer than five weather working days, Sundays and holidays excepted, charterers to pay demurrage at the rate of 800 dollars per day or *pro rata* . . . " The New Orleans longshoremen on the public elevator worked 24 hours per day and seven days per week. It was held that a weather working day consisted of the number of hours worked at standard (as distinct from overtime) rates of pay. In this respect the judge adopted the views of the Court of Appeal in *Alvion SS. Corporation of Panama* v *Galban Lobo Trading Co. S.A. of Havana*.[13] Since the House of Lords decision in the *Reardon Smith* case the distinction between standard and overtime rates would probably be ignored in arriving at a definition of normal working hours. Elwes J. agreed that it might not in all circumstances be decisive, saying[14] that payment of overtime was a major factor, and added:

> " . . . it is not open to me, even if I were disposed—and I am not—to construe these words as a matter of law in such a way as to find that the working day at New Orleans is a 24-hour day wholly irrespective of the fact that the men who worked the 24 hours were paid at different rates . . . "

---

[7] At p. 725.
[8] At p. 729.
[9] At pp. 725–726.
[10] *Ibid.*
[11] For the methods of applying the fraction, see § 7–32 below.
[12] [1962] 1 Lloyd's Rep. 52.
[13] [1955] 1 Q.B. 430 (*The Rubystone*); see §§ 2–34 and 7–34 below.
[14] [1962] 1 Lloyd's Rep. 52 at p. 59.

7–29   **Part of day once counted as whole day.** Part of a day once counted as a whole day if any of it was used for working. The rules applied to the day when notice of readiness was given[15] and to the subsequent lay days. Days were whole days, and in the absence of some charterparty provision or a subsequent agreement to the contrary, the law took no notice of parts of days. As Quain J. put it[16]:

> "The charterers are entitled to a fair working day, but if, for the convenience of all parties, a portion of a day is used, it may be counted. It was a question for the jury. . . ."

7–30   *Application of the rule.* The application of the rule so far as it affected the ordinary lay days was exemplified in *Hough* v. *Athya & Son.*[17] Loading occupied four and a half days and discharging took five and a half days. Charterers were not obliged to use a broken day; they were entitled to a fair working day. They could use the day on which notice had been given, though there might be no inference to be drawn from the provisions of the particular charterparty as to when time should begin. The parties would then try to agree whether this early starting varied the common law presumption that time began at midnight of the same day.[18]

7–31   *Reason for the rule.* The reason for the rule that part of a day counted as a whole day was explained by Lord Devlin in *Reardon Smith Line Ltd.* v. *Ministry of Agriculture*[19]:

> "It is important to see how in this respect the law has developed. In the beginning a day was a day—a Monday, a Tuesday or a Wednesday, as the case might be. Work began, one may suppose, some time in the morning and ended in the evening, the number of hours that were worked varying from port to port and in different trades. But whatever the number was, at the end of the Monday one lay day had gone and at the end of the Tuesday another; and if the work went into Wednesday, that counted as a whole day because of the rule that a part of a day was to be treated as a day. For this reason the charterer was not obliged to use a 'broken' day. If notice of readiness was given during the day he could, if he chose, wait till the following day so that he could start with a whole day; see *The Katy.*[20] But this general rule had to yield to any inference to be drawn from the provisions of the particular charterparty."

Here he deals not only with the rule that part of an ordinary lay day must be treated as a whole day, but also with the problems raised when notice is given.[21] So part of a day counted as a whole day, if it was used. But charterers were not obliged to use the part, especially as the whole day would count.

7–32   *Modification of the rule; the arrival of fractions.* The rule as to the indivisibility of lay days was modified in *Branckelow* v. *Lamport & Holt.*[22] As a result half-days came to be considered in laytime calculations. The matter was not governed by authority until that case. A fixing note, for the carriage of wheat and/or maize from the Plate to Europe, stated: "The steamer is to be loaded at the rate of 175 tons per weather working day, Sundays and holidays excepted. . . . " At Rosario rain interrupted loading on several days but in each case only for a few hours, in the morning or in

---

[15] See § 4–47 above.
[16] In *Commercial SS. Co.* v. *Boulton* (1875) 3 Asp.M.L.C.(N.S.) 111 at p. 112. This view was cited with approval by Lord Esher M.R. in *The Katy* [1895] P. 56 (C.A.) at pp. 62–63.
[17] (1879) 6 Ct. of Sess. (4th Ser.), 961.
[18] For the effect of work before laytime, see § 4–46 above.
[19] [1963] A.C. 691 at pp. 738–739 (H.L.) (*The Vancouver Strike Case*).
[20] [1895] P. 56 (C.A.), *per* Lord Esher M.R. at p. 63. See also § 4–47 above.
[21] For these see § 5–18 above.
[22] [1897] 1 Q.B. 570.

the afternoon. Sometimes a considerable quantity of work was done during the other half of the day. The shipowners wanted to treat the rainy days on which a substantial amount of work had been done as whole weather working days; the charterers contended that they should only count as portions of days. The Commercial Court held that the charterers were right; the time occupied in loading cargo on those days was to be counted as a part only of each weather working day. Rejecting the shipowners' contention that the days should be counted as whole weather working days, Lord Russell of Killowen C.J. said[23]:

> "There might be many days on which work was begun in the morning but stopped in a short time because of rain, and, if effect were given to the plaintiffs' contention, the charterer might not in a given case have half the number of days for loading to which he was entitled under the charter[24] . . . the most equitable view is to charge half a day against the charterers where substantial work is done, though not amounting to half a day, and to charge a full day against them where substantially a full day's work, though not amounting to twelve hours, is done; no smaller fraction than half a day should, however, be taken into consideration, and if the time worked is quite insignificant it should not be charged at all."

In spite of the reference by Lord Russell to "no smaller fraction than half a day" such fractions are now calculated.

An understandable modification. As a result of the decision in the **7–33** *Branckelow* case[25] a day was not always treated as a whole. It had become acceptable to calculate the effect of bad weather on part of a day; no sacrifice of principle would be involved in dealing with smaller fractions. As Lord Devlin said[26] of the former rule:

> "It must now be a matter for speculation as to why commercial men wanted the day to count as a whole since weather so often affects a day intermittently. Possibly they wanted to make up their minds at the beginning of the day whether it was to be treated as a working day or not so that if it was not the crew need not stand by but might have shore leave. At any rate, the time came when it was felt to be unreasonable to treat the day as a whole. Lord Russell of Killowen C.J. thought so in the *Branckelow* case . . ."

Which hours were to be apportioned? **7–34**

Effect of the Rubystone decision. The principle of apportionment laid down in the *Branckelow* case[27] was discussed by the Court of Appeal in *Alvion SS. Corporation Panama* v. *Galban Lobo Trading Co. S.A. of Havana.*[28] A charterparty for the carriage of sugar from Cuba to Piraeus stated: "Lay days at the average rate of [here there was inserted a formula by which the rate depended on the number of bags of varying weights and the position of the loading port] . . . provided vessel can receive at these rates per weather working day. Sundays and holidays and Saturdays afternoons excepted, shall be allowed to the said charterers . . . " By custom normal working periods at the loading ports were eight hours on a weekday and four hours on a Saturday. The parties differed as to whether a weather

---

[23] At p. 573.
[24] *e.g.* a laytime of 10 weather working days (with eight working hours on each day) would be exhausted in 10 days of four actual working hours each, *i.e.* 40 working hours, if each day on which there was work counted as a full day.
[25] [1897] 1 Q.B. 570; and see § 7–32 above.
[26] In *Reardon Smith Line Ltd.* v. *Ministry of Agriculture (The Vancouver Strike Case)* [1963] A.C. 691 (H.L.) at p. 740.
[27] [1897] 1 Q.B. 570.
[28] [1955] 1 Q.B. 430 (*The Rubystone*).

working day was one of 24 hours and, if so, whether these hours should be taken from the beginning of work or from midnight on the first day.[29] In the High Court McNair J. quoted Lord Russell C.J., who had said in *Branckelow*[30]:

> "the most equitable view is to charge half a day against the charterers where substantial work is done, though not amounting to half a day, and to charge a full day against them where substantially a full day's work, though not amounting to twelve hours, is done . . . "

7–35   McNair J. added[31]:

> "Lord Russell is saying that the question whether a particular day is to be considered a weather working day has to be determined by seeing to what extent the weather interfered with working during the 12 hours—12 hours clearly being the normal working hours at that time; and it would be quite inconsistent with his judgment to say that one has to look, not at the working hours, but at the 24 hours of the day."

Thus, if in applying the principle of apportionment one took all 24 hours into account, the absence of rain during eight working hours, combined with rain during the 16 non-working hours, would result in charterers being debited with only one third of a day. If only the working hours were considered, the question bound to arise[32] was whether such actual interruption should be stated in the timesheet, or translated so that (for example) a four-hour interruption of the eight-hour working period would result in the charterers being debited with 12 hours.[33]

7–36   **Disapproval of Branckelow.** In the Court of Appeal in *Alvion* v. *Galban Lobo*[34] Lord Goddard C.J. described[35] the rule applied in the *Branckelow* case[36] as:

> " . . . a somewhat rough-and-ready rule, or a rule-of-thumb . . . With great respect to that great Lord Chief Justice, I cannot agree that that is a proper way of applying this particular clause. I do not see any ground upon which one can lay down a rule-of-thumb (if I may put it in that way) in the way in which he did. I think that the way in which the umpire has done it in this case is the right way: that is to say, he has taken the actual time on any particular day on which the weather has stopped work, and has deducted it from the day; so that he has taken a day, we will say a Monday on which, in the ordinary way, the charterers would be entitled to eight hours, and he has said: 'Yes, but then you were stopped for [say] an hour, and therefore your day was only seven hours, and therefore you get the advantage of that, and that will prevent demurrage running against you which otherwise might.' I think that the umpire has calculated it rightly in this case, and I find it impossible to agree with the way in which the Lord Chief Justice dealt with the matter in *Branckelow's* case. I think that is importing into a contract an arbitrary rule which is not provided for in this contract. I dare say it might work substantial fairness between the parties, but the right way, I think, is to deal with the matter in the way in which the umpire has in this case . . . "

The view of the High Court in *Branckelow's* case, described by the judge as "the most equitable view," was that there should be an apportionment

---

[29] The meaning of the phrase "weather working days" as defined in *The Rubystone* is discussed in §§ 2–34–2–37 above. The moment from which the 24 hours must count is discussed in § 2–23 above.

[30] *Branckelow* v. *Lamport & Holt* [1897] Q.B. 570 at p. 573. See § 7–32 above.

[31] [1955] 1 Q.B. 430 at p. 439.

[32] As it did in *Reardon Smith Line Ltd.* v. *Ministry of Agriculture* [1963] A.C. 691 (H.L.); and see § 7–37 below.

[33] See § 7–37 below.

[34] [1955] 1 Q.B. 430 (*The Rubystone*). See § 2–34 and § 7–34.

[35] At pp. 447–448.

[36] [1897] 1 Q.B. 570.

of the day between time counted and time excepted. The decision in *Alvion* v. *Galban Lobo*[37–38] represented a refinement by the Court of Appeal of that view. Lord Goddard C.J., as we have seen,[39] described the earlier rule as "rough-and-ready," and favoured a more precise system of debiting the charterers.[40] A weather working day was assumed to comprise the number of hours customarily worked at the port in question.

Method of apportionment today   **7–37**

The method of calculation was put on a new basis by the House of Lords in *Reardon Smith Line Ltd.* v. *Ministry of Agriculture*.[41] In that case one of the charterparties[42] provided for loading in "six weather working lay days (Sundays, holidays, and rainy days not to be counted as lay or working days . . .) to commence 24 hours after the receipt by charterer's agents at loading port of the Captain's written notice of readiness." Lord Devlin referred to *Branckelow's* case[43] as having held that there should be an apportionment, adding[44]:

> "Since then it appears that in practice the rough division of the day into halves has been replaced by some more precise method of calculating the fraction."

The reasons given by Lord Devlin and the other Law Lords for regarding a working day and a weather day as days of 24 hours have been stated earlier.[45]

It is necessary to give some guidance as to how to deal with periods of   **7–38** bad weather. Where the lay days are "weather working days"[46] there must first be ascertained the length of the working day, including overtime, usually worked in that trade at that port at that time. One next determines the number of hours during which the weather was good enough to permit work, whether any was done or not. This period is expressed as a proportion of the total working hours and then applied to the 24 hours of the "weather working day." The result represents the number of hours which count against charterers. An abbreviated version of this formula has been stated by McNair J.[47]: "the time lost is to be calculated at the ratio which the actual time lost bears to the normal working hours of the port."

As Viscount Radcliffe said in the *Reardon Smith* case[48]:   **7–39**

> "Thus, if those hours" [the normal working hours] "are decided by the arbitrator to have been 16 hours out of the 24, and of those 16, four have been obstructed by bad weather, three-quarters of the whole day, that is 18 hours, are for the shipper's account. If there was bad weather in the day outside those 16 hours, say in the off hours of the night or early morning, but no weather interruption during the working hours, the whole

---

[37–38] [1955] 1 Q.B. 430 (*The Rubystone*).
[39] At § 7–36.
[40] For the effect, see § 2–37 above.
[41] [1963] A.C. 691 (*The Vancouver Strike Case*).
[42] Five were originally under discussion in the High Court but most were on similar terms.
[43] [1897] 1 Q.B. 570.
[44] At p. 741.
[45] In connection with working days, in § 2–24 above.
[46] Not "days of twenty-four hours"; see §§ 7–40–7–45 below.
[47] In *Reardon Smith Line Ltd.* v. *Ministry of Agriculture* (*The Vancouver Strike Case*) [1960] 1 Q.B. 439 at p. 516.
[48] [1963] A.C. 691 at p. 724 (H.L.) (*The Vancouver Strike Case*).

day would be chargeable: if it was fine in the off hours but weather obstructed all the working hours, no fraction of the day would be chargeable at all."

Lord Keith of Avonholm expressed his view[49] in similar terms:

> "If the amount of interference, or interruption, by weather with work during working hours is applied proportionally to the period of 24 hours a reasonable and equitable result is, I consider, achieved. Thus where there is total interference by weather with work being done during working hours which might otherwise have been done the day will not be computed as a lay day. Any lesser degree of interruption will be applied in like proportion to the period of 24 hours. When interruption becomes zero, that is when there is no interference by weather during working hours, the day will fall to be considered as a weather working day of 24 hours. I would add that I think there may be circumstances in which local custom at a port may introduce other considerations into the treatment of weather working days."

This refinement of the method of apportionment, when contrasted with the system adopted in *Branckelow's* case[50] may be attributed, in part, to the increased value attached to the time of a ship and the resultant need of the parties to define that value. In the *Reardon Smith* case the method was explained.

7–40   *2. Working days of 24 hours*

A laytime clause may refer to working days of 24 hours in either of the following forms:

(a) working days of 24 hours[51] (weather permitting[52]);
(b) weather working days of 24 hours.[53]

7–41   **(a) Working days of 24 hours[51] (weather permitting[52]).** If bad weather prevents work during all or part of the normal working hours, or would have prevented it if work were intended or contemplated,[53] then where the laytime clause refers to "working days of 24 hours" the laytime calculation is unaffected. If the words "weather permitting"[54] are also included, laytime is interrupted to the extent that the weather prevented any ship of the same general type from working. It is not relevant that, owing to the presence of another ship in the berth, the prevention was not the operative cause as to the ship not working,[55] provided that the time in question is time that counts as part of the day of 24 hours.[56]

7–42   **(b) Weather working days of twenty-four hours.[57]** The effect of bad weather during part or all of the normal working hours, in a "weather working day of 24 hours," depends upon whether the day, in the context of

---

[49] At p. 726.
[50] [1897] 1 Q.B. 570. See § 7–32 above.
[51] For this expression, see § 2–41 above.
[52] *i.e.* with or without the addition of the words "weather permitting," for the modern meaning of which, see § 7–16 above.
[53] *Compania Naviera Azuero S.A.* v. *British Oil & Cake Mills Ltd.* [1957] 2 Q.B. 293. See § 7–05 above.
[54] See § 7–10 above, and the cases then discussed.
[55] See *Dow Chemical (Nederland) B.V.* v. *B.P. Tanker Co. Ltd.* [1983] 1 Lloyd's Rep. 579 (C.A.) (*The Vorras*); and § 7–14 below.
[56] For different views as to the interpretation of the clause, see § 2–41 above.
[57] For this expression, see § 2–42 above.

the laytime clause, is treated as a conventional (or notional) day or as a day of 24 consecutive hours.[58] If it is treated as a conventional day, then bad weather which prevents work for part or all of such a day.[59] or would have interrupted it if work were intended or contemplated,[60] interrupts laytime. If it is treated as a day of 24 consecutive hours,[61] then laytime is interrupted during all hours in which work is prevented, or would have been prevented if work was intended or contemplated.

3. *Working days of 24 consecutive (or running) hours*   **7–43**
The laytime clause may refer to working days of 24 consecutive (or running) hours in either of the following forms:

(a) weather working days fof 24 consecutive (or running) hours[62]:
(b) working days of 24 consecutive (or running) hours (weather permitting[63]).

(a) Weather working days of 24 consecutive (or running) hours. If there is   **7–44**
bad weather at any time, so that work is prevented[64] or would have been prevented if work had been intended or contemplated,[65] then laytime is interrupted. It is interrupted for a period equal to the duration of the bad weather; it is not necessary to adopt the method of apportionment used in the case of "weather working days."[66]

**(b) Working days of 24 consecutive (or running) hours (weather permit-   7–45
ting.**[67]) If there is bad weather at any time preventing work, or preventing any ship of the same general type from working,[68] laytime is interrupted. No apportionment is needed. In the absence of the words "weather permitting" bad weather has no effect on the laytime calculation.

II. Bad weather at night or otherwise outside normal working hours   **7–46**
The effect of bad weather at night, or otherwise outside normal working hours, depends, as it does in the case of bad weather during normal working hours,[69] upon the wording of the laytime clause.
This may refer to:

1. Weather working days;

---

[58] For the different views as to the interpretation of the clause, see § 7–39 above. In *Forest SS. Co.* v. *Iberian Iron Ore Co.* (1899) 5 Com.Cas. 83 (H.L.) (see § 2–44) and *Watson Brothers* v. *Mysore Manganese Co.* (1910) 15 Com.Cas. 159 (see § 2–45), a working day of 24 hours was held to be a conventional day; in *Orpheus SS. Co.* v. *Bovill & Sons* (1916) 114 L.T. 750 (see § 2–46), Scrutton J. held that "working days of twenty-four hours each" were "days of twenty-four consecutive hours."

[59] For such a day only consists of normal working hours.

[60] *Compania Naviera Azuero S.A.* v. *British Oil & Cake Mills Ltd.* (*The Azuero*) [1957] 2 Q.B. 293. See § 7–05 above.

[61] This seems more probable but there is no direct modern authority on the subject. See § 2–42–2–49 above.

[62] For this expression, see § 2–50 above.

[63] For "weather permitting," see § 7–10 above and the cases then discussed.

[64] Whether the interruption is during normal working hours or not.

[65] *Compania Naviera Azuero S.A.* v. *British Oil & Cake Mills Ltd.* (*The Azuero*) [1957] 2 Q.B. 293. See also § 7–05 above.

[66] See § 7–37 above.

[67] For "weather permitting," see § 7–10 above, and the cases then discussed.

[68] See *Dow Chemical (Nederland) B.V.* v. *B.P. Tanker Co. Ltd.* [1983] 1 Lloyd's Rep. 579 (C.A.) (*The Vorras*); and § 7–16 below.

[69] See §§ 7–23 and 7–24 above.

2. Working days of 24 hours[70];

3. Working days of 24 consecutive hours.[71]

7–47 1. *Weather working days*[72]

If there is bad weather at night and the normal working hours do not extend to night-time, laytime is not interrupted. The decision of the House of Lords in *Reardon Smith Line Ltd.* v. *Ministry of Agriculture*[73] modified the position[74] as it was after the Court of Appeal decision in *Alvion SS. Corporation of Panama* v. *Galban Lobo Trading Co. S.A.*[75] Although the House said that a weather working day was, prima facie, a day of 24 hours, it can to a limited extent be regarded as a day no greater than its number of normal working hours. No account is taken, therefore, of bad weather at night, if the period is outside the normal working hours.[76]

7–48 It may seem illogical that, in accordance with the rule in *Compania Naviera Azuero S.A.* v. *British Oil and Cake Mills Ltd.*,[77] time should be interrupted during the day even when no work is contemplated or intended, but not during night hours when work is not intended. If the night is wet and the day is fine, there being eight normal working hours in the day, charterers are debited with one day. If, say, four of the eight hours are unworkable owing to bad weather, charterers are debited with one half of a day.[78] This is so even where work would not have been possible in any event, because, for example, the elevators could not be worked. Where the bad weather takes place at night the laytime calculation is unaffected; but where it takes place during normal working hours charterers receive credit for it, in terms of laytime. But in each case no work is interrupted. Lord Devlin said in *Reardon Smith*[79] that he was not startled, as were McNair J. and the Court of Appeal in *Alvion*,[80] by the thought that, if the fraction were based upon the full calendar day, the charterers might conceivably be debited with only a third of a day when in fact the day's work had not been interfered with at all. As he put it[81]:

> " . . . the charterers might conceivably be debited with only a third of a day[82] when in fact the day's work had not been interfered with at all. If the night is wet and the day is fine, that is what may happen. But this sort of artificiality is inherent in the concept of the weather working day. If, as in the present case, there can be no loading any way because the elevators cannot be worked, the weather cannot matter at all, but admittedly the lay days still have to be computed according to whether or not they are wet. If the charterer can obtain relief for the whole of a wet day which he is not using, why should he not obtain a portion of that relief for a wet night which he is not using?"

[70] See § 7–49 below.

[71] See § 7–52 below.

[72] This expression is defined in § 2–59 above. For "weather permitting working day" see § 7–14 above.

[73] [1963] A.C. 691 (*The Vancouver Strike Case*). For its treatment of a "weather working day" see § 7–37 above.

[74] See § 7–37 above.

[75] [1955] 1 Q.B. 430 (*The Rubystone*). See § 2–34 and § 7–34 above. For its definition of a "weather working day," see § 7–30 above.

[76] For Lord Devlin's comments, see § 7–27 above.

[77] [1957] 2 Q.B. 293 (*The Azuero*). See § 7–05 above.

[78] For the principles of apportionment in such a case, see § 7–37 above.

[79] [1963] A.C. 691 (H.L.).

[80] [1955] 1 Q.B. 430 (C.A.).

[81] At pp. 743–744.

[82] *i.e.* if the night and other non-working hours (16 in all) were wet and the working day (8 hours) was fine.

Though tempted to solve the problem in that way, Lord Devlin decided to follow the Court of Appeal decision to the extent that it held that one need only look to the normal working hours. Similarly, Viscount Radcliffe, dealing with the question of apportionment, said[83]:

> "If there was bad weather in the day outside those 16 hours[84] say in the off hours of the night or early morning, but no weather interruption during the working hours, the whole day would be chargeable; if it was fine in the off hours but weather obstructed all the working hours, no fraction of the day would be chargeable at all."

2. *Working days of 24 hours*   **7–49**
A laytime clause may refer to working days of 24 hours in either of the following forms:

   (a) Working days of 24 hours[85] (weather permitting[86]);
   (b) weather working days of 24 hours.

(a) Working days of 24 hours (weather permitting[86]). If the laytime   **7–50**
clause refers to "working days of 24 hours," and the words "weather permitting" do not appear in the clause, then bad weather for part or all of the night[87] or otherwise outside normal working hours does not interrupt laytime. This is so (a) whether the days are being treated as conventional days or as days of 24 consecutive hours[88]; and (b) whether the bad weather actually prevents work or, merely, would have prevented it if work had been contemplated or intended.

If the words "weather permitting" are included then any period during which weather prevents work, or prevents any ship of the same general type from working,[89] during the "working days of twenty-four hours" must be considered. A "working day of twenty-four hours" has been held[90] to be, in certain circumstances,[91] a conventional day as opposed to a calendar day, and to comprise 24 normal working hours which need not be consecutive. Where it is treated as a conventional day of 24 working hours[90] and the words "weather permitting" appear in the laytime clause, bad weather outside normal working hours interrupts laytime if it interrupts those working hours and prevents work, or prevents any ship of the same general type from working.[89] Occasionally the expression "working days of twenty-four hours, weather permitting" is held to indicate days of 24 consecutive hours.[92]

---

[83] At p. 724.
[84] *i.e.* if there were 16 normal working hours.
[85] For this expression, see § 2–42 above.
[86] *i.e.* with or without the addition of the words "weather permitting," as to which see § 7–10 above, and the cases then discussed.
[87] If no night hours are normal working hours. If they are, then the case falls within the rule set out at § 7–40 above; nevertheless the weather has no effect, owing to the absence of the words "weather" and "weather permitting."
[88] For the different views as to the interpretation of the expression "working days of twenty-four hours," see § 2–42 above.
[89] Subject to what is said in *Dow Chemical (Nederland) B.V.* v. *B.P. Tanker Co. Ltd.* [1983] 2 Lloyd's Rep. 579 (C.A.) (*The Vorras*); see § 7–16 above.
[90] See *Forest SS. Co. Ltd.* v. *Iberian Iron Ore Co. Ltd.* (1895) 5 Com.Cas. 83 (H.L.) and *Watson Brothers* v. *Mysore Manganese Co. Ltd.* (1910) 15 Com.Cas. 159. See § 2–42 above.
[91] In the two cases cited there also appeared the words "weather permitting" and provisions for the counting of time used in excepted periods.
[92] For days of 24 consecutive hours, see § 7–53. As to whether it should be so treated, see §§ 2–41–2–49 above, and *Orpheus SS. Co.* v. *Bovill & Sons* (1916) 114 L.T. 750. For that case, see § 2–46 above.

7–51 **(b) Weather working days of 24 hours.**[93] The effect of bad weather during part or all of the night or otherwise outside normal working hours, when the laytime clause refers to "weather working days of twenty-four hours,"[94] depends upon whether the day is treated as a conventional day or as a day of 24 consecutive hours.[94]

If it is treated as a conventional (or notional) day, consisting of 24 working hours, collected from different days,[95] then bad weather outside such hours does not affect the laytime calculation. This is because a conventional day consists only of normal working hours, so that bad weather outside such hours can make no difference.

If the day is treated as a day of 24 consecutive hours,[96] then bad weather at night or outside normal working hours which prevents work, or would have prevented work if it were intended or contemplated, interrupts the laytime.

7–52 3. *Working days of 24 consecutive (or running) hours*

A laytime clause may refer to working days of 24 consecutive (or running) hours which are prima facie calendar days of 24 actually consecutive hours, in either of the following forms:

(a) weather working days of 24 consecutive (or running) hours[97];
(b) working days of 24 consecutive (or running) hours (weather permitting).[98]

7–53 **(a) Weather working days of 24 consecutive (or running) hours.** Bad weather at night or otherwise outside normal working hours interrupts laytime if work is prevented or would have been prevented if it were contemplated or intended.[99] Laytime is interrupted for a period equal to the duration of the bad weather, and no apportionment[1] is necessary.

7–54 **(b) Working days of 24 consecutive (or running) hours (weather permitting).** Where the clause contains the words "weather permitting,"[2] and bad weather at night or otherwise outside normal working hours prevents work, or prevents any ship of the same general type from working,[3] laytime is interrupted. No apportionment is necessary. If the clause does not contain the words "weather permitting," the laytime calculation is unaffected.

---

[93] For this expression, see § 2–42 above.
[94] For this expression, see § 2–50 above.
[95] They will have to be collected from different days unless it is normal for a calendar day at the port to consist of 24 working hours.
[96] As to whether it should be so treated, see the contrasting decisions in, on the one hand, *Forest SS. Co. Ltd.* v. *Iberian Iron Ore Co. Ltd.* (1899) 5 Com.Cas. 83 (H.L.) and *Watson Brothers* v. *Mysore Manganese Co. Ltd.* (1910) 15 Com.Cas. 159 (day treated as a conventional day), and, on the other hand, *Orpheus SS. Co.* v. *Bovill & Sons* (1916) 114 L.T. 750 (day treated as a day of 24 consecutive hours.)
[97] For this expression, see § 2–50 above.
[98] For "weather permitting," see § 7–10 above, and the cases then discussed.
[99] See *Compania Naviera Azuero S.A.* v. *British Oil & Cake Mills Ltd.* (*The Azuero*) [1957] 2 Q.B. 293. See also § 7–05 above.
[1] For apportionment, see § 7–37 above.
[2] For "weather permitting," see § 7–10 above, and the cases then discussed.
[3] See *Dow Chemical (Nederland) B.V.* v. *B.P. Tanker Co. Ltd.* [1983] 1 Lloyd's Rep. 579 (C.A.) (*The Vorras*); and § 7–16 above.

As Lord Trayner said in *Turnbull, Scott & Co.* v. *Cruickshank & Co.*[4]:

> "in every twenty-four consecutive hours from the commencement of the loading or discharging, 500 tons were to be loaded or discharged if the weather did not hinder it or a holiday or Sunday intervene."

In that case the laytime clause referred to "working days of twenty-four consecutive hours (weather permitting)."

III. Bad weather on Saturdays   7–55

Bad weather on Saturdays[5] is usually treated in the same way as bad weather on other working days, unless the charterparty provides to the contrary. As Lord Radcliffe put it in *Reardon Smith Line Ltd.* v. *Ministry of Agriculture*[6]:

> "Saturday counts among the lay days that are imputed to the charterers and it counts as a whole day, since the parties have made no stipulation for charging fine working days by any more meticulous scale."

In the absence of such a provision as "Saturday after 1 o'clock shall be excepted,"[7] Saturday must be treated as a working day. If it is a working day, then the principles applicable when there is bad weather depend upon whether the clause refers to weather working days, weather working days of 24 hours, weather working days of twenty-four consecutive hours, and so on.

The effect of bad weather on Saturdays thus depends upon whether it takes place during[8] or outside the normal working hours,[9] and upon the wording of the laytime clause.

IV. Bad weather when part of Saturday excepted   7–56

Part of Saturday may be excepted from laytime, by the use of such words as "Saturday after 1 o'clock shall be excepted." If so, Saturday is treated like any other working day, but as a working day with normal working hours which end at 1 p.m. Thus in the case of bad weather during normal working hours, where the laytime clause provides for weather working days, there is an apportionment.[10] If, for example, the normal working hours begin at 8 a.m. and bad weather prevents work[11] for 2 hours and 30 minutes, charterers are debited with 12 hours as they have used half of a weather working day. The rules applicable thus depend upon whether bad weather takes place during normal working hours[12] or not,[13] and upon the laytime clause.[14]

---

[4] (1904) 7 Ct. of Sess., 5th Ser., 265 at p. 273; see also § 2–50 above.
[5] For Saturdays generally, see § 8–15 below.
[6] [1963] A.C. 691 (H.L.) at p. 723 (*The Vancouver Strike Case*).
[7] As in *Hain SS. Co.* v. *Sociedad Anonima Comercial de Exportacion e Importacion (The Trevarrack)* (1934) 49 Ll.L.Rep. 86.
[8] For bad weather during normal working hours, see § 7–23 above.
[9] For bad weather outside the normal working hours, see § 7–46 above.
[10] See § 7–46 above.
[11] Or would have prevented work if it were contemplated or intended; *Compania Naviera Azuero S.A.* v. *British Oil & Cake Mills Ltd. (The Azuero)* [1957] 2 Q.B. 293. See § 7–05 above.
[12] See § 7–23 above.
[13] See § 7–46 above.
[14] The different laytime clauses are set out under the headings (I) bad weather during normal working hours (§ 7–23) and (II) bad weather at night or otherwise outside normal working hours (§ 7–46) respectively.

7–57 V. Bad weather on Sundays and holidays

Where Sundays and holidays are excepted by the laytime clause, bad weather on these days has no effect. Provisions that time should count on those days when work has been done fall into two categories[15]: (a) those which cause the whole day to count, if any time is used; (b) those which cause only the time used to count. In the case of the first category the day is treated as an ordinary working day, so that the effect of bad weather depends upon the laytime clause, and upon whether the bad weather occurred during normal working hours[16] or not.[17] In the case of the second category only time used counts, so that bad weather does not affect the laytime calculation.

7–58 VI. Bad weather during other specially excepted periods such as "Friday after 5 p.m. to Monday at 8 a.m."

A charterparty may provide that laytime shall not run from, say Friday at 5 p.m. to Monday at 8 a.m. The complete exclusion of individual days appears to present no problem. In the example given, Saturday and Sunday would not count. It is the partial exclusions, of 7 hours on Friday and 8 hours on Monday, which may produce difficulties. The following situation might arise:

Monday 0000 to 0800 hours	Time not to count.
0600 to 1800 hours	Normal working hours, of which 6 hours, from 0800 to 1400 hours, could not be worked owing to rain.

In the absence of the exceptions clause, there would, in the case of laytime clause referring to weather working days, be an apportionment in respect of the 12 normal working hours,[18] so that charterers would be debited with one half of a day. Ten normal working hours are left as the period from 0600 to 0800 hours is not to count. Four of those hours (1400 to 1800 hours) could be worked, so that four tenths or two fifths of the available non-excepted working period was available to charterers. They are debited with two fifths of a day. So also in the case of other laytime clauses the calculation depends upon the number of normal working hours, which in this case are fewer, and whether the bad weather occurs during these hours[19] or not.[20]

---

[15] The provisions are discussed in greater detail at § 8–02 below.
[16] See § 7–23 above.
[17] See § 7–46 above.
[18] See § 7–37 above.
[19] See § 7–23 above.
[20] See § 7–46 above.

CHAPTER 8

SUSPENSION OF LAYTIME—OTHER THAN BY BAD WEATHER

ONCE laytime has begun[1] it runs continuously against charterers unless cus-   **8–01**
tom or express words in the charterparty provide to the contrary or unless
the shipowners remove the ship for their own purposes or to suit their own
convenience.[2] In the absence of such a provision charterers cannot prevent
time from running. This is so even where the delays have been caused by
circumstances beyond their control, such as bad weather,[3] congestion,
strikes,[4] or shortage of cargo, provided that shipowners were not responsible for any of those circumstances. A custom might have the effect of
interrupting laytime if, for example, the charterparty spoke of running
days but there was a custom not to work on Sundays,[5] or a custom not to
count time taken in moving between discharging places.[6] Laytime is often
interrupted by express words by which Sundays, holidays and other periods
are to be omitted from the calculations.[7] It may also be interrupted, or in
some other way affected, by a clause stating that time lost by reason of
various cases shall not count.[8]

A. Exclusion of Sundays and holidays   **8–02**
The phrases commonly used to exclude Sundays and holidays from lay-
time include the following:
"Sundays and holidays excepted."[9]
"Saturdays[10] after noon, Sundays, general and local holidays shall be
    excepted, unless used,[11] in which event actual time used to
    count."[12]
"Sundays and holidays excepted, unless used,[11] in which case only actual
    time used shall count."[13]

---

[1] As to when time begins, see § 4–01 above. For the possible interruption of laytime or
demurrage by a fault or other action on the part of shipowners, see §§ 10–63–10–68 below.
[2] See *Cantiere Navale Triestina* v. *Russian Soviet Naphtha Export Agency* [1925] 2 K.B. 172
(C.A.) (§ 8–53 below) and *Ricargo Trading S.A.* v. *Spliethoff's Bevrachtingskantor B.V.*
[1983] 1 Lloyd's Rep. 648 (*The Tassos N*) (§ 8–49 below).
[3] Thus frost prevented the loading of a ship at London; but the charterers were held to be
liable for delay; *Barret* v. *Dutton* (1815) 4 Camp. 333.
[4] For strikes, see § 8–30 below.
[5] *Nielsen & Co.* v. *Wait* (1885) 16 Q.B.D. 67 (C.A.). See § 2–20 above.
[6] As in *Nielsen & Co.* v. *Wait, ibid.* See § 2–20 above.
[7] For interruptions caused by weather conditions, and such phrases as "weather permitting"
and "weather working day," see §§ 7–10 and 7–24 above. For Sundays, see §§ 8–06 and
8–07 below. For holidays, see § 8–08 below.
[8] See § 8–27 below.
[9] Found in many charterparties.
[10] For Saturdays, see § 8–15 below.
[11] For the meaning of the words "unless used," see §§ 8–04, 8–05 below.
[12] Baltic Wood Charter Party 1964 (Nubaltwood).
[13] Soviet Wood Charter Party 1961 (Sovietwood).

197

8–03 *Sundays and holidays excepted*

The phrase "Sundays and holidays excepted"[14] is inserted in charterparties in favour of charterers so that time shall not run against them on these days when usually they may not want to or cannot work. Even if the charterers and other parties are willing and able to work the words prevent time from running. If work is done in an excepted period time is still not counted, unless such words as "unless used"[15] are added to the exceptions clause, or unless there is a subsequent agreement to count such time. Such an agreement must amount to a variation of the original charterparty. It is not inferred merely because the parties have worked the ship during part or all of the times in question.[16]

The requirements which have to be satisfied, if time is to count in this otherwise excepted period, were explained by the House of Lords in *Nelson (James) & Sons Ltd.* v. *Nelson Line, (Liverpool) Ltd.*[17] The laytime clause said that "Seven weather working days (Sundays and holidays excepted)" were "to be allowed by shipowners to charterers for loading." The loading was continued during holidays. There was no evidence that this arrangement amounted to an agreement to vary the charterparty.[18] The House of Lords held that no inference of law could be drawn that the terms had been varied; the charterers were entitled to the dispatch which they had claimed for "each clear day saved in loading."[19] As Lord Loreburn L.C. put it[20]:

> " . . . there were some holidays during which one of the ships was loaded by the charterers with consent of the master. No special arrangement was made. But the Court of Appeal held (apparently regarding it as a point of law) that an agreement to treat the holiday as a working day, and so to count it among the lay days, ought to be inferred from the mere fact of working by consent . . . In my view it is a question, not of law, but of fact . . . I am unable to see any evidence of such an agreement. Very likely, it was convenient to both sides to do what was done. I do not believe it entered into the head of either that they were making such an agreement as is suggested. At all events, there is no proof of it, and therefore the charterparty, which excludes holidays, must prevail . . . "[21]

8–04   **"Unless used."**[22] Sometimes a laytime clause providing for Sundays and holidays to be excepted goes on to add such words as "unless used," or "unless used, in which event only actual time used to count."

---

[14] The Charterparty Laytime Definitions 1980 (see Appendix to this book) state: "19. 'EXCEPTED'—means that the specified days do not count as laytime even if loading or discharging is done on them."

[15] See §§ 8–04, 8–05 below.

[16] *Pteroti Compania Naviera S.A.* v. *National Coal Board* [1958] 1 Q.B. 469. See also § 4–46 above.

[17] [1908] A.C. 108.

[18] Such an agreement must involve an offer and an acceptance, with an intention to affect the legal relationship of the parties, just as in the case of an ordinary contract. So also in *Pteroti Compania Naviera S.A.* v. *National Coal Board* [1958] 1 Q.B. 469 there was no agreement that time should count before laytime began; see § 4–46 above.

[19] As to the dispatch dispute, see §§ 12–14, 12–15 below.

[20] At p. 113. The House of Lords reversed the Court of Appeal, which by a majority had found in favour of the shipowners.

[21] In *Whittall & Co.* v. *Rahtkens Shipping Co. Ltd.* [1907] 1 K.B. 783 the High Court held in a similar situation that the proper inference to be drawn was that the parties had, despite the express terms of the charterparty, agreed to include the day worked among the lay days. It seems that such an inference would not be drawn from the mere fact that work took place.

[22] The Charterparty Laytime Definitions 1980 (see Appendix to this book) state: "20. 'UNLESS USED'—means that if work is carried out during the excepted days the actual hours of work only count as laytime."

Where the first of these phrases "unless used," is employed,[23] it seems that if any time is used, the whole day should count as a day of the type which the charterparty treats as lay days. If the laytime clause refers to " . . . weather working days (Sundays and holidays excepted unless used) . . . " then, if any time at all is used on the otherwise excepted days, they count as weather working days. In the circumstances the applicability of the expression "weather working days" is limited. Though a weather working day has been held[24] to be, prima facie, a calendar day of 24 hours, the effect of bad weather is only considered so far as it takes place during the normal working hours.[25] Where, as is usual, there are no normal working hours on Sundays and holidays, but parts of the days are used, how is bad weather to be treated in the laytime calculation? It is possible, though there appears to be no authority on the subject, that one day has to be debited to the charterers, with the exception only of periods when work was actually prevented, and when work would have been prevented if intended or contemplated.[26]

Where the second of the above phrases, "unless used, in which event **8–05** only actual time used to count," is used, the incidence of weather can have no effect on the laytime calculation as the time cannot be used at all if weather prevents work.

In the absence of any clause providing that time used in excepted periods should count, it is a question of law in each case as to whether the parties have varied the charterparty, by agreeing subsequently that it should count.

Sundays   **8–06**

Charterparties usually provide expressly that Sundays shall not count. It is probably enough for there to be a reference merely to "working days"[27] for Sundays to be excluded from the laytime, but in practice Sundays are specifically mentioned. The practice avoids confusion. Mere exclusion of Sundays is not sufficient to except holidays from the laytime as well.

Non-Christian countries. When the ship is in a country where work is **8–07** usually done on a Sunday, that day not being recognised as a holy or non-working day, Sundays are nevertheless excluded from laytime if the parties have so agreed. Occasionally such a contingency is foreseen, as when the ship is going to a place where the Moslem religion prevails. The expressions used include: "Fridays and holidays excepted" and "Fridays at loading ports, Sundays at discharging ports, and all holidays excepted."

If holidays only are specifically excluded, then Sundays will not be excluded thereby as they are not holidays: the result is the same if the laytime clause refers to working or weather working days, as Sundays count in such countries because they are working days. As Lord Devlin said in *Reardon Smith Line Ltd.* v. *Ministry of Agriculture*[28]:

> "But there may, of course, be days in some ports, such as the Mahomedan Friday, which are not working days and yet cannot well be described as Sundays or holidays."

---

[23] See the cases discussed in §§ 2–42 and 2–43.
[24] In *Reardon Smith Line Ltd.* v. *Ministry of Agriculture, Fisheries & Food (The Vancouver Strike Case)* [1963] A.C. 691 (H.L.). See also §§ 7–24 and 7–26 above.
[25] See § 7–38 above.
[26] See *Compania Naviera Azuero S.A.* v. *British Oil & Cake Mills Ltd.* (*The Azuero*) [1957] 2 Q.B. 293. See also § 2–62 above.
[27] As in *Nielsen & Co.* v. *Wait* (1885) 16 Q.B.D. 67 (C.A.).
[28] [1963] A.C. 691 at p. 736 (H.L.).

8–08 *Holidays*

A holiday has been defined[29] as " a day on which work is suspended; a day of recreation or amusement." Whether a day is a holiday or not for the purpose of the laytime calculation is a question of fact, depending upon the law, practice or custom applicable in the port. All three factors have to be considered, as they were in *A/S Westfal-Larsen & Co.* v. *Russo-Norwegian Transport Co. Ltd.*[30] A charterparty for a voyage from Leningrad stated: "Cargo to be loaded and stowed in nine weather working days, Sundays and holidays excepted whether used or not." When the shipowners claimed demurrage the charterers contended that three of the days were Russian holidays, and that they had earned dispatch. The days were December 25 and 26, 1929, and January 1, 1980. The only question before the High Court was, as Wright J. put it,[31]

> "one of fact, namely, whether those days were holidays according to the regulations or the practice or the custom or the law applicable in the port of Leningrad . . . "

Of these four factors, "the regulations" can be regarded as a facet of "the law" so that in effect there must be considered the practice, the custom and the law. The judge considered both a number of decrees of the U.S.S.R. relating to the working days and holidays and the evidence given by officials. He said[32]:

> "I think it is clear that in the port of Leningrad work went on, or rather holidays were recognised, according to the traditional religious festivals and feasts which they continued in the Russian Calendar and which had been preserved in the Russian Calendar. [A witness] produced the calendar of the year 1929 in which Christmas Day and Boxing Day are entered as holidays in red, indicating that they were what we call red-letter days—and I have no doubt from the evidence of those two Russian witnesses who were called . . . that that was the position in Leningrad up to 1929 at least."

The judge then considered the attempt of the government in the middle of 1929 to introduce the so-called uninterrupted or continuous week. This scheme involved the abolition of pre-existing holidays and a system whereby there would be no general interruption of work. He concluded[33] that the uninterrupted week had not then been introduced, although work had been done on all three days. He noted that there was some evidence that people working then were paid double wages because the days were holidays. The charterers won. This shows how mixed a question of law, practice and custom can be involved in deciding whether days are holidays.

8–09   **Local holidays.** A holiday need not be a national holiday; a local holiday may be sufficient to enable the charterers to interrupt the laytime.

In *Hain SS. Co.* v. *Sociedad Anonima Comercial*[34] a ship was to be "loaded at the rate of two hundred and twenty-five tons per running day up

---

[29] *Shorter Oxford English Dictionary* (3rd ed.). The Charterparty Laytime Definitions 1980 (see Appendix to this book) state: "13. 'HOLIDAY'—means a day of the week or part(s) thereof on which cargo work on the ship would normally take place but is suspended at the place of loading/discharging by reason of:
    (i) the local law; or
    (ii) the local practice."
[30] (1931) 40 Ll.L.Rep. 259.
[31] At p. 261.
[32] At p. 261.
[33] At p. 263.
[34] (1932) 43 Ll.L.Rep. 136 (*The Tregantle*). The charterparty was the River Plate Charterparty 1914 (Centrocon).

to the first three thousand tons, and at the rate of four hundred tons per running day for any quantity above three thousand tons, Sundays and holidays excepted, otherwise demurrage shall be paid . . . " A dispute arose as to whether two days, November 19 and December 6, were holidays. The umpire found that neither day was a national holiday, though by a decree of the government of Buenos Aires Province it had been declared that November 19 was an official holiday. The day was accordingly observed as a holiday in the port of San Nicolas. Stevedores insisted on double pay on that day and no work was done in the port. A Ministry of Finance decree had ordered that national departments in a Province should not observe holidays other than those declared nationally. As a result federal government offices (including the customs office) at San Nicolas did not close on November 19. December 6 was not a holiday throughout Buenos Aires Province, but it was a holiday in the town and port of San Nicolas, and had been so declared by the municipal authority. The Ministry decree also applied to December 6.

It was held that both days were holidays for the purpose of the laytime clause. As MacKinnon J. put it[35]:

> "I do not think that under this charterparty it is necessary to show that it is a holiday universally recognised or decreed or obtaining throughout the whole territory of the Argentine; and I think that must be so, having regard to what one knows as to the nature of holidays all over the world . . . things such as bank holidays notoriously are quite different in England from those which are recognised in Scotland, and for various other reasons holidays really are a local institution[36] and only very exceptionally a national institution."

A local holiday was also held to have been established in *Government* **8–10** *of India* v. *Central Gulf Steamship Corporation*.[37] A ship loaded rice at Lake Charles, Louisiana, for India, under a charterparty which stated: "Steamer to be loaded at the average rate of 1,000 tons per weather working day of twenty-four consecutive hours Saturday afternoon, Sundays and holidays excepted." A dispute arose as to whether Saturdays were holidays at Lake Charles and whether Saturday mornings should be counted. A Louisiana State Act of 1958, providing for "Days of public rest, legal holidays and half-holidays," and referring to the parishes in certain districts (within which area Lake Charles was situated), stated: " . . . the whole of every Saturday shall be a holiday for all banking institutions." There was uncontradicted evidence from a practising Louisiana attorney that the disputed Saturdays "were full legal holidays." While accepting that Saturdays in the port were in practice working days,[38] and that Saturday morning was a normal overtime working day, Donaldson J. said that the result of the legislation was that Saturdays were holidays. He added[39]:

> "It may well be that the purpose of the legislation is to ensure that there is a weekly break in the daily round of work, but I do not think that it is in any way limited to banks

[35] At p. 139.
[36] In one American case, *Tweedie Trading Co.* v. *Pitch Pine Lumber Co.* 156 Fed. 88 (1907), it was held that the general observance of the Welsh Eisteddfod was enough, even though there was no legal holiday.
[37] [1968] Lloyd's Rep. 173 (*The Mosfield*).
[38] See also § 8–15 below.
[39] At p. 179.

and such institutions. Furthermore I do not consider that it matters what is the purpose of the legislation, if the chosen method is to declare certain days to be holidays."[39a]

A local holiday interrupts time, however, if it extends to certain aspects of business at the port[40] but not to the type of work contemplated by the charterparty. Nor are the holidays observed by the ship and her crew,[40a] or the nation to which they belong, relevant. Holidays are allowed for the benefit of charterers, and not for the benefit of shipowners.

Holidays may be of different types.[41] The exceptions clause may refer to: "General and/or local holidays,"[42] "Non-working holidays,"[43] or "Official and local holidays,"[44] rather than merely to "holidays."

8-11   **"General or local holidays."** In *Love and Stewart Ltd.* v. *Rowtor SS. Co. Ltd.*[45] the House of Lords held that this phrase did not exclude from laytime wet days,[46] even where no work can be done, or Saturday afternoons,[47] even where the latter are not usually worked. A charterparty[48] for the carriage of pit props from Kristinestad, Finland, to Newport, Monmouthshire, stated that loading and discharging were to be "according to the custom of the respective ports, Sundays and general or local holidays (unless used) in both loading and discharging excepted." The main issue was whether the parties intended there to be a fixed number of lay days. According to the custom of Newport the discharge of Baltic pit props was suspended during wet weather and during half of each Saturday. A question arose as to whether the charterers could exclude from laytime Sundays, holidays, the time during which work was suspended owing to wet weather, and the Saturday half-holidays. Lord Summer discussed the scope of the expression "Sundays, general or local holidays" and said[49]:

> "I think that time during which the weather is wet, which is time that may be measured by minutes or hours, and the half of each Saturday, which though half of a calendar day may not be the same as a moeity of the number of working hours on an ordinary day, cannot be brought within the exception of 'Sundays, general or local holidays.' They are not days within the exception in the clause . . . I do not think the term extends to the latter part of a week-day, on which it is usual not to work, although we call it and enjoy it under the name of a Saturday half-holiday."

The phrase "general or local holidays" may have some effect other than that contained in the word "holidays." A holiday might not be local; but

---

[39a] In a London arbitration shipowners contended successfully that at Lake Charles the birthday of Thomas M. Gleason, a union leader, was not a legal holiday. See LMLN 209, November 7, 1987. It was common ground that labour was available only at overtime rates.

[40] In *Pacific Carriers Corporation* v. *Tradax Export, S.A. (The North King)* [1971] 2 Lloyd's Rep. 460, the High Court considered the situation where notice of readiness was given on a Saturday which was All Saints' Day and a Louisiana public holiday. In the special circumstances it was held to be a good notice. See § 5–21 above at n. 94.

[40a] Or by stevedores. See LMLN 209, November 7, 1987, on longshoremen's holidays and Clarence Henry's birthday.

[41] An extensive list, which is not binding on English courts or arbitrators, is set out annually by the Baltic and International Maritime Conference in its Holiday Calendar.

[42] White Sea Wood Charter 1933 (Russwood).

[43] Azoff Berth Contract 1910 (Azcon).

[44] See § 8–14 below.

[45] [1916] 2 A.C. 527 (H.L.).

[46] The effect of wet and other inclement days is discussed in § 7–19 above.

[47] For Saturdays, see § 8–15 below.

[48] The 1899 Wood Charter from Scandinavia and Finland to the United Kingdom.

[49] At p. 536.

the existence of a general holiday, with no practical effect on local activities, would entitle charterers to stop time from running.

"Non-working holiday." The phrase "non-working holiday" has been   **8–12**
held to include a public holiday on which only extra pay will normally produce work.

In *Panagos Lyras (Owners)* v. *Joint Danube and Black Sea Shipping Agencies of Braila*[50] a charterparty[51] for the carriage of grain from the Danube stated: "Cargo shall be loaded at the average rate of 400 units per running day (Sundays and non-working holidays excepted)." The parties disagreed as to whether Good Friday, Holy Saturday and Easter Tuesday were non-working holidays at Galatz, though it was agreed that they were holidays. The charterers produced evidence that public offices (including the custom house and the offices of the harbour-master, harbour police and sanitary authorities) were closed and that men only worked then for extra pay. The shipowners said that the days were not holidays for the workers; that the ship (and other ships) loaded on Good Friday and Holy Saturday; and that then and on Easter Tuesday labourers worked without extra pay. The arbitrator held as facts that the days were public holidays and that it was possible to load ships then without paying extra wages. The court took the view, in favour of the shipowners, that the days were not "non-working holidays." Roche J. said[52] that this phrase arose because in some foreign ports there were both the old church holidays and new political holidays. Rejecting the charterers' argument that the phrase "non-working" was mere surplusage, he said[53]:

> "I think it is intended to divide up holidays and to make some of them fall into the category of working holidays and others to fall into the category of non-working holidays."

As for extra payment he said[54] of the finding that men worked without   **8–13**
extra pay:

> "That is the kind of test which I think ought to be imposed—whether it is ordinarily a working day where people work without any real addition to their ordinary pay. I will not say that the mere fact that if one party or the other wanted to engage men and had to pay some small extra fee would make it different, but broadly speaking it is whether they ordinarily work for ordinary wages."

This last sentence shows that the enquiry may not be limited to the question of extra pay to the labourers in the ship. As the judge said[55]:

> "The mere fact of some extra payment need not make all the difference, but on the other hand, if the payments were of any large amount it might make all the difference."

The charterers asked that the arbitrator should be told to consider the men working at the silos or elevators. This might be relevant in deciding whether days were "non-working holidays" or "holidays." This case has

---

[50] (1931) 40 Ll.L.Rep. 83.
[51] The form is not stated in the law reports though Roche J. said (at p. 85) that the document before him had been in existence since 1911. It was probably the Danube Berth Contract 1911 (Dancon).
[52] At p. 85.
[53] At p. 86.
[54] *Ibid.*
[55] *Ibid.*

been cited[56] in support of the proposition that in modern conditions a finding that a day is a working day does not exclude the possibility that it is also a holiday. In countries without many holidays it would be almost invariably true that only substantial extra pay would normally produce work. If a laytime clause governing operations in such a country excepted only non-working holidays, then even so nearly all holidays would be excepted. As MacKinnon J. said in *Hain SS. Co. Ltd.* v. *S.A. Comercial de Exportacion e Importacion* when speaking of holidays[57]:

> " . . . they are non-working days, but you can get people to work if you pay them excessive wages—as, no doubt, it is possible to get people to work on the most universally recognised holidays in London, such as Bank holidays, if you pay them sufficiently to make it worth their while."

8–14   **"Official and local holidays."** This phrase has been held by the High Court in *Z SS. Co. Ltd.* v. *Amtorg, New York*[58] not to include a day when stevedores will not (as the result of a 40-hour week) work except for higher wages. A charterparty for the carriage of coal from the Azov Sea to Boston, U.S.A., said that the ship was "to be discharged at the average rate of 800 tons per weather working day, Sundays, official and local holidays excepted whether used or not." Goddard J. held that Saturday in Boston was not an official or local holiday. He described the point[59] as "a very, very difficult one." The charterers relied on the Code of Fair Competition for the Coal Dock Industry made in pursuance of the National Recovery Act 1933. The Code had the force of law. Under it people in the industry were only required to work a limited number of hours weekly at the basic rate. When working in excess of those hours they were entitled to a higher rate of pay. As a result Boston shippers, importers and retailers agreed with the unions that Saturday was to be treated as an official holiday in the coal industry. Any person could work on Saturdays if he liked, but he was then entitled to the higher rate of pay. Goddard J. said[60]:

> "Saturday is not an official holiday. Saturday has not been proclaimed to be a non-working day by any officials, if by officials is meant, as I think, Government officials or under Government powers."

As to whether Saturday was a local holiday, he said[61]:

> " . . . I cannot see how it can be said that because one particular trade for its own arrangement have said 'We will work five days a week and treat everybody who works on Saturday as though they had worked five days that week quite irrespective of whether they had or not,' that creates a local holiday."

and[62]:

> "If it could be said the evidence shows that Saturdays are regarded in the port of Boston as a *dies non*—a non-working day—unless you choose to pay higher wages, I think a great deal might be said for the view that that would come within the term 'local holiday.' If it could be shown that certain trades shut their doors, a number of trades—I do not

---

[56] In *Government of India* v. *Central Gulf Steamship Corporation* (*The Mosfield*) [1968] 2 Lloyd's Rep. 173, by Donaldson J. at p. 178. See § 8–10 above. By local law Saturdays were holidays. See also LMLN 212, December 19, 1987, as to holidays in India.

[57] (1932) 43 Ll.L.Rep. 136 at p. 139 (*The Tregantle*).

[58] (1938) 61 Ll.L.Rep. 97. For discussion there of the phrase "weather working day" see § 2–30 above.

[59] At p. 102.

[60] At p. 103.

[61] *Ibid.*

[62] At pp. 103 and 104.

think one would be enough—a certain number of trades had closed their doors in Boston on Saturdays so that a large number of working people regarded Saturday as a holiday, although you might persuade somebody to work on that day, more might be said. . . . "

Such trade arrangements may have the effect of creating local holidays if they are reasonably widespread. It is possible that it would be sufficient for all or most of those concerned in the business of shipping to be affected by such an arrangement.

B. Saturdays   8–15

Saturday as a working day. Saturday must be treated for laytime purposes like any other working day if there is no contrary reference in the charterparty, provided that it does not fall within the definition of a holiday.[63]

It is sometimes suggested that a Saturday differs from a weekday and a working day on the one hand and a Sunday or a holiday on the other hand. The confusion arises because the rules or the manner of working, and the payment,[64] are often different on Saturday. In the absence of special words to the contrary, the day will be a working day if it does not comply with the definition of a holiday.[65]

Relevance of overtime. Mere payment of overtime is insufficient to prevent Saturday being a working day rather than a holiday.   **8–16**

In *Corrado S.A. di Navigazione* v. *Exporthleb*[66] Sundays and holidays were excepted from the laytime. At the Soviet loading port there was a continuous working week of seven days at 24 hours a day, each day being worked in three eight-hour shifts. On Saturdays each worker's working day was of six hours; they had by law to be paid overtime for the extra two hours. The charterers argued that the total overtime period of six hours should not count. The High Court rejected this contention. Branson J. said[67]:

> "It seems to me that in order to show that the day is a holiday or not you must regard the question as to whether at the time concerned it is customary that work should be done. There is no doubt on the findings in this case that Saturday is not a holiday in that sense, because work goes on continuously for the whole 24 hours . . . The custom was to work in three shifts, so that there would be three periods of two hours after the men had done their work when they would be entitled to extra remuneration for the two hours. I do not see how these periods can be picked out as coming within the word 'holidays' in the charter-party."

This conclusion, that the payment of overtime was not sufficient to prevent

---

[63] For the circumstances in which Saturday might be a holiday, see below in § 8–19; and see *Z SS. Co. Ltd.* v. *Amtorg, New York* (1938) 61 Ll.L.Rep. 97 at pp. 103–104. See also *Government of India* v. *Central Gulf Steamship Corporation* [1968] 2 Lloyd's Rep. 173, and § 8–10 above.

[64] In the case of the Polcoalvoy Charter there is an optional Free Saturdays Clause. With the exception of 13 special Saturdays which are ordinary working days, Saturdays are termed Free Saturdays. The optional Clause states: "At loading port, on Free Saturdays, time from 0001 hours to 2400 hours shall not count, unless used, in which event actual time used shall count. However, notice of readiness as per Clause 3(a) may be tendered on such days."

[65] For which see § 8–08 above.

[66] (1932) 43 Ll.L.Rep. 509.

[67] At p. 510.

Saturday being a working day,[68] was affirmed by the House of Lords in *Reardon Smith Line Ltd.* v. *Ministry of Agriculture, Fisheries & Food.*[69]

8–17   **Local laws.** Saturday does not become a holiday or an excepted period merely because it is contrary to the local law to work the ship on a Saturday after 1 p.m.[70] In *Hain SS. Co.* v. *Sociedad Anonima Comercial de Exportacion e Importacion*[71] Sundays and holidays were excepted from the laytime, which was expressed in running days. The umpire found tha loading at San Lorenzo, Rosario and La Plata was contrary to local law after 1 p.m. on Saturday. The High Court held that Saturday should be computed as a full day. MacKinnon J. said[72]:

> "It would have been perfectly easy to say 'Sundays and holidays and Saturday after 1 o'clock shall be excepted.' They have not done so . . . quite clearly the period on Saturday from 1 p.m. onwards is not included in the Sundays and holidays and must not be taken to be impliedly included merely because in the Argentine a holiday is sanctioned by something more stringent than custom or usage, namely, by a local law which says that it is illegal to work."

8–18   **Effect of custom.** Nor does Saturday become a holiday or an excepted period merely because it is customary not to work on a Saturday afternoon. The decision to this effect in *Love & Stewart Ltd.* v. *Rowtor SS. Co. Ltd.*[73] was followed in *Robert Dollar Co.* v. *Blood Holman & Co. Ltd.*[74] A charterparty for the carriage of barley from San Francisco stated: "Sundays, holidays and rainy days not to be counted as lay days or working days." Saturday at Sharpness on the Bristol Channel had for some time past been a half-day only. As McCardie J. said[75]:

> "The usual working day is eight hours, but only four hours are worked on Saturdays."

Stating that he was bound by the House of Lords decision in *Love & Stewart Ltd.* v. *Rowtor SS. Co. Ltd.*,[76] he said:

> "in the present case, Saturdays, though in practice only half days, count as working days within the meaning of this charterparty."

8–19   In *Reardon Smith Line Ltd.* v. *Ministry of Agriculture*[77] the House of Lords considered, among many other topics in the field of laytime, the status of Saturdays at Vancouver. The disputes arose out of a strike of elevator personnel in February 1953. Thirty-one tramp ships chartered to load full cargoes of wheat, and arriving after the strike began, were delayed. Of

---

[68] The charterparty may, however, link the payment of overtime with the exclusion of Saturdays from laytime: see § 8–21 below.

[69] [1963] A.C. 691. See § 8–19 below.

[70] But the local law may declare Saturdays to be holidays; see *Government of India* v. *Central Gulf Steamship Corporation* [1968] 2 Lloyd's Rep. 173, and § 8–10 above.

[71] (1934) 49 Ll.L.Rep. 86 (*The Trevarrack*).

[72] At p. 88.

[73] [1916] 2 A.C. 527 (H.L.) and see § 8–11 above. This House of Lords decision does not appear to have been cited in *Aktieselskabet Dampskibet Gimle* v. *Garland & Roger Ltd.*, 1917, 2 S.L.T. 254. "Sundays, general or local holidays (unless used)" were excepted from laytime; the Court of Session held that, as no work could be done on Saturday afternoon at Leith, Saturday was a half holiday. Lord Salvesen said (at p. 256) that he was influenced by the consideration that the rate of discharge stipulated contemplated a whole working day. Such a conclusion would not be reached today.

[74] (1920) 4 Ll.L.Rep. 343.

[75] At pp. 349–350.

[76] [1916] 2 A.C. 527.

[77] [1963] A.C. 691 (*The Vancouver Strike Case*).

the three charterparties considered by the House of Lords, when hearing the demurrage and dispatch claims, all contained a laytime clause in the following terms: "Lay days. Six weather working lay days (Sundays, holidays and rainy days not to be counted as lay or working days) . . . are to be allowed the charterers for loading . . . "

One issue was whether the Saturdays, which, it was agreed by the parties, were not disturbed by weather, should count as weather working days. The charterers argued that they should not count as Saturday was not a working day. For the elevator men Saturday did not form any part of their usual working hours, just as night work and Sunday work did not form such a part. They normally worked a five-day, 40-hour week; they would work overtime if necessary to get a ship out, at time and a half on Saturdays and double time on Sundays. It was held that the Saturdays were working days.

The House of Lords upheld the principle, expounded in *Corrado Soc. Anon. di Navigazione* v. *Exporthleb*,[78] that mere payment of overtime was insufficient to deprive Saturday of its status as a working day. Lord Radcliffe said[79]:

> "I think it is quite beside the point to ask whether Saturday working was within the normal working hours of an individual employee at the port, because it seems to me that the line which divides an individual's hours at normal rate from his hours at an overtime rate has no relevance at all to the question whether a day is or is not a working day . . . Saturday counts among the lay days that are imputed to the charterers and it counts as a whole day, since the parties have made no stipulation for charging fine working days by any more meticulous scale."[80]

Lord Devlin on Saturdays. Apart from a brief reference to Saturdays by **8–20** Lord Keith[81] the only other Law Lord who discussed Saturdays was Lord Devlin. He considered first the meaning of the expression "weather working day."[82] Since it was not claimed that the weather had affected Saturday work the question was whether the lay days consisted of days or working days. If he had decided that they were merely days or calendar days, it could not have been contended by charterers that Saturdays were other than days or calendar days. He decided that the lay days were working days, so that the question which then arose was whether Saturday was a working day. His conclusion may be summarised in the statements that the word "working" did not define a part of a day but described the character of the day as a whole; and that the character of a working day could not be determined by enquiring whether on that day or on a part of it work was done at standard rates.

It followed that Saturday was not a non-working day merely because for the elevator personnel it was not a day on which they usually worked, or not a day on which they would work for the normal rate of pay. The same conclusion would, he said, be drawn even if all classes of worker were in

---

[78] (1932) 43 Ll.L.Rep. 509; and see § 8–16 above.
[79] [1963] A.C. 691 at p. 723.
[80] For a "more meticulous scale," see § 8–23 below ("Saturday afternoons excepted.").
[81] At p. 726; "In the present cases no question of interruption by weather on a Saturday arises and Saturday was, therefore, a working day at the port of Vancouver even though wheat may not generally have been loaded from elevators on that day. The whole of Saturday then falls to be computed as a lay day."
[82] A discussion also conducted by Lord Radcliffe (pp. 722–724); and Lord Keith (pp. 725–726). Lord Devlin's views on the subject, which were endorsed by the other members of the House of Lords, are set out in §§ 7–26 and 7–27 above.

the same situation as the elevator men, so far as Saturdays afternoons were concerned.[83] Nor could a Saturday afternoon be treated as a non-working part of a day. This conclusion resulted, in his view, both because the absence of work at standard rates on Saturday afternoons would not make Saturday a non-working day, and because there was nothing in the charterparty to justify splitting the working day into fractions.

8–21   Exclusion of Saturdays

If the charterparty provides expressly that Saturdays are not to count, without such a qualifying expression as "unless used,"[84] then the whole day is excluded.

Charterparties on the Baltimore Form C contain the following clause, sometimes known as the B.F.C. Saturday clause:

"(1) Notwithstanding any custom of the port to the contrary, Saturday shall not count as laytime at loading or discharging port or ports where stevedoring labour and/or grain handling facilities are unavailable on Saturday or available only at overtime and/or premium rates.

(2) In ports where only part of Saturday is affected by such conditions as described under '1' above, laytime shall count until expiration of the last straight time period.

(3) Where six or more hours of work are performed at normal rates, Saturday shall count as a full layday."

8–22   Questions have arisen, particularly with reference to the discharge of bulk grain at Rotterdam,[84a] as to whether (a) "available," as in (1) above, means available in the port in general or to the ship in question and (b) the words "stevedoring labour and/or grain handling facilities are . . . available only at overtime and/or premium rates" refer to what the customer pays the elevator operators or what those operators pay the stevedores. In *Primula Compania Naviera S.A.* v. *Finagrain Cie. Commerciale Agricole et Financière S.A.*[85] the reduced labour force available on Saturdays was paid at premium rates of 150 per cent. for the Saturday day shift and 200 per cent. for the Saturday night shift. There was a premium rate of $137\frac{1}{2}$ per cent. for weekday night shifts. The bulk grain operators made a flat rate charge to their customers for all shifts other than Saturday night shifts, averaging the rate out for the three types of shift. The *Point Clear* had carried grain to Rotterdam. A question arose as to whether laytime counted on Saturday January 5, 1974, when the ship was lying at anchor at the Hook of Holland, awaiting her turn to move to the suction elevators, and having given an effective notice of readiness.

Donaldson J., finding for the shipowners, said that the clause was intended to classify ports by reference to the existence of certain conditions

---

[83] Presumably it would also be drawn if all classes of workmen were in that situation throughout Saturday; but no Law Lord dealt with that point.

[84] See § 8–04 above.

[84a] See, in addition to the English case summarised in this section, a New York arbitration, *Fairfield Shipping Corporation* v. *Bunge Corporation* (*The Stephanie*) Society of Maritime Arbitrators Award No. 706 (1972). The panel concluded that there was insufficient labour or equipment available to work the ship on the Saturday in question. In their view, para. (1) of the B.F.C. Saturday clause excluded that day from laytime, in the circumstances prevailing, for that ship.

[85] [1975] 2 Lloyd's Rep. 243 (*The Point Clear*).

and not to determine whether any particular ship could or could not discharge. He added[86]:

> "The approach is similar to that which is adopted in deciding whether a particular day is or is not a weather working day, when it is irrelevant that the charterer is unable to use that day . . . On this particular Saturday, like other Saturdays, there was a substantial reduction in the availability of labour and grain discharging facilities, but neither was unavailable."

He then considered whether, as the charterers argued, "labour and/or grain handling facilities" were available only at "overtime and/or premium rates." It was common ground and was clear from paragraph (3) of the B.F.C. clause that what was in question was the Saturday day and not the Saturday night shift.

Donaldson J. concluded[87]:

> "In my judgment, the clause is clear. In the context of grain handling facilities, the reference to overtime or premium rates must be to the charges paid by the customers to those who supply the facilities. A similar approach should be adopted in relation to labour. In Rotterdam the customers pay the same rates for the labour and for the grain handling facilities on Saturdays as they do on weekdays. In the circumstances it cannot be said that the labour and/or grain handling facilities are available only at overtime and/or premium rates."

Saturday afternoons excepted **8–23**

In the absence of express words to the contrary, a Saturday is a working day, or a holiday if it satisfies the criteria of a holiday.[88] Without apt words it cannot be a half-holiday, even though it is usual not to work on Saturdays, especially in the afternoon.[89] A "more meticulous scale"[90] can be devised by the use of the appropriate words. An example was given by MacKinnon J. in *Hain SS. Co.* v. *S.A. Comercial de Exportacion e Importacion*[91] when he suggested the words "Sundays and holidays and Saturday after 1 o'clock shall be excepted." A more restricted example is contained in the Baltic Wood Charter-Party 1973 (Nubaltwood). This states: "Saturdays afternoon, Sundays, general and local holidays excepted, unless used, in which event actual time is to count."

Other examples are "Saturdays and days preceding general or local holidays to count only as three-quarters of a day whether used or not[92]; "Saturday afternoon, Sundays and holidays excepted"[93]; and "Saturdays and

---

[86] *Ibid.* at p. 248.

[87] *Ibid.*

[88] For these criteria see § 8–15 above.

[89] See Lord Sumner in *Love & Stewart Ltd.* v. *Rowtor SS. Co. Ltd.* [1916] 2 A.C. 527 (H.L.) at p. 536; and see § 8–11 above. It seems that this must be so, despite the decision in *Atkieselskabet Dampskibet Gimle* v. *Garland & Roger Ltd.*, 1917, 2 S.L.T. 254, see n. 69 above.

[90] The words used by Lord Radcliffe in *Reardon Smith Line Ltd.* v. *Ministry of Agriculture* [1963] A.C. 691 (H.L.) at p. 723 (*The Vancouver Strike Case*). See also § 8–19 above. As to bad weather when such a scale is used, see § 7–55 above.

[91] (1934) 49 Ll.L.Rep. 86 at p. 88 (*The Trevarrack*).

[92] Used in a charterparty for the carriage of coal from Mariupol, U.S.S.R., to Boston, U.S.A. in *Z SS. Co. Ltd.* v. *Amtorg, New York* (1938) 61 Ll.L.Rep. 97. See §§ 2–30 and 2–31 above.

[93] *Government of India* v. *Central Gulf Steamship Corporation* [1968] 2 Lloyd's Rep. 173 (*The Mosfield*). For the facts see § 8–10 above. The whole of Saturday was held to be a holiday as a result of local law.

days preceding holidays shall each count only as three-quarters of a day, unless used."[94]

8–24   **The Rubystone.** The Court of Appeal in *Alvion SS. Corporation of Panama* v. *Galban Lobo Trading Co. S.A. of Havana*[95] defined a working day[96] as a length of time consisting of a number of hours which, according to the custom of the port, were usually worked at the port. The effect was that in a time-sheet the period inserted in respect of a Saturday, where there were no deductions to be made, was the total number of hours usually worked in that port on a Saturday. Where, as in many ports, eight-hour days were worked from Mondays to Fridays and four-hour days were worked on Saturdays, a period of four hours would be inserted, deductions being made from that. The decision of the House of Lords in *Reardon Smith Line Ltd.* v. *Ministry of Agriculture*[97] resulted in that approach becoming incorrect except where the charterparty specifically allowed for it.

8–25   C. Time lost for various reasons

General exceptions clause. While laytime may be interrupted, by custom or as the result of express words, for certain periods, such as Sundays[98] and holidays,[99] it may also be affected where time is lost by reason of various named causes. The charterparty may refer to incidents more far-reaching in their effects in various terms.

8–26   In the *Asbatankvoy* form there are the words: " . . . where delay is caused to Vessel getting into berth after giving notice of readiness for any reason over which Charterer has no control, such delay shall not count as used laytime."[1] It can be seen that the parties may agree that divers causes, if they result in time being lost, bring about interruptions in the laytime. Clauses of this sort may be found in a number of charterparties; the Centrocon[2] Strike Clause and the Gencon General Strike Clause[3] are considered separately.[4]

---

[94] Soviet Wood Charterparty 1961 (Sovietwood).
[95] [1955] 1 Q.B. 430 (*The Rubystone*). See §§ 2–34 and 7–34 above.
[96] See § 2–22 above.
[97] [1963] A.C. 691.
[98] See § 8–06 above.
[99] See § 8–08 above.
[1] In a New York arbitration, *Burmah Oil Tankers Ltd.* v. *Marc Rich & Co. Inc. (The Atlantic Empress)* (Society of Maritime Arbitrators Award No. 1506, (1981)) the charterers relied on these words and said that bad weather had prevented berthing. The panel found that the evidence suggested congestion "and/or" unavailability of cargo to be the primary reason for the delay in berthing. The charterers had been aware, they said, that there was only one supplier of cargo; they could not pass on their charterparty obligations to that third party. See also, as to the words "reachable on her arrival" in this charterparty, § 4–33 above. See also Shellvoy 5, at cl. 13(1)(a), for a restricted list of situations in which a berth "shall be deemed inaccessible," so that laytime does not run.
[2] River Plate Charter-Party 1914.
[3] Uniform General Charter 1922.
[4] The Centrocon strike clause, which applies to a number of causes of delay in addition to strikes and lock-outs, in § 8–39 below; and the Gencon General Strike Clause, which also extends to lock-outs, in §§ 8–44–8–45 below.

Effect of exceptions clause. Charterers must bring themselves within an **8–27** exceptions clause[5] by showing that time has been lost by reason of one of the causes named, and that the causes were beyond their control. The time must have been lost in the operation of loading or discharging. Congestion which delays the ship in securing a berth may cause time to be lost.[6] If the discharge could have taken place, only the removal of the cargo from the quay thereafter being subject to delay by a named cause in the exceptions clause, time is not considered to be lost.[7]

If two or more causes contribute to a loss of time, so that the delay is not entirely attributable to an excepted cause, charterers are not allowed to benefit from any delay which they have caused. Thus in *Elswick SS. Co.* v. *Montaldi*[8] discharge was to be at the rate of 500 tons per day; the excepted causes "which prevent or delay the discharging" included strikes. The charterers were discharging at less than the agreed rates when a strike occurred. It was held that they could rely on the exceptions clause only to the extent that the strike would have caused delay if the discharging had been at the agreed rate.

Just as the cause must be beyond charterers' control, so also they cannot rely on the exceptions clause if they could with reasonable diligence have found another method of loading or discharging. An enquiry as to the reason for the loss of time may be necessary. For example, after or during a strike it may be difficult to ascertain how far any delay was due to the strike itself and how far it was due to congestion of ships, which would have arisen in any event but was aggravated by the strike. Both parties must therefore obtain as mush information as possible, as soon as possible, about any delays.

Charterers may contend successfully that time is lost by a cause beyond **8–28** their control although they are responsible for the loading or the discharging, and something goes wrong during one of those operations. In *Ferrum G.m.b.H.* v. *The Owners of the Mozart*[9] petroleum coke was carried from Port Arthur to Rotterdam on the Americanized Welsh Coal charterparty. Clause 3 stated: " . . . any time lost . . . by reason of accidents to . . . machinery . . . or any cause beyond the control of the charterers affecting . . . loading of the petcoke not to be computed as part of the loading time . . . No deduction of time shall be allowed for stoppage unless due notice be given at the time to the master or owners." Clause 4 read: "The cargo to be loaded and spout trimmed by men appointed by the charterer free of risk and expense to the vessel."

The charterers' United States agents entered into an agreement with an independent contractor, described specifically as not being the agents' agent or employee, who was to receive, store and load the cargo. During

---

[5] Where there is a clause dealing specifically with the effect of certain excepted causes on demurrage, and another clause dealing with excepted matters generally, the latter may not be apt to relieve the cargo interests from liability for demurrage: see the decision of the New South Wales Supreme Court in *Caltex Oil (Australia) Pty. Ltd.* v. *Howard Smith Pty. Ltd.* [1973] 1 Lloyd's Rep. 544.

[6] See also *N.V. Reederij Amsterdam* v. *President of India* [1961] 2 Lloyd's Rep. 1 (C.A.) (*The Amstelmolen*) as to congestion amounting to an obstruction under the Centrocon Strike Clause where the congestion delayed the ship in securing the berth. See § 7–42 below.

[7] *Granite City SS. Co.* v. *Ireland & Son* (1891) 19 R.Sess.Cas. (4th) 124.

[8] [1907] 1 K.B. 626.

[9] [1985] 1 Lloyd's Rep. 239 (*The Mozart*).

loading a feeder belt at the independent contractor's terminal came to a halt twice. As a result charterers said that laytime was interrupted for four days. It was held that clause 4 relieved the shipowners from responsibility for loading; but it did not mean that anything which went wrong was to be treated as not being, for the purpose of Clause 3, beyond their control.

As Mustill J. put it,[10] finding in favour of the charterers:

> " . . . it does not follow that anything which goes wrong before or during the act of loading is to be treated as the charterers' 'fault' for the purpose of cl. 3. Nor do I consider that a 'fault' can be ascribed to the charterers on the ground that, in the words of the arbitrators' reasons, 'they cannot escape from their own (vicarious) negligence' . . . I cannot see how fault on the part of TOPCO [the independent contractors] can be treated as fault on the part of Wolff [the agents], and a fortiori on the part of the charterers."

The judge went on to consider the provision in Clause 3 for "due notice," and in this respect also found in favour of the charterers. He said[11]:

> "One must therefore enquire what was the purpose of including lines 40 to 41 [the due notice provision]. It must, I think, have been to ensure that disputes were minimised by ensuring that the charterer could not seek to rely on an excepted peril, after the event and at a time when it was too late for the shipowner to carry out an investigation. One must then ask whether it would be necessary, in order to serve this purpose, that notice should be given in every case, not only of the occurrence itself, but also of the fact that the charterer was proposing to rely on it as a reason for not paying demurrage. I do not find any such necessity. *Ex hypothesi*, loading is stopped, for otherwise there would not be 'any time lost.' The master (who knows about the stoppage) or the owners, are also given notice of the occurrence which brought it about. What more do they need?"[12]

8–29   *"Any other cause" and the ejusdem generis rule*

Time can be lost by reason of a cause which is not specified, as, for example, congestion. A question may then arise as to whether such a cause is covered by the words "or any other cause beyond control of Charterers"[13] or some similar expression.[13a] The *ejusdem generis*[14] rule of construction applies where a particular description is followed by a general description. As Pollock C.B. said in *Lyndon* v. *Standbridge*[15]:

> "It is a general rule of construction that where a particular class is spoken of, and general words follow, the class first mentioned is to be taken as the most comprehensive, and the general words treated as referring to matters *ejusdem generis* with such class.

If therefore the list of causes constitutes a distinct category or *genus*, the words "any other cause" can only be taken to refer to causes in the same category.[16] If the list does not constitute a distinct category or *genus*, the

---

[10] *Ibid.* at p. 242.

[11] *Ibid.* at p. 56.

[12] This reasoning was cited, and followed, in *Valla Giovanni & C. S.p.A.* v. *Gebr. Van Weelde Scheepvaartkantoor B.V.* [1985] 1 Lloyd's Rep. 563 (*The Chanda*), by Bingham J. at p. 566. The relevant phrase was: "No deduction of time shall be allowed for stoppage, unless due notice be given at the time to the Master or Owner."

[13] Which appear in the C. (Ore) 7 Mediterranean Iron Ore Charter Party.

[13a] Thus: "Force majeure: . . . or any other . . . hindrances happening without the fault of the Charterers . . . delaying . . . discharging . . . of the cargo are excepted and neither the charterers nor the shippers should be liable for any loss or damage resulting from any such exempted clause and time lost by reason thereof shall not count as laydays or days on demurrage." In *Navrom* v. *Callitsis Ship Management S.A.* [1987] 2 Lloyd's Rep. 276 (*The Radauti*) the charterers relied successfully on these words, and congestion at Tripoli, Libya, was treated as being a hindrance. See also § 6–16 above.

[14] "of the same kind."

[15] (1857) 2 M. & N. 45 at p. 51.

[16] They need not be like those causes.

ejusdem generis rule does not apply, and the charterers are able to rely on any cause. The use of the word "whatsoever," as in the phrase "or any other cause whatsoever," or of similar words[17] may also prevent the application of the *ejusdem generis* rule. Thus in *Larsen* v. *Sylvester & Co.*[18] charterers were not liable if "frost, flood, strikes . . . and any other unavoidable accidents or hindrances of what kind soever beyond their control" delayed loading. The House of Lords held that the parties must have intended to keep the category of exceptions open.

Strikes   **8–30**
Strikes may delay loading or discharging, but the charterers cannot exclude such delay from the computation of laytime in the absence of apt provision in the charterparty.[19] They are considered here to the extent that they affect the calculation of laytime, and not as events which may excuse performance of duties under the charterparty.

Meaning. The term "strike" includes, but need not be restricted to, "a **8–31** general concerted refusal by workmen to work in consequence of an alleged grievance." So in *Williams Bros. (Hull) Ltd.* v. *Naamlooze Vennootschap W.H. Berghuys Kolenhandel*[20] a Dutch ship's crew had refused to carry a cargo of coal from Hull to Rouen in 1915 because the German government had announced its intention to sink neutral ships in the North Sea. The High Court held that the shipowners were entitled, when faced with a claim for damages by the charterers, to rely on a strike clause in the charterparty. Sankey J. said[21]:

> "A strike does not depend merely upon the question of wages. At the same time I do not think it would be possible to say that abstention of a workman from mere fear to do a particular thing or perform a particular contract would necessarily constitute a strike. I think the true definition of the word "strike" which I do not say is exhaustive, is a general concerted refusal by workmen to work in consequence of an alleged grievance."

The grievance need not concern wages[22] or even the conditions of the workmen themselves. A strike therefore includes a sympathetic strike. Thus in *Seeberg Bros.* v. *Russian Wood Agency*[23] receivers of timber said that loading in Leningrad in 1933 had been delayed by a strike of stevedores and other dock labourers. Owners of the ship, which was Latvian,

---

[17] If wide enough; the words *et cetera* have been held to be too vague to exclude the *ejusdem generis* rule; *Herman* v. *Morris* (1914) 35 T.L.R. 574 (C.A.) (ship sale and repairing contract; vendor not to be liable for delay from "strikes, lock-outs, *et cetera*, or any cause beyond the vendor's control").
[18] [1908] A.C. 295 (H.L.).
[19] For an example of such a clause, see § 8–37 below.
[20] (1916) 21 Com.Cas. 253.
[21] At p. 257.
[22] Despite the decision in *King* v. *Parker* (1876) 34 L.T. 887, where Kelly C.B., at p. 889, held that a strike meant a refusal by the whole body of workmen to work either because the employers had refused an increase in wages or because the workmen had refused to accept a diminution of wages; and depite also the comment by Lord Coleridge C.J. in *Stephens* v. *Harris & Co.* (1887) 56 L.J.Q.B. 516 at p.517: "When one hears of persons striking, it does not mean a refusal to work because the weather happens to be hot, but a standing out for higher wages." It is unlikely that this restricted view would now be adopted. The members of the Court of Appeal in that case refrained from any attempt to define a strike: (1887) 57 L.J.Q.B. 203.
[23] (1934) 50 Ll.L.Rep. 146.

said that the charterers were a state organisation and could at any time obtain labour to load. MacKinnon J. said[24]:

> " . . . it was said that it was a strike in sympathy with some labour grievance of some alleged unions of seamen or other workers on or connected with Latvian ships in Latvian and other ports. That was the nature of the strike . . . it appears to be established that there was a strike declared with all the due formality of a resolution of the trade union and so forth whereby the Leningrad stevedores agreed to abstain from loading timber upon Latvian ships."

He said that he was not satisfied that there was any practical means by which the charterers could have ended the strike or obtained labour.

8–32   A sympathetic strike was also considered, and the decision in the *Seeberg* case followed in *Vermaas' (J.) Scheepvaartbedrijf N.V.* v. *Association Technique de l'Importation Charbonnière.*[25] A charterparty, providing for the carriage of coal from Swansea to Nantes, stated: "Any time lost through existing strikes, lock-outs, civil commotions, frosts, floods, storms or accidents beyond the control of the Receivers, preventing or delaying the discharging, not to count unless the Vessel is already on demurrage." Port workers at Nantes refused to work ships carrying coal, in the hope that this would help French coal-miners who were on strike. On arrival the ship was sent to a waiting berth where she waited for 23 days before the ban was removed. McNair J. held that laytime had been suspended as time had been lost because of an existing strike. He said that a strike had once been regarded as a concerted effort by workmen either to obtain an increase in wages or to resist an attempt by employers to reduce their wages.[26] It had later[27] been defined more widely to include general concerted refusals to work in consequence of an alleged grievance. The most relevant case was that of *Seeberg Bros.* v. *Russian Wood Agency,*[28] where the facts were strikingly similar. McNair J. said[29]:

> "It seems to me that it is quite impossible for me in this case now to hold that the withdrawal of labour at Nantes arose because there was a grievance between the men refusing to work and their employers. Accordingly, it seems to me that the word 'strike' is a perfectly good, appropriate word to use to cover a sympathetic strike and a general strike and there is no need for it today to have any ingredient of grievance between those who are refusing to work and their employers."

It was irrelevant that the port labour was working ships other than those carrying coal; as in the *Seeberg* case there was a refusal to work the ship in question and as a result she lost time.

8–33   A refusal to work may constitute a strike although the abstention is limited only to a portion of the day, and even though the employees were not in breach of their contract of employment. In *Tramp Shipping Corporation* v. *Greenwich Marine Inc.*[30] the *New Horizon* was chartered to carry grain or soya beans from Norfolk, Virginia, to St. Nazaire. The charterparty stated, in the words of its Centrocon strike clause: " . . . If the cargo cannot be discharged by reason of . . . a strike . . . of any class of workmen essential to the discharge, the time for . . . discharging . . . shall not

---

[24] At p. 149.
[25] [1966] 1 Lloyd's Rep. 582. (*The Laga*).
[26] It had thus been defined in *King* v. *Parker* (1876) 34 L.T. 887.
[27] In *Williams Bros. (Hull) Ltd.* v. *Naamlooze Vennootschap W.H. Berghuys Kolenhandel* (1916) 21 Com.Cas. 253. See § 8–31 above.
[28] (1934) 50 Ll.L.Rep. 146. See § 8–31 above.
[29] *Op. cit.* at p. 591.
[30] [1975] 2 Lloyd's Rep. 314 (C.A.).

count during the continuance of such causes." At Norfolk the ship used up part of her laytime, which was "six weather working days of 24 consecutive hours, Sundays and holidays excepted," for loading and discharging. At St. Nazaire it was normal for such a ship to be discharged all round the clock for 24 hours in three shifts. When she arrived on April 30, however, the sucker drivers had begun action to improve their conditions, and refused to do shift work. Laytime began on May 2. From May 8 to 18 they did no work at all. They resumed for a few hours on May 19, but stopped again till May 24. Discharging ended on May 25. The charterers said that a strike existed when laytime began. The disponent owners agreed that the strike began only on May 8, by which time the ship was already on demurrage, which therefore continued to be payable.

The Court of Appeal upheld the Commercial Court decision[31] that the charterers were right. Lord Denning M.R. cited the words of Sankey J. in the *Williams Bros.* case,[32] to the effect that a strike was "a general concerted refusal by workmen to work in consequence of an alleged grievance." He amplified this definition by saying[33]: " . . . I think a strike is a concerted stoppage of work by men done with a view to improving their wages or conditions, or giving vent to a grievance or making a protest about something or other, or supporting or sympathising with other workmen in such endeavour. It is distinct from a stoppage brought about by an external event such as a bomb scare or by apprehension of danger." Applying that test, he considered that when the men refused to work 24 hours, but worked only for 8 hours, there was a strike, though they were not in breach of contract. A strike did not have to be continuous.

Charterers' default. Charterers can prevent time from running only to the extent that the strike rather than any action or inaction on their part caused the delay.[34] So also if a strike causes delay because they have failed in a duty, they are not relieved from their liability for delay by the exceptions clause. In *Dampskibsselskabet Danmark* v. *Poulsen & Co.*[35] the charterers had not made adequate arrangements for the supply of a cargo of coal; had they done so, the delay resulting from a strike would have been avoided. They were held liable for delay. **8–34**

Strikes of essential workmen. An exceptions clause may refer not merely to strikes but to strikes of workmen essential to the loading or discharging operations.[36] Thus in *Dampskibsselskabet Svendborg* v. *Love & Stewart Ltd.*[37] time was not to count during any delay caused by strikes of workmen essential to the discharge. As a result a strike of workmen in the charterers' yard the railway company restricted the supply of wagons, so that they would not be detained. This in turn delayed the discharge, but it was held that the charterers could not rely on the exceptions clause, as there had not been a strike of workmen essential to the loading or discharging operations. **8–35**

---

[31] By Ackner J., [1974] 2 Lloyd's Rep. 210.
[32] (1916) 21 Com.Cas. 253 at p. 257. See § 8–31 above.
[33] *Op. cit.* at p. 317.
[34] *Elswick SS. Co.* v. *Montaldi* [1907] 1 K.B. 626. See also § 8–27 above.
[35] 1913 S.C. 1043.
[36] As in the cases of the C. (Ore) 7 Mediterranean Iron Ore Charter Party in § 8–29 above.
[37] 1915 S.C. 543.

8–36   **Strike must cause delay.** Charterers can only obtain protection from an exceptions clause to the extent that the delay was caused by the strike. This view is supported by decisions in four similar cases.[38] In *Leonis SS. Co. Ltd.* v. *Joseph Rank Ltd. (No. 2)*,[39] a railway strike before the arrival of the ship caused congestion on the railway and in the harbour, and there was delay consequent on the strike in the transit of the cargo intended to be shipped. Time lost was not to be counted as part of the lay days if the cargo could not be loaded by reason of any dispute, between masters and men, occasioning a strike of railway employees or other labour connected with the working and loading or delivery of cargo proved to be intended for the ship. The Court of Appeal held that the charterers could rely on the strike clause. Vaughan Williams L.J. said[40] that the question of fact was:

> "Is it true to say that, by reason of that strike, the cargo proved to be intended for the steamer could not be loaded within the lay days?"

He answered the question in the affirmative.

In *London & Northern SS. Co. Ltd.* v. *Central Argentine Railway Ltd.*[41] the exceptions clause stated: "In case of strikes, lock-outs, civil commotions, or any other causes or accidents beyond the control of the consignees which prevent or delay the discharging, such time is not to count unless the steamer is already on demurrage." Scrutton J. held that the clause meant not that time did not count at all during a strike, but that it did not count in respect of delay caused by the strike. The words "such time" referred to the length of the delay to the ship and not the length of the strike.

In *Central Argentine Railway Ltd.* v. *Marwood*[42] the charterparty contained the same clause. Discharging was entirely prevented by a strike for a fortnight, and then slowed up for 19 days during which work was partially resumed. During the 19 days other ships discharged a quantity of coal equivalent to six days' normal work; the ship then berthed. The House of Lords held that "such time" meant the time for which the discharging was prevented or delayed by the strike; the shipowners were entitled to count the six days as lay days.

8–37   In *Reardon Smith Line Ltd.* v. *Ministry of Agriculture*[43] laytime was not to count "during any time when . . . the loading of the cargo . . . is delayed by . . . force majeure . . . strikes . . . or any other hindrance of whatsoever nature beyond the charterers' control. . . . " As a result of a strike of most of the elevator personnel loading was delayed in the case of some, but not all, ships. The Canadian Wheat Board directed that some wheat should be loaded as parcel cargoes into liners. The Court of Appeal held that the charterers were entitled to rely on the exceptions clause. Sellers L.J. said[44]:

---

[38] *London & Northern SS. Co. Ltd.* v. *Central Argentine Railway Ltd.* (1913) 108 L.T. 527; *Central Argentine Railway Ltd.* v. *Marwood* [1915] A.C. 981 (H.L.); and *Reardon Smith Line Ltd.* v. *Ministry of Agriculture* [1962] 1 Q.B. 42 (C.A.).
[39] (1908) 13 Com.Cas. 295 (C.A.).
[40] At p. 297.
[41] (1913) 108 L.T. 527.
[42] [1915] A.C. 981 (H.L.).
[43] [1962] 1 Q.B. 42 (C.A.). (*The Vancouver Strike Case*).
[44] At p. 74.

" . . . when a reasonable and sensible arrangement was made for loading what could be loaded and distributing small parcels between the liners, I think those who are shut out from receiving cargo can probably be said to be shut out by the strike."

He said[45] that even if this conclusion were incorrect,

"the charterers could rely on the loading having been delayed by a hindrance beyond their control, especially as they can rely on a hindrance of whatsoever nature."

The shipowners had relied on the House of Lords decision in *Central Argentine Railways Ltd.* v. *Marwood*,[46] which the Court of Appeal distinguished, pointing out that it seemed clear in the case before it that the strikers would not have permitted any grain, wheat or barley, to be loaded through the two working elevators. Moreover, the earlier case, though it applied the principle that a strike must have some causative effect upon the operations of the ship concerned, was based on different facts and a narrower exceptions clause. The decision in *Leonis SS. Co. Ltd.* v. *Joseph Rank Ltd. (No. 2)*[47] more closely resembled the present case and tended more to support the charterers' argument.

No claim for "damages." Some strike clauses provide that time lost shall **8–38** not be computed in the loading or discharging time.[48] Other strike clauses state that in case of delay "by reason of" strikes no "claim for damages" should be made by shipowners; such a clause was held in *Moor Line, Ltd.* v. *Distillers Co. Ltd.*,[49] where laytime and the demurrage rate were fixed, to exempt charterers from liability for demurrage caused by a strike. The ship was detained at the discharging port for four days beyond the lay days owing to congestion which followed the end of a strike. It was held that the detention was "by reason of" a strike. Claims for damages were therefore excluded, and a claim for demurrage was such a claim.

Centrocon Strike Clause. The strike clause in the Centrocon charter- **8–39** party[50] is wider in its effect than a clause[51] which provides merely that lay-time shall not count where the loading or discharging operations are interrupted by strikes. The clause names a number of excepted causes in addition to strikes.

The first two sentences of the clause are:

"If the Cargo cannot be loaded by reason of Riots, Civil Commotions or of a Strike or Lock-out of any class of workmen essential to the loading of the Cargo, or by reason of obstructions or stoppages beyond the control of the Charterers on the Railways, or in the Docks, or other loading places, or if the Cargo cannot be discharged by reason of Riots, Civil Commotions, or of a strike or Lock-out of any class of workmen essential to the discharge, the time for loading or discharging as the case may be, shall not

---

[45] At p. 75.
[46] [1915] A.C. 981. See § 8–36 above.
[47] (1908) 13 Com.Cas. 295 (C.A.). See § 8–36 above.
[48] As in the case of C. (Ore) 7 Mediterranean Iron Ore Charter Party in § 8–29 above.
[49] [1912] S.C. 514. A similar clause was held to be inoperative in *Westoll* v. *Lindsay*, 1916 S.C. 782, because the strike had ended before the ship's arrival. See § 10–40 below.
[50] River Plate Charter Party 1914.
[51] *e.g.* see § 8–45 below.

count during the continuance of such causes, provided that a Strike or Lock-out of the Shippers' and/or Receivers' men shall not prevent demurrage accruing if by the use of reasonable diligence they could have obtained other suitable labour at rates current before the Strike or Lock-out. In case of any delay by reason of the before-mentioned causes, no claim for damages or demurrage, shall be made by the Charterers, Receivers of the Cargo, or Owners of the Steamer.

8–40   The clause was discussed by Donaldson J. in *Navico A.G.* v. *Vrontados Naftiki Etairia P.E.*[52]:

> "The charterers's shield is in three parts. First, the laytime parking meter cannot begin to record the passage of time until notice of readiness has been given and twelve further hours have elapsed . . . Second, the meter will be stopped for the duration of excepted time (Sundays, holidays, etc.). Third, the meter will be stopped if and for so long as the loading of the cargo is prevented (. . . Part 1) or delayed (. . . Part 3) by any of the specified causes. It is only if and when the meter, despite these pauses, reaches 'Excess' that demurrage is payable."

These two first sentences have, for convenience, been judicially analysed[53] in three parts, *i.e.* the first eight lines of the first sentence as shown above,[54] up to and including the words "of such causes" (Part 1); the remaining part of or proviso to the first sentence (Part 2); and the second sentence (Part 3). The third sentence[55] has for convenience been treated as Part 4 of the clause. The effect of these sentences where a strike or other excepted event occur when the ship is already on demurrage is discussed elsewhere.[56]

8–41   As for inability to load or discharge during laytime, the clause states that time "shall not count during the continuance of such causes." The "causes" are (in the cases of loading and discharging) riots, civil commotions, strikes or lock-outs of essential workmen and, in the case of loading only, obstructions or stoppages beyond the charterers' control on the railways, in the docks, or other loading places. The Court of Appeal has held that congestion which delays the ships in securing a berth may amount to an obstruction for this purpose.[57] In *N.V. Reederij Amsterdam* v. *President*

---

[52] [1968] 1 Lloyd's Rep. 379 at p. 386. The dispute turned on Part 4 of the clause; for the facts see § 12–20 below. The parts were also analysed by the various tribunals in *Compania Naviera Aeolus S.A.* v. *Union of India (The Spalmatori)* [1962] 2 Lloyd's Rep. 175 (H.L.) where the strike occured when the ship was already on demurrage; see § 10–55 below.

[53] By McNair J. in *Union of India* v. *Compania Naviera Aeolus S.A. (The Spalmatori)* [1960] 1 Lloyd's Rep. 1121; the Court of Appeal in the same case at [1962] 1 Q.B. 1: the House of Lords in the same case, *sub nom. Compania Naviera Aeolus S.A.* v. *Union of India* [1964] A.C. 868 (for the facts see § 10–55 below); and by Donaldson J. in *Navico A.G.* v. *Vrontados Naftkiki Etairia P.E.* [1968] 1 Lloyd's Rep. 379 (see § 12–20 below).

[54] In § 8–39.

[55] See § 12–20 below.

[56] See § 10–54 below.

[57] In *Marrealeza Compania Naviera S.A.* v. *Tradax Export S.A.* [1982] 1 Lloyd's Rep. 52 (*The Nichos A*) an arbitrator considered the effect of Part 1 of the Clause when there was also a force majeure clause, stating: "Any delays caused by . . . events of force majeure will not count as demurrage unless the vessel is already on demurrage." He held that the Strike Clause only protected charterers when the cause of the delay affected the operation of loading; but that the force majeure clause applied to that operation and also to the provision of the cargo for loading, and that a large part of the demurrage claim should be disallowed. Lloyd J., without forming a view as to whether the arbitrator was right, declined an application for leave to appeal under the Arbitration Act, 1979, s.1, as the force majeure clause could be categorised as a one-off case.

of India[58] a charterparty on the "Approved Baltimore Berth Grain Charterparty—Steamer" form, for the carriage of wheat from New Orleans to
Madras, provided that the ship was "to be loaded according to berth terms,
with customary berth dispatch, and if detained longer than 5 weather working days of 24 consecutive hours, Saturdays after noon, Sundays and holidays excepted. Charterers to pay demurrage . . . provided such detention
shall occur by default[59] of Charterers or their Agents." A Centrocon strike
clause was attached to the charterparty. Notice of readiness was given at
New Orleans on July 21, the notice period expiring on July 22, but, as
other ships were occupying the berths, no berth was available until August
4. Loading began then, and ended on August 6. The charterers contended
that (a) there was no obligation to load in a fixed time, but only a duty to
employ "customary berth dispatch"; and (b) they were exempted from any
liability for demurrage by the Centrocon strike clause.

The High Court held that, as to (a) the charterparty was a fixed laytime
one, and, as to (b) the strike clause prevented demurrage from accruing,
because the congestion was not the charterers' fault. In the Court of
Appeal there was no argument as to (a) but it was held, dismissing the
appeal by the shipowners, that the congestion amounted to "obstructions"[60] for the purpose of the Centrocon strike clause. The lay days were
in other respects able to begin when the notice period expired but "there
was an obstruction within the meaning of the charterparty which stopped
the clock, which was not able to tick again until there was a berth available."[61] This was so in spite of the presence of the words "whether in berth
or not."

Lord Denning M.R. in a later case[62] noted that the word "obstructions"

---

[58] [1961] 2 Lloyd's Rep. 1 (C.A.). (*The Amstelmolen*). The decision was followed in *Pagnan
(R.) & Fratelli* v. *Finagrain Compagnie Commerciale Agricole et Financière S.A.* [1986] 2
Lloyd's Rep. 395 (*The Adolf Leonhardt*), where sellers failed in their contention that the
Centrocon strike clause, which applied to the sale contract, exempted them from liability
for demurrage because the cargo could not be loaded by reason of obstructions beyond
their control.
[59] For the construction of the word "default," see § 10–23 below.
[60] The court felt itself bound, though reluctantly, by the construction given to the word
"obstruction" by the Court of Appeal in *Leonis SS. Co. Ltd.* v. *Joseph Rank Ltd. (No. 2)*
(1908) 13 Com.Cas. 295, where it was held to include the obstruction caused by ships preventing access to berths. See § 8–36 above. Staughton J., in *Pagnan (R.) & Fratelli* v. *Finagrain Compagnie Commerciale Agricole et Financière S.A.* [1986] 2 Lloyd's Rep. 395 (*The
Adolf Leonhardt*) said of *The Amstelmolen*, at p. 401: "The new point in their case (so far
as the Court of Appeal was concerned) was that time was to count 'whether in berth or
not.' It could be argued that, since the only or main reason why a vessel should wait for a
berth would be congestion, it must have been intended that congestion should not be
treated as an obstruction and that time should still count. However, the Court of Appeal
unanimously decided that the words 'whether in berth or not' made no difference." See
also *Navrom* v. *Callitsis Ship Management S.A.* [1987] 2 Lloyd's Rep. 276 (*The Radauti*)
where Staughton J. said, at p. 280: "It has been held by the Court of Appeal since 1908
[*Leonis SS. Co. Ltd.* v. *Joseph Rank Ltd. (No. 2)*; see § 8–36 above], and again in *The
Amstelmolen*, that congestion in the port which prevents the vessel obtaining a berth is an
obstruction within that clause, at all events if it is unusual congestion." The Judge then
referred to his own decision in *Pagnan (R.) & Fratelli* v. *Finagrain Compagnie Commerciale Agricole et Financière S.A.* [1986] 2 Lloyd's Rep. 395 (*The Adolf Leonhardt*), where
he had held that the same was true even in a port where the congestion was endemic and
notorious.
[61] [1961] 2 Lloyd's Rep. 1 (C.A.) *per* Ormerod L.J. at p. 10.
[62] *Ionian Navigation Company Inc.* v. *Atlantic Shipping Company S.A. (The Loucas N.)*
[1971] 1 Lloyd's Rep. 215 (C.A.) at p. 218. See also § 6–04 above.

had thus been determined by the Court of Appeal to cover congestion at a port by reason of which a berth was not available, and commented:

> "I pause to say that that is an unsatisfactory decision which merchants and lawyers try to get out of. But, for present purposes, we must accept it as correct, although Mr. Mustill [counsel for the shipowners] reserved the right to challenge it, if need be, at some future time."

8–42   As a result of this Court of Appeal decision charterers and shipowners would occasionally add to the charterparty, where a Centrocon strike clause has been incorporated, a provision that the clause shall be construed as it was construed before the decision.[63] There is no reason in principle why they should not make this agreement, by which they refer to an earlier understanding of the law. There is a risk, however, that such a provision would be unenforceable as a result of its uncertainty,[64] for a court might not find it possible to ascertain how the clause was previously construed. Another course which the contracting parties can adopt, if they wish the scope of the clause to be limited to strikes and lock-outs, is to use a clause which refers solely to strikes and lock-outs[65]; or to amend the Centrocon strike clause itself.[66]

Speaking of *The Amstelmolen* decision a quarter of a century later, Staughton J. said[67]:

> "It has been said that *The Amstelmolen* decision was unsatisfactory or unpopular . . . But on reflection I find it is hard to believe that it is universally disliked. Otherwise one would not now, after 25 years, still find the Centrocon strike clause appearing in charterparties."

8–43   In *Venizelos A.N.E. of Athens* v. *Société Commerciale de Céréales et Financière S.A. of Zürich*[68] the *Prometheus* had been chartered on the Centrocon form to carry heavy grain or sorghums in bulk from one or two safe ports in the River Parana not higher than San Lorenzo and the remainder at Buenos Aires or Bahia Blanca. The charterparty's Centrocon strike clause[69] stated: "If the cargo cannot be loaded . . . by reason of obstruction beyond the control of the Charterers . . . in the Docks . . . the time for loading . . . shall not count during the continuance of such causes." She loaded at Rosario and, having been ordered to Buenos Aires to load the rest of her cargo, arrived at the Intersection anchorage on May 28,

---

[63] "It is sometimes said that this decision has proved unpopular in commercial circles; and I seem to recollect seeing a subsequent contract which provided expressly that the Centrocon strike clause should be deemed to mean what it was thought to mean before the Court of Appeal decided otherwise": *per* Staughton J. in *Pagnan (R.) & Fratelli* v. *Finagrain Compagnie Commerciale Agricole et Financière S.A.* [1986] 2 Lloyd's Rep. 395 (*The Adolf Leonhardt*) at p. 401.

[64] Of an obscure clause in a hire purchase contract Lord Wright said, in *Scammell* v. *Ouston* [1941] A.C. 251 (H.L.), at pp. 268–269: " . . . the language used was so obscure and so incapable of any definite or precise meaning that the Court is unable to attribute to the parties any particular intention."

[65] Such as the strike clause contained in the Australian Grain Charter 1928 (Austral) the Australian Grain Charter 1972 (Austwheat) and the uniform General Charter 1976 (Gencon). For the Gencon General Strike Clause, see §§ 8–44 and 8–45 below.

[66] As by the insertion of the words "caused by riots, civil commotions, a strike, or a lock-out" after the words "by reason of obstructions or stoppages beyond the control of the Charterers."

[67] In *Navrom* v. *Callitsis Ship Management S.A.* [1987] 2 Lloyd's Rep. 276, at pp. 280–281 (*The Radauti*).

[68] [1974] 1 Lloyd's Rep. 350.

[69] For the Centrocon strike clause see § 10–54 below.

1971. She was within the legal limits of the port of Buenos Aires, at a place where ships customarily waited their turn for admission to a berth, and effectively at the disposal of the charterers. On the 29th the charterers ordered her to a berth, but it was congested and she was told to wait. The ship left her anchorage on May 31. The period from May 28 to May 31 was in dispute. The disponent owners said that laytime included the time from arrival at Intersection until she left the anchorage. Applying *Oldendorff (E.L.) & Co. G.m.b.H.* v. *Tradax Export S.A.*[70] Mocatta J. held that the ship had arrived at Intersection.

The charterers had the right and the duty to name a berth. He said that such authority[71] as there was seemed to regard the choice of a berth under a port charter as well as under a berth charter as an election. It would not be right for him to hold that the selection of a berth, once notified to ship-owners or their agents, was something that charterers could change unilaterally. The nomination of a berth on May 29 was a valid one, not-withstanding that the berth was not to be available until May 31. This was an election, so that the charterers were able to rely on the exceptions clause with respect to the period from May 29 to May 31. As for the period from May 28 (when the ship arrived at the anchorage) until May 29 (when the charterers named a berth) he decided that laytime ran and that the charterers failed to show that the exceptions clause applied. The charterers could have arranged for the ship to be loaded in part (at the South Dock) and a loading berth would, had the charterers made such an arrangement, have been available so that the ship could have proceeded to it on arrival at Intersection without anchoring and waiting there.

Centrocon and Gencon Strike Clauses Compared. The General Strike **8–44** Clause of the Gencon charterparty[72] is confined to strikes or lock-outs, whereas the Centrocon strike clause[73] makes provisions for strikes, lock-outs, riots, civil commotions and (in the case of loading) obstructions and stoppages beyond the control of charterers on the railways or in the docks or other loading places. On the other hand the Gencon clause extends its application to occasions on which the excepted causes are "affecting the loading of the cargo, or any part of it," or "affecting the discharge of the cargo," whereas the Centrocon clause is restricted to occasions on which, as a result of the excepted causes, "cargo cannot be loaded" or "cargo can-not be discharged." In the first the clause will apply if work is affected but not prevented. In the second case it is clear that the clause applies if work is halted entirely, but the position is not so clear where work is delayed, as where (say) a smaller quantity than usual is loaded on a particular day. Charterers may say that "the cargo cannot be loaded," by which they mean the part which cannot be loaded on that day. Shipowners may argue that the clause only applies to a total stoppage on that day.

---

[70] [1973] 2 Lloyd's Rep. 285 (H.L.) (*The Johanna Oldendorff*). See § 4–21 above.

[71] For example: *Anglo Danubian Transport Co. Ltd.* v. *Ministry of Food* (1949). 83 Ll.L.Rep. 137; and *Reardon Smith Line Ltd.* v. *Ministry of Agriculture, Fisheries and Food* [1962] Q.B. 42 (*The Vancouver Strike Case*); see § 8–19 and 8–37 below). He also referred to *Matheos (Owners)* v. *Louis Dreyfus & Company* [1925] A.C. 654 (H.L.) and *Lewis* v. *Louis Dreyfus & Company* (1926) 24 Ll.L.Rep. 333 (C.A.).

[72] Uniform General Charter (Gencon), as revised in 1976. The wording is the same as in the 1922 revision.

[73] See § 8–39 above.

8–45   Wording of Gencon Strike Clause. The Gencon General Strike Clause[74] states: [Part 1] "Neither Charterers nor Owners shall be responsible for the consequences of any strikes or lock-outs preventing or delaying the fulfilment of any obligations under this contract.[75]

[Part 2] "If there is a strike or lock-out[75a] affecting the loading of the cargo, or any part of it, when vessel is ready to proceed from her last port[76] or at any time during her voyage to the port or ports of loading or after her arrival there, Captain or Owners may ask Charterers to declare, that they agree to reckon the laydays as if there were no strike or lock-out. Unless Charterers have given such declaration in writing (by telegram, if necessary) within 24 hours, Owners shall have the option of cancelling this contract. If part cargo has already been loaded, Owners must proceed with same, (freight payable on loaded quantity only[76a]) having liberty to complete with other cargo on the way for their own account.

8–46   [Part 3] "If there is a strike or lock-out affecting the discharge of the cargo on or after the vessel's arrival at or off port of discharge and same has not been settled within 48 hours, Receivers shall have the option of keeping vessel waiting until such strike or lock-out is at an end against paying half demurrage after expiration of the time provided for discharging, or of ordering the vessel to a safe port where she can safely discharge without risk of being detained by strike or lock-out. Such orders to be given within 48 hours after Captain or Owners have given notice to Charterers of the strike or lock-out affecting the discharge. On delivery of the cargo at such port, all conditions of this Charterparty and of the Bill of Lading shall apply and vessel shall receive the same freight as if she had discharged at the original port of destination, except that if the distance of the substituted port exceeds 100 nautical miles, the freight on the cargo delivered at the substituted port to be increased in proportion."

---

[74] Quoted in full, since " . . . the general strike clause must be construed, as one whole . . . " *per* Lord Denning M.R. in *Salamis Shipping (Panama) S.A.* v. *Edm. van Meerbeeck & Co. S.A.* [1971] 2 Lloyd's Rep. 29 (C.A.) (*The Onisilos*) at p. 33. See § 10–59 below. So also Bingham J. in *Superfos Chartering A/S* v. *N.B.R. (London) Ltd.* [1984] 2 Lloyd's Rep. 366, at p. 369 (*The Saturnia*), when analysing the three parts of the clause: " . . . it is convenient to approach the clause in this way provided one bears in mind the need for a consistent and coherent construction of the clause as a whole." See § 10–60 below.

[75] In *Armada Lines Continent-Mediterranean Service Ltd.* v. *Naviera Murueta S.A. (The Elexalde)* [1985] 2 Lloyd's Rep. 485 discharge was delayed by a dock labour strike. Shipowners said that the strike period should be disregarded because the strike ended within 48 hours and was over before laytime ended. The arbitrator decided that the charterers were not liable for delay caused by the strike. The High Court was concerned with his alleged excess of jurisdiction in answering a further question, but Hobhouse J. said of the first paragraph of the Gencon General Strike Clause, at p. 486: "The correct application of that wording has never been covered, I understand, by direct authority, although it has been indirectly referred to in cases which dealt with paragraphs of the general strike clause."

[75a] The clause does not cover a prospective strike; but in a London arbitration it was found on the evidence that an *ad hoc* agreement had been made between the parties that it would apply prospectively: LMLN 91, April 28, 1983.

[76] Presumably her last port of discharge on the previous voyage.

[76a] A problem had arisen where cargo was partly loaded and the charterers had chosen to sail, but the freight was on a lump sum basis. A London umpire held that charterers' obligation to pay lump sum freight without deduction was paramount without clear and umambiguous words excusing them from the obligation. There were no such words. (LMLN 91, April 28, 1983.)

Effect on laytime. As for loading laytime, under Part 2 of the Gencon **8–47** clause charterers can be asked to agree to count time as if there were no strike or lock-out. If they fail to do so, shipowners can cancel the charter-party.

A London arbitrator has considered[76b] what would happen if charterers did not agree that time should count, and shipowners did not elect to cancel the contract. He held that, as a result of the Part 1 of the clause, laytime did not count until the strike ended. He said: "The commercial objection . . . to the Owners' argument in this case is in my view that it deprives the Charterers of the entire benefit of the time which it was agreed they were to have for the loading and discharging of this vessel. That the laytime clock should be treated as running at a time when the laytime is, in practice, unusable appears to me to be an improbable consequence for the parties to have intended. Moreover when that was their intention—as it was in relation to the different situation covered by the third part of the clause— the intention was clearly spelled out. And the result for which the Owners here contend could equally well have been spelled out by some appropriate addition to the wording of the second part of the clause, *e.g.* 'If the Charterers are not requested to declare as above or if the Owners do not elect to cancel, the existence of such strike or lock-out shall not prevent the running of laytime but the Charterers' responsibility for demurrage (if any) shall be governed by the first sentence of this clause.' "

It has been said of Part 2[77]: "It seems plain that its intention is to modify or derogate from the blanket exemption apparently granted by Part 1 where the strike or lock-out affects the loading of the vessel. Part 2 substitutes what appears to be, in effect, a commercial bargain. The charterer has a choice. He can, if asked, declare that he agrees to reckon the laydays as if there were no strike or lock-out. If he does so, he runs the risk that his demurrage obligation, whatever it is, may accrue without his having the agreed, or even any, time to load the vessel. Or he can decline so to declare, in which event he runs the risk that the owner may cancel the charter-party. The owner also has an option, and possibly two. He may, but need not, seek a declaration from the charterer, and if such a declaration is sought and not given, he may, but need not, cancel the charter-party." Under the first sentence of the Centrocon clause[78] loading laytime automatically ceases to count during the continuance of the excepted causes, subject to the proviso as to demurrage where reasonable diligence might have secured the suitable labour. Nor can there be any claim for damages or demurrage by charterers, receivers or shipowners.[79]

As for discharging laytime,[80] under Part 3 of the Gencon clause the charterers have the option, where the strike or lock-out has not been settled within 48 hours, of keeping her waiting until the strike or lock-out has ended, against paying half demurrage after laytime ends, or of ordering her

---

[76b] LMLN 94, June 9, 1983.
[77] By Bingham J. in *Superfos Chartering A/S* v. *N.B.R. (London) Ltd.* [1984] 2 Lloyd's Rep. 366 (*The Saturnia*), at p. 369. See also § 10–60 below.
[78] See § 8–39 above.
[79] See *Union of India* v. *Compania Naviera Aeolus S.A. (The Spalmatori)* [1962] 2 Lloyd's Rep. 175 (H.L.); see also § 10–51 below.
[80] For the effect on demurrage and "half demurrage," see § 10–52 below.

to a port unaffected by strike or lock-out.[81] As to Part 3, it has been said[82]: "The basic mechanism of the clause is clear. If there is a strike or lock-out at the discharge port which affects, or will prospectively affect, the discharge of the vessel, the owner may give the charterer notice to that effect. The charterer then has an option. He can either keep the vessel waiting at that discharge port paying demurrage at half the contractual rate 'after expiration of the time provided for discharging,' or he can order the vessel to another port where she can discharge without risk of strike or lock-out, paying additional freight if the deviation involves more than 100 additional nautical miles. At such port, it would seem, any demurrage would have to be paid at the full rate." Under the first sentence of the Centrocon clause, discharging laytime is affected in the same way as loading laytime, save that the exceptions of obstructions and stoppages are omitted.

The ship need not be at the loading port to claim the benefit of the Gencon clause; thus, the captain or shipowners can ask the charterers to make their declaration when she is "ready to proceed from her last port[83] or at any time during her voyage to the port or ports of loading or after her arrival there . . . " Under the Centrocon clause the ship must be at the loading port, so that her cargo "cannot be loaded," for the laytime to be interrupted. As for the discharge, under the Gencon clause, once more the excepted causes can operate even though the ship has not begun to discharge; she may be "at or off port of discharge." Under the Centrocon clause she must be at the discharging port so that her cargo "cannot be discharged."

8–48   *Shifting—and other movements*

The cost of shifting falls upon the charterers, as the shipowners are not bound to shift at their own expense, unless there is a custom[84] or a provision to that effect, or unless it follows from the charterparty terms and the circumstances that the cost should not fall upon the charterers. As Goddard L.J. said in *King Line Ltd.* v. *Moxey, Savon & Co. Ltd.*[85]:

> " . . . the ship is not bound, once she has arrived and made fast to a berth to which she has been ordered, to shift again from that berth for the purpose of taking on board part of the cargo which is the subject-matter of the charter."

In *Cosmar Compania Naviera S.A.* v. *Total Transport Corporation*[86] the charterparty, on the Shellvoy 3 form,[86a] stated: "11. Charterers shall have the right of requiring the vessel to shift at ports of loading . . . on payment of all additional expenses incurred." Loading at Bejaia, Algeria, was inter-

---

[81] In *Salamis Shipping (Panama) S.A.* v. *Edm. van Meerbeeck & Co. S.A.* [1971] 2 Lloyd's Rep. 29 (C.A.) (*The Onisilos*), which concerned a Gencon strike clause, the parties agreed that by failing to give orders for the ship to proceed to an alternative port the charterers exercised the option of keeping her waiting until the strike ended. See § 10–59 below.

[82] Also by Bingham J. in the *Superfos Chartering* case (see n. 74 above), at p. 370.

[83] Presumably her last port of discharge on the previous voyage.

[84] *M'Intosh* v. *Sinclair* (1877) I.R. 11 C.L. 456; *The Alhambra* (1886) 6 P.D. 68 (C.A.); *Nielsen & Co.* v. *Wait* (1885) 16 Q.B.D. 67 (C.A.); and *A/S Inglewood* v. *Millar's Karri & Jarrah Forests* (1903) 8 Com.Cas. 196.

[85] (1939) 62 Ll.L.Rep. 252 at p. 253; a laytime dispute does not appear to have arisen.

[86] [1982] 2 Lloyd's Rep. 81 (*The Isabelle*) for the High Court judgment, and [1984] 1 Lloyd's Rep. 366, for the short Court of Appeal judgment, upholding the decision of the court below.

[86a] For an appraisal of the Shellvoy 5 form (in part influenced by this decision) see an article by Stan Bonnick in Charterparty International, December, 1987.

rupted by a heavy swell, and the ship had to leave her berth, and wait at an anchorage until loading could resume. The shipowners contended that the charterers were liable for the shifting expenses. Robert Goff J. rejected their claim, and said that the obligation of the charterers to pay shifting expenses under the clause presupposed that the charterers had required the ship to shift. He added[87]:

> "I am satisfied on the evidence before me that the order to shift was in fact given by the port authority . . . I have no doubt that the port authority was acting in pursuance of its function as administrator of the port, and was not acting as the charterers' agent. I am satisfied that cl. 11 contemplates some positive order by the charterers or their agents. . . ."

So also time spent in shifting from one place of loading or discharging to another is counted against the charterers, since, in the absence of a custom[88] or an express provision in the charterparty to the contrary, or a shift for the shipowners' own purposes (if the ship is withdrawn from the immediate and effective disposition of the charterers), laytime runs continuously. The same principle applies, provided that laytime has begun, to a shift from a waiting anchorage to either a loading or a discharging berth or to a layby berth, and to a shift from a layby berth to a loading or a discharging berth. But in *Breynton* v. *Theodoridi & Co.*[89] the ship, in the Danube, used up all the laytime at the first loading port, and the question was whether time counted while she moved to the second loading port. Rowlatt J. said, at p. 411:

> " . . . I apprehend that in common cases if there is one set of lay days to be distributed between two ports the time of the transit between the ports of loading is not included in the lay days. That is not because there is any exception that takes them out, but because she is not then loading but is going from one port to another port."[90]

Buckley L.J., in *Surrey Shipping Co. Ltd.* v. *Compagnie Internationale (France) S.A.*,[91] distinguishing *Breynton's* case, said: "It seems to me that a two-port charter is clearly distinguishable from a two-berth charter. In the case of a two-port charter there are two distinct carrying voyage stages, one from the loading port to the first port of discharge, and the other from the latter port to the second port of discharge. Both voyages are clearly contractual obligations of the owners. A charter to discharge at one or more berths in a single port is a very different thing. The movement from one berth to another within the port is for the convenience of the charterers. It would be eminently reasonable to construe the charterparty in such a case so as to reckon shifting time from one berth to another, or, if laytime has started to run, from anchorage to berth of discharge, as counting against laytime or demurrage and not as part of the carrying voyage." Thus charterers can direct the ship to her initial place of working; thereafter time runs whether the ship is being worked or not, and when it is being shifted, even if the shift is ordered by the port authority. In one case[92] both expense and laytime were dealt with in the following terms: "Charterers have the option of loading and discharging at two safe berths

---

[87] *Ibid.* at p. 87.
[88] *Nielsen & Co.* v. *Wait* (1885) 16 Q.B.D. 67 (C.A.). The terms prevail over custom.
[89] (1924) 19 Ll.L.Rep. 409.
[90] For his ensuing remarks as to the position when demurrage had begun at the first port, see § 10–49 below.
[91] [1978] 2 Lloyd's Rep. 154 (C.A.) at p. 163 (*The Shackleford*) See also § 5–33 above.
[92] *W.I. Radcliffe SS. Co. Ltd.* v. *Exporthleb* (1939) 64 Ll.L.Rep. 250.

in one port without extra charge and time for shifting not to count." So also the Centrocon charterparty states: " . . . time occupied in shifting between the loading ports or places . . . not to count as lay days."

8–49   It has been held, on an unusual set of facts, that demurrage may continue to run between an original discharging port and a substituted discharging port. In *Ricargo Trading S.A.* v. *Spliethoff's Bevrachtingskantor B.V.*[93] shipowners let their ship on a time charter trip, the time charterers in turn sub-chartering for a voyage from Sörnas, Finland, to Aqaba, Jordan. Aqaba was congested, and laytime expired after about 10 days, although discharge had not begun. Six weeks later it was agreed between the shipowners, the time charterers and the voyage charterers that the ship would be diverted to Mersin, Turkey, and that the voyage charterers would pay demurrage direct to the shipowners, and pay for the cost of the diversion. The shipowners, claiming demurrage for 90 days, included the period of the voyage from Aqaba to Mersin.

Lloyd J., deciding in favour of the shipowners, said[94] that the case did not fall precisely within either *Breynton* v. *Theodoridi*[95] or the *Surrey Shipping* case.[96] It did not fall within the first case because there the charterparty provided for loading at one or two safe places: "The cost of the voyage from the first to the second safe place must therefore have been taken into account in calculating the freight rate, whereas in the present case there is only a single port of discharge named in the charter-party." As for the second case, he said: "There the shifting all occurred within the confines of a single port, whereas here two separate ports were involved." He said that he had to approach the case as one depending on principle. On that basis the shipowners seemed to be correct.

The carrying voyage[97] had been completed when the ship reached Aqaba, and thereafter it was for the charterers to discharge the ship within the laydays. He then stated[98] the general principle as to laytime:

"Once time starts to run under a voyage charter-party, it continues to run, subject to any relevant exception, unless the owners remove the vessel for their own purposes or to suit their own convenience. It was not suggested that that had happened here."

The contractual carrying voyage, as the judge described it, came to an end at Aqaba, although in one sense the carrying voyage was resumed, from Aqaba to Mersin. It did not matter where the ship was or what she was doing after the end of the contractual carrying voyage, provided that she was not taken away by the shipowners for their own purposes.[99] Concluding his judgment in favour of the shipowners, Lloyd J. said[1]:

"The facts of the present case are unusual; it is perhaps unlikely that the Courts will ever

---

[93] [1983] 1 Lloyd's Rep. 648 (*The Tassos N*).
[94] *Ibid.* at p. 651.
[95] (1924) 19 Ll.L.R. 409. See § 8–48 above.
[96] [1978] 2 Lloyd's Rep. 154 (C.A.) (*The Shackleford*). See § 8–48 above.
[97] The Judge referred to Lord Diplock's division of the maritime adventure, in *The Johanna Oldendorff* [1973] 2 Lloyd's Rep. 285 (see § 4–21 above), into the loading voyage, the loading operation, the carrying voyage and the discharging operation.
[98] *Op. cit.* at p. 651. See also § 8–01 above.
[99] He said that support could be found for that view in *Cantiere Navale Triestina* v. *Russian Soviet Naphtha Export Agency* [1925] 2 K.B. 172 (C.A.), which concerned a temporary enforced removal; see § 8–53 below.
[1] *Op. cit.* at p. 652.

have to consider again,[2] whether time runs continuously between two ports of loading or discharging, as the case may be where the charter provides for a single port only. But on principle the answer must be that it does." It was, he said, a true case where one would apply the phrase "Once on demurrage, always on demurrage."[3]

Where the breach by the shipowners of a term of the charterparty causes **8–50** a delay in working the ship, the charterers can contend successfully that the time lost does not count as laytime.[3a] In *Mobil Shipping and Transportation Co. v. Shell Eastern Petroleum (Pte.) Ltd.*[4] the master had failed to sign the triplicate copy of the bill of lading, which he had carried with him on the voyage, on which oil was carried from Singapore to Madras. The original and duplicate bills had been signed before the voyage began. The charterers had to arrange for the original duplicate bills to be sent to Madras. The ship had to leave her berth, and further delay resulted as no berth was available when the duplicates arrived. The charterparty provided that time spent or lost as a result of a breach of the charterparty by the shipowners should not count as laytime. The shipowners' claim for demurrage therefore failed; and they were unable to rely on a clause by which the charterers were to indemnify them in respect of claims, demands, losses, and expenses against the ship arising by reason of delivery of the cargo without original bills of lading being presented to the master.

And not shifting   **8–51**

A provision that shifting time is not to count does not prevent time from counting after a berth has become available but before the shifting has begun. In *Compania Naviera Termar S.A. v. Tradax Export S.A.*[5] a charterparty for the carriage of corn from a United States port to London or Hull provided: "In the event of the vessel being ordered to Hull and being unable to berth immediately upon arrival on account of congestion, time to count from next working period after vessel's arrival at Spurn Head[6] anchorage but time used in shifting from such anchorage to discharging berth in Hull not to count as laytime." The port authority ordered the ship to anchor at Spurn Head, no berth being available at Hull; laytime began at 0800 hours on November 22. A berth becoming available, she was given permission by the port authority to go upstream at 2144 hours that day, but could not do so, as the water was not deep enough, until 2240 hours on November 26. She berthed at Hull at 0200 hours on November 27. The House of Lords, upholding the Court of Appeal,[7] which had reversed the decision of Mocatta J.[8] in favour of the shipowners, decided that the delay

---

[2] For an unsuccessful attempt by shipowners to distinguish this case, and to collect freight rather than demurrage, on the ground that two later calls occurred as part of contractual voyages, see *Associated Bulk Carriers Ltd. v. Shell International Petroleum Co. Ltd.* [1984] 2 Lloyd's Rep. 182 (*The Nordic Navigator*), at p. 186.

[3] For this phrase see also § 10–50 below.

[3a] For the possible interruption of laytime or demurrage by a fault or other action on the part of shipowners, see §§ 10–63–10–68 below.

[4] [1987] 2 Lloyd's Rep. 655 (*The Mobil Courage*).

[5] [1966] 1 Lloyd's Rep. 566 (H.L.) (*The Ante Topic*).

[6] For two cases involving the problem of arrival and demurrage at Spurn Head, see § 6–20 above.

[7] [1965] 2 Lloyd's Rep. 79; Sellers L.J. had dissented, at pp. 83–84, on the ground that risks such as bad weather or insufficiency of water were "ship's risks" as opposed to congestion for which the charterers would be liable. The period of compulsory lying at anchor had ended and the period of shifting had begun.

[8] [1965] 1 Lloyd's Rep. 198.

after the berth was available, but before the shift was possible, counted as laytime. As Viscount Simmonds put it[9]:

> "The word 'shift' is a verb transitive or (less commonly) intransitive, meaning to move or transfer from one place to another. It denotes at least an activity. There could not well be a less appropriate word to describe a period during which a vessel, having anchored, lies at anchor (in this case for several days) with no intention of raising anchor until the depth of water in the river permits passage . . . whether the charterers knew or not of a tidal hazard which might hold the vessel at Spurn Head, they committed themselves in unequivocal language to an agreement by which laytime began when she reached her anchorage and continued until she started to move from it to her discharging berth in Hull."

8-51A   This case was followed in *Clerco Compania Naviera S.A.* v. *Food Corporation of India.*[9a] The *Savvas* was chartered on the Baltimore Berth Grain Form to carry wheat in bulk to one or two safe berths, Bombay. Cargo was to be discharged "free of risk and expense to vessel at the average rate of 1500 tons of 2,240 lbs. per weather working day of 24 consecutive hours Saturday afternoon, Sundays and holidays excluded even if used. . . . " Lightening was said to be "at Owner's risk and expense and time used not to count as laytime." The ship arrived in Bombay on October 18, 1974, notice of readiness being given and accepted subject to the terms of the charterparty on October 19, a Saturday. Lightening began on November 6 and continued, with two interruptions, for which no reasons were available to the Court, until November 13. The charterers contended that time did not run against them until lightening had been completed and that they were entitled to have lay days calculated on the basis of the amount of the cargo before lightening.[9b] The shipowners said that time began to count on receipt of the notice of readiness but that the charterers were entitled only to laytime calculated on the reduced tonnage after lightening. The High Court held that the shipowners were right as to the moment at which laytime began but that the charterers were right as to its calculation. The provision as to time counting was a simple and straightforward one and was followed by a provision that if any time was used in lightening that time was not to count. As Parker J. said in the High Court[9c]:

> "That presupposes that the clock will have started ticking before the lightening process begins for there would otherwise appear to be little point in providing that time is not to count. It also appears to be in accordance with the words employed in this charterparty because what is envisaged is that time *used* is not to count and the words 'time used' refer to time in lightening, just as the words 'even if used' in cl. 18 [the laytime calculation clause] refer to use of the time for actual active discharging."

In a reference to the *Compania Naviera Termar S.A.* decision,[9d] the judge said[9e]:

> "As a matter of language, time sitting at Bombay from October 20 to November 6 doing nothing is not time used in lightening, any more than Sundays, holidays and Saturday afternoons, are times used in discharging unless discharging operations are taking place. In the case of the somewhat curiously named vessel *Ante Topic*[9f] . . . a somewhat

---

[9] At pp. 570–1.
[9a] [1982] 1 Lloyd's Rep. 22 (C.A.).
[9b] On this second issue see also *Hain Steamship Co. Ltd.* v. *Minister of Food* [1949] 1 K.B. 492 (C.A.) and § 2–15 above.
[9c] [1981] 1 Lloyd's Rep. 155 at p. 157.
[9d] [1968] 1 Lloyd's Rep. 566 (.H.L.) (*The Ante Topic*). See § 8–51 above.
[9e] At p. 158.
[9f] Perhaps not so curious. Ante is a first name, similar to Anthony, and commonly found among coastal people in Yugoslavia. Topic is the name of a well-known shipowning family.

similar situation occurred . . . the question was whether a time during which a vessel was immobile, albeit congestion had ceased and a berth was available, could be regarded as time used in shifting . . . [The judge then quoted the substance of a passage in the judgment of Viscount Simmonds which is set out earlier in this book][9g] I find it difficult to see that there could be a more inappropriate description for time used in lightening than a time at which this vessel was immobile in Bombay with no intention of moving until lighters could be arranged into which she might discharge. Accordingly, the argument that time does not count until the vessel has been sufficiently lightened, in my judgment, fails."

The Court of Appeal, upholding the decision in the High Court, held[9h] that (1) if it had been intended to extend the word lightening to cover that which was not normally included in its ordinary meaning clear words would have been required, and "time used" for lightening did not include time spent waiting for lightening; (2) it would be prejudicial to the shipowners to allow the charterers to raise on appeal the issue that the notice of readiness was invalid because the ship was unable physically to discharge at the berth, when that issue had not been raised in the arbitration or in the High Court; (3) the charterers were right to contend that laytime should be calculated on the basis of the full cargo before lightening.

The Court of Appeal decision in *The Savvas* was followed in *N.Z.* **8–52** *Michalos* v. *Food Corporation of India.*[10] Wheat was carried in bulk to Bombay and the charterparty again stated: "Any lightening at discharge port at Owner's risk and expense and time used not to count as laytime. . . . " Between the two periods during which the ship was lightening she was at anchor, awaiting a berth. Charterers contended that there should be excluded from laytime all time from the beginning of the first period to the end of the second period. Bingham J. said of the clause[11]:

"That language, in my judgment, means precisely what it says . . . time is not to be excluded from the calculation of laytime if it is not used for lightening. If it is used for lightening then it is to be excluded."[12]

Enforced removal of ship **8–53**
Mere removal of the ship, in the absence of some fault on the part of shipowners, and where the removal is not for their convenience, does not necessarily help charterers[13]; an enforced removal of the ship, however, presents, a different problem. A temporary enforced removal was considered in *Cantiere Navale Triestina* v. *Russian Soviet Naphtha Export Agency*[14] where an Italian ship chartered to carry lubricating oil from Batoum was ordered by the Soviet government to leave its waters. The

[9g] See § 8–51 above.
[9h] [1982] 1 Lloyd's Rep. 22.
[10] [1983] Lloyd's Rep. 409 (*The Apollon*). *The Savvas* was also followed in *The Apollon* as an authority for the proposition that readiness to discharge into lighters was sufficient to enable a notice of readiness to be validly tendered. *The Apollon* also dealt with the meaning of the words "having been entered at the Custom House"; see also §§ 5–10 and 6–23 above.
[11] *Ibid.* at p. 415.
[12] But it would not be excluded from demurrage, even if used for lightening; *Food Corporation of India* v. *Carras Shipping Co. Ltd. (The Delian Leto)* [1983] 2 Lloyd's Rep. 496, following the House of Lords decision in *Dias Compania Naviera S.A.* v. *Louis Dreyfus Corporation* [1978] 1 Lloyd's Rep. 325. See § 10–51 below.
[13] *Tyne Blyth Shipping Co. Ltd.* v. *Leech, Harrison & Forwood* [1900] 2 Q.B. 12 See § 10–59 below.
[14] [1925] 2 K.B. 172 (C.A.). For delay in berthing not caused by the charterers, see *Good & Co.* v. *Isaacs* [1892] 2 Q.B. 555 (C.A.); § 3–17 above.

enforced departure, which took place immediately after laytime began, lasted 17 days, and was ordered as the result of a dispute between Italy and the U.S.S.R. The shipowners claimed demurrage, contending that the 216 running hours allowed for laytime[15] expired during the absence from Batoum. The Court of Appeal held that they were right. Atkin L.J. said[16]:

> " . . . it appears to me that unless the defendants can show that the absence of the ship arose from a default of the shipowners—and that they clearly have not done—or unless they show that the absence of the ship is covered by an exception in the charterparty— and I think they have failed to do that also—then they are liable in this case, unless they can succeed upon the further ground of illegality . . . [17] It appears to me to make no difference whether the vessel is in harbour fifty yards away from berth and cannot get to it, or whether she is fifty miles away."

8–54   *Lightening*

Where a ship has to lighten to reach the place at which the rest of the cargo has to be discharged, it has to be decided whether laytime begins at the lightening place and, if so, whether it continues or is interrupted while the ship is going from there to the final discharging place.

If the ship has already arrived when the lightening takes place then laytime begins in the absence of any custom or contractual provision to the contrary[18] and continues to run during the move.[19] The situation was summarised by Pollock B. as follows[20]:

> "The point to bear in mind is, What was the substantial character of the act? Was it a port discharge in the ordinary acceptation of those words, or was it a discharge made solely with the view of lightening the ship? On the other hand, it is equally clear as a general rule, and apart from the custom of any particular port, that once a ship has arrived at the place within the port of discharge where such vessels are usually discharged and is ready to discharge her cargo, she is an arrived vessel, and although the consignee may be entitled to order her for the purpose of discharge to different places within the same port, the lay days commence when she is ready to discharge at the first place to which she is ordered, and continue without intermission until her discharge is completed."

It seems that arrival is the relevant criterion, and that where a ship has arrived laytime must begin and continue to run, even if she is lightening. Though the discharge may be made "solely with the view of lightening the ship," in the words of Pollock C.B., nevertheless laytime runs if she has arrived, subject to any custom or contractual provision to the contrary.

The presumption that laytime continues to run is rebuttable. There may be a custom or a charterparty term that time shall not run during the move. In *Nielsen & Co.* v. *Wait*[21] a ship was to discharge at Gloucester "or so near thereto as she may safely get." She could not get up the canal to Gloucester until part of her wheat cargo was discharged at Sharpness Dock, about 17

---

[15] For the effect of an enforced removal when demurrage is running, and a distinction between temporary and permanent removals, see § 10–64 below.

[16] At pp. 206–207.

[17] It was argued for the charterers that the ban on loading made the performance of the charterparty illegal during the continuance of the ban. This contention was rejected by the Court of Appeal on the ground that there was no proof of illegality, as opposed to mere executive action. A difficult situation might still arise if governmental action made the performance illegal, even if only temporarily. It might be argued that the contract as a whole was tainted by illegality and so void.

[18] For such a custom see *Nielsen & Co.* v. *Wait* (1885) 16 Q.B.D. 67 (C.A.).

[19] *Caffarini* v. *Walker* (1876) I.R. 10 C.L. 250; *M'Intosh* v. *Sinclair* (1877) I.R. 11 C.L. 456.

[20] In *Nielsen & Co* v. *Wait* (1885) 14 Q.B.D. 516 at p. 523. His judgment was affirmed by the Court of Appeal: (1885) 16 Q.B.D. 67.

[21] (1885) 16 Q.B.D. 67 (C.A.).

miles from the basin at Gloucester. Evidence was given of a custom by which the usual place to discharge grain was the basin, grain ships were lightened at Sharpness, and laytime counted during the lightening but not during the journey up and down the canal.[22] The Court of Appeal held that the custom was not inconsistent with the charterparty provision for "running days" and that the time taken by the move did not count.

As Lord Esher M.R. said, in an illuminating passage[23]:

> " . . . I myself treat, at all events for the purposes of this case, Sharpness as being within the port. Then what does the custom come to? It seems to me that within the port of Gloucester for a ship laden with a grain cargo there are two places of discharge. The ship begins to discharge so far as is necessary to lighten her to enable her to go up the canal at Sharpness. She then goes up to the basin and finishes the discharge. Therefore there is a double discharge, it taking place partly in one place and partly in another. If there was no custom, the lay days would commence at the beginning of the delivery at Sharpness, and would go on consecutively . . . But the custom adds this term, namely, that for the intermediate traversing of the canal in the same port, between the two places of delivery within the same port, although the running days are to be consecutive, part of them is to be cut out, and they are to be resumed when the ship arrives in the basin."

Evidence of a custom to lighten was held to be inadmissible in *Reynolds & Co.* v. *Tomlinson*.[24] but there the master refused to go up the canal and discharged all the cargo at Sharpness. The charterers held to be in breach of their obligation to name "a safe port," as the ship could not reach Gloucester safely with a full cargo. Day J. distinguished the Court of Appeal decision in *Nielsen* v. *Wait*,[25] saying[26]:

> "The question whether Gloucester was or was not a safe port under such circumstances" [*i.e.* where a ship had to lighten] "was never considered. The point was not taken. I cannot, therefore, regard that case as any authority upon the question which we have to decide."

If lightening takes place outside the port, then the ship, in the absence of **8–55** such words as "so near thereto as she can safely get," must be regarded as having been prevented from reaching her destination. Indeed where the charterparty provides for the ship to go to a "safe port, always afloat" charterers would be in breach of contract but for the lightening. In any event the ship has not arrived, and the delay during lightening is a type of detention, unless there is a custom that the time counts as laytime; thus in *Nielsen & Co.* v. *Wait*[27] Lord Esher M.R. said that even if Sharpness were not part of the port of Gloucester time would count during laytime. If the time at the lightening place is counted as laytime, then the voyage can be regarded as having been completed, so far as concerns the cargo discharged at the lightening place. This was the approach adopted by the Court of Session in *Dickinson* v. *Martini & Co.*[28] A ship was chartered to "proceed to a safe port in the United Kingdom, or so near thereunto as she may safely get always afloat at any time of the tide." Owing to her draught she had to discharge part of the cargo at Greenock before going to Glasgow, to which she had been ordered. It was held that the voyage was com-

---

[22] The custom was proved before Pollock C.B., the judge of first instance (14 Q.B.D. 516) and the case went to the Court of Appeal on the questions of law.
[23] At p. 74.
[24] [1896] 1 Q.B. 586.
[25] [1885] 16 Q.B.D. 67 (C.A.).
[26] [1896] 1 Q.B. 586 at p. 590.
[27] (1885) 16 Q.B.D. 67 (C.A.) at p. 74.
[28] (1874) 1 R. (Ct. of Sess.) 1185.

pleted at Greenock, so far as the cargo discharge there was concerned; time spent in lightening there was to be included in the lay days. In such situation the time taken to move from the lightening place to the final discharging place would not count.

CHAPTER 9

RELATIONSHIP OF LOADING AND DISCHARGING TIMES

Averaging, reversing and similar provisions   **9–01**
   Two separate calculations are usually made, one for loading and the
other for discharging,[1] any demurrage or dispatch moneys being worked
out separately at the appropriate rates. The parties may combine the two
calculations and consider as a whole the extent to which the ship has been
released early or detained. They may agree to set off loading or discharging
demurrage time against loading or discharging dispatch time, in the process
of averaging[2]; or to form one pool from all the laytime available, when laytime is reversible.[3] In the absence of such special agreements, described by
Scrutton L.J.[4] as containing: "The very inappropriate terms of 'averaging'
or 'reversible days,' neither of which phrases in any ordinary sense of the
word expressed the meaning of the parties," the loading and discharging
calculations are made separately. Of the various clauses Devlin J. said in
Alma Shipping Co., S.A. v. *V.M. Salgaoncar E Irmaos Ltda.*[5]:

> "I attach great importance to there being, not more authorities, but the reverse in
> matters of this kind. If it were possible to give one common meaning to all these clauses I
> feel that there would be a great deal of advantage in so doing."

Averaging[6]   **9–02**
   Where charterers have the right to average, they may set off days on dispatch in one operation, be it loading or discharging,[7] against any days on
demurrage in the other operation. This is to their advantage, where, as is
usual, the demurrage rate is twice the dispatch rate.[8] Where, for example,
there are three days of loading dispatch and three days of discharging
demurrage, no demurrage or dispatch is due if the charterers exercise their
option to average. If the operations were dealt with separately at the
appropriate rates, the difference in rates would result in their being debited
with demurrage. If the time saved to shipowners were twice as much (*e.g.*
six days) as the excess time used by charterers (*e.g.* three days), the latter
could by averaging cause dispatch money to be paid where otherwise the
liabilities would cancel out.

---

[1] See *Marshall* v. *Bolckow, Vaughan & Co.* (1881) 6 Q.B.D. 231.
[2] See below.
[3] See §§ 9–09–9–24 below.
[4] *Rederiaktiebolaget Transatlantic* v. *La Compagnie Française des Phosphates de l'Océanie*
(1926) 32 Com.Cas. 126 at p. 131.
[5] [1954] 2 Q.B. 94 at p. 104.
[6] The Charterparty Laytime Definitions 1980 (see Appendix to this book) state: "21. 'TO
AVERAGE'—means that separate calculations are to be made for loading and discharging
and any time saved in one operation is to be set against any excess time used in the other."
[7] Each of these operations must be taken as a whole, without separate demurrage and dispatch calculations for each of the loading or discharging ports: *Compania Naviera Azuero
S.A.* v. *British Oil & Cake Mills Ltd.* [1957] 2 Q.B. 293 (*The Azuero*). See also § 12–04
below.
[8] See § 12–02 below.

The right to average is expressed in such terms as: "Charterers to have the right to average the days allowed for loading and discharging."[9] Where the words "to avoid demurrage" are used,[10] it seems that charterers cannot use their right to make dispatch money payable to them. If no qualification as to the purpose of averaging is imposed, then their right to average is not affected by their motives.

9–03   *The cases on averaging*

Since the decisions in *Watson Brothers Shipping Co. Ltd.* v. *Mysore Manganese Co. Ltd.*[11] and *Alma Shipping Co. S.A.* v. *V.M. Salgaoncar E Irmaos Ltda.*,[12] a clear meaning can be attached to the words "to average." It was not always so.

In *Molière SS. Co. Ltd.* v. *Naylor, Benzon & Co.*,[13] which has since been distinguished,[14] an iron ore cargo was carried from Bilbao to Newport, Monmouthshire, under a charterparty which stated: "Charterers to be at liberty to average the days for loading and discharging in order to avoid demurrage. . . . " The ship was to be loaded and discharged at rates of "400 tons per clear working day, weather permitting" and "400 tons per like day, weather permitting" respectively. The charterers deducted the total time allowed from the total time used for two operations while admitting liability for some demurrage. The shipowners contended that the charterers could only take credit at the loading port for the laytime allowed for that port, and could not credit themselves with any of the laytime available for discharging. Instead, the dispatch time at the discharging port should be deducted from the demurrage time at the loading port. On this calculation the ship was on demurrage for an amount greater than that admitted by the charterers. Kennedy J. held that the charterers were right. In his view the averaging clause was ambiguous, so that evidence to construe it was admissible. According to the charterers the clause had been in common use for 10 years and had received the interpretation which they put on it. Kennedy J. was clearly much influenced by the evidence as to current practice, for he said[15]:

> "I do not say that without the evidence called by the defendants their construction of the words would be an impossible one, but it would certainly be doubtful whether it was correct. . . . There is satisfactory evidence to my mind that the defendants' contention gives a fair meaning to the clause, and one which is recognised and accepted by business men."

As a result of this decision a clause which would now be regarded as an averaging clause, and which expressly gave the charterers "liberty to average," was construed in a manner which would now only apply to a clause providing for reversible laytime. The argument successfully used by the charterers could probably be used against them now, as the practice "recognised and accepted by business men" is to treat a liberty to average

---

[9] C. (Ore) 7 Charterparty.
[10] As in *Watson Brothers Shipping Co. Ltd.* v. *Mysore Manganese Co. Ltd.* (1910) 15 Com. Cas. 159.
[11] (1910) 15 Com.Cas. 159.
[12] [1954] 2 Q.B. 94 (*The Rubystone*).
[13] (1897) 2 Com.Cas. 92.
[14] By Devlin J. in *Alma Shipping Co. S.A.* v. *V.M. Salgaoncar E Irmaos Ltda.* [1954] 2 Q.B. 94 (*The Rubystone*).
[15] At p. 100.

in the manner adopted in later cases. Devlin J. has said[16] of the *Molière* decision that he did not regard it as an authority upon construction. It was a case in which the judge had thought that the clause was ambiguous and that it would be better for him to be guided by the evidence.

The first of the modern cases was *Watson Brothers Shipping Co. Ltd.* v. **9–04** *Mysore Manganese Co. Ltd.*[17] A charterparty for the carriage of ore from Mormugao to England stated that the cargo was "to be shipped at the rate of 500 tons per clear working day of 24 hours (weather permitting), Sundays and holidays always excepted; and to be discharged at 500 tons per like day, except in the case of . . . scarcity of workmen, epidemics . . . or any cause beyond the personal control of shipper, charterer, or consignees, which may hinder the loading or discharge of the said vessel." It also stated: "Days to be averaged over all voyages performed under and during the entire currency of this charter to avoid demurrage." Plague at Mormugao earlier, though it had ended before the ship arrived, caused a scarcity of workmen, and the shipowners claimed demurrage. It was held that the charterers were not excused by the exception of scarcity of workmen or epidemics as it had not been shown that these hindered the loading, but that they could abate the amount of the demurrage by taking credit for dispatch at the port of discharge. Hamilton J. said[18]:

> "The defendants then contend that they are entitled to take 10 days for loading, and add to that 10 days for discharging, and interpret them as 20 clear working days of 24 hours."

This would have been their right if the laytime had been reversible[19] but, as the judge said, the charterparty did not provide that a number of days should be allowed for both loading and discharging. He added[20]:

> "In my opinion the meaning of the average clause is that a number of days for shipment having been stipulated and then a number of like days for discharge having been stipulated, the vessel's right to demurrage must be determined upon the events which happen at the port of loading and according to the number of days allowed for loading there, though subsequent events at the port of discharge may entitle the charterers to abate the amount of demurrage incurred at the port of loading by taking credit for the number of days saved, if any, at the port of discharge . . . my view is that, as a matter of construction at the end of ten charterparty days for loading at Mormugao, the vessel was on demurrage."

Whereas in the *Watson* case the relevant words were "Days to be aver- **9–05** aged . . . to avoid demurrage," in *Alma Shipping Co. S.A.* v. *V.M. Salgaoncar E Irmaos Ltda.*[21] they were: "Charterers to have the right to average the days allowed for loading and discharging." The court had the opportunity to explain averaging. A ship carried ore from Mormugao to Rotterdam, the charterparty providing for daily loading and discharging rates of 500 tons and 1,500 tons respectively. Loading took nearly four weeks and discharging one day; in neither case were there any holidays, non-working days (except for periods from noon on Saturdays to 8 a.m. on Mondays) or interruption by excepted perils. The charterers exercised the

---

[16] In *Alma Shipping Co. S.A.* v. *V.M. Salgaoncar E Irmaos Ltda.* [1954] 2 Q.B. 94 at p. 103 (*The Rubystone*).
[17] (1910) 15 Com.Cas. 159. The court also discussed the meaning of the expression "working day of 24 hours." See § 2–45 above.
[18] At p. 166.
[19] See § 9–09 below.
[20] At pp. 167–168.
[21] [1954] 2 Q.B. 94 (*The Rubystone*).

right to average and claimed dispatch money. They said that they were entitled to aggregate or pool the total laytime available for loading and discharging, and then to deduct from that the total time used. This is the method usually employed where laytime is reversible.[22] The shipowners deducted their loading demurrage from the time allowed for discharging. They said that the charterers must be regarded as having an overdraft on the loading laytime which had to be deducted from the discharging laytime. As the time used in discharging, though short, was longer than the time left, this resulted in their making a claim for demurrage. The parties agreed that an alternative method of calculation was one by which loading demurrage and discharging dispatch were set off against each other, thus:

	D	H	M
Time on demurrage at loading port	4	5	12
Time saved to ship at discharging port	5	19	59
Deduct loading demurrage	4	5	12
Net time saved	1	14	47

9–06   It was held that the alternative method, as set out above, was correct. Devlin J. said that the decision of Hamilton J. in 1910[23] was the one authority which was clearly applicable. He regretted the distinctions which had arisen between the various wordings, saying that there was much to be said in principle for treating all the clauses as if they were intended to achieve the same thing. He added[24]:

"... I reach the conclusion that a distinction must be drawn when the word 'average' is used in a clause of this type from a clause which, though no doubt with similar intent, is phrased so as to use other terms which are quite as commonly used."

The strong view held by Devlin J. as to the avoidance of a multiplicity of interpretations may be a useful guide as to the approach of the courts when other disputes arise. For example, he touched on the possibility of yet another method of calculation, by which the pooling or aggregation of loading and discharging times (favoured by the charterers) would be followed by a division into two parts. As he said[25]:

"What might be regarded as the stricter way of doing it by averaging (that is, dividing the aggregate by two) would, I am told, produce quite a different result and is not in fact a method that is relied upon by either side in this case."

By that method the different rates would still be reflected in the total laytime, but, as Devlin J. said, it is better to restrict the number of interpretations, except where the parties by express words have shown that they desire a particular new method of calculation.

9–07 *Waiver*

Charterers may lose their liberty to average if they act in a manner inconsistent with the intention to exercise such a liberty. If they obtain a payment for loading dispatch, as they might do, for example, by deducting it from freight, they may find themselves unable to insist that the dispatch

---

[22] See § 9–09 below. Indeed the charterers argued that averaging and reversible provisions produced the same result.

[23] In *Watson Brothers Shipping Co. Ltd.* v. *Mysore Manganese Co. Ltd.* (1910) 15 Com.Cas. 159. See § 9–04 above.

[24] At p. 104.

[25] At p. 99.

shall be averaged against discharging demurrage.[26] They should either refuse to accept the payment or accept it on condition that they retain their liberty to average. If, for example, the number of days saved equals the number of days on demurrage the averaging would result in no dispatch or demurrage being due. Should charterers fail to exercise their liberty to average they will have on balance to pay as demurrage a sum equal to half the demurrage amount taken on its own, provided that, as is usual, dispatch runs at half the demurrage rate.

It is not always easy to say whether the charterers have failed to exercise **9–08** their liberty to average. Much depends on the charterparty wording, which may be clumsy. It was so described by Bigham J. in *Oakville SS. Co., Ltd.* v. *Holmes*.[27] A charterparty for the carriage of iron ore from Cartagena, Spain, to Maryport, England, stated: "Charterers have the option of averaging days for loading and discharging in order to avoid demurrage." Loading and discharging were to be at the rate of 200 tons per working day of 24 hours. Time was saved at Cartagena but at Maryport the discharging time exceeded the stipulated period. The charterparty provided for dispatch money "to be settled in loading and discharging ports respectively." The Cartagena agents (who acted for shippers and charterers) made up an account with the master which included an item for dispatch, disbursements and loading charges. They paid the master, who wrote on the account: "Loading charge and dispatch money to be finally adjusted on quantity discharged at Maryport." This last remark was made because there was a minor dispute as to the amount loaded. The charterers contended, in defence to a claim by the shipowners for discharging demurrage, that they were entitled to reduce the claim by averaging. Bigham J. rejected this contention, admonished the parties,[28] and said[29]:

> "I think that when the defendant asked for and obtained his dispatch money at Cartagena, claiming and getting his 3 per cent.[30] upon the amount of it, he exercised once for all his option as to averaging the loading and discharging days—that is to say, he elected not to average; and it was too late for him to change his mind after the discharge at Maryport."

Of the provision that dispatch money was "to be settled" at the loading port he said that, although the amount was settled there, the charterers were entitled to refuse to accept payment, except on terms that their liberty to average was preserved. They did not impose such terms and they had thus elected not to average.

Reversing[31] **9–09**

Meaning. The word "reversible," when used of laytime, means that the loading and discharging periods can be aggregated or pooled.

---

[26] Compare with this, the waiver of the cesser clause by charterers paying loading demurrage; *Fidelitas Shipping Co.* v. *V/O Exportchleb* [1963] 2 Lloyd's Rep. 113 (C.A.). See § 11–45 below.

[27] (1899) 5 Com.Cas. 48.

[28] At p. 51: "If merchants and ship-owners would take a little more care about settling the terms of such documents they would save themselves much loss of time and money."

[29] At pp. 52–53.

[30] Interest and insurance.

[31] The Charterparty Laytime Definitions 1980 (see Appendix to this book) state: "22. 'REVERSIBLE'—means an option given to the charterer to add together the time allowed for loading and discharging. Where the option is exercised the effect is the same as a total time being specified to cover both operations."

Both averaging[32] and reversing have as their object the pooling of loading and discharging times, so that the total laytime used for loading and discharging is contrasted with the total laytime allowed. The methods of achieving the object are different.

Where charterers choose to average the total times on demurrage and dispatch are calculated, in accordance with the demurrage and dispatch clauses, which may refer to all time saved or to all working time saved.[33] The times are then set off against each other. Where time is reversible, and the charterers take advantage of the permission to reverse,[34] there is a pooling or aggregation of the days which in the charterparty count as lay days.

9–10   Charterers may be bound to decide whether to reverse within a limited period, as in the provision: "Time allowed for loading and discharging to be reversible or to be settled at each end if required by charterers, such option declarable before breaking bulk at discharing port." Their decision may depend on whether, for example, loading dispatch is payable on "all time saved" but discharging dispatch on "working time saved." If there are such contrasting provisions, and they decide to reverse, it seems that all dispatch would be payable as if it were discharging dispatch. Sometimes pooling or aggregation is achieved by the use of explicit directions as to the debiting or crediting of laytime[35]; but much depends on the words used, and a result may be achieved which does not constitute true "reversing."[36]

9–11   Crediting saved time

Provisions that "any days or parts of days not consumed in loading may be added to the time for discharging" and that "any extra time consumed in loading may be deducted from the time for discharging" were discussed in *Rederiaktiebolaget Transatlantic* v. *La Compagnie Française des Phosphates de l'Océanie.*[37] On the basis of two separate calculations the ship was on demurrage at the loading port but owed dispatch money in respect of the discharging port. The charterers denied any liability for demurrage, saying that deduction of the extra loading time from the discharging laytime resulted in their being owed dispatch money. Scrutton L.J., agreeing, as did the other members of the Court of Appeal, with the charterers' interpretation, discussed the expressions "averaging" and "reversible," saying[38]:

" . . . the charter contains a clause enabling the charterer at his option to 'pool' loading and discharging days, or to regard them as a whole fund or source out of which to satisfy the loading and discharging obligations. This process used to be described in

---

[32] See § 9–02 above.

[33] See §§ 12–07 and 12–08 below.

[34] This view, as expressed in the first edition (at p. 96), and repeated here, that the word "reversible" confers a choice upon the charterers, was noted with approval by Mocatta J. in *Fury Shipping Co. Ltd.* v. *State Trading Corporation of India Ltd.* [1972] 1 Lloyd's Rep. 509 at p. 512 (*The Atlantic Sun*). For the facts see § 9–23.

[35] As in *Rederiaktiebolaget Transatlantic* v. *La Compagnie Française des Phosphates de l'Océanie* (1926) 32 Com.Cas. 126 (C.A.); see § 9–11.

[36] As in *Rowland & Marwood's SS. Co. Ltd.* v. *Wilson, Sons & Co. Ltd.* (1897) 2 Com.Cas 198, where the clause was "Any hours saved in loading to be added to the hours allowed for discharging."

[37] (1926) 32 Com.Cas 126 (C.A.) See also below, in § 12–22, in connection with dispatch money.

[38] At p. 131.

charters by the very inappropriate terms of 'averaging' or 'reversible days,' neither of which phrases in any ordinary sense of the words expressed the meaning of the parties."

Though the expressions "averaging" and "reversible" are not usually   **9–12** employed for the same purpose, it is clear that in such cases, and in the case of the clause being considered by Scrutton L.J., there is an intention to set off time saved (or used) either against time used (or saved) or against laytime. The logical difficulty which can arise was then considered by Scrutton L.J. for it is evident that like days will not always be compared or set off. A ship is detained for running or consecutive days; laytime may not consist of such days. As he put it[39]:

> "If you have loaded the ship in 5 days less than the end of the loading time allowed you, but of those 5 days one is a Sunday and one a day on which working is prevented by weather, are you to credit the discharging time with five days, or three days? Similarly if you have taken five consecutive days more than the allowed loading time in loading, but one of the days is a Sunday, and one a non-weather working day, do you reduce the original discharging time by five days or three days? The discharging time excludes Sundays and non-weather working days; if you reduce it by consecutive days, including Sundays, are you using a day on which the charterer is not bound to work, to deprive him of a working day? It would seem reasonable that if you have saved days from your loading time, you should only add to your discharging time so many of these days as you would be bound to work on, and, therefore, not add such days as were Sundays or non-weather working days. For the days you add to discharging time must be of the same quality as the discharging days, and a Sunday or non-weather working day does not count as a discharging day. To give yourself five extra working days in discharging, because you have not used in loading three working days and two non-working days, does not look right. This, the charterers say, they avoid by treating the 'days not consumed'[40] and 'the extra days consumed'[41] as the same sort of days as compose the 'time for discharging,' to which they are to be added or from which they are to be deducted."

In this example Scrutton L.J. dealt with the problem of time saved; he went on[42] to discuss the question of "extra days consumed": " . . . you can only increase or decrease the 'pool' of lay days by adding or deducting days of the same character; and cannot use a non-weather working day on which neither the charterer nor the ship is bound to work to deprive the charterer of a day for discharging which he is entitled to require to be a weather working day." The charterparty provisions in this case took effect as if the provision had been for "reversible lay days."

As Viscount Dilhorne put it in *Aldebaran Compania Maritime S.A.*   **9–13** *Panama* v. *Aussenhandel A.G. Zürich,*[43] speaking of the *Rederiaktiebolaget Transatlantic* decision: "The question at issue was whether in calculating the time to be added or deducted, Sundays and holidays and days which were not weather working days which were not to be counted in calculating the loading time and the discharging time, were to be counted for the purpose of calculating the time to be added or deducted." He quoted with approval the passage cited above from the judgment of Scrutton L.J. and added[44]: "So in the present case it does not look right that there should be deducted from the permitted discharging time by virtue of the time lost provision periods of time which would not be counted under the discharg-

---

[39] At p. 132.
[40] *i.e.* the days saved.
[41] *i.e.* the excess day used.
[42] At p. 133.
[43] [1977] A.C. 157 at p. 173. (*The Darrah*) See § 6–09 above.
[44] At p. 174.

ing provision when determining whether the time allowed for discharge had been exceeded and if so, to what extent."

9–14 Reversing further explained

So, if the lay days are reversed the aggregation or pooling can be achieved by transferring the unused laytime,[45] or excess laytime used at loading, to the credit or debit of the discharging laytime. Thus:

Place	Laytime allowed (Days) (see *Note* below)	Laytime used (Days) (see *Note* below)	Comment
Loading Port(s)	8	5	Credit discharging time with 3 w.w.d.
Discharging Port(s)	8	12	1 day on demurrage
Totals	16	17	1 day on demurrage

(*Note*: For the purpose of the above table, a "day" is one of the "weather working days, Sundays and holidays excepted," stipulated in the charterparty.)

9–15 Whether the days are transferred in the way shown above, or merely added up so that the two totals can be compared, the process must not result in excepted days being added to or subtracted from the laytime. For example, loading may finish three calendar days before the end of loading laytime, but one of these days may be a Sunday. There are only two spare loading lay days to be moved into the other part of the pool, and they are added to the discharging laytime.[46] The fact that three calendar or running days have been saved to the ship would only be relevant if loading dispatch time were being calculated separately for the purpose of payment or as part of the averaging process, and then only if dispatch was in respect of "all time saved." In the reversing process the dispatch cannot be said to "crystallise" at this stage; the only question is as to the number of unused lay days. Alternatively, loading may take three days longer than the loading laytime, one of the extra three days being a Sunday. Charterers have begun, in effect, to draw on a supply of discharging laytime which, had they not exercised their option to reverse, would not have been available to them. Should two or three days be subtracted from the weather working days available to them for discharging laytime? It appears from the decided cases[47] that only two days should be deducted, as, in the case of the Sunday, charterers have not held the ship during a day of the type which would count against them when laytime is running. It is not relevant that, had the demurrage "crystallised," the day would have counted against them. One of the remaining two days, before the completion of loading, may have

---

[45] As in *Love & Stewart Ltd.* v. *Rowtor SS. Co. Ltd.* [1916] 2 A.C. 527 (H.L.) see § 9–16 below.

[46] Shipowners might contend that, of these two days, one was a non-weather working day, so that only one should be added to the discharging laytime; the contention would be incorrect because the loading laytime would in such a case end one day later, thus bringing the total of transferable days to two.

[47] Such as *Reardon Smith Line Ltd.* v. *Ministry of Agriculture* [1960] 1 Q.B. 439 at p. 517 (*The Vancouver Strike Case*), per McNair J. " . . . you draw on the days of that quality available for discharge to meet the excess . . . " See also § 9–21 below.

been a non-weather working day. If so, it should not be counted against charterers, and only one day is taken from the discharging laytime.[48]

The cases on reversible laytime   **9–16**

A provision that discharging time was reversible was held by the House of Lords in *Love & Stewart Ltd.* v. *Rowtor SS. Co. Ltd.*[49] to mean that laytime saved in loading could be added to the discharging time. Loading was to be "at the rate of 125 fathoms daily" and discharging "at the rate of 125 fathoms daily reversible . . . during the ordinary working hours of the respective ports, but according to the custom of the respective ports, Sundays, general or local holidays (unless used) in both loading and discharging excepted." The charterparty was for the carriage of pit props from Finland to Wales. Nine lay days were used in loading,[50] or four working days less than the loading laytime of 13 days, but the discharging time was more than the discharging laytime, which was also 13 days. There appears to have been no dispatch clause in the charterparty, but the shippers secured the agreement of the master to an allowance for dispatch money for each of the four days saved in loading. Dispatch money was therefore deducted from the freight. The bill of lading, which was filled in after this transaction, stated: "thirteen days used for loading." This was untrue. There had been no agreement at the time of the transaction that such a statement should appear. The charterers were receivers and knew of this "sale" by the shippers.

The House of Lords held that the charterers were not estopped by the false statement in the bill from claiming as discharging time, by virtue of the word "reversible," the four working days saved in the loading. Lord Sumner delivered the only reasoned judgment and dealt with the meaning of the term "reversible" in the following words[51]:

> " . . . at Kristinestad the whole cargo was loaded in nine days, and the effect of the word 'reversible' in the charter is that the receivers were entitled to seventeen lay days[52] under the charter for discharging the ship at Newport. The pursuers[53] claim (and the burden is on them) to be able to show that in the circumstances only thirteen days were available for the receiver."

The master had tried to have inserted on the bill of lading a statement indicating that only 13 days were left for discharging, but the charterers' representative stood out successfully for the words "thirteen days used for loading." The statement was incorrect to the knowledge of all the parties. The charterers were not estopped from claiming, in respect of the discharge, the four days saved in the loading.

It was apparently accepted by Lord Sumner as axiomatic, and agreed by   **9–17**
the parties,[54] that the use of the word "reversible" entitled the charterers to add loading time saved to the discharging laytime—and vice versa. The number of days saved seems merely to have been added to the discharging

---

[48] See the remarks of Scrutton L.J. in *Rederiaktiebolaget Transatlantic* v. *La Compagnie Française des Phosphates de l'Océanie* (1926) 32 Com.Cas. 126 (C.A.) at p. 133. See also § 9–11 above.

[49] [1916] 2 A.C. 527.

[50] Ten calendar days, but one of these was a Sunday.

[51] At p. 536.

[52] Four days saved in loading plus 13 days discharging time.

[53] The shipowners. This was an appeal from the Scottish Court of Session.

[54] *Ibid.* at p. 530.

laytime, without any suggestion that some allowance should be made to the extent that the days saved might have been excepted from laytime.

A provision for "cargo to be loaded and discharged together within five reversible working days" was considered in *Verren* v. *Anglo-Dutch Brick Co. (1927) Ltd.*[55] A ship was chartered for 15 to 20 trips, at charterers' option, to carry bricks from Belgium to London. The charterparty stated: "any days saved on this charter are to be deducted from the claim which the owners have for demurrage," *i.e.* on an earlier charterparty. The ship-owners made a claim for demurrage which the charterers resisted, arguing that delays by the ship amounted to deviations. The charterers also argued that as there were to be 15 to 20 trips they would read the reversible clause as if it read: "Cargoes to be loaded and discharged together within 100 reversible days," and that they could use any working day as a matter of accounting for any voyage. The Court of Appeal rejected their contentions. Scrutton L.J. said of the provision for "five reversible days"[56]:

> " . . . I do not know who was the ingenious person who first thought the word 'reversible' might possibly express what he meant to say. 'Reversible' seems to mean that you may use days for either loading or discharging. The case of *Love & Stewart, Ltd.* v. *Rowtor Steamship Company, Ltd.*[57] . . . appears to show that that is the meaning."

9–18   *Reversibility only on one voyage*

He then disagreed with the charterers' argument that the days could be used for any voyage[58]:

> " . . . if you want a day saved on one voyage to be applied to another, you must say so."

So also, as to the meaning of the word "reversible," Roche J. said in the High Court[59]:

> "It was also argued that the word 'reversible' was redundant if it meant no more that loading days and discharging days were to be reversible or set off one against another, which is its ordinary meaning. . . . I hold that 'reversible' relates only to the interchange or counting of days as between loading and discharging, and does not have reference to the counting of days as between the various voyages."

It can be seen that the judgment did not add to the views as to the meaning of reversibility already expressed in *Love & Stewart Ltd.* v. *Rowtor SS. Co. Ltd.*[60]

9–19   *"Time allowed for loading and discharging . . . to be reversible."*

The words "Time allowed for loading and discharging as per Clauses 5 and 6 to be reversible," inserted in a Gencon form of charterparty, were considered in *Z SS. Co. Ltd.* v. *Amtorg, New York.*[61] Coal was to be carried from Mariupol, U.S.S.R., to Boston, U.S.A. The loading and discharging laytime clauses (Clauses 5 and 6) stipulated that the cargo was to be loaded and discharged at the average rates of 600 and 800 tons respectively "per weather working day. Sundays, official and local holidays excepted." The dispatch money clause stated: "Owners to pay charterers

---

[55] (1929) 34 Ll.L.Rep. 210 (C.A.).
[56] At pp. 212–213.
[57] [1916] 2 A.C. 527 (H.L.); see § 9–16 above.
[58] At p. 213.
[59] (1929) 34 Ll.L.Rep. 56 at p. 58.
[60] [1916] 2 A.C. 527 (H.L.); see § 9–16 above.
[61] (1938) 61 Ll.L.Rep. 97. See § 2–30 above in connection with the meaning of the words "weather working day."

£15 (fifteen pounds) per day or *pro rata* dispatch money for all time saved in loading and discharging, to be settled at each end if required by charterers." Both loading and discharging were completed within the times allowed. Goddard J. said[62]:

> "Is the time saved at Mariupol reversible for the purpose of calculating dispatch money or for the purpose of calculating demurrage? That makes quite a substantial difference, I am told, in the calculation."

The charterers, whose contentions were rejected, said that the word "reversible" meant that one could add loading time saved to the discharging time allowed for the purpose of calculating dispatch money. One then took the enlarged discharging time, and the difference between that and the days used (if the latter were fewer in number) was the number of days for which dispatch money was due. The charterers relied on a passage to this effect from the speech of Lord Sumner in *Love & Stewart Ltd.* v. *Rowtor SS. Co. Ltd.*[63]

Dispatch allowed twice?   **9–20**

For the charterers there was the awkward question of the dispatch money clause, by which settlement for all time saved in loading and discharging was to be "at each end if required by charterers." How was this to be reconciled with the construction put upon "reversible" by the charterers? As Goddard J. said, the charterers had a right to say, directly loading was finished: "We have saved you four days; pay us four days dispatch money." He went on[64]:

> "If that is paid there is an end of the claim for dispatch money. It is quite true that in calculating the number of days that the ship had got to discharge you can add those four days on to the discharging time, because the charter says they are reversible; but it does not mean that you can get paid over again, and Mr. Willmer[65] does not suggest that it means that you are to be paid twice over. I think Mr. Brightman's contention[66] was right here, in view of the plain language of Clause 20. You have to calculate how many days have been saved in fact on the loading and pay the dispatch money in respect of that. You have then to consider how many days were actually saved in the discharging and pay the dispatch money in respect of that. In my opinion, in view of Clause 20[67] of the charterparty, the dispatch money has to be calculated independently[68]; that is to say, loading time has got to be paid for separately from discharging time, although in fact demurrage will not be incurred if having saved time at the loading port she exceeds the time granted at the port of discharge but does not exceed it by more than the time that she has saved at the loading port."

The effect of a provision for reversible laytime was one of the many   **9–21** issues concerning laytime which were considered by the High Court in *Reardon Smith Line Ltd.* v. *Ministry of Agriculture.*[69] The charterparty included the provisions: "Loading and discharging time shall be reversible"; "Dispatch money (which is to be paid to charterers before vessel sails) shall be payable for all working time saved in loading"[70]; and "Dis-

---

[62] At p. 102.
[63] [1916] 2 A.C. 527 (H.L.) at p. 536. See also § 8–16 above.
[64] (1938) 61 Ll.L.Rep. 97 at p. 102.
[65] Henry Gordon Willmer, counsel for the charterers.
[66] Eustace Webster Brightman was counsel for the shipowners.
[67] The dispatch money clause.
[68] "if required by charterers."
[69] [1960] 1 Q.B. 439.
[70] McNair J. is quoted in the available judgments as saying that the dispatch clause referred to "time saved including Sundays and holidays," but in the factual summary of the case, set out before the judgment, the words are said to be "all working time saved in loading."

patch money and/or demurrage . . . to be adjusted on completion of discharge." McNair J. dealt with the problem encountered by Scrutton L.J. in an earlier case,[71] namely, that of the quality of the days to be credited or debited. He stressed that his comments applied to a case, like that before him, where dispatch was payable on "time saved including Sundays and holidays."[70] The solution advanced by McNair J.[72] may be summarised as follows:

1. "First you ascertain the number of days of the particular quality specified in the charter which are allowed for loading and discharging, which days so ascertained form a pool. For example, eight weather working days for loading; 12 weather working days for discharging; total 20 weather working days."[72]

2. (a) If time is saved at the loading port, carry forward the balance of days of that quality (say, three weather working days) to the discharging port. This may involve the omission of some days saved, such as Sundays and holidays, if they occur between the end of loading and the end of laytime and are excepted from laytime.[73]
(b) If the eight weather working days for loading are exceeded (say, by five days) you draw on the 12 days of that quality available for discharge to meet the excess, so that fewer days of that quality (12 days less five) are left for discharging.

3. Ascertain the number of days of the specified quality used for discharging:
(a) If days used exceed the amended number of days available for discharging, whether the original number has been increased (12 plus three; see 2 (a)) or decreased (12 less five; see 2 (b)), then demurrage is payable on such excess.
(b) If days used are less than the number of days available for discharging whether that number has been increased or decreased, then dispatch money is due on the number of days unused.

9-22   What happens if the number of hours per working day at the loading port is different from the number at the discharging port? One is still comparing like with like. As McNair J. said[74]:

" . . . the factor that the working day is a period of eight hours at the loading port and a period of 24 hours at the discharging port is only brought into play in determining how many working days or parts have been used at the loading and discharging port respectively. What is carried forward or drawn on is a number of weather working days or parts of such days."

9-23   The right of charterers to exercise their option where the relevant words were "Laytime allowed for loading and discharging to be reversible" was emphasised in *Fury Shipping Co. Ltd.* v. *State Trading Corporation of India Ltd.*[75] Bulk sulphur was carried from Vancouver to Bhavnagar, India, under a charterparty which stated: " . . . dispatch money for all time saved each end to be paid to Charterers at half demurrage rate." Loading

[71] *Rederiaktiebolaget Transatlantic* v. *La Compagnie Française des Phosphates de l'Océanie* (1926) 32 Com.Cas. 126 (C.A.). See § 9-11 above.
[72] [1960] 1 Q.B. 439 at p. 517.
[73] See the remarks of Scrutton L.J. in *Rederiaktiebolaget Transatlantic* v. *La Compagnie Française des Phosphates de l'Océanie* (1926) 32 Com.Cas. 126 (C.A.) at pp. 131–132. See § 9-11 above.
[74] [1960] 1 Q.B. 439 at p. 517.
[75] [1972] 1 Lloyd's Rep. 509 (*The Atlantic Sun*).

and discharging were exceptionally fast. The ship used 5½ hours laytime out of 2 days 19 hours 11 minutes allowed for loading, and 7 days 21 hours 9 minutes out of 21 days 13 hours 20 minutes allowed for discharging. The shipowners contended that the words "to be reversible" meant that there must be one time sheet to cover loading and discharging. The charterers said that the words entitled them to separate the time sheets; the incidence of a week-end at Vancouver would then result in increased dispatch for them. Mocatta J., holding that the charterers were right, said[76] that the use of the word "reversible" to achieve some form of pooling or aggregation of laytime was "a strange and somewhat forced use of the word." Its use in the phrase "to be reversible," however, rather than the phrase "to be reversed," suggested some element of choice. He considered the four decided cases and decided that the words "for all time saved each end" were inconsistent with the shipowners' obligatory argument as to the construction of "to be reversible," since then dispatch would not be payable for time saved "each end," but only for the time ultimately found at the completion of discharge to have been saved. But if there were an option and the charterers elected not to reverse dispatch could arise at each end.[77]

Special provisions   **9–24**

Sometimes there is provision for dealing with time lost and time saved which does not amount to full reversing. The Socotroisem[78] Mineral Charter-Party, for example, states: "Charterers have the option of adding any time for which dispatch money is payable[79] at the loading port to the total time allowed for discharging; or to deduct any time vessel is on demurrage at the loading port from the total time allowed for discharging." As for the first part of the clause, it is doubtful if charterers could claim dispatch money and add the time to the discharging time. The option would seem to be between these two courses of action, rather than between the first of them and both of them.

A charterparty with special terms as to the transference of time saved, and where time was not truly reversible, was considered by the High Court in *Rowland & Marwood's SS. Co. Ltd.* v. *Wilson, Sons & Co. Ltd.*[80] Clause 5 of a charterparty for the carriage of coal from South Wales to Montevideo stated: "Any hours saved in loading to be added to the hours allowed for discharging." Clause 21 contained the words: "If sooner dispatched than time allowed steamer to pay £8 . . . for every day saved on the time allowed for discharging." In the unamended printed form of the charterparty the words "loading and" appeared before the word "discharging" in Clause 21. Loading and discharging both took less time than that allowed. The shipowners allowed dispatch for the discharging time saved

---

[76] At p. 511.

[77] He said (at p. 513) that his conclusion received "some slight support" from the words "and/or" between "loading" and "discharging." If the obligatory argument were correct one would have expected the words "time allowed for loading *and* discharging"; but he added: "I do not derive more than slight support from this because the words 'and/or' are so freely scattered about charterparties and other shipping documents."

[78] Société Commerciale des Mines, Minéraux et Métaux of Brussels; see also § 12–22, n. 79 below, under "Carrying forward dispatch time."

[79] But not paid. This wording might also result in a divergence from true reversibility, as, where a dispatch clause refers to "all time saved," the discharging time could be augmented by non-lay days, such as Sundays and holidays.

[80] (1897) 2 Com.Cas. 198.

but not in respect of the loading. The High Court held that the shipowners were right; Clause 5 only applied where there was discharging demurrage which could be eliminated or reduced by adding the hours saved in loading. Bruce J. said[81]:

> "I think that clause 5 is intended to have application to the demurrage clause. The hours saved in loading may be added to the hours allowed for discharging for the purpose of calculating the demurrage . . . in mercantile documents it is not always reasonable to expect everything to be expressed with absolute clearness, and I think from the general tenour of the charterparty it may be gathered with sufficient certainty that clause 5 was intended only to be applied to the calculation of the time when demurrage was to begin to run. Had another meaning been intended, I think different words would have been used in clause 5. The words would not have been 'any hours saved in loading to be added to the hours allowed for discharging' but would have been 'any hours saved in loading to be treated as if they were hours saved in discharging' because what the defendants[82] really contend in the present case is that the days saved[83] in loading shall be added to the days *saved* in discharging.[84] . . . The provision with regard to dispatch-money applies only to the days saved on the time allowed for discharging. . . . "

This decision depended to a considerable extent on the wording of the charterparty, on the fact that time was saved at each end, and especially on the deletion of the words[85] "loading and" in the dispatch clause.

---

[81] At pp. 199–200.

[82] The charterers.

[83] The judge's italics.

[84] But the summary of their counsel's argument, as set out in the law report, says, at p. 199: "the 'time allowed for discharging' means the fourteen days allowed by clause 13" [the lay-time clause] "and any time saved in loading."

[85] Where a charterparty is ambiguous the deletion of words in the printed form can be taken into consideration: *Baumvoll* v. *Gilchrest* [1892] 1 Q.B. 253 (C.A.) *per* Lord Esher M.R. at p. 256. See also *London & Overseas Freighters Ltd.* v. *Timber Shipping Co. S.A.* [1971] 1 Lloyd's Rep. 523 (H.L.).

CHAPTER 10

DEMURRAGE

Meaning   **10–01**
Demurrage[1] is an amount payable by charterers[2] to shipowners in respect of delay to the ship as a result of her being kept beyond the agreed[3] or a reasonable time for loading or discharging. As one High Court Judge[4] has said:

> "All the overhead and a large proportion of the running of a ship are incurred even if the ship is in port. Accordingly the shipowner faces serious losses if the processes take longer than he had bargained for and the carrying of freight on the ship's next engagement is postponed. By way of agreed compensation for these losses, the charterer usually contracts to make further payments, called demurrage, at a daily rate in respect of detention beyond the laytime."

The word "demurrage" is used to describe not only the amount but the delay itself. A demurrage stipulation in a charterparty is usually indefinite in nature, as in the words, "demurrage at the rate of £150 per day and *pro rata*." In some rare cases the period on demurrage will be limited. Any delay after the demurrage period, or any delay after the laytime, where there is no demurrage provision, entitles shipowners to damages for detention[5] at a rate assessed by reference to the current trading value of the ship rather than to a previously agreed amount.[5a]

Extension of meaning of demurrage   **10–02**
The term "demurrage" can be extended in its meaning to cover delay other than delay in the physical processes of loading and discharging.[5b] Thus in *Trading Society Kwik-Hoo-Tong of Java* v. *Royal Commission on Sugar Supply*[6] a dispute arose as to demurrage on a contract for the sale of

---

[1] The expression derives from the verb "to demur," *i.e.* "to tarry"; from the French *demeurer,* to stay, stop, remain. The Charterparty Laytime Definitions 1980 (see Appendix to this book) state: "27. 'DEMURRAGE'—means the money payable to the owner for delay for which the owner is not responsible in loading and/or discharging after the laytime has expired." It is essential with loss of freight (Tiberg, "Law of Demurrage," 3rd. ed., 1979, p. 540) and somethimes regarded as a surcharge on freight.
[2] Or other persons, *e.g.* consignees. As to their liability for demurrage, see § 11–01. The word "charterers" is intended here to include other persons who may be liable for demurrage.
[3] For the nature of the breach of contract, see § 10–07 below.
[4] Donaldson J. in *Navico A.G.* v. *Vrontados Naftiki Etairia P.E.* [1968] 1 Lloyd's Rep. 379 at p. 383.
[5] See § 10–38 below.
[5a] In *Mineral ol Handelgesellschaft m.b.H.* v. *Commonwealth Oil Refining Co.*, 734 F.2D 1079, a decision of the U.S. 5th Circuit Court of Appeals, the court acknowledged that demurrage was sometimes referred to as being a form of extended freight. Sellers who had reimbursed the charterers for demurrage sought to recover it from the buyers, but the sale contract imposed liability for "freight" and not for demurrage. The court rejected the argument that in this context the sellers should recover the demurrage as a kind of freight.
[5b] There may be express provision for laytime or demurrage to end when some other event has occurred, as in one London arbitration (LMLN 80, November 25, 1982); see § 1–19 above.
[6] (1924) 19 Ll.L.Rep. 90.

Cuban sugar. Ships provided by the buyers were kept waiting outside the loading port. The question was whether the buyers were entitled to demurrage at the rate agreed in the sale contract or were bound to prove their damages. Roche J. said that the meaning of the word "demurrage" had also been discussed in litigation[7] concerning another ship operating under the same sale contract. In that case Rowlatt J. had pointed out that demurrage in origin did not mean a sum payable for breach of contract. It meant a sum payable under a contract for unjustifiably detaining a ship at the port of loading or port of discharge. Cleasby B. in *Lockhart* v. *Falk*[8] had said:

> "The word 'demurrage' no doubt properly signifies the agreed additional payment (generally per day) for an allowed detention beyond a period either specified in or to be collected from the instrument; but it has also a popular or more general meaning of compensation for undue detention, and from the whole of each charterparty containing the clause in question we must collect what is the proper meaning to be assigned to it."

Roche J. then said that in the case before him the word "demurrage" was undoubtedly used to mean damages for breach of contract. The question was: for what breach or breaches were the damages due?

10–03   The sale contract had provided that if there was delay in bringing up the sugar the sellers should pay demurrage; that had been fixed at £200 per day. The sellers argued that the word was only applicable to damages for delay in loading and had no application where there was a default in naming or selecting the loading port or delay in beginning loading. The buyers said that the demurrage covered such default. Concluding that the buyers were right, Roche J. said[9] that for many years demurrage had had a tendency to extend its meaning:

> " . . . people use demurrage very often as expressing aptly and conveniently damages for delay in connection with either the loading or discharging of a ship or for matters such as railway trucks."

The difference between the technical and the wider definitions of demurrage was also emphasised in *The Varing*.[10] During congestion at Garston Dock, timber receivers insisted on discharge into "domestic" rather than main line railway wagons. Scrutton L.J. commented[11]:

> " . . . unless a certain state of facts existed[12] . . . the consignees were preventing, and wrongfully preventing, the ship from reaching the place provided for in the charter. The result would not be demurrage, technically, but it would be damages for preventing the ship from reaching her place of discharge—which would have practically the same result as if there was a claim for demurrage."

So also Greer L.J.[13]:

> "She is not entitled to demurrage properly so-called, because after she got to the place of discharge she was discharged within the contract time. What she is entitled to is damages for detention during the four days in which she was prevented, by the wrongful attitude taken up by the receivers, from getting into the place of discharge."

---

[7] A case of the same name; (1920) 15 Ll.L.Rep. 24.
[8] (1875) L.R. 10 Ex. 132 at p. 135.
[9] At p. 92.
[10] [1931] P. 79. See § 4–42 above.
[11] At p. 89. At p. 83 he spoke of "the claim being for either demurrage, or what I may call quasi demurrage."
[12] *i.e.* unless, as alleged by the receivers, delivery could not have been made without sorting on the quay or the storing ground.
[13] At p. 93.

The sum awarded was in fact based on the demurrage rate of £30 per day and *pro rata*.

It has been agreed between the parties that a ship may be on demurrage although discharge has not begun and she is waiting at a considerable distance from the discharge port. In *Islamic Republic of Iran Shipping Lines v. The Royal Bank of Scotland*[14] a ship carrying coal from Emden, West Germany, to Bandar Khomeini, Iran, waited off Bandar Abbas, 600 miles to the south, for nearly four months before discharging. The charterers had been content for her to wait, in view of the hostilities between Iran and Iraq; after two months they ordered her to join a northbound convoy but most of the officers and crew refused to go. The charterers eventually ordered the ship into Bandar Abbas to discharge. It was common ground between the parties that laytime ended about two weeks after arrival off Bandar Abbas.

A question arose as to whether an exceptions clause, providing that waiting time should not count as laytime, ceased to be relevant when laytime expired, about two weeks after arrival off Bandar Abbas; the charterers said that it ceased to be relevant only after the refusal to join the convoy. It was held that the shipowners' contention, that the principle "once on demurrage, always on demurrage,"[15] came into operation when laytime expired, was correct.

Steyn J., referring to the word "demurrage," said[16]:

> "That term is sometimes extended to cover delays other than delay in the physical processes of loading and discharging. The present case is an example of such an extended meaning, because it is common ground that the vessel was on demurrage while waiting off Bandar Abbas. And Bandar Abbas is a port in the vicinity of the Straits of Hormuz, and several hundreds of miles to the south of Bandar Khomeini."

Charterparty provisions   **10–04**

In most charterparties there is a provision for demurrage. It will usually put no term on the demurrage period; but it may limit it by stating, for example, a number of days.

Unlimited demurrage period   **10–05**

These are examples of provisions for demurrage where no term is put on the demurrage period:

"If the Vessel be detained beyond her loading time the Charterers to pay Demurrage at the rate of . . . per running hour."

" . . . demurrage shall be paid at the rate of threepence British Sterling per gross register ton per running day and *pro rata* for any part of a day. Such demurrage shall be paid day by day, when and where incurred."[17]

"Charterers shall pay demurrage at . . . % of the demurrage rate applicable to vessels of a similar size to the vessel as provided for in Worldscale current at the date of commencement of loading per running day and pro rata for part of a running day for all time by which the allowed laytime specified in clause 13 hereof is exceeded by the time taken to load and discharge and which under the provisions of this charter counts as laytime or for demurrage."

The demurrage rate may be calculated by reference to Worldscale, as

---

[14] [1987] 1 Lloyd's Rep. 266 (*The Anna Ch.*).
[15] See § 10–50 below.
[16] *Ibid.* at p. 269.
[17] Australian Grain Charter 1928 (Austral).

"by applying the London Tanker Brokers Panel's Monthly Average Freight Rate Assessment (AFRA) published in the month of loading applicable to vessels of a similar size to the demurrage rate appropriate to the size of vessel provided for in . . . Worldscale."[17a]

10–06 *Limited demurrage period*

This is an example of a provision for demurrage where the demurrage period is limited:

"Ten running days on demurrage at the rate stated in Box 18 per day or *pro rata* for any part of a day, payable day by day, to be allowed Merchants altogether at ports of loading and discharging."[18]

10–07 Nature of breach of contract[19]

Charterers are in breach of the charterparty where the loading or discharging has not been completed before the expiry of the laytime, but the breach is not (in the absence of some exceptional circumstances or charterparty terms to the contrary) one which entitles shipowners to treat the contract as at an end, and to sail away. The exceptional circumstances which would justify such a course include cases where there is such inordinate delay that shipowners are entitled to regard the charterparty as terminated.[20] The distinction here is similar to that made, in the case of other contracts, between breaches of condition and breaches of warranty.[21] As conditions are terms which go to the root of the contract, their breach usually entitles the aggrieved party to treat the contract as repudiated,[22] and at an end, and to claim damages. Warranties being collateral terms, their breach entitles the aggrieved party only to claim damages. So also in the case of the charterparty (unless there are other terms to the contrary) detention of the ship beyond the lay days is a breach of warranty. Time is not of the essence of the contract.[23] The effect of such a breach may depend upon whether the charterparty provides for demurrage, and, if it provides for demurrage, whether a demurrage period is stated or not.

10–08 *Delay as a permissible breach*

In the case of a consecutive voyage charterparty for a fixed period of time, where the number of voyages has not been agreed, it has been argued

---

[17a] A ship may be chosen which is too large for the contractual consignment. A London panel of arbitrators held, by a majority, that this would be unjust and inequitable, and not in accordance with usual practice. It was necessary to imply a term that sellers, under the sale contract, should not be liable for demurrage at a rate exceeding that applicable to a ship of the necessary size "plus a margin of X%." They then calculated demurrage on that basis, adding about four per cent. (LMLN 160, January 2, 1986.)

[18] Uniform General Charter 1976 (Gencon).

[19] For the nature of the damages resulting from the breach, see § 10–25 below.

[20] *Universal Cargo Carriers Corporation* v. *Citati* [1957] 2 Q.B. 401. See § 10–21 below.

[21] Though there may be intermediate stipulations: *Cehave N.V.* v. *Bremer Handelgesellschaft m.b.H.* [1976] Q.B. 44 (C.A.).

[22] As in *Behn* v. *Burness* (1963) 3 B. & S. 751; inaccurate statement in a charterparty that a ship was "now in the port of Amsterdam" held to be a condition, breach of which entitled the charterers to repudiate the contract.

[23] *Atkieselskabet Reidar* v. *Arcos Ltd.* [1927] 1 K.B. (C.A.) *per* Bankes L.J. at p. 361; "I prefer to rest the necessity for remaining upon the ground that, time not being of the essence of the contract, the shipowner will not, except under some exceptional circumstances, be in a position to assert that the contract had been repudiated unless the vessel does remain a sufficient time to enable that question to be tested." See § 10–29 below.

unsuccessfully[24] by shipowners that charterers must perform such number of voyages as prevents the ship from going on demurrage. In this way, shipowners contended, they could be assured of a profit on a greater number of voyages. As an alternative argument they said that the loss of earnings under the voyages that would have been performed constituted special damages not covered by demurrage. This contention was also rejected.[25]

Charterers can keep the ship throughout the laytime provided that they **10–09** need the ship for loading or discharging[26]; the question then arises as to the nature of their rights after laytime ends. The days which follow are not lay days, or even, in the absence of a fixed demurrage period, "lay days that have to be paid for."[27] It may be argued that charterers have a right to detain the ship beyond the lay days if they have work for the ship. A truer picture is presented if it is said that shipowners do not necessarily have the right to take their ship away, merely because the lay days have ended. Where persons—in this case charterers—break a contract, it is incorrect to describe them as exercising a right. But as they are only in breach of a warranty, they have the right to insist that shipowners should not as a result treat the contract as being at an end.[28] Time is not, in the absence of express terms or special circumstances, of the essence; a right to rescind therefore only accrues to shipowners if there is such a delay after the expiry of laytime (or after the expiry of laytime combined with any limited demurrage period agreed in the charterparty) as amounts to frustration, or such conduct by charterers in addition to mere delay as constitutes a fundamental breach of contract. In either of those events shipowners can sail away and claim unliquidated damages. Until that event occurs, and the ship has sailed away,[29] they are restricted, so far as they complain that charterers have delayed the ship, to their demurrage claim for liquidated damages at the daily rate stipulated in the demurrage clause. Where there is an agreed number of days for demurrage, shipowners are entitled to damages for detention from the expiry of the demurrage period until there is frustration, or such conduct by charterers in addition to mere delay as constitutes a fundamental breach.

The expiry of laytime does not therefore entitle shipowners to sail. The **10–10** same principle applies where laytime is not fixed, so that the ship comes on demurrage after the expiry of a reasonable time for loading or discharging. In *Wilson & Coventry Ltd.* v. *Otto Thoresen's Line*[30] a charterparty for the carriage of straw from Calais to Las Palmas contained no fixed time for laytime or demurrage. It stated: "Cargo to be loaded and discharged as fast as steamer can receive and deliver as customary at respective ports and during

---

[24] In *Suisse Atlantique Société d'Armement Maritime S.A.* v. *N.V. Rotterdamsche Kolen Centrale* [1966] 1 Lloyd's Rep. 529 (H.L.) (*The General Guisan*). See § 10–31 below.
[25] This alternative argument is considered at § 9–29 in connection with the decision in *Atkieselskabet Reidar* v. *Arcos* [1927] 1 K.B. 352 (C.A.).
[26] *Petersen* v. *Dunn* (1895) 1 Com.Cas. 8; *Margaronis Navigation Agency Ltd.* v. *Henry W. Peabody & Co. of London Ltd.* [1964] 1 Lloyd's Rep. 173; and *Shipping Developments Corporations S.A.* v. *V/O Sojuzneftexport* [1971] 1 Lloyd's Rep. 506 (*The Delian Spirit*) per Lord Denning M.R. at p. 509; and see §§ 1–06–1–08 above.
[27] As they were described by Lord Trayner in *Lilly* v. *Stevenson* (1895) 22 R. 278 at p. 286. There was a fixed demurrage period.
[28] See *Aktieselskabet Reidar* v. *Arcos* [1927] 1 K.B. 352 (C.A.) *per* Bankes L.J. at pp. 360–361. See also § 10–29 below.
[29] For the nature of the breach, see § 10–22 below.
[30] [1910] 2 K.B. 404.

customary working hours thereof"; and: "If vessel be longer detained to be paid at the rate of four pence per gross register ton per day." It was found that a reasonable time for loading would have been two and a half days; the master, anxious to arrive at Las Palmas in time to leave with a return cargo on the advertised date, left Calais before the two and a half days expired. Had he waited about 24 hours longer the shippers, who did not have all the cargo ready, could have loaded a full cargo. It was held that the ship was not entitled to sail when she did or even at the end of the laytime. As Bray J. said[31]:

> "I think it must be taken as settled since *Dimech* v. *Corlett*[32] that if the charterparty provides a fixed number of demurrage days the ship must wait for those days if the charterer requires it and there is ground for believing that further cargo will be loaded. In this charterparty demurrage is provided for, but not for any fixed time. It seemed to me and I suggested during the argument that in such a case it is the duty of the ship to wait for a reasonable time."[33]

He then adopted the words of Lord Trayner in *Lilly* v. *Stevenson*[34]:

> "Where the days on demurrage are not limited by contract they will be limited by law to what is reasonable[35] in the circumstances, as circumstances may happen to exist or to emerge,"

and said that the charterers were entitled to keep the ship at least till the further period of about 24 hours had expired.

10–11   Absolute nature of laytime warranty

Although a fixed laytime provision in a charterparty is a warranty rather than a condition,[36] so that its mere breach does not entitle shipowners to treat the contract as at an end, it is nevertheless an absolute warranty.[37] Proof by charterers that they exercised due diligence to load the cargo in time, for example, will not excuse them from liability for demurrage. Such liability can only be avoided where charterers can show that the delay was caused by the fault[38] of shipowners or of the employees, servants or other agents of shipowners,[39] or where the charterers are assisted by exceptions

---

[31] At p. 408.

[32] (1858) 12 Moo.P.C. 199 at p. 231.

[33] At the expiry of the reasonable time shipowners may take the ship away, if the charterparty can then be regarded as repudiated by the charterers or frustrated, but until then the demurrage rate applies. As to whether it applies thereafter, if the ship is not removed, see the same judge's remarks in *Western SS. Co.* v. *Amaral Sutherland & Co.* [1913] K.B. 366 at p. 371; see also § 10–16 below.

[34] (1895) 22 R. 278 at p. 286.

[35] But the mere expiry of a reasonable time does not permit the shipowners to sail; see § 10–22 below.

[36] *Atkieselskabet Reidar* v. *Arcos* [1927] 1 K.B. 352 (C.A.); and see § 10–07 above.

[37] Whether the laytime is expressly stated or calculable by reference to the tonnage or in some other way; *Alexander* v. *Aktieselskabet Hansa* [1920] A.C. 88 (H.L.).

[38] Not by their mere act. See *Houlder* v. *Weir* [1905] 2 K.B. 267. See also § 10–12 below. But in a Californian case it has been held that shipowners could not recover demurrage where the notice of readiness was given but the ship had then to wait for longshoremen to load a cargo being carried under a different contract of shipment. No damage had been suffered by shipowners: *D'Amico Mediterranean Pacific Line Inc.* v. *Proctor and Gamble Manufacturing Co.* [1975] 1 Lloyd's Rep. 202 (U.S. District Court for Northern District of California). Different facts and terms may lead to other results. In *Randall* v. *Sprague* 74 F. 247 (1st Cir. 1896) shippers sought unsuccessfully to avoid payment of demurrage on the ground that the ship could not sail after loading because the harbour was blocked by ice.

[39] See *Budgett* v. *Binnington* [1891] 1 Q.B. 35; and see § 9–12 below.

in the charterparty,[40] or where working the ship is made illegal by the law of the place of performance.[41]

Thus where receivers are prevented by bad weather[42] or by other receivers from moving their goods, they will still be held liable for demurrage.[43] So also where there is congestion of ships, receivers may be liable for demurrage even though they are not to blame for the congestion[44]; and they are liable even where the ships are controlled by the same shipowners whose responsibility it is to provide "as nearly as possible a steamer a month."[45]

Absolute warranty modified by shipowners' fault, etc.   **10–12**

Despite the absolute nature of the laytime warranty,[46] charterers may not be liable for demurrage where they can show that the delay was attributable to shipowners or to the employees, servants or agents of the shipowners,[46a] or that they are protected by exceptions in the charterparty; or that the loading or discharging was illegal by the law of the place of performance.[47]

In *Houlder* v. *Weir*[48] ballast was taken towards the end of the discharge for the safety of the ship and of the cargo remaining on board. As a result the laytime was exceeded. The charterers were held liable for demurrage. Channell J. said[49]:

"The remaining question is whether the days on which the vessel was taking in ballast as well as discharging cargo should be reckoned as whole days or not. I think they ought. When Lord Esher in *Budgett* v. *Binnington*[50] said that 'if the shipowner by any act of his

---

[40] Such as the strike clause in the River Plate Charter-Party 1914 (Centrocon). See § 10–57 below.

[41] *Overseas Transportation Company* v. *Mineralimportexport* [1971] 1 Lloyd's Rep. 514 (*The Sinoe*). See § 11–43 below.

[42] As in *Thiis* v. *Byers* (1876) 1 Q.B.D. 244. The master was prevented by bad weather from putting timber cargo over the side into the Tees, and forming rafts with it, so that the receivers could tow the timber away. They were held liable for demurrage though they were willing and able to perform their part of the work.

[43] As in *Porteus* v. *Watney* (1878) 3 Q.B.D. 534 (C.A.). The shipowners claimed three days' demurrage from the receivers, including one who had been prevented, by delay on the part of the others, from collecting his cargo. That one was held liable for demurrage despite having done everything possible to secure the goods.

[44] As in *Randall* v. *Lynch* (1810) 2 Camp. 352. Discharging laytime at the London Docks was 40 days; the ship was kept on demurrage thereafter for 41 days as the docks were congested, and the charterers were held liable.

[45] As in *Potter* v. *Burrell* [1897] 1 Q.B. 97. The arrival of two ships at once, in a port with limited facilities, was caused by excepted perils. As the shipowners were not responsible the liability of the charterers for demurrage was unaffected.

[46] See § 10–11 above.

[46a] There may be a breach of contract by shipowners which results in damages not reasonably foreseeable. In a London arbitration (LMLN 134, December 20, 1984) a ship was delayed in sailing from the loading port by the temporary absence, for personal reasons, of the chief engineer. She was therefore unseaworthy. As a result the New Year holiday and an adjacent week-end occurred while she was on demurrage, at the discharging port; otherwise they would have passed during laytime, and would have been excepted periods. It was held that at the date of the contract this was not "reasonably foreseeable, on the cards or not unlikely to occur." It might be otherwise if it had been reasonably expected that discharging would take longer than the 48 hours allowed.

[47] See *Overseas Transportation Company* v. *Mineralimportexport (The Sinoe)* [1971] 1 Lloyd's Rep. 514 at p. 519.

[48] [1905] 2 K.B. 267.

[49] At p. 271.

[50] [1891] 1 Q.B. 35 (C.A.) at p. 38.

had prevented the discharge, then, though the freighter's contract is broken, he is excused,' he was referring to a case in which the shipowner's act preventing the discharge was in breach of his obligation to give the charterer all facilities for the discharge. But here the act of the shipowner which delayed the discharge was not a breach of any obligation of his. The taking in of ballast in the course of the discharge was a thing necessary to be done."

10–13   This comment by Lord Esher M.R. in *Budgett* v. *Binnington*,[50] cited above in *Houlder* v. *Weir*,[48] was also considered in *Overseas Transportation Company* v. *Mineralimportexport*.[51] Inefficient stevedores were appointed by the charterers but under the charterparty they were the shipowners' servants. They were responsible for the delay beyond the laytime. Donaldson J. said[52]:

"Mr. Lloyd [Counsel for the shipowners] also relied upon a passage in the judgment of Lord Esher M.R. in *Budgett & Co.* v. *Binnington & Co.*[50] . . . which suggested that the class of persons for whom the owners were responsible in the context might be very limited indeed—perhaps extending no further than the master. Whatever the basis for this suggestion Lord Esher M.R. had revised his view two years later in *Harris* v. *Best, Ryley & Co.*[53] . . . when he held that charterers were not liable to pay demurrage in respect of delay caused by stevedores employed by the shipowners."

The charterers were responsible for employing and paying the stevedores; they were exempted from liability for the negligence of the stevedores, and charterers' agents had to be notified of stevedore damage. On the other hand stevedores were to be considered as shipowner's servants and were subject to the master's orders and directions. Donaldson J. concluded[54]:

"If I had to decide this point, I should hold that the charterparty does not sufficiently clearly make the owners responsible for the fault of the stevedores to rebut the prima facie liability of the charterers to pay for the detention of the vessel. Fortunately I do not have to decide it because even if I were to be in the charterers favour on that point, they have, in my judgment, no answer to the owners' rejoinder, that in employing or causing or allowing these particular stevedores to be employed, the charterers were in breach of their duty[55] to the owners. If this is right, the charterers are unable to rely upon the neglect of the stevedores as barring the owners' claim to demurrage or alternatively are liable to the owners in a like amount as damages for breach of their obligation to employ competent stevedores."

10–14   *Demurrage not succeeded by detention damages*
    A question may arise as to the rights of shipowners after the expiry of a reasonable time on demurrage. They may be concerned as to whether after a time on demurrage they may claim damages for detention (perhaps at a higher rate than the demurrage rate) and as to whether they may treat the charterparty as being at an end. Where the charterparty does not stipulate a fixed period for demurrage,[56] then so long as the contractual relationship subsists they can only claim demurrage, which is recoverable at the agreed rate.[57]

[51] [1971] 1 Lloyd's Rep. 514 (*The Sinoe*). See § 11–43 below.
[52] *Op. cit.* at p. 519.
[53] (1892) 68 L.T. 76.
[54] *Op. cit.* at p. 520. In *Blue Anchor Line Ltd.* v. *Alfred C. Toepfer International G.m.b.H.* [1982] 2 Lloyd's Rep. 432 (*The Union Amsterdam*) Parker J. said that Donaldson J. appeared to have accepted that delay by act or omission of the shipowners which did not amount to a breach of contract or duty remained the liability of the charterers. In his view that conflicted with the Court of Appeal decision in the *Ropner Shipping* case [1927] 1 K.B. 879; see § 10–68 below.
[55] As for the charterers' duty to nominate good stevedores, see § 1–14 above.
[56] As in the words "ten days on demurrage."
[57] *Western SS. Co.* v. *Amaral Sutherland & Co.* [1913] 3 K.B. 366; *Inverkip SS. Co. Ltd.* v. *Bunge & Co.* [1917] 2 K.B. 193 (C.A.). See also § 10–18 below.

There is thus no intermediate stage between the expiry of the demurrage **10–15** period and the moment at which shipowners can regard the charterparty as having been terminated by repudiation or frustration. There is no middle period during which they can merely claim damages for detention.

In *Inverkip SS. Co. Ltd.* v. *Bunge & Co.*[58] a charterparty for the carriage of grain from Galveston to the Mediterranean stated: "Steamer to be loaded according to the berth terms, with customary berth dispatch, and if detained longer than five days, Sundays and holidays excepted, charterers to pay demurrage at the rate of fourpence British sterling, or its equivalent, per net register ton per day, or *pro rata*, payable day by day, provided such detention shall occur by default of charterers or their agents." As Galveston port had been damaged by a tidal wave the ship was ordered to load at Newport News. After the five lay days had passed, 16 days of demurrage were incurred and loading had not begun. The shipowners claimed damages for detention from then on, at a rate substantially higher than the demurrage rate. They argued that where demurrage days were not limited by contract they were limited by law to what was reasonable in the circumstances, and that damages for detention then became due. The Court of Appeal rejected this argument. Scrutton L.J. said[59]:

> "To enable the ship to abandon the charter without the consent of the charterer I think the shipowners must show either such a failure to load as amounts to a repudiation of or final refusal to perform the charter, which the shipowner may accept as a final breach and depart claiming damages[60]—*Mersey Steel & Iron Co.* v. *Naylor, Benzon & Co.*[61]—or such a commercial frustration of the adventure by delay under the doctrine of *Jackson* v. *Union Marine Insurance Co.*[62] as puts an end to the contract . . . "

He concluded[63]:

> "The truth is the shipowners have made a bad bargain as to demurrage rate in loading, emphasised by their having secured an agreement for a much higher demurrage rate for discharging, and are anxious to get out of it. I can see no valid legal or business reasons for helping them to do so."

Similarly, in *Western SS. Co. Ltd.* v. *Amaral Sutherland & Co.*[64] the **10–16** High Court had held that "in the absence of an express provision in the charterparty that the demurrage rate should only apply to a reasonable

---

[58] [1917] 2 K.B. 193 (C.A.); see also *Western SS. Co.* v. *Amaral Sutherland & Co.* [1913] 3 K.B. 366.

[59] At p. 201.

[60] It seems doubtful whether shipowners could stay and claim damages for detention in respect of the period following the time at which they became entitled to depart.

[61] (1884) 9 App.Cas. 434 (H.L.); a House of Lords decision concerning a sale contract. Lord Selborne L.C. said at pp. 438–439; "You must look at the actual circumstances of the case in order to see whether the one party to the contract is relieved from its future performance by the conduct of the other; you must examine what that conduct is, so as to see whether it amounts to a renunciation, to an absolute refusal to perform the contract, such as would amount to a rescission if he had the power to rescind, and whether the other party may accept it as a reason for not performing his part."

[62] (1874) L.R. 10 C.P. 125; an Exchequer Chamber decision concerning a freight insurance policy and the frustration of a voyage. At p. 141 Bramwell B. repeated with approval the finding of the jury, saying: " . . . the finding of the jury that the time necessary to get the ship off and repairing her so as to be a cargo-carrying ship was so long as to put an end in a commercial sense to the commercial speculation entered into by the shipowner and charterers' is all important."

[63] [1917] 2 K.B. 193 at p. 203 (C.A.).

[64] [1913] 3 K.B. 366. The appeal by the shipowners, [1914] 3 K.B. 55, succeeded on a technical point, concerning an earlier order for trial of this preliminary point of law. The Court of Appeal refrained from commenting on the views of Bray J.

number of days, it applies as long as the ship is in fact detained."[65] Although the same principles arose as were to be discussed by the Court of Appeal in the *Inverkip*[66] case the judgment contains some comments on the situation arising where the ship could, but does not, sail away. Even if the landing of the cargo is possible, the circumstances which brought the delay would make such a proceeding difficult. The shipowners might also wish to take steps to preserve their lien. Two ships carrying coal had to wait at Rio de Janeiro for about six weeks after laytime had ended for their discharge to be completed. The shipowners contended that a reasonable time on demurrage would in each case have been 10 days, and that thereafter they were entitled to damages for detention at a higher rate. Discharging was to be at an average rate of 500 tons per day; "if longer detained consignees to pay steamer demurrage at the rate of fourpence per net register ton per running day or pro rata thereof." The charterers said that no provision, either express or implied, was contained in either of the charterparties that the agreed rate of demurrage should only apply to a reaonable number of days over and above the lay days. Upholding the charterers' argument, Bray J. said[67]:

> "So long as the steamer is in fact detained at the agreed rate of demurrage is what the charterer has to pay. . . . The shipowner has his choice which remedy he will adopt. In this case, if he had thought that the demurrage rate would be insufficient to recoup him for the detention, he could have landed the coals and taken his ship away. But he did not do that, and under those circumstances he is only entitled, by way of compensation for the detention, to the demurrage rate and no more."

In the case of a delayed discharge it would seem that if shipowners neither sail away nor take their own steps to land the cargo, they may be limited to a claim for demurrage. They have not accepted the conduct of charterers as amounting to a repudiation, and the contract therefore subsists.[68] Where a ship is awaiting a cargo, it would seem that the mere fact that the ship remains at the port does not disentitle shipowners from claiming damages for detention. They could only do so, however, if the conduct of charterers was equivalent to a repudiation of the charterparty, and if they treated it as such.

10–17   **Time waiting for orders.** Demurrage time, where the demurrage period is not fixed, does not yield to a time for which detention damages are payable, unless the contract itself has been repudiated or frustrated.[69] So also where a rate has been agreed for delay while awaiting orders[70] or where a specific period is to be treated as laytime and then demurrage[71]; the damages are treated as liquidated damages and the shipowners' claim is restricted accordingly. Similarly, where there is delay in ordering a port of discharge, the ship must await orders until the delay becomes such as to frustrate the voyage.[72]

---

[65] The words used by Bray J. at p. 371.
[66] [1917] 2 K.B. 193.
[67] At pp. 370 and 371.
[68] As was the case in *Chandris* v. *Isbrandtsen-Moller Co. Inc.* [1951] 1 K.B. 240; see § 10–37 below.
[69] *Inverkip SS. Co. Ltd.* v. *Bunge & Co.* [1917] 2 K.B. 193 (C.A.); see § 10–15 above.
[70] *Ethel Radcliffe SS. Co. Ltd.* v. *W. & R. Barnett Ltd.* (1926) 31 Com.Cas. 222 (C.A.).
[71] *Britain SS. Co. Ltd.* v. *Donugol of Charkoff* (1932) 44 Ll.L.Rep. 123. See § 10–18.
[72] *Zim Israel Navigation Ltd.* v. *Tradax Export S.A.* [1970] 2 Lloyd's Rep. 409 (*The Timna*). But damages for detention may be recoverable; see n. 64 below.

In *Ethel Radcliffe SS. Co. Ltd.* v. *W. & R. Barnett Ltd.*[73] a ship chartered to carry grain from the River Plate to Europe was kept for 13 days at St. Vincent, in the Cape Verde Islands, waiting for orders. The charterparty provided that for any such detention (after the first twenty-four hours) the charterers were to pay 30 shillings per hour. It was held that the shipowners could only claim this amount; as Atkin L.J. said,[74] comparing the provisions before him with those more commonly met:

> " . . . it appears to me that the 24 hours are the lay days and the 30s. per hour is the demurrage, and that the shipowner cannot say that the provision for 30s. per hour only applies to a reasonable time, after the lapse of which he can claim damages for detention."

10–18 The shipowners were also held to be restricted to the amount set out in the charterparty, and not entitled to damages at large, in *Britain SS. Co. Ltd.* v. *Donugol of Charkoff.*[75] They claimed damages for a period during which the ship was detained by ice, en route to the loading port of Mariupol, owing to the breach of chaterparty by the charterers in failing to provide adequate ice-breaking assistance. The charterparty stated: " . . . any detention caused by ice to the steamer in reaching the said port of loading . . . shall in the first case count as time for loading and in the second case as time on demurrage to be paid by the charterers at charter rate, from which time days saved in loading shall be deducted. . . . " Roche J. held that this provision was effective notwithstanding the breach by the charterers. He compared the claim to that made by the shipowners in *Inverkip SS. Co. Ltd.* v. *Bunge & Co.*[76] In that case only demurrage was recoverable in spite of a breach of contract by the charterers who had failed to provide a cargo.[77]

10–19 **When is the contract at an end?** When a ship is on demurrage a stage may be reached at which the contract can be regarded as at an end.[78] That stage is reached when either (1) the charterers by conduct or by words show that they are unable to perform, or say that they are willing to perform but that they are unable to do so: such conduct or words amount to a repudiation of the contract; or (2) the frustration of the venture has put an end to the contract.[79] The charterers are thus not entitled to delay the ship indefinitely. If their conduct is equivalent to a repudiation the shipowners may accept it as such, and sail away,[80] claiming damages. Alternatively the shipowners may choose to leave the ship where she is; if so, they are restricted to demurrage at the agreed rate. Of the intention of the charterers to repudiate, it has been said[81]:

---

[73] (1926) 31 Com.Cas. 222 (C.A.).
[74] At p. 237.
[75] [1932] 44 Ll.L.Rep. 123.
[76] [1917] 2 K.B. 193 (C.A.). See § 10–15 above.
[77] So also in *Shipping Developments Corporation S.A.* v. *V/O Sojuzneftexport* [1971] 1 Lloyd's Rep. 506 (C.A.) a failure by charterers to name a place reachable on the arrival of the ship did not entitle shipowners to damages if in respect of the same period of delay time was counting. See § 4–20 above.
[78] *Inverkip SS. Co. Ltd.* v. *Bunge & Co.* [1917] 2 K.B. 193 (C.A.); and see § 10–15 above.
[79] See § 10–22 below.
[80] *Inverkip SS. Co.* v. *Bunge & Co.* [1917] 2 K.B. 193 (C.A.) at § 10–15; *Ethel Radcliffe SS. Co.* v. *Barnett* (1926) 31 Com.Cas. 222 (C.A.) at p. 223; *Chandris* v. *Isbrandtsen-Moller Co. Inc.* [1951] 1 K.B. 240 at p. 253.
[81] By Devlin J. in *Universal Cargo Carriers Corporation* v. *Pedro Citati* [1957] 2 Q.B. 401 at p. 436.

> "The test of whether an intention is sufficiently evinced by conduct is whether the party renunciating has acted in such a way as to lead a reasonable person to the conclusion that he does not intend to fulfil his part of the contract."

10–20   The principles in such cases are similar to those which apply where a ship is waiting to load and is not yet on demurrage. In *Universal Cargo Carriers Corporation* v . *Pedro Citati*[82] a charterparty for the carriage of scrap from Basrah to Buenos Aires stated: "Cargo to be brought alongside in such a manner as to enable vessel to . . . load . . . the cargo at the rate of 1000 tons per weather working day. . . . " Attempts by the shipowners to get in touch with the shippers at Basrah were unsuccessful. Six days after the arrival of the ship, and three days before the lay days expired, the shipowners re-chartered her and ordered her away. They then claimed damages and argued that they could treat the charterparty as at an end before the lay days expired, as the charterers had committed an actual or an anticipatory breach of their obligations. The charterers were willing but unable to perform their duties within the lay days or a reaonable time thereafter; but they could have done so before the delay was so long as to frustrate the charterparty. The issue was summarised by Devlin J. in the Commercial Court[83]:

> "This case gives rise to a difficult question. How long is a ship obliged to remain on demurrage, and what are the rights of the owner if the charterer detains her too long?"

In this type of contract time is not of the esssence,[84] so that mere failure to load in the lay days is not a breach of a condition but a breach of warranty. The judge confirmed this settled view of the law saying[85]:

> "It is well settled, and not in this case disputed, that the obligation to load within the lay days is a warranty only and not a condition. Its breach does not entitle the owner to rescind but gives rise to a claim for damages only, and in this charterparty, as in most others, those damages are liquidated damages paid in the form of demurrage. It would be strange if, when the main obligation to load is only a warranty, preliminary obligations[86] should be given the status of a condition."

10–21   **Delay must go to root of contract.** Mere failure to load within the lay days is not a breach of contract entitling shipowners to treat the contract as at an end.[87] They can regard the contract as being at an end either where the charterers by conduct or words can be taken to have renounced the charterparty; or where the charterparty is impossible of performance. Where delay is the occasion of the renunciation or the impossibility, then such delay is said to have gone to the root of the contract. In the case of renunciation charterers are then in breach of a condition as opposed to a warranty.[88] In the case of impossibility the object of the contract is frustrated

---

[82] [1957] 2 Q.B. 401.
[83] At p. 426.
[84] *Atkieselkabet Reidar* v. *Arcos Ltd.* [1927] 1 K.B. 352 (C.A.); and see § 10–07 above.
[85] At pp. 429–430.
[86] In that case: (1) to nominate shippers; (2) to nominate a berth; (3) to have a cargo available, as opposed to the main obligation, which is to load it, and (4) to finish loading before the expiry of the lay days.
[87] *Universal Cargo Carriers Corporation* v. *Pedro Citati* [1957] 2 Q.B. 401.
[88] A condition and a warranty were distinguished in *Behn* v. *Burness* (1863) 3 B. & S. 751. The charterparty stated that the ship was "now in the port of Amsterdam." This was not so; the Court of Exchequer Chamber held that the statement was a breach of condition, so that repudiation was justified.

although charterers are not in breach.[89] Devlin J. said in *Universal Cargo Carriers*[90] that it was not relevant to consider whether a reasonable time had elapsed, and to apply such a period as a yardstick. Either the delay is such that it justifies merely the claim for breach of warranty, or it is such that it goes to the root of the contract, whether or not the charterers are at fault. The theory that shipowners are entitled to remove the ship after a reasonable time has elapsed is only correct if the expiry of a reasonable time occurs at the moment when the delay goes to the root of the contract. Thus Devlin J.[91]:

> "The truth is that there is nothing wrong in using a reasonable time as a yardstick provided you determine what is reasonable by considering whether or not there has been unreasonable delay in the light of the object which the parties had in mind. It is only when the two yardsticks have in effect been shown to be the same that the Courts have accepted the test of reasonableness. Where they have been contrasted, as in *Clipsham* v. *Vertue*[92] and *Tarrabochia* v. *Hickie*,[93] the test of reasonable time has been rejected."

The mere expiry of a reasonable time on demurrage or of a fixed demurrage period does not entitle the shipowners to sail away. Thus Bray J. spoke in *Wilson & Coventry Ltd.* v. *Otto Thoresen's Linie*[94] of "the duty of the ship to wait for a reasonable time." But Scrutton L.J. criticised these words in *Inverkip SS. Co. Ltd.* v. *Bunge & Co.*,[95] saying that he could not agree with the decision so far as it allowed the ship to sail at a reasonable time after the expiry of the lay days.

In *Unitramp* v. *Garnac Grain Co. Inc.*[96] a ship had been delayed after leaving Destrehan, Louisiana, by congestion, the grounding of two other ships and lack of water in a channel. Roskill L.J. said: "It is now clear law since the *Citati* case that a shipowner cannot throw up a charterparty merely because there has been (to use the phrase used in the special case here) 'commercially unacceptable delay,' that is to say, delay exceeding a reasonable time. The delay in such a case must, before he can seek to rescind and treat the charterer's conduct as a repudiation of the charterer's obligation to load, be such as will frustrate the adventure."

Detention by default of charterers   **10–22**
Normally demurrage is due because mere detention beyond the agreed laytime is sufficient to impute a breach of contract to the charterers. Where the charterparty is appropiately worded the existence of such a breach may be negatived so that demurrage is only due in certain circumstances. A proviso, by which demurrage is only due if detention occurred by default of the charterers, is frequently used to achieve this object.

---

[89] Self-induced frustration is not frustration: *Maritime National Fish Ltd.* v. *Ocean Trawlers Ltd.* [1935] A.C. 524 (H.L.) and *Bank Line* v. *Arthur Capel & Co.* [1919] A.C. 435 (H.L.).
[90] [1957] 2 Q.B. 401. See § 10–20 above.
[91] At pp. 434–435.
[92] (1843) 5 Q.B. 265. Ship chartered at London as "bound to Nantes" went to Newcastle before going to load at Nantes. The court distinguished between unreasonable delay and frustration.
[93] (1856) 1 H. & N. 183.
[94] [1910] 2 K.B. 405 at p. 408.
[95] [1917] 2 K.B. 193 at p. 203 (C.A.).
[96] [1979] 1 Lloyd's Rep. 212 at p. 218 (C.A.) (*The Homine*).

To be in "default," as that word is used in such a proviso, does not mean that the charterers must have been negligent or morally blameworthy. It is enough that there has been a breach of contract on their part. In *Argonaut Navigation Co. Ltd.* v. *Ministry of Food*[97] a proviso to the demurrage clause stated "provided such detention shall occur by default of charterer or his agents." The Court of Appeal appeared to treat default, detention and breach of contract as identical concepts, the default giving rise to the detention and so a breach of contract. Sellers J.[98] in the High Court had said:

> " . . . the charterers were in default in not completing the loading whithin the lay days. To detain the vessel beyond the lay days was a breach of the contract by the charterers; *Aktieselskabet Reidar* v. *Arcos Ltd.* They remained in default and without any protection under the charterparty until the loading was completed."

In the Court of Appeal Bucknill J. considered that this judgment was right. So also Singleton L.J.[99]:

> "The default of the charterer lay in not providing the cargo at the proper time and place. It was through that default that the detention occurred. The detention was due to the default of the charterer."

10–23   Another example of a proviso relating to the default of charterers arose in *N.V. Reederij Amsterdam* v. *President of India*.[1] A charterparty for the carriage of wheat from New Orleans to Madras stated: "Steamer to be loaded according to berth terms with customary berth dispatch[2] and if detained longer than five weather working days of 24 consecutive hours, Saturday after noon, Sundays and holidays excepted, charterers to pay demurrage . . . provided such detention shall occur by default of charterers or their agents." A further provision, described as the Centrocon Strike Clause (Amended),[3] exempted both parties from liability for "damages or demurrage" in the event of inability to load or delay in certain circumstances. The charterers contended that the lack of an available berth did not result from "default" on their part, and that they were not liable to pay demurrage. The Commercial Court held that this contention was incorrect. Pearson J. said[4]:

> " . . . the word 'default' does not necessarily involve moral fault or negligence; it means a breach of contract . . . the mere detention of the ship beyond the specified lay-time consitutes a breach of contract, and therefore a default of the charterers, unless the detention has been caused by an excepted risk or a breach of contract by the owners."

10–24   Where there is a reference to "default" it seems that charterers will nevertheless be exempted from liability in cases of *vis major* or fault of shipowners. Where the proviso applies, if detention arose from conduct of shipowners amounting to a breach of the charterparty, charterers would not be liable for demurrage. Cases might occur in which the conduct of shipowners did not amount to a breach; the proviso would then give charterers an additional protection.

[97] [1949] 1 K.B. 14 in the High Court: [1949] 1 K.B. 572 in the Court of Appeal (*The Argobec*).
[98] At p. 21.
[99] At p. 585.
[1] [1960] 2 Lloyd's Rep. 82 (*The Amstelmolen*).
[2] For "customary berth dispatch," see § 3–01 above.
[3] For the Centrocon Strike Clause generally, see § 10–57 below.
[4] [1960] 2 Lloyd's Rep. 82 at p. 94.

As for *vis major*[5] Pearson J. in the *N.V. Reederij Amsterdam* case[6] cited an American case[7] which contained a reference to "default." There the court, speaking with approval of an earlier American case[8] and dealing with English authorities, said[9]:

> "In *Crossman* v. *Burrill*[10] . . . it is declared that the one qualification of the absolute liability of the charterer is that of a *vis major* amounting to a sudden and unforeseen interruption or prevention of the act itself of loading or discharging, not occurring through the connivance or fault of the charterers."

Nature of damages[11]   **10–25**

Where there is a demurrage provision. Delay to the ship beyond the lay days, whether or not the demurrage period is limited by the charterparty, is a breach of contract.[12] Even if the parties expected the ship to be kept beyond the laytime, the conduct of charterers remains a breach for which the damages are liquidated[12a]; in other words the damages have been agreed in advance by the parties.[13] In *Lilly* v. *Stevenson*[14] Lord Trayner said:

> " . . . days stipulated for by the merchant, on demurrage, are just lay days, but lay days that have to be paid for."

It seems that this view would not be adopted where the demurrage period is not a fixed one. As Atkin L.J. said in *Aktieselskabet Reidar* v. *Arcos*[15]:

> "It appears to me to be incorrect to say that days on demurrage are extended lay days, unless the contract is so drawn."

It is possible that where the charterparty stipulates a fixed period on demurrage a court might say that the days were "extended lay days." This may have been the situation envisaged by Atkin L.J. when he spoke of a contract being "so drawn." The two other Lords Justices did not express a view as to whether the statement by Lord Trayner would apply to a fixed period.

---

[5] "Irresistible violence," according to Lord Campbell C.J. in *Walker* v. *British Guarantee Association* (1852) 18 Q.B. 277 at p. 286.

[6] [1960] 2 Lloyd's Rep. 82 at p. 93.

[7] *The Marpessa* 292 Fed. 957 (1923).

[8] *Crossman* v. *Burrill* (1900) U.S. 100.

[9] In *The Marpessa* 292 Fed. 957 at p. 969 (1923).

[10] (1900) 179 U.S. 100.

[11] For the nature of the breach itself, see § 10–07 above.

[12] Clear words would be needed to exempt charterers from liability for the breach; see *Leeds Shipping Co. Ltd.* v. *Duncan Fox & Co. Ltd.* (1932) 37 Com.Cas. 213 at pp. 222–223, *per* MacKinnon J. For the nature of the breach, and its status as a breach of warranty and not a breach of condition, see § 10–07 above.

[12a] "The effect of such a claim was to liquidate the damages payable; it did not alter the nature of the charterer's liability which was and remained a liability for damages, albeit liquidated damages"; thus Lord Brandon in *Lips Maritime Corporation* v. *President of India* [1987] 2 Lloyd's Rep. 311 at p. 315 (*The Lips*). There was no such thing as a cause of action in damages for late payment of damages. See also *Food Corporation of India* v. *Mosvolds Rederi A/S* (*The Arras* and *The Hoegh River*) [1986] 2 Lloyd's Rep. 597.

[13] Of the expression "liquidated damages," Cotton L.J. said in *Wallis* v. *Smith* (1882) 21 Ch.D. 243 at p. 267: "in terms of course that means that it shall be taken as the sum which the parties have by the contract assessed as the damages to be paid, whatever may be the actual damage." They are due though there is no loss; *Jamieson* v. *Lawrie* (1796) 6 Bro.P.C. 474.

[14] (1895) 22 R. 278 at p. 286.

[15] [1927] 1 K.B. 352 at p. 363 (C.A.).

10–26 Shipowners argue for two laytimes
Where the ship is the subject of two charterparties, and delay occurs in respect of both cargoes at the same port, the court may decide to read the two charterparties together, so that charterers do not have to pay a demurrage rate consisting of the total of the two separate demurrage rates. This will depend upon the wording of and the relationship between the two charterparties.

In *Sarma Navigation S.A.* v. *Sidermar S.p.A.*[16] Italian charterers entered into two agreements with the owners of the *Sea Pioneer*. The first charterparty provided for the carriage of steel bars, from Catania, Sicily, to La Guaira, Venezuela. Under the second charterparty the ship, after loading the steel bars, was to go to Taranto or Bari to load steel coils for Puerto Cabello, Venezuela. Both cargoes were, by later agreement, to be discharged at Puerto Cabello. There was a delay of over three weeks before discharge began. The total discharging time occupied over three weeks more, including a period of a few hours when both cargoes were being discharged at once. The shipowners contended that there were two laytimes, beginning at the same time and then running concurrently. As the laytimes were of different length demurrage (at the daily rate of $3,000 in each charterparty), they said, began at a different time in each case. When both demurrages were running the charterers should pay the combined rate. The High Court held that these contentions failed. There were references in the second charterparty which showed that the parties had tried to ensure that there was no conflict or overlap. As Lloyd J. put it[17]: " . . . if the provisions of the second charter-party had been contained in an addendum to the first charter-party instead of in a separate charter-party, there could really have been no possible answer to the charterer's contentions. It does not seem to me that the result is different merely because the contract between the parties is contained on two separate Gencon forms." It followed, he said,[18] that the demurrage rate "must be treated as the agreed rate for the ship as a whole and not as a rate which could, as it were, be doubled up by regarding the cargo under each charterparty separately . . . The only way in which the two charter-parties can be read sensibly together is to treat the permitted lay time as being consecutive and not concurrent." The judge distinguished the decision in *Agios Stylianos Compania Naviera* v. *Maritime Associates International Ltd. of Lagos*,[19] saying that the facts were different in two important respects. First, the cement could not be discharged until the vehicles had been discharged, whereas in the present case there was no physical reason why the two cargoes could not have been discharged simultaneously. Secondly, there had been two different charterers.

The Court of Appeal,[20] rejecting the shipowners' appeal, agreed that the charterparties were to be treated as complementary one to the other. The charterers ought not to be deprived of the benefit of laytime by the fact that it was convenient for both cargoes to be discharged at the same berth at the same port. Lord Denning M.R.,[21] declining to adopt what he called "the

---

[16] [1979] 2 Lloyd's Rep. 408 and [1982] 1 Lloyd's Rep. 13 (C.A.).
[17] *Op. cit.* at p. 410.
[18] *Op. cit.* at p. 411.
[19] [1975] 1 Lloyd's Rep. 426; see § 6–12 above.
[20] [1982] 1 Lloyd's Rep. 13.
[21] *Ibid.* at p. 16.

strict constructionist approach," said: "In this case it is as plain as can be that, under each of the charters, the compensation which was payable to the shipowners for the vessel being delayed was $3,000 a day. Nothing more was contemplated by the parties when the two charters were executed. By no stretch of the imagination—nor of construction—could it be extended so as to award the vessel $6,000 a day for being delayed."

In *Transamerican Steamship Corporation* v. *Tradax Export S.A.*,[22–23] **10–27** however, it was decided that there was no basis upon which two charter-parties, which were otherwise closely related, could be read together. Under the first charterparty a ship, to be nominated, was to carry rice from the U.S. Gulf to Basrah, with daily demurrage at $3,000 at loading and discharging. General cargo could also be loaded. Under the second charterparty, to the same charterers, a ship, to be nominated, was also to carry rice on the same route, with daily demurrage at $2,000 at loading and discharging. The shipowners nominated the Oriental Envoy in both cases, the nominations taking place, under the first charterparty, four days after the second charterparty, and, under the second charterparty, nearly three weeks after it was concluded.

At Basrah time ran under the first charterparty from December 27. Receivers of the second cargo only accepted notice after discharge of the overstowed general cargo had been completed, on March 6. The rice cargoes were then discharged simultaneously, until May 2. The shipowners said that when laytime under both charterparties had expired they were entitled to demurrage in each case. The charterers contended that laytime in both cases began on March 8, and that only the demurrage stipulated by the first charterparty was payable.

Parker J. held that the obligation to discharge the general cargo before the rice was not a condition precedent to the giving of a valid notice. As a result, time began under the first charterparty on December 27. The next question was whether the shipowners were entitled to demurrage under both charterparties, as charterers' Counsel referred to the problem as being "one of double demurrage."[24] Contrasting the *Sarma Navigation* case with this, Parker J. mentioned the following differences[25]:

(A) "There was the same named vessel in each charter. Here in each case the vessel was to be nominated, and it is expressly found in the case[26] that at the time when each of the two charters was concluded it was not in the contemplation of the charterers that the same vessel would be nominated under both fixtures, or that any particular vessel would be nominated under either fixture."

(B) "Furthermore, in as much as owners made no nomination under the June charter until four days after the July charter, and no nomination under the July charter until 14 days later, it appears that the owners also had nothing specific in mind at the date of either charter."

(C) "Again, in *The Sea Pioneer* the demurrage and laytime provisions

---

[22–23] [1982] 2 Lloyd's Rep. 266 (*The Oriental Envoy*).
[24] *Op. cit.* at p. 271.
[25] *Ibid.* at p. 270. Parts (A) to (C), though set out separately here, were part of one continuous sequence.
[26] The arbitrators had stated their award in the form of a special case, under the procedure applicable before the Arbitration Act 1979 came into force.

were the same, whereas here the demurrage rates are different, and there is a difference in the laytime provisions."

He concluded: "There is thus no basis here upon which the two charters could be read together. This being so, *The Sea Pioneer* is of little assistance to the charterers."

The Judge, rejecting charterers' contention that shipowners were being unduly recompensed, said that as the two charterparties should not be read together, the charterers had to pay demurrage under each charterparty. He added[27]:

> "In the present case, had the charterers been different instead of the same, there is no way that the July charterer could have avoided his obligation to pay the demurrage stipulated unless he could establish some implied term which, in the events which happened, would absolve him. No attempt was made to establish such a term, and, indeed, it would be quite impossible to do so within any known principle relating the implication of terms.
>
> It can make no difference that the charterers were in fact the same unless it were possible, as it was in *The Sea Pioneer*, to conclude that the two charters should be read as one. It is not so possible."[27a]

10–28 Is demurrage the sole remedy?

As the damages for delay have been arranged in advance by the parties, the general rule is that this agreement, as represented by the demurrage rate, prevents shipowners from claiming additional damages. Special circumstances may arise, however, as a result of which shipowners recover special damages as well as or instead of demurrage. It is not easy to extract a clear statement of principle from the two leading cases as to when shipowners may recover such special damages. It appears that they sometimes succeed even where there is no breach of the charterparty by charterers other than a breach of the obligation to load or discharge in a certain time.

10–29 In *Atkieselskabet Reidar* v. *Arcos*[28] a ship carried timber from Archangel to England. If charterers had loaded within the time stipulated for loading she would have taken on board a full summer cargo of 850 standards by October 17. By October 23 she had only loaded 544 standards. By then it was impossible to arrive in England before October 31; the carriage of any further cargo within the winter months would have exposed the master to a fine under section 10 of the Merchant Shipping Act 1906.[29] The shipowners claimed dead freight on 306 standards; the charterers contended that their only liability was for demurrage, the cargo having constituted a full and complete winter deck load. The Court of Appeal held that the charterers were liable in damages and were not entitled as of right to detain the ship beyond the laytime. As Atkin L.J. put it[30]:

> "The provisions as to demurrage quantify the damages, not for the complete breach, but only such damages as arise from the detention of the vessel."

So also Bankes L.J.[31]:

---

[27] *Op. cit.* at pp. 271–272.

[27a] For a similar problem see also *Transgrain Shipping B.V.* v. *Global Transporte Oceanico S.A.* [1988] 2 Lloyd's Rep. 149 at p. 158 (*The Mexico 1*) and § 5–33A above.

[28] [1927] 1 K.B. 352 (C.A.).

[29] For later equivalent provisions see the Merchant Shipping (Safety and Load Lines Conventions) Act 1932 and the Merchant Shipping (Load Lines) Act 1967.

[30] At p. 363.

[31] At pp. 360–361.

"I see no sufficient reason for construing the provision for demurrage as contained in the charterparty in the present case as a contractual extension of the lay days either for a reasonable time or for any other time, or as an implied term of the contract that the vessel shall remain for any time. I prefer to rest the necessity for remaining upon the ground that, time not being of the essence of the contract, the shipowner will not, except under some exceptional circumstances, be in a position to assert that the contract has been repudiated unless the vessel does remain a sufficient time to enable that question to be tested. If this is the correct view it follows that where a charterparty is in the terms of the present charterparty, and the charterers fail to load or to discharge, as the case may be, within the agreed lay days, or at the stipulated rate, they do commit a breach of contract."

The reasons given for awarding damages in the four judgments delivered **10–30** by Greer J. and by the Court of Appeal[32] were very different. As Mocatta J. said in a later case,[33] the difference in freight between a summer and a winter deck load was held recoverable by Bankes L.J. "as damages for failure to load in the agreed time"; by Atkin L.J. "as damages for failure to load a full and complete cargo in the agreed time"; and by Sargant L.J. "as damages for failure to load a full and complete cargo." The reasoning of Greer J. was similar to that of Sargant L.J. Viscount Dilhorne, also speaking in the case in which Mocatta J. was concerned, said[34] that Bankes L.J. had come to the same conclusion as Atkin L.J. and Sargant L.J., but "on somewhat different grounds"; Lord Hodson[35] said that Atkin L.J. and Bankes L.J. "were agreed that damages were payable as for dead freight beyond the sum due for demurrage"; and Lord Upjohn said[36] that Bankes L.J. "reached the same result [as the other two Lord Justices] by a different route on the particular facts of that case," though his *ratio decidendi* did not help the shipowners in the instant case.[37]

The liquidated damages payable as demurrage may be the sole remedy. **10–31** In *Suisse Atlantique Société d'Armement Maritime S.A.* v. *N.V. Rotter-*

---

[32] Of the Court of Appeal judgments Diplock L.J. said incisively in *Suisse Atlantique Société d'Armement Maritime S.A.* v. *N.V. Rotterdamsche Kolen Centrale (The General Guisan)* [1965] 1 Lloyd's Rep. 533 at p. 541 (C.A.): "But for the fact that the judgment appears to have been delivered 21 days after the hearing I should have thought that the judgments were extempore, for they seem to bear the *indicia* of extemporaneousness. At any rate, it is not easy to discover what the *ratio decidendi* of the majority or of the individual Lord Justices was upon the assessment of damages."

[33] *Suisse Atlantique Société d'Armement Maritime S.A.* v. *N.V. Rotterdamsche Kolen Centrale* [1965] 1 Lloyd's Rep. 166 at p. 176 (*The General Guisan*).

[34] *Ibid.*

[35] *Ibid.* at p. 549.

[36] *Ibid.* at p. 555.

[37] In *Chandris* v. *Isbrandtsen-Moller Co.* [1951] 1 K.B. 240 Devlin J. said, at p. 255, that the *ratio decidendi* in the *Reidar* case was to be found in the judgments of Bankes L.J. and Atkin L.J. There is an analysis of the Court of Appeal judgments, and a summary of the interpretations in *MacGregor on Damages* (14th ed.), at p. 344, and in *Scrutton on Charterparties* (19th ed.), art. 153, n. 2, at p. 308, by Webster J. in *Total Transport Corporation* v. *Amoco Trading Co.* [1985] 1 Lloyd's Rep. 423 (*The Altus*) at pp. 432–435. He concluded (at p. 435) that he must treat the *ratio decidendi* as being "that where a charterer commits any breach, even if it is only one breach, of his obligation either to provide the minimum contractual load or to detain the vessel for no longer than the stipulated period, the owner is entitled not only to the liquidated damages directly recoverable for the breach of the obligation to load (deadfreight) or for the breach of the obligation with regard to detention (demurrage), but also for, in the first case, to the damages flowing indirectly or consequentially from any detention of the vessel (if it occurs) and, in the second case, to damages flowing indirectly or consequentially from any failure to load a complete cargo if there is such failure."

damsche Kolen Centrale[38] the shipowners contended that they were entitled to damages which were not covered by the demurrage provision, but failed in their claim. A ship incurred demurrage while loading and discharging on all of eight voyages, carrying coal from the U.S.A. to Europe, with the exception of the loading on the first voyage. The charterparty, on an amended Amwelsh form,[39] provided: "This Charter is to remain in force for a total of two years' consecutive voyages . . . vessel always returning in ballast between trips. . . . " The charterparty did not state the number of voyages to be performed but stipulated certain loading and discharging rates, with demurrage to be paid at the rate of $1,000 per day if those rates were not attained. The shipowners, giving credit for the demurrage, claimed the profit which they would have made on extra voyages, had the ship not been delayed. The House of Lords, upholding the Court of Appeal and the High Court, rejected the claim. In the High Court Mocatta J. had said[40]:

> "Were it not for *Reidar* v. *Arcos*,[41] I would readily have accepted Mr. Donaldson's argument[42] that the loss suffered by the owners was indistinguishable in principle from that suffered by a shipowner under a single voyage charter when his ship is detained beyond her lay days. In consequence, I would have decided without much doubt that, just as the consequential loss of future freight in such a case would be a loss by detention covered by the demurrage provisions, so should losses of freight under the additional voyages that could have been performed under the charter be treated as covered by demurrage."

He went on to distinguish[40] the earlier case:

> " . . . it had the special feature, absent here, that the delay in loading affected the quantity of cargo that could be carried on the very voyage in which the delay in loading arose."

The demurrage rate could not compensate for the special damage, which was different in substance from damages for detention. In the absence of such a special element:

> " . . . the general principle, agreed by all members of the Court of Appeal must apply, namely that, for a claim for detention by a shipowner due to the laytime provisions in a charter being exceeded, the demurrage provisions quantify the damages recoverable."

10–32 The Court of Appeal unanimously affirmed the judgment of Mocatta J. Sellers L.J. said[43]:

> "It cannot, I think, be said that any breach of contract has been established except the failure on all but the first occasion to load and discharge within the laytime. I can find no other contractual obligation expressed or to be implied. That means that there was delay only and that the vessel was detained. The remedy for that delay is the liquidated damages which had been agreed and fixed by the demurrage rate."

Of the *Reidar* case he said[44]:

> "The damages recovered for dead freight were for a separate breach of contract and were wholly independent of the detention of the vessel . . . "

---

[38] [1966] 1 Lloyd's Rep. 529 (H.L.) (*The General Guisan*).
[39] Americanised Welsh Coal Charter.
[40] [1965] 1 Lloyd's Rep. 166 at p. 177.
[41] [1927] 1 K.B. 352 (C.A.).
[42] *i.e.* the argument of counsel for the charterers.
[43] [1965] 1 Lloyd's Rep. 533 at p. 538.
[44] At p. 539.

Harman L.J., saying that he agreed with the reasons given by Sellers L.J., said[45]:

> " . . . there is no room for saying that damages are at large. The parties have agreed that they should not be at large, but should be, in order to make it easier to assess them, a conventional figure. I cannot see how you can stretch this bargain any further than that. That is the bargain which the parties have made. It may be a bad one. It is not one that this Court can mend."

In the House of Lords[46] Viscount Dilhorne also distinguished the *Reidar* **10–33** case, saying[47]:

> "If in this case the appellants[48] had been able to establish a breach of the charter-party other than by the detention of the vessel, then *Reidar* v. *Arcos* . . . is authority for saying that the damages obtainable would not be limited to the demurrage payments. In my opinion, they have not done so."

So also Lord Hodson said of *Reidar*[49]:

> "There was a breach separate from although arising from the same circumstances as the delay, and it was in these circumstances that damages were awarded."

Lord Upjohn said[50]:

> " . . . there were in that case breaches of two quite independent obligations; one was demurrage for detention (as here) the other was a failure to load a full and complete cargo, which had become impossible owing to the onset of winter conditions and, therefore, entirely different considerations applied to that case."[50a]

The two other Law Lords, adopting the reasoning of the High Court and the Court of Appeal, did not deal with the *Reidar* case, but only with the contention by the shipowners, not advanced in the court below, that there had been a fundamental breach of contract by the charterers.[51]

The most that could be said in the *Suisse Atlantique* case was that the **10–34** delays affected the total voyages that could be carried out during the two years. But the shipowners were not entitled to expect any particular number of voyages, unless they could show an implied obligation to this effect.[52] In the *Reidar* case, on the other hand, they complained about the size of the cargo but it was a full and complete cargo, though admittedly smaller, being a winter cargo, than they would have liked. In neither case was there any breach of contract other than the failure to comply with the laytime clause. The demurrage covered the detention, but not a claim for non-feasance which was a by-product of a breach of contract.

The non-feasance in the *Reidar* case was the failure to load a summer as opposed to a winter cargo, and the shipowners won; in the *Suisse Atlantique* case it was the failure to perform more voyages, and the shipowners lost.

---

[45] *Ibid.* at p. 540.
[46] [1966] 1 Lloyd's Rep. 529.
[47] At p. 539.
[48] The shipowners.
[49] At p. 549.
[50] At p. 555.
[50a] See also *President of India* v. *N.G. Livanos Maritime Co.* (*The John Michalos*) [1987] 2 Lloyd's Rep. 188, at p. 191. The *Reidar* case was cited as showing that it was possible to obtain more than demurrage payments for detention. But Leggatt J. distinguished it, referring to the dicta of Viscount Dilhorne, Lord Hodson and Lord Upjohn in *Suisse Atlantique*.
[51] All the Law Lords held that even if there was such a breach the shipowners had affirmed the charterparty.
[52] And they failed to show that there was such an obligation; see § 10–36 above.

10–35 *Right to damages other than demurrage*

Where the only breach of contract is failure to load or discharge the cargo within the laytime, shipowners are restricted in their claim to the liquidated damages, as agreed in the demurrage clause.[53]

This will be so, whether the demurrage period is stated to be a limited one, or, as is more commonly the case, it is not limited. In the former case, shipowners can claim damages for detention after the limited period has expired; in the latter case such damages would only become due where the charterparty had come to an end because the delay was equivalent to a repudiation by charterers, and had been accepted as such by shipowners. Where the charterparty does not provide for a limited demurrage period, shipowners are limited in their claim to the demurrage rate until the contract has come to an end.[54]

10–36 As time is not usually of the essence of the contract,[55] mere detention beyond the laytime or beyond any fixed demurrage period does not give shipowners the right to repudiate. If the delay is such that the enterprise is frustrated, then the charterparty is at an end. It is not only the delay that will give rise to this situation. Other breaches of conditions as opposed to warranties may bring it about, and may entitle shipowners to treat charterers' conduct as a repudiation. In such a case, damages at large in addition to demurrage may be claimed.[56]

10–37 In *Chandris* v. *Isbrandtsen-Moller Co. Inc.*[57] dangerous cargo (turpentine) was loaded, with the knowledge of the master and charterers, at Jacksonville, Florida, for Liverpool. At Liverpool the ship was ordered out of the dock after two days of discharging because of the nature of her cargo. She had to unload into barges in the Mersey, so that the unloading took 16 days longer than it otherwise would have taken. The shipowners claimed damages for detention for those days, arguing that they were not limited to the demurrage rate. They also claimed demurrage for the days, previous to the 16, on which the ship would have been on demurrage in any event. The Commercial Court held[58] that they were not entitled to damages for detention. Devlin J. said[59]:

> "There is an express obligation on the charterer under this charterparty to furnish a full and complete cargo of lawful merchandise. He has broken that obligation, and it is not disputed that thereby he broke a fundamental obligation, by which I understand to be meant a condition going to the root of the contract the breach of which entitled the owner

---

[53] "Where there is a breach of a duty to name a place reachable on arrival, but laytime has begun, the shipowner may have similarly to rely only on the laytime provisions." See *Shipping Developments Corporation S.A.* v. *V/O Sojuzneftexport* [1971] 1 Lloyd's Rep. 506 (C.A.) (*The Delian Spirit*), and § 4–20 above. For "reachable on her arrival" see § 4–35 above.

[54] *Western SS. Co.* v. *Amaral Sutherland & Co.* [1913] 3 K.B. 366; *Inverkip SS. Co. Ltd.* v. *Bunge & Co.* [1917] 2 K.B. 193 (C.A.). See §§ 10–15, 10–16 above.

[55] *Aktieselskabet Reidar* v. *Arcos Ltd.* [1927] 1 K.B. 352 (C.A.), *per* Bankes L.J. at pp. 360–361. See also § 10–29 above.

[56] The laytime and demurrage clauses may be wide enough to cover breaches of contract for which damages would otherwise be recoverable independently; *Britain SS. Co. Ltd.* v. *Donugol, of Charkoff* (1932) 44 Ll.L.Rep. 123; and see § 10–18 above.

[57] [1951] 1 K.B. 240.

[58] Among other things; an important issue was whether the provision for the carriage of lawful merchandise, "excluding acids, explosives, arms, ammunition or other dangerous cargo" excluded turpentine. It was held that it did.

[59] At pp. 251–252.

to rescind. No doubt in the circumstances of this case, as they were explored in the arbitration, that was the proper view to take . . . the owner himself chose to affirm.[60] The result of the affirmation is that the breach of condition is to be treated as if it were a breach of warranty.[61] I can see nothing in principle to suggest that the damages for the breach of warranty ex post facto,[62] as it is sometimes called, should be any different from those for the breach of warranty ab initio, nor can I see any reason in principle why a liquidated damage clause should not apply with equal efficacy to both . . . ''

Damages for detention   **10–38**

Where damages are due. Damages for detention are the unliquidated damages[63] which accrue in respect of the wrongful detention of the ship. The mere fact that a ship has to wait does not give rise to a claim for breach of contract as she must wait for the agreed time or for a reasonable time. Wrongful detention can result from failure by charterers to load or to give orders for a loading or a discharging place[64] or some other breach by them; the failure is considered here in connection with the obligation of charterers to load or unload the ship in a fixed, calculable or reasonable time. Such damages become due either where there is no demurrage stipulation, the laytime (whether fixed, calculable or reasonable) having been exhausted, or where there is the now rare stipulation that demurrage should run for a fixed time, that fixed time having expired. Damages for detention do not become due where as in most cases, there is an exhaustive demurrage stipulation, covering all delay.[65] The word demurrage[66] is sometimes used to describe damages for detention or the period in respect of which these damages are due.[67] This usage is incorrect if demurrage be regarded as liquidated damages for detention beyond the laytime,[68] as damages for detention are unliquidated, not being agreed in advance.

In many cases, however, the demurrage rate is applied in order to calculate the detention damages[69] and then the use of the word demurrage can be justified.

---

[60] In view of this the judge, as he said, did not have to consider the practical problems which would have arisen if the shipowners had at the end of the voyage, and on discovering that cargo outside the contract description had been shipped, repudiated the contract.

[61] In accordance with the rule in *Wallis Son & Wells* v. *Pratt & Haynes* [1911] A.C. 394 (H.L.) where Lord Loreburn L.C. said of an aggrieved party, at p. 395: "He may treat the breach of a condition as if it were a breach of warranty, that is to say, he may have the remedies applicable to a breach of warranty."

[62] A term which became a warranty, having started life as a condition.

[63] For the duty to mitigate such damages, see § 10–45 below.

[64] As in *Zim Israel Navigation Company Ltd.* v. *Tradax Export S.A.* [1970] 2 Lloyd's Rep. 409 (*The Timna*), where charterers failed to give orders for the first discharging port within 48 hours of the master's application. For the measure of damages, see § 10–42 below.

[65] *Western SS. Co. Ltd.* v. *Amaral Sutherland & Co.* [1913] 3 K.B. 366. See § 10–16 above. Thus in *Shipping Developments Corporation S.A.* v. *V/O Sojuzneftexport* [1971] 1 Lloyd's Rep. 506 (C.A.) (*The Delian Spirit*) damages for detention were not awarded, although the charterers were in breach of a provision other than the laytime clause, as that clause already dealt with the delay. See § 4–20 above.

[66] For the meaning of the word see § 10–01 above.

[67] For the confusion which may arise as to whether shipowners have a lien both for demurrage and for detention damages, see § 11–25 below, and the line of cases which includes *Gray* v. *Carr* (1871) L.R. 6 Q.B. 522 and *Sanguinetti* v. *Pacific Steam Navigation Co.* (1877) 2 Q.B.D. 238 (C.A.).

[68] It was so regarded by the Court of Appeal in *Atkieselskabet Reidar* v. *Arcos* [1927] 1 K.B. 352. See also § 10–29.

[69] For the measure of detention damages see § 10–42 below.

10–39 *Payment in the nature of demurrage*

Damages for detention have been described[70] as a payment "in the nature of demurrage."[71] This description indicates the similarity in function of the two payments, which are both designed to compensate the shipowners for delay, and may be calculated at the same rate, Numerous cases as to whether a lien may be exercised both for demurrage and for detention damages make it clear that the two expressions normally have different meanings.

In *Harris and Dixon* v. *Marcus Jacobs Co.*[71] the shipowners had been given a lien on the cargo for all freight and demurrage. Cargo was "to be delivered as fast as steamer can deliver per working day . . . "; it was also stipulated: "demurrage to be at the rate of £30 per running day." The ship to discharge at London dock but when she arrived there was no quay berth ready, though she was to proceed "to London or Tyne dock to such ready quay berth as ordered by the charterers." She was consequently detained one day beyond the time needed for discharging her had she been able to get alongside a quay berth on arrival in the dock. The Court of Appeal held that shipowners were entitled to a lien for demurrage, the damages for the detention being sufficiently in the nature of demurrage to come within the demurrage clause. Brett M.R. said[72]:

> "Demurrage is the agreed amount of damage which is to be paid for the delay of the ship caused by a default of the charterers at either the commencement or the end of the voyage. Here such a delay so caused by the charterers took place at the end of the voyage. It is true that the damage in this case is not strictly demurrage, but in the nature of demurrage, and the clause as to demurrage in a charterparty is elastic enough in the ordinary construction of a charterparty to comprise such a damage as this. Then £30 is what the shipowners would be entitled in the present case to claim from the charterers for a detention in the nature of a demurrage in consequence of the default of the charterers to name a ready quay berth for the vessel. . . . "

10–40 **Effect of exceptions clause.** The expression "damages" may however, be so construed that an exceptions clause can relieve the charterers from liability not only for detention damages but also for demurrage. Thus in *Moor Line Ltd.* v. *Distillers Co. Ltd.*[73] a charterparty[74] for the carriage of grain from Russia to Scotland allowed 10 days on demurrage at a certain rate; it also provided that the days for discharging should not count during the continuance of a strike, and that "in case of any delay by reason of" a strike "no claim for damages" shall be made. The ship was detained at the discharging port for four days beyond the lay days, not as a result of the continuance of the strike, but owing to congestion after the end of the strike. The shipowners claimed demurrage for the four days. It was held that the detention was a delay "by reason of" a strike,[75] so that a claim for damages was excluded; it was also held that claims for damages for delay were not limited to claims for detention beyond the demurrage period, and that this claim for demurrage was a claim for damages and therefore failed. Lord Salvesen said[76]:

[70] By Brett L.J. in *Harris and Dixon* v. *Marcus Jacobs & Co.* (1885) 15 Q.B.D. 247 at p. 251 (C.A.).
[71] (1885) 15 Q.B.D. 247 (C.A.).
[72] At p. 251.
[73] 1912 S.C. 514.
[74] In the form known as "The 1890 Black Sea Charter-Party."
[75] Following *Leonis SS. Co. Ltd.* v. *Rank Ltd. (No. 2)* (1908) 13 Com.Cas. 295 (C.A.).
[76] At p. 520.

"The whole basis of the argument,[77] however, depends on the view that 'demurrage' in the strict sense is not a claim for damage, but is in the nature of a payment in respect of the continued use or hire of the vessel for the charterer's purposes after the expiry of the lay days. That is a theory of demurrage which at one time received some countenance, and which is certainly supported by Lord Trayner's opinion in the case of *Gardiner* v. *Macfarlane, M'Crindell, & Co.*[78] In my opinion, however, the more correct view is that demurrage is 'agreed damages to be paid for delay of the ship in loading or unloading beyond an agreed period.' In other words, the distinction between 'demurrage' and damages for detention is that the one is liquidated damages and the other unliquidated. A claim under either head is a claim in respect of detention, and is in the nature of a claim of damages. Amongst mercantile men, indeed, 'demurrage' is often used in a wider sense as including both demurrage strictly so called and damages for detention[79] although it is not necessary in order to affirm the decision of the Sherrif-substitute to hold that the term is so used in this particular clause. If, then, demurrage is regarded as liquidated damages for detention, I think there is no difficulty in holding that it is not excluded from the third part of clause 13[80] but is covered by the words 'no claim for damages.' "

In *Westoll* v. *Lindsay*[81] the Scottish Courts, considered a clause substantially similar to that discussed in *Moor Line Ltd.* v. *Distillers Co. Ltd.*[82] Grain had been carried from Russia to Scotland; owing to congestion at the port of discharge, which resulted from a strike which had ended before the ship arrived, the ship did not get a berth until the expiry of the lay days, and 10 days were then needed for her discharge. The shipowners claimed demurrage for these 10 days; it was held that as the strike had ended before the ship's arrival, the exceptions clause was inapplicable. The Lord President pointed out[83] that the facts in the *Moor Line* case were different. When the Moor Line ship arrived at Leith a strike was actually in progress, and continued for eight days after her arrival during which time she was unable to discharge. When the partial discharge had finished she completed discharge at Glasgow, using the last three days of laytime and going on to demurrage for four days. The principles enunciated in the *Moor Line* case supported the view favourable to the shipowners which the court took in *Westoll* v. *Lindsay*, for in the earlier case Lord Salvesen had said,[84] when speaking of the part of the clause which contemplated a strike occurring before the expiry of laytime: **10–41**

"If such a strike occurs, the running of the lay-days is suspended during its continuance, but when it ceases, the lay-days again commence to run."

The Lord President said[85] that in the case before him:

" . . . there was no strike of men essential to the discharge which prevented the ship being discharged. The men were all there, but there was no berth available. That is the charterer's risk and not the shipowner's."

---

[77] The shipowners' argument.

[78] (1889) 16 Rettie (Ct. of Sess., 4th Ser.) 658 at p. 660. Lord Trayner also said, in *Lilly* v. *Stevenson* (1895) 22 Rettie (Ct. of Sess., 4th Ser.) 278 at p. 286: "Days stipulated for by the merchant, on demurrage, are just lay days, but lay days that have to be paid for."

[79] The lien clause of the 1976 Gencon charterparty uses the words "demurrage (including damages for detention)."

[80] The clause which excluded any "claim for damages."

[81] 1916 S.C. 782.

[82] 1912 S.C. 514. See § 10–40 above.

[83] *Op. cit.* at p. 788.

[84] *Op. cit.* at p. 519.

[85] *Op. cit.* at p. 788.

10–42   **Measure of damages**

Damages for detention are unliquidated damages, since no sum is agreed in advance. Nevertheless, the demurrage rate, where there is one, is sometimes applied, since it represents an estimate by the parties of the daily value of the ship. So in *Zim Israel Navigation Company Ltd.* v. *Tradax Export S.A.*[86] charterers detained the ship by failing to give orders for the first discharging port. It was agreed that the measure of loss was the demurrage rate. There was no evidence that the ship could not have been used as a profit-earning chattel. It is open to the parties to show that the demurrage rate does not truly represent the damages suffered by the shipowners,[87] as they are entitled to be recompensed for such damages.[88]

10–43   Shipowners may find that their entitlement to demurrage has been increased (or their liability for dispatch reduced) because the laytime is less than that which the charterparty contemplated. The laytime may be one which is calculated by reference to the cargo actually loaded or delivered.[89] If charterers have loaded less than the amount promised by them, shipowners have a dead freight claim. In making that claim they would have to take into account the corresponding benefit which they had received in respect of the altered demurrage or dispatch.

In *Bedford Steamship Co. Ltd.* v. *Navico A.G.*[90] the *Ionian Skipper* was chartered to carry wheat from Antwerp to Alexandria. Charterers were to load a full and complete cargo of "19,500 tonnes in Bulk, 5% more or less in owner's option." Loading was to be at "the average rate of 3,000 metric tons per weather working day of 24 consecutive hours . . . " and the discharging rate was to be "1,500 metric tons per weather working day of 24 consecutive hours . . . " The Master called for 20,255.50 tonnes but 18,685.50 tonnes were loaded. The day after the ship sailed the charterers made a payment to the shipowners in respect of freight, making no deduction for dead freight. When after the end of discharge the charterers made a final payment they calculated demurrage and dispatch on the basis of laytime calculated as if a full cargo had been loaded. As a result laytime was longer. In the High Court it was common ground between the parties that the laytime should be calculated by reference to the cargo actually shipped. A question to be decided was whether the shipowners had to give credit, in making their dead freight claim, for any increase in demurrage and saving in dispatch money occasioned by the diminished laytime. Parker J. referring to the dead freight, which is a form of damages, said[91]: "Prima facie such damages would have been payable on the quantity short-loaded but there would have to be deducted from that any benefits to the owner *e.g.* by having his vessel available earlier as a result of having had to load and discharge a smaller quantity or any increased demurrage or saving in dispatch money which might result from the smaller quantity of cargo actually loaded and discharged. Any savings in dispatch and any increase in demurrage so resulting would be dependent upon two things. Firstly, the time at which laytime would have expired had the full cargo been loaded and dis-

---

[86] [1970] 2 Lloyd's Rep. 409 (*The Timna*).
[87] *Moorson* v. *Bell* (1811) 2 Camp. 616. See also *Nolisement (Owners)* v. *Bunge y Born* [1917] 1 K.B. 160 (C.A.).
[88] *Randall* v. *Lynch* (1810) 2 Camp. 352.
[89] See § 2–15 and *Hain Steamship Co. Ltd.* v. *Minister of Food* [1949] 1 K.B. 492 (C.A.).
[90] [1977] 2 Lloyd's Rep. 273.
[91] *Ibid.* at p. 277.

charged, and secondly, how long it would have taken to load and discharge the full cargo." He remitted the case to the arbitrators for a finding as to these matters.[92]

Interest also allowable **10–44**

Though demurrage is a form of liquidated damages, shipowners are not prevented from claiming interest as well.[92a] Such interest could be held to run from the time at which the demurrage fell due. As demurrage becomes due day by day such an approach would make calculations exceedingly difficult. In practice interest is not usually claimed unless there has been a dispute followed by an arbitration or court proceedings.[93] The rate of interest and period for which it is payable are then in the discretion of the tribunal.[94] There is a tendency in arbitrations to let interest run from the time at which the parties might reasonably be expected to have agreed their accounts, in the absence of dispute, until the date of the award.[95] Authority for the proposition that interest is due in respect of demurrage can be found in the High Court report of *Agrimpex Hungarian Trading Corporation* v. *Sociedad Financiera de Bienes Raices S.A.*[96] There Ashworth J. said:

> "So far as interest is concerned I wish to make it clear that I regard it as a case where interest at 4 per cent. would normally have been awarded, and it is only because the sum

---

[92] In *Kawasaki Steel Corporation* v. *Sardoil S.p.a.* [1977] 2 Lloyd's Rep. 552 shipowners were able to claim dead freight and demurrage, but the laytime was fixed in advance ("72 running hours . . . for loading and discharging") and was not reduced by the shortfall in cargo loaded. The main question, decided against the charterers, was as to whether the obligation to load a certain quantity had been frustrated by a Saudi Arabian government rationing policy.

[92a] In *Lips Maritime Corporation* v. *President of India* [1987] 2 Lloyd's Rep. 311 (H.L.) (*The Lips*) shipowners tried unsuccessfully to recover loss suffered by a change in exchange rates between the bill of lading date and the date of the award. Demurrage was expressed in dollars in the charterparty but was to be paid in sterling, converted at the exchange rate prevailing on the bill of lading date. The only remedy which the law afforded to shipowners was interest. The decision was applied in *Food Corporation of India* v. *Mosvolds Rederi A/S* [1986] 2 Lloyd's Rep. 597 (*The Arras* and *The Hoegh River*). See also *Mosvolds Rederi A/S* v. *Food Corporaton of India*, LMLN 231, September 10, 1988 (*The Arras* and *The Hoegh River*). For the currency of payment see *Mosvolds Rederi A/S* v. *Food Corporation of India* (the *Damodar General T. J. Park* and *King Theras*) [1986] 2 Lloyd's Rep. 68.

[93] *Edwards* v. *G.W. Ry.* (1851) 11 C.B. 588; *Chandris* v. *Isbrandtsen-Moller Co. Inc.* [1951] 1 K.B. 240.

[94] Law Reform (Miscellaneous Provisions) Act 1934, s.3: "(1) In any proceedings tried in any court of record for the recovery of any debt or damages, the court may, if he thinks fit, order that there shall be included in the sum for which judgment is given interest at such rate as it thinks fit on the whole or any part of the debt or damages for the whole or any part of the period between the date when the cause of action arose and the date of the judgment . . . "

[95] Thereafter the arbitration tribunal only has discretion as to whether interest shall run and not as to the rate; see Arbitration Act 1950, s.20 and *London & Overseas Freighters Ltd.* v. *Timber Shipping Co. S.A.* [1971] 1 Lloyd's Rep. 523 at pp. 531, 532. For example, Lord Brandon in *Lips Maritime Corporation* v. *President of India* [1987] 2 Lloyd's Rep. 311 at p. 317 (*The Lips*) said: " . . . on the basis that demurrage is usually settled and paid for within two months of the completion of discharge, . . . [the umpire] was . . . right to make interest payable only from the day following the expiry of that period . . . " See also *Mosvolds Rederi A/S* v. *Food Corporation of India*, LMLN 231, September 10, 1988 (*The Arras* and *The Hoegh River*).

[96] [1957] 2 Lloyd's Rep. 423 at p. 439; (*The Aello*).

eventually involved[97] before me is so small that I have not made any award of interest here."

10–45 Mitigation by shipowners

The common law rule is that where one party to a contract is in breach of it the other party must mitigate its damages[98]; it must take such steps as may reduce the measure of any damages which it might suffer as a result of the breach. This rule does not apply generally[99] in demurrage cases; there is not, for example, a duty upon shipowners to load or discharge cargo which is not being loaded or discharged by charterers at the agreed rate. The reason for this alteration of the general rule is that the parties have agreed in advance that the demurrage payment shall constitute the damages.

In certain cases, however, there is a duty to mitigate. Where a ship is detained because receivers have not paid a charge, shipowners cannot claim detention damages if the master could have released her by payment.[1] If she is detained to exercise a lien over goods which could have been discharged and put under lien in a warehouse, there is no right to detention damages.[2] So also, if a ship is kept, as if on demurrage, after both the expiry of laytime and refusal by charterers to load, no demurrage can be recovered.[3]

10–46   In *Hick* v. *Rodocanachi*[4] the bills of lading contained no stipulation as to the time within a cargo of Russian grain was to be discharged at London, so that the receivers were entitled to a reasonable time. They stated: "The goods are to be applied for within twenty-four hours of ship's arrival and reporting at the Custom House, otherwise the master or agent is to be at a liberty to put into lighters or land the same at the risk and expense of the owners of the goods . . . The master or agent shall have a lien on the goods for freight and payments made (if any) or liabilities incurred in respect of any charges stipulated herein to be borne by the owners of the goods." Discharge was delayed by a strike. The Court of Appeal rejected the shipowner's claims for demurrage and damages for detention. Lindley L.J. considered whether the receivers were relieved from all obligation to pay damages by reason of the clauses empowering the master to put the cargo into lighters or land it. He said[5]:

---

[97] £25.

[98] *British Westinghouse Electric & Manufacturing Co.* v. *Underground Electric Railways Co. of London* [1912] A.C. 673 at p. 689 (H.L.), *per* Lord Haldane: "The fundamental basis is thus compensation for pecuniary loss naturally flowing from the breach; but this first principle is qualified by a second, which imposes on a plaintiff the duty of taking all reasonable steps to mitigate the loss consequent on the breach, and debars him from claiming any part of the damage which is due to his neglect to take such steps."

[99] For cases in which it does not apply, see § 10–47 below.

[1] *Möller* v. *Jecks* (1865) 19 C.B.(N.S.) 332. See § 1–10 above.

[2] *Mors-le-Blanch* v. *Wilson* (1873) L.R. 8 C.P. 227. See § 10–48 below. See also *Lyle Shipping Co.* v. *Cardiff Corporation* (1889) 5 Com.Cas. 87 (C.A.); and *Smailes & Son.* v. *Hans Dessen & Co.* (1906) 12 Com.Cas. 117.

[3] *Blight* v. *Page* (1801) 3 B. & P. 295n.; *Dimech* v. *Corlett* (1858) 12 Moo.P.C. 199; *Hick* v. *Tweedy & Co.* (1890) 63 L.T. 765; *Inverkip SS. Co.* v. *Bunge & Co.* [1917] 2 K.B. 193 (C.A.). The Charterparty Laytime Definitions (see Appendix to this book) state: "28. 'ON DEMURRAGE'—means that the laytime has expired. Unless the charterparty expressly provides to the contrary the time on demurrage will not be subject to the laytime exceptions."

[4] [1891] 2 Q.B. 626 (C.A.).

[5] At p. 632.

"But these clauses are obviously inserted in the interest and for the benefit of the ship-owner, and they give him an additional remedy for the recovery of what is due to him, and not a remedy in substitution for any which he would have apart from these clauses. The master is under no obligation to land the goods and assert his lien instead of allowing the consignee to land them, and leaving him to be sued for the payments he ought to make."[6]

It seems that shipowners are not obliged to expedite the discharge by **10–47** adopting another method, even where the contract of affreightment expressly entitles them to do so. The authority usually cited in this connection, *The Arne*,[7] concerns a claim not for demurrage but for damages for detention; but in view of what was said in the case and has been said elsewhere[8] the proposition seems to be correct. Discharge by other methods, at the expense and risk of receivers, is a privilege given to the shipowners by the contract, and not a duty imposed by common law. In *The Arne*[9] the bill of lading stipulated that the goods were "to be taken from the ship by the consignees at their expense immediately after arrival, and as fast as steamer can deliver or the same will be transhipped into lighters, or landed, or warehoused at the expense and risk of the proprietors of such goods." The master and time charterers said that on each of two voyages from Antwerp to Swansea with pig iron and old rails the receivers took delivery more slowly than was reasonable; they claimed damages for detention. The Probate, Divorce and Admiralty Divisional Court held that the claim succeeded although the option of transhipment or warehousing had not been exercised. Jeune P. said[10]:

"Supposing the sole cause of the non-delivery was that the trucks were not ready, it would be hard to throw upon the master the responsibility of saying that the delay was so great that he could not allow it to continue . . . It would be far more reasonable to say that the ordinary remedy of the shipowner remained the same, but that he had an alternative option which he could have exercised."

The common law duty to mitigate damages seems not to have been considered; the discussion there largely concerned the receivers' defence that the delay arose from a dearth of railway wagons which was beyond their control. It is just possible that the receivers might argue successfully, in a like case, that there was a failure to mitigate damages. Where demurrage is claimed, however, the shipowners might argue that the damages have been agreed in advance, whether or not they excercise one of their options.

The expense of mitigation   **10–48**

Where shipowners step in to speed up the discharge[11] they are entitled to claim their expenses. Thus in *Cazalet* v. *Morris*[12] a shortage of railway wagons prevented the receivers from maintaining the agreed discharging rate. After demurrage began the shipowners discharged the cargo into lighters and so completed the discharge. It was held that as the shipowners had reduced the period of demurrage by their action they were entitled to

---

[6] This conclusion was not essential to the decision because the goods were applied for within 24 hours of the ship's arrival and reporting at the custom house, but it can be regarded as authoritative.
[7] [1904] P. 154.
[8] As in *Hick* v. *Rodocanachi* [1891] 2 Q.B. 626 at p. 632 (C.A.), *per* Lindley L.J.
[9] [1904] P. 154.
[10] At p. 160.
[11] Though the cases cited concern the discharging of ships, there seems to be no reason why the same principle should not apply to the loading operations.
[12] 1916 S.C. 952.

recover their expenses from the receivers, up to the amount of the demurrage saved.

The exercise of a lien for freight where the cargo is still on the ship may result in a claim by shipowners for damages for detention. Thus in *Mors-le-Blanch* v. *Wilson*[13] consignees failed to appear at Buenos Aires to claim a cargo of coal, and the master waited four weeks before landing it. The shipowners claimed detention damages from the shippers. The jury found that the shippers were liable. A new trial was ordered as the jury's assessment of the damages might have been affected by a statement by the trial judge.[14] The foreman of the jury had asked whether the captain would have lost his lien for freight if he had landed the coal at once. The judge replied that he could, there being no evidence as to the availability of warehouses such as existed at Liverpool, London and other large commercial cities, for the purpose of exercising a lien. Perhaps the questioner only meant to ask whether if a master landed goods at an ordinary landing place, and put them into an ordinary warehouse, a lien was thereby lost.[15] If so, an affirmative answer would have been correct. The Court of Common Pleas held that as the answer was too general in its terms, and might have affected the assessment of damages, the shippers were entitled to a new trial.[16] It seems that, although there was no "statutable" warehouse (that is, a warehouse where a lien could be exercised in a manner similar to that provided by the Merchant Shipping Act 1894, Pt. VII), the master might still have landed the coal without losing possession and control of it, placing it in a warehouse belonging to or hired by the shipowners, and so have preserved the lien.

10–49 How demurrage runs

Charterparties may provide that the liability for demurrage shall accrue daily, by such words as " . . . per day or *pro rata* for any part of a day, payable day by day,"[17] or even hourly, as " . . . per like hour demurrage."[18] In practice the money due is not paid until after the loading and discharging have been completed and the voyage accounts agreed. In a London arbitration it was held that shipowners were entitled to an interim award for demurrage, on account, although the calculation was made as at a time when the discharge had not yet been completed. The arbitrators limited themselves to awarding demurrage for a period of 57 days as against the 80 days which had elapsed since laytime expired. The shipowners cited in their favour a statement by Lord Diplock in *Dias Compania Naviera S.A.* v. *Louis Dreyfus Corporation*[18a]:

> "It is the almost invariable practice nowadays for these damages to be fixed by the charterparty at a liquidated sum per day and pro rata for part of a day (demurrage) which accrues throughout the period of time for which the breach continues."

Most charterparties provide that parts of days on demurrage shall be counted proportionately. A demurrage clause may state, for example:

---

[13] (1873) L.R. 8 C.P. 227.
[14] Brett J.
[15] See the remarks by Grove J. at p. 238.
[16] Though in fact they agreed to pay a reduced amount.
[17] Uniform General Charter 1976 (Gencon).
[18] In *Rayner* v. *Rederiaktiebolaget Condor* (1895) 1 Com.Cas. 80.
[18a] [1978] 1 Lloyd's Rep. 325 (H.L.) (*The Dias*), at p. 328.

"Charterers to pay Owners demurrage at the rate of . . . per day or *pro rata* for part of a day." The Shellvoy 5 form, for example, provides for demurrage to be paid at a rate related to Worldscale or the Worldwide Tanker Nominal Freight Scale "per day (or pro rata)."[19] The charterparty may be silent as to whether parts of days shall count proportionately. The presumption is that on those occasions a part of a day is counted as a whole one,[20] but the presumption may be negatived by express or implied terms. The old rule that parts of lay days counted as whole days gave way to the division of days[21]; the rule that demurrage days count as whole days still exists but it seems that it would not be difficult for that presumption to be negatived.

"Once on demurrage,[22] always on demurrage"   **10–50**

The expression "once on demurrage, always on demurrage"[23] is usually, but not invariably, true. Demurrage runs continuously except where express words or custom prevent it from doing so. This is so whether or not the demurrage time is limited. The periods excepted from laytime do not generally interrupt demurrage. The reason for the difference is that after laytime ends charterers are in breach of the contract; shipowners can then say with justice that, but for the breach, the ship would not be detained during the otherwise excepted period, whether it be a Sunday, a holiday or a period of bad weather or a strike.[24] When the ship is travelling between two ports, the demurrage period begun at one port does not continue to run, as she is on the voyage contemplated by the parties.[25] So in *Breynton* v. *Theodoridi & Co.*,[25] the ship came on demurrage at the first port and a question arose as to whether demurrage ran while she was moving to the second port. Rowlatt J. said, at p. 12 " . . . as to when she is on demurrage at the first port, I still think that while she is going from that port to the

---

[19] Baltimore Form C.

[20] So Lush J. in *Commercial SS. Co.* v. *Boulton* (1875) L.R. 10 Q.B. 346 at p. 349: "There is no ground for saying that in the case of demurrage there can be any division of a day, without express stipulation to that effect." For his refusal to divide a day, see § 2–18 above.

[21] *Branckelow SS. Co.* v. *Lamport & Holt* [1897] 1 Q.B. 570; and see §§ 7–32 and 7–33.

[22] See the Charterparty Laytime Definitions (in the Appendix to this book), at Definition 28, and n. 3 above.

[23] One sometimes finds judicial use of this common expression. In *Salamis Shipping (Panama) S.A.* v. *Edm. van Meerbeeck & Co. S.A.* [1971] 2 Lloyd's Rep. 29 at p. 34 (C.A.) (*The Onisilos*), Fenton Atkinson L.J. said: "The arbitrators accepted the charterers' contention of 'once on half demurrage' always on 'half demurrage.' " See § 10–59 below. It was also cited and applied in *Islamic Republic of Iran Shipping Lines* v. *Royal Bank of Scotland* [1987] 1 Lloyd's Rep. 266 (*The Anna Ch.*), where demurrage ran, and was not interrupted, though the ship was 600 miles from the intended discharging port; see § 10–03 above. In *Superfos Chartering A/S* v. *N.B.R. (London) Ltd.* [1984] 2 Lloyd's Rep. 366, at p. 371 (*The Saturnia*), Bingham J. said: "Once on full demurrage, always on full demurrage." See § 10–60 below. And in *Ricargo Trading S.A.* v. *Spliethoff's Bevrachtingskantor B.V.* [1983] 1 Lloyd's Rep. 648 (*The Tassos N.*) Lloyd J. said, at p. 652: "Although catch phrases seldom help and sometimes confuse legal analysis, this is, as it seems to me, a true case where one can apply the phrase 'Once on demurrage, always on demurrage.' " See § 8–49 below.

[24] On strikes, see the judgment of Lord Reid in *Compania Naviera Aeolus S.A.* v. *President of India (The Spalmatori)* [1962] 2 Lloyd's Rep. 175 at p. 182 (H.L.): " . . . the owner might well say: 'if you had fulfilled your contract the strike would have caused no loss because my ship would have been on the high seas before it began: so it is more reasonable that you should bear the loss than that I should."

[25] (1924) 19 Ll.L.R. 409.

other port she is not being detained by the charterers. She is going on the voyage contemplated and she is not being detained by the charterers in loading at all. It is a fallacy in my judgment to apply the expression 'Once on demurrage, always on demurrage' so as to bring in this time of transit, because as I have already pointed out,[26] the exclusion of the transit from the lay days in the first instance is not an exception at all. It is never within so as to be taken out." In the absence of words to the contrary demurrage will begin again on arrival at the destination, be it a port or a berth, irrespective of any notice period, as such a period relates usually only to laytime and its commencement or re-commencement.[27]

10–51   The principle, therefore, is that demurrage is to run continuously in the absence of express provision to the contrary. It has been upheld where there was a dispute as to whether the words "time so used to not count" had the effect of interrupting laytime. In *Dias Compania Naviera S.A.* v. *Louis Dreyfus Corporation*[28] the House of Lords held that these words had no further application once laytime had expired. The *Dias* had carried wheat, under a voyage charterparty on the Baltimore Form C, from Philadelphia to Hsinkang, China. Clause 15 stated: "At discharging, Charterers . . . have the option at any time to treat at their expense ship's holds/compartments/hatchway and/or cargo and time so used to not count. . . . " She arrived at Hsinkang roads on October 3, 1973. Laytime began on October 4 and expired on October 26. Between November 9 and 25 the receivers had the cargo fumigated, the ship still being in the roads. She berthed on December 6 and completed discharge on December 10. The charterers contended that they could exclude from demurrage the period occupied by fumigation. They relied particularly upon the phrase "at any time" in clause 15, saying that the words "time so used to not count" related back to these earlier words. Lord Diplock, in the House of Lords,[29] pointed out that with dry cargoes the actual discharging was an operation which could be carried on not continuously for 24 hours in each successive day, but only intermittently, as weather and working days at the port permitted. There had to be an agreed formula to enable the time allowed to the charterers to be calculated; it would provide for exceptions in respect of various periods, such as Sundays and holidays, and times used for various stated purposes. If laytime, so calculated, ended before charterers had completed the discharge (or loading) operations there was a breach of contract, daily demurrage constituting the liquidated damages due for that continuing breach. He then said[30]:

> "Since demurrage is liquidated damages, fixed by agreement between the parties, it is possible by apt words in the charter-party to provide that, notwithstanding the continuance of the breach, demurrage shall not be payable in respect of the period when some event specified in the charter-party is happening . . . As was said by Lord Justice Scrutton in a passage in his work on charter-parties[31] that was cited by Lord Reid in the *Union*

---

[26] See § 8–48 above.
[27] *Pagnan & Fratelli* v. *Tradax Export S.A.* [1969] 1 Lloyd's Rep. 150. See also the cases as to the six hours clause, set out in §§ 10–52 and 10–53 below.
[28] [1978] 1 Lloyd's Rep. 325, reversing a majority decision of the Court of Appeal, [1977] 1 Lloyd's Rep. 485, and so upholding a judgment by Mocatta J. in the Commercial Court, [1976] 2 Lloyd's Rep. 395, in favour of the shipowners.
[29] *Op. cit.* at p. 328. All the other Law Lords agreed with him.
[30] *Ibid.*
[31] *Scrutton on Charterparties*, 16th ed. (1955) at p. 353.

of India case[32] . . . 'When once a vessel is on demurrage no exceptions will operate to prevent demurrage continuing to be payable unless the exceptions clause is clearly worded so as to have that effect.' "[33]

Turning to the phrase "time so used to not count" he added[34]:

" . . . my immediate reaction, like that of Mr. Justice Mocatta, is that the answer to the question: For what purpose is time used in fumigation 'not to count'? would be: 'for the purpose of calculating laytime.' These words do not seem to me to be an apt way of saying that the time so used is not to be taken into account in assessing the damages payable by the charterer for breach of contract for failing to complete the discharging operation within the stipulated time."

The prima facie rule that demurrage runs continuously may also apply **10–52** where the ship has been on demurrage at an earlier port, and arrives at another port; a charterparty notice period which would delay the beginning of laytime is not effective to prevent the continuance of demurrage. This was confirmed by the decision in *Nippon Yusen Kaisha* v. *Société Anonyme Morocaine de l'Industrie du Raffinage*.[35] The *Tsukuba Maru* was chartered on the Exxonvoy 69 form to carry petroleum from Khor al Amaya, Iraq, to Mohammedia, Morocco. Clause 6[35a] of the charterparty stated: "Notice of readiness: Upon arrival at customary anchorage at each port of loading or discharge the Master . . . shall give the Charterer . . . notice . . . that the vessel is ready to load or discharge the cargo berth or no berth and lay time . . . shall commence upon the expiration of six (6) hours after receipt of such notice, or upon vessel's arrival in berth . . . whichever first occurs. However, where delay is caused to vessel getting into berth after giving notice of readiness for any reason over which the charterer has no control, such delay shall not count as used laytime."[36] Demurrage was payable " . . . for all time that loading and discharging and used laytime . . . exceeds the allowed laytime." At her loading port the ship used all 72 hours of laytime available for loading and discharging and a further period of 2 hours 10 minutes on demurrage. When the ship arrived off Mohammedia she gave notice of readiness but because of bad weather could not moor at the terminal for another nine days. The charterers said that they were entitled to the benefit of the six hours before demurrage recommenced.

Mocatta J. held that there was nothing to indicate that the laytime exceptions applied once the ship was on demurrage. He cited a passage from the judgment of Lord Guest in *Union of India* v. *Compania Naviera Aeolus*

---

[32] *Union of India* v. *Compania Naviera Aeolus S.A.* [1964] A.C. 868 (H.L.) at p. 879. See § 6–04 above.

[33] For an example of an application of the principle, see *Food Corporation of India* v. *Carras Shipping Co. Ltd.* (*The Delian Leto*) [1983] 2 Lloyd's Rep. 496. The words were: "Lightening . . . to be at owners' risks and expense and time used not to count as laytime." Lloyd J. said (at p. 499) that the case was "even clearer than was the case which reached the House of Lords," because of the reference to laytime.

[34] *Op. cit.* at pp. 328–329.

[35] [1979] 1 Lloyd's Rep. 459. (*The Tsukuba Maru*). See also *Mosvolds Rederi A/S* v. *Food Corporation of India* [1982] 2 Lloyd's Rep. 569, (*The King Theras*) where Staughton J. said, at p. 573: "Counsel are agreed that a notice period is like an exception and does not apply to a vessel already on demurrage." That result, he added, was said to flow from *Pagnan & Fratelli* v. *Tradax Export S.A.* [1969] 1 Lloyd's Rep. 150 (see § 10–50, n. 27, above), the *Nippon Yusa Kaisha* case, and the *Dias Compania Naviera S.A.* case (see § 10–51 above).

[35a] For a brief history of this and related clauses see § 4–33 above.

[36] For this last sentence see the cases discussed at § 4–36–4–38 above.

S.A.[37] to the effect that during demurrage the charterers were in breach and had to bring themselves within an exception to prevent demurrage arising. He referred also to the judgment of Lord Diplock in *Dias Compania Naviera S.A.* v. *Louis Dreyfus Corporation*[38] in which he said that it was possible by apt words to provide that demurrage should not be payable in respect of the period when some specified event was happening. The charterparty was inconsistent in its use of the phrase "used laytime"; it seemed that no technical distinction was intended between allowed laytime and used laytime, and that the latter phrase was not a term of art.[38a]

10–53　　The judge had been referred to a New York arbitration involving a charterparty also on the Exxonvoy 69 form, concerning the *Atlantic Monarch*.[39] The arbitrators had considered similar circumstances, the ship having had to wait at least six hours at anchorage at each discharging port. They had decided that the sentence referring to delay for reasons over which the charterers had no control was effective to interrupt demurrage. Mocatta J., noting that it said that such delay should "not count as used laytime," disagreed[40]: "The last sentence . . . can be given full effect when the ship in question is not on demurrage, but there is nothing contained within it or in the remainder of that clause to indicate that it applies when a vessel is on demurrage." There was also cited to the Court another New York arbitration award[41] in which, on similar facts and words, another tribunal came to an opposite decision and in favour of the shipowners.

This decision was followed in *Total Transport Corporation* v. *Amoco Trading Co.*[42] Webster J. referred[43] to the earlier case as one " . . . where the charterparty was in precisely the same terms (Exxonvoy 1969 form), where permitted laytime had been wholly used at the loading port, and where the charterers claimed in an arbitration to be entitled to the benefit, *inter alia*, of six hours after notice of readiness at the discharge port." Here the *Altus* had carried crude oil from Ashtart, Tunisia, to Genoa. Notice of readiness was given at Genoa, but the ship did not move from her anchorage to the berth for five days. The charterers argued that the six hours after the notice, and the time spent moving to the berth, should be excepted from the demurrage. Webster J. agreed with the judgment of Mocatta J. in

---

[37] [1964] A.C. 868 at p. 869 (*The Spalmatori*), set out at § 10–55 below.
[38] [1978] 1 Lloyd's Rep. 325 at p. 328 (H.L.) (*The Dias*). See § 10–50 above.
[38a] A view echoed in a London arbitration (LMLN 160, January 2, 1986) where, under the Asbatankvoy form, charterers contended unsuccessfully that time spent shifting from a customary place of anchorage to a discharging berth should interrupt demurrage. The provision that the time should "not count as used laytime" was not sufficiently clear to interrupt demurrage. Another panel decided (on cl. 11 of the STB VOY form) that demurrage stopped when ballasting began (LMLN 72, August 5, 1982).
[39] *Atlantic Monarch Shipping Co.* v. *Hess Oil & Chemical Division* (1975) A.M.C. 1991.
[40] *Op. cit.* at p. 473.
[41] *Glara Steamship Company* v. *Sun Oil Company* (1975) A.M.C. 2643. The 1977 Report of the United Kingdom Freight, Demurrage and Defence Association Ltd. referred, at p. 23, to an award in favour of the shipowners, in a dispute as to the Exxonvoy 69 form, *Red. A/B Sally* v. *Amerada Hess Shipping Corporation*, Society of Maritime Arbitrators, Award No. 1015 (1976) (*The Pegny*). It added: " . . . the position would probably be the same in England . . . this point has frequently been considered in New York arbitration and there are at least seven reported decisions in favour of the owners and two in favour of charterers. Until, therefore, a court has to decide the matter, the position cannot be stated authoritatively." But see now the *Tsukuba Maru* decision at § 10–52 above.
[42] [1985] 1 Lloyd's Rep. 423 (*The Altus*).
[43] *Ibid.* at p. 431.

the *Nippon Yusen Kaisha* case, and concluded that the two periods counted against demurrage.[44]

Demurrage interrupted by express words

Express words may be used to limit or to interrupt demurrage, as where demurrage is agreed to be due only in respect of such days as would have qualified as lay days. One clause[45] read: "The cargo to be loaded in 72 hours (from 5 p.m. Saturday to 7 a.m. Mondays, colliery holidays, play days, and general holidays excepted) . . . and to be discharged as fast as steamer can deliver as customary; and if longer detained charterers to pay 16s. 8d. per like hours demurrage . . . " Other clauses, linking the demurrage and the laytime provisions, may use such words as "per like day," or even state specifically the various exceptions, which may or may not be the same as those in the laytime clause. In the Fiji Charterparty[46] some of the exceptions are the same: "Sundays and holidays are not to count as lay or demurrage days under this charter." In *Lilly* v. *Stevenson*[47] the exceptions were different and demurrage was payable at "12s. 6d. per hour unless detention arises from a lock-out, strikes, etc."

The Asbatankvoy form, for example, is also drafted so that demurrage is affected when one of various events occurs. Thus: "If, however, demurrage shall be incurred at ports of loading and/or discharge by reason of fire, explosion, storm[47a] or by a strike, lockout, stoppage or restraint of labour or by breakdown of machinery or equipment . . . the rate of demurrage shall be reduced one-half . . . "[47b]

An example of the use of express words to limit both laytime and demurrage is to be found in the STB voyage charterparty.[47c] Clause 11 states: "Laytime, or, if the Vessel is on demurrage, time on demurrage shall continue until the hoses have been disconnected, or until ballasting begins at the discharge port(s), whichever occurs first." The ship might begin to ballast while some cargo remains to be discharged. If so, laytime or demurrage would no longer count, although work remained to be done. This situation arose in a London arbitration,[47d] where crude oil had been carried from Das Island, United Arab Emirates, to Mohammedia, Morocco. The shipowners contended that, in addition to the apparent anomaly of work continuing after time ended, the ship might be topping up its permanent ballast, rather than preparing its other ballast system for the next voyage. However, there was no evidence of the existence of permanent

---

[44] He cited (at p. 432) Atkin L.J. in *Aktieselskabet Reidar* v. *Arcos Ltd.* [1927] 1 K.B. 352 (C.A.), at p. 363, who said that he conceived it to be " . . . the well established principle that, unless by express stipulation, exceptions that would protect the charterer during lay days no longer protect him during demurrage days." In *Shipping Corporation of India* v. *Sun Oil Company* [1986] A.M.C. 2752 (*The Maharshi Dayanand*) the Eastern District Court of Pennsylvania decided that demurrage did not count during the six hours period; the form was Asbatankvoy 1977.

[45] In *Rayner* v. *Rederiaktiebolaget Condor* (1895) 1 Com. Cas. 80.

[46] For the carriage of sugar in bulk from Fiji to the U.K.

[47] (1895) 22 R. 278.

[47a] In a London arbitration (LMLN 166, March 13, 1986) the arbitrator considered whether bad weather amounted to a storm. He felt that in the particular case he should be guided by the Beaufort Scale, and the deck log figures, though there would have been an interesting question of construction as to the meaning of the word "storm."

[47b] Perhaps to the extent that it has been increased.

[47c] As to its obsolescence, see § 4–33 above.

[47d] LMLN 72, August 5, 1982.

water ballast or of ballast water being freshened up. The panel felt bound to apply the precise words of Clause 11, and decided against the shipowners. It was not a sensible clause, but the parties had accepted it.

10–55   The STB voyage charterparty contains two other clauses relating to the interruption of laytime and demurrage. These were considered by the House of Lords in *Société Anonyme Marocaine de l'Industrie du Raffinage* v. *Notos Maritime Corporation*.[48] The case is also interesting for what it had to say about the expressions "berth or no berth"; and "any other cause of whatsoever nature." The parts of the clauses which were relevant to the case were:

> "6. Upon arrival at customary anchorages at each port of loading or discharge, the master shall give the charterer notice . . . that the vessel is ready to load or discharge cargo, berth or no berth, and laytime, or, if the vessel is on demurrage, time on demurrage shall commence upon the expiration of six hours after receipt of such notice, or upon the vessel's arrival in berth.[49] However, where delay is caused to vessel getting into berth after giving notice of readiness for any reason whatsoever over which charterer has no control, such delay shall not count as laytime or as time on demurrage."

and:—

> "8. Charterer shall pay demurrage per running hour and pro rata . . . at the rate specified . . . for all time that laytime . . . is exceeded . . . If, however, demurrage shall be incurred at ports or loading and/or discharge for delays by reason of fire, explosion, storm or by a strike, lockout, stoppage or restraint of labor or by breakdown of machinery or equipment in or about the plant of the charterer, supplier, shipper or consignee of the cargo, such demurrage shall be calculated at one-half the rate specified . . . Laytime shall not run or, if the vessel is on demurrage, demurrage shall not accrue, for any delay caused by strike, lockout, stoppage or restraint of labor of master, officers and crew of the vessel or tugboats or pilots or any other cause of whatsoever nature or kind over which the charterer has no control."

The *Notos* carried crude oil from Ras Tanura, Saudi Arabia, to Mohammedia, Morocco. She arrived, gave notice of readiness, and went to the customary anchorage; there was such a swell, for nearly three weeks, that no ship could discharge at the charterers' customary sea-line. This time was called Period A. When the swell abated, however, another tanker was discharging there, so that the *Notos* could only make its sea-line connection three days later, when the tanker had finished (Period B). As a result of another heavy swell she was ordered away for five days (Period C).

As for Period A, the shipowners contended that as a result of Clause 6 the charterers were responsible for ensuring that a berth was available for the ship on her arrival,[50] and that its last sentence, interrupting demurrage, only operated when delay was caused to the ship getting into the berth to which she had been ordered to proceed. They relied strongly on the words "berth or no berth" in the first sentence of the clause. Lord Goff, in a speech with which the other Law Lords agreed, said[51] of the words "berth or no berth":

> "Their function, as I see it, is no more than to provide that notice of readiness can be

---

[48] [1987] 1 Lloyd's Rep. 503.

[49] Which was to include the completion of mooring when the ship was at a sea loading or discharging terminal.

[50] They relied on what their Counsel called the similar provisions of the charterparty considered by the House of Lords in *Nereide S.p.A. di Navigazione* v. *Bulk Oil International Ltd.* [1982] 1 Lloyd's Rep. 1 (*The Laura Prima*), but this submission failed; see § 4–38 above.

[51] *Op. cit.* at p. 507.

given upon arrival at the customary anchorage, and can take effect whether or not a berth is then available for the vessel."

He did not accept the view that the only excepted delay was that suffered while the ship went from the anchorage to the berth, and said[52]:

"As I read the words, the delay there referred to is postponement of the time (for any reason whatsoever over which the charterers have no control) when the vessel, having arrived at the port and given notice of readiness, can get into her berth."[53]

In the case of Period B, when the *Notos* was waiting for the other tanker to discharge, the arbitrators and the High Court had upheld the shipowners' claim for demurrage. The charterers accepted the decision of Leggatt J., so that this matter did not go to the Court of Appeal and the House of Lords.

The House of Lords held that no demurrage accrued during Period C, during which the *Notos* had been ordered away from the sea-line connection owing to heavy swell. Lord Goff summarised his views[54]:

"The Judge reached the conclusion that, just as delay caused by swell fell within the exception in the concluding sentence of cl. 6, so also it fell within the concluding sentence of cl. 8, as a cause of delay over which the charterers had no control. The Court of Appeal agreed with that conclusion; and I myself feel that, once the conclusion is reached that the exception in cl. 6 is wide enough to embrace swell, it is inevitable that the exception in cl. 8 should likewise be so construed."

The immediately subsequent words of Lord Goff are important for what he said about the word "whatsoever":

"Mr Rix [Counsel for shipowners] struggled to convince your Lordships that, despite the presence of the word 'whatsoever' in the exception, a limited meaning should be placed upon it, derived from the events expressly excepted in the last sentence, restricted to cause, relating to the vessel or her owners or those for whom they are responsible. I can only say that I can see no basis for so limiting an exception which is expressed to exclude delay caused by—
    . . . any other cause of whatsoever nature or kind over which the charterer has no control."

The words on which reliance is placed, with a view to the interruption of **10–56** demurrage, may be expressed in more general terms. In the Centrocon charterparty clause 36 provides:

"The act of God, restraint of Princes and Rulers, the Country's enemies, fire, floods, droughts and all and every dangers and accident of the seas, river and navigation of whatsoever nature and kind, riots, strikes or stoppages at seaboard and all and every other unavoidable hindrances which may prevent the loading and discharging and delivery during the said voyage always mutually [excepted]."

In *Marc Rich & Co. Ltd.* v. *Tourloti Compania Naviera S.A.*[55] this clause appeared in a charterparty for the carriage of steel scrap from Rotterdam to "one safe berth Bombay or so near thereto as she may safely get and lie always afloat and there deliver the cargo." The shipowners were entitled to give notice of readiness whether the ship was in berth or not. As

---

[52] *Ibid.*
[53] He added, also at p. 507, that he was fortified in his view because a similar meaning was placed on the words by "three experienced commercial arbitrators, by an experienced commercial Judge [Leggatt J.], and by a Court of Appeal of which two members were also experienced commercial judges" (Sir John Donaldson M.R. and Parker L.J., the other being Balcombe L.J.). In addition his four colleagues in the House of Lords agreed. The time of 12 persons acting in a judicial capacity was thus occupied in deciding this case.
[54] *Op. cit.* at p. 507.
[55] [1988] 2 Lloyd's Rep. 101 (*The Kalliopi A*) (C.A.).

a result of congestion, no berth was available when the ship arrived, and notice was given when she was anchored at the pilot station. After two months she moved to the inner anchorage, where she was able to discharge some cargo into lighters for 15 days. She went to her discharging berth a few days later. The charterers relied on clause 36, in defence to a claim for demurrage, though they agreed that the time spent discharging into lighters should count. They won in the High Court but failed in the Court of Appeal.

Evans J., finding for charterers, said that the words "all and every other unavoidable hindrance which may prevent the loading and discharging" covered congestion. He rejected a contention by shipowners that, since clause 36 did not include words such as "of what kind soever," the *ejusdem generis* rule should apply. He said[55a]: " . . . apart from the difficulty of identifying the supposed *genus* in the earlier part of the clause, the words themselves are wide enough to include at least a well-recognised kind of 'hindrance,' as congestion is." The argument that the clause only applied when the cause of delay was exceptional or abnormal had been rejected in *Pagnan (R.) and Fratelli* v. *Finagrain Compagnie Commerciale Agricole et Financière S.A.*[56] The suggestion was that the exception did not operate if the congestion was "endemic and notorious."[57]

The judge concluded[58]: "The central issue is whether clause 36 operates so as to exclude the charterer's liability for demurrage. To have that effect the clause must be clearly intended to do so. Short of identifying 'demurrage' by name, the words are clear: 'unavoidable hindrance [sc. congestion] which may prevent the . . . discharging . . . always mutually excepted.' This must be commercial shorthand for 'neither party to be liable for the consequences of,' . . . So the clause purports to exempt charterers from their liability for what will be put forward as a demurrage claim . . . it is permissible to give effect to clause 36 as an exception to the liability otherwise imposed by clause 13[59] . . ." He said that this conclusion gave effect to the words of clause 36 without infringing the undoubted rule that any demurrage exception must be clearly worded.[60]

The Court of Appeal, finding in favour of the shipowners, held that interpretation of the charterparty could not be conducted solely on the basis of the ordinary meaning of the contractual words; regard should be had to what the same or similar words had been held to mean in the past. It was established law that an exceptions clause had to be clearly worded if it was to operate to prevent demurrage continuing to be payable. As Staughton L.J. said of clause 36[60a]: "There is no doubt that the clause can have some effect quite apart from any liability of the charterers for demurrage. Thus it would provide exemption if there were a total ban on the export of scrap at the loading port, or on the import of scrap at the discharging port;

[55a] [1987] 2 Lloyd's Rep. 263 at p. 267.
[56] [1986] 2 Lloyd's Rep. 395. (*The Adolf Leonhardt*).
[57] The words used by Staughton J. in *The Adolf Leonhardt*.
[58] [1987] 2 Lloyd's Rep. 263 at p. 267.
[59] The clause imposing liability to pay demurrage.
[60] He concluded by saying that he had been provided by counsel with an agreed note of the judgment of Leggatt J. in *President of India* v. *N.G. Livanos Maritime Co.* [1987] 2 Lloyd's Rep. 188 (*The John Michalos*) (see § 10–57 below at n. 60d), decided a few weeks earlier. He considered that there was nothing in that case which was inconsistent with his conclusion, though it was concerned with materially different facts and a different clause.
[60a] *Op. cit.*, at pp. 106–107.

or if all available scrap were destroyed by enemies, fire or flood." He concluded[60b] by citing the words of Lord Edmund-Davies in *The Dias*[60c]:
" . . . the authorities . . . established that no exceptions clause will prevent demurrage from continuing to be payable unless such is clearly the effect of its language . . ."

Strike clauses   **10–57**

Exceptions clauses may exclude Sundays and holidays from the demurrage period or may have a more prolonged effect, by excluding periods longer than a day. In the event of strikes, for example, demurrage may cease to run until normal work is resumed, but only if the exceptions clause so provides.[60d]

The Centrocon Strike Clause

The Centrocon Strike Clause[61] refers, in its first sentence, to inability to load or discharge by reason of riots, civil commotions, strikes, lock-outs, or to load by reason of obstructions or stoppages beyond the control of the charterers on the railways or in the docks or other loading places. Laytime does not count during the continuance of such causes; the first sentence of the clause concludes with the following proviso: " . . . provided that a strike or lock-out of the Shippers' and/or Receivers men shall not present demurrage accruing if by the use of reasonable diligence they could have obtained other suitable labour at rates current before the Strike or Lock-out." There follows the second sentence: "In case of any delay by reason of the before-mentioned causes, no claim for damages or demurrage shall be made by the Charterers, Receivers of the Cargo, or Owners of the Steamer.[62]

These two sentences thus provide that: (a) laytime does not count during the continuance of certain causes,[63] but nevertheless demurrage may still accrue if shippers and/or receivers could with reasonable diligence have obtained suitable labour at rates previously current; (b) no one shall claim demurrage or damages if there is any delay by reason of the said causes. As for (b) it has been held[64] that delay by strikes which occur after laytime has ended does not entitle the receivers to repudiate a demurrage claim. The

---

[60b] *Ibid.*, at p. 107.
[60c] *Dias Compania Naviera S.A.* v. *Louis Dreyfus Corporation* [1978] 1 Lloyd's Rep. 325 (H.L.), at p. 329. See § 10–51 above.
[60d] For example, the typed clause "Charterers shall not be liable for any delay in . . . discharging . . . which delay . . . is caused in whole or in part by . . . strikes" appeared in the charterparty in *President of India* v. *N.G. Livanos Maritime Co.* [1987] 2 Lloyd's Rep. 188 (*The John Michalos*). It was held that demurrage was interrupted.
[61] Part of the River Plate Charterparty 1914 (Centrocon), but sometimes added, not always with satisfactory results, to other forms of charterparty. The first two sentences of the Clause are set out at § 8–39 above; the third sentence appears at § 12–20 below.
[62] For the third sentence see § 12–20 below.
[63] An arbitrator has held that whereas this provision may only help the charterers when the cause of the delay affects the operation of loading, an appropriately worded force majeure clause may apply, where the delay affected the provision of cargo for loading. See *Marrealeza Compania Naviera S.A.* v. *Tradax Export S.A.* [1982] 1 Lloyd's Rep. 52 (*The Nichos A*) and § 8–41, n. 57, above.
[64] *Compania Naviera Aeolus S.A.* v. *Union of India* [1962] 2 Lloyd's Rep. 175 (H.L.) (*The Spalmatori*); distinguished in *Navico A.G.* v. *Vrontados Naftiki Etairia P.E.* [1968] 1 Lloyd's Rep. 379 at p. 385, by Donaldson J., as being a case which dealt with a strike breaking out at discharging port after expiry of laytime and while ship was on demurrage.

effect of strikes which occur before laytime has ended is discussed else-where.[65]

10–58 The Centrocon Strike Clause was construed by the House of Lords in *Compania Naviera Aeolus S.A.* v. *Union of India*.[66] A charterparty on the Baltimore Form C, for the carriage of wheat from a United States port to Bombay, had attached to it the Centrocon Strike Clause.[67] Three days after laytime had expired discharge was prevented for eight days and ten hours by a strike which fell within the clause. The receivers said that they were not liable to pay demurrage for that period.

The courts were thus asked to decide whether demurrage which had already started to run should be interrupted.[68] The House of Lords held by a majority[69] that it was not interrupted. As to the proviso at the end of the first sentence, Lord Reid said[70]:

> "The reference to preventing demurrage accruing is not happy, but I think that the meaning is clear enough. The existence of the strike is not to prevent demurrage from beginning to accrue at the end of the stipulated laytime if other labour was available. Without the proviso demurrage would not have begun to accrue then; the first part of the clause would have prevented that and demurrage would only have begun to accrue at the end of the stipulated laytime *plus* the time during which the strike prevented work."

As for the apparent exclusion, in the second sentence, of claims for demur-rage or damages if there was any delay[71] by reason of the said causes (the strike in this case), the receivers argued that they came within the clause. Lord Reid said that the first and third sentences of the Centrocon Strike Clause,[72] and the third sentence dealing with dispatch,[73] could only apply where a strike occurred before the end of the laytime. The receivers con-tended that there was no such limitation as regards the second sentence. He continued:

> "If you read the provision literally then if there were one day's delay by reason of a strike but 10 days' demurrage there could be no claim at all for the demurrage. . . ."

He concluded that the receivers' contention was misconceived as it would, if upheld, produce insuperable contradictions[74] within the strike clause as a whole. The second sentence was thus inapplicable to this case where the

---

[65] See § 8–37 above; and for dispatch see § 12–20 below.
[66] [1962] 2 Lloyd's Rep. 175 (H.L.) (*The Spalmatori*). It was also construed by the High Court in *Navico A.G.* v. *Vrontados Naftiki Etaria P.E.* [1968] 1 Lloyd's Rep. 379. See §§ 8–40 above and 12–20 below.
[67] The effect of the first sentence of the clause, so far as it referred to the suspension of lay-time, is discussed in § 8–40 above.
[68] This was also the case in *Superfos Chartering A/S* v. *N.B.R. (London) Ltd.* (*The Saturnia*) [1984] 2 Lloyd's Rep. 366, which, however, involved the Gencon Strike Clause; see § 10–60 below.
[69] Three (Lord Reid, Lord Hodson and Lord Guest) to two (Lord Cohen and Lord Morris of Borth-y-Gest).
[70] At p. 181.
[71] In *Marc Rich & Co. Ltd.* v. *Tourloti Compania Naviera S.A.* [1987] 2 Lloyd's Rep. 263 (*The Kalliopi A*) Evans J. said, at pp. 267–8, that Lord Reid's analysis of the Centrocon Strike Clause made the distinction between "prevent," meaning a stoppage of work, and "delay," meaning that the operation was prolonged and completed later, without a stop-page at any time.
[72] See § 8–40 above.
[73] See § 12–20 below.
[74] Discussed in detail in [1962] 2 Lloyd's Rep. 175 at pp. 181–182 (H.L.).

strike began after the end of the lay days. Of the functions of the first part of the first sentence and of the second sentence, he said[75]:

> "As I said when dealing with the first part, that part does not cover two kinds of case (1) where the strike does not stop work, but merely slows down the loading or unloading and (2) where the after-effects of the strike stop or slow down the work. The third part[76] may well have been intended to cover such cases: it is unnecessary to decide whether or not it does so. Then the third part alone contains any reference to claims for damages by the charterers or receivers of the cargo. But Counsel were unable to suggest any likely case in which such a claim could arise out of any of the 'before-mentioned causes,' and I think therefore that this reference must have been inserted simply as a precaution and should not influence the decision of this case . . . There is no wholly satisfactory interpretation or explanation of the third part of the clause and one must choose between two almost equally unsatisfactory conclusions."

His choice was in favour of the shipowners, in that he held that the demurrage was uninterrupted. Stating that the conclusion was not an arbitrary one, he stressed that where a strike occurred during the demurrage period the charterers or receivers were already in breach of contract for having delayed the ship. But for this breach, the strike would have had no effect, for the ship would already have departed. As Lord Hodson put it[77]:

> " . . . the respondents" [the receiver] "are in breach already and on demurrage so that they have reached a position of vulnerability to delay caused by strikes which they would never have reached if they had complied with the terms of their contract."

The Gencon Strike Clause **10–59**

The Gencon Strike Clause[78] was construed by the Court of Appeal in *Salamis Shipping (Panama) S.A.* v. *Edm. van Meerbeeck & Co. S.A.*[79] The *Onisios* was chartered on the Gencon form to carry mixed cargo from Antwerp to Charleston, Mobile and Houston. At Charleston there was already a strike "affecting the discharge" when she arrived, with six days of laytime left for the three ports. This time was exhausted at Charleston in waiting for the strikes to end. It was agreed that the charterers, by failing to give orders for an alternative port, had exercised their option of keeping her waiting until the strike ended. The shipowners said that the "half demurrage after expiration of the time provided for discharging"[80] was payable (1) while the ship was waiting for the strike to end, with full demurrage thereafter; or (2) until completion of discharge at Charleston with full demurrage thereafter; or (3) until the end of the strike and thereafter for any periods of delay presumably caused by a strike. The charterers claimed half demurrage for all time after laytime ended, *i.e.* while the ship waited for the strike to end; while she discharged at Charleston after the strike ended; while she discharged at Mobile; and while, at Houston, she waited for a berth and then discharged.

The Court of Appeal held that the charterers were right. The opening sentence of the clause, by which neither party was to be "responsible for

---

[75] At p. 182.
[76] *i.e.* the second sentence.
[77] At p. 190.
[78] For the wording of the clause see § 8–45 above.
[79] [1971] 2 Lloyd's Rep. 29.
[80] Of these words, in Part 3 of the Gencon Strike Clause (see § 8–45 above for the full wording) Bingham J. in *Superfos Chartering A/S* v. *N.B.R. (London) Ltd.* [1984] 2 Lloyd's Rep. 366, at p. 371 (*The Saturnia*), said: " . . . the reference to paying half demurrage after expiration of the time provided for discharging does suggest that the draftsman had in mind a strike or lock-out taking effect before laytime had expired." For a strike starting after laytime had expired, see § 10–60 below.

the consequences of any strikes or lock-outs preventing or delaying the fulfilment of any obligations," meant that the charterers were not liable for demurrage from the expiry of laytime until the end of the strike. It was agreed by the shipowners that the charterers were liable for half demurrage during that period. They could not be liable for full demurrage for the period from the end of the strike till the end of congestion if the provision as to "consequences" was to have any effect. But they were liable for half demurrage not only then, but also from the end of congestion until the end of the discharge. The only alternative for these last two periods was that there should be no demurrage and then full demurrage. That would have meant drawing a line between the two periods. As Lord Denning M.R. said,[81] it was:

> "a very uncertain and difficult line to draw . . . It seems to me that when this strike clause was framed, the parties must have foreseen that complications would arise if they tried to divide up the periods—and that it was entirely a matter of chance how it would turn out. So they cut the Gordian Knot on a 50–50 basis. That is to say, in case of a strike, after the laytime expires the charterers are to pay half demurrage until the discharging is complete."

This view that the Gencon Strike Clause should be taken as a whole, and treated as an attempt to spread responsibility and expense fairly between shipowners and charterers, was shared by the two other appeal judges. Fenton Atkinson L.J. said[82]:

> " . . . the shipowners' construction of clause 3, far from achieving a fair apportionment of loss, must in almost any circumstances, operate gravely to the charterers' disadvantage. As I see it, it involves them paying half demurrage during the strike itself and full demurrage during a period of delay caused by the consequences of the strike after the strike itself is over, instead of paying nothing during either of these periods under par.[83] 1 of the clause."

So also Sir Gordon Willmer[84]:

> "By opting to pay demurrage at half rate, instead of nothing, during such time as the strike might last, the charterers would reap the corresponding advantage of continuing to pay at only half the rate until the completion of discharge at the final port. This would be a sensible and reasonable return for the sacrifice they made by opting to pay demurrage at half the rate during the continuance of the strike."

10–60   In *Superfos Chartering A/S* v. *N.B.R. (London) Ltd.*[85] the Gencon Strike Clause was again considered, but laytime had expired before the strikes began. The situation was thus factually similar to that considered by the House of Lords in the *Compania Naviera Aeolus* case[86] but, as the Judge said: " . . . they did so when construing the Centrocon strike clause and the speeches of the majority were closely based on the detailed provision of that clause. The present problem of construction is accordingly novel."

The shipowners had chartered the Saturnia on the Gencon form to carry sugar and general cargo from Antwerp to Lagos. The charterparty provided for 19 days for loading and discharging. Laytime at Lagos ended, and demurrage began to run, on May 21, 1982. There were then strikes for three periods of from six to nine days each before discharge was com-

---

[81] *Ibid.* at p. 33.
[82] *Ibid.* at p. 34.
[83] This must mean the opening sentence, or cl. 1.
[84] *Op. cit.* at p. 35.
[85] [1984] 2 Lloyd's Rep. 366 (*The Saturnia*).
[86] [1962] 2 Lloyd's Rep. 175 (H.L.) (*The Spalmatori*); see § 10–58 above.

pleted, on June 29. The shipowners claimed demurrage without interruptions. The charterers contended that as a result of the Gencon Strike Clause they were liable to pay only half demurrage from the beginning of the first strike. Bingham J., finding for the shipowners, held that the "half demurrage" provision had no application where laytime had expired before the discharge was affected by the strike.

He discussed, as did the Court of Appeal in the *Salamis* case,[87] the effect of Part 1, the opening sentence of the clause, relieving the parties from responsibility "for the consequences of any strikes or lock-outs preventing or delaying the fulfilment of any obligations." He accepted as sound the shipowners' submission that when the first strike began the charterers were already in breach of contract, and that, accordingly, the shipowners had an accrued right of demurrage at the full rate; and that the charterers were not prevented or delayed in fulfilling their obligation to pay demurrage by the strikes. But the payment of demurrage was not their only duty; they remained under an obligation to discharge the ship, and the strike affected that obligation.

Saying that the analysis could not begin and end with consideration of Part 1, the Judge referred next to Part 2, which deals with the loading, and said[88]:

" . . . Parts 1 and 2 seem to me to represent a coherent commercial bargain. If a strike or lock-out affects the loading of the vessel at the loading port after expiry of the agreed laytime, the charterer has no relief from his obligation to pay demurrage at the full rate.
It is his fault that the vessel has not been loaded. There is no reason why the owner should suffer loss of his contractual demurrage when, but for the charterer's breach, the loading of the vessel would not have been affected by the strike or lock-out. If the strike or lock-out affects the loading of the vessel during the agreed laytime, and the owner does not seek a declaration from the charterer,[89] the charterer can rely on the exemption in Part 1. He is not in breach, no obligation to pay demurrage has occurred, and if the owner is worse off as a result of failing to seek a declaration of agreement, then he only has himself to blame."

Bingham J. then turned to Part 3, saying[90] that it seemed clear, as in the *Salamis Shipping* case,[91] that it represented:

"a commercial bargain attempting fairly to apportion the loss between the parties. The owner would suffer through losing the use of his ship for only half the contractual compensation, but he would at least recover that. The charterer would suffer either by paying demurrage at a half rate when his inability to discharge was due to no fault of his or by taking the risk of paying full demurrage at an alternative port, but at least his potential liability at the original port would be mitigated."

He said that he did not find in Part 3, or in the clause as a whole, or in the charterparty as a whole, any single and decisive indication of the correct answer to the problem.

He concluded by saying[92]:

" . . . this is a standard clause and it is not unreasonable to attribute to the draftsman the intention to ensure that once laytime had expired, charterers should be subject to their full demurrage obligation. Once on full demurrage, always on full demurrage. I accord-

---

[87] See § 10–59 above.
[88] *Op. cit.* at p. 370.
[89] As is the shipowners' entitlement; see Part 2, set out at § 8–45 above.
[90] *Op. cit.* at p. 370.
[91] See § 10–59.
[92] *Op. cit.* at p. 371. His judgment was upheld in the Court of Appeal: [1987] 2 Lloyd's Rep. 43.

ingly conclude that the half rate provision has no application where laytime has already expired before the discharge of the vessel is affected by the strike or lock-out."

10–61 Comments on:

(a) Centrocon Strike Clause. It is clear from some of the judgments in *Compania Naviera Aeolus S.A.* v. *Union of India*[93] that the Centrocon Strike Clause was considered to be obscure, and it is therefore not surprising that people should have had genuine differences of opinions as to its meaning. The Centrocon charterparty[94] was first published in 1914. It is described in its heading as having been "Arranged and agreed with The Centro de Céréales of Buenos Ayres," the body representing the chartering interests. The form was amended in 1934, 1937, 1950 and 1974.[95]

In his judgment Lord Reid was concerned only with the strike clause, as the charterparty was on the Baltimore Form C, to which the clause was attached. He said[96] of the so-called third part of the clause (by which damage and demurrage claims were said to be available in certain circumstances):

"It is fairly obvious that the third part is not an original part of the Clause, but it is a later addition: I cannot imagine even the least legally minded draftsman drafting the Clause as a whole in its present form. We were informed that the cases show that 50 years ago the Clause was in use without the third part, but I prefer to base my conclusion on the Clause as it stands now."

10–62 **(b) Centrocon charterparty.** In lighter vein, Atkin J. spoke of the Centrocon charterparty generally in 1926, when giving judgment in the Court of Appeal[97]:

"This is one of the numerous and regular disputes upon the terms of the Chamber of Shipping River Plate Charterparty, 1914, a charterparty which must have resulted in the payment of law and other costs in disputes of this kind which, if put together, would, I imagine, be such as to cause an appreciable difference in the price of the quartern loaf."[98]

And Donaldson J. said in 1968[99]:

" . . . the rights of the parties turn upon the construction of the strike clause in the 'Centrocon' form of charter-party. Despite the fact that this charter-party in general and this clause in particular have kept lawyers in congenial employment for years, there is no reported decision bearing directly on the point in issue."

10–63 *Ship unavailable: effect on demurrage*

The rule that demurrage runs continuously is qualified not only where there are express words to the contrary but also where the ship moves away for the convenience of shipowners, or is otherwise unavailable, generally as a result of some action on their part. Thus in *Budgett & Co.* v. *Binn-*

---

[93] [1962] 2 Lloyd's Rep. 175 (H.L.) (*The Spalmatori*). See § 10–52 above.
[94] River Plate Charter-Party 1914.
[95] It is understood that the strike clause as introduced in 1914 was not affected by the amendments. For a possible amendment by the contracting parties, see § 8–42 above.
[96] At p. 181.
[97] In *Ethel Radcliffe SS. Co. Ltd.* v. *Barnett (W. & R.) Ltd.* (1926) 31 Com.Cas. 222 at p. 234 (H.L.). See § 10–17 above.
[98] A four-pound loaf.
[99] In *Navico A.G.* v. *Vrontados Naftiki Etairia P.E.* [1968] 1 Lloyd's Rep. 379 at p. 382. See § 8–40 above.

ington & Co.[1] the Court of Appeal held that it was material to ascertain whose default was responsible for a ship not being available. As Lord Esher M.R. said[2]:

> "If, for instance, the master refused to discharge the cargo, the owner would be responsible."

It must be a question of fact as to whether shipowners must be regarded as responsible for the actions of those who cause the delay. From this decision it appears that the mere fact that labourers on strike are jointly employed by shipowners and charterers does not make shipowners responsible for the delay. But in *Harris* v. *Best, Ryley & Co.*,[3] where the stevedores were appointed by the charterers, but employed and paid for by the shipowners, the latter were held to be liable for delay; the delay had been caused by the re-stowage of cargo which had shifted.

Mere inability on the part of the ship to load or discharge, in the absence of any default on the part of shipowners, does not necessarily assist the charterers. In *Tyne & Blyth Shipping Co. Ltd.* v. *Leech, Harrison & Forwood*[4] a ship was chartered to carry ore from Poti, U.S.S.R, to the U.S.A. Owing to the inability of the charterers to provide a quay berth the ship went on demurrage at anchor, where she was run into by another ship. While she was being repaired at Constantinople a berth fell vacant but she could not take it. On her return to the loading port she was kept waiting a further six weeks for a quay berth. It was held that this period counted as demurrage. The charterers contended that no demurrage was due because the loss of a quay berth arose from a cause (the collision) over which they had no control. They further relied on a general exceptions clause of which the material words were " . . . all causes beyond the control of the . . . charterers which might prevent or delay the delivery of the ore at port of shipment and/or the loading . . . are always mutually excepted." The Commercial Court held that the shipowners were right. Kennedy J. said[5]:

> " . . . when once the shipowners were in a position to say, 'Our vessel is on demurrage, and you are bound under the charterparty to pay us 15s. an hour,' from that time, unless some default could be attributed to the shipowners, the demurrage obligation was enforceable against the charterers . . . the fact that another cause prevented the vessel from getting her berth no more affects the question than if the ship had been driven to sea by a gale of wind, in which case the loss of time could not be attributed to the owners' default."

The shipowners had made no demurrage claim for the period of the repairs, so that the case is not in itself an authority for allowing or excluding such a claim. Nevertheless, the decision can be regarded as being con-

---

[1] [1891] 1 Q.B. 35. Followed in numerous cases, including *Gatoil International Inc.* v. *Tradax Petroleum Ltd.* [1985] 1 Lloyd's Rep. 350 (*The Rio Sun*), where Bingham J. said, at p. 363: "It is questionable whether notice of readiness was given to the refinery on January 2, but whether it was or not the inescapable fact is that the vessel was not ready and willing to discharge at that time . . . It cannot be suggested that Tradax could recover demurrage from Gatoil during a period when the vessel was either unwilling or unable for lack of bunkers to discharge. See *Straker* v. *Kidd & Co.*, (1878) 3 Q.B.D. 223; *Budgett & Co.* v. *Binnington & Co.* [1891] 1 Q.B. 35."
[2] At p. 38.
[3] (1892) 68 L.T. 76 (C.A.).
[4] [1900] 2 Q.B. 12.
[5] At pp. 16–17.

sistent with the other authorities[6] by which only the default of the ship-owners interrupts demurrage. The exceptions clause was of no avail to the charterers; a clause in such terms affects the obligation to load but not the calculation of demurrage.

10–64 *Removal of ship*

Mere removal of the ship, in the absence of some fault on the part of shipowners and where the removal is not for shipowners' convenience, does not necessarily help charterers.[7] Demurrage has been held to be inter-rupted where an enforced removal was final.[8] Such a removal was dis-cussed in *Petrinovic & Co. Ltd.* v. *Mission Française des Transports Maritimes*,[9] where a ship trying to discharge solidified bulk pitch and general cargo at Bordeax in 1940 during the German invasion of France was sent to Glasgow by the shipowners. Their demurrage claim, for the two ports, was allowed only up to the point at which the ship left Bor-deaux. Atkinson J. said[10]:

> "It is quite true that a Charterer may continue to be liable to pay demurrage, although the discharging is interfered with by, for example, temporary or by voluntary departures of the ship, such as being driven out to sea, or some temporary inability of the ship to discharge, if, for instance, she is damaged by a collision[11]; but I think it is perfectly clear that the obligation to pay demurrage cannot continue if the ship is taken away finally for her own purpose, for her own safety, under such circumstances as to make it quite clear that there is no intention whatever of her coming back to the port of discharge to enable the discharge to be completed."

After mentioning four authorities for this proposition,[12] Atkinson J. continued[13]:

> "On these authorities it seems to me to be perfectly hopeless for the claimants [the shipowners] to contend that demurrage continued to run during this very long period when the ship was away from Bordeaux—purely in the interests of the ship and the cargo, because it was of no interest whatever to the charterers—and I have no difficulty in com-ing to the conclusion that the claim for demurrage must fail."

---

[6] Including *Cantiere Navale Triestina* v. *Russian Soviet Naphtha Export Agency* [1925] 2 K.B. 172 (C.A.) (see below); *Re Ropner Shipping Co. Ltd. and Cleeves Western Valleys Anthra-cite Colliers Ltd.* [1927] 1 K.B. 879 (C.A.) (see § 10–66 below); and *Petrinovic & Co. Ltd.* v. *Mission Française des Transports Maritimes* (1941) 71 Ll.L.Rep. 208 (see § 10–64 below). In *Rashtriya Chemicals and Fertilizers Ltd.* v. *Huddart Parker Industries Ltd.* [1988] 1 Lloyd's Rep. 342 (*The Boral Gas*) Evans J. referred to the *Cantiere Navale* and *Ropner* cases, and others which he said were cited in Scrutton on Charterparties, 19th ed., art. 154, and in the 3rd edition of *Summerskill on Laytime*, at § 9–59 (now § 10–63). He said, at p. 349: "The cases are well-known but not always easy to reconcile, and the mean-ing of 'default' in this context is unclear." He held that demurrage did not cease to accrue merely by reason of the shipowners' reasonable and lawful exercise of their lien.
[7] *Tyne & Blyth Shipping Co. Ltd.* v. *Leech, Harrison & Forwood* [1900] 2 Q.B. 12. See § 10–63 above.
[8] For enforced removal where laytime is running, see *Cantiere Navale Triestina* v. *Russian Soviet Naphtha Export Agency* [1925] 2 K.B. 172 (C.A.) and § 8–53 above.
[9] (1941) 71 Ll.L.Rep. 208.
[10] At pp. 215–216.
[11] As in *Tyne & Blyth Shipping Co.* v. *Leech, Harrison & Forwood* [1900] 2 Q.B. 12; and see § 10–63 above.
[12] *Budgett & Co.* v. *Binnington & Co.* [1891] 1 Q.B. 35 (C.A.); *Houlder* v. *Weir* [1905] 2 Q.B. 267; *Cantiere Navale Triestina* v. *Russian Soviet Naphtha Export Agency* [1925] 2 K.B. 172 (C.A.); *Re Ropner Shipping Co. Ltd. and Cleeves Western Valleys Anthracite Collieries Ltd.* [1927] 1 K.B. 879 (C.A.), see § 10–66 below.
[13] At p. 217.

If work is prevented by some action by shipowners, and that action **10–65** amounted to a fault, then laytime will be interrupted. If charterers show that the ship left her berth while loading or discharging, shipowners then have to justify their action or show that it was involuntary. In *Gem Shipping Co. of Monrovia* v. *Babanaft (Lebanon) S.A.R.L.*[14] the *Fontevivo* had been chartered to carry petroleum from Tutunciftlik, Turkey, to Lattakia, Syria. On the day of the ship's arrival at Lattakia there was aircraft activity and anti-aircraft gunfire. At midnight that day the master yielded to pressure from his officers and crew and took the ship outside territorial waters for two days. The charterers resisted a demurrage claim, saying that time did not run while the ship was absent.

Donaldson J., holding that the charterers were right, referred to the charterers' obligation to load and discharge within the lay days; but this was subject to the qualification, applicable to all contracts, that a party was not liable for a breach which arose because the other party prevented performance of the contract and did so without lawful excuse.[15] Referring to the decisions in *Houlder* v. *Weir*[16] and *Compania Crystal de Vapores of Panama* v. *Herman & Mohatta (India) Ltd.*,[17] he said that the reason underlying those cases was that the mere fact that shipowners prevented the continuous loading or discharging was not enough to interrupt the running of the lay days; it was necessary to show also that there was some fault on the part of shipowners. He continued[18]:

> "The fundamental distinction between these cases and *Petrinovic*[19] lies in the fact that in the latter case, the departure of the vessel was intended to be permanent. Such a departure must bring the contract of carriage to an end, whether it be a justified or an unjustified repudiation or whether it merely recognises that in the events which were unfolding the contract had been frustrated. Once the contract of carriage is at an end, laytime must also cease to run."

Donaldson J. then concluded[20]:

> "The long and the short of it is that the crew of this Somali vessel had a severe attack of cold feet in a hot climate and the master decided that the cure was to leave Lattakia. There is no finding[21] that this was necessary for the safety of the ship or cargo or that, had he left the ship at the discharging berth, she would not have been at the disposal of the charterers for the purpose of discharging."

It followed that laytime did not run during the ship's absence from Lattakia.

Where shipowners perform some action for their own convenience, **10–66** demurrage may also be interrupted. Thus in *Houlder* v. *Weir*[22] Channell J.

---

[14] [1975] 1 Lloyd's Rep. 339.

[15] He referred to *Budgett & Co.* v. *Binnington & Co.* [1891] 1 Q.B. 35 (C.A.). See the comment in that case by Lord Esher M.R. cited at § 10–13 above.

[16] [1905] 2 K.B. 267. See § 10–12 above.

[17] [1958] 2 Q.B. 196. See § 7–03 above, as to the threat of bad weather. As to the burden of proof being on charterers to establish fault, see the reference to the *Compania Crystal* case in *Blue Anchor Line Ltd.* v. *Alfred C. Toepfer International G.m.b.H.* (*The Union Amsterdam*) [1982] 2 Lloyd's Rep. 432 at p. 434.

[18] *Op. cit.* at p. 342.

[19] See § 10–64.

[20] *Op. cit.* at p. 343.

[21] He said (at p. 342): "The arbitrator studiously refrains from finding that the discharging berth in particular or Lattakia in general had become dangerous to ship or cargo or that the master acted reasonably in the interest of either in leaving the berth."

[22] [1905] 2 Q.B. 267.

held that demurrage ran continuously while ballast was being put into a ship to enable her to discharge in safety. The interference was temporary and necessary for the safe discharge of the cargo. The question of bunkering for the convenience of shipowners was discussed in *Re Ropner Shipping Co. Ltd. and Cleeves Western Valleys Anthracite Collieries Ltd.*[23] A charterparty for the carriage of coal from Swansea to Vancouver provided for cargo to be loaded in 150 running hours (with various exceptions, including Sundays, local holidays and bunkering time) and demurrage thereafter at a fixed rate "for every running hour." While the ship was on demurrage, and when no cargo was available for shipment, the shipowners shifted her to a bunkering position. After five days she was shifted so that one cargo hatch could receive cargo, and on the sixth day bunkering was completed. The shipowners made no demurrage claim for the time (less than six days) occupied in the operation of bunkering. The Court of Appeal held that demurrage was interrupted for the whole time during which the ship was at a bunkering position.[23a] Bankes L.J. said[24]:

> "In my opinion, this being a claim for demurrage in respect of the detention of the vessel . . . it does not lie in the mouth of the owners to say that the vessel was being detained by the charterers during the time that they, the owners, for their own convenience, were bunkering . . . "

So also Sargant L.J.[25]:

> "In order that demurrage may be claimed by the owners they must at least do nothing to prevent the vessel being available and at the disposal of the charterers for the purpose of completing the loading of the cargo."

10–67   Circumstances may be such that shipowners' demurrage claim may fail, even though the ship is sent away as a result of some irresistible constraint. Much depends upon the facts. In *Silver Coast Shipping Co. Ltd.* v. *Union Nationale des Co-opératives Agricoles des Céréales*[26] the *Silver Sky* was chartered to carry 10,250 metric tons of wheat from Bordeaux to Moçamedes, Angola. The charterparty contained a restraint of princes clause. The ship arrived at Moçamedes on September 3, 1975, tendering notice of readiness. On October 1 laytime expired but discharging began only on October 7, proceeding very slowly until January 10, when 750 tonnes remained on board. Unrest in Angola had interrupted the discharge. On January 10 the ship was taken over by members of the F.N.L.A. The master was made to take about 1,600 Portuguese refugees to Walvis Bay. Their disembarkation was completed on January 28; on the next day the shipowners fixed the ship for a further voyage, and on January 30 the remaining cargo was found to be unfit for human consumption. It was later jettisoned. The shipowners claimed demurrage or alternatively damages for detention from January 10 to January 30.

The High Court held that when the master left it was with the positive

---

[23] [1927] 1 K.B. 879 (C.A.).

[23a] In a London arbitration (LMLN 71, July 22, 1982) it was said that the *Ropner Shipping* case would have been decided in favour of the shipowners if it had been shown that the charterers were unable to work the ship during her period of unavailability. See § 5–13A above.

[24] At pp. 887–888.

[25] *Ibid.* at p. 888.

[26] [1981] 2 Lloyd's Rep. 95.

intention not to return and complete the unloading. This conclusion was supported by the fact that the shipowners made a new fixture on January 29 before they knew of the unfitness of the cargo. The claim for demurrage therefore failed. The claim for damages also failed. The delay from January 10 to January 30 resulted from the master's compliance with F.N.L.A. orders; it was neither the natural consequence of the charterers' breach nor the probable or foreseeable consequence of that breach.[27]

10–68 A question has arisen as to whether actionable fault by the shipowners is required to stop demurrage running. It appears that this need not be the case. In *Blue Anchor Line Ltd.* v. *Alfred C. Toepfer International G.m.b.H.*[28] the ship had gone on to demurrage while waiting for a berth. When a berth became available two pilots took her in, but she grounded, and remained aground for five days. The charterers said that demurrage was interrupted during this period, but the shipowners, relying on an exceptions clause in the charterparty,[29] said that the absence of contractual liability on their part meant that demurrage was not interrupted. Holding that the exceptions clause could not help the shipowners, Parker J. said[30]:

> "It excuses them from liability for delay. It is, however, said that the clause makes negligent navigation not actionable and that to stop demurrage running, actionable fault is required. There appears to be no direct authority on the point, although in *The Sinoe*[31] . . . Mr. Justice Donaldson[32] appears to have accepted that delay by act or omission of the owners which does not amount to a breach of contract or duty remains the liability of the charterers."

The Judge said that the approach adopted by Donaldson J. conflicted with the decision of the Court of Appeal in the *Ropner Shipping* case.[33] In the latter case it appeared to have been accepted that although a period of bunkering while the ship was on demurrage did not involve a breach of the charterparty, demurrage was nevertheless interrupted. He then referred with approval to the judgments of Bankes L.J. and Sargant L.J., including the passages cited above.[34] A breach of duty, he concluded, remained a breach of duty, and therefore fault, not withstanding that liability for the breach was excluded.

10–69 Shipowners may contend that the removal did not prejudice the charterers, since the latter were not able or proposing to work the ship during that time. If they say this, they must prove it. It is their duty to have the ship available and at the disposal of charterers to complete the loading or

---

[27] It was also held that the cause of the loss of the ship for those 20 days was the master's compliance (which would otherwise have been a breach) with the F.N.L.A. orders. The F.N.L.A. leader had for this purpose to be regarded as a prince, so that the restraint of princes clause excused the master.

[28] [1982] 2 Lloyd's Rep. 432 (*The Union Amsterdam*).

[29] The clause stated " . . . neither the vessel nor the Master or Owners shall be or shall be held liable for any loss of or damage or delay to the cargo for causes excepted by the U.S. Carriage of Goods by Sea Act 1936 . . . " Among the causes excepted by s.4(2) of the 1936 Act were act, neglect or default of the master mariner, pilot or the servants of the carrier in the navigation or in the management of the ship.

[30] *Op. cit.* at p. 435.

[31] *Overseas Transportation Company* v. *Mineralimportexport* [1971] 1 Lloyd's Rep. 514. See § 10–13 above and § 11–43 below.

[32] *Ibid.* at p. 519.

[33] As to which see § 10–66 above.

[34] At § 10–66.

the discharge. Thus in *Re Ropner Shipping Co. and Cleeves Western Valleys Anthracite Collieries Ltd.*[35] Sargant L.J. said[36]:

> "It seems to me that when it is shown that, by the act of the owners, the vessel has been placed in a position which renders her unavailable for the charterers' purposes in loading the cargo, it is for the owners who claim demurrage to show that the charterers had not in fact cargo available for loading during the period the vessel was used for bunkering."

If shipowners could show that work was not interrupted, as it was not proposed or possible throughout the period of absence, then they might succeed in establishing a claim to continuous demurrage. Thus Bankes L.J. in the *Ropner Shipping* case[37]:

> "Here I do not say what my decision would be if the case had been presented to the umpire on the footing that bunkering at the time it took place was either done then in order to trim the vessel, or for some equally good reason, or was done then because no cargo was available for loading. Nothing of that kind arises here. We have to deal with the case on the footing that the owners selected the particular time for bunkering for no reason at all except that it was the most convenient time for them."

---

[35] [1927] 1 K.B. 879 (C.A.). The only finding of fact before the Court of Appeal on this point was that when the ship was sent to be bunkered "no more cargo was then available for shipment." There was no finding that cargo was not or could not have been available during the days spent in bunkering.

[36] At p. 888.

[37] *Ibid.* at p. 887.

CHAPTER 11

LIABILITY FOR DEMURRAGE

Liability of charterers 11–01

Any liability for demurrage under a charterparty may in the absence of words to the contrary be assumed to fall upon charterers.[1] Thus in the Gencon charterparty[2] the demurrage clause merely states: "Ten running days on demurrage at the rate stated in Box 18 per day or *pro rata* for any part of a day, payable day by day, to be allowed Merchants altogether at ports of loading and discharging." Despite the use of the word "Merchants" (meaning here shippers and receivers) who are not parties to the charterparty unless charterers were also the merchants in question, liability for demurrage would, without further words, fall on charterers.[3]

This liability of charterers may in certain circumstances be modified or come to an end, in which case attempts are usually made to transfer it[4] to the receivers of the cargo. The modification or termination is achieved by the use of the cesser or lien clause, by which the parties agree that responsibility for demurrage and some other items such as freight and damages for detention (except so far as they were incurred at the loading port) are to be borne by receivers. For example, the lien clause[5] in the Gencon charterparty[6] states: "Owners shall have a lien on the cargo for freight, deadfreight, demurrage and damages for detention. Charterers shall remain responsible for dead-freight and demurrage (including damages for detention) incurred at port of loading. Charterers shall also remain responsible for freight and demurrage (including damages for detention) incurred at port of discharge, but only to such extent as the Owners have been unable to obtain payment thereof by exercising the lien on the cargo." The Exxonvoy 1969 charterparty states: "The Owner shall have an absolute lien on the cargo for all freight, deadfreight, demurrage and costs, including attorney fees, or recovering the same, which lien shall continue after delivery of the cargo into the possession of the Charterer, or of holders of

---

[1] Discharging port demurrage has been held to be due from a firm named as charterers and shippers as well as from receivers, although the charterparty also stated that it was concluded on behalf of receivers, and that they were to pay the demurrage. See *Tudor Marine Ltd.* v. *Tradax Export S.A.* (*The Virgo*) [1976] 2 Lloyd's Rep. 135 (C.A.) and *Etablissement Biret et Cie S.A.* v. *Yukiteru Kaiun KK and Nissui Shipping Corporation* (*The Sun Happiness*) [1984] 1 Lloyd's Rep. 381.

[2] Uniform General Charter (Gencon) 1976 revision.

[3] The charterparty provisions for freight and for demurrage may be expressed in different terms. In *George Veflings Rederi A/S* v. *President of India* [1979] 1 Lloyd's Rep. 123 (C.A.) freight was payable "at exchange rate ruling on Bill of Lading date" but demurrage was due "at U.S. $2,800 per day." It was held that the bill of lading date did not apply to the demurrage, for which the moneys of account and payment were U.S. dollars, the rate of exchange being taken at the date of payment. The decision in *Miliangos* v. *George Frank (Textiles) Ltd.* [1976] A.C. 433 (H.L.) was applied.

[4] For the methods used, see § 11–20 below.

[5] For liens, see § 11–22 below.

[6] Uniform General Charter (Gencon) 1976 revision.

any Bills of Lading covering the same or of any storageman." Lord Diplock said of this wording[7]:

> " . . . I deliberately refrain from expressing any view upon the effect of this curiously drafted lien clause,[8] except to say that the time may be ripe for this House to re-examine this and other standard forms of lien clauses around which there seems to have accumulated a mystique which cries out for clarification and simplification."

A more simply worded clause, in the Welsh Coal Charter,[9] states: "The Charterers' liability shall cease as soon as the Cargo is shipped, and the advance of Freight, Dead Freight, and Demurrage in loading (if any) are paid, the Owners having a lien on the Cargo for Freight, Demurrage and Average."

11–02   Liability of others

The shippers[10] of the cargo; any persons who present the bill of lading to obtain the goods, if from their conduct there can be implied an agreement to pay demurrage[11]; any consignees named in the bill to whom property in the goods has passed by virtue of the consignment[12]; and the indorsees of the bills of lading to whom property has passed by the indorsement or subsequent delivery[13]; all these groups are the persons other than charterers who may be liable to pay demurrage. This does not always mean that they are liable. For example, although a bill of lading states that the terms of a charterparty are incorporated, it does not automatically follow that every consignee is liable to pay the full amount of the loading and discharging demurrage.[14] Their liability in these capacities, as opposed to their liability where any of them are charterers, arises from their having been originally or having become subject to the rights and duties in the contract evidenced by the bills of lading. It is usual for the bills of lading to make no express reference to demurrage. Liability for demurrage under the bill of lading thus arises in most cases where the bill incorporates the terms of a charterparty[15] which itself provides for demurrage. Some bills of lading do however refer to demurrage expressly, as in the cases of the Conlinebill[16] and

---

[7] In *Miramar Maritime Corporation* v. *Holborn Oil Trading Ltd.* [1984] 2 Lloyd's Rep. 129, (*The Miramar*) at p. 134. See § 11–07 below.

[8] The reason was that the question of a lien for demurrage, although it arose at the trial (before Mustill J., [1983] 2 Lloyd's Rep. 319, at p. 324), was not the subject of appeal to the Court of Appeal ([1984] 1 Lloyd's Rep. 142) or to the House of Lords. See also one judge's description of cesser clauses as "these curious animals" at § 11–21 below.

[9] 1896.

[10] See §§ 11–03–11–06.

[11] See § 11–16 below.

[12] See § 11–08 below.

[13] See § 11–10 below.

[14] Lord Diplock spoke of " . . . a whole host of questions as to how the liability is to operate as between different consignees of different parts of the cargo . . . To give some examples: is any personal liability for demurrage incurred by consignees of cargo which has been discharged before the expiring of laytime? If the discharge of a consignee's cargo takes place after the vessel is on demurrage is his liability to pay demurrage limited to the amount of demurrage accrued after the expiring of laytime and up to the time when the discharge of his part of the cargo is complete? Is each consignee liable for all demurrage accrued while his cargo remains on board?" See *Miramar Maritime Corporation* v. *Holborn Oil Trading Ltd.* (*The Miramar*) [1984] 2 Lloyd's Rep. 129, at p. 132; and § 11–07 below.

[15] See §§ 11–07 and 11–09 below.

[16] Liner Bill of Lading (an optional clause).

the Conlinethrubill[17]; "The Carrier shall be paid demurrage at the daily rate of . . . per ton of the vessel's gross register tonnage. . . . "

Liability of shippers   **11–03**

Where bill of lading not assigned. The contract of shipment[18] evidenced by the bill of lading[19] is concluded between shipowners[20] and shippers. Shippers are usually liable for demurrage only where there is an express demurrage clause or where the charterparty is incorporated[21] by reference in the bill of lading.[22] Even in those cases it is rare for them to be held liable, for the bill of lading rights and duties are usually assigned, so that the shipowners look to assignees, or to charterers, for payment of demurrage.[23]

Where the word "demurrage" is not used, and where there is no reference to a charterparty, the wording of the bill of lading may be such as to impute liability for demurrage to shippers. In *Cawthron* v. *Trickett*[24] a ship carried a cargo of stone to Maidstone where unloading was delayed owing to a misunderstanding between consignors and consignees. The bill of lading stated: "the vessel to take her regular turn in unloading" but there was no express reference to demurrage. The master and the part-owners of the ship sued the consignors for demurrage. Erle C.J. said[25]:

> "Now, it is clear that the master may sue the consignor upon any contract that is contained in the bill of lading: and it seems to me that there is in the bill of lading in question that which amounts to a contract on the consignor's part that the ship shall take her regular turn in unloading. . . . There is a confusion of ideas in saying, that, because the consignee is not liable upon an implied contract, therefore this action against the consignor cannot be maintained."

The importance of this case lies in its emphasis on the right of shipowners to sue shippers for demurrage. The entitlement of the master to sue, and the contrast between implied and express contracts, are to be distinguished from this right of shipowners.

---

[17] Liner Through Bill of Lading (an optional clause).

[18] For the position where the shippers are parties to another contract by being also charterers, see § 11–06 below.

[19] The preamble to the Bills of Lading Act 1855, refers to "all rights in respect of the contract contained in the bill of lading." Lord Bramwell, in *Sewell* v. *Burdick* (1884) 10 App.Cas. 74 (H.L.) at p. 105, said of the Act: "It speaks of the contract contained in the bill of lading. To my mind there is no contract in it. It is a receipt for the goods, stating the terms on which they were delivered to and received by the ship, and therefore excellent evidence of those terms, but it is not a contract. That has been made before the bill of lading was given." So also A.C. 272 (H.L.) at p. 278, speaking of a bill of lading: " . . . it is somewhat inaccurately described as a contract in the Bills of Lading Act . . . "

[20] Or in some cases by the time charterers, especially where their bills of lading are used.

[21] For incorporation, see § 11–09.

[22] A party named as charterer and as shipper has been held to be liable for discharging port demurrage, even though the charterparty also said that it was signed on behalf of the receivers, and that the receivers were to pay this demurrage. As Lloyd J. said, in *Etablissement Biret et Cie S.A.* v. *Yukiteru Kaiun K.K. and Nissui Shipping Corporation* [1984] 1 Lloyd's Rep. 381 (*The Sun Happiness*), at p. 384: "It is a fallacy to suppose that a person cannot be a party to a contract in two capacities, both as principal and as agent. Clearly, Lord Justice Megaw, in *The Virgo* [*Tudor Marine Ltd.* v. *Tradax Export S.A.* [1976] 2 Lloyd's Rep. 135] contemplated that Gasco [the receivers in both cases] might be liable as well as Tradax. See also Bowstead on Agency, art. 112 . . . "

[23] As to whether the shippers remain liable, see § 11–05 below.

[24] (1864) 15 C.B.(N.S.) 754.

[25] At pp. 757–758.

11–04 Right of master to claim demurrage
Much of the argument in *Cawthron* v. *Trickett*[26] concerned cases[27] in which the question was whether the master could sue the consignees upon an implied contract for delay in removing the goods. Nevertheless it seems from the judgment of Erle C.J. that he regarded the master as being entitled to claim demurrage in the circumstances there arising even where he was not an owner or part-owner of the ship. Willes J. said[28]:

> "The bill of lading amounts to a contract[29] to take the cargo from the captain in the ship's regular turn. It is clear, therefore, that this is an action upon a contract made with the plaintiff."

The question of the part-ownership of the ship by the master was not mentioned in the judgments, but in discussion with counsel Willes J. compared the position of the master to that of a tenant in common "letting his part for years or at will to his companion." Although it is not possible to say with certainty what view the court would have taken if the master had had no interest in the ship, it seems that he would have had a claim. This view finds support in *Evans* v. *Forster*,[30] to which Willes J. referred. There general cargo had been carried from Limerick to London where the ship was delayed waiting for the consignees; it was argued that there was an implied contract that the consignees should pay demurrage. Lord Tenterden C.J. rejected the claim, and said of his decision[31]:

> "The inconvenience resulting from it may be obviated by the insertion of a few words in the margin of the bill of lading, as is often done, and as was done in the case of *Jesson* v. *Solly*,[32] in which it was held that the master might maintain the action."

11–05 *Shippers' liability where bill of lading assigned*
Where rights and duties under the bill of lading have been assigned,[33] shipowners usually look to the assignees for performance of the duties thereunder. Difficulties may arise, however, where for some reason they are unable to exercise their rights against assignees, and it may be asked whether the shipper remains liable. At common law obligations can only be assigned with the consent of the person entitled to enforce them.[34] The shippers are freed from liability for freight only if there is an express con-

---

[26] (1864) 15 C.B.(N.S.). See above.
[27] *Brouncker* v. *Scott* (1811) 4 Taunt. 1 (no action by master, who was not the owner, on implied promise in bill of lading not to detain ship); followed in *Evans* v. *Forster* (1830) 1 B. & Ad. 118; *Stinott* v. *Roberts* (1848) 5 D. & L. 460 was also mentioned by Willes J. at p. 758. As to whether the master can give up the shipowners' demurrage claim, see *Portofino (Owners)* v. *Berlin Derunaphtha* (1934) 49 Ll.L.Rep. 62 (C.A.), where Scrutton L.J. said, at p. 69: "I therefore start with this . . . that the master had no authority to make a contract giving up the claim for demurrage, and did not in fact make a contract giving up the claim for demurrage."
[28] At p. 759.
[29] Or is evidence of such a contract. See the comments by Lord Bramwell in *Sewell* v. *Burdick* (1884) 10 App.Cas. 74 (H.L.) at p. 105; and see n. 19 to § 11–03 above.
[30] (1830) 1 B. & Ad. 118.
[31] At pp. 121–122.
[32] (1811) 4 Taunt. 52; a claim by the master against consignees for discharging demurrage. The bill of lading bore the clause: "ship to be cleared in sixteen days, and £8 per day demurrage to be paid after that time."
[33] For the position where shippers are parties to another contract by being also charterers, see § 11–06 below.
[34] "You have a right to the benefit you contemplate from the character, credit and substance of the party with whom you contract"; *per* Lord Denman C.J. in *Humble* v. *Hunter* (1848) 12 Q.B. 310 at p. 317.

tract to this effect, or where there is a release of the shippers by the ship-owners or the master after the issue of the bill.[35] It seems that the same common law principles apply in the case of demurrage.

Under statute law it is arguable that the liability of shippers for demurrage is transferred by assignment of the bill of lading. Section 2 of the Bills of Lading Act 1855,[36] states:

> "Nothing herein contained shall prejudice or affect any right of stoppage in transitu, or any right to claim freight against the original shipper or owner. . . . "

This section, with its preservation of the right to claim freight from the shippers, follows section 1 which provides that every indorsee and named consignee "shall have transferred to and vested in him all rights of suit, and be subject to the same liabilities" as if the bill of lading contract had been made with himself. But the argument, that the demurrage claim against the shippers ends when the bill is assigned,[37] would be difficult to maintain in view of the failure of section 1 to provide for the transference of the liabilities in the way in which it transfers rights of suit.

Shippers as charterers **11–06**

The shippers to whom the bill of lading is issued may also be the charterers. If so the bill has the properties attached to it by common law and by the Bills of Lading Act 1855, but so far as its terms differ from those of the charterparty it yields to the charterparty.[38] Indeed the charterers are generally obliged to submit bills of lading which are consistent with the charterparty. The only exception to the rule, that the terms of the charterparty must prevail, arises where the shipowners and the shippers-charterers are shown to have intended to vary the terms of the charterparty, recording that variation in the bill of lading. The mere issue of the bill, and its signature by the master or shipowners' agents, is not sufficient evidence of such an intention.

As the Earl of Halsbury said, in *Kruger & Co. Ltd.* v. *Moel Tryvan Ship Co. Ltd.*[39]:

> "The bill of lading cannot control what has been agreed upon before between the shipowner and the merchant and what has been expressed in a written instrument which is the final and concluded agreement between the parties. It is in truth a bill of lading."

It follows that where shippers are also charterers the rights of shipowners to claim demurrage are those set out in the charterparty, combined with any set out in the bill of lading so far as it is consistent with the charterparty, unless it is shown that by the issue of the bill the parties intended to vary the charterparty. Whether the rights in the bill of lading have been assigned or not, the shippers' liability for demurrage does not then depend on the general rules laid down by common law and by the Bills of Lading Act 1855.[40] In most cases only the terms of the charterparty are relevant,

---

[35] *Lewis* v. *M'Kee* (1868) L.R. 4 Ex. 58; *Watkins* v. *Rymill* (1883) 10 Q.B.D. 178.
[36] The position of indorsees, so far as it is governed by the Act, is discussed at § 11–10 below.
[37] Just as the liabilities of assignees come to an end when they indorse the bill of lading: *Smurthwaite* v. *Wilkins* (1862) 11 C.B.(N.S.) 842, where the 1855 Act was applied. See also §§ 11–10 and 11–11 below.
[38] As to the incorporation of the charterparty arbitration clause in the bill of lading, and the position when shippers are charterers, see the cases cited in note 51 to § 10–08 below.
[39] [1907] A.C. 272 (H.L.) at p. 278.
[40] For these rules see § 11–05 above.

special attention being paid to the cesser clause,[41] though of course the bill of lading must also be considered.

11–07 Liability of consignees, indorsees and receivers

Those liable for demurrage under a bill of lading may include not only the shippers[42] but also the consignees, the indorsees of the bill, and other persons presenting the bill in return for the goods. This liability may exist if the bill of lading incorporates[43] provisions for demurrage either expressly or by referring to the terms of a charterparty which contains such provisions. Alternatively such liability may exist by virtue of an agreement implied in the contract of shipment, of which the bill of lading is evidence, by which the shippers agree to discharge the goods with reasonable dispatch. The consignees, indorsees and other persons presenting the bill may also incur this liability.

The liability does not always exist. In *Miramar Maritime Corporation* v. *Holborn Oil Trading Ltd.*[44] the *Miramar* had carried diesel oil from Singapore to Trincomalee, Sri Lanka. The charterparty was on the Exxonvoy 1969 form and the bill of lading was on the form stipulated for use in conjunction with that charterparty. The bill stated: "This shipment is carried under and pursuant to the terms of the Charter . . . all the terms whatsoever of the said charter . . . apply to and govern the rights of the parties concerned in this shipment." As substantial discharging demurrage was incurred the shipowners exercised a lien on the cargo until the receivers promised to pay whatsoever was held to be due by an English court. The charterers were insolvent. The receivers contended that the demurrage provisions in the charterparty referred to the liability of the charterers, and that they should not be manipulated so as to create a liability for the holders of the bills of lading.

The House of Lords, upholding the decision of the High Court[45] and the Court of Appeal,[46] held that the receivers were right. There was no business reason for verbal manipulation of the designation "charterer" in any of the 26 clauses in the charterparty in which the word appeared, so as to substitute for it, or to include within it, "the consignee" or "holder of a bill of lading." Lord Diplock agreed with the reasons set out by Sir John Donaldson M.R.,[47] but added[47a]:

> "I regard it, however, as more important that this House should take this opportunity of stating unequivocally that, where in a bill of lading there is included a clause which purports to incorporate the terms of a specified charter-party, there is not any rule of construction that clauses in that charter–party which are directly germane to the shipment,

---

[41] See § 11–20 below.
[42] See § 11–03 above.
[43] For incorporation see § 11–09 below.
[44] [1984] 2 Lloyd's Rep. 129 (H.L.)(*The Miramar*).
[45] [1983] 2 Lloyd's Rep. 319. Mustill J. said, at p. 324: "In my view, the expression 'the charterer' should be understood as meaning what it says. It should not be rewritten so as to confer a new contractual right against the bill of lading holders."
[46] [1984] 1 Lloyd's Rep. 142. In the House of Lords, Lord Diplock (*op. cit.* at p. 134) described Sir John Donaldson M.R. as having relied particularly upon "the semantic argument based upon the presence of the express reference to 'consignee' distinguishing him from 'Charterer' in the sentence of cl. 8 itself [the demurrage provision], under which the owners' claim for demurrage was brought, and he relied also upon the inclusion of cl. 20, issuance and terms of bills of lading . . . "
[47] See n. 46.
[47a] *Op. cit.*, at p. 134.

carriage or delivery of goods and impose obligations upon the 'charterer' under that designation, are presumed to be incorporated in the bill of lading with the substitution of (where there is a cesser clause), or inclusion in (where there is no cesser clause), the designation 'charterer,' the designation 'consignee of the cargo' or 'bill of lading holder.' "

Liability of consignees   **11–08**

Bills of lading usually state the name of the consignees. Thus one bill,[48] after describing the goods, says that they "are to be delivered in the like apparent good order and condition at the said port of . . . unto . . . or . . . Assigns . . . " A consignee of cargo has been described[49] as "a person residing at the port of delivery to whom the goods are to be delivered when they arrive there." The insertion of the consignees' name in the bill constitutes an instruction by the shippers to the master. At any moment before delivery of the goods to the consignees the shipper may cancel this instruction,[50] as no contract between shipowners and consignees is created by the insertion.

Consignees can be held liable for demurrage where the bill of lading **11–09** expressly provides for demurrage or incorporates,[51] by reference to the charterparty, its demurrage provisions, or where it may be implied from the contract of shipment that the shippers agree to discharge the goods with reasonable dispatch.[52] Their liability arose at common law, before the Bills of Lading Act 1855, by virtue of their presentation of the bills of lading with a view to obtaining the cargo. The principles governing the transaction at that stage were similar to those which apply wherever receivers, even though they were not the consignees, presented bills of lading in return for cargo.[53]

The Bills of Lading Act 1855 states[54]:

> "Every consignee of goods named in a bill of lading[55] . . . to whom the property in the goods therein mentioned shall pass, upon or by reason of such consignment . . . shall have transferred to and vested in him all rights of suit, and be subject to the same liabilities in respect of such goods as if the contract contained in the bill of lading had been made with himself."

The liability of consignees for demurrage is thus contingent not on their presentation of the bill of lading and demand for the goods[56] but on the passing of the property in the goods "upon or by reason of such consignment." The property would rarely if ever pass either upon or by reason of

---

[48] General Home Trade Bill of Lading 1928 (Britcont).

[49] In *Wolff* v. *Horncastle* (1798) 1 B. & P. 316 at p. 322 by Buller J.

[50] Or perhaps at any moment before the delivery of the bill to the consignees; *Mitchel* v. *Ede* (1840) 11 Ad. & El. 888.

[51] For an extended note as to a number of cases on the subject of incorporation of a charterparty in a bill of lading, see the end of this chapter, § 11–51.

[52] The decision in *Hogarth's* case (see n. 51) was applied in *Astro Valiente Compania S.A.* v. *Government of Pakistan Ministry of Food and Agriculture* (*The Emmanuel Colocotronis (No. 2)*) [1982] 1 Lloyd's Rep. 286, where the history of the cases is set out. The bill of lading said: "All other conditions, exceptions, demurrage, general average and for disbursements as per above-named charter-party." It was held that the charterparty arbitration clause was one of the "conditions" included in the bill of lading, the charterparty clearly providing that the clause was to be incorporated. However, in *Skips A/S Nordheim* v. *Syrian Petroleum Co. Ltd. and Petrofina S.A.* (*The Varenna*) [1983] 1 Lloyd's Rep. 416, Hobhouse J. declined to follow the *Astro Valiente* decision.

[53] See § 11–06 below.

[54] s.1.

[55] The reference to indorsees, omitted here, is discussed in § 11–10 below.

[56] As in the case of receivers generally; see § 11–16 below.

the consignment, as the sale contract between shippers and consignees is unlikely to provide that property should pass at the moment of the act of consignment, *i.e.* the insertion of a name in the bill of lading. Even then the property would be said to have passed upon the consignment but by reason of the pre-existing contract of sale.[57] As the special jury summarised its finding in *Lickbarrow* v. *Mason*[58]:

" . . . by the custom of merchants, bills of lading, expressing goods or merchandises to have been shipped by any person or person to be delivered to order or assigns, have been and are, at any time after such goods have been shipped, and before the voyage performed . . . negotiable and transferable by . . . indorsing . . . and that by such indorsement and delivery, or transmission, the property in such goods . . . is transferred to such other person . . . "

As a rule the passing of the property only occurs "by such indorsement and delivery or transmission" if the parties to the sale contract so intend. The use of the word "negotiable" in this context does not mean that the bill resembles a cheque in that its negotiation (unless it is marked "not negotiable") in holders obtaining a better title than that of those who passed it. Any such general rules are of course subject to the terms of the particular contract of sale, the terms of which govern the passing of property. As section 17 of the Sale of Goods Act 1979[59] provides:

"(1) Where there is a contract for the sale of specific or ascertained goods the property in them is transferred to the buyer at such time as the parties to the contract intend it to be transferred. (2) For the purposes of ascertaining the intention of the parties regard shall be had to the terms of the contract, the conduct of the parties, and the circumstances of the case."

11–10 *Liability of indorsees*

An indorsee of a bill of lading is one to whom the shippers, consignees or earlier indorsees have purported to assign the rights and duties under the contract evidenced by the bill, where the cargo has not been surrendered to receivers, indicating this by putting the name of the assignees on the bill. In the case of a bill under which goods are deliverable "to order" or "to order or assigns," property in the cargo passes, as and when intended by the sale contract, from the assignors to the assignees.

At common law the liability of indorsees for demurrage depended upon their being also receivers who presented a bill of lading demanding the cargo in return.[60] Indorsement of the bill combined with payment of the sale price had the effect of transferring the property in the goods, if that

---

[57] See § 10–10 below for the comments by Lord Bramwell in *Sewell* v. *Burdick* (1884) 10 App.Cas. 74 (H.L.) at p. 105, as to whether property passes "by reason of" an indorsement.

[58] (1794) 5 T.R. 683 at pp. 685–686. Of this decision Alderson B. said in *Thompson* v. *Dominy* (1845) 14 M. & W. 403 at p. 408: "Because, in *Lickbarrow* v. *Mason*, a bill of lading was held to be negotiable, it has been contended that that instrument possesses all the properties of a bill of exchange . . . The word 'negotiable' was not used in the sense in which it is used as applicable to a bill of exchange, but as passing the property in the goods only." Though in the *Thompson* case it was held that the indorsees, the owners of the cargo, could not sue on the contract for non-delivery of the part of the cargo, it seems that they would have had sufficient title to maintain an action for conversion: *Howard* v. *Shepherd* (1850) 9 C.B. 297. As Parke B. said in *Legg* v. *Evans* (1840) 6 M. & W. 36 at p. 41: "Any person having a right to the possession of goods may bring trover in respect of the conversion of them."

[59] c. 54.

[60] For the liabilities of such receivers see § 11–16 below.

was the intention of the parties, but did not transfer to the indorsees the rights and duties created by the contract of affreightment.

The Bills of Lading Act 1855 states[61]:

> " . . . every endorsee[62] of a bill of lading to whom the property in the goods therein mentioned shall pass, upon or by reason of such . . . endorsement, shall have transferred to and vested in him all rights of suit, and be subject to the same liabilities in respect of such goods as if the contract contained in the bill of lading had been made with himself."

The liability of indorsees for demurrage is thus said to depend, as in the case of consignees,[63] not upon their being the receivers who present the bill of lading and demand the goods, but upon the passing to them of the property in the goods "upon or by reason of such . . . indorsement." The property is unlikely to be regarded as passing by reason of the indorsement, but it may pass, if the parties to the sale contract so intend, at the time of the indorsement. As Lord Bramwell said in *Sewell* v. *Burdick*[64]:

> "I take this opportunity of saying that I think there is some inaccuracy of expression in the statute. It recites that, 'by the custom of merchants a bill of lading being transferable by indorsement the property in the goods may thereby pass to the indorsee. . . . ' Now the truth is that the property does not pass by the indorsement, but by the contract in pursuance of which the indorsement is made. If a cargo afloat is sold, the property would pass to the vendee, even though the bill of lading was not indorsed. I do not say that the vendor might not retain a lien, nor that the non-indorsement and non-handing over the bill of lading would not have certain other consequences. My concern is to show that the *property* passes by the contract."

Upon the indorsement of the bill the indorsees thus become liable for demurrage. This will be so whether or not such liability has accrued at that time, for the Act refers simply to "liabilities in respect of such goods" and does not limit its own application to accrued liabilities.

If the indorsees themselves indorse the bill of lading, they and the next **11–11** party intending that the property should pass, and if the property does then pass, their liability for demurrage ceases and is transferred to the new indorsees. In *Smurthwaite* v. *Wilkins*[65] goods had been carried from Odessa to England under a bill of lading making them deliverable to a London firm "or their assigns." The London firm sold the goods during the voyage to the defendants, indorsing the bill to them. Later, still during the voyage, the defendants sold them and indorsed and delivered the bill to the new buyers. Rejecting the shipowners' claim for freight from the defendants, Erle C.J. said[66] of their contention:

> "The consequences which this would lead to are so monstrous, so manifestly unjust, that I should pause before I consented to adopt this construction of the Act of Parliament.[67] . . . Looking at the whole statute, it seems to me that the obvious meaning is, that the assignee *who receives the cargo* shall have all the rights and bear all the liabilities of a contracting party; but that, if he passes on the bill of lading by indorsement to another, he passes on all the rights and liabilities which the bill of lading carries with it."

He considered the preamble to the Act and continued[68]:

---

[61] s.1.
[62] The reference to consignees, omitted here, is discussed in § 11–09 above.
[63] See § 11–09 above.
[64] (1884) 10 App. Cas. 74 (H.L.) at p. 105.
[65] (1862) 11 C.B. (N.S.) 842.
[66] At p. 848.
[67] The Bills of Lading Act 1855, s.1, and in particular the words: " . . . every endorsee . . . shall . . . be subject to the same liabilities in respect of such goods as if the contract contained in the bill of lading had been made with himself."
[68] At pp. 848–849.

> "When the assignee assigns over to another, does he retain all the rights and liabilities of the original contracting party? He clearly has no right to the cargo. Is he, then, by the indorsement, to pass on his rights to the indorsee, and to retain all his liabilities in respect of the goods? Such a construction might be very convenient for the shipowner, but it would be clearly repugnant to one's notions of justice."

He said that the origin of the common law liability of assignees was that the master had a lien, and receipt of the goods was assumed to be made under an implied bargain,[69] that if the master would forego his lien, the assignees would pay freight and demurrage. That could not apply in the smallest degree to one who did not receive the goods.

11–12 **Indorsees as charterers.** If charterers are the indorsees of a bill of lading,[70] a question may arise as to whether their rights are governed by the charterparty or by the bill of lading. Of the three cases described below,[71] the first held that charterers took the goods under the bill of lading. For many years that decision was used to support the proposition that charterers who were indorsees could not say that contradictory charterparty terms overrode the bill of lading. The answer to the question is now regarded as depending upon the facts in each case. In the second case the court decided that the charterparty was the governing document. The decision appears to have gone unnoticed by courts and textbooks for many years, until the arguments in the Court of Appeal in the third case, in which it was held that charterers' rights were governed by the charterparty.

11–13 1. *SS. Calcutta Co. Ltd.* v. *Andrew Weir & Co.*[72] Shipowners were able to rely on bill of lading exceptions, in defence to a claim for cargo damage, although the claimants and indorsees were the charterers, against whom the charterparty exceptions would have been insufficient as a defence. Under the charterparty, dates were part of a cargo carried from Busreh[73] to London for a lump sum freight to be paid at London. Bills of lading were to be signed "without prejudice to this charterparty."[74] The bill of lading was indorsed to the charterers in return for an advance which they made to the shippers. The dates, partly damaged, were discharged to the charterers, who presented the bill of lading. At that time they were pledgees and also agents of the shippers for the sale. They claimed to deduct from the lump sum freight a sum equal to the depreciation in value of the goods. It was held that they were liable for the freight in full, it being assumed that the goods were damaged by causes for which the bill of lading, as distinct from the charterparty, exempted the shipowners from liability. Hamilton J. explained[75] the meaning of the words "without prejudice to this charterparty":

> "When the charterparty provided that the captain should so sign bills of lading without prejudice to the charterparty the intention was that neither charterers nor shipowners

---

[69] See § 11–16 below.

[70] For the position where the charterers are the shippers, see § 11–06 above.

[71] *SS. Calcutta Co. Ltd.* v. *Andrew Weir & Co.* [1910] 1 K.B. 759; *Love & Stewart Ltd.* v. *Rowtor Steamship Co. Lt.* [1916] 2 A.C. 527 (H.L.); and *President of India* v. *Metcalfe Shipping Ltd.* [1969] 2 Lloyd's Rep. 476 (C.A.) (*The Dunelmia*).

[72] [1910] 1 K.B. 759.

[73] Now known as Basrah.

[74] Which words, said shipowners' counsel, only meant "without prejudice to the rights and liabilities of the parties of the charterparty in respect of acts done under the charterparty": *ibid.* at p. 766.

[75] At p. 770.

should thereby be prejudiced in mutual relations touching any acts done under the charterparty. But in the present case there never was any shipment of these goods by the charterers under the charterparty, neither did they acquire them under the charterparty."

He concluded[76]:

" . . . when the defendants demanded delivery of the goods under the bill of lading at the end of the voyage they did so upon production of the bill of lading and as parties interested by virtue of it, and thereupon, under the Bills of Lading Act 1855,[77] the contract expressed or evidenced by the bill of lading would become binding upon them as between themselves and the shipowner . . . "

2. *Love & Stewart Ltd.* v. *Rowtor Steamship Co. Ltd.*[78] Purchasers **11–14** agreed to buy pit props from a Finnish seller for delivery f.o.b. at Kristinestad, Finland. They chartered a ship to carry them to Newport, Monmouthshire. The charterparty allowed 13 days for loading and 13 days for discharging. The time was reversible.[79] Loading was completed in 9 days but the bill of lading was wrongly claused "thirteen days used for loading," in an endeavour to limit the discharging days to 13 instead of 17. The shippers, having indorsed the bill, presented it to the charterers, who paid the invoice and took delivery. As it took seventeen and a half days to discharge, the shipowners claimed four and a half days' demurrage, *i.e.* the excess over 17 days. The House of Lords, reversing the decision of the Court of Session,[80] held that the shipowners could only claim half a day's demurrage. They were bound by the reversible provision in the charterparty, and could not rely on the "thirteen days" clause in the bill of lading. Lord Sumner said:

"Nothing had occurred by which any contract for the carriage of the goods arose between them and the shipowners other than the charter itself."[81]

3. *President of India* v. *Metcalfe Shipping Ltd.*[82] The Indian government **11–15** chartered a ship to carry bagged urea from Ravenna and Ancona to Madras. The charterers had previously agreed to buy urea from sellers, f.o.b. stowed port of exit. The sellers indorsed the bill of lading to the charterers. A dispute as to the shortage on discharge was found by Megaw J.[83] to fall under the charterparty arbitration clause. The Court of Appeal, upholding his decision, agreed that property in the goods remained in the sellers until after the goods were loaded. Relations between charterers and shipowners were prima facie governed by the charterparty, and signature by the master of a bill of lading was not a modification or variation of the charterparty. Lord Denning M.R. said[84]:

"The bill of lading here was not separate or severable from the charter-party. It was issued in pursuance of it. The Italian sellers A.N.I.C. had already contracted to sell the

---

[76] At p. 771.

[77] *i.e.* s.1. Perhaps the law report should read "therefore" and not "thereupon." The rights and duties pass by virtue of the indorsement and passing of property, and not upon the demand for delivery. See § 11–10 above.

[78] [1916] 2 A.C. 527. For the aspects concerning "reversible laytime" and "general or local holidays," see §§ 9–16 and 8–11 above, respectively.

[79] See § 8–09 above.

[80] Which had followed *SS. Calcutta Co.* v. *Andrew Weir & Co.* [1910] 1 K.B. 759.

[81] *Op. cit.* at p. 540.

[82] [1969] 2 Lloyd's Rep. 476 (C.A.) (*The Dunelmia*).

[83] [1969] 1 Lloyd's Rep. 32.

[84] At p. 482. He said (also at p. 482) that this view was supported by *Love & Stewart Ltd.* v. *Rowtor Steamship Co. Ltd.* [1916] 2 A.C. 527 (H.L.) and added (at p. 483): "I see no difference between the House of Lords case and this case."

fertiliser to the Government of India: and the Government had chartered the ship to carry it. The bill of lading was a mere instrument to carry out these contracts. It did not evidence any separate contract at all. As between charterers and shipowners, it was only a receipt for the goods."

As a result charterers' claim in respect of cargo shortage was subject to a time limit of six years, rather than to a limit of one year, as would have followed from the bill of lading alone.

11–16 *Liability of receivers*

When holders of a bill of lading, who are neither the consignees[85] named therein nor indorsees to whom ownership has passed by indorsement, present it with a view to obtaining the goods, they are usually deemed to be making an offer to shipowners. They offer to become bound by the terms set out or referred to in the bill, in return for the right to receive the cargo. If the shipowners accept the offer and deliver the cargo, then they become liable for freight and demurrage, and for other incidents attaching to the cargo, where the bill so provides, unless at the time of the offer they protested against such liability. Such persons will not necessarily have vested in them the ownership of the goods, which can pass by virtue of the consignment or by virtue of the indorsement of the bill, or delivery following indorsement.

The principle was stated by Cave J. in *Allen* v. *Coltart & Co.*[86] He referred to various cases in which the rule had been applied[87] and said[88]:

" . . . where goods are deliverable to the holder of a bill of lading on certain conditions being complied with, the act of demanding delivery is evidence of an offer on his part to comply with those conditions, and the delivery accordingly by the master is evidence of the acceptance of that offer."

The liability of receivers in these circumstances does not arise as a matter of law; it is a question of fact whether such an agreement can be said to exist. It seems probable, though each case depends also on its own facts, that such an agreement will be inferred unless the bill of lading holders disclaim liability.

In *Wegener* v. *Smith*[89] timber was carried from Stettin to Sunderland under a charterparty providing for demurrage. The bill of lading made the goods deliverable to order "against payment of the agreed freight and

---

[85] The same principles applied to consignees at common law (see § 11–09 above) but their position is now governed by s.1 of the Bills of Lading Act 1855 (see § 11–09 above).

[86] (1883) 11 Q.B.D. 782.

[87] *Stindt* v. *Roberts* (1848) 5 D. & L. 460, where the bill of lading stipulated for the payment of demurrage and it was held that the taking of the goods under it by the indorsees was evidence of an agreement to pay demurrage: *Wegener* v. *Smith* (1854) 15 C.B. 285, for which see below; and *Young* v. *Moeller* (1855) 5 El. & Bl. 755, where taking was regarded as evidence of an agreement to be bound by the terms of the bill whatever they were. See also *Scotson* v. *Pegg* (1861) 6 H. & N. 295.

[88] *Op. cit.* at p. 785. This statement by Cave J. was cited in *Skips A/S Nordheim* v. *Syria Petroleum Co. Ltd. and Petrofina S.A. (The Varenna)* [1983] 1 Lloyd's Rep. 416, at p. 420, by Hobhouse J. He said of the use of the word "conditions" in incorporation clauses:
"It has throughout been consistently interpreted as meaning the conditions which have to be performed on the arrival of the ship by the consignee who is asserting his right to take delivery of the goods. Typically such a condition is the discharge of any lien on the goods or the performance of any unloading obligations. The commercial situation which this reflects is well stated by Mr. Justice Cave" [there followed the above-mentioned citation].

[89] (1854) 15 C.B. 285.

other conditions as per charterparty." The indorsees refused to pay what was apparently discharging demurrage and it was held that they were liable. Maule J. said[90]:

> "As the defendant received the goods under the bill of lading, the demurrage was clearly a matter of just charge against him."

The manner in which receivers become parties to a contract, on the terms set out in the bill of lading, was explained in *Brandt* v. *Liverpool, Brazil & River Plate Steam Navigation Co. Ltd.*[91] Bags of zinc ashes were shipped at Buenos Aires for Liverpool. Owing to their wet and heated condition the master discharged most of them into a warehouse at Buenos Aires. After an unnecessary delay they were reconditioned and reshipped on another ship.   **11–17**

She arrived three months after the first ship and the value of zinc ashes had fallen. The indorsees of the bill of lading were pledgees who had made an advance to the shippers, and were not indorsees to whom the property in the goods had passed under section 1 of the Bill of Lading Act 1855.[92] On their claim for damages for delay and repayment of the forwarding costs, which they had paid under protest to prevent a lien, it was held that a contract between them and the shipowners could be inferred, and that the shipowners were liable. Their rights did not and could not arise under the 1855 Act, but a contract had to be inferred from their presentation of the bill, payment of the freight, and delivery and acceptance of the goods. Bankes L.J., speaking of earlier cases,[93] said[94]:

> "By those authorities it has been clearly established that where the holder of a bill of lading presents it and offers to accept delivery, if that offer is accepted by the shipowner, the holder of the bill of lading comes under an obligation to pay the freight and to pay the demurrage, if any. . . . "

So also Scrutton L.J.[95]:

> " . . . the contract to be inferred in cases such as this is that the holder of the bill of lading and the shipowner make a contract for the delivery and acceptance of the goods on the terms of the bill of lading, so far as they are applicable to discharge at the port of discharge."

Disclaimer of liability by receivers. If bill of lading holders are neither consignees nor indorsees to whom property in the goods has passed by indorsement, they cannot be held liable for freight and demurrage if they have disclaimed such liability before or when receiving the goods. A disclaimer prevents a request for the goods from being regarded as an offer subject to the liabilities forming part of the bill of lading contract.   **11–18**

An example of a disclaimer made before the goods reached their desti-

---

[90] At p. 289. In *Smith* v. *Sieveking* (1855) 5 El. & Bl. 589 (see n. 96 below) Jervis C.J. distinguished the *Wegener* case, saying that it concerned discharging demurrage, which had thus accrued from the indorsees' own delay. He applied the same distinction to *Jesson* v. *Solly* (1811) 4 Taunt. 52; see § 11–04 above.
[91] [1924] 1 K.B. 575 (C.A.).
[92] This passes rights of suits and liabilities under the bill to consignees and to "every endorsee of a bill of lading to whom the property in the goods therein mentioned shall pass, upon or by reason of such consignment or endorsement . . . " See also § 11–10 above.
[93] *Stindt* v. *Roberts* (1848) 5 D. & L. 460; *Young* v. *Moeller* (1855) 5 El. & Bl. 755; *Allen* v. *Coltart & Co.* (1883) 11 Q.B.D. 782. See also n. 87 to § 11–16 above.
[94] [1924] 1 K.B. 575 (C.A.) at p. 589.
[95] *Ibid.* at p. 600.

nation is to be found in *Sanders* v. *Vanzeller*[96] The shipowners claimed freight and not demurrage but the principle is the same. A ship carried wool from the Danube to London under a charterparty. The bills of lading stipulated that delivery should be at London to the charterers "or to their assigns, he or they paying freight for the said goods as per charter party." The charterers sold the cargo to English buyers who, by the sale contract, agreed "to perform and fulfil all charter parties and agreements for freight . . . made, or to be made, by the sellers, excepting any charges that may be made for demurrage, of which the buyer is in no case to be liable to pay." The bills of lading were indorsed and delivered to the buyers. There was a dispute about the quality of the wool and the shipowners claimed freight from the buyers. Holding that the buyers were not liable, Tindal C.J. said[97]:

> " . . . the question referred by the jury to the Court is one of law: *viz.* whether the law would, upon these facts, imply a contract by the defendant with the plaintiff to pay the freight at the rate specified. We are satisfied that it would not . . . there would have been no promise implied by law, though there would have been evidence to warrant the jury in finding that there was such a contract; and it has been so much the practice for the indorsee of such a bill of lading to pay the specified freight, if he accepts the goods under it, that there is little or no doubt that the jury would, on such a question, have found in favour of the shipowner if the indorsee received the goods without a disclaimer of his liability to the freight."

As for the reference to charterparty freight in the bills of lading, he said[98]:

> " . . . the reference in the bill of lading to the charter party is, in the opinion of some of us, introduced for the purpose of keeping the charter party unvaried, and preserving the lien for the charter party freight, and not for the purpose of creating a new contract, *viz.* to deliver the goods in each bill of lading on the payment of a freight for each according to the rate in the charter party."

11–19   It is a question of fact as to whether bill of lading holders have disclaimed liability for freight and demurrage. So in *SS. County of Lancaster Ltd.* v. *Sharp & Co.*[99] the consignees took delivery of part of the cargo, the shipowners exercising a lien for demurrage over the residue. Property had not passed to the consignees by reason of the consignment, within the meaning of the Bills of Lading Act 1855,[1] and they were known by the shipowners to be acting as agents. It was held that there was no evidence of a contract by the consignees to pay demurrage. Mathew J. said of them[2]:

> " . . . it appears that they took delivery on the express understanding that they agreed to pay freight, but did not agree to pay demurrage. *Wegener* v. *Smith*[3] was relied on as shewing that the receipt of the goods and the payment of freight for them by the consignee at the bill of lading rate constituted conclusive evidence of a contract on his part to be bound by all the terms of the bill of lading."

---

[96] (1843) 4 Q.B. 260. In *Smith* v. *Sieveking* (1855) 4 El. & Bl. 945 London consignees offered to pay freight but refused to pay loading demurrage incurred at Memel. The bill of lading, after naming the consignees, used the words "paying for the said goods as per charterparty"; it was held and affirmed on appeal ((1855) 5 El. & Bl. 589), that the consignees were not liable.

[97] At pp. 294–295.

[98] At pp. 296–297.

[99] (1889) 24 Q.B.D. 158.

[1] s.1. See § 11–09 above.

[2] At pp. 161–162.

[3] (1854) 15 C.B. 285. See § 11–16 above.

The judge said that the *Sanders* case was distinguishable; the indorsees had taken delivery under a bill of lading which made demurrage payable, and then repudiated liability; in the case before him the consignees had said plainly that they would not pay the demurrage.

Cesser clause   **11–20**
    A cesser clause is a provision, found in most charterparties, by which the liability of charterers is stated to cease upon the shipment of the cargo. It may be expressed briefly, as in the words: "Charterers' liability under this Charter to cease on cargo being shipped"[4]; or in some detail, as in the Gencon charterparty[5]: "Owners shall have a lien on the cargo for freight, dead-freight, demurrage and damages for detention. Charterers shall remain responsible for dead-freight and demurrage (including damages for detention), incurred at port of loading. Charterers shall also remain responsible for freight and demurrage (including damages for detention) incurred at port of discharge, but only to such extent as the owners have been unable to obtain payment thereof by exercising the lien on the cargo." In this case the clause purports primarily to grant a lien and to state certain responsibilities which remain those of charterers; only then does it qualify this responsibility by limiting it in proportion to the inability of shipowners to exercise a lien for the items named.[6] A cesser clause may be particularly apt where charterers are also party to a sale contract, the chartering of the ship being for them a subsidiary operation. They may have arranged with buyers, who may be indorsees of the bills of lading, or consignees, that they shall assume certain responsibilities, including the liability to pay demurrage. Whatever the motive for the insertion of the clause in a particular charterparty, the question of cessation of liabilities depends primarily upon the cesser clause and the laytime provisions.

Which liabilities cease?   **11–21**
    In the majority of clauses ("these curious animals," as they have been called)[7] it is provided merely that charterers' liability, with or without the addition of the words "under this charterparty," shall cease on shipment. Their range of liabilities is wide; it is necessary to find out whether they cease to be liable for all freight, dead freight, demurrage and damages for detention. The cesser clause could apply to all liabilities, whether arising before or after shipment, or only to those which have accrued by the end of the shipment. The shipowners may be particularly concerned as to whether loading demurrage, the liability for which has accrued when shipment is completed, ceases to be the responsibility of charterers.
    It would be an exaggeration if it were said that a logical and simple set of rules could be extracted from the many cases which the courts have decided on the subject of cesser clauses and liens. The changing demands of the mercantile community, as evidenced for example by its gradual

---

[4] Baltimore Form C Berth Grain Charter-Party.
[5] Uniform General Charter 1976 revision.
[6] As to the efficacy of the lien, see § 11–32 below.
[7] By Donaldson J. in *Overseas Transportation Co.* v. *Mineralimportexport* [1971] 1 Lloyd's Rep. 514 at p. 516 (*The Sinoe*). See also § 11–01 above, for a judicial description of the Exxonvoy 1969 charterparty lien clause as "this curiously drafted lien clause."

abandonment of a fixed number of days on demurrage; the alterations in the views of the judges, who have in turn been affected by the wishes of the merchants; and the sheer variety and often bad drafting[8] of laytime, cesser, lien and demurrage clauses; all these have contributed over a period of a hundred years to the uncertainty which still exists in this branch of the law.

There has been criticism of earlier cases, combined with unpredictability as to the results of modern cases. In *Miramar Maritime Corporation* v. *Holborn Oil Trading Ltd.*[9] Lord Diplock referred[10] to the nineteenth century decisions in *Gray* v. *Carr*[11] and *Porteus* v. *Watney.*[12] In the first of these cases the consignee who held the bill of lading was held to be liable for demurrage accrued at the loading port before the cargo had been loaded as well as for discharging demurrage. Lord Diplock spoke of the application there of "a literalist construction to the actual words appearing in particular clauses in a charter-party and a bill of lading," and said that he had little doubt that the two cases would, "in the last two or three decades," have been decided differently. It is however possible to state certain general propositions, as to which there is broad agreement.

11–22   Three general propositions concerning liens

1. Cesser clause applies to obligations accruing before and after shipment. A clause generally applies, where it applies at all,[13] in the absence of other charterparty terms to the contrary, both to obligations which accrue before or at the completion of shipment and to those which accrue after shipment.[14] The words "charterers' liability to cease" are thus not interpreted as meaning merely "charterers' liability to cease to be augmented or extended after shipment": instead they are generally taken to mean that the charterers cease thenceforth to be liable at all, subject to the provision of a lien, unless it was clearly intended that they should remain liable.

11–23   Thus in *Francesco* v. *Massey*[15] a ship chartered to carry coal from Birkenhead to Genoa was to load "in fifteen working days," and "to be discharged, weather permitting, at the rate of not less than thirty-five tons of coal per working day . . . and ten days on demurrage, over and above her said lay-days, at £8 per day . . . Charterer's liability to cease when the ship is loaded, the Captain having a lien upon the cargo for freight and demurrage." The shipowners claimed demurrage and damages for detention at the loading port. It was held that the charterers were not liable for the loading demurrage.

---

[8] As Bramwell B. said in *Gray* v. *Carr* (1871) L.R. 6 Q.B. 522 at p. 549: " . . . it is to be observed that every case such as this, where no general principle of law is involved, but only the meaning of careless and slovenly documents, must depend on its own particular words." Or as Donaldson J. said in *Overseas Transportation Co.* v. *Mineralimportexport* [1971] 1 Lloyd's Rep. 514 at p. 520 (*The Sinoe*): "have words any meaning in this charterparty?"

[9] [1984] 2 Lloyd's Rep. 129 (H.L.) (*The Miramar*).

[10] At pp. 132–133.

[11] (1871) L.R. 6 Q.B. 522. See also § 11–27 below.

[12] (1878) 3 Q.B.D. 534 (C.A.).

[13] As to whether the cesser clause comes into operation, see § 11–32 below.

[14] Despite doubts expressed in *Kish* v. *Cory* (1873) L.R. 8 Ex. 101. See § 11–24 below.

[15] (1873) L.R. 8 Ex. 101.

Cleasby B. said[16]:

> " . . . the language is general, that the charterer's liability should cease, and for the cessation of liability a corresponding benefit is obtained by the shipowner in having a lien upon a full cargo for demurrage, which he would not have unless expressly agreed."

So also Bramwell B. said of the cesser clause[17]:

> "It is impossible to say that this would not give a lien for demurrage incurred as well at the port of loading as at the port of discharge, and so for the demurrage sued for; and it seems impossible to hold that the matters as to which the liability was to cease were not the same as the matters as to which the lien was given."

It is important to note the use by Cleasby B. of the expression "a corresponding benefit" and the reference by Bramwell B., with approval, to an earlier case[18] where the judge had said:

> "If there were any provision giving the shipowner an equivalent advantage[19] that would be a very good reason for his absolving the defendant altogether."

A similar conclusion to that in *Francesco v. Massey*[20] was reached in **11–24** *Kish v. Cory*[21] where the cesser clause read: "Charterer's liability to cease when the ship is loaded, the captain or owner having a lien on cargo for freight and demurrage." Coal was carried from Hull to Alexandria; the loading took longer than the agreed time, so that the shipowners claimed five days' loading demurrage, out of the 10 days' demurrage stipulated by the charterparty. It was held, following *Francesco v. Massey*,[20] that the charterers were, upon loading the cargo, discharged from liability for loading demurrage. Objections were expressed (by Lord Coleridge C.J., Brett J. and Grove J.) to the principle by which the liability of the charterers ceased in respect of all breaches; but the court felt that the earlier decisions should not be overruled, as mercantile documents were often drawn up with those decisions in mind.[22] Had the matter been free from authority they would have been inclined to hold that the clause kept alive the liability of the charterers for breaches committed before completion of loading. Cleasby B. said[23]:

> "So far as the position of the shipowner, as well as of the charterer, is concerned, it makes no difference whatever whether the demurrage accrues at the port of loading or at the port of discharge. In either case the shipowner has his lien, and it does not appear to be reasonable to hold that, if the demurrage accrued at the port of discharge, the char-

---

[16] At p. 104. He said that the case of *Bannister* v. *Breslauer* (1867) L.R. 2 C.P. 429 was similar and that the court should accept its authority. There also it was provided that charterers liability was to cease when the cargo was shipped, and that the captain was to have a lien for freight, dead freight and demurrage. It was held that the cesser clause applied to damages for detention at the loading port, but the charterparty did not provide for demurrage there; the ship had "to load and unload with all dispatch."

[17] At p. 106. He said that *Bannister* v. *Breslauer* (1867) L.R. 2 C.P. 497 was in point.

[18] *Christoffersen* v. *Hansen* (1872) L.R. 7 Q.B. 509 at p. 516, *per* Lush J.

[19] On the efficacy of the lien, see § 11–32 below.

[20] (1873) L.R. 8 Ex. 101. See § 11–23 above.

[21] (1875) L.R. 10 Q.B. 553.

[22] As Lord Esher M.R. (formerly Brett L.J.) said in a later case: "It is a wholesome rule that has been often laid down, that when a well-known document has been in constant use for a number of years, the court, in construing it, should not break away from previous decisions, even if in the first instance they would have taken a different view, because all the documents made after the meaning of one has been judicially determined are taken to have been made on the faith of the rule so laid down." *Dunlop & Sons* v. *Balfour Williamson & Co.* [1892] 1 Q.B. 507 at p. 518 (C.A.).

[23] At p. 561.

terer should be released, as the shipowner could look to his lien, but if it occurred at the port of loading he could not."

This first general proposition, that the cesser clause applied to liabilities arising both before and after shipment, was also approved by the Court of Appeal in *Fidelitas Shipping Co. Ltd.* v. *V/O Exportchleb.*[24] Pearson L.J. said[25]:

> "the cessation of liability on shipment involves not only not incurring liability in respect of events occurring after shipment, but also a release from liability incurred before shipment."

11–25   **2. Liens for demurrage and detention damages distinguished.** The second broad proposition which can be extracted from the cases is that a lien for demurrage cannot, generally speaking, be taken to be the same as a lien for damages for detention. In most charterparties there is an exhaustive stipulation for demurrage, in that although there may be a fixed laytime the number of days on demurrage is not fixed.

11–26   *Unlimited demurrage period (exhaustive stipulation)*
    If there is a lien clause in such words as "Vessel to have a lien on the cargo for all freight, dead freight, demurrage or average," the shipowners have a lien for demurrage[26] but not for damages for detention.

11–27   *Limited demurrage period (partial stipulation)*
    The same rule applies where there is a fixed demurrage period, as in the words "six days to load and six days on demurrage"; there also a lien clause has the effect of giving the shipowners a lien for demurrage but not for damages for detention.
    In *Gray* v. *Carr*[27] it was held that the shipowners had a lien for demurrage, but not for damages for detention, where there was a contractual lien only for demurrage. The charterparty, for the carriage of staves and/or grain from Sulina, Romania, to London, also stated: "fifty running days . . . are to be allowed the said merchant (if the ship is not sooner dispatched) for loading, and to be discharged as fast as ship can put the cargo out, and ten days on demurrage over and above the said laying days at £8 per day. . . . " The cesser clause read: "The owners to have an absolute lien on the cargo for all freight, dead freight, demurrage, and average; and the charterer's responsibilities to cease on shipment of the cargo, provided it be of sufficient value to cover the freight and charges on arrival at port of discharge . . . " The bills of lading provided for delivery "unto order, or to his or their assigns,[28] he or they paying freight *and all other conditions*[29] or demurrage (if any should be incurred) for the said goods, as per the aforesaid charterparty." The ship was detained at the loading port throughout the lay days and the demurrage period of 10 days, and for a further 18 days. A full and complete cargo was not shipped. At London the shipowners claimed the right to lien the cargo for dead freight, demurrage and detention damages.

---

[24] [1963] 2 Lloyd's Rep. 113. See § 11–37 below.
[25] At p. 122.
[26] As in *Sanguinetti* v. *Pacific Steam Navigation Co.* (1877) 2 Q.B.D. 238 (C.A.); see § 11–47 below.
[27] (1871) L.R. 6 Q.B. 522.
[28] The shippers' assigns.
[29] The words in italics were inserted in writing on the printed form of the bill.

The court held that the shipowners could exercise a lien for demurrage   **11–28**
but not for dead freight[30] and detention damages. This was so in spite of
the reference in the clause to a lien for dead freight; it was silent as to
detention damages. The dead freight claim was regarded by the court as
being more properly a claim for damages for short loading, so that it was
not a claim for which a lien was given. As Brett J said[31]:

> "It seems to me that a charterparty which leaves damages to be recovered in respect of
> short loading unspecified, and therefore at large, gives no claim for dead freight properly
> so called. Such a claim for unliquidated damages is not dead freight. . . . "

The cesser clause spoke of the cessation of the responsibilities of the charterers but made no provision for a lien for detention damages. Brett J.,
dealing with this clause and with the reference to the charterparty in the
bill of lading, said[32]:

> " . . . no liability other than such as naturally attaches in respect of the carriage of the
> particular goods is to be held to be imposed on a consignee of goods mentioned in a bill of
> lading, unless such liability is clearly imposed by plain words."

In his view the reference in the bill of lading to "conditions or demurrage"
could be taken as intentionally alternative. It was specially relevant to the
discharging port, for which there were no laytime or demurrage provisions.
There was thus no lien for detention damages at the loading port.

Much depends on the exact wording of the charterparty and bill of lading. In *Gray* v. *Carr*[33] the special factors included the fixed loading laytime,
the provision for discharging "as fast as ship can put the cargo out," the
partial demurrage stipulation ("ten days on demurrage") and, especially,
the reference in the bill of lading to "all other conditions or demurrage."

A similar conclusion was reached in *Lockhart* v. *Falk*.[34] There was an   **11–29**
"absolute lien on cargo for freight and demurrage, the charterer's liability
to any clauses in this charter ceasing when he has delivered the cargo
alongside ship." The shipowners had to claim damages for detention at the
loading port, there being no provision for loading demurrage although
there was one for discharge of demurrage. It was held that the lien did not
extend to the damages for detention, for which the charterers remained
liable.

In *Gardiner* v. *Macfarlane, M'Crindell & Co.*[35] the Court of Session considered a situation similar to that in *Lockhart* v. *Falk*.[34] There was a provision for "days on demurrage" at the discharging port, but no such
provision for the loading port. The lien for demurrage was not a lien for
detention damages, and the charterers remained liable for such damages.

---

[30] The court distinguished the decision of the House of Lords, in the same year, in *McLean* v.
Fleming (1871) L.R. 2 H.L. (Sc.) 128. There it was held that a lien for dead freight, granted
by the charterparty, was enforceable although that a lien for dead freight, granted by the
charterparty, was enforceable although it was in respect of a claim for unliquidated
damages. The House of Lords in *Kish* v. *Taylor* [1912] A.C. 604 confirmed its earlier
decision. Lord Atkinson said at p. 614: "an agreed lien does cover such damages though
they be unliquidated."
[31] At p. 535.
[32] At p. 540.
[33] (1871) L.R. 6 Q.B. 522. See § 11–27 above.
[34] (1875) L.R. 10 Ex. 132.
[35] (1889) 26 Sc.L.R. 492.

11–30   The situation considered in *Lockhart* v. *Falk*[34] and *Gardiner* v. *Macfarlane, M'Crindell & Co.*[35] arose again in *Clink* v. *Radford & Co.*,[36] where the cesser clause read: "the charterers' liability under this charterparty to cease on the cargo being loaded, the owners having a lien on the cargo for the freight and demurrage." There were provisions for discharging laytime and demurrage, but none for loading. The shipowners contended that the ship was kept at the loading port of Newcastle, New South Wales, for 16 days beyond what was usual and customary. The shipowners claimed damages for detention from the charterers for this delay. The charterers said that their liability for damages for detention ceased "on the cargo being loaded." The Court of Appeal held that it did not. In spite of the wording of the first part of the cesser clause, it was to be read in connection with its second part, relating to a lien for freight and demurrage. The cessation of liability thus occurred only in respect of those items—freight and demurrage—for which the shipowners had a lien. Lord Esher M.R. said[37]:

> " . . . the main rule to be derived from the cases as to the interpretation of the cesser clause in a charterparty, is that the Court will construe it as inapplicable to the particular breach complained of, if by construing it otherwise the shipowner would be left unprotected in respect of that particular breach, unless the cesser clause is expressed in terms that prohibit such a conclusion . . . "[38]

As for the second part of the clause, relating to the lien for freight and demurrage, he said[39]:

> "The word 'demurrage' must mean demurrage as used in the charterparty; that is, as I have just stated, demurrage at the port of discharge, and the shipowner has no lien according to this charterparty in respect of detention of the ship at the port of loading. If that be the true construction of those words in the charterparty, then in respect of detention at the port of loading, if the cesser clause is construed so as to cover that breach, the shipowner will be left without remedy."

11–31   The proposition that a lien for demurrage was not a lien for damages for detention was again upheld by the Court of Appeal in *Dunlop & Sons* v. *Balfour, Williamson & Co.*[40] A charterparty stated: "All liability of charterers to cease on completion of loading, provided the value of the cargo is sufficient to satisfy the lien, which is hereby given for all freight, dead freight, demurrage, and average (if any) under this charterparty. . . . " Loading was to be "as customary," and discharging also as customary but at a mimimum average rate. The laytime clause added: "Demurrage to be at the rate of £20 per day." The shipowners claimed detention damages for delay at the loading port. The Court of Appeal held that the cesser clause did not protect the charterers against a claim for detention damages Lord Esher M.R. said[41]:

> "If there were nothing else in the charterparty to which the word demurrage would be applicable,[42] it may be—though I do not say it would be—that the Court would then be obliged to say that the lien for demurrage must apply to such uncalculated damages. But

---

[36] [1891] 1 Q.B. 625 (C.A.). Followed in *Jennesen, Taylor & Co.* v. *Secretary of State for India* [1916] 2 K.B. 702.

[37] At p. 627.

[38] These words were cited, and described as being directly applicable, in *Action S.A.* v. *Britannic Shipping Corporation Ltd.* [1987] 1 Lloyd's Rep. 119 (C.A.) (*The Aegis Britannic*), by Dillon L.J. at p. 121, where *Clink* v. *Radford & Co.* was described as the "leading authority" as to cesser clauses. See also § 11–33 below.

[39] At p. 629.

[40] [1892] 1 Q.B. 507.

[41] At p. 519.

[42] If, for example, there were no demurrage provision at all.

there is in the charterparty a matter to which the lien can apply, and it cannot be a proper mode of construction to say that, where there is that to which the lien can fitly apply it is also to be applicable to something to which in ordinary circumstances it would not be applicable."[43]

3. Cesser clause correlative with the lien. The third basic proposition on this subject is that a cesser clause is effective, generally, to the extent that shipowners are given a lien[44] on the cargo in respect of the claim which would otherwise lie against charterers.

11–32

It has been said[45] that if any provision gives the shipowners "an equivalent advantage," that would be a very good reason for exempting the charterers from liability. So also one judge referred[46] to "a corresponding benefit" given to shipowners in having a lien for demurrage and, in another case,[47] said: " . . . if the demurrage accrued at the port of discharge, the charterer should be released, as the shipowner could look to his lien. . . . " Lord Esher M.R. pointed out that this relationship of the lien to the cesser clause might not exist, when he said of such a clause[48]:

" . . . the Court will construe it as inapplicable to the particular breach complained of, if by construing it otherwise the shipowner would be left unprotected in respect of that particular breach, unless the cesser clause is expressed in terms that prohibit such a conclusion. . . . "

Three years later Lord Esher M.R. again emphasised that charterers were released from liability so far as that liability was replaced by a lien. In *Hansen* v. *Harrold Brothers*[49] oats were carried from New Zealand to London for a lump sum freight under a charterparty by which the liabilities of the charterers were "to cease on the vessel being loaded, the master and owners having a lien on the cargo for all freight and demurrage under this charterparty." The charterers were entitled to re-charter the ship at any rate of freight, the captain signing bills of lading at any rate required without prejudice to the charterparty. They did so, and bills of lading were given by which freight was payable in London at a certain rate per ton on the delivered cargo. The cargo lost weight on the voyage and the bill of lading freight, for which the shipowners had a lien, did not cover the amount due for the lump sum freight. The Court of Appeal held that the shipowners could recover the difference from the charterers. Lord Esher M.R. pointed out that the master was obliged to sign the bills of lading, and said[50]:

11–33

" . . . according to the principle laid down in *Clink* v. *Radford*,[51] on the true construction of that clause, it only relieves the charterers from so much of their liability under the charterparty as is co-extensive with or equivalent to the lien given to the shipowner."

See also Goddard J. in *Z SS. Co.* v. *Amtorg New York*[52]: "The doctrine

---

[43] He cited *Lockhart* v. *Falk* (1875) L.R. 10 Ex. 132. (see § 11–29 above) and *Clink* v. *Radford & Co.* [1891] 1 Q.B. 625 (C.A.). (See § 11–30 above).

[44] As to what is meant when a lien is given, see § 11–34 below.

[45] *Christoffersen* v. *Hansen* (1872) L.R. 7 Q.B. 509 at p. 516, *per* Lush J.

[46] Cleasby B. in *Francesco* v. *Massey* (1873) L.R. 8 Ex. 101 at p. 104. See § 11–23 above.

[47] *Kish* v. *Cory* (1875) L.R. 10 Q.B. 553 at p. 561. See § 11–24 above.

[48] In *Clink* v. *Radford & Co.* [1891] 1 Q.B. 625 at p. 627 (C.A.). See § 11–30 above.

[49] [1894] 1 Q.B. 612 (C.A.). Followed in *Jennesen, Taylor & Co.* v. *Secretary of State for India in Council* [1916] 2 K.B. 702 and in *Overseas Transportation Company* v. *Mineralimportexport* [1972] 1 Lloyd's Rep. 201 (*The Sinoe*) (C.A.) (see § 11–43 below).

[50] At pp. 619–620.

[51] [1891] 1 Q.B. 625 (C.A.). See § 11–30 above.

[52] (1938) 61 Ll.L.Rep. 97 at p. 100.

is now well settled that the lien, or rather the exemption granted to the charterer against liability for freight, must be co-extensive with the lien which is conferred on the shipowner, and if the lien which is conferred on the shipowner does not cover the whole of the matters which may materialise, then the charterer will be liable."

In a later case[53] the Court of Appeal again discussed the relationship of the cesser and lien clauses. Pearson L.J. said[54]:

> "The cessation of liability incurred before shipment should be construed as co-extensive with the lien, because it is not reasonable to suppose that the shipowner gives up his accrued right *in personam* against the charterer except in return for a corresponding lien on the goods."

In the same case Harman L.J. said[55]:

> "I am content for the purpose of the present argument to accept the view that the cesser clause will only avail the charterers to the extent to which they can show that they did provide the owners with a proper lien on the freight."

So also Donaldson J. agreed[56] that a cesser clause meant that charterers' liability would cease if and to the extent that shipowners are given an effective right to a lien on the cargo for demurrage, and added:

> "Rights which are unaccompanied by effective remedies have much less attraction for mercantile men than for lawyers. . . ."

This proposition was expressed in similar terms by Kerr J. in *Japan Line* v. *Australian Wheat Board*[57]: " . . . it is also settled law that the operation of the cesser clause is coextensive with the existence of an effective lien for demurrage at the port of discharge. In other words it only releases the charterers from liability for discharging port demurrage if and to the extent that the owners could have enforced payment of such demurrage by exercising a lien over the cargo."

So also Dillon L.J. in *Action S.A.* v. *Britannic Shipping Corporation Ltd.*[58]:

> " . . . where the question has arisen in a context of reconciling a cesser clause and a lien clause, the Court has held that the reconciliation is to be effected by holding that the cesser clause only applies in so far as the lien is effective"[59]

and, speaking[59a] of the particular case before the Court of Appeal[60]:

> "If the owners had no alternative remedy against the receivers of the cargo or, for that

---

[53] *Fidelitas Shipping Co. Ltd.* v. *V/O Exportchleb* [1963] 2 Lloyd's Rep. 113 (C.A.) (See § 11–37 below).

[54] At p. 122.

[55] At pp. 120–121.

[56] In *Overseas Transportation Company* v. *Mineralimportexport* [1971] 1 Lloyd's Rep. 514 at p. 518 (*The Sinoe*). See § 11–43.

[57] [1977] 2 Lloyd's Rep. 261 (*The Cunard Carrier, Eleranta and Martha*), at p. 263; see also § 11–43.

[58] [1987] 1 Lloyd's Rep. 110 (C.A.) (*The Aegis Britannic*), at p. 122.

[59] Here he referred to *Hansen* v. *Harrold Brothers* [1894] 1 Q.B. 612 (C.A.) (see earlier in this section) as the first case so to hold, though perhaps some earlier cases suggested the same principle (see § 11–32 above).

[59a] Also at p. 122.

[60] The charterparty said that charterers were to remain responsible only for dead freight and demurrage at the loading port, and freight and demurrage incurred at the discharging port; and that charterers' liability was to cease upon shipment, except as to freight, dead freight and demurrage. The receivers obtained judgment against the shipowners in respect of cargo damage, the judgment being enforced in part because the shipowners had put up a guarantee. The shipowners claimed an indemnity from the charterers. They succeeded.

matter anyone else, the cesser clause cannot be construed as immediately cutting out and extinguishing the charterers' primary liability under cl. 5 [the clause which stated that cargo was to be loaded, stowed, and discharged 'at the expense and risk of shippers/charterers . . . receivers/charterers']."

Creating a lien   **11–34**

In the charterparty it may be agreed expressly that shipowners are to have a lien over the cargo, and further agreed, either expressly or impliedly, that the liability of charterers shall cease to the extent that shipowners have a lien. A lien is a right; it has been defined as a "Right to retain possession of property until a debt due to the person detaining it is satisfied."[61]

At the time of the charterparty there is thus an agreement that shipowners will be in a position to exercise this right to hold the cargo. It is not necessary to say that the lien exists at that date, when indeed there are no goods in respect of which it can be exercised, as the cargo has not been loaded. As Bowen L.J. put it in *Clink* v. *Radford & Co.*[62]:

> "reasonable persons would regard the lien given as equivalent for the release of responsibility which the cesser clause in its earlier part creates, and would expect to find the lien commensurate with the release of liability."

Though the right arises on shipment, it is necessary to study the bill of   **11–35** lading to find whether the contract of shipment, of which the bill is evidence, provides for a lien. In the absence of such a provision the shipowners may have to look to charterers for payment of demurrage because a lien for demurrage, unlike a lien for freight, does not arise at common law and must be expressly given.[63]

The creation of a lien was discussed by Davey L.J. in *Hansen* v. *Harrold Brothers*[64]:

> "It is to be observed that the words 'the master and owners having a lien, &c.,' do not create a lien; the lien arises subsequently on the goods shipped, and could only in this case come into operation when the vessel was rechartered. There are no goods on which a lien can be created at the time of the execution of the charterparty. . . . The words, therefore, do not themselves create a lien, but point to a lien to be created hereafter. They import, in my opinion, a contract to give or procure a lien."

So also Harman L.J. in *Fidelitas Shipping Co. Ltd.* v. *V/O Exportchleb*[65]:

> " . . . they[66] are not apt to *create* a lien. . . . They are, however, in my judgment apt to operate as a proviso, that is to say, you are to look and see whether in the hands of the receiver of the goods the owner will have, by virtue of the bill of lading or some other subsequent document, a comparable lien operative against the receiver."

And in the same case Pearson L.J. said[67]:

> "The second part of the Clause, even when it is expressed in participial form ('the

---

[61] *Shorter Oxford English Dictionary* (3rd ed.).
[62] [1891] 1 Q.B. 625 (C.A.) at pp. 629–630. These views were adopted by Davey L.J. in *Hansen* v. *Harrold Brothers* [1894] 1 Q.B. 612 (C.A.) at p. 620; and by Harman L.J. in *Fidelitas Shipping Co. Ltd.* v. *V/O Exportchleb* [1963] 2 Lloyd's Rep. 113 (C.A.) at p. 120.
[63] *Birley* v. *Gladstone* (1814) 3 M. & S. 205.
[64] [1894] 1 Q.B. 612 (C.A.) at pp. 620–621 (C.A.). See § 11–33 above.
[65] [1963] 2 Lloyd's Rep. 113 at p. 120 (C.A.).
[66] The words of the cesser clause: "the owner or his agent having a lien." Compare *French* v. *Gerber* (1877) 2 C.P.D. 247 (C.A.): "the owners of the ship to have an absolute lien on the cargo for all demurrage."
[67] *Ibid.* at p. 122.

owner or his agent having a lien on the goods') creates a lien prospectively, in the sense of providing that a lien shall arise upon shipment of the goods.''

11–36   The bill of lading may refer to the charterparty generally, giving its date and stating that its terms are to be regarded as incorporated therein, in which case such terms as are not "insensible and inapplicable"[68] would be incorporated; or it may provide expressly that shipowners shall have a lien for demurrage. If the shipowners are responsible for drawing up the bill, it is not possible for them to criticise the charterers for the failure of the bill to give a lien.[69] If on the other hand shipowners are unable to prevent the issue of such a bill, as where the master has to sign bills of lading as presented, then charterers are responsible for the failure of the bill effectively to incorporate a lien clause. In the event of such a failure, no lien arises and the cesser clause does not operate.[70]

11–37   Where the lien clause in the bills of lading does not refer to demurrage, there may nevertheless be a lien if the charterparty has been incorporated in the bill, since lien clauses in bill and charterparty need not be contradictory. This proposition is supported by the decision in *Fidelitas Shipping Co. Ltd.* v. *V/O Exportchleb.*[71] A charterparty for the carriage of grain from the Black Sea to England provided for charterers' liability to cease when the cargo was shipped, "the owner or his agent having a lien on the cargo for freight, dead-freight, demurrage, lighterage at port of discharge and average." The bill of lading bore the words: "All terms and conditions as per charterparty": it also stated that the carriage was subject to "all conditions terms and clauses inserted into this bill of lading," and gave the carriers a lien in respect of "freight and all other charges and expenses due under the contract of carriage." A dispute arose as to whether the cesser clause protected the charterers from liability for loading demurrage. The Court of Appeal held that the cesser clause was effective and that the charterers were not liable, since a lien for loading demurrage had been created.

11–38   Harman L.J. discussed[72] the difference between an agreement to create a lien and the creation of a lien.[73] He noted that although the bill of lading purported to incorporate the charterparty, and thus on the face of it provided for a lien, the lien clause in the bill did not refer expressly to loading demurrage. Nevertheless there was not necessarily any contradiction, though in fact he thought that it covered loading demurrage, by its reference to "other charges and expenses."[74]
     Pearson L.J. said[75] that in spite of differing provisions and surrounding

---

[68] The words used by Brett L.J. in *Porteus* v. *Watney* (1878) 3 Q.B.D. 534 at p. 542 (C.A.): " . . . if taking all the conditions to be in the bill of lading, some of them are entirely and absolutely insensible and inapplicable, they must be struck out as insensible; not because they are not introduced, but because being introduced they are impossible of application."

[69] See the remarks of Pearson L.J. to this effect in *Fidelitas Shipping Co. Ltd.* v. *V/O Exportchleb* [1963] 2 Lloyd's Rep. 113 at p. 124 (C.A.).

[70] *Argonaut Navigation Co. Ltd.* v. *Ministry of Food* [1949] 1 K.B. 572 (*The Argobec*) at p. 583.

[71] [1963] 2 Lloyd's Rep. 113 (C.A.).

[72] At p. 120.

[73] See § 11–34 above.

[74] If demurrage were not "charges" there was no reason why it should not be regarded as "expenses." See *Rederactieselskabet Superior* v. *Dewar & Webb* [1909] 1 K.B. 948 at p. 952, *per* Bray J, on what the word "charges" means: "Primarily I think it means sums which the master or the ship has had to pay; it does not mean sums which the ship is entitled to receive."

[75] [1963] 2 Lloyd's Rep. 113 (C.A.) at p. 122.

circumstances there were certain basic propositions which could be derived from the decided cases, and which could be appropriately applied to this case. He also discussed the creation of the lien[76] and added[77]:

> "On shipment of the goods the lien comes into existence and the charterer is relieved of his personal liability,[78] even if he is and remains the owner of the goods: in such a case the shipowner must rely on his lien, and, if he loses his lien by parting with the goods without receiving payment, he cannot successfully sue the charterers. . . . Thus the lien arises in the first instance under the charter-party."

As to the existence of a right of lien for demurrage, in spite of there being no express reference thereto in the bill of lading, he said[79]:

> "The introduction of the charter-party lien for demurrage at the port of loading would not be inconsistent with the express provisions of the bill of lading. . . . "

The bill provided that there should be a lien for "freight and all other charges and expenses due under the contract of carriage"; it also incorporated the charter-party by reference. He added[80]:

> "The lien for demurrage at the port of loading is brought in from the charter-party and that demurrage is one of the 'charges' which the receiver has to pay. I find no difficulty in regarding demurrage as a 'charge.' "

Inability to exercise the lien   11–39

The cesser clause does not operate if charterers have failed to create a lien in favour of shipowners; what happens if the lien, though created, is not or cannot be exercised? Goddard J. said of a shipowner's claim for freight in *Z SS. Co. Ltd.* v. *Amtorg. New York*[81]:

> " . . . the shipowner never exercised his lien and therefore there is no extent to which the charterers' liability can remain."

A lien, though created in favour of shipowners by charterers, may prove **11–40** to be ineffective because it is illegal to exercise it, as where it is against the law to exercise a lien over government cargo; because its exercise is prevented as a matter of administrative discretion, as where the port authority refuses to make suitable premises available; because the security is inadequate, as where the value of the cargo is less than the sum for which the lien is exercised; or for some other reason.

Where the exercise of a lien is illegal, it has been argued that shipowners must rely on their remedy *in personam* against receivers, as neither shipowners nor charterers are at fault; alternatively it may follow from the doctrine of co-extensiveness that charterers should remain liable. The latter view is correct.

If the exercise of a lien is administratively impossible, the cesser clause is **11–41** inoperative. It is possible for the parties to anticipate such a situation by agreeing that the liability of charterers ceases, provided that the exercise of a lien is possible. Thus in the Gencon[82] charterparty the lien clause states

---

[76] See § 11–34 above.
[77] At p. 122.
[78] Provided that the lien is effective; see §§ 11–39–11–43 below.
[79] At p. 125.
[80] At p. 126.
[81] (1938) 61 Ll.L.Rep. 97 at p. 101. See § 8–14 and § 9–19. The charterers were to remain responsible for freight "only to such extent as the owners have been unable to obtain payment thereof by exercising the lien on the cargo." These words are similar to those considered in *Bravo Maritime (Chartering) Est.* v. *Alsayed Abdullah Mohamed Baroom* [1980] 2 Lloyd's Rep. 481 (*The Athinoula*). See § 11–43 below.
[82] Uniform General Charter 1922 and 1976 revisions.

that charterers' responsibility for freight and discharging demurrage remains in existence "only to such extent as the Owners have been unable to obtain payment thereof by exercising the lien on the cargo."

11–42   Where a lien is ineffective because the security (*i.e.* the value of the cargo) is inadequate, it seems that the liability of charterers continues to the extent of the inadequacy. Nevertheless here also it is possible for the parties to anticipate the situation by using such words as: " . . . the Charterers' liability shall cease upon the shipment of the Cargo and payment of deadfreight, difference in freight and demurrage provided such Cargo be worth the Bill of lading freight at the port of shipment."[83] In *Hansen* v. *Harrold Brothers*[84] the security proved inadequate, as a diminution in weight of the cargo resulted in the bill of lading freight (payable on outturn weight) being insufficient to provide for the freight due under the charterparty. The Court of Appeal held that the cesser clause was inoperative to the extent of the insufficiency of the lien.

11–43   The exercise of a lien was found to be impossible for a combination of reasons in *Overseas Transportation Company* v. *Mineralimportexport.*[85] A ship had been chartered on the Gencon form to carry bagged cement from Constantza to Chittagong. The charterparty provided[86]: "Stevedores to be employed by Charterers in loading and by Shippers[86] in discharging who shall be considered as Owners servants and subject to the orders and directions of the Master. Charterers not to be responsible for any negligence default or error in judgment of Stevedores employed . . . "; and "Demurrage . . . at loading port to be settled[87] directly between . . . Owners and Receivers." The cesser clause stated: "Charterers' liability shall cease as soon as the cargo is on board. Owners having an absolute lien on the cargo for freight, dead freight, demurrage and average." The charterparty also provided: " . . . Charterers to remain ultimately responsible for freight, deadfreight and demurrage at loading port." The ship went on demurrage at Chittagong because the stevedores were slow, incompetent and too few. The shipowners claimed demurrage or alternatively damages for detention, blaming the charterers for having appointed the stevedores. The charterers relied on the cesser clause; on the other clauses referring to demurrage as indicating that they were not liable for discharging port demurrage; and on the provision that the stevedores were shipowners' servants. The combined effect of local law and practice in Chittagong was such that no lien for demurrage could be exercised by or on behalf of the shipowners either on shore[88] or on board.

---

[83] River Plate Charter-Party 1914 (Centrocon).
[84] [1894] 1 Q.B. 612 (C.A.). See § 11–33 above.
[85] [1972] 1 Lloyd's Rep. 201 (*The Sinoe*).
[86] The parties agreed that "Shippers" meant "Charterers."
[87] A question arose in *Gerani Compania Naviera S.A.* v. *Alfred C. Toepfer* [1982] 1 Lloyd's Rep. 282 (*The Demosthenes V*) *(No. 2)* as to whether "settled," in the phrase " . . . demurrage . . . is to be settled directly between Owners and Receivers . . . ," meant "paid," as contended by charterers. Shipowners, however, agreed, so that the Court adopted the construction and the issue was not argued.
[88] As for a lien on shore, Goddard J. said in *Z SS. Co. Ltd.* v. *Amtorg, New York* (1938) 61 Ll.L.Rep. 97, at p. 100: "You can if you wish land your cargo without handing it over to the receivers . . . " This may be impossible by virtue either of the physical circumstances at the port or the charterparty provisions, as in *Bravo Maritime (Chartering) Est.* v. *Alsayed Abdullah Mohamad Baroom* [1980] 2 Lloyd's Rep. 481 (*The Athinoula*). See § 11–46 below.

The Court of Appeal, upholding a judgment by Donaldson J.[89] in favour of the shipowners, decided that, because the lien was not effective, charterers were not relieved by the cesser clause from liability for demurrage. It was not enough that the shipowners were given a right of lien in the charterparty. Lord Denning M.R. said[90]: "It seems to me that, once it is accepted that the two parts of the clause are to be co-extensive, then it is sensible to require that the lien should be an effective lien. It is no use for a shipowner to be given a right of lien unless he can exercise it so as to get the money due to him. A right without a remedy is a vain thing." Megaw L.J. said[91]: "In my view, following what I understood to be the guidance given in *Hansen* v. *Harrold Brothers*[92] . . . this clause . . . involves a contract that the owners will have an effective lien at the port of discharge. If not—if the owners do not have an effective lien at the port of discharge—then there is no cessation of the charterers' liability in respect of the claim for freight, dead-freight, demurrage or average, as the case may be . . . It is not enough for the shipowners to show merely commercial inconvenience or difficulty. It must be impossibility. In my view, the lesser clause does not avail the charterers in this case."

As Kerr J. said in *Japan Lines* v. *Australian Wheat Board*[93]: "The mere **11–44** presence of a lien clause in the charter is not enough; the lien must be effective. Any remaining doubts about this were laid to rest by the decision of the Court of Appeal in *Overseas Transportation Company* v. *Mineralimportexport* . . . " In the case before him, which involved primarily applications for extensions of time for demurrage claims in arbitrations against charterers, no effective lien could be exercised on grain discharged at Basrah or Beirut because the receivers were government departments, and also possibly because of the civil disorder in Beirut.

The charterparty terms may make it impossible for shipowners to **11–45** demand demurrage until after the cargo has been discharged. In such a case no lien is impossible and charterers remain liable.

In *Bravo Maritime (Chartering) Est.* v. *Alsayed Abdullah Mohamed Baroom*[94] the Athinoula had carried cement on three voyages from Eleusis, Greece, to Jeddah. The charterers were also shippers and consignees. The printed cesser clause stated: "Owners shall have a lien on cargo for . . . demurrage . . . Charterers shall also remain responsible for . . . demurrage . . . incurred at port of discharge, but only to such extent as the Owners have been unable to obtain payment thereof by exercising the lien on the cargo." The typed demurrage clause stipulated: "Demurrage at the rate of U.S. $2,000 per day or pro rata for any part of a day . . . at . . . discharging port is payable to the Owners by the Charterers every 15 days where and when due. In any case demurrage to be paid by Charterers to Owners within 1 week after presentation of Statement of Facts and Time Sheet of each voyage. . . . " The shipowners did not try to lien the cargo

---

[89] [1971] 1 Lloyd's Rep. 514. He said (at p. 518): "Rights which are unaccompanied by effective remedies have much less attraction for mercantile men than for lawyers . . . "

[90] At p. 204.

[91] At p. 206.

[92] See §§ 11–33 and 11–42 above. Donaldson J. had said (*op. cit.* at p. 519) that the facts were much closer to the situation in the *Hansen* case than to that in the *Fidelitas* case.

[93] [1977] 2 Lloyd's Rep. 261 (*The Cunard Carrier, Eleranta and Martha*), at p. 263. See also § 11–33.

[94] [1980] 2 Lloyd's Rep. 481.

for demurrage; they contended that it was impossible or impractical to lien the cargo at Jeddah. Statements of facts and time sheets could not be presented to the charterers until after the completion of discharge.

The High Court held that the shipowners were entitled to demurrage. Relying especially on the second sentence[95] in the typed demurrage clause, they had said that as discharge had to be completed before each statement of facts and timesheet could be prepared, and the charterers only had to pay demurrage within one week thereafter, they could not exercise a lien, as the cargo would already have been discharged. Mocatta J. said[96] that it was well established that where there was a conflict between a printed clause and a typed clause the latter should prevail. It was therefore not necessary to investigate whether at Jeddah cargo could be discharged into warehouses and subjected to a lien, since such action would have been inconsistent with the provision of the second sentence in the demurrage clause. He concluded[97]:

> "It seems to me that under that clause [the demurrage clause] demurrage cannot be demanded until after the statement of facts and the timesheet for the voyage have been prepared. These things cannot take place until after the cargo has been discharged and by then the possibility of the exercise of a lien will have vanished."

11–46 The decision in the *Overseas Transportation* case had been followed in *Granvias Oceanica Armadora S.A.* v. *Jibsen Trading Co.*,[98] in which Kerr J. said[99] of the earlier case: "It decided and settled the test which is equally applicable here . . . It decided that the mere provision of a right of lien over the cargo for discharging port demurrage is not sufficient to relieve the charterers. They are only relieved if the lien is effective in the sense that the owners can exercise it in practice." As in the case before him, a charterparty may contain a cesser clause, though the bill of lading may not incorporate the charterparty but contain different demurrage and lien provisions. If so charterers cannot rely upon the cesser clause; furthermore, unless the discharging time as stipulated in the bill of lading was exceeded, they may not even be able to make the shipowners reduce their claim by the extent to which the bill of lading provision would have entitled shipowners to claim demurrage from receivers. In the *Granvias* case the *Kavo Peiratis* had been chartered on the Gencon form to carry cement from Poro Point, Philippines, to Zanzibar, Tanzania. The lien clause stated[1]: "Owners shall have a lien on the cargo for . . . demurrage. Charterers shall remain responsible for . . . demurrage incurred at port of discharge but only to such extent as the Owners have been unable to obtain payment thereof by exercising the lien on the cargo." The charterers' agents, with the shipowners' agreement, issued a bill of lading which did not incorporate the provisions of the charterparty. It provided for a lien for demurrage. As to discharging time, however, the bill said: "The consignees . . . must be ready to take delivery immediately on steamer's arrival at discharging port . . . and must so continue ready and receive their goods as fast as

---

[95] This second sentence is, as was pointed out by Mocatta J. in this case, similar to that used in the charterparty considered in *Z SS. Co. Ltd.* v. *Amtorg, New York* (1938) 61 Ll.L.Rep. 97. See § 11–39 above, at n. 81.
[96] *Ibid.* at p. 487.
[97] *Ibid.* at p. 488.
[98] [1977] 2 Lloyd's Rep. 344.
[99] *Ibid.* at p. 351.
[1] It was in the standard unamended Gencon form.

steamer can deliver . . . " Kerr J. held that the charterers had deprived the shipowners of their ability to exercise a lien. There had been no finding that a reasonable time for discharging was exceeded. The charterers were therefore liable for demurrage at Zanzibar in the manner and to the extent stipulated in the charterparty.

The *Overseas Transportation* decision[2] was also applied in *Maritime* **11–47** *Transport Operators G.m.b.H.* v. *Louis Dreyfus et Cie.*[3] Sellers sold about 11,000 metric tons of rice c. & f. Bandar Shahpour, Iran. Under a charterparty shipowners let their ship be nominated to the charterers to carry the rice from Orange, Texas, to Bandar Shahpour. Demurrage was to be paid by the charterers. Shipowners were given a lien for demurrage; charterers were stated to be "responsible for freight and demurrage incurred at port of discharge, but only to such extent as the Owners have been unable to obtain payment thereof by exercising the lien on the cargo." The charterers sub-chartered the ship to the sellers on identical terms. The Iranian receivers were a governmental or quasi-governmental organisation. The bill of lading incorporated all the terms, conditions and exceptions of the charterparty. While the ship was on her voyage shipowners and charterers agreed an addendum which provided, *inter alia*: " . . . demurrage at discharge port is to be paid by Receivers instead of Charterers." In consideration of this the charterers undertook to assume liability for all discharging demurrage not paid within 30 days of the shipowners' invoice being submitted to the receivers. The charterers were only to be liable if they received the invoice, time sheet and statement of facts. There was demurrage; the cargo was delivered to the receivers without any attempt by the shipowners to exercise a lien. The arbitrator found as a fact that the exercise of a lien would have been impractical and ineffective.

The charterers contended that their liability was only for such part of the demurrage as the shipowners could establish that they were unable to recover by the exercise of the lien; and that as they had not tried to exercise the lien they must show that it was legally ineffective or could not be exercised. They relied on the decision of Goddard J. in *Z Steamship Co. Ltd.* v. *Amtorg, New York*[4] and of the Court of Appeal in *Overseas Transportation.*[5] Parker J. said[6] that it was not necessary to deal with the former decision as it was merely illustrative of the general principle and did not deal with the circumstances in which, notwithstanding the failure to exercise a lien, shipowners could recover. He decided, finding in favour of the shipowners, that it followed from the arbitrator's finding of fact and the Court of Appeal decision that the shipowners' claim was not debarred.

In the *Overseas Transportation* case it had been held that the shipowners could recover although they did not try to exercise a lien. It was, he concluded,[7] "clear authority that if the owners can show that the right of lien was either legally or practically an ineffective right the failure to attempt to exercise it will not debar his claim . . . in the present case the arbitrator's

---

[2] [1971] 1 Lloyd's Rep. 514 (*The Sinoe*).
[3] [1981] 2 Lloyd's Rep. 159; and it was considered in *Gerani Compania Naviera S.A.* v. *Alfred C. Toepfer* (*The Demosthenes V*) (*No. 2*) [1982] 1 Lloyd's Rep. 282.
[4] (1938) 61 Lloyd's Rep. 97. See § 11–39 above.
[5] [1972] 1 Lloyd's Rep. 201 (*The Sinoe*). See § 11–43 above.
[6] *Op. cit.* at p. 165.
[7] *Op. cit.* at p. 166.

findings are such as to bring the owners squarely within the decision in *The Sinoe* not as to legal but as to practical ineffectiveness."

11–48 Waiver of cesser clause

Just as payment of freight by charterers may result in them being deemed to have waived the cesser clause,[8] so it seems that payment of demurrage may have this effect. The point was touched on in *Fidelitas Shipping Co. Ltd.* v. *V/O Exportchleb*[9] where the shipowners asked the High Court to consider whether they could contend that the charterers had waived their right to rely on the cesser clause, Megaw J. (whose remarks were *obiter dicta* and not considered in the appeal) said[10]: " . . . the owners' claim against the charterers is excluded by Clause 27" [the Cesser Clause] "of the charter-party so far as the owners' claim relates to demurrage alleged to have been incurred at the port of loading." He said that it followed that it was not open to the umpire, when the matter was remitted to him, to consider any alleged waiver by the charterers. To hold that there had been a waiver would be to reach a conclusion inconsistent with the answer to the question (whether the cesser clause excluded the claim) put by him to the Court. It seems that circumstances could arise in which the demurrage payment amounted to a waiver.

11–49 Charterers are consignees

Where charterers are consignees and the bill of lading incorporates the charterparty terms, they cannot rely on the cesser clause to defeat a claim by shipowners for discharging demurrage. Thus in *Gullischen* v. *Stewart Brothers*[11] a charterparty stipulated: "as this charterparty is entered into by the charterers on account of another party,[12] their liability ceases as soon as the cargo is on board, the vessel holding a lien upon the cargo for freight and demurrage." The bill of lading made the goods deliverable to the charterers at the port of discharge, "they paying freight, and all other conditions as per charterparty." The shipowners claimed discharging demurrage from the charterers, as consignees. The Court of Appeal held that the cesser clause was inapplicable and that the charterers were liable. Brett M.R. said[13] that it would be absurd to suppose that the charterers' liability upon the bills of lading would cease upon the loading of the cargo:

> "Pushed to its logical conclusion, the argument for the defendants would free them from liability for freight."

The bill of lading thus incorporated some charterparty provisions, but not the cesser clause.

11–50 If charterers are consignees, they may be able to rely on the cesser clause, so far as liability for loading demurrage is concerned, even though the bill of lading incorporates the terms of the charterparty. Thus in *San-*

---

[8] *Rederiaktiebolaget Transatlantic* v. *Board of Trade* (1924) 30 Com.Cas. 117 at pp. 125–126, *per* Roche J.: "If the cesser clause was being acted upon, all they" [the charterers] "would have paid and ought to have paid was, not the sum of £31,000 odd, but a sum of about £22,000 odd, which was the advance freight. They therefore have waived the cesser clause as to some £10,000."

[9] [1963] 1 Lloyd's Rep. 246. See § 11–37 above.

[10] At p. 255.

[11] (1884) 13 Q.B.D. 317 (C.A.). See also *Bryden* v. *Niebuhr* (1884) C & E. 241.

[12] The cesser clause was used frequently to protect charterers' brokers who acted for foreign principals.

[13] At pp. 318–319.

guinetti v. *Pacific Steam Navigation Co.*[14] the lien clause stated: "The master to have a lien on the cargo for all freight and demurrage due under this agreement. All liability of the charterers under this agreement shall cease as soon as the cargo is on board . . . and all questions, whether of short delivery, demurrage, or otherwise, are to be settled with the manager or agents of the charterers at the port of destination . . . the owners and master to have a lien on the cargo for all freight, dead freight, and demurrage." Demurrage was payable "for each day beyond the said days allowed for loading and discharging." The ship carried coal from Cardiff to Callao, Peru. The shipowners did not exercise a lien for the loading demurrage at the discharging port. They then claimed it, as demurrage or alternatively as damages for detention, from the charterers, who were also the receivers, but who relied on the cesser clause. The Court of Appeal held that the charterers' liability for demurrage and detention damages ended when the cargo was put on board. Mellish L.J. said that the shipowners were to have nothing but a lien on the cargo as a remedy for their freight, dead freight and demurrage.

The incorporation of a charterparty in a bill of lading **11–51**

This subject, though not itself a laytime problem, arises sufficiently often to justify a summary of the relevant cases. A brief reference has already been made to this problem.[15]

The mere statement in a bill of lading that the contract of shipment incorporates the charterparty does not have the effect of including an arbitration clause which refers only to disputes under the charterparty.[16] It may do so, however, if the arbitration clause refers to disputes under both charterparty and bill of lading.[17] The test prescribed by Russell L.J. in *The Merak*[18] was followed in *The Annefield*,[19] although the arbitration clause was held not to have been incorporated. Reference to arbitration may not subject the charterparty as a whole to arbitration.[20] The words "General average & arbitration to be settled according to the York-Antwerp Rules 1950 in London . . . " have been held not to be wide enough to subject the shipowners' demurrage claim to arbitration. It has been said that there are "many gradations" of the "breadth of the intention disclosed by the bill of lading."[21]

---

[14] (1877) 2 Q.B.D. 238 (C.A.).
[15] See § 11–09 above.
[16] See *Hamilton & Co.* v. *Mackie & Sons* (1889) 5 T.L.R. 677 (C.A.); *Thomas & Co.* v. *Portsea SS. Co.* [1912] A.C. 1 (H.L.); *The Njegos* [1936] P. 90; *Atlas Levante Linie Aktiengesellschaft* v. *Gesselschaft fuer Getreidhandel A.G. & Becher* [1966] 1 Lloyd's Rep. 150; and *Federal Bulk Carriers Inc.* v. *C. Itoh & Co. Ltd.* [1989] 1 Lloyd's Rep. 103. In this last case the bill of lading clause incorporated "all terms, conditions and exceptions as per charterparty dated 20 January 1986 and any addendum thereto . . . as fully written." It was held by the Court of Appeal that the arbitration clause was not thereby incorporated in the bill of lading.
[17] *The Merak* [1964] P. 223 (C.A.).
[18] *Ibid.* at p. 260.
[19] [1971] 1 Lloyd's Rep. 1.
[20] *Transamerican Ocean Contractors Inc.* v. *Transchemical Rotterdam B.V.* [1978] 1 Lloyd's Rep. 238 (C.A.).
[21] *Skips A/S Nordheim* v. *Syrian Petroleum Co. Ltd. and Petrofina S.A.* (*The Varenna*) [1983] 1 Lloyd's Rep. 416 *per* Hobhouse J. at p. 419. For incorporation see also *Hogarth Shipping Co. Ltd.* v. *Blyth Greene, Jourdain & Co. Ltd.* [1917] 2 K.B. 534 (C.A.). In *Miramar Maritime Corporation* v. *Holborn Oil Trading Ltd.* [1984] 2 Lloyd's Rep. 129 (*The Miramar*) Lord Diplock referred to *The Merak* and *The Annefield*, and what was said there by Russell L.J. and by Lord Denning M.R., respectively. He said, at p. 131: " . . . those dicta drew a

The effectiveness of general words of incorporation and the nature of the master's duty to sign the bill of lading were discussed in *Garbis Maritime Corporation* v. *Philippine National Oil Co.*.[22] Many of the cases were reviewed in *Astro Valiente Compania Naviera S.A.* v. *Government of Pakistan Ministry of Food and Agriculture* (*The Emmanuel Colocotronis*) (*No. 2*)[23] in which the bill of lading said: "All other conditions, exceptions, demurrage, general average and for disbursements as per above named charter-party"; it was held that the charterparty arbitration clause was one of the "conditions" to be incorporated.

clear distinction as respects incorporation in the bill of lading between an arbitration clause in the charterparty and a clause therein 'which is directly germane to the shipment, carriage and delivery of goods.' A clause that falls within this latter category, it was said, is to be treated as incorporated in the bill of lading even though it may involve a degree of 'manipulation' of the words in order to fit exactly a bill of lading."

[22] [1982] 2 Lloyd's Rep. 283 (*The Garbis*).
[23] [1982] 1 Lloyd's Rep. 286.

CHAPTER 12

DISPATCH

Definition   **12–01**

Dispatch money is money due from shipowners to charterers[1] if the charterers complete the loading or the discharging before the laytime ends.[2] It
becomes due in return for the early release of the ship. If demurrage can be
looked upon as a surcharge on freight,[3] rather than as damages, then dispatch money can be regarded as a discount on freight or a rebate of
freight.[4] Alternatively, it may be seen as a reward to charterers for performing more than their duty, or, as it were, a work of supererogation. The
amount due will depend on the wording of the dispatch clause and the rate
stipulated. The following are examples of dispatch clauses found in charterparties:

"Despatch Money (which is to be paid to Charterers before Steamer
sails) shall be payable for all time saved in loading (including Sundays and
Holidays saved) at the rate of £10 sterling per day for Steamers up to 4,000
tons Bill of Lading weight, and £15 sterling per day for Steamers of over
4,000 tons Bill of Lading weight. . . . "[5]

"If sooner dispatched Owners to pay Charterers dispatch at . . . per day
or *pro rata* for part of a day for all laytime saved."[6]

Rates and calculations for each port   **12–02**

The rate stipulated is usually, though not necessarily, one half of the
demurrage rate.[7] "Since the shipowner may have difficulty in obtaining
another engagement at short notice or in advancing the date of the ship's
next voyage, he stands to gain less by unexpected expedition in loading and
discharging than he stands to lose by delay. Accordingly dispatch is usually

---

[1] Or shippers or receivers, according to the provisions of the contract.
[2] The Charterparty Laytime Definitions 1980 (see Appendix to this book) state: "29. 'DES-
PATCH MONEY' or 'DESPATCH'—means the money payable by the owner if the ship
completes loading or discharging before the laytime has expired."
[3] For its meaning, see § 10–01 above.
[4] Donaldson J. in *Navico A.G.* v. *Vrontados Naftiki Etairia P.E.* [1968] 1 Lloyd's Rep. 379 at
p. 383 said: " . . . the shipowner, in theory at least, reaps the advantage of being able to
proceed earlier upon the ship's next freight earning engagement. In recognition of this
advantage provision is usually made for the payment by the owners of a rebate of freight at
a daily rate for all time saved."
[5] River Plate Charter-Party 1914 (Centrocon).
[6] Baltimore Form C.
[7] See the comment by McNair in *Thomasson Shipping Co. Ltd.* v. *Peabody & Co. of London
Ltd.* [1959] 2 Lloyd's Rep. 296 at p. 303: " . . . it is almost the universal practice (as is
shown by the cases and one's own experience) that the rate of dispatch is one half the rate
of demurrage—not invariably but almost universally . . . " See also § 12–10 below. And
see *United British SS. Co. Ltd.* v. *Minister of Food* [1951] 1 Lloyd's Rep. 111 (as to which
see § 12–03 below), where the dispatch rate was one third of the demurrage rate.

payable at half the demurrage rate. . . . "[8] Although charterparties almost invariably provide for demurrage, fewer charterparties, and practically no tanker charterparties, provide for dispatch. Among dry cargo charterparties, for example, the Gencon[9] charterparty, for example provides for demurrage but not for dispatch.

The dispatch money due for loading or discharging should be calculated, in the absence of words to the contrary, for all the loading ports together and all the discharging ports together, and not for each port separately.[10] Unless this is done, any difference in demurrage and dispatch rates could produce an inequitable result. Separate calculations at each of two loading ports, for example, might show that demurrage was due for three days at the first port, and dispatch due for a like period at the second port. The total loading time would thus be that permitted by the laytime clause. A calculation of the financial position at each port would give shipowners an unfair profit if the demurrage rate were, as is usual, greater than the dispatch rate.

12–03   In *United British SS. Co. Ltd.* v. *Minister of Food*[11] a charterparty for the carriage of wheat from one Australian to two English ports stated: "Cargo to be discharged at the average rate of 1,000 tons for bulk and 750 tons for bags per weather working day, (Sundays and holidays excepted) (provided vessel can deliver at this rate). Vessel to pay dispatch money at one-third of the demurrage rate for all time saved in discharging. Dispatch or demurrage, if any, at discharging port(s) to be settled in London." The lay days, based on the cargo discharged at each port, were exceeded at Southampton but not at London. The shipowners contended that the two discharging times should be taken separately. The dispatch money at London would then be deducted from the demurrage due at Southampton.

The charterers argued that the total time allowable for discharge at both ports should be the basis. The High Court held that the charterers were right. Croom-Johnson J. said[12]:

> "If the parties wanted to make an agreement under which they were going to pay demurrage for delay at one point and only get one-third[13] of the demurrage back, so to speak, or credit for the equivalent of one-third of the demurrage, for any time they saved at the other port, they could no doubt have framed an appropriate clause which would have produced that result. It is quite plain that they have not done it, and it seems to me that, looking at this charter-party as a whole, when I see 'cargo to be discharged at the average rate of' so-and-so, I think those words really mean what they say. It looks to me as if it would have been so simple to say, 'Cargo to be discharged at the average rate of so-and-so at each port.' But they never did it."

If the parties had used a clause of the type mentioned by Croom-Johnson J. there would have been separate calculations at each port, with dispatch at London and demurrage at Southampton. If the charterer had the right to average, the time saved and extra time used could have been set off against each other. In the absence of such a right there would have been separate financial calculations for each port, of the type requested by the unsuccessful shipowners.

---

[8] Donaldson J. in *Navico A.G.* v. *Vrontados Naftiki Etairia P.E.* [1968] 1 Lloyd's Rep. 379 at p. 383.
[9] Uniform General Charter 1976.
[10] See also § 9–01 above.
[11] [1951] 1 Lloyd's Rep. 111.
[12] At p. 115.
[13] The dispatch rate in this case was one third of the demurrage rate.

The question of separate calculations for each port was also mentioned **12–04** in *Compania Naviera Azuero S.A.* v. *British Oil & Cake Mills Ltd.*[14] The laytime clause stated: "Cargo to be received at destination at an average rate of not less than 1,000 tons per weather working day. . . . " Discharging was carried out at a higher average rate than this at Belfast and a lower average rate at Avonmouth. The shipowners claimed that laytime should be calculated separately for each port and dispatch money or demurrage paid separately. Pearson J. rejected this contention and said that there could only be one calculation for both ports. The clause did not say "each destination"; it spoke not of "average rates" but of "an average rate." He said[15]:

> "If some delay at one port is exactly offset by the expedition at the other port, the unloading will be completed and the ship will be released for further employment at the proper time. In that case, it would seem unreasonable that the shipowners should pay dispatch money at one port and charge demurrage at the other port, and make a profit out of the difference of rates."

Furthermore, time began after a notice period at Belfast but upon the giving of notice of readiness at Avonmouth. Separate calculations would discriminate unfairly in favour of the Belfast receivers. He cited with approval the decision in *United British SS. Co. Ltd.* v. *Minister of Food.*[16]

Time for which dispatch is payable   **12–05**
The length of time for which dispatch money is payable depends upon the charterparty terms. Disputes arise as to whether the calculation should be based on the lay days or on the calendar days saved. Dispatch money is frequently agreed to be payable for "all time saved." This means time saved to shipowners. It thus means actual time or calendar days, but a slight variation either in the words themselves or in their position in the charterparty may produce a different interpretation.

Summary of the rules   **12–06**
The rules which relate to this apparently simple task have been summarised thus[17]:

1. The object of a dispatch clause is presumed to be that shipowners will pay money to charterers for all time saved to the ship, on the same basis as charterers would pay demurrage to shipowners, that is, ignoring the lay day exceptions.
2. This presumption (a) may be, but is not necessarily, rebutted by shipowners where lay days and dispatch are dealt with in one clause and demurrage in another clause[18]; and (b) is rebutted where lay days, dispatch and demurrage are dealt with in the same clause but

---

[14] [1957] 1 Lloyd's Rep. 312 (*The Azuero*). The case is also reported at [1957] 2 Q.B. 293, but the part of the judgment printed there only relates to the question of weather working days (see § 6–05 above). On separate calculations, see also § 9–01 above.
[15] At p. 324.
[16] [1951] 1 Lloyd's Rep. 111. See § 12–03 above.
[17] There follows a paraphrase of part of the judgment of Bailhache J. in *Mawson Shipping Co. Ltd.* v. *Beyer* [1914] 1 K.B. 304 at p. 312; see § 12–09 below.
[18] In his judgment in *Mawson Shipping Co. Ltd.* v. *Beyer* [1914] 1 K.B. 304 at p. 312. Bailhache J. said that the presumption would be rebutted in these circumstances. It is submitted that the above statement of the law is correct: see the dissenting judgment of Fletcher Moulton L.J. in *The Glendevon* [1893] P. 269 (C.A.).

the wording is such that the lay day exceptions can be taken to apply also to the dispatch period.

12–07 **"All time saved"**[19]**; "any time saved"; "every hour saved"; and similar expressions**

Even phrases as apparently unambiguous as "all time saved," "any time saved" or "every hour saved" may be so placed in the charterparty or so affected by immediately adjacent words that the presumption, that dispatch is calculated on the same basis as demurrage, is rebutted.[20] If such phrases are not so placed or affected, then the words will mean that all calendar time saved, and not merely laytime saved, is to be counted in favour of charterers where they load or discharge within the laytime.

12–08 *Actual time saved*

It is presumed that "time saved" means all time, without the exceptions which apply to laytime. The presumption was held to be justified in *Laing* v. *Hollway*.[21] A charterparty for the carriage of ore from Elba to Wales provided that cargo was to be loaded at 200 tons per running day and discharged at 200 tons per working day. It also stated: "Demurrage, if any, at the rate of 20s. per hour . . . Dispatch money 10s. per hour on any time saved in loading or for discharging." Four days were saved in loading and five days in discharging. At 24 hours a day the charterers were entitled to 216 hours dispatch. At 12 hours a day they would have been entitled to 108 hours dispatch. There was no reference to 12 hours in the laytime clause. The Court of Appeal said that there was no ground for the suggestion that the length of a day saved was 12 hours. It held that the charterers were right and that dispatch was due for 216 hours. Bramwell L.J. said[22]:

> "There is a maximum of obligation on the charterer of 200 tons for loading and discharging on each working day, but the maximum of obligation on the ship to receive and discharge has no limit except 'as rapidly as possible'; and the charterers have the whole twenty-four hours round in which they may unload the 200 tons . . . It is admitted on both sides, and is clear, that 'time saved' means if the ship is ready earlier than she would be if the charterers worked up to their maximum obligation only, all the time by which she is the sooner ready is time saved within the meaning of the charterparty. Then the question is by how much time is she sooner ready? The answer is in nine times twenty-four hours. Really the reason of the thing is that way."

12–09 *Sundays usually count as "saved"*

As it is presumed that, in the absence of contrary words, dispatch money is payable for all time saved, Sundays count in the time saved. In *Mawson Shipping Co. Ltd.* v. *Beyer*[23] a charterparty for the carriage of wheat from Novorossisk provided that the cargo should be "loaded at the average rate of 500 units per running day of twenty-four consecutive hours (Sundays and non-working holidays excepted)." Demurrage was payable at a certain rate per running day. The dispatch clause stated: "Owners agree to pay

---

[19] The Charterparty Laytime Definitions 1980 (see Appendix to this book) state: "30. 'ALL TIME SAVED'—means the time saved to the ship from the completion of loading/discharging to the expiry of the laytime including periods excepted from the laytime."

[20] In *Nelson (James) & Sons Ltd.* v. *Nelson Line, Liverpool, Ltd.* [1907] 2 K.B. 705 (C.A.) the words were "each clear day saved in loading"; it was held (Fletcher Moulton L.J. dissenting) that the charterers were not entitled to dispatch money for a Sunday or a holiday after the end of loading. See § 12–16 below.

[21] (1878) 3 Q.B.D. 437 (C.A.).

[22] At p. 441.

[23] [1914] 1 K.B. 304.

charterers £10 (say ten pounds) per day for all time saved in loading." The shipowners and charterers disagreed as to one day's dispatch money deducted by charterers. The time between the end of loading and the expiry of laytime included a Sunday. The charterers claimed that this day should be included in the dispatch calculation. The shipowners said that the definition of the word "day," as used in the dispatch clause, was to be found in the laytime clause. It meant a "running day of twenty-four consecutive hours (Sundays and non-working holidays excepted)." The High Court held that the charterers were right. Bailhache J. said[24]:

> "1. Prima facie the presumption is that the object and intention of these dispatch clauses is that the shipowners shall pay to the charterers for all time saved to the ship, calculated in the way in which, in the converse case, demurrage would be calculated; that is, taking no account of the lay day exceptions . . .
> 2. This prima facie presumption may be displaced, and is displaced,[25] where either (i) lay days and time saved by dispatch are dealt with in the same clause and demurrage in another clause: *The Glendevon*[26]; (ii) lay days, time saved by dispatch, and demurrage are dealt with in the same clause, but upon the construction of that clause the Court is of opinion, from the collocation of the words or other reason, that the days saved are referable to and used in the same sense as the lay days as described in the clause, and are not used in the same sense as days lost by demurrage: *Nelson & Sons Ltd.* v. *Nelson Line, Liverpool, Ltd.*"[27]

The judge said that application of those rules brought the case before him within the first class: the prima facie rule applied and the charterers succeeded.

"All working time saved"[28] and dispatch "per day"   **12–10**

In *Thomasson Shipping Co. Ltd.* v. *Henry W. Peabody & Co. of London Ltd.*[29] a charterparty for the carriage of maize from Capetown to Europe stated: "Dispatch money . . . shall be payable for all working time saved in loading and discharging at the rate of £100 per day, or *pro rata* for part of a day saved." To calculate the loading dispatch, the shipowners first took the number of working hours saved and divided it by 24.[30] The charterers divided the same number by the number of hours customarily worked each day.[31] In each case the result was multiplied by the daily rate of £100. The High Court held that the charterers were right. McNair J. said[32]:

> " . . . the true effect of this clause, as a simple matter of construction, is that dispatch money is payable at the rate of £100 per day and *pro rata* for each day upon which working time is saved."

---

[24] At p. 312.
[25] If the laytime exceptions clearly apply to the time saved; but the mere presence of these provisions in the same clause may not always be enough. See the dissenting judgment of Fletcher Moulton L.J. in *Nelson (James) & Sons, Ltd.* v. *Nelson Line, Liverpool, Ltd.* [1907] 2 K.B. 705 at pp. 719 and 721 (C.A.). See also § 12–17 below.
[26] [1893] P. 269; and see § 12–15 below.
[27] [1907] 2 K.B. 705 (C.A.); and see § 12–16 below.
[28] The Charterparty Laytime Definitions 1980 (see Appendix to this book) state: "31. 'ALL WORKING TIME SAVED' or 'ALL LAYTIME SAVED'—means the time saved to the ship from the completion of loading/discharging to the expiry of the laytime excluding any notice time and periods excepted from the laytime."
[29] [1959] 2 Lloyd's Rep. 296.
[30] Thus: 76 hours 10 minutes divided by 24 = 3 days 4 hours 30 minutes (shipowners' calculation).
[31] Thus: 76 hours 10 minutes divided by 8 hours 40 minutes = 8 days 7 hours 10 minutes (charterers' calculation).
[32] At p. 304.

The words "all working time saved" meant, in the view of the judge,[33] that Sundays and holidays should be excluded from the time saved.[34] He rejected the shipowners' contention that "time saved" meant hours saved. The expression "day" signified a calendar day of 24 hours and not merely a period of 24 hours made up of separate periods of working hours. If the shipowners were right, the charterers would, in the case of an eight-hour working day, have to complete the ship three days before laytime ended in order to earn one day's dispatch.

12–11 Dispatch for same days twice

The ship may be so expeditiously handled by charterers that they become entitled to dispatch in respect of the same days twice. The laytime at one port may so far exceed the time used that the work at the next port is completed within that same period of laytime. If so, and if the work at the second port is completed also within the laytime at the second port, dispatch may be payable at each port for the same days. There is no reason why the charterparty provisions should not produce this unusual effect. This situation arose in *The Themistocles*.[35] Under a charterparty for the carriage of phosphate from Sfax and Casablanca to Finland the ship was to be loaded at the rate of 750 tons per weather working day. Another clause provided for loading demurrage "at the rate of U.S. $1,000 per running day or *pro rata*" and stated: "On all time saved at port of loading, owners to pay to shippers dispatch money at half of demurrage rate per day (portions of a day *pro rata*)." Loading at Casablanca, the second port, ended before laytime would have expired at Sfax, if the shippers had exercised their right to use all the time allowed. The issue was whether, as the owners contended, dispatch money should be calculated by reference to the allowable time saved. If the charterers were right they were entitled to dispatch in respect of three of the days, both at Sfax and at Casablanca. The High Court held that they were right. Morris J., speaking of earlier cases,[36] said[37]:

> "In considering them, it is essential, in my judgment, to recognise that they are decisions which have been given in regard to particular words in particular contracts."

Of the words "all time saved at port of loading" in the case before him he said[38]:

> " . . . those words have reference to the whole time which is saved as a result of the vessel being able to leave the port of loading on some date or at some time earlier than she would have left had the shippers kept the vessel as long as they could have kept her . . . The words 'on all time' are, in my judgment, wide and embracing."

He rejected the argument that the charterers were wrongly counting certain days twice. The ship could have been kept by them for loading several days longer at each port. She had been saved that time; it was immaterial

---

[33] He cited *Laing* v. *Hollway* (1878) 3 Q.B.D. 437 (C.A.). See § 12–08 above.
[34] And possibly, though he expressed no conclusion, rainy days.
[35] (1949) 82 Ll.L.Rep. 232.
[36] *Laing* v. *Hollway* (1878) 3 Q.B.D. 437 (C.A.); *The Glendevon* [1893] P. 269; *Nelson & Sons, Ltd.* v. *Nelson Line, Liverpool, Ltd.* [1907] 2 K.B. 705 (C.A.); *Re Royal Mail Steam Packet Co. Ltd. and River Plate SS. Co. Ltd.* [1910] 1 K.B. 600; and *Mawson Shipping Co. Ltd.* v. *Beyer* [1914] 1 K.B. 304.
[37] (1949) 82 Ll.L.Rep. 232 at p. 238.
[38] At p. 239.

that some of the days which could have been used at Sfax, had the ship been kept there, were the days which were used in Casablanca.

Exclusion of notice time   **12–12**

Notice time or free time may be specifically excluded from consideration in the calculation of time saved. A question may arise as to whether the notice time should be dispensed with so that laytime begins earlier. In such a case laytime would end correspondingly earlier and the dispatch period, between the end of the loading or discharging and the end of laytime, would be reduced. Alternatively the notice time might be included in order to establish when laytime begins, and its specific exclusion will only arise where work has been completed within the notice time. Much will depend on the wording, but in one case the High Court has held that the latter alternative is correct.

In *Sir R. Ropner & Co., Ltd.* v. *W.S. Partridge & Co.*[39] charterparties   **12–13**
for the carriage of coal from the U.S.A. to England[40] provided that laytime should begin "48 hours after written notice is given of vessel being completely discharged of inward cargo and ballast in all her holds and ready to load, whether in berth or not . . . unless commenced earlier." Dispatch was due for each running day saved, and *pro rata*, and the clause contained the words: "No dispatch to be paid on the 48-hours free time." The shipowners contended that laytime ran from the giving of the written notice of readiness, as if the reference to 48 hours had been deleted. The charterers said that laytime ran from the end of 48 hours after notice of readiness or from the beginning of loading if that was earlier. In their view the exclusion clause meant that if loading was completed within 48 hours after notice of readiness dispatch was not payable on any part of such 48 hours remaining after completion of loading. Branson J., holding that the charterers were right, said[41] that on their construction "you do not get the peculiar circumstance of having to apply to lay days for the purpose of demurrage a different calculation from that (applying to the same lay days) for the purposes of dispatch."

The differing effects of the parties' contentions can be seen in the following list[42] of hypothetical cases put before the umpire, whose award was upheld. The figures were based on a cargo of 6,000 tons to be loaded at an average rate of 1,500 tons per day, *i.e.* in four days.

> "(1) Vessel *A* commenced loading 48 hours after notice of readiness and loaded in two days. The owners contended that in such a case no dispatch would be payable. The charterers contended that two days' dispatch would be payable.
>
> (2) Vessel *B* commenced loading immediately on notice of readiness being given and loaded in 24 hours. The owners contended that in such a case three days' dispatch would be payable. The charterers contended that two days' dispatch would be payable, laytime running from commencement of loading, but no dispatch being payable on the 24 hours' balance of the 48 hours.
>
> (3) Vessel *C* commenced loading 24 hours after notice of readiness and loaded in three days. The owners contended that in such case no dispatch would be payable. The charterers contended that one day's dispatch would be payable."

[39] (1929) 33 Ll.L.Rep. 86.
[40] The printed forms of charterparty were, as Branson J. put it (at p. 87): " . . . adapted to somewhat unusual conditions during the time when British ships were going to the United States to bring coal from there while the coal strike was dislocating the supply of coal in this country."
[41] At p. 88.
[42] *Ibid.* at p. 87.

12–14 A clearer dispatch clause

Difficulties surrounding the use of such dispatch provisions as "all time saved" may be avoided by the use of different words. "All time" may be taken to mean laytime, and be subject to the same exceptions. The word "days" is sometimes ambiguous.[43] The phrase "running days" is clearer[44] and is usually taken to mean all calendar days, subject of course to any exceptions expressly stated.

So in *Re Royal Mail Steam Packet Co. Ltd. and River Plate SS. Co. Ltd.*[45] a charterparty for a voyage from England to South America allowed 20 running days for discharge, with certain periods excepted, and stated: "the owners of the ship to pay £10 per day dispatch money for each running day saved." The High Court held that the charterers were entitled to dispatch for all running days (*i.e.* all calendar days), and not merely for all lay days saved. Bray J. said[46]:

> "I think the word 'saved' must be construed as meaning saved to the shipowner, as it was construed in *Laing* v. *Hollway*.[47] I am of opinion that the words 'running day' in clause 8 mean consecutive days, and that it is not correct to say that, because the clause says that holidays and week-ends are for the purpose of loading and discharging to be excepted from the running days, that is a definition of 'running day.' It is clear that for the purpose of demurrage the running days include Sundays and week-ends, and I think that for the purpose of calculating dispatch money they must also be counted, as they are days saved to the shipowners."

Here the clear words of the dispatch provision enabled the charterers to recover dispatch money for time which would have been excepted from the laytime. The laytime, demurrage and dispatch provisions were all in the same clause, but the excepted periods were inserted immediately after and only referable to the laytime provision.

12–15 Do the laytime exceptions apply?

The presumption that shipowners must pay dispatch for all time saved may be rebutted.[48] It can be rebutted where lay days and dispatch are dealt with together or in some other manner which makes the laytime exceptions apply to the time saved. The wording is important and one decision may not be an authority in another case. One such decision is that of the Probate Divorce and Admiralty Divisional Court in *The Glendevon*.[49] Though it has frequently been relied upon by shipowners,[50] its authority is not strong except perhaps with respect to charterparties containing similar words in a similar form.

A charterparty for the carriage of coal from Newcastle to Lisbon stated: "The steamer to be discharged at the rate of two hundred tons per day weather permitting (Sundays and Fête Days excepted) according to the custom of the port of discharge and if sooner discharged to pay at the rate of 8s. 6d. per hour for every hour saved . . . Demurrage twenty pounds for every day's detention in discharging and in same proportion for any part of

---

[43] See § 2–15 above.
[44] See § 2–20 above.
[45] [1910] 1 K.B. 600.
[46] At pp. 608 and 609.
[47] (1878) 3 Q.B.D. 437 (C.A.); and see § 12–08 above.
[48] See § 12–07 above.
[49] [1893] P. 269.
[50] For example in *Re Royal Mail Steam Packet Co. Ltd.* v. *River Plate SS. Co. Ltd.* [1910] 1 K.B. 600, where Bray J. distinguished it; there the laytime clause provided for running days, while dispatch was payable "for each running day saved." See § 12–14 above.

such day over and above the days allowed. . . . " The dispute was as to whether a Fête Day and a Sunday, occurring between the end of discharging and the end of laytime, should be counted in the calculation of "every hour saved." The Divisional Court held that they should be excluded. The President, Sir Francis Jeune, described[51] one argument advanced by the successful shipowners:

> "they point out that days, during which the weather does not permit discharge, stand on the same footing as regards the charterers' right as Sundays and fête days; that is to say, the charterer need not discharge on Sundays and fête days, and need not discharge if the weather does not permit on other days, but if Sundays and fête days are to be reckoned in as time saved for the purpose of the payment of dispatch money, then the days during which the weather does not permit discharge ought to stand on the same footing. I confess I am unable to see any answer to that argument, and the results would be so extraordinary as to be unintelligible. It would come to this, that after the ship was discharged, the charterer would have the right to say that on a large number of days, it might be even weeks or months, he was prevented by the weather from discharging, and therefore he was entitled to add these in as days of twenty-four hours, for each hour of which he was entitled to have 8s. 6d. That is an absurdity."

Criticism of The Glendevon **12–16**

The judge appears to be summarising the shipowners' argument as follows:

> "Sundays and fête days are on the same footing as days when weather does not permit work. This results from the exception in the laytime provision and the words 'weather permitting.' It follows that the charterers should claim dispatch money not only for Sundays and fête days saved but also for days saved when weather would not have permitted work anyhow. There might be many such days, or weeks, or months. The end of laytime would be postponed and time saved correspondingly. But this is ridiculous: therefore charterers cannot even claim for the Sundays and fête days."

This argument may be criticised on the ground that, contrary to the view held by the shipowners, it does not follow that all the excepted periods should apply to the dispatch time. The case might still have been decided in their favour and "Sundays and Fête Days" excepted on the ground that "every hour saved" meant "all laytime saved." Nevertheless a case could occur, where the expression "weather working days" is used, in which there was a claim for dispatch for bad weather days and days otherwise excepted, so that the dispatch period was inflated.

The decision in *The Glendevon*[52] was followed by a majority of the Court of Appeal in *Nelson (James) & Sons Ltd.* v. *Nelson Line, Liverpool Ltd.*[53] An agreement in the nature of a charterparty for the carriage of frozen meat from the River Plate to Liverpool and London stated: "Seven weather working days (Sundays and holidays excepted) to be allowed by owners to charterers for loading . . . For any time beyond the periods above provided the charterers shall pay to the owners demurrage at the rate of £40 per day . . . For each clear day saved in loading the charterers shall be paid or allowed by the owners the sum of £20."

In the case of certain ships loaded under the agreement the charterers, **12–17** by loading within a shorter period of time than that allowed, let the ship sail two days earlier than the date to which she might have been kept without earning demurrage. One of the days was a Sunday or holiday, on which the charterers were not bound to work. When the charterers claimed dis-

[51] At p. 273.
[52] [1893] P. 269.
[53] [1907] 2 K.B. 705.

patch money for the two days, the shipowners said that the only days which could be saved were days on which the ship could be required to work. The reasons for the court's decision in favour of the shipowners were given by Buckley L.J.[54]:

> "Suppose that a vessel begins to load on a Wednesday, and completes her loading on Saturday, thus occupying four days, how many clear days have been saved in loading? The appellants[55] say that they have utilised four out of seven, and have saved the remaining four."[56]

The problem can thus be presented, where a charterparty provides for seven weather working days, Sundays and holidays excepted, and there occurs the sequence of events envisaged by Buckley L.J.:

Wednesday 1st	Lay time begins; loading begins.
Saturday 4th	Loading completed; four days have been occupied in loading.
Sunday 5th	An excepted day.
Monday 6th	One clear day saved.
Tuesday 7th	One clear day saved.
Wednesday 8th	End of laytime, *i.e.* of seven weather working days, the Sunday being excepted. This clear day has also been saved.

Buckley L.J. continued[57]:

> "In this lies a delightful touch of humour. It is as if an Irishman[57a] were to say that, having only half-a-crown in his pocket, he had spent two shillings of it, and saved the remaining shilling. Of course the appellants do not put their contention in this bald form. They adopt the not uncommon device of forgetting, or seeking to distract attention from, the language of this contract, and arguing that, if the language had been different, that would have been the result. They say, and quite truly, that the departure of the ship has been accelerated, not by three days, but by four, because she got the benefit of Sunday; that the charterers might have occupied until the end of the next Wednesday in loading; and that, had they done so, the ship would have left four days later than in fact she did. If the contract had been that the charterers should have so much a day for each day saved to the ship, this would have been right, but it does not so provide. The provision is that they shall have so much for each clear day saved in loading."

He said that his conclusion was in accordance with the decision in *The Glendevon*,[58] which in his view was rightly decided.

12–18   The judge thus distinguished a mere saving in delay to the ship from time "saved in loading," which he equated to laytime. The payment, in his view, was to be for any saving effected in the seven days allowed for loading. In his dissenting judgment Fletcher Moulton L.J. said that he considered the decision in *The Glendevon*[59] to be wrong in law and that the Court of Appeal was bound by the principles which it had laid down in *Laing* v. *Hollway*.[60] If the laytime clause had referred to "seven working days (Sundays and holidays excepted)" he would have been satisfied that the charterers were right. They would have been entitled to spread their loading over the whole of a period containing neither Sundays nor holidays, and

---

[54] See pp. 724–725.

[55] The charterers.

[56] Though they would have said that while they had used four out of the seven lay days there remained four calendar days of which three were lay days.

[57] At p. 725.

[57a] It is doubtful whether a Court of Appeal (or High Court) judge would use a nationalistic or racist analogy today. But this was 1907.

[58] [1893] P. 269. See § 12–15 above.

[59] [1893] P. 269. See also § 12–15 above.

[60] (1878) 3 Q.B.D. 437, where Bramwell L.J. had said, at p. 441: " . . . all the time by which she is the sooner ready is time saved within the meaning of the charterparty. Then the question is by how much time is she sooner ready?" See § 12–08 above.

would have recovered dispatch for the shortening of that period. It had been argued by the shipowners that where "seven weather working days" were allowed the use of the full time might have brought the ship into a period of bad weather when the days would not count. They said that this was a *reductio ad absurdum* because the number of days saved would become far greater. But it was not necessary to interpret the phrase "days saved" as including such possible future prolongations of the period allowed for loading. As Fletcher Moulton L.J. concluded[61]:

> "I think that the services and the payment for them must be determined at the moment when the ship is freed by the charterers, and put at the disposal of the shipowners, and that the payment must be determined *rebus sic stantibus* for the services so rendered. Accordingly, the period must be taken as it stood at the moment when the vessel was given over to the shipowners at the termination of the loading, and the charterer must be paid for the unexpired portion."

Need The Glendevon be reconciled with other cases?   **12–19**

The Glendevon decision may be regarded as one which depends on its particular facts. The proximity of the words "for every hour saved" to the laytime provision, with its exceptions, may be taken to explain this decision in favour of the shipowners. Any theory which sought to reconcile all the principles uttered in these cases would be artificial and precarious. As Morris J. said in *The Themistocles*[62]:

> "I doubt how far any question of principle is involved in what I have to decide or was involved in the various reported cases."

Even the analysis made by Bailhache J. in *Mawson Shipping Co. Ltd.* v. *Beyer*[63] has to be qualified, in part, by a reference to the possible idiosyncracies of particular charterparties. In that case he said[64] that it

> "would serve no useful purpose and would perhaps be hardly respectful to criticise the judgment of the Court in *The Glendevon*."

The Centrocon Strike Clause and dispatch   **12–20**

The third sentence of the Centrocon Strike Clause[65] states:

"For the purpose, however, of settling dispatch money accounts, any time lost by the Steamer through any of the above cases[66] shall be counted as time in loading." For example, a strike of a "class of workmen essential to the loading of the Cargo" may prevent cargo from being loaded, so that laytime is interrupted as a result of the first sentence of the Clause. If loading is completed before the extended laytime ends, dispatch is, prima facie, due.[67]

The reason for the insertion of this third sentence, or Part 4,[68] was given by Donaldson J. in *Navico A.G.* v. *Vrontados Naftiki Etairia P.E.*[69] He

---

[61] [1907] 2 K.B. 705 at p. 271 (C.A.).
[62] (1949) 82 Ll.L.Rep. 232 at p. 239.
[63] [1914] 1 K.B. 304; and see § 12–09 above.
[64] At p. 312.
[65] In the River Plate Charter-Party 1914. For the first two sentences, see § 8–38 above.
[66] *i.e.* riots, civil commotions, a strike or lock-out of any class of workmen essential to the loading or discharging, or obstructions or stoppages beyond the control of the charterers on the railways, or in the docks, or other loading places.
[67] The Centrocon charterparty provides that dispatch is due "for all time saved in loading (including Sundays and Holidays saved)."
[68] The other Parts being Pts. 1 and 2, forming the first sentence, and Pt. 3, forming the second sentence. This division has been judicially adopted in two cases; see § 8–39 above.
[69] [1968] 1 Lloyd's Rep. 379 at p. 384.

pointed out that the clause was designed to reduce or eliminate charterer's liability to pay demurrage, if the delay was caused by specified circumstances beyond their control, and that it achieved that result by extending the laytime. He then said:

> "Such an extension could, of course, not only eliminate all liability to pay demurrage, but even give rise to a right to receive dispatch from the shipowner, notwithstanding that the ship had been delayed for a considerable time beyond that for which he had bargained. The clause therefore ends with a sentence which is intended to give the shipowner some protection from what, from his point of view, is so undesirable a result."

In that case a ship was to carry wheat from Necochea, Argentina, and Bahia Blanca, Brazil. When she anchored off Neochea she was in all respects physically ready to load but could not berth owing to the congestion. After five days she was granted free pratique, and after four more days her holds were declared to be fit for loading. Notice of readiness was given on the next day. Loading took place later, in a period shorter than the agreed laytime. The charterers claimed dispatch, saying, as their Counsel put it[70]:

> "Once the clock started after the end of the confusion, the loading was completed in that amount of time [the dispatch time] less than the permitted loading time."

Donaldson J., holding that the charterers were right, accepted their submission that their entitlement arose under a calculation which started with the giving of notice of readiness; Part 4 of the Clause was a defence to a claim so calculated. "Accordingly," he said,[71] there is no reason why it should be concerned with matters occurring before laytime began." He rejected the shipowners' argument that the period from the anchoring to the notice of readiness was to "be counted as time used in loading." He said of this third sentence[72]: "Part 4 protects the shipowners by preventing the charterer from using his shield[73] against a claim to demurrage as a spear with which to extract dispatch money from the shipowner. . . . The owners contend that their protection under Part 4 . . . should be co-extensive with that afforded to the charterers under Clause 13 (time not to count before the expiry of 12 hours from the giving of notice of readiness) and Parts 1, 2 and 3 of Clause 30. The charterers contend that Part 4 is to be construed as being co-extensive with Parts 1, 2 and 3 of the same Clause." He decided that the charterers' argument should prevail. Clause 30 was a self-contained code; just as Part 3 had been held not to extend forward in time beyond the period affected by Parts 1 and 2, so Part 4 was similarly limited and did not extend backwards in time before that period.

The application of the third sentence of the Clause appears to result in the otherwise excluded time being counted, so that laytime ends earlier and the dispatch period is reduced or eliminated. The reference in the third sentence to the list of causes[66] set out in the first sentence might be taken to affect discharging as well as loading dispatch accounts. But the closing words of the third sentence provide that the time lost "shall be counted as time used in loading." It seems that the sentence only affects loading dispatch.

---

[70] *Ibid.* at p. 382.
[71] At p. 385.
[72] At p. 386.
[73] *i.e.* the provisions for the beginning of laytime, exceptions to laytime and Pts. 1 and 3. As to the shield, see § 8–39 above.

Relationship of loading and discharging dispatch   **12–21**

Dispatch clauses usually make separate provisions for loading and discharging ports. They may depart from this pattern by providing that the time saved to shipowners in loading shall in some way be carried forward to benefit charterers during discharging. This will be an alternative to translating the loading time saved into dispatch money payable to charterers. Other methods of combining the loading and discharging times include averaging,[74] when charterers have the right to set off dispatch time against demurrage time, and reversibility,[75] when they can add together loading and discharging laytimes.

Carrying forward dispatch time   **12–22**

A typical clause for the lengthening of discharging laytime by the time saved in loading may read: "Any hours saved in loading to be added to the hours allowed for discharging"[76]; or any "days or parts of days not consumed in loading may be added to the time for discharging, and any extra time consumed in loading may be deducted from the time for discharging"[77]; or "For the purpose of calculating demurrage and/or dispatch money Charterers have the option of adding any time for which dispatch money is payable at the loading port to the total time allowed for discharging; or to deduct any time vessel is on demurrage at the loading port from the total time allowed for discharging."[78] Each of these provides for an addition to discharging laytime; and two of them allow the charterers to subtract loading demurrage from the discharging laytime.

A charterparty may provide that laytime is to be interrupted by various excepted causes, and that time lost thereby shall, for the purpose of dispatch calculations, be added to the loading time used. One such provision[79] stated that if the cargo could not be loaded or discharged by reason of certain excepted causes, no claim for damages or demurrage should be made by the charterers, receivers of the cargo, or the shipowners. It continued: " . . . but for the purpose, however, of settling dispatch money accounts any time lost by the steamer through any of the above causes shall be counted as time lost in loading." It has been held[79] that such a clause does not entitle shipowners to reopen a settled loading dispatch account when time is lost by an excepted cause at the port of discharge. The presence in the charterparty of a cesser clause may have a special significance in such a case.

In *Chadwick, Weir & Co. Ltd.* v. *Louis Dreyfus & Co.*[80] a ship had been chartered on the Centrocon form to carry grain from Buenos Aires to Spain. The charterparty was worded in the manner described above.[81] The charterers earned dispatch at the loading port and were paid it; the shipowners claimed it back because a strike at the discharging port had con-

---

[74] See § 9–02 above.
[75] See § 9–09 above.
[76] As in *Rowland & Marwood's SS. Co.* v. *Wilson, Sons & Co. Ltd.* (1897) 2 Com.Cas. 198.
[77] As in *Rederiaktiebolaget Transatlantic* v. *Compagnie Française des Phosphates de l'Océanie* (1926) 32 Com.Cas. 126; and see § 9–11 above.
[78] Socotroisem Mineral Charter-Party (Société Commerciale des Mines, Minéraux et Métaux of Brussels). See also § 9–24 above.
[79] In *Chadwick, Weir & Co. Ltd.* v. *Louis Dreyfus & Co.* (1923) 14 Ll.L.Rep. 108.
[80] (1923) 14 Ll.L.Rep. 108.
[81] *i.e.* as set out in the last paragraph.

sumed a greater amount of time. Greer J. held that the shipowners' claim failed. He said[82]:

> " . . . this clause with regard to the time lost by the steamer through any of the above causes being set up against the dispatch money only applies to the settlement of dispatch money accounts which had to be settled by the charterers at the port of loading, where it is impossible to deduct anything except time which has been lost by any of those causes at the port of loading. That view of the clause is, to my mind, assisted to some extent by the fact that there is the usual cesser clause in this contract. . . . "

The cesser clause stated that charterers' liability was to cease upon shipment and payment of dead freight, difference in freight and demurrage.

12–23   Payment of dispatch money

It is sometimes agreed that dispatch money should be paid before the ship leaves her loading port. If charterers submit their account before the departure they are not necessarily estopped from saying later that, contrary to their earlier statement, a certain day is or is not a holiday.

In *Hain SS. Co. Ltd.* v. *Sociedad Anonima Comercial de Exportacion e Importacion*[83] a ship was chartered on the Centrocon form to load at San Nicolas, Argentina. The dispatch clause stated: "Dispatch money (which is to be paid to charterers before steamer sails) shall be payable for all time saved in loading (including Sundays and holidays saved). . . . " The laytime clause provided for the ship to be "loaded at . . . tons per running day . . . Sundays and holidays excepted." A time sheet prepared by the charterers before the ship sailed was made out on the basis that one day was a holiday and another a working day. The master signed the time sheet under protest. A second time sheet, submitted by the charterers after the ship sailed, treated both days as holidays. Holding that the charterers were entitled to rely on the second time sheet, MacKinnon J. said[84]:

> " . . . I think unless there is some defence available on the ground that there was a settled account or that the charterers in some way are estopped by the representation which they made before the steamer sailed that a certain day was a holiday, I can see no reason why they should not after the steamer sailed say: 'We made a mistake of fact in calculating our claim and we find that something more is due' . . . I think it is quite clear there was no estoppel. It was found by the learned umpire that there was nothing in the shape of a settled account, and, in the circumstances, I see no reason whatever why the charterers should not subsequently avow the mistake they had made and ask to be paid the true amount due to them upon the correct calculation."

Charterers who wish to withdraw a representation that a certain day is not a holiday may therefore be estopped from so doing if there exists a document "in the shape of a settled account."[85] A settled account, often described as an account stated, is an account which has been agreed between the parties and which is relied upon by one party in defence to an action by the other. There must be an agreement; the mere submission of a statement[86] by one party is insufficient to raise an estoppel.[87]

---

[82] At p. 110.
[83] (1932) 43 Ll.L.Rep. 136; (*The Tregantle*).
[84] At p. 138.
[85] The words used by MacKinnon J., *op. cit.* at p. 138.
[86] As in the case of the time sheet in the *Hain SS. Co. Ltd.* case, *op. cit.*
[87] *Irvine* v. *Young* (1823) 1 Sim. & St. 333.

APPENDIX

CHARTERPARTY LAYTIME DEFINITIONS 1980

A 1974 report by the secretariat of the United Nations Conference on Trade and Development (UNCTAD), entitled "Charterparties,"[1] stated, in a section headed "Charterparty clauses": "In sum, therefore, it would appear that, whilst on the one hand most of the chartering interests consulted are generally satisfied with the present structure and content of standard charterparties in current use, on the other, a sizeable group among them are of opinion that further standardisation of terms and clauses is desirable, so as to inject a greater measure of certainty as to their operation and application." The report also expressed concern as to the delay and expense involved in disputes. The Executive Council of the Comité Maritime International (CMI) decided, in 1976, to ascertain whether it would be possible, by drafting definitions, to reduce the number of disputes. Although the ideal would be to have definitions covering all aspects of charterparties, it was decided that laytime should be the first subject for consideration.

The Executive Committee of the CMI felt that the project should have the widest support and that the views of as many people as possible in the shipping industry should be canvassed. The Baltic and International Maritime Conference (BIMCO) and the General Council of British Shipping (GCBS) agreed to help. A working group was set up in January 1977, under the auspices of these three bodies and under the chairmanship of William A. Wilson, a partner in Messrs. Richards Butler, London solicitors. A first draft of a set of definitions was considered at a plenary meeting of the CMI in Rio de Janeiro at the end of September 1977.

The amended draft was returned to the working group, which now included the Federation of National Associations of Ship Brokers and Agents (FONASBA).

A set of 31 definitions of words and phrases was then published by the four sponsoring bodies under the title "Charterparty Laytime Definitions 1980." The definitions have sometimes been called the Rio laytime definitions. The announcement stated:

CHARTERPARTY LAYTIME DEFINITIONS 1980

Issued jointly by The Baltic and International Maritime Conference (BIMCO), Copenhagen, Comité Maritime International (CMI), Antwerp, The Federation of National Associations of Ship Brokers and Agents (FONASBA), London, and the General Council of British Shipping (GCBS), London, December, 1980.

PREAMBLE
The definitions which follow (except such as are expressly excluded by the deletion or otherwise) shall apply to words and phrases used in the charterparty, save only to the extent that any definition or part thereof is inconsistent with any other express provision of the charter-

---

[1] Published by the United Nations, Sales Number E.74.II.D.12.

343

party. Words used in these definitions shall themselves be construed in accordance with any definition given to them therein. Words or phrases which are merely variations or alternative forms of words or phrases herein defined are to be construed in accordance with the definition (*e.g.* "Notification of Vessel's Readiness," "Notice of Readiness").

LIST OF DEFINITIONS

1. "PORT"
2. "SAFE PORT"
3. "BERTH"
4. "SAFE BERTH"
5. "REACHABLE ON ARRIVAL" or "ALWAYS ACCESSIBLE"
6. "LAYTIME"
7. "CUSTOMARY DESPATCH"
8. "PER HATCH PER DAY"
9. "PER WORKING HATCH PER DAY" or "PER WORKABLE HATCH PER DAY"
10. "AS FAST AS THE VESSEL CAN RECEIVE/DELIVERY"
11. "DAY"
12. "CLEAR DAY" or "CLEAR DAYS"
13. "HOLIDAY"
14. "WORKING DAYS"
15. "RUNNING DAYS" or "CONSECUTIVE DAYS"
16. "WEATHER WORKING DAYS"
17. "WEATHER WORKING DAYS OF 24 CONSECUTIVE HOURS"
18. "WEATHER PERMITTING"
19. "EXCEPTED"
20. "UNLESS USED"
21. "TO AVERAGE"
22. "REVERSIBLE"
23. "NOTICE OF READINESS"
24. "IN WRITING"
25. "TIME LOST WAITING FOR BERTH TO COUNT AS LOADING/DISCHARGING TIME" or "AS LAYTIME"
26. "WHETHER IN BERTH OR NOT" or "BERTH NO BERTH"
27. "DEMURRAGE"
28. "ON DEMURRAGE"
29. "DESPATCH MONEY" or "DESPATCH"
30. "ALL TIME SAVED"
31. "ALL WORKING TIME SAVED" or "ALL LAYTIME SAVED"

DEFINITIONS

1. "PORT"—means an area within which ships are loaded with and/or discharged of cargo and includes the usual places where ships wait for their turn or are ordered or obliged to wait for their turn no matter the distance from that area.
   If the word "PORT" is not used, but the port is (or is to be) identified by its name, this definition shall still apply.

2. "SAFE PORT"—means a port which, during the relevant period of time, the ship can reach, enter, remain at and depart from without, in the absence of some abnormal occurrence, being exposed to danger which cannot be avoided by good navigation and seamanship.

3. "BERTH"—means the specific place where the ship is to load and/or discharge.
   If the word "BERTH" is not used, but the specific place is (or is to be) identified by its name, this definition shall still apply.

4. "SAFE BERTH"—means a berth which, during the relevant period of time, the ship can reach, remain at and depart from without, in the absence of some abnormal occurrence, being exposed to danger which cannot be avoided by good navigation and seamanship.

5. "REACHABLE ON ARRIVAL" or "ALWAYS ACCESS-

IBLE"—means that the charterer undertakes that when the ship arrives at the port there will be a loading/discharging berth for her to which she can proceed without delay.

6. "LAYTIME"—means the period of time agreed between the parties during which the owner will make and keep the ship available for loading/discharging without payment additional to the freight.

7. "CUSTOMARY DESPATCH"—means that the charterer must load and/or discharge as fast as is possible in the circumstances prevailing at the time of loading or discharging.

8. "PER HATCH PER DAY"—means that laytime is to be calculated by multiplying the agreed daily rate per hatch of loading/discharging the cargo by the number of the ship's hatches and dividing the quantity of cargo by the resulting sum. Thus:

$$\text{Laytime} = \frac{\text{Quantity of Cargo}}{\text{Daily Rate} \times \text{Number of Hatches}} = \text{Days}$$

A hatch that is capable of being worked by two gangs simultaneously shall be counted as two hatches.

9. "PER WORKING HATCH PER DAY" or "PER WORKABLE HATCH PER DAY"—means that laytime is to be calculated by dividing the quantity of cargo in the hold with the largest quantity by the result of multiplying the agreed daily rate per working or workable hatch by the number of hatches serving that hold. Thus:

$$\text{Laytime} = \frac{\text{Largest Quantity in one hold}}{\text{Daily rate per hatch} \times \text{Number of Hatches serving that hold}} = \text{Days}$$

A hatch that is capable of being worked by two gangs simultaneously shall be counted as two hatches.

10. "AS FAST AS THE VESSEL CAN RECEIVE/DELIVER"—means that the laytime is a period of time to be calculated by reference to the maximum rate at which the ship in full working order is capable of loading/discharging the cargo.

11. "DAY"—means a continuous period of 24 hours which, unless the context otherwise requires, runs from midnight to midnight.

12. "CLEAR DAY" or "CLEAR DAYS"—means that the day on which the notice is given and the day on which the notice expires are not included in the notice period.

13. "HOLIDAY"—means a day of the week or part(s) thereof on which cargo work on the ship would normally take place but is suspended at the place of loading/discharging by reason of:
  (i) the local law; or
 (ii) the local practice.

14. "WORKING DAYS"—means days or part(s) thereof which are not expressly excluded from laytime by the charterparty and which are not holidays.

15. "RUNNING DAYS" or "CONSECUTIVE DAYS"—means days which follow one immediately after the other.

16. "WEATHER WORKING DAY"—means a working day or part of a working day during which it is or, if the vessel is still waiting for her turn, it would be possible to load/discharge the cargo without interference due to the weather. If such interference occurs (or would have occurred if work had been in progress), there shall be excluded from the laytime a period calculated by reference to the ratio which the duration of the interference bears to the time which would have or could have been worked but for the interference.

17. "WEATHER WORKING DAY OF 24 CONSECUTIVE HOURS"—means a working day or part of a working day of 24 hours during which it is or, if the ship is still waiting for her turn, it would be possible to load/discharge the cargo without interference due to the weather. If such interference occurs (or would have occurred if work had been in progress) there shall be excluded from the laytime the period during which the weather interfered or would have interfered with the work.

18. "WEATHER PERMITTING"—means that time during which weather prevents working shall not count as laytime.

19. "EXCEPTED"—means that the specified days do not count as laytime even if loading or discharging is done on them.

20. "UNLESS USED"—means that if work is carried out during the excepted days the actual hours of work only count as laytime.

21. "TO AVERAGE"—means that separate calculations are to be made for loading and discharging and any time saved in one operation is to be set against any excess time used in the other.

22. "REVERSIBLE"—means an option given to the charterer to add together the time allowed for loading and discharging. Where the option is exercised the effect is the same as a total time being specified to cover both operations.

23. "NOTICE OF READINESS"—means notice to the charterer, shipper, receiver or other person as required by the charter that the ship has arrived at the port or berth as the case may be and is ready to load/discharge.

24. "IN WRITING"—means, in relation to a notice of readiness, a notice visibly expressed in any mode of reproducing words and includes cable, telegram and telex.

25. "TIME LOST WAITING FOR BERTH TO COUNT AS LOADING/DISCHARGING TIME" or "AS LAYTIME"—means that if the main reason why a notice of readiness cannot be given is that there is no loading/discharging berth available to the ship the laytime will commence to run when the ship starts to wait for a berth and will continue to run, unless previously exhausted, until the ship stops waiting. The laytime exceptions apply to the waiting time as if the ship was at the loading/discharging berth provided the ship is not already on demurrage. When the waiting time ends time ceases to count and restarts when the ship reaches the loading/discharging berth subject to the giving of a notice of readiness if one is required

by the charterparty and to any notice time if provided for in the charterparty, unless the ship is by then on demurrage.

26. "WHETHER IN BERTH OR NOT" or "BERTH NO BERTH"—means that if the location named for loading/discharging is a berth and if the berth is not immediately accessible to the ship a notice of readiness can be given when the ship has arrived at the port in which the berth is situated.

27. "DEMURRAGE"—means the money payable to the owner for delay for which the owner is not responsible in loading and/or discharging after the laytime has expired.

28. "ON DEMURRAGE"—means that the laytime has expired. Unless the charterparty expressly provides to the contrary the time on demurrage will not be subject to the laytime exceptions.

29. "DESPATCH MONEY" or "DESPATCH"—means the money payable by the owner if the ship completes loading or discharging before the laytime has expired.

30. "ALL TIME SAVED"—means the time saved to the ship from the completion of loading/discharging to the expiry of the laytime including periods excepted from the laytime.

31. "ALL WORKING TIME SAVED" or "ALL LAYTIME SAVED"—means the time saved to the ship from the completion of loading/discharging to the expiry of the laytime excluding any notice time and periods excepted from the laytime.

INDEX

Index